Lecture Notes in Computer Science

Lecture Notes in Artificial Intelligence   **14140**

Founding Editor

Jörg Siekmann

Series Editors

Randy Goebel, *University of Alberta, Edmonton, Canada*
Wolfgang Wahlster, *DFKI, Berlin, Germany*
Zhi-Hua Zhou, *Nanjing University, Nanjing, China*

The series Lecture Notes in Artificial Intelligence (LNAI) was established in 1988 as a topical subseries of LNCS devoted to artificial intelligence.

The series publishes state-of-the-art research results at a high level. As with the LNCS mother series, the mission of the series is to serve the international R & D community by providing an invaluable service, mainly focused on the publication of conference and workshop proceedings and postproceedings.

Cédric Buche · Alessandra Rossi ·
Marco Simões · Ubbo Visser

Editors

RoboCup 2023:
Robot World Cup XXVI

 Springer

Editors
Cédric Buche
ENIB/Naval Group Pacific
Plouzané, France

Marco Simões (iD)
Bahia State University
Salvador, Brazil

Alessandra Rossi (iD)
University of Naples Federico II
Naples, Italy

Ubbo Visser
University of Miami
Coral Gables, FL, USA

ISSN 0302-9743 ISSN 1611-3349 (electronic)
Lecture Notes in Artificial Intelligence
ISBN 978-3-031-55014-0 ISBN 978-3-031-55015-7 (eBook)
https://doi.org/10.1007/978-3-031-55015-7

LNCS Sublibrary: SL7 – Artificial Intelligence

Cover photo by Maëlic Neau, ENIB, France/Flinders University, Australia, used with his kind permission.

This Springer imprint is published by the registered company Springer Nature Switzerland AG
The registered company address is: Gewerbestrasse 11, 6330 Cham, Switzerland

Paper in this product is recyclable.

Preface

RoboCup is the world's largest robotics and artificial intelligence competition. The 2023 edition took place in Bordeaux at the Parc des Expositions. For more than 20 years, this event has been bringing together more than 2,500 competitors, the best researchers in these fields, and a large number of visitors to a different country every year. Co-organized by the University of Bordeaux and its partners, the Nouvelle-Aquitaine Region, Bordeaux Métropole and the Bordeaux Academic Region, the 26th edition took place from 4 to 10 July 2023 in Bordeaux.

This book highlights the approaches of champion teams from the competitions and the proceedings of the 26th annual RoboCup International Symposium that was held at the Présidence de l'Université de Bordeaux on July 10, 2023. Due to the complex research challenges set by the RoboCup initiative, the RoboCup International Symposium offers a unique perspective for exploring scientific principles underlying advanced robotic and AI systems.

For the RoboCup 2023 Symposium, a total of 47 submissions were received. The submissions were reviewed by the 55 members of the International Program Committee who helped to read and evaluate each of the submissions. Each paper was scored and discussed by at least three reviewers per submission in a single-blind review. The committee decided to accept 20 regular papers and 5 papers for a special track on development for an overall acceptance rate of 57%. Among the accepted papers, 7 were selected for oral presentations (acceptance rate 15%), and the remainder were presented as posters.

Among the 20 accepted research papers, three papers were nominated as best paper award finalists. The awards committee evaluated the finalists based on the paper as well as their associated reviews and presentations, and selected one best paper: Vincenzo Suriani, Emanuele Musumeci, Daniele Nardi and Domenico Daniele Bloisi, *Play Everywhere: A Temporal Logic based Game Environment Independent Approach for Playing Soccer with Robots*

The RoboCup 2023 Symposium was fortunate to have three invited keynote talks:

- **Cynthia Breazeal**, Massachusetts Institute of Technology, USA: *Social Robots: Reflections and Predictions of Our Future Relationship with Personal Robots*
- **Laurence Devillers**, Sorbonne University, France: *Socio-affective robots: ethical issues*
- **Ben Moran** and **Guy Lever**, DeepMind: *Learning Agile Soccer Skills for a Bipedal Robot with Deep Reinforcement Learning*

We thank the members of the Program Committee and the additional reviewers for their time and expertise to help uphold the high standards of the Symposium Program, as well as the members of the awards committee for their work in selecting the best paper award.

January 2024

Cédric Buche
Alessandra Rossi
Marco Simões
Ubbo Visser

Organization

Symposium Co-chairs

Cédric Buche   ENIB/Naval Group Pacific, France
Alessandra Rossi   University of Naples Federico II, Italy
Marco Simões   Universidade do Estado da Bahia, Brazil
Ubbo Visser   University of Miami, USA

Program Committee

Hidehisa Akiyama   Tamagawa University, Japan
Sven Behnke   University of Bonn, Germany
Reinaldo A. C. Bianchi   Centro Universitario FEI, Brazil
Joydeep Biswas   University of Texas at Austin, USA
Ansgar Bredenfeld   Dr. Bredenfeld UG, Germany
Xieyuanli Chen   University of Bonn, Germany
Jorge Alberto De Campos   UNEB - State of Bahia University, Brazil
Christian Deppe   Festo Didactic SE, Germany
Klaus Dorer   Hochschule Offenburg, Germany
Vlad Estivill-Castro   Universitat Pompeu Fabra, Spain
Farshid Faraji   Bonab Azad University, Iran
Thomas Gabel   Frankfurt University of Applied Sciences,
                            Germany
Katie Genter   Red Ventures, USA
Reinhard Gerndt   Ostfalia University of Applied Sciences, Germany
Justin Hart   University of Texas at Austin, USA
Masahide Ito   Aichi Prefectural University, Japan
Tetsuya Kimura   Nagaoka Univ. of Tech., Japan
Nuno Lau   University of Aveiro, Portugal
Pedro U. Lima   Instituto Superior Técnico, U. Lisboa, Portugal
Luis José López Lora   Federación Mexicana de Robótica, Mexico
Patrick MacAlpine   University of Texas at Austin, USA
Sebastian Marian   Elrond Network, Romania
Seyed Ehsan Marjani   Bajestani Polytechnique Montréal, Canada
Ana P. M. Magalhães   UNEB - State of Bahia University, Brazil
Alex Mitrevski   Hochschule Bonn-Rhein-Sieg, Germany
Seyed Mohammad Reza Modaresi University Sorbonne Paris Nord, France

Arne Moos	TU-Dortmund, Germany
Fagner De Assis Moura Pimentel	Centro Universitário FEI, Brazil
Daniele Nardi	Sapienza University of Rome, Italy
Luis Gustavo Nardin	Mines Saint-Étienne, France
Asadollah Norouzi	LeddarTech, Canada
Oliver Obst	Western Sydney University, Australia
Hiroyuki Okada	Tamagawa University, Japan
Tatiana F. P. A. T. Pazelli	Federal University of Sao Carlos, Brazil
Luis Paulo Reis	APPIA, University of Porto/LIACC, Portugal
A. Fernando Ribeiro	University of Minho, Portugal
Robson Marinho Da Silva	Bahia State University (UNEB), Brazil
Gerald Steinbauer-Wagner	Graz University of Technology, Austria
Frieder Stolzenburg	Harz University of Applied Sciences, Germany
Peter Stone	University of Texas at Austin / Sony AI, USA
Flavio Tonidandel	Centro Universitario da FEI, Brazil
Rudi Villing	Maynooth University, Ireland
Arnoud Visser	University of Amsterdam, The Netherlands
Oskar von Stryk	TU Darmstadt, Germany
Maike Paetzel-Prüsmann	Disney Research, Switzerland

Additional Reviewers

Simon Bultmann	University of Bonn, Germany
Angel Villar-Corrales	University of Bonn, Germany
Lasse van Iterson	University of Amsterdam, The Netherlands
Théo Massa	ENSTA Bretagne, France
Vincenzo Suriani	Sapienza University of Rome, Italy
Elena Umili	Sapienza University of Rome, Italy

Contents

Best Paper Award

Play Everywhere: A Temporal Logic Based Game Environment Independent Approach for Playing Soccer with Robots

Vincenzo Suriani[1]([✉]) [iD], Emanuele Musumeci[1] [iD], Daniele Nardi[1] [iD],
and Domenico Daniele Bloisi[2] [iD]

[1] Department of Computer, Control, and Management Engineering,
Sapienza University of Rome, Rome, Italy
{suriani,musumeci,nardi}@diag.uniroma1.it
[2] Department of Mathematics, Computer Science, and Economics,
University of Basilicata, Potenza, Italy
domenico.bloisi@unibas.it

Abstract. Robots playing soccer often rely on hard-coded behaviors that struggle to generalize when the game environment change. In this paper, we propose a temporal logic based approach that allows robots' behaviors and goals to adapt to the semantics of the environment. In particular, we present a hierarchical representation of soccer in which the robot selects the level of operation based on the perceived semantic characteristics of the environment, thus modifying dynamically the set of rules and goals to apply. The proposed approach enables the robot to operate in unstructured environments, just as it happens when humans go from soccer played on an official field to soccer played on a street. Three different use cases set in different scenarios are presented to demonstrate the effectiveness of the proposed approach.

Keywords: semantic mapping · multi-agent planning · robot soccer

1 Introduction

The development of robots that can perform complex tasks in dynamic and unstructured environments is an open research problem. One of the challenges of this research area is to design control architectures that can adapt to changing conditions and generalize to new and unseen situations.

In this paper, we focus on autonomous robots playing soccer. In the domain of robot soccer, the majority of existing approaches rely on hard-coded behaviors that are specifically designed for certain game scenarios (e.g., using green carpets in indoor environments). While these methods can be effective in well-structured environments, they often fail to cope with unexpected situations or variations in the game conditions. Moreover, they are typically difficult to transfer to other domains or tasks, as they rely on a fixed set of rules and assumptions.

To address the above listed limitations, we propose a dynamic approach to robotic soccer, in which the robot derives the rules of the game from the

C. Buche et al. (Eds.): RoboCup 2023, LNAI 14140, pp. 3–14, 2024.
https://doi.org/10.1007/978-3-031-55015-7_1

Fig. 1. Different scenarios where robots can play using the same architecture. The agent establishes the goal for the task from the semantics of the environment.

semantics of the playing environment. Specifically, we suggest a hierarchical representation of soccer that allows the robot to choose the level of operation based on the perceived characteristics of the game scenario. In this way, the robot can select the appropriate set of rules to follow and dynamically modify its goal function accordingly. Our approach enables the robot to operate in unstructured and dynamic environments, such as street soccer fields (see Fig. 1), where the traditional hard-coded approaches fail. Furthermore, our method is highly adaptable to different domains and tasks, as it does not rely on fixed rules or assumptions.

In the context of the RoboCup, adapting robot strategy to the environment can be hard to achieve given the fact that, in most leagues, state-machine behaviors are still predominant [1], and, even when the deployed behavior is learning-based, the resulting policies can suffer in challenging and dynamic environmental conditions.

To enable a robot to operate in unstructured environments, we propose a hierarchical representation of the rules of the RoboCup agent controlled by a planning system capable of accepting constraints in real-time from the external environment. We believe that creating a mechanism for deploying robotic agents in environments where not all the semantic elements are constituted is preparatory to deal with the RoboCup 2050 challenge.

Our goal is to create a software architecture that can be used in every scenario, spanning from simple (i.e., a robot playing alone) to complex scenarios (i.e., two teams playing in a regular field using a specific set of rules). In particular, to exploit the task adaptation capabilities in RoboCup SPL, we present an architecture to deduce the goal of the robotics system while preserving the full capability of the software, based on a planned strategy. In particular, we deployed online conditioning through Pure-Past Linear Temporal Logic (PPLTL) rules on finite traces, also known as $PLTL_f$ rules, expressing temporally extended goals and non-Markovian properties over traces, natively. Our application allows for real-time generation of non-deterministic policies that are able to fit different situations in which robots have to spot the semantic relevant elements in an environment and play using a goal deduced from them, as shown in Fig. 1.

The contribution of this work is three-fold.

1. A hierarchical representation of the goal capable to adapt to the complexity level of the operational environment, based on a measure of the perceived semantics that can be extracted from the robot sensors.
2. An SPL-related conceptual layer capable to generalize and to map ordinary objects to semantically equivalent entities, decoupled from the sensory level.
3. An approach to FOND planning for temporal goals, enabling the system to model the uncertainty of the environment and to manage such uncertainties, by encoding non-Markovian properties on the resulting finite traces, as mixed sets of predicates and $PLTL_f$ rules.

The rest of the paper is organized as follows. In Sect. 2, we survey the current state-of-the-art; in Sect. 3, we expose a brief theoretical background to introduce the concepts expressed in the paper; in Sect. 4, we show more in detail the proposed method; in Sect. 5, we illustrate three use cases of the presented system. Finally, in Sect. 6, we draw the conclusions and the possible future developments of this work.

2   Related Work

Traditional approaches to programming robot soccer behavior often rely on hard-coded rules that struggle to generalize when the game location changes [1]. To address this issue, recent research has explored the use of machine learning techniques to develop more adaptive robot soccer players by creating new environments based on real soccer scenarios as in [7].

However, these approaches still are leading to very specific robotic behaviors and policies capable to behave properly in a structured scenario with a standardized set of elements and a fixed set of rules. We propose a dynamic approach in which the rules of the game are derived from the semantics of the environment and extracted from the full standard set of rules.

To let the robots deal with the semantics of the environments, in [10] a semantic mapping system is divided into four layers on three levels, spanning from a sensory layer, to a categorical and a place layers is presented. In [2], an online approach enables online semantic mapping, that permits adding elements acquired in long-term interaction with the users to the representation. None of these approaches tacked a peculiar field as the robotic soccer.

Our approach is specifically tailored to the game of soccer, and we present a hierarchical representation of soccer in which the robot selects the level of operation based on the perceived characteristics of the environment. The hierarchical representation helps to scale in different scenarios, adapting to new goals. In place of temporal constraints, the online generation of plans can be time-consuming. To this end, [5] proposes FOND Planning with Linear Temporal Logic over finite traces (LTL_f) in Fully Observable Non-Deterministic (FOND) domains. [4] extends the previous approach to $PLTL_f$ goals by suitably modifying standard FOND planning domains. In [9], PLTLf was used to condition a RoboCup team's behavior based on high-level commands from a human coach, encoded as additional temporal constraints in the original goal for the FOND planning problem at hand (in this case, the task specific to the robot role in the multi-agent team).

Our approach differs from previous work because the set of $PLTL_f$ rules is automatically chosen based on the perceived characteristics of the environment. The $PLTL_f$ goal function is dynamically modified to adapt to changing conditions enabling the robot to operate in unstructured environments, like a street soccer field, where the characteristics of the environment may change rapidly and require complex properties to be expressed without restructuring the whole planning domain. In summary, the proposed approach has the potential to enable more adaptive and robust robot players, and could also be applied to other domains where environmental cues can be used to determine robot behavior.

3 Background

Among the tools we used to automatically scale the robot policy based on the environment semantics, we need to introduce planning with a $PLTL_f$ goal formula. In [6] and [5], a plan that entails an LTL goal formula is obtained by checking the non-emptiness of the product of a deterministic automaton (modeling the planning domain) and a non-deterministic automaton modeling the goal formula. In FOND planning, a DFA game is to be solved on said cross-product, to obtain a policy.

Following [4], given a pre-existing, non-deterministic planning domain $\mathcal{D}$ and a PPLTL planning goal G, a new domain D' and a new goal G' can be compiled, so that any off-the-shelf non-deterministic planner can compute a plan for the new goal, treating the problem as a typical FOND planning problem. Given the set $\mathbf{sub}(G)$ of logical sub-formulae recursively obtained by the original goal G, a minimal subset $\Sigma_G \subseteq \mathbf{sub}(G)$ of sub-formulae of G can be computed.

Then, given the a formula $g \in \Sigma_G$, a propositional interpretation s_i over the set of predicates $\mathcal{P}_{deduced}$ in the current planning domain, in the current state at instant i, and a specific interpretation $\sigma_i : \Sigma_G \to \{\top, \bot\}$, keeping track of the truth values of sub-formulas in Σ_G in the current state at instant i, a predicate $\mathbf{val}(g, \sigma_i, s_i)$ can be defined for each sub-formula $g \in \mathbf{sub}(G)$ to track recursively the truth value of the $PLTL_f$ sub-formula g at the current state.

Given a trace τ over $\mathcal{P}_{deduced}$, the satisfaction of the original goal G is equivalent to the truth value in the final state of the predicate $\mathbf{val}(\cdot)$:

$$\tau \models G \text{ iff } \mathbf{val}(G, \sigma_f, s_f) \tag{1}$$

where σ_f is the interpretation of Σ_G in the final state and s_f is the set of predicates of $\mathcal{P}_{deduced}$ verified in the final state of the trace. At this point, each predicate $\mathbf{val}(g, \sigma_i, s_i)$ can be included as an additional propositional variable in the state of the planning domain, obtaining a new planning domain $\mathcal{D}'$. According to equivalence 1, the new planning problem Γ' will feature a new goal $G' = \mathbf{val}(G, \sigma_f, s_f)$. Given the original planning problem Γ with a PLTL$_f$ goal G and the new planning problem Γ', featuring the new planning domain $\mathcal{D}'$, with the new goal G', then Γ has a winning strategy π if and only if Γ' has a winning strategy π'.

4   Proposed Approach

Our approach consists of three main components: 1) A perception module that extracts relevant features from the environment, 2) A hierarchical representation of the task (the soccer game), and 3) A decision-making module that selects the appropriate level of operation and goal function. To model the hierarchical representation and the decision-making module, we start from the definition of a *Semantic Map* in the formalization introduced in [3], with some modifications. Specifically, we consider a representation composed by a tuple of three elements

$$\mathcal{SM} = \langle R, \mathcal{M}, \mathcal{P} \rangle \tag{2}$$

where:

- R is the global reference system in which all the elements of the semantic map are expressed;
- $\mathcal{M}$ is a set of geometrical elements obtained from sensor data, expressed in the reference frame R, describing spatial information in mathematical form.
- $\mathcal{P}$ is a set of predicates, describing the environment.

Here, the definition of a unique reference frame R allows associating the elements of $\mathcal{M}$ with those in $\mathcal{P}$. Then, given two semantic maps $\mathcal{SM}_1 = \langle R_1, \mathcal{M}_1, \mathcal{P}_1 \rangle$ and $\mathcal{SM}_m = \langle R_m, \mathcal{M}_m, \mathcal{P}_m \rangle$ generated as an expected model of the environment, an evaluation metric can be defined as

$$\delta(\mathcal{SM}_1, \mathcal{SM}_m) = f(|\mathcal{M}_1 \ominus \mathcal{M}_m|, |\mathcal{P}_1 \boxminus \mathcal{P}_m|), \tag{3}$$

where R_1 and R_m must coincide (e.g., through a simple geometrical transformation). It is important to notice that, since Eq. 3 assumes a unique reference frame, it is particularly suitable for the analysis of different semantic maps which are used to distinguish different semantic contexts in which the robot has to operate. In fact, it allows reformulating the problem of semantic maps comparison as the problem of anchoring their representation to a common reference frame. In the deployed environment, objects and their semantic characterization have to belong to the same reference frame as the robotic agent maps them. Such metrics can be applied at multiple levels of abstraction, spanning from the low sensory level ($\ominus$) to a conceptual level ($\boxminus$), as presented in [3].

The set $\mathcal{M}$ is related to the environmental elements that can be perceived by the agent. In the case of the soccer environment, the set of field elements is finite and represented by the field elements:

$$\mathcal{M}_m = \{Ball, GoalPosts, Players, Field\} \tag{4}$$

But it can also include referees, gestures, and any other element of the game that can be perceived by the agent. The set of predicates contains the full set of rules of the game that can be relaxed. In fact, $\mathcal{P}$ is derived by the set of rules of the soccer game using the semantic evaluation δ as a metric. Only the predicates referring to $\mathcal{M}$ and coherent with the global $\mathcal{R}$ are taken into account:

$$\mathcal{P}(\delta) \subseteq \mathcal{P}_{\mathcal{SPL}} \tag{5}$$

Being $P_i(\delta)$ the $i - th$ level in the rule selection hierarchy and indicating it as $\mathcal{P}_i$ for clarity of notation, the subsequent goals hierarchy is expressed as

$$\mathcal{G}_m = \bigcup_{i=1}^{n} G(\mathcal{P}_i) \supseteq \bigcup_{i=1}^{n-1} G(\mathcal{P}_i) \supseteq \cdots \supseteq G(\mathcal{P}_1), \tag{6}$$

where G_i represents the set of goals for the i-th level of the rules, and n is the total number of stages.

As we progress through the inclusion of new rules, each set of goals (represented by G_i) builds upon the previous set of goals. The notation $\bigcup_{i=1}^{n} G_i$ represents the union of all the sets of goals up to the n-th stage, while $\bigcup_{i=1}^{n-1} G_i$ represents the union of all the sets of goals up to the (n-1)-th stage.

Each set of goals is a subset of the next set of goals, with the final set of goals (G_1) being the most basic and foundational. For example, for a single robotic soccer player, if the only perceived element of the environment is the ball, the fundamental goal is to reach and hold the ball. Perceiving a set of goal posts, the agent's goal is extended in reaching and holding the ball and scoring to the goal. If in the semantics of the environment, the robot spots a couple of goals, the agent goal will be extended in order to take into account the presence of two teams and, hence, a goal that have to be defended and one that has to be used for scoring. Finally, in the case of perceived full robotic fields the robot refers to the full set of rules of the SPL.

In the presented architecture, when dealing with the robot behavior, the $\mathcal{SM}$ influences the policy generated for the FOND planning problem through the constraints expressed on the set of deduced predicates made available by the conceptual layer. In fact, $\mathcal{SM}$ conditions the behavior of the robot assembling a goal based on the set of rules that are related to items of the Semantic Map.

$$\pi = (U|S, \mathcal{SM}) = (U|S, (\mathcal{R}, \mathcal{M}_R S, \mathcal{P}_{deduced})) \tag{7}$$

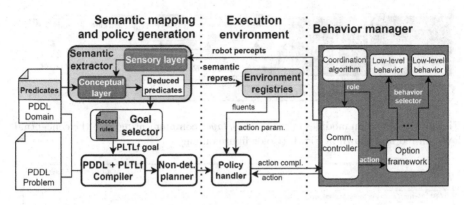

Fig. 2. Functional architecture. The *sensory layer*, here highlighted in green, is shown in Fig. 3, while the conceptual layer, in red, is shown in Fig. 4. (Color figure online)

$\mathcal{P}_{deduced}$ is a subset of the planning domain $\mathcal{D}$ predicates. The FOND policy conditioned by the semantic mapping leads automatically to a new policy:

$$\pi_{\bigcup_{i=1}^{n} G_i} = (U|S, \mathcal{P}_{deduced}) \tag{8}$$

This approach aims at the deployment of the robotic agent in an unstructured environment where the goal is defined by a $PLTL_f$ formula ϕ activated by the set of elements that the robot can perceive.

As shown in [4], $PLTLf$ goals are computationally advantageous with respect to $LTLf$ when temporal goal specifications are naturally expressed with respect to finite past traces. With those premises, the policy π is the solution for a corresponding *FOND* planning problem Γ with a $PLTL_f$ goal defined in [5] as

$$\Gamma := \langle \mathcal{D}, s_0, \phi \rangle \tag{9}$$

where $\mathcal{D}$ is a FOND domain model, s_0 is the initial state and ϕ is a $PLTL_f$ formula. In the proposed approach, the equation above becomes

$$\Gamma := \langle \mathcal{D}', s_0, \phi(\bigcup_{i=1}^{n} G_i) \rangle \tag{10}$$

where $\mathcal{D}'$ is a planning domain where each sub-formula is represented by fluents, s_0 is the initial state common to all the traces of the robot behavior and the goal depends on the sum of the n sets of goals G_i deduced in the current context.

4.1 Functional Architecture

Figure 2 shows the three main components of our architecture: 1) The perception module, which extracts relevant features from the environment, 2) the hierarchical and conceptual representation of the task (the soccer game), and 3) the decision-making module that selects the appropriate level of operation and goal function. The architecture relies on the B-Human Team SPL framework [11].

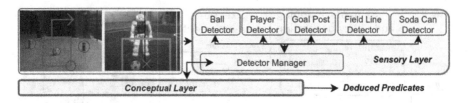

Fig. 3. The detection modules in the *sensory layer* communicating with the conceptual layer, in red and shown in Fig. 4. (Color figure online)

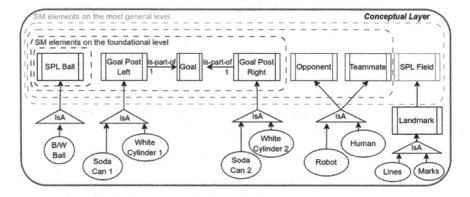

Fig. 4. Hierarchical architecture showing the relationships between the perceived objects and the semantic map in the conceptual layer.

Sensory Layer and Perception Modules. The classification of the environment starts from the perception modules. We rely on different classifiers to percept the field elements of the environment in order to reactive the unused ones (see Fig. 3). To be able to play in every scenario, we created classifiers able to detect common objects, easy to retrieve. In particular, for the use-cases presented, we used:

- a *Ball Perceptor* capable to detect the SPL ball on any background and under any light conditions, based on a OpenCV Haar Cascade Classifier.
- a *Field Perceptor* to identify the official SPL field and its elements.
- a *Goal Perceptor* capable to detect official SPL goal posts on any terrain.
- a *Soda Can Perceptor* to perceive soda can as elements representing goal posts, developed with an OpenCV Haar Feature-based Cascade classifiers.
- a *Player Perceptor*, Deep Learning based.

The perception module is responsible for extracting relevant features from the environment and providing them to the decision-making module.

Hierarchical Representation and Conceptual Layer. Figure 4 shows the hierarchical representation of the soccer game. It consists of multiple levels, each representing a possible abstraction of the game and a goal that depends on the semantic reconstruction of the environment. This is based on the conceptual

layer, which compromises common-sense knowledge about concepts, and relations (mainly *IsA* and *IsPartOf* relations) between those concepts, and instances
of spatial entities. The conceptual layer is built based on a pre-defined list of
possible objects but it can be easily extended in order to include equivalences
between entities belonging to official SPL fields and other heterogeneous environments. Here, the elements are hierarchically classified, and from this representation, the set of predicates extracted $\mathcal{P}_{deduced}$ are used to condition the planner
in the next module.

Decision-Making Module Using PLTLf Goals over PDDL Domains.
The uncertain set of features made available by the conceptual layer determines
the level of operation of the agent and the planning goal that is dynamically
adapted to it. The problem is modeled as a FOND planning problem in which
the goal is formulated as a PLTL_f formula using predicates in $P_{deduced}$ made
available by the *conceptual layer* of the Semantic Extractor. Following [4], this
formalism allows to have generated traces satisfy temporal constraints, to model
RoboCup SPL rules or the goal G required at the current level of operation.

Given the goal G and a pre-existing PDDL domain $\mathcal{D}$, describing the actions
that the agent can execute in the RoboCup SPL setting, with a set of predicates
containing the set of deduced predicates $P \supseteq P_{deduced}$, we can obtain the new
problem Γ', featuring the new domain $\mathcal{D}'$, such that any off-the-shelf planner
will produce a policy that realizes the original goal G, by realizing a new goal
G' that is compatible with the original one. Following [4], the evaluation of the
new goal G' is equivalent to the evaluation of the predicate $\mathbf{val}(G, \sigma_f, s_f)$.

For each predicate $g_i \in \mathbf{sub}(G)$, a new predicate $\mathbf{val}_{g_i} = \mathbf{val}(g_i, \sigma_i, s_i)$
is added to the planning domain $\mathcal{D}$. The evaluation of all such propositions
will depend on the evaluation of a reduced set of propositional predicates
$g_i \subseteq \Sigma_G \subseteq \mathbf{sub}(G)$. Using some features currently well-supported by most
off-the-shelf planners, the new set of propositional rules is embedded in the
pre-existing PDDL planning domain. For each sub-formula $g \in \mathbf{sub}(G)$, a corresponding predicate $\mathbf{val}_g$ is embedded into the original PDDL domain as a
derived predicate, so that the result of its evaluation is equivalent to the result
of $\mathbf{val}(G, \sigma_i, s_i)$.

Domain actions are also modified accordingly: using the PDDL construct for
conditional effects, the effects of each domain action are populated with rules
for the update of the new set of derived predicates, of the form:

$$\mathbf{val}_g \;\to\; f(g) \in \Sigma_g \qquad\qquad \neg\mathbf{val}_g \to \neg f(g) \in \Sigma_g \qquad (11)$$

where $f(g)$ is a propositional formula in the reduced set Σ_g that is relevant
for the evaluation of $\mathbf{val}_g$. These rules are added to the effect of all domain
actions, so that the truth values of each $\mathbf{val}_g$ are updated every time an action
is performed. As shown in [4], the size of the new planning problem is polynomial
in the size of the original problem and, in particular, the number of additional
predicates introduced is linear in the size of the PPLTL goal G.

The resulting PDDL problem will have a new goal $G' = \{\mathbf{val}_G\}$. Given the
original planning problem Γ with a PLTL_f goal G and the new planning problem

Γ' with the new goal G', then Γ has a winning strategy π if and only if Γ' has a winning strategy π'. In this case, any sound and complete planner returns a policy π' generating robot behaviors that are compliant with the original temporal goal.

In scenarios where fluents from the environment are needed to model conditions that are not known at planning time, *"oneof"* constructs are used in the post-conditions of actions to enumerate their possible unpredictable results, featuring predicates whose value will depend on the agent's own world model and percepts at runtime. Policies generated with non-deterministic planners from the provided PDDL domain are therefore robust for a set of unpredictable outcomes. The generated policy is not yet ready to be executed with temporally-extended actions. To overcome this problem, a pipeline composed by a set of *"environment registries"*, used to ground policy fluents, actions and their arguments, to elements made available by the conceptual layer, similarly to the architecture presented in [9].

5   Use-Cases

In order to test the presented approach, we propose three scenarios, in which the agent has to gather data from the environment, extract the set of elements belonging to the environment, determine the level of operation given the available elements, assemble the corresponding goal and compute a policy accordingly.

The three use-cases present a progressively increasing number of features made available by the conceptual layer, leading to an increasing level of complexity in the resulting goal, in the number of temporal constraints. The MyND planner [8] was used for the presented experiments.

Reaching the Ball. First, only the ball is made available by the conceptual layer. The goal is $G_0 = O(isat\ robot1\ ballposition)$, where the PLTL$_f$ operator $O(\cdot)$ (*"once"*) was used to require that any generated trace satisfies the predicate *"isat robot1 ballposition"* at least once. The resulting policy, shown in Fig. 5a, features only one action that moves the robot to the ball position.

Scoring a Goal. At the conceptual layer, *"Score a goal"* and *"Score in the Opposite Goal"* are different (in the first case two goal posts are required to identify a goal, while in the second case four goal posts are required to identify two different goals and discern which one is the opponent goal), while at the decision-making level, the policy will be the same. The conceptual layer will provide at runtime the correct fluents to determine if a goal is available and the grounded position of the opponent goal. The resulting goal $G_1 = G_0 \wedge O(goalscored)$ leads to a more complex policy: the additional PLTL$_f$ rule $O(goalscored)$, requires that the goal is scored at least once along any generated trace. Given that the policy enumerates all possible combinations of predicates representing runtime fluents, only a single branch of the policy is show in Fig. 5b.

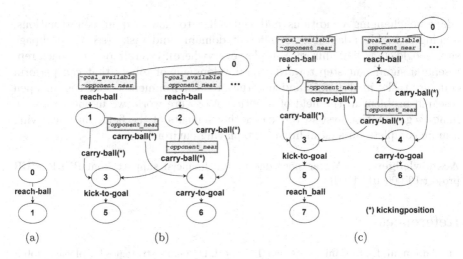

Fig. 5. Policies generated from goals of increasing complexity. From left to right: $G_0 = O(isat\ robot1\ ballposition)$, $G_1 = G_0 \wedge O(goalscored)$, $G_2 = G_{SPL} = G_1 \wedge O(ballsafe\ S\ isat\ robot1\ ballposition)$. Rectangular boxes contain fluents for the overlapped branch.

Scoring a Goal on the SPL Field. In case the full field is perceived (including the field lines), it is safer for the agent to assume the presence of the opponents on the field, adopting a safer strategy in order to ensure that a goal is scored. The goal is $G_2 = G_{SPL} = G_1 \wedge (ballsafe\ S\ isat\ robot1\ ballposition)$, where the additional PLTL$_f$ construct $(ballsafe\ S\ isat\ robot1\ ballposition)$ requires the traces to keep the predicate "$ballsafe$" verified in all states in the states following the state in which the predicate $isat\ robot1\ ballposition$ is verified for the first time: the agent will execute domain actions that keep the ball protected (these actions have the predicate $ballsafe$ in their post-conditions). Result is partially shown in Fig. 5c.

The webpage sites.google.com/diag.uniroma1.it/play-everywhere contains videos and images of NAO robots playing soccer in the wild. The page contents will be extended in the future with novel use-cases.

6 Conclusions and Future Directions

In this paper, we have presented a novel approach to robot soccer, which enables the robot to adapt its behavior and goals to the semantics of the environment in real-time. The proposed approach is based on a hierarchical representation of soccer and uses Pure-Past LTL rules to express temporal goals on finite traces.

Our method aims at being effective in unstructured and dynamic environments, where traditional hard-coded approaches fail. We have demonstrated its effectiveness through three different use-cases, conducted in different scenarios. Experimental results show that the proposed method can adapt to changing conditions and generalize to new and unseen situations, making it highly adaptable to different domains and tasks (see the webpage sites.google.com/diag.uniroma1.it/play-everywhere). Overall, our approach represents a significant step towards the development of robots that can perform complex tasks in dynamic and unstructured environments, which is an open research problem in the field of robotics. As future work, we intend to use an image segmentation system to extract the elements of the field, thus achieving a more complete understanding of the playing environment.

Acknowledgement. We acknowledge partial financial support from PNRR MUR project PE0000013-FAIR.

References

1. Antonioni, E., Suriani, V., Riccio, F., Nardi, D.: Game strategies for physical robot soccer players: a survey. IEEE Trans. Games **13**(4), 342–357 (2021)
2. Bastianelli, E., et al.: On-line semantic mapping. In: ICAR, pp. 1–6 (2013). https://doi.org/10.1109/ICAR.2013.6766501
3. Capobianco, R., Serafin, J., Dichtl, J., Grisetti, G., Iocchi, L., Nardi, D.: A proposal for semantic map representation and evaluation. In: 2015 European Conference on Mobile Robots (ECMR), pp. 1–6. IEEE (2015)
4. De Giacomo, G., Favorito, M., Fuggitti, F.: Planning for temporally extended goals in pure-past linear temporal logic: a polynomial reduction to standard planning (2022)
5. De Giacomo, G., Rubin, S.: Automata-theoretic foundations of fond planning for LTLF and LDLF goals. In: IJCAI, pp. 4729–4735 (2018)
6. De Giacomo, G., Vardi, M.Y.: Linear temporal logic and linear dynamic logic on finite traces. In: Proceedings of the Twenty-Third International Joint Conference on Artificial Intelligence, IJCAI 2013, pp. 854–860. AAAI Press (2013)
7. Kurach, K., et al.: Google research football: a novel reinforcement learning environment. In: Proceedings of the AAAI Conference on Artificial Intelligence, vol. 34, pp. 4501–4510 (2020)
8. Mattmüller, R., Ortlieb, M., Helmert, M., Bercher, P.: Pattern database heuristics for fully observable nondeterministic planning. In: Proceedings of the International Conference on Automated Planning and Scheduling, vol. 20, no. 1, pp. 105–112 (2021). https://doi.org/10.1609/icaps.v20i1.13408
9. Musumeci, E., Suriani, V., Antonioni, E., Nardi, D., Bloisi, D.D.: Adaptive team behavior planning using human coach commands. In: Eguchi, A., Lau, N., Paetzel-Prüsmann, M., Wanichanon, T. (eds.) RoboCup 2022. LNCS, vol. 13561, pp. 112–123. Springer, Cham (2022). https://doi.org/10.1007/978-3-031-28469-4_10
10. Pronobis, A., Jensfelt, P.: Large-scale semantic mapping and reasoning with heterogeneous modalities. In: 2012 IEEE International Conference on Robotics and Automation, pp. 3515–3522. IEEE (2012)
11. Röfer, T., et al.: B-Human team report and code release 2021 (2021). http://www.b-human.de/downloads/publications/2021/CodeRelease2021.pdf

Oral Presentations

Neural Network and Prior Knowledge Ensemble for Whistle Recognition

Diana Kleingarn[✉] and Dominik Brämer

Robotics Research Institute, Section Information Technology,
TU Dortmund University, 44227 Dortmund, Germany
`diana.kleingarn@tu-dortmund.de`

Abstract. Whistle recognition is becoming an increasingly crucial aspect of RoboCup. Therefore neural networks are being utilized in this field more frequently. They are typically more effective than straightforward conventional approaches but still have flaws in fields that require prior knowledge, as conventional approaches do. In this work, we present an approach that can outperform standalone variants of both methods by fusing prior knowledge of traditional methods with a neural network. Additionally, we were able to keep the composite system runtime efficient on the integrated hardware of the NAO Robot.

Keywords: Whistle recognition · Convolutional neural network · Classical audio processing

1 Introduction

Robots, in general, have a primary purpose, like, in our case, playing soccer. However, on top of their main goal, they have to react to specific events, such as a whistle. Although it is clear that whistle recognition is not the main focus of soccer robots, not reacting to this referee command is usually punished. Whistle recognition was first introduced in the Standard Plattform League (SPL) to indicate the start of a game in 2015. However, in the beginning, the disadvantage in form of a time delay of 15 s of the game controller signal compared to the whistle was only implemented for quarterfinals and onwards. Since then, this time delay has been installed for all whistle signals during the games. Furthermore, with the recent in-Game Visual Referee Challenge [6], reliably recognizing the whistle becomes more and more crucial.

One of the biggest challenges RoboCup teams face for audio processing is noise. Just like humans, soccer robots are supposed to react reliably to a whistle, independent of the surrounding, the room impulse response, or the cheering crowd, including children. Loud people, especially children, bring additional challenges to audio processing. This is described in detail in Sect. 2 in combination with the dataset we use.

D. Kleingarn and D. Brämer—These authors contributed equally to this work.

C. Buche et al. (Eds.): RoboCup 2023, LNAI 14140, pp. 17–28, 2024.
https://doi.org/10.1007/978-3-031-55015-7_2

Since whistle recognition is relevant for all RoboCup teams, a variety of solutions are already presented or published within the teams' code release. The already existing solutions, described in Sect. 1.1, all have their advantages but, at the same time, do not cover all critical situations. While some solutions are good at detecting soft whistles, they are also likely to detect loud noise as a whistle. Robustness against noise, however, usually causes a lot of false negatives. Moreover, if a whistle is supposed to be detected in a noisy environment, keeping the balance between false positives and false negatives is more challenging. False recognitions are for sure never desirable during a soccer game, especially with the described disadvantage of not hearing a whistle. These include reducing the time robots have to return to their own half of the field after scoring a goal from 45 s to 30 s or waiting 15 s to receive the referee command for kick-off or a penalty kick. Nevertheless, recognizing something, for example the cheering crowd, as a whistle, which was not a whistle, is even worse because a whistle during a robot soccer game means a goal was scored, so the robots would start returning to their starting position.

In order to create a whistle recognizer that works more independently of the surroundings or the used whistle, we combine a neural network with prior knowledge, such as the pattern in the frequency domain created by a whistle or the overall noise over all frequencies. This approach is promising since the advantages and disadvantages of the neural network and the prior knowledge method compensate each other. In addition, the dampening factor ensures that the system is less likely to detect false positives in very loud environments, in which it is also hard for humans to differentiate the sounds. The setup of the proposed solution is described in Sect. 3. For the evaluation, in Sect. 4, we test our solution simultaneously with the code release of two other SPL teams and our old whistle recognizer, which uses a neural network. The final section summarizes the results and provides an overview of future projects.

1.1 Related Work

Even though whistle recognition is a pretty specific topic, it is not completely new. For example, the whistle recognizer presented by Bonarini et al. [3] was designed to detect not only a whistle event but also the pattern to identify referee commands. Although pattern recognition is not yet needed in the SPL, other requirements, such as robustness of the detection and against noise or runtime, are similar. They use a frequency mask followed by a neural network approach. In addition, they provide a software tool to help the user to tune the system.

In 2014 Poore et al. [13] introduced two real-time sound recognition approaches designed for the NAO Robot in various noisy environments. The first approach uses a frequency/band-pass filter to isolate the fundamental frequency of the whistle in a permitted error range. This idea is comparable to the frequency mask in [3]. The second approach uses a logistic regression with l2-norm regularization. According to the paper, the second approach outperforms the first in all datasets.

Fig. 1. Spectrogram of different whistles.

The SPL Team from Hamburg, the HULKs [9], are also using a frequency mask. However, instead of just filtering for the fundamental frequency, they also check if the first overtone exists. Since all whistles we examined had this clear pattern in the frequency domain, having at least one prominent overtone is a good indicator of a whistle. The spectrogram of different whistles is shown in Fig. 1. The most dominant feature is the fundamental frequency, but also its multiple are visible.

The SPL team from Bremen, B-Human [1], uses a correlation to capture this unique pattern. Furthermore, to consider that different whistles have a different fundamental frequency, they have a sample of every whistle they tested. So their whistle recognizer can give the additional information which whistle was recognized.

In recent years neural networks are increasingly popular, so naturally, this approach deserves attention. For example, the HTWK Robots published their whistle recognizer [8], which uses a neural network after the Fourier transformation instead of a frequency mask. Another example of a neural network approach can be found in our code release from 2022 [12]. The main idea of using a neural network is to teach the network to recognize the characteristic whistle pattern shown in Fig. 1. As can be seen in the evaluation, Sect. 4, this approach worked for us in most cases, but the neural network correlated sound volume with a whistle event. Since the human eye can easily spot this pattern of a whistle in the frequency domain, we did some research on adding prior knowledge to the system. Forssell and Lindskog's work about combining semi-physical and neural network modelling [7] inspired the new approach we present in this paper. Their method was explained by the example of a water tank system with the suggestion to modify it for sound in the future.

2   Dataset

For training a neural network, preparing the dataset is one of the most critical steps. Since the idea is to use the neural network as a pattern recognizer in the frequency domain, the audio samples must be prepared accordingly. This process involves buffering the audio stream to get windows containing 1024 samples. In the second step, we use a window function, the Hamming window, to avoid the Leakage-Effekt of a rectangular window. Following this, we compute the spectrogram of this window. Due to the symmetry of the Fourier transformation, we only need one half of the result plus the Nyquist frequency. After a Fourier transformation, the result contains complex numbers. However, we only use the real part of these complex numbers. For a more informative visualization, the volume/amplitude per frequency is shown in decibel (dB). This is not only justified by the concept of human hearing, but tests without the squared amplitude's logarithmic representation showed that the characteristic pattern, described in Sect. 1.1, was not as visible to the human eye.

In general, we use two different types of datasets, one to train, test and validate the neural network and one to tune parameters like the threshold for recognizing a whistle and benchmark how the whistle recognizer works in our framework. In both cases, we recorded the data with NAO Robots. For the first dataset, we extracted the audio data from log files. These log files were recorded during soccer games, tests and competitions, and explicit whistle tests. In addition, we cut off most redundant parts, like silence or robots walking, to have a slightly more balanced ratio between the events 'whistle' and 'no whistle'. However, we kept audio sequences which produced false positives. So in total, we have 369680 non-whistle and 18052 whistle samples after the adjustment, which makes a 20:1 ratio between the non-whistle and whistle samples.

The second dataset contains two log files. One was recorded during a show game at the Maker Faire in Rome. Again, due to the cheering crowd directly around the field, we noticed more false positives than in any other game, especially since at least one kid hit the fundamental frequency of the whistle. To further increase the difficulty, we used the log file of the goalkeeper, who was constantly near the spectators, instead of the field players. In addition, the referee, who holds the whistle, is moving around the field, so a whistle blown near the opponent's goal has the maximum distance. Unfortunately, real games contain fewer whistles compared to whistle tests. This log, in particular, contains only three whistles, a single whistle to indicate the start and two short whistles for the end of the game. The other log was a whistle test recorded in our lab in three steps. First, we only tested whistles where we control the airflow through the whistle. Since most teams and referees use handwhistles nowadays, the intensity and length of the sound highly depend on how fast and hard the currently whistling person is pressing on the air-filled ball attached to the whistle. Then, as a second step, we tested different types of noise to see what triggers false positives. And lastly, we combined both tests to get a more realistic benchmark where the desired sound is masked by noise. For the different types of noise, we went through a list of potential sounds caused by the robots, spectators, or other leagues. The list of sounds contains a robot falling and standing up in both directions, a whistle, a plastic bag for candy, finger-snapping, clapping, a human whistling, 'hit the pot', a circular saw, an angle grinder, a drilling machine, a vacuum cleaner robot and birds' twittering. In contrast to the first dataset, where we extracted the audio, we kept the second dataset as log files, which is an advantage and disadvantage at the same time. The argument for doing that was that we can replay these logs in our simulator and have the exact same conditions for every test. But unfortunately, our simulator is incompatible with

other frameworks and extracting the audio to use loudspeakers would distort
the result.

3   Whistle Recognition Architecture

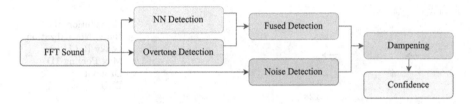

Fig. 2. Overview of our whistle recognition pipeline where red arrows indicate the flow
of FFT information of the current audio and blue arrows indicate the confidence flow.
(Color figure online)

Our whistle recognition architecture is divided into three main parts, firstly a
neural network, then a traditional method, and finally a damping factor that
takes the ambient noise and volume into account. All the parts just mentioned
generate a confidence value from an audio sample processed by a fast Fourier
transformation (FFT). Figure 2 shows a simplified overview of the architecture
and the dependencies of the modules we use in our whistle recognition pipeline.
The complete recognition architecture runs in real-time on the NAO Robot.

3.1   Neural Network

In this section, we present our neural network approach in detail. It contains four
convolution blocks of two types and a dense layer that merges the information
and returns a confidence value, indicating whether a whistle is present. The
first convolution block type consists of a one-dimensional convolution, a batch
normalization layer, a leaky Rectified Linear Unit (ReLU), a one-dimensional
max-pooling layer, and a dropout layer at the end. This combination should
ensure that the neural network reacts less strongly to loud noises like our old
approach, which is also visible in Sect. 4 and is thus more focused on the actual
whistling patterns. The second convolution block type consists of only a one-
dimensional convolution with an Exponential Linear Unit (ELU) as an activation
function. Even without performing another computationally expensive batch
normalization, this combination achieves a similar effect [5] as the previous block.
Every convolution layer also uses a bias vector which is added to the output.
The first three convolution blocks use a filter size of 32, 64, and 128 with a
kernel size of 5 and a stride of two. After this, the second convolution block type
uses a filter size of 64, a kernel size of 5, and a stride of one. The last stage
of our neural network is a dense layer with one unit and a sigmoid function as

an activation, which processes the flattened output of the second convolution block. As a result, the output of the last layer forms the confidence of our neural network c_{nn}. Furthermore, hyperparameters used for this architecture will be discussed in Sect. 4. Figure 3 shows a high-level perspective of the previously mentioned network design.

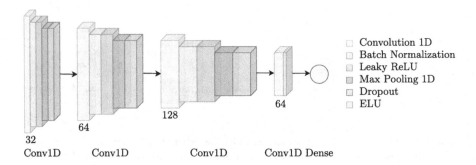

Fig. 3. Overview of our proposed whistle recognition neural network architecture where the numbers indicate the filter count of the convolution part of the current block and a step indicates that the input is reduced by half.

For the training of our neural network, we use the dataset described in Sect. 2, which is split into training- and validation data. Each dataset entry consists of 1024 samples of sound, which are Fourier transformed. This results in 513 amplitudes that are refined by $20 \cdot \log (amplitude)$ for further processing. Since our data still has a significant imbalance around 20:1 between background noise and real whistles, we further process our training data after splitting. Therefore we use the Imbalanced-learn Python library [10] to over-sample our training data with the synthetic minority over-sampling technique (SMOTE) [4] and then under-sample it with our variant of the edited nearest neighbors (ENN) algorithm [14]. We use the combination of SMOTE+ENN because, according to Batista et al. [2], this combination is well suited to balancing data for machine learning algorithms. This also gives better results in our empirical tests than using a loss specialized on imbalanced data like a focal loss [11]. The validation data used while training is not affected by this and still shows an imbalance typical for these data. To train our network with the training data generated in this way, we use the TensorFlow implementation of Rectified Adam (RAdam) as an optimizer in combination with the TensorFlow implementation of the lookahead mechanism; this combination is also referred as Ranger [15]. We then train our network for a maximum of 45 epochs with early stopping enabled to avoid overfitting because our neural network converges very fast.

3.2 Prior Knowledge Acquisition

Acquiring prior knowledge is a crucial part of our whistle recognition architecture. The acquisition is divided into two parts: a physical model-based detection of the whistle and a detection of the ambient volume and frequencies, which is treated as a noise indicator.

The model-based detection uses, just like the neural network, 1024 samples of sound, which are Fourier transformed as input. The resulting 513 amplitudes are then used to find a peak in a predefined range of frequencies. We define a peak as a whistle candidate if the amplitude of the peak is greater or equal to the average of the last 200 maximum amplitudes. After this, our model-based detection searches for the first overtone peak in the doubled frequencies range. If the amplitude of the overtone peak is greater or equal to the average amplitude of all samples, the whistle candidate is verified as a whistling sound.

Since all our detectors must output a confidence, a reasonable value must also be generated here. For this purpose, we use a gradient map that reflects the gradients between the amplitudes. Therefore, we extract the upward and downward gradient of the peak of the current whistle candidate. If the whistle candidate has been confirmed, the maximum absolute value of these two gradients, normalized by the current maximum amplitude, forms the confidence c_{pm}. Otherwise, the minimum absolute value of these two gradients, normalized by the maximum amplitude, forms the confidence. The ratio between the whistle candidate amplitude A and the current maximum amplitude A_{max} then weights the confidence. The strategy to compute the confidence of the model-based detection is shown in Eq. 1.

$$c_{pm} = \begin{cases} \dfrac{A}{A_{max}} \cdot \max\left(\left|\dfrac{\delta_{max}}{A_{max}}\right|, \left|\dfrac{\delta_{min}}{A_{max}}\right|\right), \text{ if the whistle candidate} \\ \qquad\qquad\qquad\qquad\qquad\qquad\quad \text{ is confirmed} \\ \dfrac{A}{A_{max}} \cdot \min\left(\left|\dfrac{\delta_{max}}{A_{max}}\right|, \left|\dfrac{\delta_{min}}{A_{max}}\right|\right), \text{ otherwise.} \end{cases} \tag{1}$$

Whistle recognition is especially difficult when a loud crowd and children are involved. Therefore, it is important to consider the volume and frequency that results from a crowd cheering or children. For this reason, we are introducing our noise detection. The problem is that the louder and larger the crowd that cheers is, the more frequencies become dominant. Therefore, we define our noise confidence as the ratio between the frequencies $\#f_c$ whose amplitudes exceeds a predefined limit and the number of all frequencies $\#f$, as shown in Eq. 2.

$$\sigma = \frac{\#f_c}{\#f}. \tag{2}$$

In order to further improve the accuracy of the model-based whistle recognition, we have also added an automatic calibration of the frequency range in which we search for a peak. The automatic calibration is implemented as follows: each time a whistle is detected via the combined confidence, the corresponding whistle frequency, determined via the model-based whistle recognition, is stored in a buffer. That buffer holds the last ten detected whistle frequencies because this amount of detections is sufficient to compute an estimation of the current whistle frequency. The average f_{avg} of these frequencies is then used to determine the absolute deviation of the boundaries f_{min} and f_{max} of the frequency range, used to detect the whistle candidate. Due to the hardware and environmental fluctuation of the whistle frequency, it is mandatory to maintain a certain margin for the detection of the whistle. A margin of 250 Hz allows the whistle to be detected even if it deviates more strongly from the expected whistle frequency. Equation 3 shows the update strategy of our boundaries, where the 250 Hz grants a minimum distance between the expected whistle frequency and the boundaries.

$$
\begin{aligned}
f_{min} &= \min \left(f_{avg} - \frac{|f_{avg} - f_{min}|}{2}, f_{avg} - 250\,\mathrm{Hz} \right) \\
f_{max} &= \max \left(f_{avg} + \frac{|f_{avg} - f_{max}|}{2}, f_{avg} + 250\,\mathrm{Hz} \right).
\end{aligned}
\tag{3}
$$

3.3 Combining Information

Combining all acquired information is an essential part of every ensemble. Our combination strategy is divided into two steps; the first one fuses the whistle recognition confidences, and the second one dampens the resulting confidence to consider the environmental conditions.

$$
c_{nn/pm} = \frac{w_{nn} \cdot c_{nn} + w_{pm} \cdot c_{pm}}{w_{nn} + w_{pm}}.
\tag{4}
$$

We implement the fusion of our whistle confidences $c_{nn/pm}$ by a weighted average of the individual confidences. The weights w_{nn} and w_{pm} control whether the neural net or the physical model approach is more trustworthy, so prior knowledge is also introduced at this point. Equation 4 shows this process in detail.

$$
c = c_{nn/pm} \cdot (1 - (w_\sigma \cdot \sigma)).
\tag{5}
$$

To ensure a trustworthy confidence even in different noisy environments, the fused confidence is attenuated by the sigma factor of Eq. 2. For this purpose, the fused confidence is multiplied by the sigma factor, as shown in Eq. 5.

4   Evaluation

The evaluation has several objectives: on the one hand, we compare the approach proposed here with different methods of other SPL teams and our old whistle recognition as an example of a neural network approach. On the other hand, we show the impact the three presented main components have on the whistle recognition accuracy as well as their impact on the false positive rate.

As shown in Fig. 4, we have chosen an experimental setup to compare our new approach with that of other SPL teams and our old approach. Therefore, each of the four approaches runs on a separate robot, and all robots sit close to the center line at the edge of the field. Afterwards, we disturb each robot (close) five to ten times per object with a cordless drill on different speed settings, a vacuum cleaner, and an angle grinder without whistling a whistle to see which

Fig. 4. Whistle comparison evaluation setup. Frameworks from left to right B-Human, the method presented here, our old approach and HULKs.

approach falsely detected a whistle from this kind of noise. In addition, all robots are disturbed by selected noise objects from the other half of the field (far).

We then tested how well the different approaches could detect a whistle without additional noise. To do this, we blew a whistle ten times at different intensities, from soft to loud, and from various locations on an SPL robot soccer field in a quiet environment. Subsequently, we repeated this test five to ten times, again with different intensities of the airflow through the whistle, but this time masked with noise.

In addition, we performed an ablation study on a laboratory and an event dataset, described in Sect. 2. Here, we investigate the influence of the two detection components alone, how the combination of both components affects the result, and finally, what influence the inclusion of noise has.

For the first part, we use the False Positive Rate, i.e., how many interfering noises are falsely detected as whistles, and the True Positive Rate, i.e., how many whistles are detected despite interfering noises, as a metric, with the first one being slightly more important, as described in Sect. 1. For the second part, we use precision and recall as a metric to demonstrate the influence of our approach's different factors on the resulting score.

Table 1. A comparison of how different noise from different approaches is detected as a whistle (False Positive Rate). Lower is better.

	B-Human	HULKs	Old Approach	Our
Cordless Drill Level 1	0.2	0.0	0.0	0.0
Cordless Drill Level 2	0.2	0.0	0.0	0.0
Vacuum Cleaner (close)	0.6	0.0	0.0	0.0
Angle Grinder (far)	0.0	0.0	0.0	0.0
Angle Grinder (close)	1.0	0.0	0.8	0.0

As shown in Table 1, the whistle recognition of B-Human is prone to most of our tested noise types. Our old neural network approach is vulnerable to loud noise from an angle grinder. In contrast, our approach presented here and HULKs whistle recognition is resistant against all noise types.

Table 2. A comparison of how different noise affects the performance of varying whistle recognition frameworks (True Positive Rate). Higher is better.

	B-Human	HULKs	Old Approach	Our
None	0.6	0.9	0.9	**1.0**
Vacuum Cleaner (far)	0.7	0.7	**0.9**	**0.9**
Angle Grinder (far)	**1.0**	0.2	1.0	**1.0**

The effect of different types of noise on the True Positive Rate is shown in Table 2. As the table shows, most whistle recognition approaches work well in a quiet environment. The only exception to this is the whistle recognition of B-Human. However, this can probably be attributed to the fact that the B-Human framework is not able to handle weaker whistles well. Based on this baseline, the table shows that the framework of the HULKs has problems detecting a whistle as soon as noise is involved. However, the B-Human framework also has problems recognizing the whistle next to noise. This only changes significantly with the loudest noise, the angle grinder, because only then exclusively loud whistles whistled. Only our old approach, as well as our new approach, performed similarly well in this experiment. The second objective of our evaluation is to analyze the impact of the different components of our detection approach on the result.

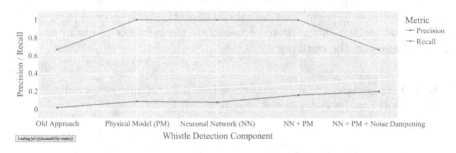

Fig. 5. Comparison of the influence of the different components of our approach on precision and recall during the Maker Faire Rome plus our old system since it proved to be promising in the previous tests.

Therefore, Figs. 5 and 6 show, from left to right, the precision and recall of our old approach, the model-based detection alone, the neural network detection alone, our whistle recognition without the noise dampening component, and our whole whistle recognition architecture.

As already discussed in Sect. 2, the Maker Faire Rome dataset is quite tricky due to the cheering crowd directly around the field. The results of this dataset are shown in Fig. 5, where our old approach has completely failed with a precision of practically zero. In contrast, our model-based method and our new neural network have a slightly higher precision on this dataset. The precision is further increased when the model-based method and the new neural network work together. The attenuation depending on the ambient noise increases the precision even further but decreases the recall.

Figure 6 shows that the precision and recall of our old approach is outperformed by every part of our new recognition method on the lab dataset, described in Sect. 2. Moreover, it is shown that the precision of our new neural network is higher than that of the model-based method, in contrast to the recall, which is higher for the model-based approach. Furthermore, it is visible that both methods together achieve a higher precision with only a slightly lower recall. When all three main components work together, the recall significantly increases while maintaining the same high precision.

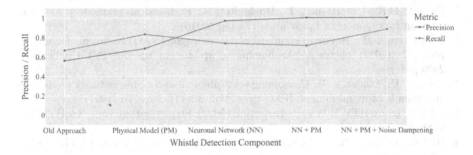

Fig. 6. Comparison of the influence of the different components of our whistle recognition on precision and recall under lab conditions plus our old system since it proved to be promising in the previous tests.

5   Conclusion and Future Work

The main goal of this work was to combine different strategies into one whistle recognizer to create a system that is more robust against various types of noise without missing whistle events. Additionally, runtime is a critical feature, especially on embedded hardware. As shown in Sect. 4, all tested approaches perform well under lab conditions. However, these conditions can't be guaranteed at all times. In addition, a varying airflow through the whistle and noise is challenging, especially in this combination. Nevertheless, we showed a significant improvement in noisy environments by combining the three described components while still creating an output in real-time. However, it would be nice to detect the third whistle on the data recorded in Rome as well, without decreasing the recall. A possible approach would be noise reduction/cancellation as a preprocessing. Another common error source are games on neighbouring fields when they are started around the same time. Right now, this difficulty is avoided by the organizers. In the future, however, it would be practical to determine the direction of the sound source.

References

1. B-Human Team: B-Human Code Release (2022). https://github.com/bhuman/BHumanCodeRelease/releases/tag/coderelease2022
2. Batista, G.E., Prati, R.C., Monard, M.C.: A study of the behavior of several methods for balancing machine learning training data. ACM SIGKDD Explor. Newsl. **6**(1), 20–29 (2004)
3. Bonarini, A., Lavatelli, D., Matteucci, M.: A composite system for real-time robust whistle recognition. In: Bredenfeld, A., Jacoff, A., Noda, I., Takahashi, Y. (eds.) RoboCup 2005. LNCS (LNAI), vol. 4020, pp. 130–141. Springer, Heidelberg (2006). https://doi.org/10.1007/11780519_12
4. Chawla, N.V., Bowyer, K.W., Hall, L.O., Kegelmeyer, W.P.: Smote: synthetic minority over-sampling technique. J. Artif. Intell. Res. **16**, 321–357 (2002)
5. Clevert, D.A., Unterthiner, T., Hochreiter, S.: Fast and accurate deep network learning by exponential linear units (ELUs) (2016)
6. Committee, R.T.: Robocup standard platform league (NAO) technical challenges, pp. 2–7 (2023). https://spl.robocup.org/wp-content/uploads/SPL-Challenges-2023.pdf
7. Forssell, U., Lindskog, P.: Combining semi-physical and neural network modeling: an example of its usefulness. IFAC Proc. Vol. **30**(11), 767–770 (1997)
8. HTWK Team: HTWK Whistle Detection (2022). https://github.com/NaoHTWK/WhistleDetection
9. HULKs Team: HULKs Code Release (2022). https://github.com/HULKs/hulk/releases/tag/coderelease2021
10. Lemaître, G., Nogueira, F., Aridas, C.K.: Imbalanced-learn: a python toolbox to tackle the curse of imbalanced datasets in machine learning. J. Mach. Learn. Res. **18**(1), 559–563 (2017)
11. Lin, T.Y., Goyal, P., Girshick, R., He, K., Dollár, P.: Focal loss for dense object detection. In: Proceedings of the IEEE International Conference on Computer Vision, pp. 2980–2988 (2017)
12. Nao Devils Team: Nao Devils Code Release (2022). https://github.com/NaoDevils/CodeRelease/releases/tag/CodeRelease2022
13. Poore, K., Abeyruwan, S., Seekircher, A., Visser, U.: Single- and multi-channel whistle recognition with NAO robots. In: Bianchi, R.A.C., Akin, H.L., Ramamoorthy, S., Sugiura, K. (eds.) RoboCup 2014. LNCS (LNAI), vol. 8992, pp. 245–257. Springer, Cham (2015). https://doi.org/10.1007/978-3-319-18615-3_20
14. Wilson, D.L.: Asymptotic properties of nearest neighbor rules using edited data. IEEE Trans. Syst. Man Cybern. (3), 408–421 (1972)
15. Wright, L.: Ranger - a synergistic optimizer (2019). https://github.com/lessw2020/Ranger-Deep-Learning-Optimizer

RoboNLU: Advancing Command Understanding with a Novel Lightweight BERT-Based Approach for Service Robotics

Sinuo Wang[1,3(✉)], Maëlic Neau[1,2,4], and Cédric Buche[1,4]

[1] CROSSING, CNRS IRL, Adelaide 2010, Australia
sinuo.wang@student.adelaide.edu.au
[2] Flinders University, Adelaide, Australia
[3] University of Adelaide, Adelaide, Australia
[4] Lab-STICC, CNRS UMR 6285, ENIB, Brest, France

Abstract. This paper proposes a novel approach to natural language understanding (NLU) in service robots called RoboNLU, which leverages pre-trained language models along with specialized classifiers to extract meaning from user commands. Specifically, the proposed system utilizes the Bidirectional Encoder Representations from Transformers (BERT) model in conjunction with slot, intent, and pronoun resolution classifiers. The model was trained on a newly created, large-scale, and high-quality GPSR (General Purpose Service Robot) command dataset, yielding impressive results in intent classification, slot filling, and pronoun resolution tasks while also demonstrating robustness in out-of-vocabulary scenarios. Furthermore, the system was optimized for real-time processing on a service robot by leveraging smaller, quantized versions of the BERT-base model and deploying the system using the ONNXruntime framework (Code and data available at https://github.com/RoboBreizh-RoboCup-Home/RoboNLU).

Keywords: Natural Language Command Understanding · BERT · Joint Slot-Filling · RoboCup@Home · Service Robotics

1 Introduction

Natural Command Understanding plays a crucial role in the field of robotics as it enables humans to interact with robots using natural language commands, without computer science or robotics prerequisite knowledge. This can make robots more accessible and user-friendly, allowing for intuitive and efficient communication between humans and machines. Natural Command Understanding involves the joint detection of the user's intentions and associated arguments, known as the task of Joint Slot-Filling in Natural Language Processing (NLP) [13]. The task is to identify the intents of the sentence and the associated information (slots) that is needed to carry out that intent.

C. Buche et al. (Eds.): RoboCup 2023, LNAI 14140, pp. 29–41, 2024.
https://doi.org/10.1007/978-3-031-55015-7_3

For instance, given the following utterance:

Go to the kitchen, leave a bowl on the storage table and a spoon in it.   (1)

the system will identify the intents such as go and put, and the task-related arguments (or slots) such as destination: kitchen and destination: storage table, object: bowl, spoon. In Service Robotics, and by extension in the RoboCup@Home competition, Joint-Slot Filing is of utmost importance as it enables any downstream modules to process formal and unambiguous information to generate an action plan and act accordingly. For instance, in the GPSR task of the RoboCup@Home, the goal is to fulfill random complex commands given in natural language by the operator, see 1.

However, there are many challenges in the learning of Natural Language Commands, such as **(1)** the inherent ambiguity of natural language and **(2)** the recognition of multiple intents in a single sentence. Regarding **(1)**, most of the user utterances are composed of multiple intents and arguments in sequences, where pronouns can be used to refer to subsequent different entities, such as the pronoun it in the example above. Traditional Joint Slot-Filling approaches in robotics [5,12,18,29] do not have pronoun disambiguation and will for instance output it as the destination slot for the intent put, leading to a strong ambiguity between storage table and bowl in 1. For **(2)**, current solutions [20,29] leverage the use of a phrase parser as a pre-processing step to break down a multi-intent sentence into a sequence of single-intent phrases. This process is efficient to process short and simple intentions but fails in more complex cases, for instance when the understanding of one intent depends on slots from a previous one [18].

Taking advantage of recent approaches in Joint-Slot Filling in NLP [2,4] and the powerful language representation of large language models such as BERT [7], we propose a novel approach, named RoboNLU, for Natural Command Understanding with pronoun disambiguation in the context of the GPSR task. Furthermore, as no existing dataset introduces pronoun annotations, we provide a novel large-scale dataset of commands annotated with fine-grained intents, slots, and pronoun references. Finally, in a set of real-world experiments, we show that our approach outperforms the state-of-the-art presented in the GPSR task by a strong margin while being faster to run. We also show the flexibility of our approach on out-of-vocabulary samples.

Our contributions can be summarized as follow:

- A new large-scale dataset of natural language commands for the task of Joint-Slot Filling with pronoun disambiguation
- A novel architecture for Joint-Slot Filling with pronoun disambiguation in natural language commands
- An ablation study on the deployment of this architecture on the constraint platform Pepper robot used in the RoboCup@Home Social Standard Platform League (SSPL)

2   Related Work

2.1   Joint-Slot Filling

In the past, conventional methods would approach the two tasks, Intention Detection (ID) [5,21] and Slot Filling (SF) [15,23,32] individually. However, more recent models that address both tasks together have shown improved performance. Utilizing the idea of multi-task learning and transfer learning, the joint model could recognise semantic relationships between intent and slots, and also alleviate the error propagation due to pipelined methods [4,11,13,14,19,33]. While these previous studies have shown promising results, they have mainly concentrated on dealing with simple single-intent situations. Their models are built on the premise that each statement contains only one single intent, but users often express multiple intents in a single statement in real life. In order to overcome the limitations of prior research, researchers proposed various methods to support multi-intent detections [2,12,24,25]. Nevertheless, there remain important issues that have yet to be fully addressed. Current multi-intent Joint Slot-Filling methods could deliver ambiguous outputs when there are two or more sub-tasks with the same semantic intent in one statement. As they only predict the semantic intent for each slot, consequently, these works fail to robustly identify the corresponding slots for each instance of the intent. This limitation is particularly evident in examples such as the two distinct tasks with the same put intent, as illustrated in 1. Furthermore, multi-intent utterances tend to consist of chains of instructions, which often leads to the co-reference of pronouns. In our work, we inherit the idea of multi-task learning and transfer learning to jointly model the relations among intent instances, slots, and also pronoun references to provide high-quality solutions to task-oriented dialogue interface.

2.2   Natural Language Command Understanding

Traditional natural language command understanding in robotics methods are rule-based grammar parsers, such as TINA [27], Gemini [8], ECG [10], which are based on formal context-free grammars and rely on a set of pre-defined rules that extract meaning from the grammatical structures. Popular approaches in service robotics [9,22] but also in the context of the RoboCup@Home [3] integrate the use of lambda-calculus to represent the user utterance in a logical form and ground it to the robot actions and world model. The theory of *frame semantics* is also used to map the input sentence into frames and arguments related to the robot world representation [1,16]. However, this kind of application is limited by the reliance on a set of pre-defined rules, and constraints to a set of specific output robotic actions. It is also inflexible in handling language constructs that deviate from standard grammatical rules or are idiomatic in nature. To mitigate these issues, later methods [20] introduced a free-form representation of user intents and slots, inspired by the popular format used in NLP, that could be further transcript into robotic action by a dedicated reasoning engine, depending on the robot platform and the context of the interaction. In this work, our goal is to follow this last direction by generating a new annotated dataset for the GPSR task and proposing the RoboNLU that transcribes complex user commands into intents and dedicated slots. As robots in the RoboCup@Home possess different capabilities, it is necessary to have a general and flexible system of intent and joint slot filling to provide a strong backbone to different kinds of reasoning engines.

3 Proposal

3.1 System Architecture

The proposed RoboNLU architecture is composed of a shared encoder and three different classifiers, see Fig. 1.

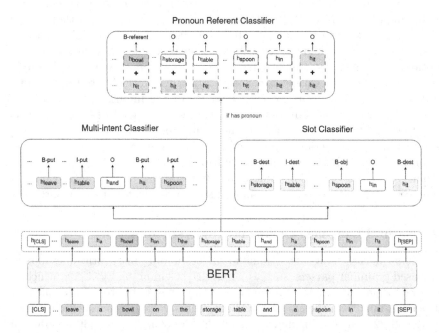

Fig. 1. Overview of our architecture composed of a shared encoder from BERT [7] (bottom), a slot classifier (right), an intent classifier (left), and a pronoun referent classifier (top). The pronoun referent classifier is activated exclusively on sentences that contain at least one pronoun, with the purpose of enhancing efficiency.

Encoder. We utilized the pre-trained language model, BERT [7], as the shared encoder in our NLU architecture. It employs self-attention to encode the relationships between different tokens within a sequence, consequently enabling the capture of complex dependencies between different parts of the text and generating contextualized embeddings of the input sentence for the downstream target tasks. We leverage the pre-trained knowledge in BERT for accomplishing the target tasks of multi-intent detection, slot classification, and pronoun disambiguation.

The input to the BERT model comprises a sequence of pre-processed token embeddings $X = (x_{cls}, x_1, x_2, \ldots, x_K, x_{sep})$, wherein each token embedding is formed by adding the word or sub-word embedding generated using the WordPiece tokenizer [31], the segment embedding, and the positional embedding. Two special tokens, [CLS] and [SEP], mark the start and end of the sentence, respectively. Following the encoding process, the output of BERT can be expressed as $H = (h_{cls}, h_1, h_2, \ldots, h_K, h_{sep})$, where $h \in \mathbb{R}^d$.

Slot Classifier and Multi-intent Classifier. Inspired by the work of JointBERT [4] and SLIM [2], we constructed an individual network for each specific downstream target task. Given a set of M possible slot labels and a set of N intent labels, the classifiers predict the probability distributions of the slot labels $y_k^s \in \mathbb{R}^M$ and intent labels $y_k^i \in \mathbb{R}^N$ for each token h_k, where $k \in \{1, \ldots, K\}$. In contracts to the intent detection approaches adopted in JointBERT [4] and SLIM [2], our method predicts the instances of the intent spans at the token level by adopting the concept of slot labeling and applying the BIO tagging scheme on the intent labels. To achieve these, each hidden embedding, h_k is fed separately into the slot classifier and the multi-intent classifier, followed by the applications of the softmax functions.

Pronoun Referent Classifier. The goal of the pronoun referent classifier is to disambiguate pronouns in sentences by identifying the antecedent tokens to which the pronoun refers. The classifier is selectively employed exclusively on sentences that comprise pronouns, such as the example given in reference 1. The proposed classifier estimates y_k^r, which indicates the probability of a given token at position k functioning as a referent. This classifier takes the concatenated embedding $h_k | h_p \in \mathbb{R}^{2d}$ as its input, where h_k represents the hidden state of the word under consideration at position k and h_p represents the hidden state of the pronoun. To represent the probability distribution, the output is transformed using the softmax function.

Multi-task Training. In our research, we adopted the concept of multi-task learning to concurrently model the associations between instances of intent, slots, and pronoun references. The overall loss is the weighted sum of the intent loss $\mathcal{L}_{CE_i}$, slot loss $\mathcal{L}_{CE_s}$, and the pronoun reference loss $\mathcal{L}_{CE_r}$, i.e.,

$$\mathcal{L}_{overall} = \alpha \mathcal{L}_{CE_i} + \beta \mathcal{L}_{CE_s} + \gamma \mathcal{L}_{CE_r}, \tag{2}$$

where the hyperparameters α, β, and γ are introduced to adjust the relative importance of each loss term during training. By adopting this approach, we jointly model the relations among intents, slots, and pronoun references to provide fine-grained solutions to task-oriented dialogue interfaces.

3.2 Implementation Details

We use the English uncased BERT-Base model, which has 12 layers, 768 hidden states, and 12 heads. The max sequence length is 32. The output layers of all three classifiers are equipped with a dropout rate of 0.1. Regarding the loss function 2, the loss weights assigned to the multi-intent detection, slot-filling, and pronoun disambiguation are set to 1, 1, and 5, respectively. The model is trained over 3 epochs, with a learning rate of 5e-5, batch size of 64, using the Adam optimizer [17].

4 Experiments

4.1 Dataset

For dataset creation, we utilized the command generator used in the RoboCup@-Home[1] and manually inserted annotations for slots, semantic intents, and pronoun references into the command grammar file. We first generated 100,000 different sentences from the Enhanced GPSR (EGPSR) task and labels using the generator. We use sentences from the EGPSR task as they are more complex and contain multiple intents. Following this, we cleansed the raw generated text by separating the labels from the command text, eliminating duplicate commands. Intent instance (task) identification within each command was accomplished by parsing the sentence by stop words, commas, and polite words. All tokens within a task span were labeled with BI-taged intent, and tokens outside of task boundaries were labeled with an intent label of 'O'. The resulting dataset consisted of 60,334 complex commands comprised of 9 different intents and 5 different slots, see Table 1. The slots classes are `object`, `source`, `destination`, `person` and `what-to-say`.

According to our dataset analysis, 54.10% of the commands in the dataset contain multiple instances of intent. Specifically, there are 30.08% commands containing multiple instances of intent but with the same semantic, such as 1. This example contains 2 different tasks of `put`, while `bowl` and `spoon` are both the object slot with the same semantic but referring to different `put` intent. Conventional methods of intent semantic labeling may cause confusion for downstream task planning by providing one `put` intent with two object slots, instead of providing the correct information of two instances of `put` intents with the object slot of `bowl` and `spoon` respectively. Additionally, multi-intent utterances tend to consist of chains of instructions, which often leads to pronoun references. It was observed that 32.08% of the command samples in the dataset have at least one pronoun reference. To support pronoun disambiguation, pronoun reference annotations were provided, such that the model would provide `bowl` instead of `it` as the destination slot in the aforementioned example 1.

---

[1] https://github.com/kyordhel/GPSRCmdGen.

Table 1. List of the different intents and associated proportions in our dataset.

Intents	greet	know	follow	take	tell	guide	go	answer	find
%	3.8	0.9	4.3	31.9	12.4	7.5	5.0	2.3	31.9

4.2 Comparison with Other Approaches

Regarding evaluation, we compared our approach with state-of-the-art models on our generated dataset. Mbot [20] has been retrained on our dataset for 5 epochs. As Mbot processes only single-intent sentences, we split our dataset using the stop-word phrase parser provided by the authors [20]. We then evaluate our model on two approaches that use the frame semantics, LU4R [1] and Grut [16]. As the format and goal of these approaches are slightly different from ours, we retrained both models using the original dataset used by the authors [30]. We then perform the evaluation on our dataset by mapping the 18 different frames and corresponding arguments used to our format of intentions and slots, following the mapping by [18]. The evaluation is performed on a set of 10,000 sentences from our test set using Accuracy for the intents, F1 for the slots, and Accuracy for the global sentence, following [2]. Sentence accuracy measures the proportion of completely accurate recognition of both slots and intents. To fairly compare with other approaches that do not perform pronoun disambiguation, we first perform the evaluation without pronoun slots.

From the results displayed in Table 2 we can see that our approach largely outperforms every other one. Mbot performs slightly well for both intents and slots whereas LU4R and Grut are having difficulties with both. This is mainly due to the mapping from *frame* objects to intents and slots that is far from optimal. For instance, frame arguments such as sough_entity from the frame Locating can be either a person or an object depending on the context. Finally, LU4R and Grut have low accuracy on our test set because they have been trained on a different dataset [30] where robotics commands are simpler than the ones generated in ours and possess a slightly different vocabulary.

Table 2. Comparison with other approaches on the test set of our generated dataset for the GPSR task. Numbers are in %.

Model	Intents Acc.	Slots F1	Full Sentence Acc.
Without pronouns			
Mbot [20]	80.87	90.28	28.3
LU4R [1]	63.58	51.40	1.3
Grut [16]	69.47	45.10	6
RoboNLU	**100**	**100**	**100**
With pronouns			
Mbot [20]	80.87	86.46	20.2
RoboNLU	**100**	**100**	**100**

These results show the advantage of our approach in processing the full sentences in an end-to-end manner. In fact, in contrast to Mbot, our architecture leverage the complex dependency between different intents at once, without splitting the utterance into single-intent phrases as a pre-processing step. On the evaluation with the pronoun disambiguation, we observed that Mbot accuracy drops consequently to the number of pronoun slots in the dataset (around 6% of the total number of slots) while our method correctly identifies all the pronoun slots as their referee. Regarding usage in the competition, Mbot is not a viable choice as it is able to fully understand only 20% of the utterance and would likely lead to a failure in the GPSR or EGPSR task.

We show a qualitative example of the advantage of our appoach in comparison to Mbot [20] in Table 3. We can see that Mbot over-predicts the `take` intent and output the pronoun as a slot, this will result in a failure to grasp the full intention and thus perform the action.

Table 3. A prediction sample from the test data of our dataset, colors indicate either an intent or a slot and corresponding arguments, in order.

Sentence	Could you please navigate to the dining room, pinpoint the orange juice, and deliver it to Jennifer
Mbot	take destination dining room, take object orange juice, take object it destination Jennifer
RoboNLU	go destination dining room, find object orange juice, take object orange juice destination Jennifer

4.3 Ablation Studies

To demonstrate the advantage of using BERT in our proposal, we conducted an evaluation of our model's performance on Out Of Vocabulary (OOV) commands. The OOV test sets comprised two distinct categories: Simple OOV and Complex OOV. The former consisted of 100 examples, which were generated using the GPSR Command Generator and involved modifications of objects, person names, and locations. Additionally, we manually created and annotated 10 domestic service robot commands that included out-of-vocabulary slots and complex utterances to further assess the model's generalization capabilities. The results of the OOV test are presented in Table 4, indicating that the model's performance remained robust in detecting intent and slot in OOV simple cases. Moreover, our observations revealed that the pronoun classifier demonstrated remarkable proficiency in accurately capturing pronoun reference relationships despite the complex variations in the different cases. The intents accuracy remains strong even in complex sentences that possess different structures than the training dataset.

Table 4. Evaluation on Out Of Vocabulary (OOV) data. Numbers are in %.

Type	Intents Acc.	Slots F1	Pronoun Acc.	Sentence Acc.
Simple	100	97.22	100	95
Complex	97.24	66.67	100	10

4.4   Real World Usage

To use our model during the RoboCup@Home competition we tested different implementations, first on a deported laptop taking advantage of latest GPU and CPU optimizations with CUDA and Pytorch. Then, we implemented our approach onboard the robot by splitting the fine-tuned BERT and the slot, intent, and pronoun classifiers. The BERT-like model inference is performed using ONNXruntime [6] while the final layers for slots, intents, and pronouns classification are implemented in plane numpy. We found out that this implementation is more optimized for the robot as well as more flexible. The original BERT-base used in our approach is unsuited for real-time processing on the robot, thus we perform different experiments with other BERT-based models. We used three different versions of the original BERT model: **(1)** the original BERT-base model [7], **(2)** DistilBERT [26], a distilled version of BERT that reduce the size of the original model by 40% while keeping 97% of its accuracy and **(3)** MobileBert [28], an optimized version of the model to run on edge devices. To further reduce the latency onboard the robot we use quantization techniques as follows: the models are first optimized using the ONNX optimization tool[2] and then the weights are quantized to Float16 and Int8 precision. We benchmark the different models' inference time on 50 commands from the test set of our dataset. We do not report the original BERT latency on the robot because the model weights are too big to be loaded on the platform. At runtime, we perform inference using the 4 available cores of the robot CPU, parallelism is managed by the ONNXruntime framework when concurrent operations are available.

Table 5 displays the results obtained, we observed that DistilBERT performs the best, followed closely by MobileBert. The main difference between DistilBert and MobileBert is the number of layers, 6 for the former and 24 for the latter as well as the hidden dim, 768 versus 512. We then observe a significant increase in the memory usage for DistilBert but no significant difference in latency on the robot hardware. This memory usage can be important in real-world scenarios as the robot only possesses 2 GB of RAM. We explain the gap between latency on the laptop CPU and the robot CPU (an average of ×37.76) by the type of hardware that does not fit anymore the recent software implementation. In fact, Pepper CPU is an x86 architecture with no AVX2 or AVX512 instructions like any recent CPU, whereas ONNX is optimized for these types of instructions.

---

[2] https://github.com/onnx/optimizer

Table 5. Inference time comparison between the different BERT models. Sentence accuracy has been computed on the full test set of our dataset.

Model	Model Size (mb)	Latency (ms)			Sen. Acc. (%)
		GPU[a]	CPU[b]	Pepper CPU[c]	
BERT [7]	440	2.63	71.98	–	100
–quant. fp16	275	6.75	176.37	5525.21	100
–quant. int8	105	21.98	47.73	3185.37	98.3
DistillBERT [26]	264	**1.66**	34.71	**654.57**	100
–quant. fp16	153	10.84	96.55	2774.27	100
–quant. int8	64	11.87	33.91	1768.53	100
MobileBERT [28]	101	8.23	35.88	1032.95	100
–quant. fp16	49	16.44	56.29	4569.35	100
–quant. int8	**25**	28.01	**33.63**	1767.89	98.3

[a] Nvidia GeForce RTX3080 8 GB
[b] 11th Gen Intel Core[TM] i7-11800H @ 2.30 GHz × 16
[c] Intel Atom[TM] E3845 @ 1.91 GHz x 4

5   Conclusion and Future Work

In this work, we presented a novel approach, named RoboNLU, that leverages the popular BERT architecture for multi-intent joint slot filling with pronoun disambiguation in the scope of natural language commands. We also propose a new large-scale and diverse dataset of natural language commands for the General Purpose Service Robot task of the RoboCup@Home competition. This dataset encompasses intents, slots, and pronoun reference annotations and can benefit the @Home and robotic community in general. Furthermore, we showed the competitive advantage of our approach against state-of-the-art solutions used in the @Home competition. Lastly, we provide an in-depth analysis of the implementation of BERT-based models on the constraint platform Pepper robot with highly limited resources. In our future work, we intend to extend the scope of our research by exploring the effectiveness of other language models and architectures for multi-intent joint slot filling with pronoun disambiguation in the context of natural language commands. Additionally, we plan to investigate the feasibility of deploying our proposed approach on resource-constrained platforms and devices, such as the Pepper robot. To achieve this goal, we will explore various techniques, including model pruning and knowledge distillation, to ensure that our approach remains effective and accurate while being deployed on such platforms.

Acknowledgment. This work benefits from the support of Britanny region.

References

1. Bastianelli, E., Croce, D., Vanzo, A., Basili, R., Nardi, D., et al.: A discriminative approach to grounded spoken language understanding in interactive robotics. In: IJCAI, pp. 2747–2753 (2016)
2. Cai, F., Zhou, W., Mi, F., Faltings, B.: SLIM: explicit slot-intent mapping with BERT for joint multi-intent detection and slot filling. In: ICASSP 2022-2022 IEEE International Conference on Acoustics, Speech and Signal Processing (ICASSP), pp. 7607–7611. IEEE (2022)
3. Chen, K., Lu, D., Chen, Y., Tang, K., Wang, N., Chen, X.: The intelligent techniques in robot *KeJia* – the champion of RoboCup@Home 2014. In: Bianchi, R.A.C., Akin, H.L., Ramamoorthy, S., Sugiura, K. (eds.) RoboCup 2014. LNCS (LNAI), vol. 8992, pp. 130–141. Springer, Cham (2015). https://doi.org/10.1007/978-3-319-18615-3_11
4. Chen, Q., Zhuo, Z., Wang, W.: BERT for joint intent classification and slot filling. arXiv preprint arXiv:1902.10909 (2019)
5. Costello, C., Lin, R., Mruthyunjaya, V., Bolla, B., Jankowski, C.: Multi-layer ensembling techniques for multilingual intent classification (2018)
6. ONNX Runtime developers: ONNX runtime. https://onnxruntime.ai/ (2021). Version: x.y.z
7. Devlin, J., Chang, M.W., Lee, K., Toutanova, K.: BERT: pre-training of deep bidirectional transformers for language understanding. arXiv preprint arXiv:1810.04805 (2018)
8. Dowding, J., et al.: GEMINI: a natural language system for spoken-language understanding. arXiv preprint cmp-lg/9407007 (1994)
9. Dzifcak, J., Scheutz, M., Baral, C., Schermerhorn, P.: What to do and how to do it: translating natural language directives into temporal and dynamic logic representation for goal management and action execution. In: 2009 IEEE International Conference on Robotics and Automation, pp. 4163–4168. IEEE (2009)
10. Eppe, M., Trott, S., Raghuram, V., Feldman, J.A., Janin, A.: Application-independent and integration-friendly natural language understanding. In: GCAI, pp. 340–352 (2016)
11. Firdaus, M., Bhatnagar, S., Ekbal, A., Bhattacharyya, P.: A deep learning based multi-task ensemble model for intent detection and slot filling in spoken language understanding. In: Cheng, L., Leung, A.C.S., Ozawa, S. (eds.) ICONIP 2018. LNCS, vol. 11304, pp. 647–658. Springer, Cham (2018). https://doi.org/10.1007/978-3-030-04212-7_57
12. Gangadharaiah, R., Narayanaswamy, B.: Joint multiple intent detection and slot labeling for goal-oriented dialog. In: Proceedings of the 2019 Conference of the North American Chapter of the Association for Computational Linguistics: Human Language Technologies, Volume 1 (Long and Short Papers), pp. 564–569 (2019)
13. Goo, C.W., et al.: Slot-gated modeling for joint slot filling and intent prediction. In: Proceedings of the 2018 Conference of the North American Chapter of the Association for Computational Linguistics: Human Language Technologies, Volume 2 (Short Papers), pp. 753–757 (2018)
14. Guo, D., Tur, G., Yih, W.T., Zweig, G.: Joint semantic utterance classification and slot filling with recursive neural networks. In: 2014 IEEE Spoken Language Technology Workshop (SLT), pp. 554–559 (2014). https://doi.org/10.1109/SLT.2014.7078634

15. Haffner, P., Tur, G., Wright, J.H.: Optimizing SVMs for complex call classification. In: 2003 Proceedings of the IEEE International Conference on Acoustics, Speech, and Signal Processing (ICASSP 2003), vol. 1, p. I-I. IEEE (2003)
16. Hromei, C.D., Croce, D., Basili, R.: Grounding end-to-end architectures for semantic role labeling in human robot interaction. In: Proceedings of the Sixth Workshop on Natural Language for Artificial Intelligence (NL4AI 2022) co-located with 21th International Conference of the Italian Association for Artificial Intelligence (AI* IA 2022) (2022)
17. Kingma, D.P., Ba, J.: Adam: a method for stochastic optimization (2017)
18. Kramer, E.R., Sáinz, A.O., Mitrevski, A., Plöger, P.G.: Tell your robot what to do: evaluation of natural language models for robot command processing. In: Chalup, S., Niemueller, T., Suthakorn, J., Williams, M.-A. (eds.) RoboCup 2019. LNCS (LNAI), vol. 11531, pp. 255–267. Springer, Cham (2019). https://doi.org/10.1007/978-3-030-35699-6_20
19. Liu, B., Lane, I.: Attention-based recurrent neural network models for joint intent detection and slot filling. arXiv preprint arXiv:1609.01454 (2016)
20. Martins, P.H., Custódio, L., Ventura, R.: A deep learning approach for understanding natural language commands for mobile service robots. arXiv preprint arXiv:1807.03053 (2018)
21. Masumura, R., Shinohara, Y., Higashinaka, R., Aono, Y.: Adversarial training for multi-task and multi-lingual joint modeling of utterance intent classification. In: Proceedings of the 2018 Conference on Empirical Methods in Natural Language Processing, pp. 633–639. Association for Computational Linguistics, Brussels (2018). https://doi.org/10.18653/v1/D18-1064, https://aclanthology.org/D18-1064
22. Matuszek, C., Herbst, E., Zettlemoyer, L., Fox, D.: Learning to parse natural language commands to a robot control system. In: Desai, J., Dudek, G., Khatib, O., Kumar, V. (eds.) Experimental Robotics. Springer Tracts in Advanced Robotics, vol. 88, pp. 403–415. Springer, Heidelberg (2013). https://doi.org/10.1007/978-3-319-00065-7_28
23. Peng, B., Yao, K.: Recurrent neural networks with external memory for language understanding. arXiv preprint arXiv:1506.00195 (2015)
24. Qin, L., Wei, F., Xie, T., Xu, X., Che, W., Liu, T.: GL-GIN: fast and accurate non-autoregressive model for joint multiple intent detection and slot filling. arXiv preprint arXiv:2106.01925 (2021)
25. Qin, L., Xu, X., Che, W., Liu, T.: AGIF: an adaptive graph-interactive framework for joint multiple intent detection and slot filling. arXiv preprint arXiv:2004.10087 (2020)
26. Sanh, V., Debut, L., Chaumond, J., Wolf, T.: DistilBERT, a distilled version of BERT: smaller, faster, cheaper and lighter. arXiv preprint arXiv:1910.01108 (2019)
27. Seneff, S.: TINA: a natural language system for spoken language applications. Comput. Linguist. **18**(1), 61–86 (1992)
28. Sun, Z., Yu, H., Song, X., Liu, R., Yang, Y., Zhou, D.: MobileBERT: a compact task-agnostic BERT for resource-limited devices. arXiv preprint arXiv:2004.02984 (2020)
29. Tada, Y., Hagiwara, Y., Tanaka, H., Taniguchi, T.: Robust understanding of robot-directed speech commands using sequence to sequence with noise injection. Front. Robot. AI **6**, 144 (2020)
30. Vanzo, A., Croce, D., Bastianelli, E., Basili, R., Nardi, D.: Grounded language interpretation of robotic commands through structured learning. Artif. Intell. **278** (2020). https://doi.org/10.1016/j.artint.2019.103181

31. Wu, Y., et al.: Google's neural machine translation system: bridging the gap between human and machine translation (2016)
32. Yao, K., Zweig, G., Hwang, M.Y., Shi, Y., Yu, D.: Recurrent neural networks for language understanding. In: Interspeech, pp. 2524–2528 (2013)
33. Zheng, Y., Liu, Y., Hansen, J.H.: Intent detection and semantic parsing for navigation dialogue language processing. In: 2017 IEEE 20th International Conference on Intelligent Transportation Systems (ITSC), pp. 1–6. IEEE (2017)

3D Multimodal Socially Interactive Robot with ChatGPT Active Listening

Katarzyna Pasternak[1]([⊠]), Christopher Duarte[1], Julio Ojalvo[1], Christine Lisetti[2], and Ubbo Visser[1]

[1] Department of Computer Science, University of Miami, Coral Gables, USA
{kwp,cduarte,jojalvo,visser}@cs.miami.edu
[2] Knight Foundation School of Computing and Information Sciences, Florida International University, Miami, USA
lisetti@cs.fiu.edu

Abstract. Independent and autonomous at-home care can solve many current societal issues. However, with increased life expectancy and the rise of aging populations, further improvements to interactive robots are needed to increase Quality-of-Life. The standalone Toyota Human Support Robot has the ability to conduct independent at-home care. However, it lacks the establishment of autonomous social behaviors. We show that, by synthesizing a 3D multi-modal social interactive agent, it is capable of performing active listening in conjunction with the physical HSR. We perform a user analysis between social behaviors of standalone HSR and proposed by us – SIA-HSR. Experimental results have shown the effectiveness of our proposed approach, enhanced user experience, and improved rapport-building with HRI.

Keywords: Human-Robot Interaction · Active listening · 3D Socially Interactive Agent · ChatGPT · Autonomous Support Robots · Multimodal Communication

1 Introduction

Given the rise of aging populations in many countries and the consequent need for independent living for older individuals and persons living with disabilities, there exists an urgent requirement for technological solutions related to at-home care. To address this issue, robotic platforms for social and assistive purposes are being designed and developed. One of these platforms is the Human Support Robot [30] (HSR) built by the Toyota Motor Corporation. A significant impediment to robot expansion into people's households is the specialized knowledge or training required for active robot use. The proposed approach is the integration of a 3D multi-modal virtual socially interactive agent (SIA) with the physical HSR, referred to as the SIA-HSR, to serve as a social extender through the detection and expression of both verbal and non-verbal cues to perform active listening.

Active listening involves "listening, engaging with, and understanding individual(s)" [24]. A practitioner of active listening must provide attention, exhibit

C. Buche et al. (Eds.): RoboCup 2023, LNAI 14140, pp. 42–53, 2024.
https://doi.org/10.1007/978-3-031-55015-7_4

reflective listening, detect and express non-verbal cues, and demonstrate empathy. It is primarily used to stimulate behavioral change in individuals through motivational interviewing, which is an empathetic, non-confrontational, and person-centered counseling approach [20,21]. An SIA is a virtually and/or physically embodied agent capable of communicating with others in a socially intelligent manner using multi-modal behaviors, specifically verbal and non-verbal cues [18]. Active listening in an SIA allows users to feel heard and understood by demonstrating attention and establishing rapport through both verbal and non-verbal behaviors.

The SIA-HSR with the inclusion of active listening is capable of both detecting and exhibiting both verbal and non-verbal behaviors. Verbal behaviors consist of appropriately spoken natural language communication through the application of speech-to-text recognition, text natural language processing, and text-to-speech audio. Non-verbal behaviors consist of physical robot gestures, movements, and autonomous object retrieval. The synthesis of both behaviors is a necessary component of the SIA-HSR as it represents a significant factor in daily human-human communication due to building understanding, trust, and rapport amongst participants. This same concept can be applied to human-robot interaction by eliminating the need for specialized knowledge and training for non-technical users through the generation of autonomous robot behaviors.

The objective of this study is to evaluate the performance of a socially interactive agent system capable of active listening in relation to human-robot interaction (HRI). We aim to answer the posed research question: Does an SIA-HSR with Active Listening social cue abilities enhance user perceptions of the SIA-HSR's social behavior (believability, usability, engagement, etc.) compared to a standalone HSR (no SIA) without Active Listening social cues?

2   Related Work

Research on social robots for establishing rapport is an ongoing topic, with various research groups investigating the synthesis of verbal [7,11] and non-verbal [22,23] behaviors for social interactions. In this regard, artificial social agents have demonstrated the capability to communicate with humans utilizing innate communication channels, such as speech, body gestures, and facial expressions, to increase user engagement with the user [3,15,27].

Reading verbal [29] and nonverbal cues [14], expressing such cues [8,13,29], exhibiting reflective listening [16], performing social gaze [2], demonstrating attention [5], and/or expressing empathy [6,10] affect the human and embodied virtual agent interaction and human-robot interaction. With the emergence of publicly available Transformer-based large language models (LLMs) [28], such as OpenAI's ChatGPT [4], Google's Bard [19,25], and Meta's LLaMa [26], generating non-scripted artificial human-like responses has become easier than ever before to produce. This paper illustrates an application of the pre-trained ChatGPT LLM as a component of the SIA-HSR for performing active listening and promoting more natural conversations within HRI.

The importance of understanding interrelations between non-verbal and verbal signals in HRI has been studied in Johal et al. [13]. Their studies found that the cues discriminating between robot conditions were mainly verbal while non-verbal cues of communication (gestures, posture, voice tone, and gaze) substituted the neutral verbal message determining the message tone. They highlight that verbal and non-verbal communication can facilitate the understanding of messages when combined appropriately.

Further, studies such as Bruce et al. [5] suggest that indicating attention with movement and having an expressive face make a robot a more interesting object of interaction. Also, robot gaze has been shown to be successful at indicating attention to people or objects, with the variation of gaze duration and frequency which affects that view of attention [1]. Per Lisetti et al. [17], an embodied conversational agent exhibits nonverbal communication by following a user's face, reflecting emotion, and anticipating if a question will be pleasant or not based on the content of the upcoming question. The mutual gaze helps with engaging the conversational partner and staying focused on the task, and in general terms, aids in building rapport.

Although there exists previous work that integrates an avatar on a robot, to the best of our knowledge no study examines how the inclusion of active listening in an SIA integrated with a robotic platform affects the user experience and HRI rapport. This is achieved through more humanistic responses and an enhanced conversational context through the inclusion of both verbal and non-verbal cues in the form of natural language processing (NLP) large language model (LLM) responses, empathy, attention, and social gaze.

3   Technical Approach

SIA-HSR is a synthesis of both a 3D virtual SIA and a service robot designed to assist individuals with disabilities and the elderly with household tasks such as cleaning or retrieving objects. The software enabling the behavior of the SIA-HSR runs using the Robot Operating System (ROS), a middleware suite to run programs called *nodes* communicate using data channels called *topics*. The hardware of the SIA-HSR includes a wide array of sensors that provide rich data of the surroundings and actuators to affect the environment based on perceived data.

Our system is composed of a ROS behavior node in union with a virtual SIA modular framework and the HSR. The inclusion of an SIA enables the creation of dynamic SIA dialogs suitable for a wide range of scenarios and the HSR allows for physical interactions with participants.

The following configuration was used: The virtual SIA was created using Unity and runs natively on the HSR, which has an Intel Core i7-4700EQ and a NVIDIA Jetson GPU. The behavior node runs on a laptop with Intel Core i7-7700HQ @ 2.80 GHz x 8 processor. Communication between the laptop and HSR was facilitated using a 5G WiFi network with an average package return time of 5 ms.

3.1   Verbal Active Listening

To enact verbal active listening conversations between participants and the SIA-HSR, a separate ROS package for verbal active listening, shown in Fig. 1, was developed and utilized in tandem with the SIA-HSR behavior node. The package utilizes Microsoft Azure's speech-to-text (STT) and text-to-speech (TTS) solutions and OpenAI's ChatGPT large language model. The participant's utterance(s) were detected and transcribed to text by the STT model, processed by ChatGPT, and NLP response spoken by the TTS model. Each conversation transaction from the user and agent (ChatGPT) response was recorded and kept as an ongoing transcript throughout the conversation. The

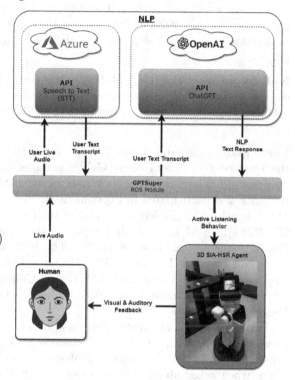

Fig. 1. Active Listening ROS Module

transcript was then included as part of each ChatGPT API prompt to allow the model to keep track of the current conversation context. The model is currently not fine-tuned for the active listening task but responses are filtered for higher relevancy within the conversation context.

3.2   Nonverbal Active Listening

The non-verbal components of active listening conversations are integrated as robot gestures within the ROS behavior node. This involves generating movements to greet the user, guide the user, retrieve objects, and signal conversation start and end. In addition, the head and eye gaze movements are incorporated within the behavior node to act as an active listening nonverbal cue aid in building rapport and generating an impression of SIA-HSR attention on the interaction participant and its awareness of its actions.

4   Experiments and Procedures

Overview. We designed two within-subject experiments based on the receptionist task from the RoboCup@Home competition [12], which are described in the following sections, to assess the impact of active listening in conversational transaction with the SIA-HSR. The study had prior Institutional Review Board (IRB) approval (no. 20230041) to conduct the experiments and discuss the results as detailed below. For the purpose of the study we establish our hypothesis as follows.

Null hypothesis H_0: The SIA-HSR with Active Listening social cue abilities does not enhance the users' perception of HSR's social behavior (believability, usability, engagement, etc.) compared to the HSR without Active Listening social cues.

Participants. Experiments were conducted with 43 participants recruited from the University of Miami Coral Gables campus with ages ranging from 18 to 64 years old. 43 participants took part in experiment A and 30 of those participants also participated in experiment B. Participants were 58.1% male and 41.9% female. The participants reported their age ranges as 18–24 (69.8%), 25–50 (27.9%), 51–64 (2.3%). They reported their race as White (81.3%), Asian (14.3%), and African Descent (4.7%). The participants reported their ethnicity as Not Hispanic/Latino (32.5%), Hispanic/Latino (67.5%). Their education level was High School Diploma (13.9%), some College (42.0%), Bachelor's Degree (16.4%), some Graduate School (6.9%), Master's Degree (13.9%), and Doctoral Degree (6.9%).

Participants also answered questions, on a 5-point Likert scale, about their previous technical experience: 6.9% claimed little experience, 23.3% had some experience, and 69.8% had a lot or professional-level experience with computers. Then, when asked about their experience with digital avatars and robots, the majority (over 62%) of participants claimed to have little or no previous experience. Thus, while most of the participants had at least some experience with computers most had little to no experience with virtual agents or robots.

Procedure. Participants were recruited on the university campus by staff members who verbally asked if they would like to participate in a study where they would interact with the SIA-HSR. Prior to the experiments, participants were asked to complete a consent form and demographics questionnaire. They were then briefed about the conversational and nonverbal behavior skills of the SIA-HSR. Both experiments were conducted using the SIA-HSR cf. Fig. 1. The SIA-HSR moved within the RoboCanes lab room to conduct the experiments. In both experiments, participants started at the entrance of the RoboCanes lab and were asked to follow the SIA-HSR to a seating area where the agent would be tasked to complete drink retrieval and then verbally interact with participants. The independent variable is the inclusion of the 3D virtual SIA with active listening on the HSR. We randomly alternated which experiment was performed first between participants to avoid a learning effect.

After each completed experiment, each participant responded to a statement regarding the interaction using a 7-point Likert-scale ranging from −3 (strongly disagree) to 3 (strongly agree) which were based on a validated questionnaire [9] created for evaluating artificial social agent interactions. The chosen statements for evaluation were the following:

S1   The SIA-HSR acts naturally.
S2   The SIA-HSR is easy to use.
S3   I like the SIA-HSR.
S4   The SIA-HSR interacts socially with me.
S5   The SIA-HSR is characterless.
S6   I can see myself using the SIA-HSR in the future.
S7   It is interesting to interact with the SIA-HSR.
S8   The interaction captured my attention.
S9   The SIA-HSR understands me.
S10 The SIA-HSR remains focused on me throughout the interaction.
S11 The SIA-HSR knows what it is doing.
S12 The SIA-HSR reciprocates my actions.

Experiment A. The SIA-HSR, with the 3D virtual SIA included, greeted the guest at the starting position of the RoboCanes lab door entrance, guided the guest to the seating area, retrieved drinks for guests, if desired, and, finally, conversed with the guest in the seating area using ChatGPT LLM verbal responses. Conversation transactions were handled through the verbal active listening ROS module enabling conversation up to five transactions. The active listening module of the SIA-HSR was evaluated via user statement(s) response after the procedure was completed.

Experiment B (Control). The SIA-HSR, without the 3D virtual SIA included, greeted the guest at the starting position of the RoboCanes lab door entrance, guided the guest to the seating area, retrieved drinks for guests, if desired, and finally, conversed with the guest(s) in the seating area using pre-defined verbal responses. The SIA-HSR did not provide responses to participants during the seating area conversation portion beyond a verbal opening and closing statement.

5   Results and Discussion

Our results consist of a total of 43 survey participants that interacted with experiment A. Out of this total, 30 participants interacted with the SIA-HSR in both experiment A and experiment B. The participants responded to the 12 questionnaire statements after each experiment to evaluate SIA-HSR performance. The mean participant evaluation based on all responses and the mean difference of each participant's response from experiment A to B (A - B) are shown in Table 1.

Table 1. Average of all survey results for experiments A, B, and difference between the two (A-B). * out of 43 participants, ** out of 30 participants ($\bar{x}$ and σ).

Survey Question	Avg. A*	Avg. B**	Avg. A-B**
SIA-HSR acts naturally	0.95 (1.32)	0.19 (1.33)	0.75
SIA-HSR is easy to use	1.86 (1.11)	1.13 (1.33)	0.84
I like SIA-HSR	2.09 (1.29)	1.53 (1.83)	0.5
SIA-HSR interacts socially with me	2.04 (0.83)	0.10 (1.81)	1.97
SIA-HSR is characterless	−1.07 (1.44)	0.57 (1.52)	−1.34
I can see myself using SIA-HSR in the future	1.37 (1.48)	0.57 (1.74)	0.91
It is interesting to interact with SIA-HSR	2.37 (0.99)	1.60 (1.35)	0.63
The interaction captured my attention	2.26 (1.18)	1.76 (1.27)	0.53
SIA-HSR understands me	0.51 (1.87)	−0.27 (1.81)	0.97
SIA-HSR remains focused on me [...]	1.72 (1.32)	0.70 (1.67)	0.88
SIA-HSR knows what it is doing	1.07 (1.48)	0.13 (1.66)	1.09
SIA-HSR reciprocates my actions	0.19 (1.69)	−0.27 (1.74)	0.63

Experiment B (control) results amongst participants are shown in Fig. 2. There was an 83% approval of the SIA-HSR capturing participant attention and 70% agreement that the SIA-HSR maintained focus throughout the interaction. Only 50% of the participants felt that the SIA-HSR engaged in social interactions and less than 47% agreed that the agent

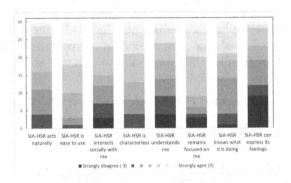

Fig. 2. Experiment B Questions.

acted naturally. *Experiment A*, results shown in Fig. 3, scored a higher approval rating compared to the control. 93% of the participants agreed that the SIA-HSR captured their attention, 91% agreed that the SIA-HSR retained focus on them through the interaction, and 70% of the participants agreed that the SIA-HSR acted more naturally as opposed to 50% agreement for experiment B. The most significant outcome was from the statement "the SIA-HSR interacted socially" which received a 95% agreement among participants with 0.83 standard deviations.

Between 13 participants that only took part in experiment A and 30 participants that took part in both experiment A and B, we noticed a difference of 0.34 point on average in results in experiment A which account for a 5.6% difference on a 7-point Likert scale. Although the 13-participant sample is not large, it hints at no bias between the inclusion of the avatar and a lack thereof.

When comparing the results of 30 participants that took part in both experiments, A and B, as shown in Fig. 4, a majority of participants (77%) found the interaction with the SIA-HSR to be more social when active listening was present. Only 6 participants (20%) found no difference in the social aspect of the interactions between A and B, and only one (3%) found that having active lis-

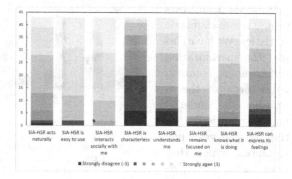

Fig. 3. Experiment A Questions.

tening was detrimental to interaction. Furthermore, 60% of the participants commented that they felt that the SIA-HSR understood them more when active listening was present, as opposed to 13% in the scripted interaction during experiment B - while 27% found no difference amongst experiments.

There was an improvement in the social robot's behavior among 17 of the 30 participants (57%), for which the natural behavior of the robot with active listening was present. 23% noticed no difference, and 20% believed that active listening on the SIA-HSR had a detrimental impact. According to 18 participants (60%), active listening module made the SIA-HSR easier to use, where 33% found no change, and 7% believed the agent was easier to use without active listening. The "SIA-HSR is characterless" statement saw a positive evaluation shift among 63% of the sample population, with participants finding active listening provided character to the agent. Seven participants (23%) found no difference between experiments A and B, and 13% agreed that the inclusion of active listening made the agent more characterless.

Equally significant was the attention and, more precisely, the perception of human subjects of the SIA-HSR's focus on them. While 17% found a lack of active listening to be more favorable for receiving attention, 57% preferred to have active listening as an avenue of receiving attention from the agent. 27% of the participants indicated no difference between interactions. With the inclusion of active listening, 18 participants (60%) found that the SIA-HSR had a heightened awareness of its actions. For 23% presence of active listening made no difference, and 5 participants (17%) found it hindering the overall experience. 77% of the participants found the SIA-HSR more expressive of its feelings in interactions using active listening. While 13% found no change in the matter, only 3 participants (10%) saw a negative influence on the expressiveness of feelings by the active listening agent.

Our null hypothesis is that there is no significant difference in means between the experiments, specifically between the presence of a 3D virtual avatar with active listening and the absence of any 3D virtual agent.

50   K. Pasternak et al.

Our data suggests using non-parametric statistics. We have chosen the permutation test over a common t-test because the t-test has the underlying assumption that the data have equal variances, which they have not. We performed a large number

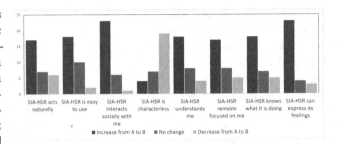

Fig. 4. Comparison between A and B.

of permutations (10,000) by randomly shuffling the combined dataset and dividing it into two new groups of the same size as the original groups. The resulting p-value is 0.013 which is less than our significance level of 0.05.

Thus, we can reject the null hypothesis and conclude that an SIA-HSR with active listening enhances user perceptions of the SIA-HSR's social behavior compared to a standalone HSR without active listening.

Overall, the described results corroborate that the inclusion of active listening in the SIA-HSR results in better overall user experience and increased rapport in HRI. These are the following statements receiving the highest scores for experiment A (w/ active listening) as illustrated in Table 1: "It is interesting to interact with the SIA-HSR", "The interaction captured my attention", "I like SIA-HSR", "SIA-HSR interacts socially with me", and "SIA-HSR is easy to use". All of these statements (in addition to others present in the table) received positive scores for experiment A individually and positive scores when compared against experiment B (Avg. A-B). When comparing against the control, all participants favored and preferred the procedure with active listening. This signifies that the inclusion of active listening generated an overall better user experience for participants.

Although the obtained results have satisfied the objective of this study, there still exist areas for improvement. These include diversifying and increasing the size of the sample population to reduce bias, diminishing inaccuracies produced by the behavior software, and finding workarounds for the hardware limitations of the HSR. Improvements in these areas are expected to result in better overall feedback when compared to the findings presented in the paper.

The video demonstration of selected fragments of the study experiments can be found at www.tinyurl.com/36kn8fyj.

6   Conclusion

The SIA-HSR serves a critical role in providing at-home care for aging individuals and those suffering from disabilities. A significant hurdle for active use of social robots is the technical expertise needed to operate them, this necessitates the creation of autonomous behaviors. The objective of this study was to evaluate the performance of the SIA-HSR capable of active listening as a means of building rapport with the user during human-robot interaction.

The study was composed of two experiments: the first would engage participants in the interaction with SIA-HSR skilled in active listening, while the second served as a control to compare the feedback on the interaction where the SIA component was disabled and the active listening module was replaced by scripted communication. The experiments revealed that, in general, the SIA-HSR with active listening enhanced user perceptions of the HSR's social behavior compared to the standalone HSR without active listening.

Occasionally, however, inaccurate responses of verbal behavior contradicted user expectations of how the system should behave and thus left a negative impression of the interaction. One potential explanation for the SIA-HSR's inaccurate verbal behavior is the limitation of the hardware such as the microphone's capability to register sound. Another is the different accents amongst participants which might make the intention harder to recognize. For future work, we plan on using an additional external microphone placed closer to or worn by the user which should partially eliminate erroneous transcriptions and therefore responses. Also, the extended response times where there was a prolonged silence after the prompt from the user had an observed negative and frustrating effect on the participants. For future work, we plan to reduce the response time and provide a smoother interaction, while retaining the user's attention throughout the experiment.

An additional novel finding from the study, learned through follow-up questions after the completed experiments, was that a participant's point of focus on the SIA-HSR depended on the presence of the virtual avatar. Regardless of their demographics and previous experience with robots and virtual avatars, participants would focus their attention on the robot's display and define it as a face of the SIA-HSR throughout experiment A, while during experiment B, participants would consider the robotic head, with two round stereoscopic cameras as eyes, as the robot's face and center their attention there during the interaction. This phenomenon is another topic we would like to investigate further and see how it might affect people's attitudes toward the SIA-HSR.

References

1. Admoni, H., Hayes, B., Feil-Seifer, D., Ullman, D., Scassellati, B.: Are you looking at me? Perception of robot attention is mediated by gaze type and group size. In: 2013 8th ACM/IEEE International Conference on Human-Robot Interaction (HRI), pp. 389–395. IEEE (2013)
2. Admoni, H., Scassellati, B.: Social eye gaze in human-robot interaction: a review. J. Hum.-Rob. Interact. 6(1), 25–63 (2017)
3. Breazeal, C.: Toward sociable robots. Robot. Auton. Syst. 42(3), 167–175 (2003). Socially Interactive Robots
4. Brown, T.B., et al.: Language models are few-shot learners (2020)
5. Bruce, A., Nourbakhsh, I., Simmons, R.: The role of expressiveness and attention in human-robot interaction. In: Proceedings 2002 IEEE International Conference

on Robotics and Automation (Cat. No. 02CH37292), vol. 4, pp. 4138–4142. IEEE (2002)

6. Charrier, L., Rieger, A., Galdeano, A., Cordier, A., Lefort, M., Hassas, S.: The rope scale: a measure of how empathic a robot is perceived. In: 2019 14th ACM/IEEE International Conference on Human-Robot Interaction (HRI), pp. 656–657. IEEE (2019)

7. Dieter, J., Wang, T., Chaganty, A.T., Angeli, G., Chang, A.: Mimic and rephrase: reflective listening in open-ended dialogue. In: Proceedings of the 23rd Conference on Computational Natural Language Learning (CoNLL), pp. 393–403 (2019)

8. Ekman, P.: An argument for basic emotions. Cogn. Emot. **6**(3/4), 169–200 (1992)

9. Fitrianie, S., Bruijnes, M., Li, F., Abdulrahman, A., Brinkman, W.P.: The artificial-social-agent questionnaire: establishing the long and short questionnaire versions. In: Proceedings of the 22nd ACM International Conference on Intelligent Virtual Agents, pp. 1–8 (2022)

10. Gonsior, B., et al.: Improving aspects of empathy and subjective performance for HRI through mirroring facial expressions. In: 2011 RO-MAN, pp. 350–356. IEEE (2011)

11. Grigore, E.C., Pereira, A., Zhou, I., Wang, D., Scassellati, B.: Talk to me: verbal communication improves perceptions of friendship and social presence in human-robot interaction. In: Traum, D., Swartout, W., Khooshabeh, P., Kopp, S., Scherer, S., Leuski, A. (eds.) IVA 2016. LNCS (LNAI), vol. 10011, pp. 51–63. Springer, Cham (2016). https://doi.org/10.1007/978-3-319-47665-0_5

12. Hart, J., et al.: RoboCup@Home 2022: rules and regulations (2022). www.athome.robocup.org/rules/2022 rulebook.pdf

13. Johal, W., Calvary, G., Pesty, S.: Non-verbal signals in HRI: interference in human perception. In: ICSR 2015. LNCS (LNAI), vol. 9388, pp. 275–284. Springer, Cham (2015). https://doi.org/10.1007/978-3-319-25554-5_28

14. Kim, J.: Bimodal emotion recognition using speech and physiological changes. Robust Speech Recogn. Underst. **265**, 280 (2007)

15. Kirby, R., Forlizzi, J., Simmons, R.: Affective social robots. Robot. Auton. Syst. **58**(3), 322–332 (2010)

16. Kobayashi, Y., Yamamoto, D., Koga, T., Yokoyama, S., Doi, M.: Design targeting voice interface robot capable of active listening. In: 2010 5th ACM/IEEE International Conference on Human-Robot Interaction (HRI), pp. 161–162. IEEE (2010)

17. Lisetti, C., Amini, R., Yasavur, U.: Now all together: overview of virtual health assistants emulating face-to-face health interview experience. KI-Kunstliche Intell. **29**(2), 161–172 (2015)

18. Lugrin, B., Pelachaud, C., Traum, D. (eds.): The Handbook on Socially Interactive Agents: 20 Years of Research on Embodied Conversational Agents, Intelligent Virtual Agents, and Social Robotics Volume 1: Methods, Behavior, Cognition, vol. 37, 1 edn. Association for Computing Machinery, New York (2021)

19. Manyika, J.: Google Bard. https://ai.google/static/documents/google-aboutbard.pdf

20. Miller, W.R., Rollnick, S.: Motivational Interviewing: Helping People Change, 3rd edn. Guilford Press (2013)

21. Resnicow, K., McMaster, F.: Motivational interviewing: moving from why to how with autonomy support. Int. J. Behav. Nutr. Phys. Act. **9**, 19 (2012)

22. Riek, L.D., Paul, P.C., Robinson, P.: When my robot smiles at me: enabling human-robot rapport via real-time head gesture mimicry. J. Multimodal User Interfaces **3**(1), 99–108 (2010)

23. Ritschel, H., Aslan, I., Mertes, S., Seiderer, A., Andre, E.: Personalized synthesis of intentional and emotional non-verbal sounds for social robots. In: 2019 8th International Conference on Affective Computing and Intelligent Interaction (ACII), pp. 1–7. IEEE (2019)
24. Rogers, C.R., Farson, R.E.: Active listening. Organ. Psychol. (1984)
25. Thoppilan, R., et al.: LaMDA: language models for dialog applications (2022)
26. Touvron, H., et al.: LLaMA: open and efficient foundation language models (2023)
27. Ulhoi, J.P., Norskov, S.: The emergence of social robots: adding physicality and agency to technology. J. Eng. Tech. Manage. **65**, 101703 (2022)
28. Vaswani, A., et al.: Attention is all you need (2017)
29. Wuth, J., Correa, P., Nunez, T., Saavedra, M., Yoma, N.B.: The role of speech technology in user perception and context acquisition in HRI. Int. J. Soc. Robot. **13**, 949–968 (2021)
30. Yamamoto, T., Terada, K., Ochiai, A., Saito, F., Asahara, Y., Murase, K.: Development of human support robot as the research platform of a domestic mobile manipulator. ROBOMECH J. **6**(1), 4 (2019)

Human Presence Probability Map (HPP): A Probability Propagation Based on Human Flow Grid

Jacques Saraydaryan[1,3](✉), Fabrice Jumel[1,3], and Olivier Simonin[2,3]

[1] CPE Lyon, Villeurbanne, France
jacques.saraydaryan@cpe.fr
[2] INSA Lyon, Villeurbanne, France
[3] CITI Lab., INRIA-INSA Chroma team, Villeurbanne, France

Abstract. Personal assistance, delivery services, and crowd navigation through robots fleet are complex activities that involve human-robot interaction and fleet coordination. Human location estimation is one of the key factors in assisting robots in their tasks. This paper proposes an efficient process for propagating human presence probability based on partial observation of humans by the robot fleet. This process provides real-time information about the most probable region on the map where humans can be found.

We propose a new problem representation allowing us to efficiently parallelize the propagation. To deal with the learned model and the real time robot observations, we propose to include a gaussian rotation probability process (VonMises [11]) combined with the previous learned observation to adapt the propagation. A set of experiments has been conduced with simulated environments that include real data allowing us to evaluate the model and to compare with the standard approaches.

1 Introduction

Building robotic systems that can interact with humans remains a challenging task today. Knowledge about human behavior is crucial to develop human-acceptable and safe solutions. Navigating in populated environments or serving humans through robot fleets requires to understand human motion.

In this paper, we propose a scalable method to predict human motions in a closed environment from the observations colleted by a fleet of robots along the time. According to [14] our approach aims at computing human presence probability at middle term (>10 s). Indeed, middle term prediction is particularly important for robot fleet tasks achievements, where a robot could benefit of other robots observation to adapt its behavior and decision. In other words, we build a Human Presence Probability Map from robot observations.

We build our approach over an existing discrete human orientation probability map [5], called Flow Grid Map, similar to [9,19]. Then we are able to propagate online human observation information which is exploited by robots to navigate efficiently and to find humans in order to serve them.

© The Author(s), under exclusive license to Springer Nature Switzerland AG 2024
C. Buche et al. (Eds.): RoboCup 2023, LNAI 14140, pp. 54–65, 2024.
https://doi.org/10.1007/978-3-031-55015-7_5

The Fig. 1 shows an example of Human presence probability propagation on an entire closed environment. Here, an existing flow grid is used to help the propagation. Each time a robot detects a human, the algorithm begins to propagate the information. The cumulative information through all robot observations results in a map highlighting the probability to meet pedestrian.

This paper is organized as follows: Sect. 2 describes related works in human flow modeling and human motion trajectory prediction. The Sect. 3 explains Human flow grid models used as computation baseline. The Sect. 4 describes our human presence probability propagation computation and associated optimizations. Finally, the Sect. 5 shows experiments and results.

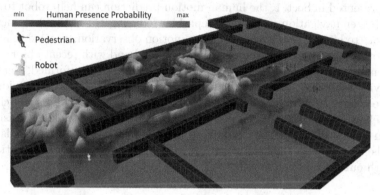

Fig. 1. HPP Map representation on closed environment

2   Related Work

Human motion prediction get a growing interest recent years. Human motion prediction could be divided into two different objectives: short term prediction (1–2 s) and long term prediction (up to 20 s) [14]. Moreover Rudenko and al. [14] propose to distinguish different kind of modeling approaches. **Physics-based modeling** aims at simulating a set of explicitly defined dynamics equation that follow a physics-inspired model. Such methods predicts human motion after sensing the environment and are mostly used in short term prediction (e.g. [7]). **Planning based** methods are more focused on long-term motion. After sensing the environment, hypothesis are used to estimate path used by human to reach their goals. Finally, **Pattern-base methods** intents to learn motion model after sensing the environment. This kind of methods (sequential methods) could learn conditional models over time and recursively apply learned transitional function for inference or model the distribution over full trajectories. In this paper we particularly focus on Pattern-based approaches and especially sequential methods. In such approaches conditional models are learned from observation and mainly used Markov models. Some works intends to model local transition such as probabilities of transition between cells on a grid map [5,8,12]. Other methods use Recurrent Neural Networks (RNN) or Long Short-term Memory (LSTM) to learn sequence of motions. Such recent methods gives good result especially on short therm prediction [20], nevertheless lots of data is needed for training such network and computed models are sensitive to motion habits changes. Other interesting approaches compute clusters on observed trajectories to predict human motion [4,21]. Despite very good prediction results, these methods suffers of same limitation as RNN or LSTM approaches. Moreover, most these methods needs either a complete trajectory monitoring (e.g. start and goal position of pedestrian) or a capacity to re-identify pedestrian. Such constraints do not fit our current hypotheses of partial pedestrian observation thought a robot fleet.

As presented in Sect. 1, the human motion prediction can help robot to compute a better navigation (socially acceptable, reducing travel time) or increase the service to human. With partial human motion observation, we need to inform the robots about human motion with learned trend and with recent observation. Furthermore, the more the map used for navigation will be informed, the more the service to human efficiency will increase. Such information is precious to help the robots to navigate [3,15]. This kind of hypotheses reduces the choose of modeling approaches. We choose to improve methods modeling transitions between cells with an efficient probability propagation process. We extends such methods [5,8,12] with the help of both learned trends and recent observation to deal with our context constraints.

3   Flow Grid Reminder

The authors in [5] defined a map reflecting the probability to meet a human with a certain direction. This map is computed as follows.

In each cell $c_{x,y}$, we discretize the possible flow directions by a set of K directions, and we note $k_i \in K$ each direction[1]. For instance, we can set $K = \{North, NorthEast, ..., South\}$. We note Z^t the set of observation performed by all the robots up to time t. An observation, in a cell $c_{x,y}$, consists in identifying a human direction, eventually none, and its duration. By hypothesis, only one human can occupy a cell at a given time. In practice, we consider cell sizes from 0,25 m² to 1 m².

Let note $R = r_1, r_2, ..., r_n$ the set of robots. We note $t_{c_{x,y}(r)}$ the sum of the durations of all observation (human observed or not) performed by the robot r on cell $c_{x,y}$. $t_{c_{x,y,k}(r)}$ is the sum of durations of the observation of a human moving in direction k in cell $c_{x,y}$.

We set $M_{flow} = \forall x \forall y \forall k (M_{c_{x,y,k}})$ the grid of human motion likelihood in every direction k of each cell $c_{x,y}$, called **Flow grid**. By considering that human flows are stationary processes, each cell value is computed (updated) as follows:

$$M_{c_{x,y,k}}(Z^t) = \frac{\sum_{n=1}^{|R|} t_{c_{x,y,k}}(r_n)}{\sum_{n=1}^{|R|} t_{c_{x,y}}(r_n)} \tag{1}$$

---

[1] When a robot detects a human in x, y pose with θ orientation $z_{x,y,\theta}$, we approximate the orientation θ to a discrete orientation k.

To deal with non stationary processes a forgetting factor could be added as is was done in [15]. By extension, the probability to meet a pedestrian in a given cell is defined by:

$$M_{pres_{c_{x,y}}}(Z^t) = \sum_{k \in K} M_{c_{x,y,k}}(Z^t) \tag{2}$$

The Flow grid could be extended if the probabilities is related to some hour of the day and day of a week as its was suggested in [19]. Thus, the likelihood to meet a human in a given orientation k is noted $M_{c_{x,y},k}^{t_{day}}$ where t_{day} represents the likelihood at a given day/week time (e.g. Monday 10h12).

4 Human Presence Probability Map (HPP Map)

4.1 Basic Computation

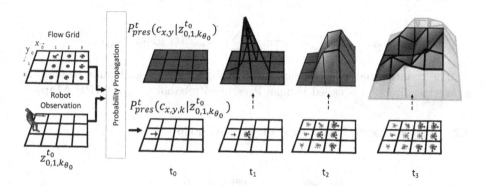

Fig. 2. Example of human presence probability propagation

Once we are able to compute information about human flow, as it was explained in Sect. 3, we have to provide a method to propagate pedestrian presence probability when these ones have been detected by robots.

To do so, we assume that this likelihood $M_{c_{x,y},k}$ gives us a transition probability between the current cell $c_{x,y}$ and the neighbor cell targeted by the given orientation k. E.g if k means north, an current cell is $c_{1,1}$, $M_{c_{1,1},North} \equiv P(c_{1,1} \rightarrow c_{0,1})$.

Without additional information finding the most likelihood human presence on a given direction could be expressed such as: $argmax(M_{c_{x,y},k})$.

This information only takes into account human presence flow model and not recent/current human observation. In order to predict the human position in next seconds and more, we have to combine pre-computed human flow grid and current set of observation.

A common probability propagation could be expressed as follows:

For each neighbor cells around the discrete observation z_{x,y,k_θ}^t, let note $P_{pres}^{t+1}(c_{x_1,y_1,k})$ the probability to meet the previously observed human on the cell c_{x_1,y_1} at $t+1$ with the orientation k.

$$P_{pres}^{t+1}(c_{x_1,y_1,k}|z_{x_0,y_0,k_\theta}^t) = \frac{M_{c_{x_1,y_1,k}}}{\sum_{i=1}^{||K||} M_{c_{x_1,y_1,k_i}}} \times \alpha \times P_{pres}^t(c_{x_0,y_0,k_c}|z_{x_0,y_0,k_\theta}^t)$$

(3)

where k_c is the orientation pointing to the current cell c_{x_1,y_1}, k_θ is the approximated orientation θ of the observation, $P_{pres}^t(c_{x_0,y_0,k_c}|z_{x_0,y_0,k_\theta}^t) = 1$ if $k_\theta = k_c$, 0 otherwise and $\alpha \in [0;1]$ represents a stationary coefficient.

The Fig. 2 illustrates this principle. On the left we find input data, the learnt flow grid and a robot observation. The probability propagation process is represented from t_0 to t_3. On the bottom, the likelihood of pedestrian presence over the time is represented. Each blue arrow on each cell defines the probability to meet human in a given direction. The total probability to meet a human on each cell is represented on the top.

For a set of observation occurring at different times, noted $Z^{1:t}$, each cell accumulates the propagated probability of each observation:

$$P_{pres}^t(c_{x,y,k}|Z^{1:t}) = \frac{1}{||Z^{1:t}||} \sum_{i=1}^{||Z^{1:t}||} P_{pres}^t(c_{x,y,k}|z_{x_i,y_i,k_{\theta_i}}^{t_i})$$

(4)

The resulted matrix representing the probability to meet human moving in a targeted direction is called Human Presence Probability Map (**HPP Map**).

4.2   Scalability and Propagation Optimization

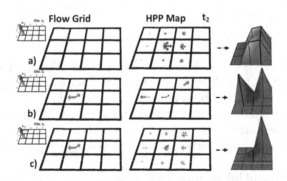

Fig. 3. Von Mises propagation optimisation: a) no information is held by the flow grid map, Von Misies coefficient are used to propagate, b) flow grid held information, propagation only used flow grid, c) both flow grid and Von Mises Coeff are used

To make easier the parallelization of the computation, we propose to reformulate the problem as follows: On one side, at a time t, a cell get the sum of cumulative probability from a set of observation $Z^{1:t}$. On the other side, the cell contributes to the probability propagation to neighbors cells. We propose to formulate the probability of presence of a human in a given cell as follows:

$$
P_{pres}^t(c_{x,y,k}|Z^{1:t}) = \frac{\alpha \times M_{c_{x,y,k}}}{\sum_{i=1}^{\|K\|} M_{c_{x,y,k_i}}} \times \sum_{j=1}^{\|N(c_{x,y})\|} P_{pres}^{t-1}(c_{x_j,y_j},k_c|Z^{1:t})
$$
$$
+ (1-\alpha) \times P_{pres}^{t-1}(c_{x,y,k}|Z^{1:t}) \qquad (5)
$$

where $\|N(c_{x,y})\|$ is the cardinality of neighbourhood of $c_{x,y}$, $\sum_{j=1}^{\|N(c_{x,y})\|} P_{pres}^{t-1}$ $(c_{x_i,y_i},k_c|Z^{1:t})$ represents the probability propagation of each neighbors cells and $(1-\alpha) \times P_{pres}^{t-1}(c_{x,y,k}|Z^{1:t})$ the previous cell value minus the current cell propagation effort to neighbor cells.

Such reformulation allows massive parallelization. At t each HPP Map cells could computes its $t+1$ value without waiting computation from neighbors. This property allows a GPU implementation of the HPP Map computation.

Moreover, some flow grid cell could be uninformed, meaning that no observation has been made in flowgrid map. In such situation, we assume that human motion follows a Gaussian orientation change model as described by Von Mises equation such as: $VonMises(\theta_k, \theta_{k_{ref}}) = \frac{e^{Ccos(\theta_k - \theta_{k_{ref}})}}{2\pi I_0(C)}$ where $\frac{1}{C} = \sigma^2$ and θ_k and $\theta_{k_{ref}}$ represents the angle of a given orientation (e.g. if K means North, $\theta_k = \frac{\pi}{2}$) respectively for a given orientation and a referent orientation. I_0 is the modified Bessel function of order 0.

Thus, for uninformed flow grid cell, the probability propagation could be defined as:

$$
P_{pres}^{t+1}(c_{x_1,y_1,k}|z_{x_0,y_0,\theta}^t) = VonMises(\theta_k, \theta_{k_c}) \times \alpha \times P_{pres}^t(c_{x_0,y_0,k_c}|z_{x_0,y_0,k_\theta}^t) \quad (6)
$$

The Fig. 3.a shows an example of application.

The flowgrid maps give a trend of human motion. In some situation, some observation not fit computed model. E.g if an observation was made from a cell to a given direction, if the targeted cell contains high probabilities to go back to the current cell, the system would not take into account the characteristic of the current observation. To avoid such behavior, we propose to use again the Von Mises function to combine current observation motion and human motion trends. This approach will temper probability propagation by combining the current observation and the learnt flow grid map. The resulting value is expressed as follows:

$$
P_{pres}^{t+1}(c_{x_1,y_1,k}|z_{x_0,y_0,\theta}^t) = \frac{VonMises(\theta_k, \theta_{k_c}).M_{c_{x,y,k}}}{\sum_{i=1}^{\|K\|} M_{c_{x,y,k_i}}}
$$
$$
\times \alpha \times P_{pres}^t(c_{x_0,y_0,k_c}|z_{x_0,y_0,k_\theta}^t) \qquad (7)
$$

The Fig. 3 shows an example of propagation using such equation. In the Fig. 3b situation only flow grid information is used to propagate probability. In such case half of probability is send back to the cell where the observation was made. Such behavior means that the human has 50 per cent to half turn. In the Fig. 3c case, we apply Von Mises coefficients to prioritize ongoing moves, reflecting a more realistic propagation.

5   Experimentation

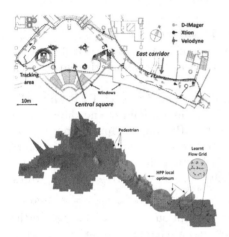 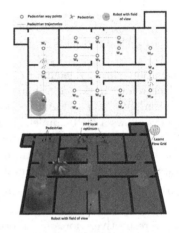

Fig. 4. Real ATC scenario. On the top, the original configuration scenario as mentioned in [2]. On the bottom, the scenario played with 3 robots following Hamiltonian path, flow grid learning and HPP computation

Fig. 5. Museum Scenario (Artificial Scenario). On the top, the scenario map and the set of way points following by 2 pedestrian groups. On the bottom, the scenario played with 4 robots following Hamiltonian path, flow grid learning and HPP computation

Our first series of experiments was made on a simulated environment using the ROS version of Pedsim simulator [1]. This experiment involved 50 pedestrians walking through pre-defined trajectories (Fig. 5). The environment is composed of several corridors and rooms. In this experiment case, we want to highlight the performance improvement of computing Human Presence Probability propagation with a standard implementation with python and numpy, and a GPU implementation using Numba [10]. For experimentation, we use the flow grid described in our previous worked [5]. In this scenario, 4 robots allowing wide-ranging observations (360° field of view with a range of 3 m) navigate across the environment according Hamiltonian path [13] (optimising the space coverage). Thus the robot fleet covers the environment and updates the human presence (z_{x,y,k_θ^t}) when a pedestrian is met (in the robot field of view). We assumed that probabilities coming on map walls are removed. This experiment was conducted during 800 seconds. The experiment was made on a laptop i7, 9th gen., 16Go RAM, graphic card NVIDIA Quatro T1000. With an average processing time of 1.632 s (to propagate the HPP of the entire environment at each processing step) for the standard implementation and 0.052 s for the GPU implementation, this gain of more than 30 times make the usage of the HPP map computing online realistic (Fig. 4).

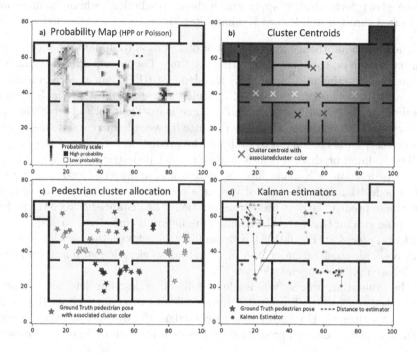

Fig. 6. Pedestrian position prediction evaluation steps

During this scenario, most probable regions to meet people are clustered (HPP clusters) and human position ground truth is used to evaluate the distance between real human position and HPP clusters. In other words, the lower the average distance is, the more the pedestrian estimation is accurate. The Fig. 6b shows the HPP Cluster centroids. To build such clusters, we first filter HPP Map (Fig. 6a) data that are above a threshold. Here we assume that probabilities below such threshold are not sufficient to be representative of Human position estimation. A DBscan [16] clustering algorithm is then applied and resulted cluster centroids are displayed by a colored cross in the Fig. 6b). At the end, tracked pedestrian are affected to the closest cluster centroid (wave front propagation from the targeted cluster center) and distance between pedestrian position and cluster centroid is measured. The error measure could be expressed by $error_{h_i} = \underset{clust \in DBscan(HPPMap)}{\arg\min} \left(dist(clust, h_i) \right)$, where $clust$ is a cluster centroid and h_i the ground truth of a pedestrian pose.

We compare our results obtained in such scenario with two other approaches:

- one long term design approach: human affordance map [18] aims at building a statistical representation of human presence (only human presence per cell is considered in such approach).
- one short term design approach: Kalman prediction, where humans are tracked through well known Kalman filter [6].

The human affordance map uses robot observation to update the probability to meet human on each map cell during the time. The human affordance map is updated all experimentation long. As it is done for HPP map, at each evaluation step, a DBscan cluster algorithm distinguishes a set of most probable human presence area based on the human affordance map. Then each observed human is affected to the closest cluster. The distance between human and its associated cluster centroid is considered to evaluate the prediction precision (Fig. 6c).

The Kalman prediction is also used to predict pedestrian pose. When robot meet a pedestrian, a Kalman filter is created and updated as long as the associated pedestrian is in the field of view of a robot. Otherwise the Kalman filter continue to predict the next pedestrian position. The distance between the pedestrian pose ground truth and the Kalman prediction is considered to evaluate the prediction precision (Fig. 6d). All Kalman filter are set with the associated pedestrian pose, an acceleration of 0.68 m.s^2 and an acceleration standard deviation of 0.2 based on recommendation of [17].

The evaluation process was made as follows: pedestrian detected by robot are tracked (ground truth position) during different time range (from 10 s to the end of experiment). For each tracked pedestrian, the distance between ground truth pose and associated prediction is measured for each evaluation process:

- HPP: Distance to the closed hpp cluster
- Human affordance: Distance to the closed human affordance cluster
- Kalman prediction: Distance to the associated Kalman filter prediction pose.

The results of the average distance of all ground truth pedestrian poses and HPP cluster centroids are available in the Fig. 7.

In the Fig. 7a, the average distance is measure during the time. Each colors refers to different pedestrian track duration. For instance, the orange curve refers to a track during of 10s meaning that over 10s of a pedestrian tracking, this one is no more tracked and its ground truth position is forgotten. We can notice that the average distance decrease over the time. This observation is due to the enrichment of the flow grid map, increasing the accuracy of the HPP. In the Fig. 7b the cumulative average distance is computed. It comes as no surprise that lower pedestrian tracking duration implies best pedestrian prediction. We can notice that tracking pedestrian during 30s (brown curve) or tracking over the whole experimentation (800s, blue curve) results of no significant difference compare to duration of 10s or 30s.

The results of the average distances (average of all ground truth pedestrian poses and cluster centroids/estimators) of each processes are available in the Table 1. In this table, we compare two versions on HPP, one with the VonMises propagation model, and one without. The capacity of the VonMises propagation model to balance current pedestrian observation/direction and the learnt flow gives better results on all different pedestrian tracking duration. The HPP with VonMises get best results on all pedestrian tracking durations except for 800s duration. In this case, Human affordance coupled with the flow grid already learnt get better results. This can be explain by the fact that the more the tracking duration is the more the pedestrian as a chance to not being met by a robot and so the static statistical Human probability representation (human affordance map) get best results. We also highlight the influence of the flow grid, both learning flow grid from the start and previously learnt flow grid at the experimentation start have been played. We can notice that concerning the Human affordance map or HPP Map results are significantly better when flow grid is already learnt.

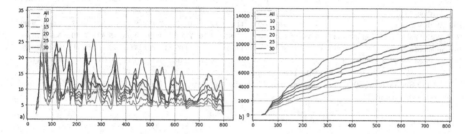

Fig. 7. Average distance from ground truth and HPP clusters during the time. The figure a shows average distance from HHP cluster using a sliding windows of 20. The figure b represents the cumulative average error distance over the time.

The second set of experiments was made on a subset of the ATC pedestrian tracking data set [2]. This dataset is the result of tracking people on an ATC shopping center in Japan over about 900 m^2 between October 24, 2012 and November 29, 2013. We extract a subset of this dataset (data of the 2012/11/14). The interaction between robot's moves and the crowd is considered by integrating real data into the pedsim simulator:

- Extract consecutive series of individual pedestrian position
- Sample individual pedestrian position
- Convert samples pose into way points
- Create pedestrian at the apparition time, following its associated way points

Between way points, each pedestrian is driven by Pedsim local planner (repulsive and attractive potential forces) and thus avoid collision between other simulated pedestrian or robot. The same evaluation process used in the first experiment is applied. The results of the average distances (average of all ground truth pedestrian poses and cluster centroids/estimators) of each processes of the ATC scenario are available in the Table 1.

The results show the same trends found the first experiment. HPP Map with VonMises get the best results no matter the pedestrian tracking duration.

Results became also better when an already learnt flow grid is used. In this set of experiment, Human affordance process do not overcome the HPP Map method for long pedestrian tracking (e.g. 800 s). This result is mainly due to the fact that in the ATC dataset pedestrian appear and disappear on quite short period meaning that a tracking no more exceed 30 s.

The experiments carried out are illustrated in the video here[2]. Our proposition outperforms other tested models by an average of 17% (and up to 40% in certain conditions).

Table 1. Average distance (in meter) of pedestrian between computed pedestrian pose estimation and ground truth from Museum scenario (artificial scenario) and Real ATC dataset

Tracking duration (in s.)	Museum Scenario						Real ATC scenario					
	10	15	20	25	30	800	10	15	20	25	30	800
HPP Without VonMises	10.60	12.57	13.96	14.96	15.66	21.31	Not Tested					
HPP With VonMises	6.58	8.54	10.20	11.50	12.53	16.12	**7.45**	**8.11**	**8.52**	**8.77**	**8.91**	**9.00**
HPP With VonMises Flow grid learnt[a]	**5.38**	**6.01**	**6.81**	**7.87**	**8.79**	13.02	**4.29**	**4.95**	**5.44**	**5.49**	**5.53**	**5.81**
Human affordance	13.46	13.86	14.01	14.04	13.96	12.99	14.63	15.06	15.84	16.44	16.55	16.55
Human affordance Flow grid learnt[a]	9.29	9.27	9.14	9.13	9.14	**9.03**	9.00	9.83	10.65	11.05	11.26	11.90
Kalman Prediction	13.01	14.83	16.582	18.05	19.11	24.01	11.69	13.67	15.21	16.16	16.57	16.63

[a] For ATC Scenario 500000 records was used to learn the flow grid, the next 500000 records are used to evaluate the model.

6   Conclusion

In this paper, we propose a new method for propagating human presence probability based on partial human observation by a robots fleet. With the help of a Flow grid Map, representing the probability to meet human in a cell in a direction, we propagate probabilities as soon as a robot observes a human. By reformulating the problem, we manage to massively parallelize computation (GPU) allowing online Human Presence Probability propagation. Thanks to the applied optimization (VonMises), our method is able to handle both learned trends and current observations. Our experimental results, conducted on two different scenarios (an artificial and a real-life dataset), demonstrate that our model outperforms existing long-term (Human Affordance Map) and short-term (Kalman estimator) human presence estimators.

References

1. Ros packages for pedsim (pedestrian simulator) based on social force model of Helbing et al. https://github.com/srl-freiburg/pedsimros
2. Brscic, D., Kanda, T., Ikeda, T., Miyashita, T.: Person tracking in large public spaces using 3-D range sensors. IEEE Trans. Hum.-Mach. Syst. **43**, 522–534 (2013)

---

[2] https://youtu.be/H7Ly9nZKNks.

3. Fulgenzi, C., Spalanzani, A., Laugier, C.: Probabilistic motion planning among moving obstacles following typical motion patterns. In: IEEE/RSJ International Conference on Intelligent RObots and Systems (2009)
4. Han, Y., Tse, R., Campbell, M.E.: Pedestrian motion model using non-parametric trajectory clustering and discrete transition points. CoRR (2020)
5. Jumel, F., Saraydaryan, J., Simonin, O.: Mapping likelihood of encountering humans: application to path planning in crowded environment. In: The European Conference on Mobile Robotics (ECMR) (2017)
6. Kalman, R.E., et al.: A new approach to linear filtering and prediction problems. J. Basic Eng. (1960)
7. Kooij, J.F.P., et al.: Context-based path prediction for targets with switching dynamics (2019)
8. Kucner, T,P., et al.: Enabling flow awareness for mobile robots in partially observable environments. IEEE Robot. Autom. Lett. (2017)
9. Kucner, T.P., et al.: Probabilistic mapping of spatial motion patterns for mobile robots. In: Cognitive Systems Monographs (2020)
10. Lam, S.K., Pitrou, A., Seibert, S.: Numba: a LLVM-based python JIT compiler. In: Proceedings of the 2nd Workshop on the LLVM Compiler Infrastructure in HPC (2015)
11. Mardia, K., Jupp, P.: Directional statistics (2000)
12. Mellado, S., et al.: Modelling and predicting rhythmic flow patterns in dynamic environments. In: Towards Autonomous Robotic Systems TAROS (2018)
13. Portugal, D., Rocha, R.: A survey on multi-robot patrolling algorithms. In: Camarinha-Matos, L.M. (ed.) DoCEIS 2011. IAICT, vol. 349, pp. 139–146. Springer, Heidelberg (2011). https://doi.org/10.1007/978-3-642-19170-1_15
14. Rudenko, A., et al.: Human motion trajectory prediction: a survey. Int. J. Robot. Res. **39**, 895–935 (2020)
15. Saraydaryan, J., Jumel, F., Simonin, O.: Navigation in human flows: planning with adaptive motion grid. In: IROS Workshop CrowdNav (2018)
16. Schubert, E., et al.: DBSCAN revisited, revisited: why and how you should (still) use DBSCAN. ACM Trans. Database Syst. **42**, 1–21 (2017)
17. Teknomo, K.: Microscopic pedestrian flow characteristics: development of an image processing data collection and simulation model. arXiv (2016)
18. Tipaldi, G.D., Arras, K.O.: I want my coffee hot! Learning to find people under spatio-temporal constraints. In: Proceedings of the IEEE International Conference on Robotics and Automation (ICRA) (2011)
19. Vintr, T., et al.: Spatio-temporal representation of time-varying pedestrian flows. In: ICRA Workshop on Long-term Human Motion Prediction (2019)
20. Xie, Z., Xin, P., Dames, P.M.: Towards safe navigation through crowded dynamic environments. In: IEEE/RSJ International Conference on Intelligent Robots and Systems, IROS (2021)
21. Zhou, B., Tang, X., Wang, X.: Learning collective crowd behaviors with dynamic pedestrian-agents. Int. J. Comput. Vision **111**, 50–68 (2014)

Neural Network-Based Joint Angle Prediction for the NAO Robot

Jan Fiedler and Tim Laue[✉]

Fachbereich 3 – Mathematik und Informatik, Universität Bremen, Postfach 330 440,
28334 Bremen, Germany
{jan_fie,tlaue}@uni-bremen.de

Abstract. One common problem in closed-loop robot motion control
is the motor response delay. When computing, for instance, a walking
step for a humanoid robot, the available state of the sensor joints comes
from the past and the newly computed actuator positions will not be set
immediately. This might lead to suboptimal motion planning, especially
for fast and dynamic motions. In this paper, we present an approach for
bridging this time gap and predicting the state of the joints of a NAO
robot by using neural networks. The training of the neural networks was
based on a dataset that covers multiple full tournaments played by the
B-Human SPL team.

1 Introduction

The motor response delay, i. e. the time between setting a desired actuator state
and the subsequent measurement of the corresponding motion, is inevitable in
robotics. The actual extent of such a delay depends on multiple factors such
as the control frequency of the installed actuators or the update frequency of
control boards or some middleware situated between the motor and the motion
planning software.

For the fifth generation of the NAO robot, Böckmann and Laue [2] determined a motor response delay of 30 ms on average. For the NAO[6], Reichenberg
and Röfer [10] found a delay of at least 36 ms. This is probably not relevant for
slow and rather stable motions, but in case of a fast closed-loop walk, which is
balancing to deal with bumps in the ground and collisions with other robots,
such delays make a difference between keeping walking or stumbling.

To overcome such problems, a prediction of the joint angles' states in the
near future is required. The contribution of this paper is a neural network-based
approach for bridging the NAO robot's motor response delay. For this purpose,
we evaluated a number of neural network architectures to determine the one that
best fits this particular problem and that is able to become executed in realtime.
The presented approach clearly outperforms different baseline approaches. This
is shown on a huge dataset that incorporates data of 11 different robots, recorded
on multiple different fields during four full RoboCup tournaments in 2019 and
2022. A publication of this dataset will become the second major contribution
of this paper.

C. Buche et al. (Eds.): RoboCup 2023, LNAI 14140, pp. 66–77, 2024.
https://doi.org/10.1007/978-3-031-55015-7_6

The work presented in this paper focuses on the NAO[6]. However, the general approach is supposed to be transferrable to similar platforms as well.

The remainder of this paper is organized as follows: In Sect. 2, an overview of related research is given. Our dataset is described in Sect. 3, the general approach in Sect. 4, followed by the evaluation in Sect. 5 and the final conclusion in Sect. 6.

2   Related Work

As the motor control delay is a general problem that more or less affects all robots, several related works providing solutions for its compensation exists, including the RoboCup Soccer domain.

Especially the RoboCup Small-Size League (SSL) faces a significant and inherent delay of over 100 ms due to its setup based on external cameras and computers. A solution to this problem has been presented by Behnke et al. [1]. Similar to the work presented in this paper, a neural network was trained. It uses recently sensed 2D robot poses as well as the most recent motion commands as input to predict a future robot pose, which is a less complex representation than the set of joint angles predicted by our approach (see Subsect. 5.1). A different approach that has been, among others, applied to the SSL scenario, was presented by Ommer et al. [8]. They developed an adaptive compensation feedforward controller to counteract non-modeled disturbances such as slippage or hardware malfunctions. As this controller is able to prevent motion errors a priori, it implicitly predicts future motor states. By evaluating different approaches, Locally Weighted Projection Regression by Vijayakumar et al. [15,16] was found to handle the task best.

In the RoboCup Standard Platform League, Böckmann and Laue [2] presented an approach for dynamic kick motions that is based on Dynamic Movement Primitives. In order to balance the robot during a kick, a mathematical motor model (a second order dynamical system based on a mass spring damper) was developed to compensate the NAO's motor control delay. The working of this approach was shown for short specific walking motions but not for general walking sequences that occur in real games. In [14], Seekircher and Visser present a closed-loop walk for the NAO robot that is based on a Linear Inverted Pendulum Model. This walk involves an online adaptation of the model parameters. Their reduction of model prediction errors implicitly predicts future joint states without an explicit model of these. The optimization is carried out by applying the CMA-ES approach by Hansen et al. [4].

A related work outside the RoboCup domain has been presented by Huang et al. [7]. They apply deep recurrent neural networks to compensate the control delay of an artificial knee joint for humans. By using measurements of inertial measurement units and muscle activity, an approach that is able to provide predictions over 50 ms and that is transferable to persons, whose data was not used for training, was found.

3 Data

The work presented in this paper is based on data that was collected on different robots during multiple official RoboCup tournaments. This section provides details about our dataset.

All data was recorded by NAO^6 robots of the *B-Human* team during official tournaments at the *RoboCup German Open 2019* in Magdeburg, the *RoboCup 2019* in Sydney, the *GORE 2022* in Hamburg, and the *RoboCup 2022* in Bangkok. The data includes official games as well as several inofficial test games. Between 2019 and 2022, no other central tournaments with full games took place. All competition sites featured similar playing fields with "8 mm artificial turf mounted on a flat wooden base" as specified by the SPL rules for 2019 [3] (and subsequent years). Although being standardized, the actual properties of the ground might still differ from site to site.

In total, eleven different robots were used. A majority of eight robots has been the same for 2019 and 2022. One robot was borrowed in 2019 and two other robots played their first major competitions in 2022. As 2019 was the first year in which NAO^6 robots were used in tournaments, this has an important implication for the composition of our dataset: It includes recordings of robots that are almost new and thus without any major joint wear as well as of (partially the same) robots that have been in use for many years and thus suffer of wear in many joints. This particular issue is further discussed in Sect. 4.

For our work, we only consider walking motions. All other motion sequences have been removed, which almost halves the size of the dataset, as shown in the overview in Table 1. Besides walking, the second most common robot state in a game is standing, which does not require any prediction as no real motion occurs besides minor adaptions to prevent joints from overheating. Special motions such as kicking or getting up have been omitted, too, as they are based on very specific and sudden motion patterns and occur rather infrequently. Due to our focus on walking, the dataset only contains measured and commanded joint angles for the NAO's eleven leg joints.

Table 1. Overview of the collected data

Year	Fields	Robots	Games	Total Time (in min)	Time Walking (in min)
2019	6	9	25	2413.30	1295.24
2022	5	10	22	2375.31	1136.92
Sum	11	11	47	4788.61	2432.16

To generate walk motions for the NAO robot, B-Human uses an implementation that is based on the concept presented by Hengst [5], which is probably the currently most popular walk approach in the SPL. The implementation used for the 2019 competitions has been released as open source and is described in a team report [12]. For 2022, an advanced version has been used, incorporating

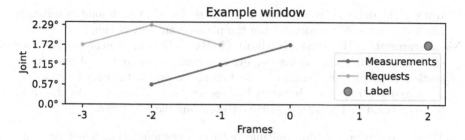

Fig. 1. An example time period for a joint angle prediction. In the current frame 0, the commanded joint angle requests of the previous three time steps, as well as the current and the previous angle measurements are known. This data is used to predict the joint angle in frame 2.

the approach by Reichenberg and Röfer [10]. This implementation has also been released as open source and is described in [13].

As depicted in Table 1, we collected data for a total of 2432.16 min walking time. As data exchange with the NAO platform is possible every 12 ms (with some slight outliers), this results in data points for 12 112 153 time steps. Each data point contains information about measured and commanded joints angles plus some additional information, which is used for data handling but not for learning. As walking is frequently interrupted by standing or other motions, the dataset is divided into 12 073 sequences of continuous walking. The lengths of these sequences vary from 0.1 s to multiple minutes (in rare cases), the median length of a walking sequence is 4.86 s.

Our dataset has been made publicly available[1].

4   Approach and Research Questions

The prediction of the future joint angles can be formulated as a supervised learning problem. Fortunately, no labeling of the desired output is necessary, as the future joint angles are already part of the dataset. Regarding the input, related works, as discussed in Sect. 2, showed that recent measurements as well as recently controlled angles provide suitable information. An example is given in Fig. 1.

To the best of our knowledge, there is no related work that provides results to which we can set our prediction results in comparison. Thus, to measure the impact of our approach, we define the following three baseline approaches to compare it against:

Measurement. This approach assumes the current joint angle measurement as the state of the joint in the moment it receives the currently computed command. This corresponds to the complete ignoring of the motor response delay.

---

[1] https://b-human.informatik.uni-bremen.de/public/datasets/joint_angles/.

Request. The delay is known and one could assume that each joint will simply reach its requested position within the planned amount of time.

Measurement + Request Gradient (MRG). To complement the first two obvious and naive approaches, we implemented a combination of both information. A prediction is computed by taking the sum of the current measurement and the difference between two recent joint commands. As shown in Subsect. 5.2, this heuristics clearly outperforms the other two.

Given this general setup, multiple research questions arise, which are supposed to be addressed by our evaluation in Sect. 5:

Network Architecture. As no directly comparable related works exists, the first major question that arises is: Which network architecture fits the given problem best? Furthermore, it has to be investigated, which model sizes are necessary or sufficient. With an increasing model size, the required computing time often increases, too. Thus, a compromise between a desired precision and the available computing time needs to be found.

Transferability. The NAO is a standardized robot. All copies of this system were manufactured under the same professional circumstances and are supposed to be very similar. However, a little bit because of manufacturing tolerances and mainly because of different states of wear in joints, no two robots move the same, especially not if you want them to walk fast. This leads to the research question: How does a learned joint angle prediction perform on a (maybe new) robot of which no data was part of the training set?

The Effect of Joint Wear. Over time, it is inevitable that a robot's joints suffer from wear. The internal gears lose material and the joint cannot reach the commanded angles precisely anymore. As aforementioned, our approach involves the usage of requested joint angles and is therefore directly affected by this problem. Thus, we have to investigate the effect on our prediction approach.

5 Evaluation

In this section, we present our results regarding a suitable neural network model for the joint angle prediction, along with an analysis of the transferability to different robots and to different states of wear. Furthermore, information about the required runtime is given.

5.1 Previously Determined Bases for the Evaluation

In this paper, we focus on the aforementioned major aspects of our joint angle prediction approach. However, multiple additional parameters have been investigated and are now described here in summarized form.

In the example window in Fig. 1, the usage of the last three joint measurements and requests is depicted. For this work, we evaluated the three alternatives

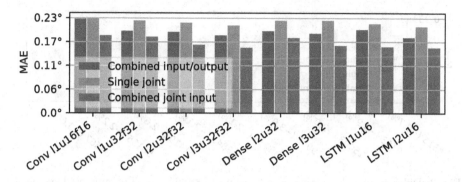

Fig. 2. Mean absolute error (MAE) of different models. For each model, the three alternative types of joint input and output were evaluated. The model names encode the network type, the number of layers, the units per layer, and the number of filters.

of using 3, 6, or 10 frames. It turned out that this parameter hardly makes a difference. Although the version with 10 frames leads to a slightly higher precision, we decided to carry out all further experiments with only 3 frames, as this has a lower effect on runtime.

All joint angles of the NAO robot can be measured and set independently from each other. Thus, training a specialized predictor for each *single joint* appears to be a reasonable choice. However, within a walking pattern, each joint's motion occurs in a context with the other joints' motions. Therefore, measurements and requests of the other joints could be used as additional input (here named *combined joint input*). Another alternative would be to use data from all joints and predict the angles for all joints with one network (*combined input/output*). We evaluated all three options. As described in the later Subsect. 5.2, for this paper, we evaluated a number of different models for prediction. In an early stage, a subset of these was used to decide which of these three options appears to be the most reasonable one. The result is depicted in Fig. 2. Overall, the *combined joint input* approach has the highest precision. However, as this means having a network for each joint, we performed a second evaluation that compares the approaches with each using a model size similar to the other two. The result is shown in Fig. 3. We draw the conclusion that when considering runtime, which roughly scales with the overall number of involved parameters, the *combined input/output* network appears to be the best choice as it has the highest precision for each model size. This comparison was also part of our runtime analysis, as described in Subsect. 5.3.

As a consequence, the further evaluation has been carried out on neural networks that use information from all joints as input and predict a full set of angles for all joints.

As listed in Table 1, the data was recorded on different fields. Our experiments did not show any impact of different fields on the prediction. Maybe, all fields were very similar or maybe the detailed structure of the ground does not affect the prediction. We can't make any clear statement about this. Thus, for the following experiments, the fields are not considered.

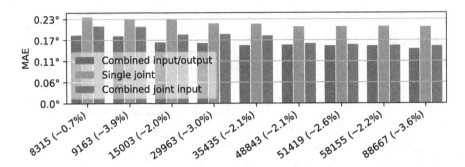

Fig. 3. Different models ranging from 8 315 up to 88 667 overall parameters have been trained for the three different approaches. As not exactly the same model sizes could be set for technical reasons, the respective maximum deviation is noted in percent. For each model size, the network that uses input from all joints to make a combined prediction for all angles has the smallest error.

5.2   Network Architecture

For this work, three different neural network architectures were evaluated along with different numbers of model parameters:

Dense. A dense network with fully connected layers. In the input layer, the joint data sequences become flattened out and the explicit temporal information is initially lost.

Conv. A dense network in which the temporal information about the joint sequence is modeled as a one-dimensional convolution in the input layer.

LSTM. A Long Short-Term Memory network [6], which has by design the capability of storing temporal information.

For all these architectures, the number of parameters per layer as well as the number of the layers may vary. To find proper solutions for our prediction problem, a grid search over the respective parameter spaces was performed. The overall result is depicted in Fig. 4.

Overall, there does not seem to be a major difference between the network architectures. The LSTM appears to perform slightly better for any number of model parameters and the *Conv* network appears to perform slightly worse. Depending on the model size, all three architectures achieve a higher reduction of the mean absolute error (MAE) the more parameters they have. However, from 40 000 parameters on, the reduction reaches a saturation. We evaluated models with sizes of up to 109 067 parameters. Due to the saturation as well as due to the required runtime for the inference on the robot (see Subsect. 5.3), no larger models were considered.

Furthermore, we compared the results of these networks to the baseline approaches described in Sect. 4. The results are shown in Fig. 5. All models achieved a lower prediction error than all three baseline approaches. While the

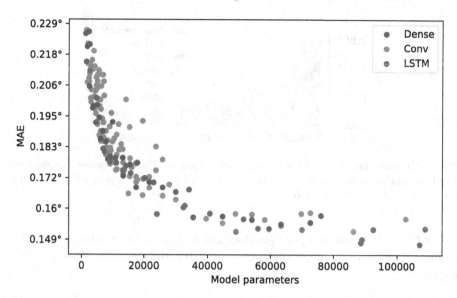

Fig. 4. Mean absolute error over all joints of different network architectures depending on the number of model parameters.

MRG approach achieves a precision that is at least close to some of the models, the other two approaches provide mean absolute errors that are many times larger than those of the worst models. In particular the results for the basic *Measurement* approach show the actual average joint angle error, as if no prediction is performed, which clearly indicates that a prediction approach makes a difference.

5.3 Runtime

Our approach was integrated into the B-Human software and is capable of running on a NAO[6] robot. For inference, we use the ONNX Runtime implementation [9]. We evaluated different models on the robot, the results are depicted in Fig. 6.

To interpret the results, one has to consider the realtime constraints of a NAO soccer robot, on which the available (and quite limited) computing power must be divided among many tasks. In the B-Human system, all subtasks related to robot motion and sensor data processing (excluding vision) are grouped within one thread that is supposed to run at 83 Hz, which is the rate at which sensor data can be read and joint request can be set. This means that within 12 ms all tasks must be completed.

Overall, all networks of the *combined input/output* type, even those with more than 100 000 parameters, require about 1 ms or less. Given the available computing time, this appears to be a reasonable and usable result. As one can

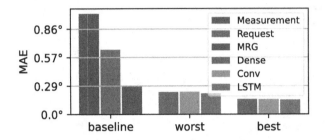

Fig. 5. Mean absolute error of the learned models compared to our baseline approaches. The best and worst models are the ones depicted in Fig. 4 in the upper left corner and the lower right corner respectively.

see, in Fig. 6, the *combined joint input* approach that uses one network per joint requires computing resources that would probably violate our realtime requirements.

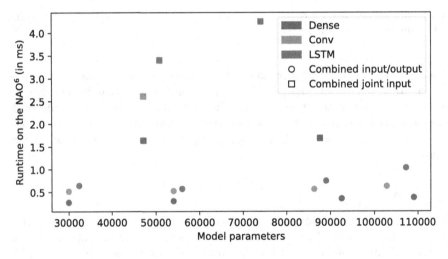

Fig. 6. Runtime of different networks on a NAO[6] robot.

5.4   Transferability

For applying the joint angle prediction on a robot, of which no previous joint data exists, one has two options: Record new data and (re-)train a model or just use a model that has been trained on data of other robots. Obviously, the latter option is more appealing, as it does not require any extra work. Thus, we performed a cross-validation over multiple robots on two subsets of our data to evaluate the transferability of our approach. The first subset includes eight robots with a total of 525 min of walking time on a single field at the RoboCup German Open 2019. The second one consists of data from nine robots with a total of 290 min of walking time on a single field at RoboCup 2022. The results are depicted in Fig. 7. In both cases, the data of each robot was validated against a model learned on data of the other robots.

For most robots in both datasets, the cross-validation does not show significant differences. However, the robot *Herta* shows a clear deviation in both years. Thus, one can conclude that a transferability is given in general but not for every robot to the same extent. Nevertheless, even in the worst cases, the mean absolute error still below the best baseline approach, which is even averaged over all robots.

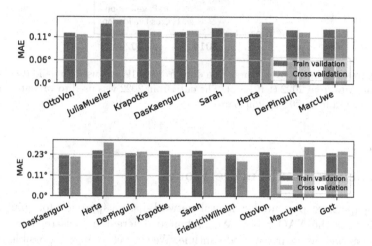

Fig. 7. Cross-validation on two datasets. The upper figure shows robots at the RoboCup German Open 2019. The lower figure shows robots at RoboCup 2022.

5.5 Joint Wear

In Fig. 7, one can see that the mean absolute error on the 2022 dataset is significantly higher than on the 2019 dataset. Both datasets include almost the same robots that have worn out over the years. To investigate the effect of the joint wear, we performed an additional cross-validation. One model was trained on data from 2019 and evaluated on data from 2022 and vice versa. The result is depicted in Fig. 8.

This evaluation, together with the results shown in Fig. 7, offers some helpful insights: A model that is trained and used on rather new robots provides by far the best results. Doing the same on older robots leads to significantly higher errors. This means that the effect of joint wear cannot be fully compensated by our approach. When evaluating a model that was trained on older robots with data from rather new robots, the error decreases. Vice versa, when evaluating a model that was trained on data of rather new robots with data from worn-out robots, the error significantly increases. This leads to the conclusion that one has to consider the general state of the used robots when learning and applying a learned prediction model, as joint wear appears to be an influencing factor.

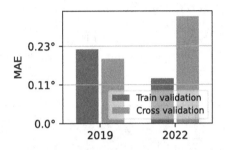

Fig. 8. Cross-validation over years. The data from 2019 was used to validate a model trained on data from 2022 (left bars). The data from 2022 was used to validate a model trained on data from 2019 (right bars).

6 Conclusion and Future Works

In this paper, we presented a neural network-based approach for joint angle prediction for the NAO robot. We evaluated different models regarding their precision as well as their required runtime. We showed that it is possible to significantly reduce the prediction error compared to different baseline approaches whilst taking into account the realtime requirements of the robot. Furthermore, we showed that it is possible to transfer learned models to new robots, of which no new joint data is required for learning. In addition, we discussed the effect of joint wear on this particular prediction task.

Although we showed the feasibility and possible precision for joint angle prediction on a NAO robot, this paper does not discuss the actual impact on playing soccer. However, in a parallel work, Reichenberg and Röfer [11] developed a novel approach for joint control on worn-out NAO robots that already makes use of our prediction approach by applying one of our LSTM models.

References

1. Behnke, S., Egorova, A., Gloye, A., Rojas, R., Simon, M.: Predicting away robot control latency. In: Polani, D., Browning, B., Bonarini, A., Yoshida, K. (eds.) RoboCup 2003. LNCS (LNAI), vol. 3020, pp. 712–719. Springer, Heidelberg (2004). https://doi.org/10.1007/978-3-540-25940-4_70

2. Böckmann, A., Laue, T.: Kick motions for the NAO robot using dynamic movement primitives. In: Behnke, S., Sheh, R., Sariel, S., Lee, D.D. (eds.) RoboCup 2016. LNCS (LNAI), vol. 9776, pp. 33–44. Springer, Cham (2017). https://doi.org/10. 1007/978-3-319-68792-6_3
3. RT Committee: RoboCup Standard Platform League (NAO) Rule Book (2019). https://spl.robocup.org/wp-content/uploads/downloads/Rules2019.pdf
4. Hansen, N., Müller, S.D., Koumoutsakos, P.: Reducing the time complexity of the derandomized evolution strategy with covariance matrix adaptation (CMA-ES). Evol. Comput. **11**(1), 1–18 (2003)
5. Hengst, B.: rUNSWift Walk 2014 report. Technical report, School of Computer Science & Engineering University of New South Wales, Sydney 2052, Australia (2014). http://cgi.cse.unsw.edu.au/-robocup/2014ChampionTeamPaperReports/ 20140930-Bernhard.Hengst-Walk2014Report.pdf
6. Hochreiter, S., Schmidhuber, J.: Long short-term memory. Neural Comput. **9**(8), 1735–1780 (1997)
7. Huang, Y., et al.: Real-time intended knee joint motion prediction by deep-recurrent neural networks. IEEE Sens. J. **19**(23), 11503–11509 (2019)
8. Ommer, N., Stumpf, A., von Stryk, O.: Real-time online adaptive feedforward velocity control for unmanned ground vehicles. In: Akiyama, H., Obst, O., Sammut, C., Tonidandel, F. (eds.) RoboCup 2017. LNCS (LNAI), vol. 11175, pp. 3–16. Springer, Cham (2018). https://doi.org/10.1007/978-3-030-00308-1_1
9. ONNX Runtime developers: ONNX Runtime (2021). https://github.com/ microsoft/onnxruntime
10. Reichenberg, P., Röfer, T.: Step adjustment for a robust humanoid walk. In: Alami, R., Biswas, J., Cakmak, M., Obst, O. (eds.) RoboCup 2021. LNCS (LNAI), vol. 13132, pp. 28–39. Springer, Cham (2022). https://doi.org/10.1007/978-3-030-98682-7_3
11. Reichenberg, P., Röfer, T.: Dynamic joint control for a humanoid walk. In: RoboCup 2023: Robot World Cup XXVI (2023, submitted)
12. Röfer, T., et al.: B-Human team report and code release 2019 (2019). http://www. b-human.de/downloads/publications/2019/CodeRelease2019.pdf
13. Röfer, T., et al.: B-Human team report and code release 2022 (2022). https:// raw.githubusercontent.com/bhuman/BHumanCodeRelease/coderelease2022/ CodeRelease2022.pdf
14. Seekircher, A., Visser, U.: A closed-loop gait for humanoid robots combining LIPM with parameter optimization. In: Behnke, S., Sheh, R., Sariel, S., Lee, D.D. (eds.) RoboCup 2016. LNCS (LNAI), vol. 9776, pp. 71–83. Springer, Cham (2017). https://doi.org/10.1007/978-3-319-68792-6_6
15. Vijayakumar, S., D'Souza, A., Schaal, S.: Incremental online learning in high dimensions. Neural Comput. **17**(12), 2602–2634 (2005)
16. Vijayakumar, S., Schaal, S.: Locally weighted projection regression: an O(n) algorithm for incremental real time learning in high dimensional space. In: Proceedings of the Seventeenth International Conference on Machine Learning (ICML 2000), vol. 1, pp. 288–293. Morgan Kaufmann (2000)

Multi-robot Path Planning with Safety Based Control Applied to the Small Size League Robots

Leonardo da Silva Costa$^{(\boxtimes)}$ and Flavio Tonidandel

University Center of FEI, São Bernardo do Campo, Brazil
`{unieleocosta,flaviot}@fei.edu.br`

Abstract. This work provides a comparison between two path planners, the coordinated Multi-Robot A Star (MRA*) and uncoordinated Dynamic Visibility Graph A Star (DVG+A*) algorithms when applied to the highly dynamic, uncertain, multi-robot environment of the RoboCup Small Size League. To consider dynamic obstacles and uncertainties, the path planners were combined with the Probabilistic Safety Barrier Certificates (PrSBC) collision avoidance algorithm. Two experiments were proposed to evaluate the performance of the algorithms: the antipodal and the marking tests. Both tests evaluated the algorithms regarding their navigation time, computational time, and minimum distance to other robots. Through the antipodal test, the influence of barrier gain and safety radius of the PrSBC for collision avoidance were analyzed, along with the benefits of using a coordinated path planner versus an uncoordinated one. The marking test explored the capacity of the navigation system to deal with dynamic obstacles. The results have shown that the PrSBC is capable of avoiding collisions in an environment where all robots use the same avoidance algorithm. Furthermore, the coordinated path planner has shown a significantly lower computational time when compared to the uncoordinated algorithms. However, it did not outperform the other algorithms in the navigation time or safety during the marking test. In conclusion, for multi-robot applications, there is a performance improvement when using coordinated path planners. Nevertheless, avoiding every collision is not trivial in the presence of dynamic obstacles, especially at velocities higher than 2 m/s.

Keywords: Multi-Robot Path Planning · Obstacle Avoidance · Safety based Controller · A Star

1 Introduction

The RoboCup Small Size League (SSL) is one of the most dynamic categories that exist within the RoboCup soccer competition. In the SSL, two teams of

This study was financed in part by the Coordenação de Aperfeiçoamento de Pessoal de Nível Superior - Brasil (CAPES) - Finance Code 001.

C. Buche et al. (Eds.): RoboCup 2023, LNAI 14140, pp. 78–89, 2024.
https://doi.org/10.1007/978-3-031-55015-7_7

robots compete in a soccer match completely autonomously. Teams are composed of six, up to eleven, omnidirectional robots each, and those robots can reach velocities up to 4 m/s. The match happens in a 9 m × 6 m field, for six robots, and a 12 m × 9 m field, for eleven robots. The ball is an orange golf ball that the robots can kick with a speed as high as 6.5 m/s. All these characteristics make the SSL a challenging environment for navigation since the obstacles are highly dynamic, unpredictable, and team coordination is needed.

As seen on [17], navigation is one of the most critical characteristics of a mobile robot since it provides the robot with the necessary skills to navigate autonomously without causing collisions and following the most optimal path considering the restrictions of the robot.

Four sub-systems compose the navigation of a robot: mapping, localization, planning, and obstacle avoidance [15]. The mapping sub-system generates a model of the environment based on the sensor's readings. Localization is the task of calculating the position of the robot. Planning is the process of, given the start and goal positions of the robot, calculating the path that the robot must take to reach its target position while avoiding static obstacles and respecting the constraints of the robot. At last, the obstacle avoidance sub-system is responsible for making local changes in the path obtained during planning to account for dynamic obstacles that may have come to interfere with it [15].

According to [1], navigation still is one of the biggest challenges for mobile robots due to the difficulties that arise when dealing with dynamic and uncertain environments, which are present in most real-world applications. Moreover, in [9, 14], it is possible to see that mobile robot navigation in dynamic and uncertain environments is a problem that still demands more research, given that there is still a gap to fill when it comes to controlling teams of mobile robots in dynamic and uncertain environments.

The same gap also was identified in the SSL. By analyzing the team description papers in the last five years [16], around 20 papers describe which technique each team uses for navigation. Except for [3,6], the rest of the papers don't use a separate obstacle avoidance algorithm, resulting in the need to recalculate everything when an obstacle interferes with the previous path. However, a previous study [20] has shown that, although the computational time to run the planning algorithm is low, collisions cannot be avoided in time. The results show that many collisions were observed during a match in the SSL [20].

Furthermore, when it comes to using some algorithm for coordination between the robots' paths, there has never been an application in the SSL. Even though the environment is sparse, there are situations where some regions of the field become crowded with robots. Also, coordinated paths can improve the team's play since all the robots would reach their destination faster.

Therefore, the objective of this paper is to apply a coordinated path planner, the Multi-Robot A Star (MRA*) [2], combined with an obstacle avoidance (OA) algorithm, the Probabilistic Safety Barrier Certificates (PrSBC) [10], in the SSL environment. With this study, we hope to improve the current state of the SSL, where numerous collisions happen every match [20], by providing teams with a robust and easy-to-use navigation system. The MRA*+OA will be compared against the Dynamic Visibility Graph + A Star (DVG+A*) [19], which is the current path planner used by our team. This paper will show the advantages of a dedicated OA algorithm and the benefits of a coordinated path planner over the uncoordinated one.

This paper is organized as follows: Sect. 2 presents the related work in the state-of-the-art for path planners and obstacle avoidance algorithms, Sects. 3, 4 and 5 briefly explains the algorithms used, Sect. 6 details the experiments and metrics used to evaluate them, Sect. 7 presents and discusses the results obtained, at last, the conclusions of the paper are in Sect. 8.

2   Path Planning Techniques

Many path-planning algorithms aim to find a set of coordinated paths [2,8,13, 20], each using different approaches. In [2], the author uses the A* algorithm to find the initial paths for a team of robots and assigns a cost, which weights the path length and collisions, to each one. Then, the algorithm searches for the optimal solution by recalculating each path and replacing them if the solution cost is lower. Although the approach is quite simple, the results obtained by the author show that the MRA* improves the coordination among several paths, thus, lowering the navigation time.

The approach seen on [8] also generates the initial paths using A*. Then, the vertices with a collision get marked as obstacles, and the A* is used again to avoid these vertices. If the A* fails to find a valid path, a co-evolutionary algorithm is used to find a solution. The search process runs until no collisions exist or the number of iterations reaches the limit. The algorithm proposed by [8] only considers collisions if they happen in an instant lower than a threshold, which relaxes the path planning problem and is a valid assumption since the robots and dynamic obstacles will likely be in a different position in the future.

A similar approach can be seen on [13], the author uses a modified potential field algorithm to generate the initial population of paths for an optimization process using an enhanced genetic algorithm (EGA). This initial step improves the convergence speed of the algorithm by providing the EGA with a set of feasible solutions. The EGA optimizes the paths by reducing their length and vertices under collision while increasing their smoothness and safety.

Concerning the approaches used in the SSL, since the environment is sparse, visibility graph-based algorithms have been gaining some popularity [11,18] since they can reduce memory consumption in such an environment. With that in mind, the DVG+A* uses the A* algorithm to find a path in a dynamic visibility graph (DVG). The DVG is a simpler version of the classic visibility graph that aims to decrease the computational complexity by ignoring obstacles that will not influence the optimal path. A previous study [19] has shown that the DVG+A* outperforms the classic Rapidly-exploring Random Trees algorithm by providing a shorter path, with a lower computational time and minimum post-processing needed.

Regarding obstacle avoidance, the analyzed algorithms are separated into two categories: velocity obstacle techniques [4] and optimization-based algorithms [10,21]. Those techniques are used due to their flexibility to deal with linear and nonlinear systems and low computational time, given that the optimization problem usually can be cast into a quadratic program (QP) [7], which can be quickly solved.

In [21], the Buffered Uncertainty Aware Voronoi Cells (BUAVC) algorithm is proposed. This technique builds the Voronoi cell of the robot and obstacle and dillates it according to the uncertainty of the state of the robots and obstacles, the time it takes to stop completely, and a probabilistic threshold. By ensuring that the robot is always inside the BUAVC, the algorithm guarantees that the robot is safe. Therefore, the robot navigates to the closest point to the target position inside the Voronoi cell until it reaches the goal. Although the experiments show that the algorithm guides the robot safely, the computational time is relatively high for the SSL.

A velocity obstacle approach can be seen on [4], in this work, the authors propose a Cooperative Collision Avoidance (CCA) algorithm. The CCA uses a set of constraints that will minimally modify the preferred velocity of the robot to avoid collisions and respect the kinematic limits of the robot. The solution of the optimization process happens in two phases. First, a QP is solved considering only the convex constraints of the problem (velocity obstacle and trajectory tracking error constraints). Second, the non-convex constraints are enforced through a grid search. The results show that the CCA avoids collisions while accounting for cooperation among robots with a low computational time.

In the SSL, it is worth mentioning the approaches seen on [3,6]. In the former, a potential field (PF) is built to push the robot away from the obstacles. Although this approach might provide satisfactory results, the PF method has a problem of local minimum, which may trap the robot in a position. In the latter, the team uses the desired path line, i.e., the beeline that connects the robot to its goal, to generate a velocity that will not lead the robot in the direction of an obstacle that intersects this line. Results show that the approach is capable of avoiding collisions with static obstacles.

Finally, in [10], it is possible to see an approach using a safety-based controller. The author proposes a Probabilistic Safety Barrier Certificate (PrSBC) to control a team of robots. The PrSBC guarantees that if the robots are initially safe, then there won't be any collisions. The guarantee is valid even in the presence of an amplitude-bounded noise in the state or input of the system. Given that the PrSBC controller can be cast into a QP, its computational time is around a few milliseconds, allowing it to run at a high frequency.

As seen in the literature, algorithms for path planning and obstacle avoidance are constantly evolving. However, most applications only cover simulated or basic environments and slow-moving robots. Because of that, and the current gap in the use of coordinated path planners and obstacle avoidance algorithms in the SSL, the purpose of this paper is to fill the gap by using the SSL environment as a testing ground for the DVG+A*, MRA* and PrSBC. Testing and comparing algorithms is of paramount importance in the evolution of obstacle avoidance and path-planning techniques to make them more robust for challenging environments by identifying the strengths and weaknesses of each algorithm. Given the characteristics of the SSL, it is the perfect challenge for navigation systems to evaluate those characteristics.

3   Dynamic Visibility Graph a Star – DVG+A*

The DVG+A* [19] is based on two algorithms, the Dynamic Visibility Graph (DVG) and the A*. The DVG is an extension of the classic visibility graph, it works by determining an Active Region (AR) and then building the graph using only the objects contained in the AR, which is a rectangle whose width is the distance from the robot to the goal, and its height is a constant distance $2d_{AR}$. Figure 1 shows an example of the DVG. The robot's and obstacle's models are polygons with 12 vertices circumscribed in a circle with a radius of 200 mm.

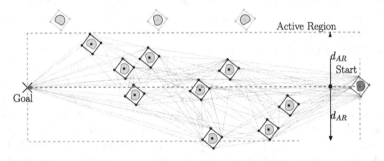

Fig. 1. The obstacles are the yellow circles, the graph edges are the red lines, the active region is the dashed rectangle and ignored obstacles vertices are gray. (Color figure online)

An A* heuristic search is performed to find a path in the resulting graph. This search is based on the evaluation function described in Eq. (1).

$$f(s) = h(s) + g(s, s') \tag{1}$$

where, s, s' are the current and parent states (the state is the x, y position of the robot), $h(s)$ is the heuristic function that guides the algorithm towards the goal, in this paper it is the Euclidean distance from the current state to the goal, and $g(s, s')$ is the cost, i.e. distance, to move from s' to s.

The algorithm works by pushing new states into an open list, then, the state with the lowest $f(s)$ is popped and put into a closed list. This state gets expanded, and its children get added to the open list. The algorithm ends when the solution appears in the open list. The final path is obtained by following the parent states of the solution until it reaches the starting state. The details about the implementation can be seen on [20].

4   Multi-robot a Star – MRA*

The A* uses an eight-connected grid map as an environment model. The first step of the MRA* starts by generating the robots' paths considering only the obstacles. Then, for each robot $i \in \{1, \dots, N\}$ where N is the maximum number of robots, the path's cost $c(i)$ is computed according to Eq. (2) [2].

$$c(i) = W \times \text{Len}_i + \beta \times \text{Con}_i + \eta \times K_i \tag{2}$$

where, Len_i is the length of the path, Con_i is the number of shared vertices and K_i is the number of robots that participates in the collisions, and W, β, η are weights that are tuned to prioritize a certain aspect of the path.

After computing the costs, the algorithm recalculates each path considering the shared vertices as obstacles. If the total cost ($\sum c(i)$) reduces, the new path replaces the old one. This process repeats until the cost stabilizes or the algorithm reaches the iteration limit. During the experiments, the value of the weights are $W = \beta = 1$, $\eta = 10$, and the grid resolution is 250 mm.

5   Probabilistic Safety Barrier Certificates – PrSBC

The Probabilistic Safety Barrier Certificate [10] extends the concept of a control barrier function (CBF) [5] to account for the uncertainty present in the system's states. The purpose of a CBF is to, given a safe set $\mathcal{C}$, enforce the invariance of the set. This means that if the safe set is composed of all states where the robot doesn't collide, the CBF will guarantee that the system never leaves $\mathcal{C}$ as long as the constraints hold, more details can be seen on [5].

In practice, the PrSBC will minimally modify the control input of the robots, which is usually generated by a path tracking algorithm, in order to avoid any possible collisions. The PrSBC is implemented as a QP as seen on Eq. (3) [10].

$$\mathbf{u}_i^* = \underset{\mathbf{u} \in \mathbb{R}^{mN}}{\arg\min} \sum_{i=1}^{N} \|\mathbf{u}_i - \mathbf{u}_i^*\|^2; \ s.t. \ \mathbf{u} \in S_{\mathbf{u}}^{\sigma} \bigcap S_{\mathbf{u}}^{\sigma_o}; \ \|\mathbf{u}_i\| \leq \alpha_i, \ \forall i \in \mathcal{I} \tag{3}$$

where, $\mathbf{u}_i$, $\mathbf{u}_i^*$ is the current and optimal control effort, respectively. N is the number of controlled robots, α_i is the maximum control amplitude, m is the number of dimensions (2), S_u^{σ} and $S_u^{\sigma_o}$ are the safe sets for the control input considering the collision avoidance between robots and between robots and obstacles, respectively. For more details see [10].

In practice, the optimization problem of Eq. (3) gets transformed into a QP of the form seen on Eq. (4). Since the cost function $\sum_{i=1}^{N} \|\mathbf{u}_i - \mathbf{u}_i^*\|^2$ is quadratic, it can be easily cast into a QP. Then, the safety constraints (S_u^{σ} and $S_u^{\sigma_o}$) are directly transformed into the linear constraint $Au \leq b$.

$$\mathbf{u}^* = \underset{\mathbf{u} \in \mathbb{R}^{mN}}{\arg\min} \ \frac{1}{2} \mathbf{u}^T P \mathbf{u} + q^T \mathbf{u}; \quad s.t. \quad Au \leq b \tag{4}$$

The parameters for the PrSBC are: $\sigma = 0.95$ and the finite support of the process and measurement noise for all robots are $\mathbf{w}_{ik} = [0.05, 0.05]$ and $\mathbf{v}_{ik} = [0.0, 0.0]$, respectively. These finite supports can also be determined using a Standard Kalman Filter. The best values for the barrier gain (γ) and safety radius (R_i) were determined in Sect. 7.

6   Methodology

During the tests, the grSim [12] simulator was used with six robots per team, and the speed of the robots was limited to 2 m/s, it is assumed that the robot has a speed controller which can track the target velocities without slipping. The robot's dimensions are constrained to a cylinder with a diameter of 0.18 m and height of 0.15 m, hence the collision threshold (CT) equals 0.18 m.

The algorithms were compared using two test scenarios[1]: antipodal position switch and team positioning under disturbance from opponents. For each experiment, three different algorithm combinations were used: DVG+A*, DVG+A* w. OA, and MRA*+OA. The algorithms were implemented using C++.

The antipodal position switch is a commonly used test in the literature [4,10] of obstacle avoidance algorithms. In this experiment, the robots are positioned along a circle of radius $r = 1$ m with their goal position as the diametrically opposite position. In this test, it is possible to see the obstacle avoidance algorithm in action, along with the effect of path coordination.

The marking experiment was proposed to test the algorithms when an adversarial obstacle is trying to block the robot's path. If the OA algorithm doesn't take the optimal action, the robots will get into a live or deadlock situation. In this test, each obstacle will try to position 0.5 m in front of each controlled robot without using any form of path planning or obstacle avoidance.

The results were evaluated using three metrics: total navigation time (T_{nav}), minimum distance (d_{min}) between the robots and obstacles, and computational time. If $T_{\text{nav}} \geq 30$ s for any test, it is considered as failed. To get a reasonable sample size each experiment was repeated 100 times. It is expected that, by using an optimal OA algorithm combined with a coordinated path planner, it will be possible to navigate the robots toward the goal in the minimum navigation time while maintaining a safe distance between robots, and a low computational time.

7   Results

During the antipodal test, the experiments have shown a significant influence of the barrier gain (γ) in the robot's behavior. A bouncing effect, also known as reciprocal dance [4], can be observed for large values of γ. The bouncing happens due to large amplitudes of the control effort. Thus, given the high speeds that the robots reach, the PrSBC isn't capable of avoiding collisions in time. Figure 2 shows the decrease in the minimum distance due to the increase in γ.

---

[1] Experiments can be seen on https://youtu.be/ItNmRY2a5Y0. Implementations are available at https://gitlab.com/leo_costa/RobotNavigation.

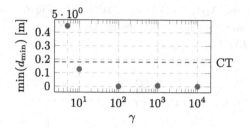
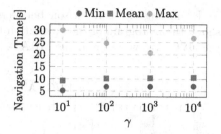

Fig. 2. Minimum distance with $R_i = 0.2$ m.   **Fig. 3.** Average, minimum and maximum navigation time with $R_i = 0.2$ m.

By analyzing Fig. 2 it is possible to see that for $\gamma = 5$ no collisions happened, and the robots were always capable of maintaining a distance higher than 0.4 m. Thus, the experiment shows that lowering the barrier gain can improve the system's safety. Also, in Fig. 3, it is possible to see that lower values of the barrier gain don't increase significantly the navigation time, which could happen since the admissible control space gets reduced. Although there are some cases of failed positioning, the average, and minimum, navigation time are slightly lower than the values obtained for larger values of the barrier gain.

Furthermore, lower values of the barrier gain allow the robots to reach higher velocities without causing collisions. Moreover, since the minimum distance is far from the collision threshold, the safety radius (R_i) can also be lowered, which helps to avoid deadlocks. Figure 4 and 5 show the minimum distance and navigation time, respectively, for different values of barrier gain and safety radius.

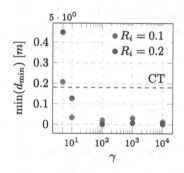
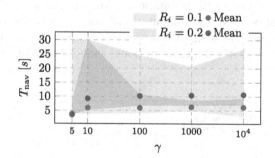

Fig. 4. Minimum distance.   **Fig. 5.** Average navigation time bounded by the maximum and minimum values.

Therefore, by analyzing Fig. 4 and 5 it is possible to see that for $\gamma = 5$ and $R_i = 0.1$ m, it is possible to achieve the best trade-off between safety and navigation time, i.e., the algorithm isn't too conservative ($\min(d_{\min}) \gg 0.18$ m) and the navigation time is the lowest and without deadlocks. Hence, these values were used throughout the rest of the experiments.

Regarding the comparison between the MRA*+OA and DVG+A*, Fig. 6 shows the histogram of the navigation time obtained when using the DVG+A*, the DVG+A* w. OA and the MRA*+OA.

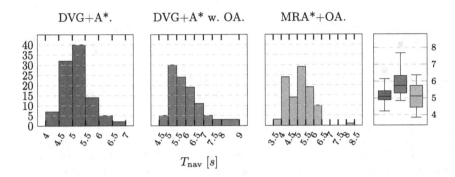

Fig. 6. Histograms and box plot of the navigation time for the antipodal test.

The results shown in Fig. 6 demonstrate that using an uncoordinated path planner without OA is similar to using a coordinated path planner with respect to the navigation time. The DVG+A*, DVG+A* w. OA, and MRA*+OA had 100%, 89% and 99% of the samples with $T_{nav} \leq 7$ s, respectively. This shows that the OA algorithm slows down the robots when the paths aren't coordinated. However, by analyzing the box plot in Fig. 6, it is possible to see that path coordination is capable of eliminating this problem, therefore, showing the importance of the coordination step in the path planner.

Along with maintaining a low navigation time, the coordinated path planner also has a low computational cost, since it generates the paths once. Figure 7 shows the boxplot comparing the computation time of each algorithm. For both DVG+A*, the computational time is accumulated for each recalculated path.

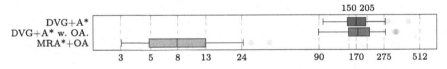

Fig. 7. Box plots of the computational time in [ms] for the antipodal test. The whiskers are samples closest, but not higher, than $\pm 1.5 \times$ Inter Quantile Range (IQR).

In conclusion, Fig. 7 shows that there is practically no advantage in using an uncoordinated path planner for multi-robot applications. For the minimum distance, the rate of samples lower than the CT are 100%, 2% and 0% for the DVG+A*, DVG+A* w. OA, and MRA*+OA, respectively. Thus, only the MRA*+OA completely avoided collisions.

When it comes to the marking test, Fig. 8 shows that the DVG+A* had 98% of the samples with $T_{nav} < 8\,$s, while the DVG+A* w. OA and MRA*+OA had 75% of samples lower than around 15 s. This confirms the results obtained during the antipodal test, in which the DVG+A* was the fastest algorithm.

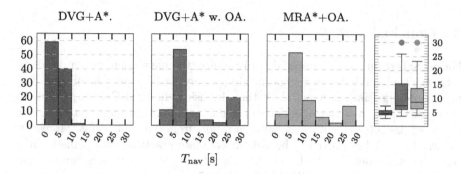

Fig. 8. Histograms and box plot of the navigation time for the marking test.

As expected from the results of the antipodal test, the minimum distance obtained in the marking experiment (Fig. 9) shows that the DVG+A* didn't complete a single test without causing collisions. For the DVG+A* w. OA and MRA*+OA, the results show that both algorithms had a similar performance, where only 21% and 27% of the samples are lower than the CT, respectively.

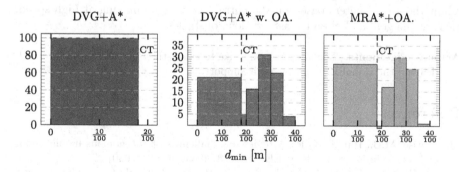

Fig. 9. Histograms of the minimum distance for the marking test.

At last, Fig. 10 shows the results regarding the computational time. During the marking test, the DVG+A*, DVG+A* w. OA. and MRA*+OA have 75% of their samples below 115 ms, 155 ms and 20 ms, respectively. Hence, the coordinated path planner is better than the uncoordinated one. The DVG+A* samples with a computational time lower than 32 ms happened when the robot quickly avoided the obstacles, and the path didn't have to be recalculated many times.

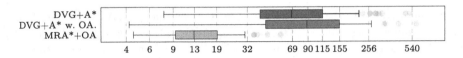

Fig. 10. Box plot of the computational time in [ms] for the marking test.

8   Conclusion

For an SSL team to have optimal performance, the navigation system needs to achieve a trade-off between navigation time, safety, and computational time. The results obtained in this paper show that, by using the PrSBC, it is possible to eliminate collisions among allied robots. Along with reducing more than 70% (see Fig. 9) of the detected collisions between robots from different teams. Moreover, the MRA*+OA has proven to be able to maintain practically the same navigation time and safety as the DVG+A* (Fig. 8 and Fig. 9) with a computational time of almost 700% up to 2100% lower (Fig. 7 and 10) on average.

For future works, it would be beneficial to perform a comparison between more collision avoidance algorithms, especially for algorithms based on different concepts, e.g., velocity obstacle-based [4]. Although the PrSBC was capable of avoiding the collisions during the antipodal test, for the marking experiment it didn't render the same results regarding the minimum distance. Beyond that, for higher speeds ($\geq 2\,\mathrm{m/s}$), the experiments suggest that the values of the barrier gain and safety radius will need to be adjusted.

Furthermore, given the influence of the barrier gain and safety radius in the PrSBC algorithm, its performance could be improved by using a technique to adapt these parameters based on the current state, e.g., moving at high speed, close to the goal and close to fast, or slow, obstacles.

Acknowledgements. The authors would like to thank the University Center of FEI, CAPES and the RoboFEI team for their support.

References

1. Alatise, M.B., Hancke, G.P.: A review on challenges of autonomous mobile robot and sensor fusion methods. IEEE Access **8**, 39830–39846 (2020)
2. Ali, H., Xiong, G., Wu, H., Hu, B., Shen, Z., Bai, H.: Multi-robot path planning and trajectory smoothing. In: 2020 IEEE 16th International Conference on Automation Science and Engineering (CASE), pp. 685–690. IEEE (2020)
3. Allali, J., et al.: NAMeC-Team Description Paper Small Size League RoboCup 2019 Application of Qualification in Division B (2019)
4. Alonso-Mora, J., Beardsley, P., Siegwart, R.: Cooperative collision avoidance for nonholonomic robots. IEEE Trans. Rob. **34**(2), 404–420 (2018)
5. Ames, A.D., Coogan, S., Egerstedt, M., Notomista, G., Sreenath, K., Tabuada, P.: Control barrier functions: theory and applications. In: 2019 18th European control conference (ECC), pp. 3420–3431. IEEE (2019)

6. Degawa, S., Kurosaki, Y., Kanyama, N., Sota, Y., Beppu, T.: MCT Susano Logics 2019 Team Description (2019)
7. Fletcher, R.: Practical Methods of Optimization. Wiley, Hoboken (2013)
8. García, E., Villar, J.R., Tan, Q., Sedano, J., Chira, C.: An efficient multi-robot path planning solution using A* and coevolutionary algorithms. Integrated Comput.-Aided Eng. 30(1), 41–52 (2023)
9. Kyprianou, G., Doitsidis, L., Chatzichristofis, S.A.: Towards the achievement of path planning with multi-robot systems in dynamic environments. J. Intell. Robot. Syst. 104(1), 1–18 (2022)
10. Luo, W., Sun, W., Kapoor, A.: Multi-robot collision avoidance under uncertainty with probabilistic safety barrier certificates. In: Advances in Neural Information Processing Systems, vol. 33, pp. 372–383 (2020)
11. Maranhão, A., et al.: ITAndroids Small Size League Team Description Paper for RoboCup 2020 (2020)
12. Monajjemi, V., Koochakzadeh, A., Ghidary, S.S.: grSim – RoboCup small size robot soccer simulator. In: Röfer, T., Mayer, N.M., Savage, J., Saranlı, U. (eds.) RoboCup 2011. LNCS (LNAI), vol. 7416, pp. 450–460. Springer, Heidelberg (2012). https://doi.org/10.1007/978-3-642-32060-6_38
13. Nazarahari, M., Khanmirza, E., Doostie, S.: Multi-objective multi-robot path planning in continuous environment using an enhanced genetic algorithm. Expert Syst. Appl. 115, 106–120 (2019)
14. Patle, B., Pandey, A., Parhi, D., Jagadeesh, A., et al.: A review: on path planning strategies for navigation of mobile robot. Defence Technology 15(4), 582–606 (2019)
15. Raj, R., Kos, A.: A comprehensive study of mobile robot: history, developments, applications, and future research perspectives. Appl. Sci. 12(14) (2022)
16. RoboCup: Robocup small size team description papers (2023). https://ssl.robocup.org/team-description-papers/. Accessed 03 Apr 2023
17. Rubio, F., Valero, F., Llopis-Albert, C.: A review of mobile robots: concepts, methods, theoretical framework, and applications. Int. J. Adv. Robot. Syst. 16(2) (2019)
18. Silva, C., et al.: Robôcin 2019 Team Description Paper (2019)
19. da Silva Costa, L., Tonidandel, F.: Comparison and analysis of the DVG+A* and rapidly-exploring random trees path-planners for the Robocup-Small size league. In: 2019 Latin American Robotics Symposium (LARS), pp. 1–6. IEEE (2019)
20. da Silva Costa, L., Tonidandel, F.: DVG+A* and RRT path-planners: a comparison in a highly dynamic environment. J. Intell. Robot. Syst. 101(3), 1–20 (2021)
21. Zhu, H., Brito, B., Alonso-Mora, J.: Decentralized probabilistic multi-robot collision avoidance using buffered uncertainty-aware Voronoi cells. Auton. Robot. 46(2), 401–420 (2022)

Poster Presentations

Improving Inertial Odometry Through Particle Swarm Optimization in the RoboCup Small Size League

Lucas Cavalcanti$^{(\boxtimes)}$, João G. Melo$^{(\boxtimes)}$, Riei Joaquim$^{(\boxtimes)}$, and Edna Barros$^{(\boxtimes)}$

Centro de Informática, Universidade Federal de Pernambuco, Av. Prof. Moraes Rego, 1235 - Cidade Universitária, Recife, Pernambuco, Brazil
{lhcs,rjmr,jgocm,ensb}@cin.ufpe.br

Abstract. Small Size League (SSL) robots require mobile navigation to interact with their surroundings. Therefore, robots may rely on odometry to track their movement from the actuator's data and navigate. The odometry is based on the robot's kinematic model, which explains how actuators influence movement. However, robot's kinematic models have parameter inaccuracy and cause systematic errors that accumulate. This study proposes to optimize odometry accuracy using Particle Swarm Optimization (PSO). The method records the robot's movement from its sensor to simulate the traveled path with different robot's kinematic models enabling parameters optimization. The proposed technique improved an SSL odometry accuracy by 76%, with less than 5 cm error in a 10-m path. With a reduced computational cost, it enables longer autonomous navigation for SSL robots and outperforms previous methods.

Keywords: odometry · navigation · kinematics · mobile robots · PSO · RoboCup

1 Introduction

The RoboCup Small Size League (SSL) motivates the development of autonomous robotics focusing on the problem of multi-robots' cooperation in adversarial, highly dynamic environments through robot soccer matches. According to Siegwart et al., an architecture for building these robotics systems should be based on four pillars: perception, localization, cognition, and mobility [1]. In this League, perception and localization are provided by SSL-Vision [2], the centralized vision software from the competition, which sends ball and robots positions to teams' off-field computers, demanding teams to build mainly cognition and mobility for commanding 6 to 11 omnidirectional mobile robots (OMR).

Supported by Centro de Informática (CIn - UFPE), Fundação de Amparo a Ciência e Tecnologia do Estado de Pernambuco (FACEPE), and RobôCIn Robotics Team.

C. Buche et al. (Eds.): RoboCup 2023, LNAI 14140, pp. 93–104, 2024.
https://doi.org/10.1007/978-3-031-55015-7_8

Typically in the SSL, off-field computers process the received information for making decisions and estimating the robots' desired movements, sending them commands through radio frequency wireless communication. However, this architecture presents latency limitations, since perception updates are limited to the cameras' capture frame rates, and commands only reach the robots after being computed and communicated. As the League improves towards more complex and dynamic strategies, with more robots, larger fields, and faster velocities, these limitations become more relevant, demanding faster solutions for tracking the robots' movements.

One approach for achieving faster robot position updates is to use embedded sensing and processing to compute self-tracking estimations. For example, research in the SSL has shown that merging SSL-Vision information with onboard inertial sensors reduces the system's latency [3]. Similarly, state-of-the-art autonomous navigation systems use multiple sensors for computing localization, as information overlap enhances the perception's quality [4].

In an OMR, the robot's odometry, i.e., its position changes over time, can be estimated using inertial sensors and its kinematics model, which describes how actuators contribute to its movement [5], being expressed from the robot's geometry and dimensions [1]. Although these parameters can be measured, their uncertainties, due to modelling inconsistencies and imprecision, may lead to critical differences between the expected and real movements, causing inertial odometry models to accumulate systematic errors over time [6].

For mitigating systematic errors from modelling limitations, authors typically propose optimization solutions based on closed-form equations, requiring analytical work, thus reducing the solution's generalization capability [6]. Sousa et al., for instance, proposed an offline approach to estimate kinematic parameters through optimization methods, learning the best values for minimizing the differences between ground-truth and odometry-estimated trajectories for multiple types of robots [7]. However, it depends on the kinematics partials derivatives for each robot measure, requiring analytical work to match the robot's design.

In this work, we propose a generic offline odometry optimization solution by learning the kinematics matrix's elements using optimization algorithms, avoiding analytic rework to adapt the technique for different robots. Our method demands recordings of the robots' navigation for training, requiring ground truth positions and wheels' movement data. This information, combined with the kinematics matrix, is used for simulating the robot's odometry and computing its error regarding the real trajectory. A Particle Swarm Optimization (PSO) [8] is employed for learning the model that minimizes the Root Mean Square Error (RMSE) between simulated odometry and ground truth translation components.

The approach was tested with an SSL robot from team RobôCIn [9], using SSL-Vision to acquire ground truth data. Results show that optimized parameters have increased its path-tracking accuracy by 76%. Therefore, this paper has the following contributions:

- A method to simulate and evaluate robots' paths.
- An odometry optimization method that optimizes kinematics parameters regardless of the robot's model.
- Optimized odometry parameters for an SSL robot.

2 Related Work

Since 1996 there has been robot parameters optimization research. It started using an analytic equation of the path robot performed, compared to a quadrilateral path it was programmed to perform with a differential robot [6]. Later, additional work extended it to explore a circular path to calibrate differential robot physical measurements [10]. Both works' optimization is a closed-formed equation built according to the robot's structure and experiment path, which narrows the application to specific robots. On the other hand, the odometry optimization achieved accuracy below 10 cm between planned and tracked positions.

Recent authors proposed an odometry optimization for a 3-wheel omnidirectional robot through the kinematic parameters [5]. The least-square error optimization depends on the robot's structure. Lins et al. propose to evaluate paths at a maximum speed of 0.8 m/s to reduce the chance of robot slippage. The experiments had a 2-m path, and besides the low speed and short path, the achieved path error after calibration was around 0.1 m.

Sousa et al. proposed the OptiOdm, a framework to optimize the robot's odometry using the predicted positions and an external vision monitoring system [7]. The methodology uses a Resilient Propagation algorithm (RProp) to optimize the odometry of four types of robots. The RProp finds the error direction between the predicted and the vision positions, so the kinematics parameters are fixed by a factor in the opposite direction of the error. With that method, the OptiOdm achieved an odometry path accuracy of 0.1 m for differential and tricycle robots and 0.2 m for 3-wheel omnidirectional and 4-mecanum wheel robots.

Although OptiOdm optimizes four different robots' structures and it results in accurate odometry, the RProp is based on kinematics equation partial derivatives, which are specific for each robot's model. Therefore, to apply it to SSL robots, it is required to build new optimization equations based on the kinematics of the partial derivatives.

Particle Swarm Optimization (PSO) is a flexible and efficient parameter optimization successfully used to fix robotics parameters [11]. PSO is suitable for multiple applications because it can optimize various parameters and accepts different evaluations, called fitness. As odometry optimization can have a variety of parameters that depend on the robot, and the generated path reveals the odometry quality, the PSO algorithm fits as an optimization solution.

3 Proposed Method

In a wheeled robot, odometry can be estimated by measuring its wheels' rotations and converting them to the robot's movements using its kinematics model. The integration of movements generates a sequence of positions that represents the

Fig. 1. Diagram with overview steps of the method proposed.

robot's path. Therefore, given a set of robot ground truth positions and wheels' movement data, we aim to learn a kinematics model that minimizes the error between predicted and real trajectories on the given data.

We propose an odometry optimization methodology for wheeled mobile robots with four high-level steps, as presented in Fig. 1. First, we collect data from the robot navigating on predefined paths, acquiring its ground truth positions, wheels' angular speeds, and timestamps between samples. Then, given a kinematics model, we simulate the robot's odometry by integrating the wheels' movements with the given timestamps. Thirdly, we evaluate the current model by computing the odometry's trajectory error compared to the ground truth.

Finally, suppose the model does not fit our requirements. In that case, we run a Particle Swarm Optimization (PSO) to generate a new set of elements for the kinematics matrix and move back to step 2. The following subsections present detailed descriptions of each step from the proposed odometry optimization method.

3.1   Data Collection

We acquire data from the robot's movements using WLAN wireless communication, typically used to control SSL robots [12]. Figure 2 presents the data collection pipeline, on which the robot transmits its wheels' speeds ($\dot{\phi}$) and gyroscope angle rotations (θ) to an external computer, where data is aggregated with robot's ground-truth (δ) position from ssl-vision, for each timestamp (t), generating a ".csv" file for each recording.

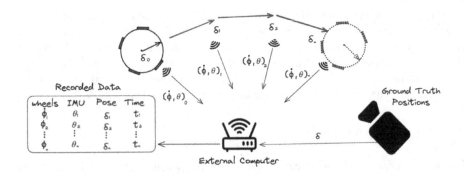

Fig. 2. Data acquisition overview.

3.2   Simulating Odometry Path

Figure 3 illustrates the process of simulating the robot's odometry path from the collected data. First, the kinematics model is applied to the wheels' movements to convert them into the robot's motion. Then, the angular movement is replaced for the IMU gyroscope measurements since it has a high accuracy in real-time movement estimate [13]. Finally, the estimated robot movement is added to its position, and the new pose is appended to the odometry path, and this process is repeated until the data is over.

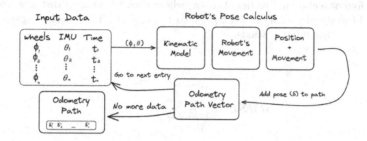

Fig. 3. Simulation overview, which robot's data is the input to the simulation. Then, each data entry is converted to robot's movement. The movement adds to the previous pose, and all poses build the odometry path. In the figure, $\dot{\phi}$ is wheels' speed, θ the IMU angular movement, δ' the robot's expected pose, and t the timestamp.

For an SSL robot with four omnidirectional wheels, as shown in Fig. 4, the analytical kinematics model for converting wheels' speeds to the global robot velocities can be expressed as Eq. 1, which requires a rotation matrix with the robot's orientation, $R(\theta)$, the J_{1f}^{-1}, which is the inverse of J_{1f}, presented in Eq. 2, the J_2, a wheel's radius identity matrix, and the wheel's speed vector, $\dot{\phi}$.

$$\dot{\xi}_I = R(\theta)^{-1} J_{1f}^{-1} J_2 \dot{\phi} \tag{1}$$

$$J_{1f} = \begin{pmatrix} -sin(\alpha_1^\circ) & cos(\alpha_1^\circ) & l \\ -sin(\alpha_2^\circ) & -cos(\alpha_2^\circ) & l \\ sin(\alpha_3^\circ) & -cos(\alpha_3^\circ) & l \\ sin(\alpha_4^\circ) & cos(\alpha_4^\circ) & l \end{pmatrix} \tag{2}$$

3.3   Odometry Evaluation

This work proposes to quantify a path quality by calculating the Root Mean Square Error (RMSE) of the Euclidean distances from the robot's odometry path to ground truth path. As described in Eq. 3, RMSE uses all samples to evaluate the path, as n is the number of samples, δ_i is the robot's ground truth position, $\hat{\delta}_i$ is the robot's odometry predicted position and i^{th} sample order.

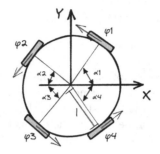

Fig. 4. A four-wheel omnidirectional robot, where each wheel has l distance from the center, and the wheel's rotation, ϕ_1, ϕ_2, ϕ_3, ϕ_4 respectively. The wheels' angles are α_1, α_2, α_3, α_4 from the robot's X axis.

$$RMSE = \sqrt{\frac{1}{n}\sum_{i=1}^{n}(\delta_i - \hat{\delta}_i)^2} \qquad (3)$$

3.4 Kinematics Model Optimization

This work proposes to use Particle Swarm Optimization (PSO) algorithm to reduce kinematic model issues. According to previous research, the PSO was chosen because it produces better and faster solutions [14]. Furthermore, the algorithm can also optimize robotics parameters [11]. For implementing PSO, two important components must be defined: the parameters to optimize, which will build the particles, and how to evaluate it, called particle fitness.

Parameters to Optimize. The goal is to optimize the odometry path fixing kinematic model issues, the parameters change towards an odometry simulation that enhances the path evaluation. As shown in Eq. 1, there are two matrices which have the robot's parameters, the J_{1f}^{-1} and wheels' radius, used in J_2, then these are the parameters to optimize. Considering a 4-wheel SSL robot, there are 12 parameters from J_{1f}^{-1}, and the wheel radius from J_2; thus, the PSO optimizes 13 parameters.

PSO Hyper-Parameters. The PSO has three hyper-parameters, the C_1, C_2, and W, and it varies according to the optimization problem; therefore, different robots will require different parameters. This work proposes to use C_1, C_2, and W as 0.5, 0.3, and 0.9, respectively, as this set of parameters produced interesting results. Also, there is the number of particles, which previous work suggests a minimum of 20 [15]. Moreover, for the number of iterations, it is suggested to test whether the last dozen iterations have stayed with the same fitness.

Optimization Diagram. As shown in Fig. 5, the process starts with the experiments data, which will go through the simulation to generate the odometry-based path, the path is evaluated and then PSO optimizes the matrix J_{1f}^{-1} and wheels' radius, used in J_2.

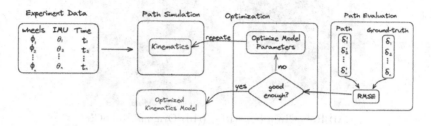

Fig. 5. Proposed optimization diagram. Where fitness function is the RMSE from the experimental data path simulation, using kinematic parameters in PSO population.

4 Evaluation

For evaluating the proposed method, two SSL robots were used. With them, it was necessary to collect data, perform the optimization process and then evaluate the optimized odometry in the soccer field.

4.1 Experiment Setup

In the experiments, two models of 4-wheeled omnidirectional cylindrical robots were used, with 180 mm of diameter. We label them by their SSL IDs, defined by the colour patterns on the top covers, being robot 5 a 150 mm tall, used by team RobôCIn in common SSL matches, and robot 0 a 220 mm tall, which is used for technical challenges in the League, also having a computing module on its top. Both are shown in Fig. 6, with robot 0 on the left and 5 on the right.

The robots are controlled by an external computer, that receives positions from SSL-Vision and communicates with the robot using a Nordic Radio Frequency module, which has low power consumption and a high data exchange rate [12].

On the robot's embedded system, there are four routines with a two milliseconds period to calculate each wheel speed based on encoder sensor pulses. The odometry routine happens every five milliseconds, and it uses the wheels' speed and IMU angular movement into the robot's kinematic equation to convert sensor readings into the robot's motion; this motion is periodically added to the robot's prior known position to build the internal path tracking. An additional communication routine occurs every five milliseconds to report the robot's current wheels' speed, and odometry predicted position to an external computer.

((a)) RobôCIn robot with   ((b)) Original RobôCIn
additional modules.   SSL robot.

Fig. 6. The RobôCIn SSL robots and their structure.

Kinematics Parameters. The kinematics equation has two components that depend on the robot structure, the J_{1f}^{-1}, the inverse of the J_{1f}, and the J_2, the identity matrix of the wheels' radius, which is 0.0248 m for the given robot.

The J_{1f} is presented in Eq. 2, and its inverse does not exist; therefore, it was necessary to use a pseudo-inverse method. So, according to Moore-Penrose method $J_{1f}^{-1} = J_{1f}^*(J_{1f}J_{1f}^*)^{-1}$ [16]. Calculating the inverse of Eq. 2 for the RobôCIn robot, with $\alpha_n = \{\frac{\pi}{3}, -\frac{\pi}{3}, \frac{3\pi}{4}, -\frac{3\pi}{4}\}$ and l as 0.081 m, the results are shown in Eq. 4.

$$J_{1f}^{-1} = \begin{pmatrix} -0,346410 & -0,282843 & 0,282843 & 0,346410 \\ 0,414214 & -0,414216 & -0,414214 & 0,414214 \\ 3,615966 & 2,556874 & 2,556874 & 3,615966 \end{pmatrix} \tag{4}$$

Movement Simulation. The simulation was implemented in Python scripts. It calculates the kinematic movement for each line at the comma-separated dataset and then aggregated it over time to produce the robot's simulated path. Although the robot reported data every five milliseconds, the period used in the conversion from speed to movement was 6.1 ms to accommodate the transmission period.

Odometry Optimization. The PSO was implemented according to the original paper [8]. It was necessary to configure the algorithm hyper-parameters, the number of parameters to optimize, 13, and the fitness function. The fitness method receives the parameters, simulates the robot's path, and returns the path evaluation against the ground truth path from RMSE calculus. For speeding up the conversion of the PSO, the initial parameters population was the original kinematic parameters added to a random value of ±0.2.

4.2 Results

The experiment data were collected in quadrilateral paths of 2×2.5 m, with the robot executing forward, side, and rotational movements; thus, there were movement variations sufficient to evaluate the kinematics components (x, y, ω). Three main experiments were conducted to evaluate the method. For each experiment, there were 4 datasets used to optimize the robot's kinematic model. After the optimization, the parameters were added to the robot's odometry for validation.

Robot 0 Optimization. In the first experiment, robot 0 odometry and ground-truth positions had an RMSE of 0.3749. Applying the optimization process at the original kinematic model, the RMSE with optimized parameters decreased to 0.0907 in the simulated path, as shown in Fig. 7. Applying these parameters to the robot's odometry, a new experiment resulted in an RMSE of 0.1765, shown in Fig. 8. In the end, the optimization reduced the error from 0.3749 to 0.1765, 53% of improvement.

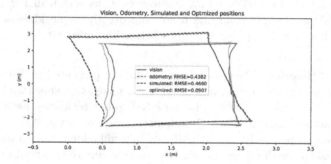

Fig. 7. Robot 0 odometry optimization.

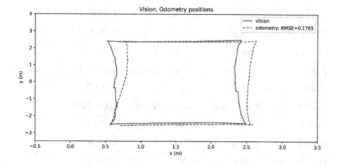

Fig. 8. Robot 0 odometry validation.

Robot 0 Optimization over Optimization. The robot 0 optimized parameters validation still shows an error in the X-axis. Then, more data was collected, now with optimized parameters, for another optimization, such as fine-tuning. The new optimized parameters validation in the robot had 0.0908 RMSE. Moreover, the first optimization achieved an RMSE of 0.1765, and the second, with 0.0908, improved the odometry by 48%. The overall improvement was from 0.3749 to 0.0908, reducing error by 76%.

Robot 5 Optimization. The robot 0 odometry path error decreased by 76%, the original and optimized parameters were applied to Robot 5. With the original parameters, the Robot 5 odometry RMSE was 0.2623; with Robot 0 optimized parameters, the Robot 5 odometry error was 0.1538. This improvement shows that the parameters optimization from one robot improved by 41% for another robot with the same kinematic model.

Finally, it was time to optimize robot 5 parameters with its data to evaluate it against robot 0 optimization. After collecting robot 5 data, its optimization had a 0.1280 RMSE, as shown in Fig. 9. The new parameters validation improved the RMSE from 0.2623 to 0.1050, a 60% improvement, as shown in Fig. 10. Then, the optimized parameters from one robot improve the same kinematic model parameters; however, its optimization has better improvement.

Consolidate Results. The experiment results are presented in Table 1. In it, there are the kinematics model and robot used, navigation speed and the path RMSE. The proposed method can improve SSL robot odometry path tracking. Evaluating methodology 10 times, the odometry error mean was 0.12 and 0.15 for robots 0 and 5, respectively. Also, the RobôCIn's embedded computational time is $156.24 \pm 0.47\,\mu s$ with odometry, $25.03\,\mu s$ more compared without odometry.

Table 1. Consolidate results for all experiments with odometry optimization.

Kinematics Parameters	Robot	Speed	Odometry RMSE
Original Kinematic	$robot_0$	1 m/s	0.37486
Original Kinematic	$robot_0$	2 m/s	0.43823
Original Kinematic	$robot_5$	1 m/s	0.26232
Original Kinematic	$robot_5$	2 m/s	0.29521
$Robot_0$ 1st Optimized	$robot_0$	1 m/s	0.17649
$Robot_0$ 1st Optimized	$robot_0$	2 m/s	0.16051
$Robot_0$ 2nd Optimized	$robot_0$	1 m/s	**0.09076**
$Robot_0$ 2nd Optimized	$robot_0$	2 m/s	0.12111
$Robot_0$ 2nd Optimized	$robot_5$	1 m/s	0.15380
$Robot_0$ 2nd Optimized	$robot_5$	2 m/s	0.16205
$Robot_5$ 1st Optimized	$robot_5$	1 m/s	**0.10501**
$Robot_5$ 1st Optimized	$robot_5$	2 m/s	0.11152

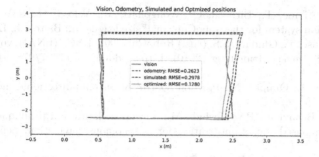

Fig. 9. Robot 5 odometry optimization.

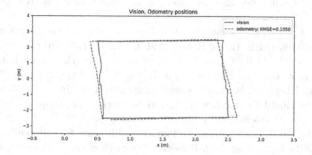

Fig. 10. Robot 5 odometry validation.

5   Conclusion

This work presents a method to improve SSL robot navigation by odometry optimization through learning the robot's kinematic model using PSO. The robot's data, simulation, and RMSE evaluator quantify the kinematic parameters error and implements the PSO fitness method.

While previous works focused on optimizing target-specific robot designs, the proposed optimization works with different kinematics models. Also, the method validation in an SSL robot improved odometry path-tracking accuracy by 76%. With the optimization, the position error for a 10-m path was less than 3 cm. It increases autonomous navigation confidence and works for different robots and navigation speeds, required at SSL competition.

Future work will extend this study to evaluate different robots' kinematic models. It is essential to evaluate the optimization with different navigation techniques. Additionally, it is important to automatize data collection and optimization, so that this method becomes applicable in SSL competition sites.

References

1. Siegwart, R., Nourbakhsh, I.R., Scaramuzza, D.: Introduction to Autonomous Mobile Robots, 2nd edn. The MIT Press, Cambridge (2011)

2. Zickler, S., Laue, T., Birbach, O., Wongphati, M., Veloso, M.: SSL-vision: the shared vision system for the RoboCup small size league. In: Baltes, J., Lagoudakis, M.G., Naruse, T., Ghidary, S.S. (eds.) RoboCup 2009. LNCS (LNAI), vol. 5949, pp. 425–436. Springer, Heidelberg (2010). https://doi.org/10.1007/978-3-642-11876-0_37

3. Abbenseth, J., Ommer, N.: Position control of an omnidirectional mobile robot (2015)

4. Kolar, P., Benavidez, P., Jamshidi, M.: Survey of datafusion techniques for laser and vision based sensor integration for autonomous navigation. Sensors **20**(8) (2020)

5. Lin, P., Liu, D., Yang, D., Zou, Q., Du, Y., Cong, M.: Calibration for odometry of omnidirectional mobile robots based on kinematic correction. In: 2019 14th International Conference on Computer Science and Education (ICCSE), pp. 139–144 (2019)

6. Borenstein, J., Feng, L.: Measurement and correction of systematic odometry errors in mobile robots. IEEE Trans. Robot. Autom. **12**(6), 869–880 (1996)

7. Sousa, R.B., Petry, M.R., Costa, P.G.: OptiOdom: a generic approach for odometry calibration of wheeled mobile robots. J. Intell. Robot. Syst. **105**, 39 (2022)

8. Kennedy, J., Eberhart, R.: Particle swarm optimization. In: Proceedings of ICNN 1995 - International Conference on Neural Networks, vol. 4, pp. 1942–1948 (1995)

9. Silva, C., et al.: Robôcin 2020 team description paper (2020)

10. Tomasi, D.L., Todt, E.: Rotational odometry calibration for differential robot platforms. In: 2017 Latin American Robotics Symposium (LARS) and 2017 Brazilian Symposium on Robotics (SBR), pp. 1–6 (2017)

11. Cao, Y., et al.: Parameter optimization of CPG network based on PSO for manta ray robot. In: Wu, M., Niu, Y., Gu, M., Cheng, J. (eds.) ICAUS 2021. LNEE, vol. 861, pp. 3062–3072. Springer, Singapore (2022). https://doi.org/10.1007/978-981-16-9492-9_300

12. Cavalcanti, L., Joaquim, R., Barros, E.: Optimized wireless control and telemetry network for mobile soccer robots. In: Alami, R., Biswas, J., Cakmak, M., Obst, O. (eds.) RoboCup 2021. LNCS (LNAI), vol. 13132, pp. 177–188. Springer, Cham (2022). https://doi.org/10.1007/978-3-030-98682-7_15

13. Baghdadi, A., Cavuoto, L.A., Crassidis, J.L.: Hip and trunk kinematics estimation in gait through Kalman filter using IMU data at the ankle. IEEE Sens. J. **18**(10), 4253–4260 (2018)

14. Kecskés, I., Székács, L., Fodor, J.C., Odry, P.: PSO and GA optimization methods comparison on simulation model of a real hexapod robot. In: 2013 IEEE 9th International Conference on Computational Cybernetics (ICCC), pp. 125–130 (2013)

15. Piotrowski, A.P., Napiorkowski, J.J., Piotrowska, A.E.: Population size in particle swarm optimization. Swarm Evol. Comput. **58**, 100718 (2020)

16. Ben-Israel, A., Greville, T.N.E.: Generalized Inverses. Springer, New York (2003). https://doi.org/10.1007/b97366

Hybrid Inverse Kinematics for a 7-DOF Manipulator Handling Joint Limits and Workspace Constraints

Maximilian Gießler$^{(\boxtimes)}$ (ID) and Bernd Waltersberger

Offenburg University of Applied Sciences, 77652 Offenburg, Germany
maximilian.giessler@hs-offenburg.de

Abstract. A manipulator with a human-like range of motion combined with adequate control strategies can increase the autonomy of humanoid robots. If we look at the motion patterns of human beings during manipulation, we see that they often combine trunk and manipulator motion to grasp objects lying outside the workspace of the manipulator itself. In this work, we introduce an approach for a hybrid inverse kinematics algorithm with a focus on avoiding joint and workspace limitations. We combine a fully analytical inverse kinematics algorithm for a redundant 7-DOF manipulator with the inverse kinematics of the robot's trunk. To handle the workspace limitations, if a desired pose lies outside the workspace, we combine the robot's trunk motion with the manipulator motion. We demonstrate the performance of our approach with the humanoid robot Sweaty, playing fully autonomously a chess game against a human while picking up chess pieces lying outside the workspace of its manipulator by a combined trunk and manipulator motion.

Keywords: 7-DOF manipulator · Hybrid inverse kinematics · Joint limit avoidance · Workspace constraints avoidance · Humanoid robot

1 Introduction

Humanoid robots have a distinct advantage over all other types of robots since they are designed to resemble the human body, making them ideal for interacting in human-made environments. To improve the autonomy of humanoid robots, it is crucial to enhance their manipulation ability to interact or avoid collisions with objects in human-made habitats. A manipulator with a human-like range of motion and implementing the mathematical foundations to control the manipulator can open new areas of application, such as household chores, elderly care, and service work.

It is generally known that we can abstract the range of motion of a human arm with seven degrees of freedom (DOF), see for example [2,8]. Due to the seven DOF, the manipulator structure is over-actuated since the pose results in a maximum of six constraints. This leads to an over-determined system of

© The Author(s), under exclusive license to Springer Nature Switzerland AG 2024
C. Buche et al. (Eds.): RoboCup 2023, LNAI 14140, pp. 105–116, 2024.
https://doi.org/10.1007/978-3-031-55015-7_9

equations for the inverse kinematic problem. Mechanically, this leads to redundancy resulting in the ability to rotate the forearm and upper arm structure around the relative vector pointing from the intersection point of the shoulder joint axes to the intersection point of the wrist joint axes without leaving the requested pose with the end effector. The elbow joint moves then on a circular trajectory around this relative vector. In the literature, this typical movement is called *self-motion* (see, e.g., [2] or [8]).

Many approaches have been published introducing algorithms to solve the inverse kinematic problem of a redundant manipulator [2,8,10]. Gong et al. showed in [2] an analytical approach to solve the inverse kinematics of a 7-DOF manipulator with two spherical joints in the z_i-, y_j-, and z_k-axis configuration for the shoulder and wrist joints. In this work, Gong et al. focus especially on using the redundancy of the manipulator for obstacle and joint limit avoidance. The subscript of the indexed axis represents the corresponding body-fixed frame. Shimizu et al. showed in [8] a similar approach for a different mechanical manipulator structure. In general, each mechanical design of a robot arm needs its approach to solve inverse kinematics. Therefore, Yu et al. published in [10] an analytical inverse kinematics solution for a redundant manipulator having a wrist joint that is not equivalent to a spherical joint.

Another point to consider is a singularity pose depending on the mechanical manipulator structure that arises in different joint settings. For example, the spherical joint typically used for industrial robots with a rotational order of z_i-, y_j-, and z_k-axis has a singularity if the y_j-axis assumes the joint position zero. Then the two z-axes z_i and z_k are collinear to each other. Moving with the y_j-axis through the null point introduces a configuration change in the joint angles of z_i- and z_k-axis. This leads to a discontinuity in the joint trajectories.

A manipulator based on the human arm typically uses rotational joints leading to a defined spatial workspace. Similarly, there are joint limits in the real world due to mechanical design. For example, humans combine the motion capability of their upper body with that of their arm to reach objects located outside of the workspace of the human's arm separately. Such whole-body motion planning is also the subject of research. Ferrari et al. demonstrated in [1] an approach for planning a whole-body motion for locomotion, loco-manipulation, and manipulation tasks.

Other aspects of manipulators used in humanoid robotics are the total mass, on the one hand, and robustness regarding mechanical loads on the other. Especially the total mass has a crucial role. The dead weight of the manipulator with given actuators reduces both the static and the dynamic working load. To reduce the total mass in combination with high robustness, we can use adapted bearing concepts. Lohmeier et al. describe in [7] a joint design of the robot *LOLA*. For this approach, Lohmeier et al. use a cross roller bearing. The crossed roller bearing is supposed to absorb forces and moments in all spatial directions and thus enable a high load carrying capacity [9]. In addition to the mechanical properties, these bearings are also characterized by their compact design and thus low space requirements [9]. This bearing concept is also used in other humanoid robots as described in [4–6].

Therefore, we introduce with this work an approach for a robust and over-actuated manipulator (7-DOF with a spherical joint as wrist realized by z_i-, y_j-, and z_k-axis), including a closed analytical inverse kinematics. To solve the over-determined system of equations analytically, we introduce an additional parameter as a seventh constraint. The parameter Φ corresponds mechanically to the angle of the elbow joint on the circular path around the connection vector to a given reference. We use the parameter Φ for collision and joint limit avoidance. Further, we show that we can avoid configuration discontinuity due to the singular configurations of the manipulator using an analytical approach. In the case, the robot recognizes that an object to be grasped lies outside the workspace, we use the approach of hybrid inverse kinematics. For this purpose, we solve the inverse kinematics of the trunk to move the manipulator as close as possible to the object under considering the robot's stability.

2 7-DOF Manipulator

The redundant manipulator used in this work has seven DOFs. We arrange the actuators of the shoulder joint in such a way that three uniaxial rotational motors are mechanically connected in series so that the respective joint axes x_1-, y_2-, and z_3- intersect at a point. This mechanical structure represents an ideal spherical joint. We represent the human elbow joint as a uniaxial rotational joint about the y_4-axis of K_4, whereby K_i denotes the i-th coordinate system with orthonormal basis vectors $e_{i\alpha}$ and $\alpha = x, y, z$. For the wrist, we deviate from the structure of the human wrist. We use a spherical joint with the uniaxial rotational axes connected in series about z_5-, y_6-, and z_7-axes concerning the three co-rotating systems K_5, K_6, and K_7. This arrangement offers advantages in terms of reducing the complexity and weight of the structure. A disadvantage of this arrangement is the singular position (zero position of the y_6-axis, z_5- and z_7-axes are collinear), and the resulting configuration change in the joint space at the zero crossing of the y_6-axis. To realize a low-weight manipulator, the manipulator segments and the crossed roller bearings are manufactured of polyamide (PA 12). The entire crossed roller bearing weighs 28 g including the needle roller and cage assemblies. By assembling the crossed roller bearing, it becomes self-supporting and can absorb forces and moments in all spatial directions [9]. We show the total mechanical design in Fig. 1.

In three-dimensional space, six minimal coordinates result in a unique description of the pose. The consequence is that the 7-DOF manipulator is over-actuated since the number of possible joint movements quantitatively exceeds the six independent DOFs in three-dimensional space. This leads to the so-called *self-motion* redundancy, seen in Fig. 1. We form the connecting vector from the intersection of the shoulder joint axes to the intersection point of the wrist joint axes. Next, we span a plane, which we form from the vectors of the upper and lower arm and the point of intersection of the shoulder joint axes (see Fig. 2). It is obvious that this plane then also contains the connecting vector pointing from the shoulder to the wrist intersection point since the wrist intersection point

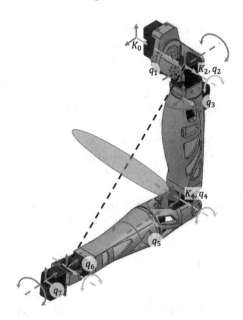

Fig. 1. Model of the 7-DOF manipulator of the humanoid robot *Sweaty*. It contains the DOF referenced with q_i, the body-fixed frames, and the respective joint axis. Further, it displays the circular trajectory of the self-motion characteristic.

is part of the straight line formed from the direction vector of the forearm and wrist intersection point. One Characteristic of redundancy is that rotation of the plane spanned by the upper and lower arm about the represented relative vector is feasible. Assuming ideal joints, a complete rotation is possible while the pose of the end effector does not change. The elbow joint, which lies at the intersection point of the upper and lower arm vector, moves on a circular trajectory around the connection vector. Each point on this circle represents a possible manipulator configuration for reaching the given pose. Provided we define a zero position of the plane, each possible configuration can be described by the parameter Φ.

2.1 Inverse Kinematics

In the following section, we show the equations of the closed-loop analytic inverse kinematic. We have to find an additional analytical constraint so that the number of degrees of freedom matches the number of constraints. The solving approach relies on computing a defined spatial point on the self-motion trajectory of the elbow joint. Starting from this spatial point, we can determine arbitrary solutions by moving along the self-motion trajectory. Therefore, we formulate mathematical conditions, which we use to describe any spatial point on the self-motion trajectory. Figure 2 shows two triangular structures. The upper and lower arm, shown in an arbitrary position, represent two sides of the triangle. The vector r_{TCP} describes the hypotenuse vectorially pointing from the intersection of the

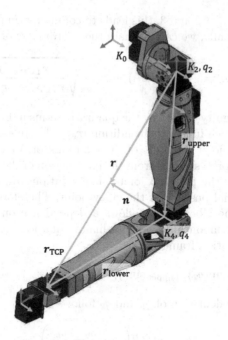

Fig. 2. Description of the vectors defining the plane, which contains the upper r_{upper} and lower arm vector r_{lower} as well as the vector r and n.

joint axes of the shoulder to the target point. The angle q_4 corresponds to the elbow joint angle. Since we know the upper and lower arm lengths in general, we can calculate the drawn angles of the triangle via the cosine theorem. The angle α describes the angle between the upper arm vector r_{upper} and the connection vector r_{TCP}. The following relationship applies to q_4

$$q_4 = \pi - \text{acos}(\frac{r_{\text{upper}} \cdot r_{\text{upper}} + r_{\text{lower}} \cdot r_{\text{lower}} - r_{\text{TCP}} \cdot r_{\text{TCP}}}{2|r_{\text{upper}}||r_{\text{lower}}|}). \qquad (1)$$

We can calculate the vectors spanning the triangle shown in Fig. 2 using the following relationships. The vector r is given thorough the projection of r_{upper} with the unit vector of e_{TCP}. It applies $r = (r_{\text{upper}} \cdot e_{\text{TCP}}) e_{\text{TCP}}$. Next, we must find a normal vector n. It must fulfill the following conditions. Its norm is defined through

$$|n| = |r_{\text{upper}} \times e_{\text{TCP}}|, \qquad (2)$$

which represents the maximum height of the triangle in Fig. 2 and

$$0 = r_{\text{TCP}} \cdot n. \qquad (3)$$

Furthermore, we must define a third condition to calculate the coordinates of the normal vector n represented in the evaluation frame K_0 unambiguously. For example, we choose the condition that the z-component of n is equal to zero.

Combining this with Eq. 2 and 3, this leads to common arm gestures of a human being in general. Finally, we can evaluate the coordinates of n with

$$0 = n_z, \quad n_y = -\left(\frac{n_y\, r_{\mathrm{TCP}_y}}{r_{\mathrm{TCP}_x}}\right), \quad n_x = \pm\sqrt{\frac{r_{\mathrm{TCP}_x}{}^2\,|n|^2}{r_{\mathrm{TCP}_x}{}^2 + r_{\mathrm{TCP}_y}{}^2}} \tag{4}$$

Because of the ambiguity caused by the quadratic terms in Eq. 4, we must choose the combination, which fulfills the condition $|r_{\mathrm{upper}}| = |r + n|$.

If we look at the joint structure of the manipulator, we see that the relative vector of the elbow joint, starting from the intersection of the shoulder joint axes, is influenced just by the first two joints. The rotation around the z_3-axis does not change the spatial position of the elbow joint. Therefore, from the forward kinematics up to the elbow joint follows a dependence on the first two joint angles q_1 and q_2. Symbolically the coordinate equations related to the body-fixed shoulder evaluation frame K_0 are

$$^0r_{\mathrm{elbow}} = [-r_{\mathrm{upper}}\sin(q_2),\ r_{\mathrm{upper}}\sin(q_1)\cos(q_2),\ -r_{\mathrm{upper}}\cos(q_1)\cos(q_2)]^T. \tag{5}$$

using Eq. 5 for the calculation of q_1 and q_2 follows directly

$$q_1 = \mathrm{atan2}\left(\frac{r_{\mathrm{elbow}} \cdot e_{0y}}{-r_{\mathrm{elbow}} \cdot e_{0z}}\right) \tag{6}$$

$$q_2 = \mathrm{asin}\left(\frac{r_{\mathrm{elbow}} \cdot e_{0x}}{-r_{\mathrm{upper}}}\right). \tag{7}$$

By knowing the vectors r_{TCP} and r_{upper} in the evaluation system, we can calculate $r_{\mathrm{lower}} = r_{\mathrm{TCP}} - r_{\mathrm{upper}}$. In the following, we use the property of the mechanical manipulator structure that only the angles from q_1 to q_4 are position-determining. We rotate the coordinates of vector $^0r_{\mathrm{lower}}$ into the coordinate system K_2 using the rotation matrix $^{20}R(q_1, q_2)$ and then set up the symbolic equations for the forward kinematics starting from K_2 to the wrist axes intersection point. This results in

$$^2r_{\mathrm{lower}} = [-r_{\mathrm{lower}}\sin(q_3)\sin(q_4),\ r_{\mathrm{lower}}\cos(q_3)\sin(q_4),\ -r_{\mathrm{lower}}\cos(q_4)]^T. \tag{8}$$

From Eq. 8 obviously follows

$$q_3 = \mathrm{atan2}\left(\frac{-r_{\mathrm{lower}} \cdot e_{2x}}{r_{\mathrm{lower}} \cdot e_{2y}}\right). \tag{9}$$

Finally, the first four joint angles are defined. The end effector now reaches the required position in space.

However, the orientation of the end effector does not yet match the orientation requested for the pose. We correct the difference between the required and actual orientation by the wrist angles. As a first step, we calculate the difference of the requested orientation ^{07}R and the current orientation of the end effector $^{04}R(q_1, q_2, q_3, q_4)$ through $^{47}R(q_5, q_6, q_7) = {^{04}R(q_1, q_2, q_3, q_4)}^T\, {^{07}R}$. We set the difference in the orientation $^{47}R(q_5, q_6, q_7)$ equal to the symbolic forward kinematics of the wrist joints. In general, it applies to the angles q_5, q_6, and q_7

$$q_5 = \text{atan2}\left(\frac{^{47}R_{23}}{^{47}R_{13}}\right) \tag{10}$$

$$q_6 = \text{atan2}\left(\frac{^{47}R_{13}\cos(q_5) + {}^{47}R_{23}\sin(q_5)}{^{47}R_{33}}\right) \tag{11}$$

$$q_7 = \text{atan2}\left(\frac{^{47}R_{32}}{-^{47}R_{31}}\right). \tag{12}$$

We choose another way to calculate q_5, q_6, and q_7, which considers the characteristics of the singularity position for $q_6 = 0$ and the corresponding discontinuity in the joint trajectories in this case. If the trajectory of the pose of the end effector requires a change in sign of q_6, we want to evaluate the joint trajectories of all wrist joint angles without discontinuity. Our algorithm solves this by evaluating two different solutions for the wrist joint angles in parallel. Therefore, it uses the following equations

$$q_{6_1} = \text{acos}(^{47}R_{33}) \tag{13}$$

$$q_{6_2} = -\text{acos}(^{47}R_{33}). \tag{14}$$

By inserting respectively the results of Eq. 13 and 14, it evaluates the Eqs. 10 and 12. This results in a set of two different solutions in the joint space for the wrist joint angles. To prevent discontinuities for q_5 and q_7 it compares both solutions in the joint space to the last applied joint angle values. It chooses the solution with smaller changes in the joint space values. Finally, through this procedure, we can ensure that we evaluate the inverse kinematics of the 7-DOF manipulator fully analytically.

If we request an orientation where q_6 needs to be exactly $q_6 = 0$, the Eqs. 10, 11, and 12 would evaluate $q_5 = 0$, $q_6 = 0$, and $q_7 = 0$. This would lead to a wrong pose of the end effector. We avoid this by evaluating the joint angle q_6 through $q_6 = \text{acos}(^{47}R_{33})$. If our algorithm detects that $q_6 = 0$, we change the calculation method for q_5 and q_7. At first, the algorithm stores the previous value of q_5 in each cycle. By evaluating the symbolic forward kinematics of the wrist joint including $q_6 = 0$ and setting q_5 to the value of the stored one $q_{5_{\text{old}}}$, it follows that we can evaluate q_7 as follows

$$q_7 = \text{atan2}\left(\frac{\cos(q_{5_{\text{old}}})\,^{47}R_{21} - \sin(q_{5_{\text{old}}})\,^{47}R_{11}}{\cos(q_{5_{\text{old}}})\,^{47}R_{11} + \sin(q_{5_{\text{old}}})\,^{47}R_{21}}\right). \tag{15}$$

By using the value $q_{5_{\text{old}}}$ for calculating the current solution, we avoid discontinuities in the joint space.

2.2   Joint Limit and Workspace Constraints Avoidance

The calculated joint angles depend directly on the defined normal vector n since it influences the position of the upper arm vector r_{upper}. Consequently, we lose the self-motion property of the 7-DOF structure. To regain this property, we use second-order rotation tensor [3]. The following relation applies

$$r_{\text{upper}_{\text{rot}}} = (\cos(\Phi)\,\boldsymbol{I} + (1 - \cos(\Phi))\,(e_{\text{TCP}} \otimes e_{\text{TCP}}) + \sin(\Phi)\,\tilde{e}_{\text{TCP}})r_{\text{upper}}. \quad (16)$$

This allows the rotation of r_{upper} around r_{TCP}. Here Φ is the rotation angle. The chosen normal vector n defines the initial position of the manipulator where $\Phi = 0$ applies. $\tilde{e}_{\text{TCP}}$ is a skew-symmetric tensor representing the cross-product multiplication. We use this characteristic to avoid joint limits. We have parameterized the joint limits in the algorithm. The algorithm checks for each calculation cycle whether the evaluated joint configuration exceeds the joint limits. If a joint limit is not met, the algorithm automatically varies the parameter Φ and generates iteratively another joint configuration. The algorithm repeats this procedure until a joint configuration is found within the joint limits and a maximum predefined deviation from the current arm configuration to avoid discontinuities.

Further, at the beginning of each calculation cycle, the algorithm compares the length of r_{TCP} to the maximum manipulator length. If it determines that r_{TCP} has a norm in the range of the maximum manipulator length, our algorithm uses the inverse kinematic algorithm for the trunk angles of the robot ahead. We try to move the trunk so that the distance to the target point is minimized and lies in the workspace of the manipulator. This process is limited by the joint limits of the trunk and by the robot's static stability, which has to be guaranteed. Finally, the robot can move its trunk angles only in a range where the tipping of the robot is avoided. We call this procedure hybrid inverse dynamics.

3   Results

We analyze the capability of our approach compared to the commonly used inverse kinematics approach. For this, we simulate a manipulator movement lifting the TCP in the z-direction of the evaluation frame K_0 with a constantly requested orientation of the TCP using both approaches simultaneously. In Fig. 3(a), we show the developments of the wrist joint angles q_5, q_6, and q_7 for the inverse kinematics using the commonly used equations (Eqs. 10, 11 and 12). In contrast, in Fig. 3(b), we show the curve developments for the wrist joint angles evaluated with our approach. If we compare the curve developments of both wrist joint angle trajectories, we see that our solution using Eq. 13 or Eq. 14 for calculating the joint angle q_6 allows positive as well as negative values. In contrast, Eq. 11 of the commonly used approach evaluates q_6 as continuous positive. Further, if we analyze the time point at 2.4 s, we see that q_6 is with both approaches evaluated as zero. At this point in time, the commonly used equations lead to a discontinuity in the joint angles development of q_5, q_6, and q_7. q_6 is not crossing the zero line. It increases for the following time points. Our approach evaluates q_6 for the time points before 2.4 s as negative and after that time point as positive. We see there is no discontinuity. Due to this, also the developments of q_5 and q_7 contain no discontinuity.

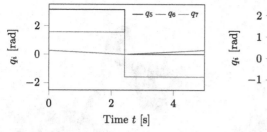
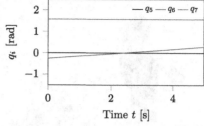

(a) Inverse Kinematic with discontinuity (b) Inverse Kinematic without discontinuity

Fig. 3. Developments of wrist joint angles using common inverse kinematics equations shown in (a) and using adapted inverse kinematics equations to prevent discontinuity shown in (b).

From the forward kinematics, it follows immediately that, provided q_6 reaches the zero position, the result for the angles q_5 and q_7, calculated by Eq. 10 and 12, respectively, are also zero. This follows because the corresponding entries of the rotation matrix $^{47}R(q_5, q_6, q_7)$ contain the term $\sin(q_6)$ as a factor. The leads at the so-called singular pose to a deviating TCP orientation compared to the requested pose. In contrast, in our approach, we use the collinear property of the z_5- and z_7-axis in the singular pose. Therefore, it is possible to set q_5 equal to the last valid value of q_5 and using only rotation matrix entries that do not contain the term $\sin(q_6)$ to evaluate q_7 with Eq. 15. Thus rotation matrix entries are generally non-zero. This leads to joint angles, which can cover the requested orientation.

In Fig. 4, we show the capability of our hybrid inverse kinematics approach. If a pose is located at the edge or outside the workspace of the 7-DOF manipulator, our algorithm uses the trunk joint angles to move the pose inside the workspace of the manipulator. For this purpose, the inverse kinematics for the trunk is used. The 7-DOF inverse kinematics of the manipulator then calculates the joint angles needed to move the pose based on the results of the inverse kinematics of the trunk. We see in Fig. 4(a) that the manipulator does not reach the pose despite maximum manipulator deflection. In contrast, we reach the pose by the resulting upper body motion from the inverse kinematics of the trunk, as seen in Fig. 4(b).

4   Discussion

Our work aimed to show an inverse kinematics approach for a 7-DOF over-actuated manipulator with a spherical joint (z_5-, y_6-, and z_7-axis rotation) as the wrist that overcomes the discontinuities due to the singularity pose. Further, we want to use the capabilities of this analytical inverse kinematics approach and combine it with a second inverse kinematics algorithm for the trunk joint angles to avoid running into mechanical joint limits and increasing the spatial space of the workspace (compared to [2] and [8]).

(a) 7-DOF inverse kinematic   (b) Hybrid inverse kinematic (10-DOF)

Fig. 4. Comparison of the evaluated joint configurations of the 7-DOF inverse kinematics in Fig. (a) and hybrid 10-DOF inverse kinematics in Fig. (b) for a pose lying outside of the workspace of the manipulator of the humanoid robot *Sweaty*.

The main findings of our work are, on the one hand, that we show a fully analytical approach that overcomes the discontinuity in the wrist joint angles, provided that the manipulator reaches its singular joint position during the movement of the manipulator on a trajectory. Therefore, we use two different calculation methods for the joint space configuration of the wrist joint angles simultaneously. This allows us to set positive as well as negative values for the joint angle q_6 of the y_6-axis of the wrist. Furthermore, this possibility leads to the fact that we do not have discontinuities in the wrist joint angles when moving on trajectories (compared to [2]). We have proven this by the results shown in Fig. 3.

If we request a pose that requires the singularity posture of the manipulator's wrist joint, our approach calculates a joint angle configuration that allows the manipulator to reach the requested pose. Here, we exploit the collinear property of the z_5- and z_7-axis in the singular pose. This allows us to set an arbitrary value for, e.g., q_5. By defining q_5, we can solve the analytical equation for q_7 extracted from the forward kinematics (see Eq. 15). Since we define q_5 equal to the previous value for $q_{5_{old}}$ in this particular case, we minimize the change between the previous and the joint angle configuration in the singular position to a minimum. In contrast, in such a case the commonly used approaches [2] evaluate the joint angle for q_5 and q_7 to zero. The manipulator fails to reach the requested pose.

Further, we show a concept to avoid exceeding the mechanical joint limits. On the one hand, the introduced parameter Φ is suitable for this purpose. If at least one joint angle of the calculated joint configuration lies outside of the joint limits ranges, the algorithm iteratively searches for the closest possible alternative joint configuration that matches the joint limits using the parameter Φ.

If the pose is outside the working range of the manipulator and therefore cannot be reached, we have combined the inverse kinematics of the 7-DOF manipulator with the inverse kinematics of the trunk. This results in a significantly larger workspace without moving the entire robot. We showed an example of the application in Fig. 4. We want to mention that this method is limited by the robot's static stability. In some configurations, the trunk angles may cause the robot to tilt. To prevent this, we evaluate the static stability of the calculated kinematic configuration (containing the trunk and arm angles) by checking whether the predicted center of mass projection lies within the support polygon of the robot's feet. If static stability is guaranteed, the robot quasi-statically actuates the joints to reach the target configuration with its trunk and arm. If static stability is not guaranteed, the algorithm rejects the kinematic configuration. In future work, we want to extend the algorithm so that the robot could additionally use a balancing movement with the hip and its other arm to reach a static stable kinematic configuration. In addition, it would also be conceivable to move bipedally in the direction of the target pose.

The real-world application of all these methods combined, we showed in the first public chess game of a humanoid robot against a human being. The humanoid robot *Sweaty* was able to compete fully autonomously in playing chess, while it moved the chess pieces autonomously using hybrid inverse kinematics. An impression of the chess game one can find at https://www.youtube.com/watch?v=ATJoprLp1iI.

5   Conclusion and Future Work

In this work, we demonstrate an approach for a hybrid inverse kinematics algorithm with a focus on avoiding joint and workspace constraints. We introduce a fully analytical inverse kinematics algorithm for a redundant 7-DOF manipulator. With this, we can handle the singularity pose of the manipulator and use its self-motion property to find iteratively joint configurations lying within the joint limits. To handle the workspace constraints, for example, if a desired pose lies outside the workspace, we move the robot's trunk toward the requested spatial position to reduce the manipulator's distance from it.

We showed the real-world application of this approach with our humanoid robot *Sweaty* playing a chess game fully autonomous against a human being. While playing chess, it picked up the chess pieces positioned out of the workspace of its manipulator through a combined trunk and manipulator motion. Further, there were no discontinuities in the joint trajectories of the wrist.

In further work, we plan to extend the approach allowing hip displacement by adjusting the leg joint angles. This should significantly increase the standing stability of the robot to expand the range of applicable trunk joint angles.

References

1. Ferrari, P., Cognetti, M., Oriolo, G.: Humanoid whole-body planning for loco-manipulation tasks. In: 2017 IEEE International Conference on Robotics and Automation (ICRA), Singapore, Singapore, pp. 4741–4746. IEEE (2017). https://doi.org/10.1109/ICRA.2017.7989550. http://ieeexplore.ieee.org/document/7989550/

2. Gong, M., Li, X., Zhang, L.: Analytical inverse kinematics and self-motion application for 7-DOF redundant manipulator. IEEE Access **7**, 18662–18674 (2019). https://doi.org/10.1109/ACCESS.2019.2895741. https://ieeexplore.ieee.org/document/8630999/

3. Itskov, M.: Tensor Algebra and Tensor Analysis for Engineers. MATHENGIN, Springer, Heidelberg (2013). https://doi.org/10.1007/978-3-642-30879-6

4. Kang, S.H., Tesar, D.: An analytical comparison between ball and crossed roller bearings for utilization in actuator modules for precision modular robots. In: Volume 2: 29th Design Automation Conference, Parts A and B, Chicago, Illinois, USA, pp. 1221–1230. ASMEDC (2003). https://doi.org/10.1115/DETC2003/DAC-48834. https://asmedigitalcollection.asme.org/IDETC-CIE/proceedings/IDETC-CIE2003/37009/1221/297675

5. Kim, I.M., Kim, H.S., Song, J.B.: Design of joint torque sensor and joint structure of a robot arm to minimize crosstalk and torque ripple. In: 2012 9th International Conference on Ubiquitous Robots and Ambient Intelligence (URAI), Daejeon, Korea, pp. 404–407. IEEE (South) (2012). https://doi.org/10.1109/URAI.2012.6463026. http://ieeexplore.ieee.org/document/6463026/

6. Lee, C.H., Choi, J., Lee, H., Kim, J., Bang, Y.: Mechanism design of exoskeletal master device for dual arm robot teaching. In: 2014 14th International Conference on Control, Automation and Systems (ICCAS 2014), Gyeonggi-do, South Korea, pp. 241–243. IEEE (2014). https://doi.org/10.1109/ICCAS.2014.6987993. http://ieeexplore.ieee.org/document/6987993/

7. Lohmeier, S., Buschmann, T., Ulbrich, H., Pfeiffer, F.: Modular joint design for performance enhanced humanoid robot LOLA. In: Proceedings 2006 IEEE International Conference on Robotics and Automation, ICRA 2006, Orlando, FL, USA, pp. 88–93. IEEE (2006). https://doi.org/10.1109/ROBOT.2006.1641166. http://ieeexplore.ieee.org/document/1641166/

8. Shimizu, M., Kakuya, H., Yoon, W.K., Kitagaki, K., Kosuge, K.: Analytical inverse kinematic computation for 7-DOF redundant manipulators with joint limits and its application to redundancy resolution. IEEE Trans. Robot. **24**(5), 1131–1142 (2008). https://doi.org/10.1109/TRO.2008.2003266. http://ieeexplore.ieee.org/document/4631505/

9. Wittel, H., Spura, C., Jannasch, D.: Roloff/Matek Maschinenelemente: Normung, Berechnung, Gestaltung. Springer Fachmedien Wiesbaden, Wiesbaden (2021). https://doi.org/10.1007/978-3-658-34160-2

10. Yu, C., Jin, M., Liu, H.: An analytical solution for inverse kinematic of 7-DOF redundant manipulators with offset-wrist. In: 2012 IEEE International Conference on Mechatronics and Automation, Chengdu, China, pp. 92–97. IEEE (2012). https://doi.org/10.1109/ICMA.2012.6282813. http://ieeexplore.ieee.org/document/6282813/

Calibration of Inverse Perspective Mapping for a Humanoid Robot

Francisco Bruno Dias Ribeiro da Silva[1]([✉]) [iD],
Marcos Ricardo Omena de Albuquerque Máximo[1] [iD], Takashi Yoneyama[2] [iD],
Davi Herculano Vasconcelos Barroso[1], and Rodrigo Tanaka Aki[1]

[1] Autonomous Computational Systems Lab (LAB-SCA), Computer Science Division,
Aeronautics Institute of Technology, São José dos Campos, SP 12.228-900, Brazil
fbrunodr@gmail.com.
[2] Electronic Engineering Division, Aeronautics Institute of Technology,
São José dos Campos, SP 12228-900, Brazil

Abstract. This paper proposes a method to calibrate the model used for inverse perspective mapping of humanoid robots. It aims at providing a reliable way to determine the robot's position given the known objects around it. The position of the objects can be calculated using coordinate transforms applied to the data from the robot's vision device. Those transforms are dependent on the robot's joint angles (such as knee, hip) and the length of some components (e.g. torso, thighs, calves). In practice, because of the sensitivity of the transforms with respect to the inaccuracies of the mechanical data, this calculation may yield errors that make it inadequate for the purpose of determining the objects' positions. The proposed method reduces those errors using an optimization algorithm that can find offsets that can compensate those mechanical inaccuracies. Using this method, a kid-sized humanoid robot was able to determine the position of objects up to 2 m away from the itself with an average of 3.4 cm of error.

Keywords: robotics · humanoid robot · inverse perspective mapping · computer vision · calibration

1 Introduction

ITAndroids is a team of students from the *Aeronautics Institute of Technology* (ITA) that participates in national and international robotics competitions. One of the leagues in which ITAndroids participates is Humanoid KidSize, which is a league of autonomous robots with a human-like body structure and senses that play soccer against each other [1]. This task involves some complex challenges, such as building and controlling the robot, as well as programming its decision making abilities.

Supported by CNPQ (Conselho Nacional de Desenvolvimento Científico e Tecnológico).

One of these challenges is the robot's autonomous localization on the field with their human-like sensors. This is especially important, as knowing their position on the field is necessary to take a variety of actions, such as determining whether they are getting out of bounds of the field or attacking the correct goal (a field is symmetric, so a robot without its localization cannot discern between his and the opponent's goal). In a higher level, the knowledge of their position is also of paramount importance in planning and adoption of complex attack and defence tactics.

On the Humanoid League, with exception of some match commands (like start the match, foul and end the match), the robot is not allowed to receive information from an external computer. Therefore, the robots need to process all the information they need to play is a manner analogous to human players, including finding their own position.

Notice that solving the problem of finding the robot's position cannot be done only with the image of their camera (the field they play is, theoretically, symmetrical). However, given an algorithm that estimates well the position of the robot relative to some field marks it sees on camera, we can use a Monte Carlo Localization technique to determine the robot's pose in the field, as described in [2] (Here, field marks refer to the intersection of field lines, as can be seen in Fig. 1).

Fig. 1. Image with annotated field markers. The field marks are the intersections between field lines. This image was generated thanks to [3].

The algorithm that is used to perform the estimation of the robot position relative to the field marks it sees on camera is the inverse perspective mapping algorithm. Section 2 describes how this algorithm is used to obtain the position of objects in a plane (in our case, the plane is the playing field and the objects are the field marks) (for further reading see [4]). Having a good estimation of the robot's position relative to some field marks we can use [2] to solve the localization problem. This is the standard approach used by teams in Robocup Humanoid KidSize competition.

However, this process is not easy to do in practice, as there is error involved in the inverse perspective mapping calculations, which can make the objects' positions estimation inadequate for the Monte Carlo Localization. Particularly, the ITAndroids humanoid robot uses the inverse perspective mapping algorithm to calculate its position relative to objects seen on camera. This process achieves good results on simulations, yet, does not perform well in real life, as the vector transformations involved in the calculations are sensitive to minor mechanical inaccuracies (for instance, a joint with a minor angle offset can output a major position difference). So, we need a calibration process capable of eliminating those mechanical errors in the calculations.

This paper contributes by developing a method to calibrate a humanoid robot inverse perspective mapping algorithm. The ideas here can be applied to other domains in which a robot performs a inverse perspective mapping to determine the position of objects relative to itself. The method developed here is based on *guessing* offsets on some of the robot's joints angles until the calculated positions of known objects are in agreement with their actual positions.

The remaining of this paper is organized as follows. Section 2 explains inverse perspective mapping (IPM). Section 3 presents detailed description of the calibration method and why it is done the way it is, so the reader can adapt our solution to their needs. Section 4 presents numerical and visual data of the results of our calibration method in a humanoid kid sized robot. Finally, Sect. 5 concludes and shares our ideas for future work.

2   Inverse Perspective Mapping

Inverse perspective mapping (IPM) is concerned with determining the 3D world position of an object seen in an image. In this context, the well-known pinhole camera model dictates that the perspective projection of a point $[x \ y \ z]^T$ represented in the world coordinate system yields an image point $[u \ v]^T$ [9] given by

$$s \begin{bmatrix} u \\ v \\ 1 \end{bmatrix} = K \begin{bmatrix} R \ t \end{bmatrix} \begin{bmatrix} x \\ y \\ z \\ 1 \end{bmatrix}, \tag{1}$$

where K and $[R \ t]$ are the intrinsic and extrinsic matrices, respectively. These matrices are defined as

$$K = \begin{bmatrix} f_x & 0 & c_x \\ 0 & f_y & c_y \\ 0 & 0 & 1 \end{bmatrix}, \tag{2}$$

$$[R \ t] = \begin{bmatrix} r_{11} & r_{12} & r_{13} & t_1 \\ r_{21} & r_{22} & r_{23} & t_2 \\ r_{31} & r_{32} & r_{33} & t_3 \end{bmatrix}, \tag{3}$$

where f_x and f_y are the focal lengths expressed in pixel units, and (c_x, c_y) is the principal point. The parameters $r_{ij}, \forall i, j \in \{1, 2, 3\}$ and $t_k, \forall k \in \{1, 2, 3\}$ encode the camera's pose w.r.t. the world coordinate system.

The intrinsic matrix depends solely on the camera and the lenses, but not on the camera's pose, therefore its parameters can be determined once by using information provided in the camera's data sheet or by a calibration process usually provided by most computer vision libraries, such as OpenCV [5]. For a mobile robot, the extrinsic matrix is always changing with the robot's motion. In our case of a humanoid robot, the extrinsic matrix may be computed using the joint positions and kinematic chain information.

There are many issues that prevent a precise kinematic model, such as manufacturing imprecision, and joint flexibility and backlash. Moreover, due to communication bandwidth limits, we are unable to read all the servo positions within one walking control cycle, so we need to use expected joint positions for the leg's joints.

These errors propagate through the kinematic chain, making the extrinsic matrix estimate very imprecise. To mitigate these effects, we compute the camera's translation using only the joint positions, but use the torso's orientation estimate together with the positions of the neck joints measured by the servos' encoders for the camera's rotation. The torso's orientation is estimated by an Extended Kalman Filter (EKF) running on IMU data [6]. Unfortunately, this is not enough for an adequate estimate, since even small angular errors can be very harmful to distances estimated by IPM. Furthermore, there is also error in IMU alignment.

Notice that (1) shows how to project a world point to the image. IPM deals with the inverse problem, but there are infinite world points which are mapped to the same image point during perspective mapping. In humanoid robot soccer, objects seldom leave the ground, so to avoid this ambiguity, a common approach is to consider that the seen object is on the ground. Therefore, assuming that the object is at a constant height $z = h$ above the ground, we may write

$$
s \begin{bmatrix} u \\ v \\ 1 \end{bmatrix} = K \begin{bmatrix} R \ t \end{bmatrix} \begin{bmatrix} x \\ y \\ h \\ 1 \end{bmatrix},
\tag{4}
$$

which is a system of linear equations with x and y as variables. Then, Eq. (4) may be solved analytically to yield the world position $[x \ y \ h]^T$ of a given pixel $[u \ v]^T$. In our system, we use $h = 0$ for field features and goalposts (we use the intersection of the goalpost with the ground as feature) and $h = r$ for the ball, where r is the radius of the ball.

3   Calibration Methodology

The robot IPM model calibration can be divided in two parts. In the first, it uses its camera to get images with ArUco [7] markers and saves the position of each detected ArUco in a file. In the second part, it passes that data to an algorithm that estimates the offsets in some of the robot's coordinate transforms.

3.1   Data Collection

In the first part of the calibration process, the robot collects data from objects in known positions. To do that, we used ArUco markers placed in known positions. An ArUco marker is a synthetic square marker composed by a wide black border and an inner binary matrix which determines its identifier (id). The black border facilitates its fast detection in the image and the binary codification allows its identification and the application of error detection and correction techniques [7]. Examples of such markers can be seen in Fig. 2.

Fig. 2. Example of 7 distinct ArUco markers [7].

The operation principle of an ArUco marker is similar to that of a QR-Code. The choice for ArUco instead of the most familiar QR-Code is based on its ease of detection [7], allowing the robot to see them further away, yielding better results.

For the calibration with ArUco markers in known positions, we developed a carpet (see Fig. 3) with 120 markers in known positions. This carpet has different size markers, according to the robot's distance detection capability. Its size (3 m by 1.5 m) allows for a good area of calibration without making it difficult to be transported, stored or set up. This approach was inspired by the solutions other teams have developed, such as Rhoban [13] and MRL [14].

During calibration, the robot is placed in the bottom center of the carpet, with its feet's center aligned with the carpet side, as Fig. 4. Then, the robot obtains images of the carpet with its neck in different angles, in such a way to map the carpet entirely. Those images are processed by an ArUco detection algorithm. Every time the robot detects some ArUco, the information necessary to perform the IPM is saved, together with the position of every detection on the image and the real positions of the ArUcos. This information is saved in a file which is later read by the calibration algorithm.

3.2   Calibration Algorithm

Comparing the calculated positions of each ArUco markers and their actual positions we notice substantial errors (see Fig. 5). That happens due to the robot's mechanical inaccuracies. To fix those inaccuracies we set offsets for the angles of some of the robot's coordinate transforms. We choose the angles that affect the

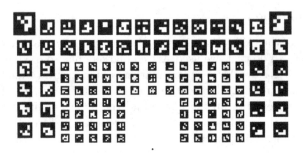

Fig. 3. Carpet with ArUcos that is used during a calibration. The real carpet is 3 m by 1.5 m.

Fig. 4. Robot collecting data for calibration.

calculation of the ArUco's positions, and they are: the three rotational degrees of freedom of the neck and the roll and pitch of the torso. The yaw of the torso was not taken into account, as the way the legs are built does not allow significant displacement in that direction. Also, length offsets were ignored. The calibration considering length offsets in the torso, legs and neck was also done, with small optimization difference. This calibration happens just before a match and must be performed as fast as possible. Adding length offsets doesn't increase the cost of computing (5), but takes longer for the optimizer to converge due to additional dimensions. Thus we conclude that adding those offsets is not worth the longer runtime.

The purpose of the calibration is to find the offsets that make the calculated positions of the ArUcos as close as possible to their actual positions. Considering that those offsets make the calculated positions sufficiently close to the real positions, we can assure that any object within a carpet of distance to the robot (up to 1.5 m in front and 1.5 m to the side) will have its distance calculated precisely, as it is equivalent to the robot detecting an ArUco marker in the same position.

Notice that, even though an area of 3 m by 1.5 m seems tiny, in comparison to a person, the Humanoid Kidsize League has robots between 40 cm and 90 cm and a field with length 9 m by 6 m of width, according to the RoboCup rules [8]. Thus, given a successful calibration, we can assure precise distance calculation in, at least, an area that corresponds to $(3 \cdot 1.5)/(9 \cdot 6) = 8.33\%$ of the area of the entire field. The calibration also generalizes well for positions out of this area because of how the IPM algorithm works. So, in practice, we have precise distance estimation for objects even out of the training area (here training area refers to the carpet area).

To find the best offsets to calculate the position of an object, we need an expression to evaluate the quality of each set of offsets. Let x be a vector containing the chosen offsets, $\mathcal{D}$ all the data collected in the first part of the calibration, we need a function $J(x, \mathcal{D})$ that outputs the cost related to the vector x given the collected data $\mathcal{D}$. In this problem, a vector x_1 is said to be better than other vector x_2 if $J(x_1, \mathcal{D}) < J(x_2, \mathcal{D})$. We have a problem of optimization of the cost function J. Let us construct J in the following way: for every ArUco detection $i \in \mathcal{D}$ we infer its position (using the IPM algorithm) and then get an error $\varepsilon_i = \hat{p}_i - p_i$. Then J is the sum of the square of the modulus of the errors:

$$J(x, \mathcal{D}) = \sum_{i \in \mathcal{D}} \|\varepsilon_i\|^2 = \sum_{i \in \mathcal{D}} \|\hat{p}_i - p_i\|^2, \tag{5}$$

where p_i is the ground truth position of the i-th detected ArUco in $\mathcal{D}$ and $\hat{p}_i$ is the calculated position of the i-th detected ArUco in $\mathcal{D}$. Remember $\mathcal{D}$ is all the collected data. In the example used in this paper, $\mathcal{D}$ is a text file with all the detected ArUcos' positions in their images, their real 3D positions and the robot joints' positions which are necessary to perform the IPM algorithm. p_i and $\hat{p}_i$ are 3 dimensional vectors, but in our case all ArUcos are in the same plane (they are on the ground, so $z = 0$), so p_i and $\hat{p}_i$ are reduced to two dimensional vectors.

Calculating $\hat{p}_i$ is done using the information of the joints' angles saved in $\mathcal{D}$, the position of the detection in the image and the IPM algorithm, as described in Sect. 2.

Knowing how to calculate $\hat{p}_i$ from the collected data and the offsets x, and the actual position of each ArUco p_i, the cost function $J(x, \mathcal{D})$ is defined. However, in practice, those definitions are not enough to optimize x, due to errors that occur during the data collecting part of the calibration. So, we need, firstly, to remove outliers from the data.

Removing Outliers from Data. Plotting $\hat{p}_i$ for each detected ArUco $i \in d$ from some benchmark collected data (this data was collected during one of the calibration tests and is used throughout this entire paper) we obtain Fig. 5.

In Fig. 5(a), blue dots have alpha $= 0.2$ (image opacity level). Hence, dark points are actually more than one detection in the same region. Decreasing the value of alpha to 0.01 it is still possible to note some dark regions, as Fig. 5(b) shows.

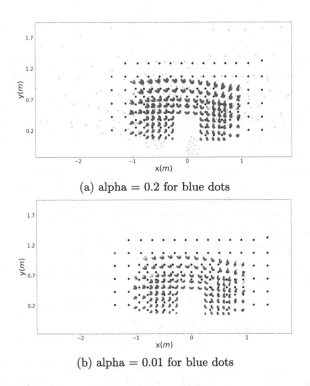

(a) alpha = 0.2 for blue dots

(b) alpha = 0.01 for blue dots

Fig. 5. ArUcos' calculated positions before calibration. Blue dots are the calculated positions while black dots are the actual positions. (Color figure online)

The difference between Fig. 5(a) and (b) suggests that all the light blue dots found on Fig. 5(a) are false positives. Those false positives are detrimental to the calibration, since some of them were detected really far away, creating a harmful bias in the optimization of x.

To remove the outliers in $\mathcal{D}$, we need to adopt a point selection criteria. The criteria we chose is described in the following steps:

- For each ArUco on the carpet, a list containing all the detections of this ArUco is made.
- For each list, we calculate the mean position and the standard deviation.
- We delete all the points in each list that are above 2 standard deviations from the mean. This value was chosen knowing that, for a gaussian distribution, approximately 95% of the data correctly detected will not be deleted. This allows us to exclude false positives without compromising the data.

The results of such selection can be seen in Figs. 6 and 7. Red points are points that were excluded in the process. Blue points are the calculated points that were not excluded. The brown dot is the mean of the calculated positions (blue and red points) and the black point is the actual ArUco position.

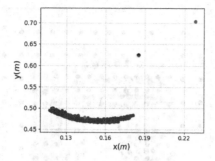

Fig. 6. Outlier removal example for an ArUco with 1 false positive.

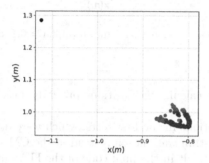

Fig. 7. Outlier removal example for an ArUco without false positives.

Even though this process may lose some true positives, such as Fig. 7, it is efficient to remove outliers, as shown in Fig. 6. The remaining data after this process is plotted in Fig. 8.

In fact, analysing Fig. 8 we can already associate each black dot with a cluster of blue points. This indicates that the outlier removal process worked correctly.

Optimizing Offsets. With the outliers removed from $\mathcal{D}$, we may optimize x through $J(x, \mathcal{D})$. Now, we need to choose an algorithm that estimates better offsets until we find the minimum of $J(x, \mathcal{D})$. This is a non-linear optimization problem. It is also hard to do some kind of gradient descent to solve this problem. Because of that, during the development of this calibration method, we used the following two optimization algorithms: Covariance Matrix Adaptation Evolution Strategy (CMA-ES) [11] and Nelder-Mead [12]. Both algorithms choose a starting value for x and, through a cost function (in this case J), they get a better x in the next iteration. The algorithms return a vector x when they reach a stop criterion, usually when $J(x, \mathcal{D})$ can not be reduced anymore by the algorithm.

It is important to highlight that neither of these algorithms guarantee convergence of $J(x, \mathcal{D})$ to its global minimum. Indeed, both algorithms can return a value of x found on a local minimum. For the purpose of this calibration, it is heuristically assumed that the values returned by these algorithms will, at least,

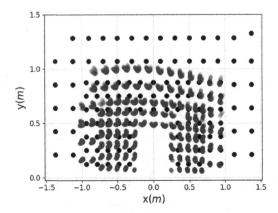

Fig. 8. Calculated positions after outlier removal (alpha = 0.1 for blue points). (Color figure online)

suffice for our goals of calculating positions precisely, even if they are not the global minimum.

Due to time restrictions in the first tests, which were done using MATLAB, the Nelder-Mead algorithm was chosen instead of the CMA-ES algorithm. This algorithm is used as default in the final code of the ITAndroids team.

To suit our time constraints, the Nelder-Mead algorithm was rewritten in C++. Using the compilation flags "-Ofast -fext-numeric-literals -fPIC" for the g++ compiler, it was possible to achieve an execution time under 3 s on average. The results of the calibration using the Nelder-Mead algorithm (implemented in C++) are shown in Fig. 9.

4   Results and Discussions

Comparing Figs. 8 and 9, we notice that the offsets found by the algorithm improved the robot's position calculation, as the blue clusters are now much closer to their respective black points. In fact, the cost before optimizing x was $J(0, \mathcal{D}) = 3{,}782.52$. After optimizing, $J(x, \mathcal{D}) = 65.69$. That is a 98.3% cost reduction. Furthermore, the average cost of each detected ArUco was 0.00118 after the calibration. As all the positions are calculated in meters and the error is the squared distance, the quadratic mean of the distance between the calculated position of an Aruco and its actual position is $\sqrt{0.00118\,\mathrm{m}^2} = 0.034\,\mathrm{m} = 3.4\,\mathrm{cm}$. So the average distance between an ArUco and its calculated position is less than 3.4 cm (remember that the arithmetic mean is less than or equal to the quadratic mean).

Finally, we need to check whether the solution found by the algorithm suits the problem conditions (even though the calibration results were good, if the solution x has a big offset, say, a 38° offset, the solution should be disregarded, as this kind of error is beyond an usual mechanical error). In the example presented

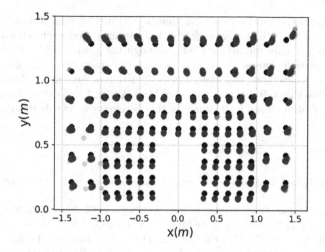

Fig. 9. Calculated positions after calibration (*alpha* = 0.1).

during this paper, the bigger offset found was the torso roll, with 7°, followed by the camera yaw with 1.4°. These values match the problem intuition of small offsets. Also, the solution must be obtained in a short time, as the robots are calibrated just before going into a match, so an algorithm that takes a long time to execute is impractical. As said in Sect. 3.2, it was possible to achieve an execution time, on average, under 3 s. This is enough for our purposes.

5   Conclusion

This paper presents a method for the calibration of the inverse perspective mapping model of a humanoid robot. The use of this calibration allows the IPM algorithm to precisely determine the robot distance to known objects in the field. This information can then be used with a Monte Carlo Localization technique, such as the one described in [2], to allow the robot to locate itself on the field.

In the example presented in this paper, the calibration reduced the costs of approximately 60 thousand object detections by 98.3%, making the average distance between estimated and real positions inferior to 3.4 cm. All those objects were placed in an area of 3 m by 1.5 m, which is around 8.3% of the field area of a RoboCup match.

For future research, we suggest:

- Use more complex models for the calibration (instead of the joint's angles).
- Use a deep neural network to optimize the offsets.
- Use the own field features to calibrate.
- Generalize this method so it can be applicable to other scenarios other than the humanoid league.

128   F. B. D. R. da Silva et al.

Acknowledgment. Francisco da Silva thanks CNPq (Conselho Nacional de Desenvolvimento Científico e Tecnológico) for his undergraduate research scholarship. Marcos Maximo is partially funded by CNPq through the grant 307525/2022-8. Takashi Yoneyama is partially funded by CNPq through the grant 304134/2-18-0. We thank the entire ITAndroids team, especially Lucas Steuernagel, for helping during data collection tests. We thank Robocup's sponsors MathWorks, FESTO, SoftBank Robotics and United Robotics Group for making all this development in robotics possible.

References

1. RoboCup. RoboCup Humanoid League. https://humanoid.robocup.org/ October 2020
2. Muzio, A., Aguiar, L., Máximo, M.R.O.A., Pinto, S.C.: Monte Carlo Localization with Field Lines Observations for Simulated Humanoid Robotic Soccer (2018)
3. Bestmann, M., Engelke, T., Fiedler, N.: TORSO-21 Dataset: Typical Objects in RoboCup Soccer (2021). https://github.com/bit-bots/TORSO_21_dataset
4. Tanveer, M.H., Sgorbissa, A.: An inverse perspective mapping approach using monocular camera of Pepper humanoid robot to determine the position of other moving robot in plane (2018)
5. OpenCV, Camera Calibration. https://docs.opencv.org/4.x/dc/dbb/tutorial_py_calibration.html
6. Maximo, M.R.O.A.: Automatic walking step duration through model predictive control. Dissertation Ph.D. thesis, Aeronautics Institute of Technology (2017)
7. OpenCV, Detection of ArUco Markers (2020)
8. RoboCup. Humanoid League Laws of the Game (2020). http://www.robocuphumanoid.org/wp-content/uploads/RCHL-2019-Rules-changesMarked.pdf
9. Szeliski, R.: Computer Vision Algorithms and Applications, pp. 42–49. Springer, Cham (2011). https://doi.org/10.1007/978-1-84882-935-0
10. Kajita, S., Hirukawa, H., Yokoi, K., Harada, K.: Introduction to Humanoid Robotics, pp. 19–42. Springer, Cham (2014). https://doi.org/10.1007/978-3-642-54536-8
11. École Polytechnique. The CMA Evolution Strategy (2020). http://www.cmap.polytechnique.fr/nikolaus.hansen/cmaesintro.html
12. Lagarias, J.C., Reeds, J.A., Wright, M.H., Wright, P.E.: Convergence properties of the Nelder-Mead simplex method in low dimensions. SIAM J. Optim. **9**, 112–147 (1998)
13. Gondry, L., Hofer, L., Laborde-Zubieta, P., et al.: Rhoban Football Club: RoboCup Humanoid KidSize 2019 Champion Team Paper (2019)
14. Mahmudi, H., Gholami, A., Delaravan, M.H., et al.: MRL Champion Team Paper in Humanoid TeenSize League of RoboCup 2019 (2019)

Using Neural Factorization of Shape and Reflectance for Ball Detection

Xavier Monté[ID], Joey van der Kaaij[ID], Rogier van der Weerd[ID],
and Arnoud Visser[(✉)][ID]

Intelligent Robotics Lab, Universiteit van Amsterdam, Amsterdam, The Netherlands
a.visser@uva.nl
https://www.intelligentroboticslab.nl/

Abstract. Visually detecting a well-defined object like a soccer ball should be a simple problem. Under good lighting conditions this problem can be claimed to be solved, but unfortunately, the lighting conditions are not always optimal. In those circumstances, it is valuable to have a shape and reflectance model of the ball, to be able to predict how its appearance changes if the lighting changes. This is a prerequisite for playing soccer outside, with direct sunlight and clouds. The predicted appearance will be used to fine-tune an existing ball detection algorithm, based on the classic Yolo algorithm.

Keywords: reflectance estimation · view synthesis · object detection

1 Introduction

In the RoboCup Standard Platform League (SPL) autonomous Nao robots are engaged in competitive soccer matches [3]. In this league no modifications are allowed on the hardware level, which forces the teams to concentrate on the robotic algorithms in the perceive-plan-act cycle [5]. To play soccer, the perception of the soccer ball should be done with high precision and recall [8]. Unfortunately, the computational resources on board the robot, even the Nao v6, limit the application of advanced neural network architectures to scaled-down versions optimized to achieve acceptable frame rates.

Yet, even scaled-down neural networks can perceive a soccer ball with high precision and recall [26] when properly trained. By extending the training set with challenging samples, rather than random ones, the algorithm's performance can be improved even further.

To extend the training set for ball detection under difficult lighting conditions this research uses a modern breakthrough in the field of Neural Factorization of Shape and Reflectance or in short reverse image rendering. Until recently it was not possible to render realistic objects using a neural network [13]. The NeRF algorithm has made it possible to properly render any object using a neural network [13]. This means that the colour, shadow, reflection, and shape can be rendered realistic. A new feature on top of the NeRF algorithm is the NeRFactor

C. Buche et al. (Eds.): RoboCup 2023, LNAI 14140, pp. 129–140, 2024.
https://doi.org/10.1007/978-3-031-55015-7_11

algorithm [28]. This feature allows for rendering unknown light conditions [28]. A constraint of NeRFactor is that there must be a rich data set of the object available, not a sparse data set. Two similar photos of the object must be exactly the same, the lighting, material, etc. NeRFactor has not been tested on round objects, such as the football used in this paper. In this paper, we will apply and generalize NeRFactor by training NeRFactor on a round object [12].

Once trained, such a model can come to aid when soccer-playing robots experience difficulties when they have to recognize the soccer ball under different light conditions. The angle of the light creates all kinds of shadows. Also, the colour changes under different lighting conditions. Moreover, a soccer ball is a perfectly round object; the symmetry makes the shape estimation both simpler and more sensitive to errors. Note that reliable shape estimation of round objects can also play a role in agriculture, for instance when apples, tomatoes, and melons have to be detected.

2   Theoretical Background

2.1   NeRF

This study will generate training sets with the NeRFactor algorithm [28], which is an extension of NeRF algorithm [13]. NeRF describes an object as a continuous 5D function. This 5D function outputs at every 3D point (x, y, z) the radiance emitted at each direction (θ, φ). The density at any point in space acts as a differential opacity on how much radiance is collected by a light beam through the point (x, y, z). In addition, a deep neural network is used to estimate the albedo, the RGB colour of the light reflected at any point, as a function of the viewpoint.

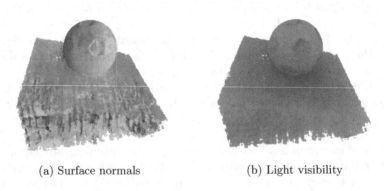

(a) Surface normals   (b) Light visibility

Fig. 1. Two aspects of the shape and reflectance of a football

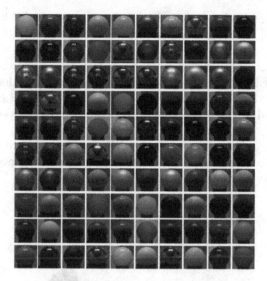

Fig. 2. The 100 BRDF balls used in the MERL dataset courtesy: MERL [15] (https://cdfg.csail.mit.edu/wojciech/brdfdatabase)

The result is a model which estimates the shape and reflectance of the ball. The shape can be represented with the surface normals of the surface points (x, y, z). A surface normal is the vector that is perpendicular to the surface and is a unit vector. In Fig. 1a NeRFactor's surface normals are shown on the football. The different colours are the directions of the surface normals. For rendering the images, the directions have been translated to RGB, if a surface normals go up, the colour is blue, orange is down, etc.

The reflectance of the ball can be represented with the light-visibility function. Light visibility is the visibility of any of the surface points (x, y, z) for any light source. In Fig. 1b the light visibility rendered by NeRFactor of the football is visible. The darker the colour, the less light is reflected from the object. The different black and white surfaces are visible on the rendering. Note that this light visibility indicates the amount of reflected light, but this value has still to be augmented with the albedo to estimate the colour of the reflected light.

The NeRF algorithm is trained with hundreds of 2D photos of the same object from different viewpoints. The Structure-from-Motion (SfM) from the COLMAP library is used to reconstruct from the 2D images a 3D object [20]. Once the reconstruction is finished, the object can be rendered from any viewpoint, generating synthetic scenes.

2.2 NeRFactor

The NeRF algorithm can generate a continuous high-resolution rendering of an object under good lighting conditions. Yet, for this study, we are interested in difficult lighting conditions. NeRFactor tried to improve NeRF by the introduction of multiple lighting conditions in contrast to the one lighting condition in NeRF [28].

NeRFactor accomplishes this by using a deep neural network that is pretrained on the MERL dataset [15], which contains the Bidirectional Reflectance Distribution Function (BRDF) which measures the amount of electromagnetic radiation, reflected or scattered from objects measured for 100 different reflections (see Fig. 2).

This is not the only improvement of NeRFactor compared to NeRF. In addition, the algorithm has an improved geometry and reflection model by dividing the volume density estimated by NeRF into surface geometry.

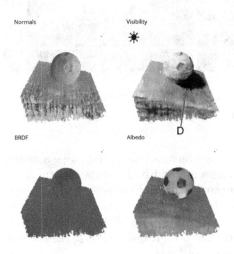

Fig. 3. NeRFactor factorization.

It also factored photos of an object into shape, reflectance, and illumination, which allows viewpoint-independent editing of lighting with shadows and material. Figure 3 gives an example of factorization in the case of a point-based lighting condition called OLAD (One-Light-At-a-Time). In the visibility model, one can see a sharp shadow (marked with D) behind the ball opposite to the light source. With these factorized models (and several visibility models) any viewpoint and lighting condition can be rendered from the soccer ball.

3   Dataset

The correct working of both the NeRF and NeRFactor algorithms was first tested on the well-known datasets that accompany the algorithms: a hot dog, a pine cone, and a vase.

For this study, an equivalent dataset was recorded at the Intelligent Robotics Lab[1] of the RoboCup Standard Platform League[2] official soccer ball. The official ball is a soft foam ball with a black and white soccer ball print (see Fig. 4a). They are 100 mm in diameter and weigh 44 g. The recorded soccer ball was well used in several competitions [1], so some wear is visible on the ball.

(a) Nao robot with ball   (b) Actual dataset recording

Fig. 4. .

To be able to reconstruct the viewpoints of the recordings, the Colmap algorithm requires that the recordings must be taken 'neatly'. This means that the recorded object should be in the centre of the frame (see Fig. 4b), the light and background must be the same for recordings taken from the same angle of the object [20]. The algorithm also works better if you walk around the object in circles of different heights. The NeRF algorithm needs around 100 recordings per scene. Still, as we used a round object with a symmetrical pattern the reconstruction could not always correctly distinguish between the different angles of the object, so the scene had to be recorded several times until we had a good dataset.

The next step is the calculation of geometry buffers [28]. Calculating geometry buffers is very resource intensive. Because the geometry buffers do not change, they can be calculated in advance. This makes it easier to execute the next steps of the algorithm. The algorithm calculates three different buffers, they are:

- The first step is the calculation of the surface points following any camera ray.
- The second step is the calculation of the surface normals.
- And the final step is the calculation of the light visibility for the whole object from each viewing angle.

The resulting light visibility map that has been made of the object shows how the light is scattered for each angle. The result can be seen in Fig. 5. The

---

[1] https://www.intelligentroboticslab.nl/.

[2] https://spl.robocup.org/.

rendering was performed with two different bounding boxes; one square and one rectangular. The render with the rectangular bounding box has more noise in the background as can be seen at the top. In addition, there should be no light visible behind the object. The geometry buffers calculated with the rectangular bounding box have more light scattering in the shadow of the ball. The calculation of the geometry buffers with the square bounding box gives a better result, so these buffers are used in the rest of the study.

(a) with a rectangular base   (b) with a square base

Fig. 5. Examples of creating a geometry buffer of the light visibility for one viewing angle. A complete buffer is calculated for each viewing angle.

The last step is the factorization of the NeRFactor algorithm. The results of the NeRF algorithm and geometry are combined with the BRDF model and the different lighting conditions. For example, we can look at the results for the sunrise and night lighting condition. For these two conditions the ball is illuminated from two opposite angles and the surface normals should point exactly in the opposite direction (indicated by the rainbow color). That is indeed the case at arrow A (see Fig. 6, 7), which is sky-blue for the sunrise condition and pink at night. The purple colors of the BRDF indicate the kind of reflection. Indeed, as can be seen at arrow B (see Fig. 7) the black areas are light purple (less reflection) and the white areas are dark purple (more reflection). The correctness of the albedo can be seen at arrow C (see Fig. 6), with the correct white and black pattern. In addition, one can see the warm colour of the sunset reflected on the white surface. The only downside is that the reflection model seems to have a metallic-like appearance, which is a known feature of the NeRFactor algorithm [28]. A more detailed analysis of the factorization results can be found in [14]. Yet, overall it is clear that the shape of the ball and the black hexagons are well preserved and the shadows & the colouring is realistic.

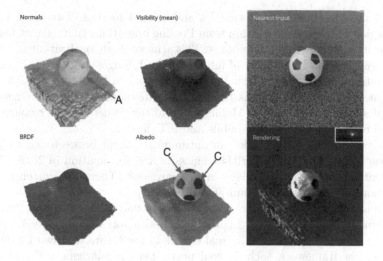

Fig. 6. Rendering of the ball at sunrise.

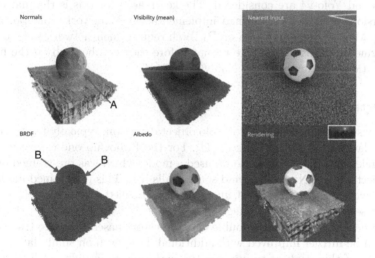

Fig. 7. Rendering of the ball at night.

The results seem to be good enough to generate a training set to fine-tune a ball detection algorithm, as the combination of YOLO and the HAAR algorithm used by the Dutch Nao Team [1].

4   Object Detection

The last 20 years have seen many breakthroughs in object detection techniques, well documented by several surveys [7,27,29]. Detection algorithms can be categorized into two-stage (R-CNNs, SPP, FPN, FCN and others) and single-stage

(SSD, Yolo, Mask R-CNN, RetinaNet and others) models. Two-stage models split Region of Interest generation from Pooling operations that extract features and specify candidate bounding boxes. This achieves high localization and recognition accuracy but at the cost of inference speed. Single-stage models combine all operations in one convolutional forward pass which leads to faster inference. In recent years, much effort has been put into developing lightweight networks (examples include SqueezeNet, MobileNet) that can be deployed in resource constrained environments such as mobile and IoT devices.

For real-time detection tasks, an optimum is sought between accuracy and inference speed. The Yolo algorithm, since its first formulation in 2016 [17] has consistently pushed the boundary in this envelope. There are currently eight generations of the Yolo algorithm [9, 17–19, 23–25].

Yolo is a clear candidate of choice as a generic and high performing detection algorithm. It is preferred over highly optimized algorithms for specific classes given the ability to include additional classes in the future that can be relevant to the soccer framework such as goal posts, penalty markers, different robot stances, etc. As a basis for our application, variants of the Darknet based versions Yolo-v3 and Yolo-v4 are considered. The key reason for this is the maturity of this version, with well-established implementation frameworks and portability options. Modern versions based on PyTorch require their network weights to be transformed to TensorFlow Lite format before they can be used on the limited computational resources of the Nao v6 robot [16].

Ball Detection

There exist pretrained models for Yolo object detection, typically trained on the COCO dataset (80 object classes) [11]. For the RoboCup one can concentrate on the relevant object classes; so we used a model which was pre-trained on only two object classes: Nao robots and soccer balls [26]. This pre-trained model was trained with datasets of RoboCup recordings labelled collaboratively [4]. The training set contained 7,500 images.

The performance of such double class detectors based on a pre-trained network can be further improved with additional data, even on small datasets [10]. The focus of this study is to improve the performance in different lighting conditions.

Synthetic Dataset

The shape, reflectance, and illumination of the ball under different lighting conditions as described in Sect. 3 can be incorporated in a virtual reality environment of the Intelligent Robotics Lab created in Unity [2]. To do this the mesh has to be recovered [22]. Once the model of the ball is part of the virtual reality environment, one can view the ball from different viewpoints, including the 2D bounding box with the label. In addition, Unity Perception contains Randomizer tools that allow random object placement, position, rotation, texture, and hue. So, not only the lighting conditions are changed, but also the background is changed (the view through the windows of the Intelligent Robotics Lab). This is comparable with the stochastic scene generation performed in the Unreal environment by Hess *et al.* [6]. An example of some of the generated images can be found in Fig. 8. For each Randomizer tool, the range can be specified. For instance, for the Intensity-range we used [135.5, 378.5] lm and for the Temperature-range [5250, 7750] K. For the Light range Ceiling we used the Intensity-range [3050–7350] lm and the Temperature-range [3600–6000] K.

Fig. 8. Synthetic images created in Unity with the mesh learned from NeRFactor

5   Training and Testing Yolo-v4/3L

The Darknet[3] can be used to train Yolo models up to version 4. Based on the previous experience [26] we concentrated on the reduced model with three scales ('Tiny Yolo-v4/3L'). Key hyperparameters that were kept constant include the input size of the images (416 × 416), anchor box dimensions (3 per grid cell), batch size (64) and optimizer settings (SGD optimizer with momentum 0.9 and weight decay of $5e^{-4}$). A learning rate of 0.00261 was used, which was reduced by 10% after steps 10k and 15k.

The previous work reported a mean average precision (mAP@50) of 84.2% on the ball detection, based on the learning curve illustrated in Fig. 9a. This was the result of training on 7,500 images recorded during RoboCup soccer matches, enriched with live scenes recorded in the Intelligent Robotics lab. This trained network was in the next step further trained with synthetic images with the mesh of the ball generated based on the model generated NeRFactor (480 images). The pretrained networked started directly with a high mAP and a low

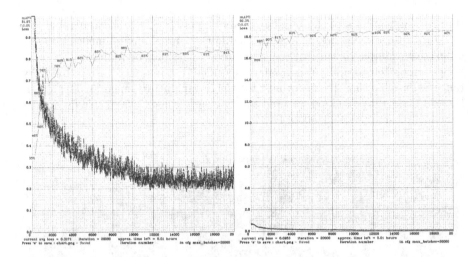

Fig. 9. Learning curves of 'Tiny Yolo-v4/3L'

loss, which was further improved in 20,000 iterations (see Fig. 9b). The resulting mean average precision improved to 92.3% on the real validation dataset.

Yet, the most important criterion is if the diversity of lighting conditions improved the robustness of the algorithm for real circumstances. When the model trained with the NeRF mesh is validated on the real validation set with recordings from live scenes (593 images) we get a mean average precision of 92.89%, outperforming the 84.2% earlier reported earlier (See Table 1). For convenience, also the results of Specchi *et al.* [21] are given, although these results were acquired on slightly different dataset with an another resolution (320×320 instead of 416×416). The number of parameters have a strong influence on the performance, so this work with 23K parameters nicely falls between the 12K and 47K results reported by [21]. Note that the focus of Specchi *et al.* [21] was to trade accuracy with speed to reach a high framerate on the Nao robot.

Table 1. Comparison of ball-detection precision results

Model	#Parameters	mAP@50
vanderWeerd [26] - Tiny Yolo-v4/3L	23K	84.2%
Specchi *et al.* [21] - Tiny Yolo-v7/YTv7_12K	12K	88.8%
our work - Tiny Yolo-v4/3L	23K	92.9%
Specchi *et al.* [21] - Tiny Yolo-v7/YTv7_47K	47K	**94.0%**

---

[3] https://github.com/AlexeyAB, maintained by Alexey Bochkovsky.

6   Conclusion

This experiment shows the value of being able to generate synthetic datasets which can boost the performance of object detectors such as Yolo. The focus of this research is the relative improvement; with more advanced algorithms (e.g., Yolo v7) or by generating much larger synthetic datasets we could have pushed the boundary even further. Yet, we could already see an impressive improvement on a small dataset, which seems to originate from the diversity which could be generated with the Randomizer tools. So, we trained with the data that challenged the object detector enough to further improve, instead of adding more of the same 'real' data. As long as the computational resources of the Nao robot do not facilitate more advanced algorithms the solution has to come from better training schemes.

References

1. Bolt, L., Klein Gunnewiek, F., Lekanne gezegd Deprez, H., van Iterson, L., Prinzhorn, D.: Dutch Nao Team - Technical report, December 2022
2. Borkman, S., et al.: Unity perception: generate synthetic data for computer vision, July 2021. arXiv preprint 2107.04259
3. Chown, E., Lagoudakis, M.G.: The standard platform league. In: Bianchi, R., Akin, H., Ramamoorthy, S., Sugiura, K. (eds.) RoboCup 2014: Robot World Cup XVIII. RoboCup 2014. LNCS, vol. 8992, pp. 636–648. Springer, Cham (2015). https://doi.org/10.1007/978-3-319-18615-3_52
4. Fiedler, N., Bestmann, M., Hendrich, N.: Imagetagger: an open source online platform for collaborative image labeling. In: Holz, D., Genter, K., Saad, M., von Stryk, O. (eds.) RoboCup 2018: Robot World Cup XXII. RoboCup 2018. LNCS, vol. 11374, pp. 162–169. Springer, Cham (2019). https://doi.org/10.1007/978-3-030-27544-0_13
5. Hayes-Roth, B.: Architectural foundations for real-time performance in intelligent agents. Real-Time Syst. **2**(1–2), 99–125 (1990)
6. Hess, T., Mundt, M., Weis, T., Ramesh, V.: Large-scale stochastic scene generation and semantic annotation for deep convolutional neural network training in the RoboCup SPL. In: Akiyama, H., Obst, O., Sammut, C., Tonidandel, F. (eds.) RoboCup 2017: Robot World Cup XXI. RoboCup 2017. LNCS, vol. 11175, pp. 33–44. Springer, Cham (2018). https://doi.org/10.1007/978-3-030-00308-1_3
7. Jiao, L., et al.: A survey of deep learning-based object detection. IEEE Access **7**, 128837–128868 (2019)
8. Kahlefendt, C.: A Comparison and Evaluation of Neural Network-based Classification Approaches for the Purpose of a Robot Detection on the Nao Robotic System. Master's thesis, Technische Universität Hamburg-Harburg, April 2017
9. Li, C., et al.: Yolov6 v3.0: a full-scale reloading, January 2023. arXiv 2301.05586
10. Li, G., Song, Z., Fu, Q.: A new method of image detection for small datasets under the framework of yolo network. In: 2018 IEEE 3rd Advanced Information Technology, Electronic and Automation Control Conference (IAEAC), pp. 1031–1035, October 2018
11. Lin, T.Y., et al.: Microsoft coco: common objects in context. In: Fleet, D., Pajdla, T., Schiele, B., Tuytelaars, T. (eds.) Computer Vision – ECCV 2014. ECCV 2014. LNCS, vol. 8693, pp. 740–755. Springer, Cham (2014). https://doi.org/10.1007/978-3-319-10602-1_48

12. Martin-Brualla, R., Radwan, N., Sajjadi, M.S.M., Barron, J.T., Dosovitskiy, A., Duckworth, D.: Nerf in the wild: neural radiance fields for unconstrained photo collections. In: Proceedings of the IEEE/CVF Conference on Computer Vision and Pattern Recognition (CVPR), pp. 7210–7219, June 2021

13. Mildenhall, B., Srinivasan, P.P., Tancik, M., Barron, J.T., Ramamoorthi, R., Ng, R.: Nerf: representing scenes as neural radiance fields for view synthesis. Commun. ACM **65**(1), 99–106 (2021)

14. Monté, X.: Neural factorization of shape and reflectance of a football under an unknown illumination. Bachelor thesis, University of Amsterdam, February 2023

15. Mungan, C.: Bidirectional reflectance distribution functions describing first-surface scattering. AFOSR Final Report for the Summer Faculty Research Program (Summer 1998)

16. Narayanaswami, S.K., et al.: Towards a real-time, low-resource, end-to-end object detection pipeline for robot soccer. In: Eguchi, A., Lau, N., Paetzel-Prusmann, M., Wanichanon, T. (eds.) RoboCup 2022:. RoboCup 2022. LNCS, vol. 13561, pp. 62–74. Springer, Cham (2023). https://doi.org/10.1007/978-3-031-28469-4_6

17. Redmon, J., Divvala, S., Girshick, R., Farhadi, A.: You only look once: unified, real-time object detection. In: Proceedings of the IEEE Conference on Computer Vision and Pattern Recognition (CVPR), pp. 779–788, January 2016

18. Redmon, J., Farhadi, A.: Yolo9000: better, faster, stronger. In: Proceedings of the IEEE Conference on Computer Vision and Pattern Recognition (CVPR), pp. 7263–7271, July 2017

19. Redmon, J., Farhadi, A.: Yolov3: an incremental improvement, April 2018. arXiv 1804.02767

20. Schönberger, J.L., Frahm, J.M.: Structure-from-motion revisited. In: Conference on Computer Vision and Pattern Recognition (CVPR), pp. 4104–4113, June 2016

21. Specchi, G., et al.: Structural pruning for real-time multi-object detection on NAO robots. In: RoboCup 2023: Robot World Cup XXVI, July 2023

22. Tang, J., et al.: Delicate textured mesh recovery from nerf via adaptive surface refinement, March 2023. arXiv preprint 2303.02091

23. Terven, J., Cordova-Esparza, D.: A comprehensive review of yolo: from yolov1 to yolov8 and beyond, April 2023. arXiv 2304.00501

24. Wang, C.Y., Bochkovskiy, A., Liao, H.Y.M.: Scaled-yolov4: scaling cross stage partial network. In: Proceedings of the IEEE/CVF Conference on Computer Vision and Pattern Recognition (CVPR), pp. 13029–13038, June 2021

25. Wang, C.Y., Bochkovskiy, A., Liao, H.Y.M.: Yolov7: trainable bag-of-freebies sets new state-of-the-art for real-time object detectors, July 2022. arXiv 2207.02696

26. van der Weerd, R.: Real-time object detection and avoidance for autonomous NAO robots performing in the standard platform league. Project report, University of Amsterdam, July 2021

27. Zaidi, S.S.A., Ansari, M.S., Aslam, A., Kanwal, N., Asghar, M., Lee, B.: A survey of modern deep learning based object detection models. Digit. Signal Process. **126**, 103514 (2022)

28. Zhang, X., Srinivasan, P.P., Deng, B., Debevec, P., Freeman, W.T., Barron, J.T.: Nerfactor: neural factorization of shape and reflectance under an unknown illumination. ACM Trans. Graph. **40**(6) (2021)

29. Zou, Z., Chen, K., Shi, Z., Guo, Y., Ye, J.: Object detection in 20 years: a survey. Proc. IEEE **111**(3), 257–276 (2023)

Hybrid Methods for Real-Time Video Sequence Identification of Human Soccer Referee Signals

Prawal Lohani and Timothy Wiley[✉]

School of Computing Technologies, RMIT University, Melbourne, Australia
s3853474@student.rmit.edu.au, timothy.wiley@rmit.edu.au
http://rmit.edu.au/ailab

Abstract. We evaluate several real-time machine learning and hybrid symbolic algorithms to identify body-gestures of Human Soccer Referees as part of the 2022 RoboCup Soccer Standard Platform League (SPL) Visual Referee Challenge. This challenge, in part, encourages development of software for effective human-robot interactions as the Nao must interpret and respond in real-time to human referee's gestures, so RoboCup can progress towards it's 2050 goal. We train and evaluate the real-time accuracy and speed of two Deep Convolutional Neural Networks architectures, OpenPose and Stacked HourGlass, against our novel hybrid machine-learning and symbolic approach on the resource constrained SoftBank Nao V6. Our results show that there remains an important trade-off between the single-image accuracy of Deep Networks, and the execution speed of hybrid when evaluating across a video sequence. Our hybrid method achieved a strong result in 2022 SPL "Visual Referee Challenge". Our work has been motivated by the requirements for methods in human-robot interaction, where the human perspective of a robot's behaviour strongly influences the evaluation criteria of software.

Keywords: Human Pose Recognition · Human-Robot Interaction · Hybrid-Symbolic Machine Learning · Deep Convolutional Neural Networks

1 Introduction

In the RoboCup Soccer Standard Platform League (SPL), communications between the human referee officiating a match are almost entirely conducted via "electronic messages" that are sent to the robots via the "Game Controller" software[1]. However, for RoboCup to achieve its 2050 goal of a team of humanoid robots defeating the FIFA World Cup champions, the electronic signals must be

---

[1] The exception to this in 2022 is the use of a whistle for Kick-off, followed by a electronic kick-off signal sent after a 15 s delay.

C. Buche et al. (Eds.): RoboCup 2023, LNAI 14140, pp. 141–153, 2024.
https://doi.org/10.1007/978-3-031-55015-7_12

replaced, in part, by hand-signals by the human referee. That is, in the course of a soccer game, the referees will indicate decisions including a goal, a corner-kick, a goal-kick, and a free-kick via a hand-gesture in addition to other verbal/audio indications. This is fundamentally a problem in the field of human-robot interaction (HRI). The human referee must be satisfied that a robot has both *quickly* and *reasonably* responded to their decisions. In 2022, the Soccer SPL introduced a "Visual Referee Challenge" to progress toward disposing of the electronic referee [5]. The challenge evaluated the *speed* and *accuracy* with which a robot could recognise one of seven different hand-gestures, featuring both one-handed static gestures, two-handed static gestures, and dynamic gestures (where both hands are moving). However, the SoftBank Nao V6 robots [15] used within the Soccer SPL are heavily resource constrained, impacting the algorithms that can effectively address this challenge. We demonstrate an effective approach to the "Visual Referee Challenge", that leverages a hybrid symbolic and neural network methodology, and use evaluation criteria that is based on requirements for human-robot interaction, where speed is an important factor. We trade single-image accuracy for processing speed with a video sequence in a methodology that approaches the accuracy of the slower single-image methods.

Since the introduction of LeNet [9], the majority of computer vision approaches are dominated by Convolutional Network Networks (CNNs). For the task of human-pose estimation in the "Visual Referee Challenge", suitable CNN architectures include OpenPose [4], Stacked HourGlass [13], and DeepPose [20]. However, the hardware constraints of the Nao V6 severely limit the applicability of these algorithms for real-time use. Therefore, we investigate hybrid CNN and symbolic methods to meet real-time constraints. These real-time requirements are further motivated by requirements in human-robot interactions. A wide body of research in HRI has shown that robots are still viewed as being unreliable, unintelligent, unresponsive, and untrustworthy [3,10]. This is partially due to the slow response of the autonomous robots, creating a dissonance to the human expectation of what makes an "intelligent" robot, even where the eventual actions of the robot are "accurate" [18]. Therefore, we favour the speed of a robot's response as an important evaluation criteria.

We present our novel hybrid symbolic and "light-weight" machine learning methodology for the 2022 Soccer SPL "Visual Referee Challenge", in which we achieved 3rd place in the Challenge. We additionally evaluate our method against two Deep Learning architectures: OpenPose [4] and Stacked HourGlass [13]. We compare the performance of all methods on both single-image use, and real-time video image sequences, using criteria motivated by HRI requirement, balancing the *speed* and *accuracy* of the robot's interpretation of the human referee signals.

2 Related Work

Extensive research in HRI shows that social element of interactions, that is, the modality and feel of an interaction is crucial. A person's perception of an autonomous robot's intelligence, competency, and the person's trust in the robot, are all heavily influenced by how the human and robot interact [7,10]. A bad interaction is likely to result in a view of a lack of intelligence and a loss of trust, even if the robot is objectively good at performing a given task. Therefore, it's critical to build autonomous robotic systems that are accepted by the people who are meant to work with them. This means, evaluating the performance of autonomous robots through the lens of the human, that is, their *expectation* of how the system should perform. Contributing factors to this human perception include the *speed* and *reasonable accuracy* of the robot's response [7]. Importantly, "reasonable" does not imply "perfect". Some error is acceptable, so long as the errors are recoverable, the overall response is sufficiently fast, and ultimately produces a preferable behaviour from the human perspective [18,22]. We hypothesise that in RoboCup soccer, the human referee will prefer such as "quick-and-reasonable" response over a slow response. Indeed, the scoring system of the SPL "Visual Referee Challenge" [5] balances accuracy and time.

The "Visual Referee Challenge" is largely a task of human pose-detection, for which various CNN approaches have been proposed. OpenPose [4], Stacked Hour-Glass [13], and DeepPose [20] focus on localizing the keypoints of the human body in an image. In particular OpenPose [4], provides a 2D estimation of human pose by computing the confidence maps affinity fields. Stacked hourglass [13], consists of multiple hourglass modules which is an encoder-decoder type CNN that are stacked up. The architecture uses both top-down and bottom-up approaches that increase the number of parameters as the hourglass blocks are piled-up, resulting in better performance. Therefore, tuning the number of hourglass blocks can assist in reducing the model execution time while compromising on accuracy. Additionally, both OpenPose and HourGlass have relative real-time performances. However, these may still be insufficient given the constraints of the Nao V6.

In recent years, vision research in RoboCup SPL has been associated with recognizing the ball, robots, and field features, for which various architectures have been proposed. UT Austin proposed a heuristic-based approach [12] that includes applying complex filters to distinguish all possible ball regions which are followed by Support Vector Machine [1]. B-Human [16] developed a CNN based encoder-decoder for deriving the segmented images to approximate the size of the ball where some parts of the ball are obscured due to lighting conditions or shadows. This is followed by two "light-weight" Deep Neural Networks (DNNs) for ball recognition. In the humanoid RoboCup leagues, JET-NET [14] identifies moving robots under varying lighting conditions, by implementing Simulation Transfer Learning that reuses existing features to estimate new features, such as distance. JET-NET uses image segmentation and augmentation for producing more training data and also prunes the filters that has the least activation which is compensated by fine tuning. Similarly, Cruz *et al.*, 2017 [6] and Szemenyei *et al.*, 2018 [19] also utilise DNNs. There also exists a trade-off between accuracy and other computational requirements of the robot on other tasks that are necessary to play a game of soccer [6,14]. However, these approaches are insufficient for the "Visual Referee Challenge" as the size of a human requires processing a much larger region of the image compared to locating a ball or robot.

Fig. 1. Example poses for the "Visual Referee Challenge": (a) Goal Kick Blue, (b) Goal Kick Red, (c) Corner Kick Red, (d) Corner Kick Blue, (e) Kick in Blue, (f) Kick in Red, (g) Pushing Freekick Blue, (h) Pushing Freekick Red, (i) Goal Blue, (j) Goal Red, (k) and (l) extremities of the Full Time signal (Color figure online)

Instead, we observe that a common features of these approaches is using "light-weight" CNNs after image pre-processing to reduce input to the CNNs. Similarly, strong results have been shown with hybrid systems that leverage both symbolic reasoning methods along with "light-weight" machine learning systems, for real-time applications on resource constrained robots [17]. Therefore, we propose the use of a hybrid symbolic and 'light-weight" machine learning, but also evaluate our approach against state-of-the-art CNN methods for human-pose detection.

3 Methodology

We describe our method for data collection, our hybrid symbolic and "light-weight" machine learning, and two CNN-based human-pose detection models (OpenPose [4] and Stacked HourGlass [13]) that we evaluate our method against.

3.1 Data Collection

We collect a training data set of referee hand signals as defined in the challenge rules [5]. Figure 1 shows a sample of poses, divided into three types: (1) one-handed signals in (a) to (f); (2) two-handed signals in (g) to (j); and (3) a dynamic signal where the referee moves their hands on a horizontal plane between two poses shown in (k) and (l). Our training data includes a diversity of lighting conditions and backgrounds as the challenge could be held in a variety of conditions. We note that challenge rules require the referee to wear red gloves.

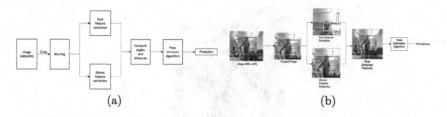

(a)   (b)

Fig. 2. Architecture of our hybrid symbolic and "light-weight" machine learning method (a) along with a visual illustration (b) of each stage.

3.2 Our Hybrid Symbolic and Machine Learning Method

The architecture for our hybrid symbolic and machine learning method is shown in Fig. 2 along with an illustration of each stage. First we down-sample and pre-process the camera image. Next we use two "light-weight" machine learning algorithms to locate bounding boxes for the face and hands of the human referee. From these bounding boxes, we compute various heuristic symbolic measurements for properties of the human pose, such as the angles between the human referee's gloved hands and face, which are passed through a rule set to determine the referee signal. These stages are described below.

Image Pre-processing. The camera image is down-sampled to a 360×480 image. Additionally, $1/4$ of the image border is trimmed as, for the purpose of the "Visual Referee Challenge", the referee must stand a set distance from and directly in front of the robot.

"Light-Weight" Machine Learning and Feature Extraction. From the pre-processed image, we search for a human face using the Viola-Jones Haar Cascade Classifier [21]. This is a sufficiently computationally efficient framework with a proven high accuracy rate, but we also further restrict the classifier to the top half of the image. The classifier provides properties for a detected human face of the centre pixel, and the height and width of a bounding box around the face. A standard colour filter is defined using OpenCV for identifying bounding boxes of red pixels to detect the red gloves, where the bounding boxes must have a size between 30 to 70 pixels. Where more than two red regions are found, the two largest are selected. We experimented with different machine learning methods for identifying the gloves, such as Support Vector Machines [1] and YOLOv5 [8], however, the colour filter was sufficient and the most computationally efficient. We then extract features for the heuristic symbolic rule set, shown in Fig. 3. The point $P(x_f, y_f)$ is the center point of the bounding box of the face while $P(x_l, y_l)$ and $P(x_r, y_r)$ are the center points for the two bounding boxes of the red gloves on left and right side of the Y-axis. L_l and L_r are euclidean distances as computed in Eq. (1), and compute angles θ_{l_x}, θ_{l_y}, θ_{r_x}, and θ_{r_y} as in Eqs. (2) and (3).

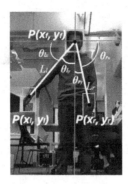

Fig. 3. Visual representation of values computed after our feature extraction.

$$L_l = \sqrt{(x_f - x_l)^2 + (y_f - y_l)^2} \qquad L_r = \sqrt{(x_f - x_r)^2 + (y_f - y_r)^2} \qquad (1)$$

$$\theta_{r_x} = \arccos \frac{|x_r - x_f|}{L_r} \qquad\qquad \theta_{r_y} = \arccos \frac{|y_r - y_f|}{L_r} \qquad (2)$$

$$\theta_{l_x} = \arccos \frac{|x_f - x_l|}{L_l} \qquad\qquad \theta_{l_y} = \arccos \frac{|y_l - y_f|}{L_l} \qquad (3)$$

Heuristic Symbolic Model for Pose Estimation. The extracted features are then passed to a heuristic symbolic rule set to classify which of the 11 poses is signaled by the referee. Each pose is defined using a set of symbolic rules, as described in Eqs. (4) to (12). While relatively simple, our results presented in Sect. 4, show that the symbolic rule set approach is sufficient for this task, and is likely to be computationally efficient. However, there are challenges to differentiating signals for "Pushing Free-Kick" and "Goal", due to both signals having the position of the gloves at a similar pose. This can result in no better than a random selection between the two signals. Although, we observe that more complex CNN-based approaches we compare against suffer similar issues.

$$goal\,kick\,blue : y_f - y_l >= 20, y_r - y_f >= 50 \qquad (4)$$

$$goal\,kick\,red : y_f - y_r >= 20, y_l - y_f >= 50 \qquad (5)$$

$$kick\,in\,blue : 0 < \theta_{l_x} < 35, 0 < \theta_{r_y} < 35, \frac{x_r}{x_f} > 1.05, 0.75 < \frac{L_l}{L_r} < 1.3 \qquad (6)$$

$$kick\,in\,red : 0 < \theta_{r_x} < 35, 0 < \theta_{l_y} < 35, \frac{x_l}{x_f} < 0.95, 0.75 < \frac{L_l}{L_r} < 1.3 \qquad (7)$$

$$corner\,kick\,blue : 30 < \theta_{l_x} < 70, 0 < \theta_{r_y} < 30, 0.75 < \frac{L_l}{L_r} < 1.3 \qquad (8)$$

$$corner\,kick\,red : 30 < \theta_{r_x} < 70, 0 < \theta_{l_y} < 30, 0.75 < \frac{L_l}{L_r} < 1.3 \qquad (9)$$

$$full\,time : 0 < y_f + y_l < 140, 0 < y_f + y_r < 140, 0.75 < \frac{L_l}{L_r} < 1.3 \qquad (10)$$

Fig. 4. Keypoints obtained using the Stacked-Hourglass architecture

$$push\,fk/goal\,blue : 0 < \theta_{l_x} < 35, \theta_{r_y} <= 25, \frac{x_r}{x_f} <= 1.1, \frac{L_l}{L_r} >= 1.5 \quad (11)$$

$$push\,fk/goal\,red : 0 < \theta_{r_x} < 35, 0 < \theta_{l_y} < 35, \frac{x_l}{x_f} >= 0.95, \frac{L_r}{L_l} >= 1.5 \quad (12)$$

3.3 Deep Convolutional Neural Network Models for Pose Estimation

We compare our approach against two relatively real-time Deep Convolutional Neural Network (DCNN) for pose estimation: OpenPose [4], and Stacked Hourglass [13]. Both DCNNs are used to obtain skeleton keypoints of a human body in an image. These keypoints are then passed through a SVM classifier [1] that is trained to identify the signals of the "Visual Referee Challenge".

OpenPose [4] uses a bottom-up approach to detect keypoints for multiple humans in an image frame and is capable of achieving real time performance, by applying part affinity fields to locate the parts of the image that contain a human. The architecture consists of 10 layers of VGG-19 which is fine tuned to the pose recognition task. The VGG-19 output is passed through the multiple blocks which consists of 2 CNN-branches for computing the confidence maps and the part affinity fields. The results are then passed through a parsing step where bipartite matching is done to acquire body parts candidates which are assembled to get full body poses. OpenPose is trained on MPII [2].

Stacked Hourglass [13], as the name suggests, stacks multiple Hourglass models in sequence to process an image and locate keypoints of a human body, and is trained with the COCO dataset [11]. The number of hourglasses must be configured for each application. We use 4 blocks due to the computational constraints of the Nao V6, which results in a reduction in accuracy. Figure 4 shows an example of the keypoints obtained from our Stacked HourGlass model.

The keypoints from both OpenPose and Stacked HourGlass are fed through an SVM classifier [1] that determines the referee signal. This SVM is trained using the same dataset of referee signals used evaluating our hybrid method. To reduce the computational requirements, we identify important keypoints located at the extremities of the body, then normalize the euclidean distance between

Table 1. Execution speed and accuracy of each method

Model	Time (sec)	Accuracy (%)
Hybrid	0.38	0.77
OpenPose	7.30	0.90
Stacked HG	5.27	0.93

the keypoints to make it consistent with the referees of different heights. Any keypoints from below the hip area are discarded as these information does not improve the accuracy.

4   Experiments and Results

We evaluate all methods on the dataset we collected as described in Sect. 3.1. We evaluate all of the methods on both single image instances, and on a video-sequence. The experiments are conducted on the SoftBank Nao V6 (ATOM E3845 1.91 GHZ CPU, Quad core, 4 GB DDR3 RAM), with all methods implemented in Python 3 for consistency. OpenPose and Stacked HourGlass are loaded with OpenCV 4.6.0. We note that the Nao V6 image is 960×1280, which is down-sampled to 360×480 pixels for our hybrid, and 256×256 for the DCNNs.

4.1   Evaluation on Single Frames

We first evaluate all of the methods on single image frames, across our dataset. Table 1 summarises the speed and the accuracy of each method. Our hybrid approach takes significantly less processing time by approximately 95% and 93% compared to OpenPose and Stacked HourGlass respectively, at a cost in accuracy. However, this general trend is not observed across all of the referee signals. Table 2 shows the F1 score of all methods for all each referee signal. We observe that like our method, OpenPose and Stacked HourGlass struggle to classify "Goal" and "Pushing Free Kick" signals. Additionally, the performance of OpenPose is only slightly better than our faster hybrid approach on these same signals. We observed that OpenPose reaches a higher accuracy if a larger image size is used, and likewise for Stacked HourGlass by increasing the number hourglass blocks. For both DCNN methods, this produces an unacceptable increase in processing time, and would fall outside the time limitation of the 2022 challenge. Our hybrid approach also struggles to distinguish between the "Goal" and "Pushing Free Kick" signals, as shown in the confusion matrix in Fig. 5. This is due to the choice of features that are extracted from the image resulting in similar measurements for angles and distances.

Different lighting conditions and the background behind the referee has varying impacts on each approach. Our hybrid method fails to identify a signal in very few images despite the lighting conditions. The face detection and colour filter are relatively robust to the lighting conditions where failures are observed

Table 2. F1-score of each referee signal for all methods

Referee Signal	Hybrid	OpenPose	Stacked HG
Kick In Blue	1.00	0.89	0.96
Kick In Red	0.90	0.93	0.96
Corner Kick Blue	0.81	0.96	0.96
Corner Kick Red	0.89	0.89	1.00
Goal Kick Blue	1.00	1.00	0.92
Goal Kick Red	0.97	1.00	0.97
Goal Blue	0.50	0.62	0.83
Goal Red	0.40	0.57	0.88
Pushing Free Kick Blue	0.30	0.55	0.84
Pushing Free Kick Red	0.47	0.86	0.89
Full Time	0.92	1.00	0.96

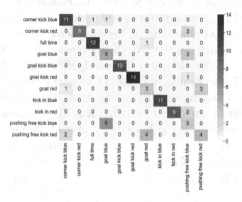

Fig. 5. Confusion Matrix for the devised hybrid approach

and are results of lack of brightness in the camera images. In these circumstances, the Haar Cascade struggles to find a face, while change in the intensity of colors makes it difficult to identify the regions-of-interest for the red gloves. Figure 6 demonstrates that in a low-light condition and intricate environment, the algorithm identifies false regions-of-interest for the gloves. Similarly, changes in lighting conditions or increasing the background complexity also impacts OpenPose and Stacked HourGlass. The number of keypoints identified under these conditions is significantly reduced as the complexity of both DCNNs are restricted for computational reasons. Consequently, the SVM classifier fails to correctly identify a referee signal. Interestingly, when omitting these challenging situations, our algorithm produces comparable results to the DCNNS, except for the "Goal" and "Pushing Free Kick" signals.

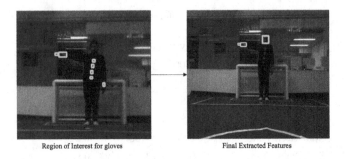

Region of Interest for gloves   Final Extracted Features

Fig. 6. False feature extraction in low light conditions using our approach.

These results show that our hybrid symbolic method is viable. Our hybrid method has limitations on the same referee signals as OpenPose and Stacked HourGlass, however, our hybrid method is substantially faster. Furthermore, it is arguable that neither OpenPose nor Stacked HourGlass could be applicable in a real-game setting. SPL games are conducted under fast-paced and real-time constraints. Therefore, we conclude that a *human* referee would be unsatisfied with the length of time required by the DCNN approaches to recognise and respond to the referee's call. A duration of 5–7 seconds is a relatively long time-frame for an SPL game. These results also do not consider the other computational work of the robot in playing an SPL game, thus, the detection of the referee signal could be longer in a real-game setting. It is likewise possible that a *human* referee may be unsatisfied by the inaccuracy of each method. However, as our hybrid method is relatively quick, we can run the method across multiple camera frames to improve accuracy. This is why it is important to evaluate all methods on video image sequences.

4.2   Evaluation on Video Sequence of Frame

We evaluate all of the methods using a video sequence of images. The Nao V6 camera operates 30 frames per second [15]. From Table 1, each DCNN method take more than 5 s to execute. This implies that by the time the DCNN methods predict a referee signal on a single image, our hybrid method is able to classify multiple frames. To demonstrate this, Fig. 7 shows an example of a referee transitioning from a signal for "goal kick" to "corner kick" across four select images of a video sequence of about 25 s. The figure also has a table listing the processing time of each method. Our hybrid model produces a signal classification in an accumulated 1.5 s across all four frames. However, both OpenPose and Stack Hourglass run into problems due to the long processing times on a single frame. As we can notice in frame (c) both the DCNN methods predicted an incorrect signal of a "corner kick" when the referee hand was still transitioning This means it's crucial to properly select the frame from which the DCNNs should predict the referee signal. Although the speed of our approach does have limitations, such as in frame (b), where an incorrect prediction is made before

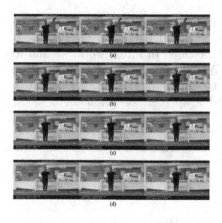

	Models	Predicted	Time
	Hybrid	Goal Kick Red	0.373
a	Stacked HG	Goal Kick Red	5.291
	OpenPose	Goal Kick Red	7.226
	Hybrid	Kick In Red	0.377
b	Stacked HG	Goal Kick Red	5.174
	OpenPose	Goal Kick Red	7.234
	Hybrid	Corner Kick Red	0.364
c	Stacked HG	Kick In Red	5.300
	OpenPose	Kick In Red	7.255
	Hybrid	Corner Kick Red	0.371
d	Stacked HG	Corner Kick Red	5.212
	OpenPose	Corner Kick Red	7.259

Fig. 7. Prediction of our Hybrid method, Stacked HG, and OpenPose (from left to right respectively) in 4 sequenced frames (a to d), where the referee transitions in pose from Goal Kick Red to Corner Kick Red. The table shows the evaluation time and prediction for each model. (Color figure online)

the referee showed final stable signal. Finally, while all methods did classify the final frame correctly, on-an-average another 5.27 and 7.30 s is required for Stacked Hourglass and OpenPose respectively. Alternatively our approach is able to self-correct from an earlier incorrect prediction in a much shorter time due to processing more frames.

Hence, our hybrid approach of combining "light-weight" machine learning with a heuristic symbolic rule set finds its advantage in real-time scenarios. In a real SPL soccer game, we conclude that our approach is more viable at continuously responding to the human referee as they are performing different gestures to indicate events in a soccer match. Further, we conclude that the robot would have the capacity to more quickly correct an error in identification of a referee signal, and this would strengthen the human referee's perception of the robot as it self-identifies and self-corrects it's mistakes.

5   Conclusions and Future Work

We present our hybrid symbolic and "light-weight" machine learning method for recognising the signals of a human referee in RoboCup Soccer in the 2022 "Visual Referee Challenge", in which we placed 3rd. We compare our method against other real-time existing CNN methods for human pose-estimation. We show that, under the resource constraints of the SoftBank Nao V6, there remains a crucial trade-off between the accuracy and speed in vision tasks; a trade-off that parallels known issues for creating meaningful human-robot interactions. We show that a symbolic approach, combined with "light-weight" machine learning, is competitive against the performance of slower CNN approaches, and provides a significant speed advantage. We further show under real-world video image sequences, our method has an ability to self-correct in a shorter time-frame to an initial error. Given our motivation from the field HRI, we view this speed advantage and self-correction as significant benefits. In future work, we aim to investigate learning the symbolic model. We also aim to evaluate influencing factors of HRI that a human referee prefers. We view this human perspective as important progress towards the 2050 RoboCup goal, for autonomous soccer robots to interact with human referees.

Acknowledgements. We acknowledge the members of our 2022 RoboCup team, Red-BackBots, who contributed to the data collection to support this work.

References

1. Alpaydin, E.: Introduction to Machine Learning. MIT Press, Cambridge (2014)
2. Andriluka, M., Pishchulin, L., Gehler, P., Schiele, B.: 2D human pose estimation: new benchmark and state of the art analysis. In: IEEE Conference on Computer Vision and Pattern Recognition (2014)
3. Anjomshoae, S., Najjar, A.: Explainable agents and robots: results from a systematic. In: 18th International Conference on Autonomous Agents and Multiagent Systems, pp. 1078–1088. Montreal, Canada (2019)
4. Cao, Z., Hidalgo Martinez, G., Simon, T., Wei, S., Sheikh, Y.A.: Openpose: real-time multi-person 2D pose estimation using part affinity fields. IEEE Trans. Pattern Anal. Mach. Intell. 7291–7299 (2019)
5. Committee, R.T.: Robocup standard platform league (NAO) rule book. Pdf, May 2022. https://spl.robocup.org/wp-content/uploads/SPL-Rules-master.pdf
6. Cruz, N., Lobos-Tsunekawa, K., Ruiz-del Solar, J.: Using convolutional neural networks in robots with limited computational resources: detecting NAO robots while playing soccer. In: Akiyama, H., Obst, O., Sammut, C., Tonidandel, F. (eds.) RoboCup 2017: Robot World Cup XXI. RoboCup 2017. LNCS, vol. 11175, pp. 19–30. Springer, Cham (2018). https://doi.org/10.1007/978-3-030-00308-1_2
7. Graaf, M.M.A.D., Allouch, S.B.: Exploring influencing variables for the acceptance of social robots. Robot. Auton. Syst. **61**(12), 1476–1486 (2013)
8. Jocher, G.: Yolov5 (v6.2) (2022). https://github.com/ultralytics/yolov5
9. Lecun, Y., Bottou, L., Bengio, Y., Haffner, P.: Gradient-based learning applied to document recognition. Proc. IEEE **86**(11), 2278–2324 (1998)
10. Leite, I., Martinho, C., Paiva, A.: Social robots for long-term interaction: a survey. Int. J. Soc. Robot. **5**(2), 291–308 (2013)
11. Lin, T., et al.: Microsoft COCO: common objects in context. CoRR (2014)
12. Menashe, J., et al., Stone, P.: Fast and precise black and white ball detection for robocup soccer. In: Akiyama, H., Obst, O., Sammut, C., Tonidandel, F. (eds.) RoboCup 2017: Robot World Cup XXI. RoboCup 2017. LNCS, vol. 11175, pp. 45–58. Springer, Cham (2017). https://doi.org/10.1007/978-3-030-00308-1_4
13. Newell, A., Yang, K., Deng, J.: Stacked hourglass networks for human pose estimation. In: Leibe, B., Matas, J., Sebe, N., Welling, M. (eds.) Computer Vision – ECCV 2016. ECCV 2016. LNCS, vol. 9912, pp. 483–499 Springer, Cham (2016). https://doi.org/10.1007/978-3-319-46484-8_29
14. Poppinga, B., Laue, T.: Jet-net: real-time object detection for mobile robots. In: Chalup, S., Niemueller, T., Suthakorn, J., Williams, M.A. (eds.) RoboCup 2019: Robot World Cup XXIII. RoboCup 2019. LNCS, vol. 11531, pp. 227–240. Springer, Cham (2019). https://doi.org/10.1007/978-3-030-35699-6_18

15. Robotics, S.: Nao - user guide - aldebaran 2.8.7.4 documentation (2022)
16. Röfer, T., et al.: B-human 2019-complex team play under natural lighting conditions. In: Chalup, S., Niemueller, T., Suthakorn, J., Williams, M.A. (eds.) RoboCup 2019: Robot World Cup XXIII. RoboCup 2019. LNCS, vol. 11531, pp. 646–657. Springer, Cham (2019). https://doi.org/10.1007/978-3-030-35699-6_52
17. Sammut, C., Farid, R., Wicaksono, H., Wiley, T.: Logic-Based Robotics. In: Human-Like Machine Intelligence, pp. 465–486. Oxford University Press, Oxford (2021)
18. Sheh, R.K.: Different XAI for different HRI. In: AAAI Fall Symposium Series, pp. 114–117. AAAI (2017)
19. Szemenyei, M., Estivill-Castro, V.: Real-time scene understanding using deep neural networks for RoboCup SPL. In: Holz, D., Genter, K., Saad, M., von Stryk, O. (eds.) RoboCup 2018: Robot World Cup XXII. RoboCup 2018. LNCS, vol. 11374, pp. 96–108. Springer, Cham (2018). https://doi.org/10.1007/978-3-030-27544-0_8
20. Toshev, A., Szegedy, C.: Deeppose: human pose estimation via deep neural networks. CoRR abs/1312.4659, 1653–1660 (2013)
21. Viola, P., Jones, M.: Rapid object detection using a boosted cascade of simple features. In: Proceedings of the 2001 IEEE Computer Society Conference on Computer Vision and Pattern Recognition, vol. 1, p. I (2001)
22. Wicaksono, H., Sammut, C., Sheh, R.K.: Towards explainable tool creation by a robot. In: IJCAI-17 Workshop on Explainable AI, pp. 63–67. Melbourne (2017)

Temporal Planning and Acting in Dynamic Domains

Marco De Bortoli$^{(\boxtimes)}$ and Gerald Steinbauer-Wagner

Graz University of Technology, Graz, Austria
mbortoli@ist.tugraz.at

Abstract. Due to increased demands related to flexible product configurations, frequent order changes, and tight delivery windows, there is a need for flexible production using AI methods. A way of addressing this is the use of temporal planning as it provides the ability to generate plans for complex goals while considering temporal aspects such as deadlines, concurrency, and durations. Drawbacks in applying such methods in dynamic environments are their high and unpredictable planning time as well as the limited ability to react to unexpected delays during the plan execution. In this paper, we address these issues with a temporal planning and execution framework that employs an online goal management strategy to deal with high and variable computational costs, and a plan dispatcher that takes the future temporal feasibility of plans into consideration. The framework has been evaluated using the RoboCup Logistics League simulation framework.

1 Introduction

Due to increased demands related to flexible product configurations, frequent order changes, and tight delivery windows, there is a need for flexible production using AI methods. A way of addressing this is the use of temporal planning as it provides the ability to generate plans for complex goals (e.g. production plans for product assembly) while considering temporal aspect such as deadlines, concurrency, and the duration of activities. Drawbacks in applying such methods in dynamic environments (e.g. autonomous mobile robots in a warehouse fulfilling on-the-fly orders) are their high and unpredictable planning time (e.g. robots need to come up with decisions in short time) as well as the ability to react to unexpected difficulties in the plan execution (e.g. failed or delayed actions).

There has been tremendous progress in the expressivity (e.g. numerical fluents) and performance of temporal planners (e.g. OPTIC [1]). Often the practical execution of plan was not considered in research, but efforts were made in bridging high-level reasoning and plan execution to allow the deployment in dynamic domains [12]. Systems like OpenPRS [11] and FAPE [2] address this but limit the reasoning by using (provided) hierarchical structures in planning and goal reasoning. The CX system [18] proposes a goal management similar to FAPE but does not limit the planning explicitly. ROSPlan [3] provides an integrated planning and execution system bridging the popular PDDL-based planning and the ROS-based robotics world, allowing supervised dispatching of plans.

In this paper, we address in particular the issues of high and variable computational cost for the planning process and the discrepancy of temporal constraints at planning and execution time. We propose a temporal planning and execution framework similar to ROSPlan that employs an online goal management strategy to deal with changing computational cost, an improved estimation of the duration of actions, and a plan dispatcher that takes the future temporal feasibility of plans into consideration. The goal manager is based on the observation that the planning time for different sets of sub-goals is different and not easily predictable. In order to be able to react in time, we plan concurrently for a given time for a multiset of goals, formed by a relaxation of the preferred goal set. Once planning is done we proceed with the plan for the goal set with the highest expected reward. Obviously, we trade the optimal plan/reward for reactivity. In order to minimize potential discrepancies between the planning and execution of actions, we employ an improved action duration estimation that is precomputed for each planning problem. This estimation is also used during plan dispatching, where a temporal graph representing the actual plan (i.e. deadlines as well as start and end of actions) is generated and updated. The consistency of this temporal graph is constantly monitored to recognize infeasible plans early, in order to trigger replanning.

We used the RoboCup Logistics League (RCLL) [17] as an example domain in the evaluation of the proposed framework. The domain was modeled as a planning problem and an experimental evaluation was conducted using the PExC simulation environment [19].

In the next section we will briefly introduce the RoboCup Logistics League. In Sect. 3 the proposed planning and execution framework is presented. An evaluation of the framework is presented in the Sect. 4. We conclude the paper in Sect. 5.

2   The RoboCup Logistics League

The RoboCup initiative aims to stimulate the development of Robotics and AI using robotics competitions. RCLL is part of this initiative and focuses on flexible approaches for production [17]. A fleet of three autonomous mobile robots cooperate to assemble a set of products, by interacting with production stations in a real world environment. The environment resembles a shop floor of the size of $14\,m \times 8\,m$. Orders (product configuration and delivery time) to accomplish are randomly generated during the game on an incremental basis. A product is mimicked by stacks of one base, zero or more rings, and a single cap. These elements may have different colors. The amount of rings basically determines the complexity of the product. In general, several refining steps of intermediate products by different machines are needed to assemble a product. Depending on the complexity of a delivered product, the corresponding amount of points is awarded. The goal is that teams develop a production strategy that maximizes

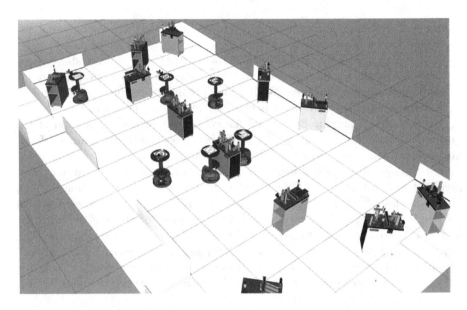

Fig. 1. Simulation of a RoboCup Logistics League game.

the points awarded in a 17 min production phase. The game field is depicted in Fig. 1. In order to challenge the flexibility of the developed approaches the layout of the shop floor may change and is not known in advance and, moreover, machines go down randomly for maintenance and are thus not available for a period of time.

3   The Planning and Dispatching Framework

The proposed Planning and Dispatching Framework implements a centralized control strategy for a multi-agent system in a dynamic domain. It is based on three main components: (1) a Goal Reasoner, (2) a Planner, and (3) a Dispatching and Monitoring system. In Fig. 2, the interaction between the components is shown. The Dispatching and Monitoring component plays the role of the main controller that invokes the Goal Reasoner, and consequently the planner, and executes the obtained plan. The plan execution is constantly monitored for issues that may require a regeneration of the goals or the plan, e.g. failed actions or deadline violations.

3.1   Modeling and Planning

The planner is responsible for finding a plan to achieve the goals selected by the Goal Reasoner while minimizing its makespan. The Goal Reasoner commits the selected goals to the planner. The planning process is performed using the temporal planner Optic [1] that provides a considerable set of features from PDDL

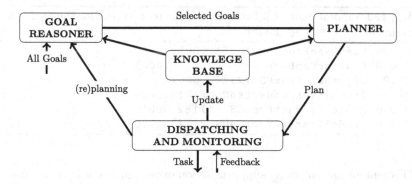

Fig. 2. Planning and Dispatching Architecture.

2.1 [9]. PDDL (Planning Domain Definition Language) was born as an attempt to standardize the existing planning languages, and it is the default language for the International Planning Competition. In its first versions it addresses classical planning. Given a PDDL description of the domain in terms of feasible actions and the specific instance, a PDDL planner calculates a plan. A plan consists of a sequence of non-interleaving actions leading to the set of provided goals, starting from a given initial situation. Temporal Planning augments the features of classical planning with handling of time, action concurrency, and temporal constraints. A temporal plan can not be represented with a sequence of action, and it consists of a map between time points and starting/ending of actions. Such features are standardized in PDDL 2.1 [9]. For further details about classical and temporal planning, we refer to [16]. Different temporal PDDL planners may be used as well, as long as an interface to parse the planner output is provided. We favor temporal planning over other approaches, like HTNs (Hierarchical Task Networks) [8], as it is able to find better plans in terms of makespan. The latter is needed to be able to serve as many orders as possible. Moreover, temporal planning makes handling temporal deadlines and coordinating multiple agents easier. The downside is the high computational cost of the planning process. In order to address this issue for the RCLL domain, we simplified the domain model and introduced a corresponding goal selection. The domain is modeled in PDDL by representing the two possible interactions with a station as abstract action: *get* and *deliver*. The former is used to retrieve a workpiece from a station after it has been processed, while the latter is needed to deliver the workpiece to a station for processing. An example is the action *deliverProductToCS(r cs p color)*. This action models the delivery of a product to a cap station, in order to mount a cap. The parameters include the robot r performing the action, the cap station cs, the partial product p, and the color of the requested cap *color*. The result of the planning process is a temporal plan, which is represented by the schedule σ, formed by a set of triples $\langle a, t_a, d_a \rangle$, where a is a grounded action, t_a is the time when the action a needs to be started, and d_a is the duration of the action. Listing 1 shows the plan to deliver a simple product in the RCLL domain.

Listing 1. Temporal plan a C_0 Product. Parameters (except for the agent) have been omitted for better readability.

```
1   0.000:(getBaseFromBS r1)[51.000]
2   0.000:(bufferCapBaseFromCS r2)[89.000]
3   89.001:(getBaseFromCS r2)[52.000]
4   141.002:(deliverProducttoCS r1)[85.000]
5   226.003:(getProductFromCS r1)[52.000]
6   278.004:(deliverProductToDS r1)[73.000]
```

This representation poorly supports action dispatching, since it is not easy to determine how delays that occurred in the execution of an action affect the other triples of the plan. To address this, we represent the plan as a temporal graph (Simple Temporal Network [6]), which encodes the temporal dependencies and the partial order between the actions, without constraining the start of actions to specific time points. It can be computed from the temporal plan and the planning domain. A temporal graph G is a directed graph $G = (V, E)$. The set of vertices V represents time points, like starting or ending of an action, while each edge (or arc) $e \in E$ is a pair of vertices $(v_1, v_2) \in V \times V$. The function $\Lambda : E \to \mathbb{N} \times \{\mathbb{N}, \infty\}$ labels each edge with a pair of natural numbers $[lb, ub]$ or with $[lb, +\infty)$. In a label $[lb, ub]$ for an arc (v_1, v_2), lb and up express the lower and upper bound of the time difference between the time points associated to v_1 and v_2. This allows to express temporal constraints between time points. The fact that (v_1, v_2) is a directed edge encodes a partial order relation from v_1 to v_2, stating that v_2 can not happen before v_1. In its less restrictive form, a label $[0, +\infty)$ encodes just a partial order relation from v_1 and v_2, without imposing any temporal constraint. Given an action a with estimated duration d_a, we denote with a_s and a_e the two vertices representing start and end of a. An edge labeled $[d_a, d_a]$ is created from a_s to a_e. Figure 3 shows the temporal graph equivalent to the plan in Listing 1.

An accurate estimation of action duration is crucial, both for appropriate planning as well as monitoring plan execution. Since the temporal planner tries to optimize the makespan of the plan, the plan is considered optimal in reality only if the estimated duration of an action is close to the real execution time. In our domain every action models a specific interaction between a robot and a station. For performance reasons, we do not model the actions to move a robot between two locations. As a consequence, in every action we need to consider the time needed for the robot to move from its actual position to the involved station. Each action is thus characterized by two cost (or time) components: (1) the movement costs and (2) the interaction costs. The interaction costs (e.g. time to input a product into a machine and mount a cap) have been estimated for each action empirically. We determined the average duration during several invocations of the action. In order to estimate the duration of the movement included in the actions, we precompute a matrix for each setup (randomly selected location of stations), containing all the estimated costs for traveling between each

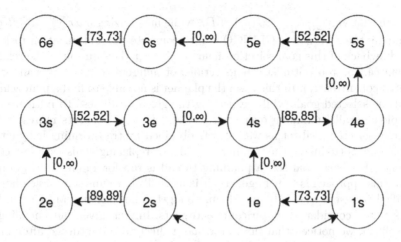

Fig. 3. Temporal graph for the plan shown in Listing 1.

pair of locations. Since the same path finding algorithm is used as in the robot's navigation skill to find the best path between locations, the estimated times are close to the real ones. To make the estimation even more precise, we are also considering costs for managing the orientation at the start and at the end of each movement action. By adopting this procedure we achieve an accurate estimation of actions duration that is incorporated into the PDDL domain.

3.2 Goal Reasoning and Multi-thread Planning

Since we are interested in dynamic domains where issues arise unexpectedly, the planning process needs to be fast, in order to be able to react to changes and opportunities in the environment in time. For this reason, the Goal Reasoner selects the most rewarding set of goals the planner may be able to obtain a plan with a given time budget (e.g., 1 min.). In the RCLL domain a single goal is an individual order (product configuration and delivery time). In general, planning for all received orders is not possible with the given time budget. Thus, we follow the idea of partial satisfactory planning [20]. The Goal Reasoner solves a relaxed version of the RCLL domain, where it is assumed that each goal can be achieved by a single agent individually, without considering cooperation or management of resources. In this simple setting the set of processing steps needed for goal g are known in advance. Using the duration estimation of actions described in the previous section, we can formulate the selection as a simple task allocation problem with an overall deadline. We denote with $M(g)$ the makespan of g (sum of process steps) and with $R(g)$ the reward for achieving it. G denotes the set of all possible goals, $SG \subseteq G$ the set of the selected goals. DL is the total remaining time for achieving said goals. Solving the relaxed problem means to find a task allocation τ, formed by a set of allocations $\langle r_i, g_j \rangle$ (robot r_i works on goal $g_j \in$

SG) such that $\forall r_i \sum_{\langle r_i, g_j \rangle \in \tau} M(g_j) < DL$ while maximizing $max \sum_{g_j \in SG} R(g_j)$. We employ the ASP solver CLINGO [10] to compute this optimization task.

A drawback of this goal selection heuristic is that the solution of the relaxed problem can be too optimistic (e.g. actions of different robots that cannot be executed concurrently). In this case, the planner is not able to find a plan achieving all the selected goals while respecting the given deadlines. To mitigate this we exploit parallel planning over multiple sets of goals. The sets represent the originally selected goal set as well as sets obtained by transforming it by either dropping goals (reducing the number of goals) or replacing goals with less complex ones. For each goal set, a planning thread is ran for 1 min. The rationale behind this approach is that in general it is more likely to find a feasible plan for simplified goal sets with a bounded time budget. The time bound of 1 min has been selected considering empirical experiments. In fact, given our encoding of the problem, we noticed that no better plan is likely to be returned after 1 min of computation, due to the combinatorial explosion of the problem. Among the returned feasible plans, we select and dispatch the one with the highest reward. Thus, we trade a higher reward for a better response time. The entire process is shown in Fig. 4.

3.3 Dispatching and Monitoring

The task of this module is to dispatch the actions of the obtained plan in time, to monitor its proper execution (in terms of state and time), and to initiate replanning when necessary. The following three events may trigger replanning: (1) failed execution of an action (task), (2) successful execution of the actual plan, (3) impossibility to achieve a goal in time.

In ROSPlan a temporal graph is dispatched starting from the root node and traversing its outgoing edges, respecting their lower and upper bound $[lb, ub]$. Nodes corresponding to the end of an action are called contingent nodes [5], since we do not have control over them. Their dispatching is notified to us by the lower levels of the software stack. In general, in order to know when it is safe to dispatch a node, all the temporal constraints encoded in all the edges must be propagated [14]. However, except for duration edges, discussed later in this section, in the temporal graphs produced by our domain there are no other types of edges going towards contingent nodes. As a consequence, a new node can be dispatched after all its incoming edges have been traversed successfully, without the need for further constraint propagation. For instance, looking at Fig. 3, we can see that action 4 (*deliverProducttoCS*) must be preceded by action 3 and 2. However, action 1 can be executed in parallel to actions 2 and 3. In this work, we use a slightly different approach to check the temporal constraint on the edges, in order to allow an earlier detection of deadline violations. As it can be seen in Fig. 3, there are two types of edges: (1) action duration edges $[d_a, d_a]$ between start and end of the action a, and (2) partial order edges $[0, +\infty)$ between the end of an action and the start of the following one. Nodes corresponding to start actions are dispatched by sending the corresponding action to the robot

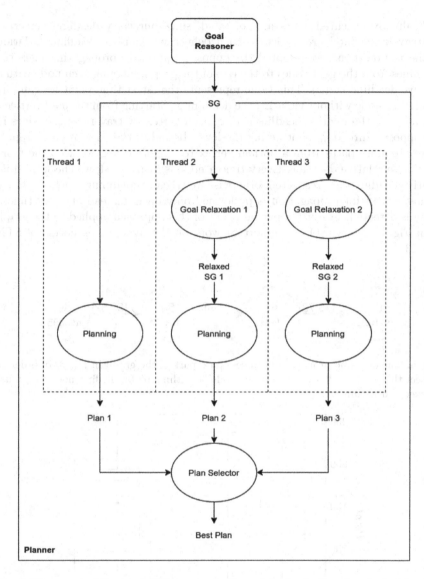

Fig. 4. Planner Architecture. SG represents the original set of goals selected by the Goal Reasoner.

for execution, while end nodes are dispatched when a feedback for the successful execution of the corresponding action is received. The partial order encoded through the edges is ensured by this dispatching process. Unfortunately, it can not be expected that the execution in the real world perfectly respects the temporal constraint $[d_a, d_a]$. The approach presented in [4] propagates the detected delay by fixing the execution times of already executed actions and updating (by constraint propagation) the remaining deadlines. In our approach, violations of such already executed edges are tolerated, since our early deadline detection strategy immediately recognizes if such delays will cause a deadline violation in the future. Thus, we adopted the opposite approach, propagating back the deadlines from the goal nodes to the rest of the graph, labeling each node with a relative deadline $rdl(x)$. This value represents the latest time point we can dispatch that node without violating the deadline x. Starting from the *goal* vertices, we calculate the relative deadlines rdl of each vertex by traversing the edges in the opposite direction, subtracting the lower bound of the edge at each step. If there are more paths from a normal vertex to a *goal* vertex, we keep the more restrictive relative deadline. Every time a node is dispatched, we check if all its relative deadlines are respected, otherwise we trigger replanning. The advantage is that constraint propagation is performed only once, instead of every time a delay is detected. In Fig. 5 a partial result of this approach applied to the graph from Fig. 3 is shown. Other important work on the dynamic execution of STN are [13–15].

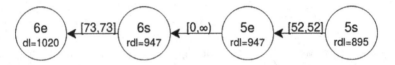

Fig. 5. The deadline propagation process on a part of the graph in Fig. 3. In order to respect the deadline dl, dispatching the node 6e within 1020 s, the first node (5 s) must be executed within 895 s.

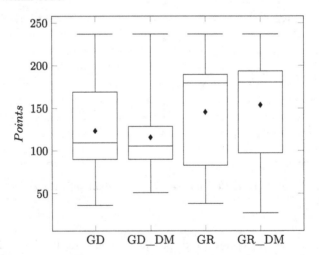

Fig. 6. System Evaluation. The rhombus is the average.

4   Evaluation

To evaluate the proposed system and the main contributions, we compare four different configurations of our approach using the PExC simulation [19]. One version uses a greedy (GD) first-in-first-served goal selection. The planner calculates the plan for the first three available orders. No deadline management strategy is used. A second version named Greedy Deadline Management (GD_DM) is similar, but replanning is triggered when a violation of a deadline is detected. In such case, the corresponding goal (order) is dropped. The third version makes use of the Goal Reasoner component to select the most viable orders, but no replanning is triggered in case of a deadline violation. We refer to it as Goal Reasoning (GR). The fourth version (GR_DM) resembles the complete proposed system.

Figure 6 shows the results of the experimental evaluation. A set of 20 games with different machine setups and order histories has been played for each system. As metric we use the awarded points that reflect well how the system was able to process the given orders. We compare the four different versions of our system (GD to GR_DM), using the skills implementation from [7]. The first noticeable result is the improvement achieved by using the Goal Reasoner. Selecting the most prominent goals from the beginning is crucial, in order to avoid wasting time with less rewarding orders, or trying to plan for too complex orders. In the latter cases, the planning process lasts too long for providing a plan in time. By comparing GD and GD_DM we see similar results for the median and the lower quartile, but a worse upper quartile for the latter. When investigation games where GD achieves good results, it can be seen that in GD_DM replanning is triggered after the relative deadline of a mostly completed complex order is violated for a few seconds. However, since the violation of the deadline has not been severe, GD sometimes still succeeds in delivering the order. Early detection of deadlines works better if supported by a decent Goal Reasoning strategy, as shown by the results obtained by GR and GR_DM. Here, even if replanning is triggered unnecessarily, such situations are compensated by the Goal Reasoner, either by rehabilitating the violated order or by replacing it with a slightly easier order. In fact, even if an order violated a relative deadline in the old plan, it may be accomplished in time in the new plan. The limited improvement of GR_DM with respect to GR can be explained by the fact that games gaining most of the points are the ones where replanning was never triggered. In this cases, GR and GR_DM result in the exact same execution, and a complex product is delivered. The opposite case applies when both GR and GR_DM are not able to achieve a complex goal. When this happens, GR_DM performs better by dropping it in advance and is able to deliver some simpler products.

5   Conclusion

In this paper an approach was presented that allows to use temporal planning in dynamic domains. Despite existing drawbacks (e.g. uncertainty of planning and execution time), we show that temporal planning can be feasible for dynamic environments. The two main contributions of the proposed framework are a Goal Reasoner and a deadline violation detection. The former uses relaxed planning problems and multi-threaded planning to address unpredictable planning times while the latter is able to detect plan violations caused by action delays in early stages of its execution. An experimental evaluation using the PExC simulation framework showed that tasks with deadlines that arrive incrementally can be served better. In the future, a more appropriate relaxation of goals will be investigated to improve the Goal Reasoning strategy. Moreover, an improvement of the deadline management will be investigated, minimizing the number of useless invocations of replanning.

References

1. Benton, J., Coles, A., Coles, A.: Temporal planning with preferences and time-dependent continuous costs. In: Proceedings of the International Conference on Automated Planning and Scheduling, vol. 22, no. 1, pp. 2–10, May 2012. https:// ojs.aaai.org/index.php/ICAPS/article/view/13509
2. Bit-Monnot, A.: Temporal and Hierarchical Models for Planning and Acting in Robotics. Ph.D. thesis, Université de Toulouse (2016)
3. Cashmore, M., et al.: Rosplan: planning in the robot operating system. In: Proceedings International Conference on Automated Planning and Scheduling, ICAPS 2015, pp. 333–341, January 2015
4. Castillo, L., Fdez-Olivares, J., González-Muñoz, A.: A temporal constraint network based temporal planner, January 2002
5. Cimatti, A., Do, M., Micheli, A., Roveri, M., Smith, D.E.: Strong temporal planning with uncontrollable durations. Artif. Intell. **256**, 1–34 (2018)
6. Dechter, R., Meiri, I., Pearl, J.: Temporal constraint networks. Artif. Intell. **49**(1), 61–95 (1991). https://doi.org/10.1016/0004-3702(91)90006-6, https:// www.sciencedirect.com/science/article/pii/0004370291900066
7. Egger, V., Fürbaz, L., Haas, S., Krickl, S., Ludwiger, J., Martin, I., et al.: Robocup logistics league Graz robust and intelligent production system grips (2018)
8. Erol, K., Hendler, J., Nau, D.S.: HTN planning: complexity and expressivity. In: AAAI, vol. 94, pp. 1123–1128 (1994)
9. Fox, M., Long, D.: PDDL2.1: an extension to PDDL for expressing temporal planning domains. J. Artif. Intell. Res. (JAIR) **20**, 61–124 (12 2003)
10. Gebser, M., Kaminski, R., Kaufmann, B., Schaub, T.: Clingo= asp+ control. arXiv preprint arXiv:1405.3694 (2014)
11. Ingrand, F., Chatila, R., Alami, R., Robert, F.: PRS: a high level supervision and control language for autonomous mobile robots. In: Proceedings of IEEE International Conference on Robotics and Automation, vol. 1, pp. 43–49 (1996)
12. Ingrand, F., Ghallab, M.: Deliberation for autonomous robots: a survey. Artif. Intell. **247**, 10–44 (2017). https://www.sciencedirect.com/science/article/ pii/S0004370214001350, special Issue on AI and Robotics
13. Morris, P.: Dynamic controllability and dispatchability relationships. In: Simonis, H. (eds.) Integration of AI and OR Techniques in Constraint Programming. CPAIOR 2014. LNCS, vol. 8451, pp. 464–479. Springer, Cham (2014). https://doi. org/10.1007/978-3-319-07046-9_33

14. Morris, P., Muscettola, N., Vidal, T.: Dynamic control of plans with temporal uncertainty. In: Proceedings of the 17th International Joint Conference on A.I. (IJCAI-01), August 2003
15. Muscettola, N., Morris, P., Tsamardinos, I.: Reformulating temporal plans for efficient execution. In: Principles of Knowledge Representation and Reasoning (1998)
16. Nau, D., Ghallab, M., Traverso, P.: Automated Planning: Theory & Practice. Morgan Kaufmann Publishers Inc., San Francisco, CA, USA (2004)
17. Niemueller, T., Ewert, D., Reuter, S., Ferrein, A., Jeschke, S., Lakemeyer, G.: RoboCup Logistics League Sponsored by Festo: A Competitive Factory Automation Testbed, pp. 605–618, October 2016
18. Niemueller, T., Hofmann, T., Lakemeyer, G.: Goal reasoning in the clips executive for integrated planning and execution. In: Proceedings of the International Conference on Automated Planning and Scheduling, vol. 29, no. 1, pp. 754–763, May 2021. https://ojs.aaai.org/index.php/ICAPS/article/view/3544
19. Niemueller, T., Karpas, E., Vaquero, T., Timmons, E.: Planning competition for logistics robots in simulation. In: International Conference on Automated Planning and Scheduling (ICAPS) - Workshop on Planning and Robotics (PlanRob) (2016)
20. Van Den Briel, M., Sanchez, R., Do, M., Kambhampati, S.: Effective approaches for partial satisfaction (over-subscription) planning. In: Proceedings of the National Conference on Artificial Intelligence (AAAI), pp. 562–569 (2004)

SUSTAINA-OP™: Kid-Sized Open Hardware Platform Humanoid Robot with Emphasis on Sustainability

Masato Kubotera[✉] and Yasuo Hayashibara

Department of Advanced Robotics, Chiba Institute of Technology,
Narashino, Chiba, Japan
masatokubotera06@yahoo.co.jp

Abstract. This paper presents the approach to designing and constructing SUSTAINA-OP™, a robot developed to participate in the RoboCup Humanoid League KidSize. The robot was developed as a humanoid hardware platform with the objective of overcoming the barrier of high hardware development costs associated with participation in the RoboCup Humanoid League. The concept of this platform is to create a "sustainable" system that is user-friendly for both new participants and software developers who employ multiple robots, facilitating long-term development. To achieve this, our design focused on enhancing robustness, minimizing resources required for repair and maintenance, and increasing versatility. Moreover, the system is equipped with a high-performance System-on-Module to support software development, considering the growing importance of deep learning-based recognition and other applications. The robot featured in this paper was utilized by the CIT Brains team from Chiba Institute of Technology, which emerged victorious in the Humanoid League of RoboCup2022. The data for the developed robot is available on GitHub.

Keywords: Open Hardware Platform · Humanoid Robot · RoboCup

1 Introduction

The RoboCup Humanoid League presents a wide variety of research challenges, such as walking control, object recognition, and self-localization in soccer competitions. To avoid the issue of high hardware development costs, teams participating in the league sometimes utilize open platform robots. DARwIn-OP [1], a notable example, is an open humanoid platform, co-developed by ROBOTIS and Virginia Tech which was released in 2011. The Humanoid League's rule [2] is updated annually according to a roadmap until 2050 [3] to foster scientific and technological advancements in robotics and artificial intelligence while gradually approximating human soccer. Therefore, open platform robots must exhibit sufficient flexibility to rapidly adapt to evolving competition rules and research challenges. DARwIn-OP has faced difficulties in adjusting to walking on artificial turf and accommodating changes in competition regulations. In recent years,

C. Buche et al. (Eds.): RoboCup 2023, LNAI 14140, pp. 166–178, 2024.
https://doi.org/10.1007/978-3-031-55015-7_14

novel open platform robots such as NimbRo-OP2X [4] and Wolfgang-OP [5] have been proposed. Despite these endeavors, the number of teams participating in the Humanoid League has been dwindling, with our research team being the sole Japanese team.

This paper presents the SUSTAINA-OP^{TM} open hardware platform humanoid robot as shown in Fig. 1 and Table 1. This platform was developed based on the concept of "sustainability" to create a user-friendly platform for both new participants and software developers who employ multiple robots, facilitating long-term development. The objective was to enhance robustness, minimize resources required for repairs and maintenance, and increase flexibility in adapting to new competition rules. As an open hardware platform, the development data for SUSTAINA-OP^{TM}is available on GitHub [6]. The release of the SUSTAINA-OP^{TM} aims to overcome the problems of high hardware development cost and continuity in research and development of humanoid robots, including for the RoboCup Humanoid League, thereby accelerating progress in humanoid research. Our research team, CIT Brains [7], achieved first place in the RoboCup2022 Humanoid League Soccer Competition for KidSize using this platform. This paper focuses on the robustness of the platform and the control circuits with high-performance System-on-Module (SoM), which contributed to the victory. It is not detailed in the champion paper [8].

Fig. 1. The SUSTAINA-OP^{TM} open hardware platform humanoid robot and its kinematics diagram.

2   Related Work

Table 2 shows a comparison of hardware specifications between well-known humanoid robot platforms and the SUSTAINA-OP^{TM}. DARwIn-OP (also known as ROBOTIS-OP), a leading platform in the Humanoid League, is widely used by researchers. While the third-generation DARwIn-OP3 (also known as ROBOTIS-OP3) is currently available, it is no longer being sold. Team DARwIn won first place in the Humanoid League Soccer Competition for KidSize during

Table 1. Specification of SUSTAINA-OP^{TM}

Type	Specification	Value	
General	Height · Weight	647 mm · 5.18 kg (Battery included)	
	Battery	LiHv 11.4 V 3S1P 2,800 mAh	
	Battery life	Max. 30 min. walking possible	
	Materials	A2017, GFRP, POM, TPU, PLA, etc.	
Actuators	Total	10 × B3M-SC-1170-A	9 × B3M-SC-1040-A
	Stall torque · current	7.6 Nm · 5.4 A	4.6 Nm · 3.6 A
	No load speed	46 rpm	54 rpm
Sensors	IMU	TDK MPU-9250 (Magnetometer not used in software)	
	Camera	e-con Systems^{TM} e-CAM50_CUNX	
	Camera lens	TOWIN S02512512524F 160°(D) · 125°(H) · 90°(V)	
	Encoders	Contactless magnetic 12bit/1round	
Control boards	System-on-Module	NVIDIA® Jetson Xavier^{TM} NX	
	Carrier board	AVerMedia EN715	
	Electronics boards	Main Board Ver. 2.2	
		EN715 Expansion Board Ver. 1.1	
		Start Stop Switch Ver. 3.0	

RoboCup2011-2012 using DARwIn-OP for two consecutive years. Furthermore, in RoboCup2014, 50% of the KidSize teams that submitted qualification material either utilized the DARwIn-OP platform or based their robot on it [9]. However, due to rule revisions such as artificial turf for the playing field and the relaxation of height restrictions, DARwIn-OP became inferior in terms of walking speed after the RoboCup2015.

In recent years, many humanoid platforms have been developed for the RoboCup Humanoid League. One such example is Sigmaban+ [10], developed by Rhoban Football Club at the University of Bordeaux, France. The team won the Humanoid League Soccer Competition for KidSize four times during RoboCup2016-2019. Sigmaban+ addresses the league's challenge "the robots should be able to withstand falls". Although equipped with a structure that partially absorbs the impact of falls, the shoulder motors are prone to failure and are described as "still not reliable enough" [11]. Furthermore, while deep learning is employed in the vision system, they stated that "none were usable in the very limited embedded computers" [12]. As a result, a custom Convolutional Neural Network (ConvNet) is used, which lacks generality.

Wolfgang-OP, developed by the University of Hamburg, Germany, shares a similar kinematic structure with the original NimbRo-OP [13]. This platform also addressed fall-related damage prevention, using passive compliances with 3D-printed thermoplastic polyurethane Series of Elastic Actuators (SEAs) and bumpers at the front and back of the robot's torso [5]. Fall-related damage prevention remains an important issue for many humanoid platforms, and "the robots of the KidSize league happens to be an interesting benchmarking environment for this subject" [11].

As described above, humanoid platform robots still require further improvement, and improving their performance and reliability continue to be a subject of research.

Table 2. Hardware specifications of well-known humanoid robot platforms and SUSTAINA-OP^{TM}

Robot	Size (cm)	Mass (kg)	DoF	Actuator	Processing unit	Senser	Battery	Cost (€)
DARwIn-OP [1]	45.5	2.8	20	RX-28	Intel® Atom Z530 1 GB RAM	Camera IMU Encoder FSR	–	–
Wolfgang-OP [5]	80	7.5	20	MX-106 MX-64 XH540	Intel® i5-8259 8 GB RAM	Camera IMU Encoder Strain Gauge	Li-Po 14.8 V 5.2 Ah	11,000
Sigmaban+ [10]	70	5.5	20	MX-106 MX-64	Intel® i5 Micro-6700T 8 GB RAM	Camera IMU Encoder Strain Gauge	–	30,000 (SP)
NimbRo-OP2X [4]	135	19	20	XH540	Intel® i7-8700T 4 GB RAM (With GPU)	Camera IMU Encoder	Li-Po 14.8 V 8.0 Ah	–
SUSTAINA-OP^{TM}	64.7	5.18	19	B3M-SC-1170 B3M-SC-1040	NVIDIA® Xavier^{TM} NX 8 GB RAM (With GPU)	Camera IMU Encoder	Li-Hv 11.4 V 2.8 Ah	7,000

SP = sale-priced

3 Design Concept

The hardware specification of the SUSTAINA-OP^{TM} open hardware platform humanoid robot is outlined in Table 1. This platform was developed, keeping the concept of "sustainability" at its core, to provide ease of use and long-term viability for both new participants and software developers who utilized multiple robots. The focus is on enhancing robustness, minimizing resources required for repair and maintenance, and increasing adaptability to new competition rules. In the current Humanoid League, four robots from each team play soccer in different roles, such as attacker and goalkeeper. Our research team utilizes the same platform with identical specification, which is versatile enough to play all roles.

As an open hardware platform, the SUSTAINA-OP^{TM} is available on GitHub [6] for mechanical and electrical design and other development data. Mechanical and electrical design processes employ Autodesk® Inventor® and Eagle. To increase flexibility in responding to new competition rules, not only intermediate file formats such as Stereo Lithography (STL) and Standard for the Exchange of Product (STEP) for mechanical components and Gerber Format for circuit boards are provided, but also data to facilitate platform modifications, such as modeling file(e.g., Inventor® part file (IPT)), schematic file (e.g., Eagle schematic file (sch)), and board layout file (e.g., Eagle board file (brd)). In addition, issues encountered in daily usage are published. The 3D CAD model of the robot is also available on Autodesk® Viewer [14] for convenient browsing.

4   Mechanical Design

All mechanical components used in the SUSTAINA-OP™ are built by student members of CIT Brains, with the exception of ready-made components purchasable through e-commerce sites such as MISUMI. Most of these components can be fabricated using the facilities at Chiba Institute of Technology. The platform is designed to enable even first-time robot developers to build, maintain, and operate it, although engineering knowledge is required. Mechanical components are primarily constructed through small CNC machining and 3D printing via Fused Deposition Modeling (FDM). Components are primarily made from Duralumin (2017 Aluminum Alloy), Glass Fiber Reinforced Plastics (GFRP), and Polyoxymethylene (POM) plates. To enhance machining accuracy, orthogonal components are not fabricated by bending, but by joining with concavo-convex joints. The exterior and bumpers are 3D printed using Poly-Lactic Acid (PLA) and Thermoplastic Polyurethane (TPU). Additionally, to comply with the competition rules, red/blue team markers must be made from polypropylene(PP) material using a laser cutting machine, dyed with anodized aluminum, and sandblasted to prevent reflections.

This chapter focuses on the mechanical structure of the platform to improve robustness and minimize the resources required for repair and maintenance.

4.1   Kinematic Structure and Actuators

The SUSTAINA-OP™ has two legs, two arms, and one head attached to its trunk as shown in Fig. 1. The legs possess three Degrees of Freedoms (DoFs) at the crotch joint (roll, pitch, and yaw), one DoF (pitch) at the knee joints, and two DoFs (roll and pitch) at the ankles. The arms have two DoFs (roll and pitch) at the shoulder joint and one DoF at the elbow joint. These joints enable the robot to walk, kick, and recover from a fall, all essential actions for soccer. In addition, the head has one DoF of yaw for panning motion, and a camera for vision to recognize objects on the field and estimate its own position. In general, humanoid platforms have one degree of freedom in pitch to perform tilt movements for the head. However, in the SUSTAINA-OP™, a camera module with a wide-angle lens is mounted at a tilt angle of 45°, providing a sufficient field of view for soccer games as shown in Fig. 2, and thus the pitch DoF is omitted. This reduction results in lower total cost and weight of the robot. All actuators are position-controlled daisy-chain command servo motors from the Kondo Kagaku B3M series.

4.2   Leg Structures Supporting Stable Walking

To achieve stable walking on artificial turf fields and to prevent falls, the leg joints must move along a computed trajectory. Falls are the most detrimental element of the robot's hardware. Therefore, stable walking is an important factor for the long-term use of the robot. This paper presents three mechanical design guidelines for stable walking.

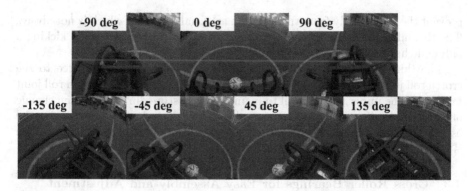

Fig. 2. Field of view in the SUSTAINA-OP^{TM} when standing on the center mark of soccer field captured at ±135° from the front at 45° intervals. (These view images are distortion-corrected.)

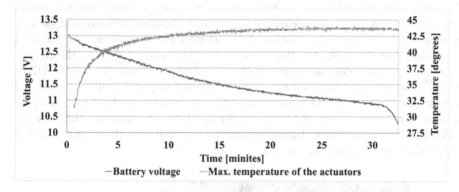

Fig. 3. Battery voltage and maximum actuator temperature. The SUSTAINA-OP^{TM} was walked around a soccer field up to the limit of battery usage. The sensor (Texas Instruments INA238) to obtain the battery voltage was retrofitted only during verification since it is not normally attached to the platform.

The first design guideline is to utilize the actuator's torque with margin. The SUSTAINA-OP^{TM} is designed with a height of 65 cm and a weight of 5.2 kg (including battery), which is lower than the allowable height of 100 cm for KidSize. Consequently, the design ensures walking stability even if the torque decreases due to heat generated by continuous operation. As a result, as shown in Fig. 3, it has been confirmed that the robot can walk continuously for up to 30 min without falls when using a battery.

The second design guideline is the use of parallel link structures for the legs. In small humanoid platforms, serial link structures for the legs are commonly used, but maintaining a constant toe posture becomes difficult when backlash increases due to the deterioration of the actuator. Therefore, the parallel link structure is used for the thigh and knee links so that the posture of the feet does not change in relation to the waist during leg extension and retraction. To prevent the upper body from tilting on an artificial turf field, which is not always flat, the ankle pitch joints have been added, which can be used when kicking a ball and changing the center of gravity.

The third design guideline is the addition of a deceleration device to the crotch roll joint. Insufficient torque and increased backlash in the crotch roll joint may cause the upper body to fail to maintain its posture during a sudden change of direction, leading to a fall. Therefore, by adding the reduction device using the oscillating slider-crank mechanism to the crotch roll joint, the maximum torque is increased and the angular error is reduced.

4.3   Cross Roller Bearings for Easy Assembly and Adjustment of Crotch Yaw Joints

The yaw joints of the crotch receive axial loads from the actuator during walking and landing. Some platforms designed to address this problem employ thrust bearings. However, while thrust bearings are relatively inexpensive and easy to obtain, adjusting the axial clearance between the housing raceway and bearing is difficult. If the gap is too narrow, the frictional force increases, and the joint does not move smoothly. On the other hand, if the gap is too wide, the rigidity of the crotch joint decreases, and walking becomes unstable. The SUSTAINA-OP^{TM} eliminates the need for gap adjustment by using cross-roller bearings, as shown in Fig. 4. Furthermore, all forces other than those in the direction of the axis of rotation are received by the cross-roller bearings, reducing not only the axial load on the actuator during walking landing but also the force applied to the motor during a kicking motion.

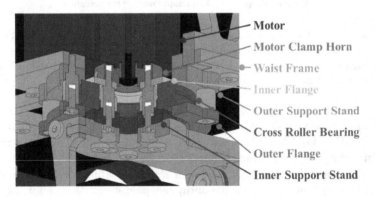

Fig. 4. Cross-sectional view of the cross-roller bearing structure for the crotch yaw axis in the SUSTAINA-OP^{TM}.

4.4   Sliding Bearings in the Legs to Cope with the Impact of Walking

The parallel link structure of the legs is fabricated using GFRP to suppress plastic deformation that may occur due to the impact of walking. Although this structure has many bearings, axial loads are applied to the joints each time the impact of walking is applied. Therefore, the ball bearings in the conventional robot [15] used by our research team were often damaged. The SUSTAINA-OP^{TM} uses plain bearings for all bearings except for the crotch yaw joint, as shown in Fig. 5, to prevent damage even when axial loads are applied. As a result of using this bearing design, no serious damage has occurred during the RoboCup2022 competition or during the software development and verification process up to that time.

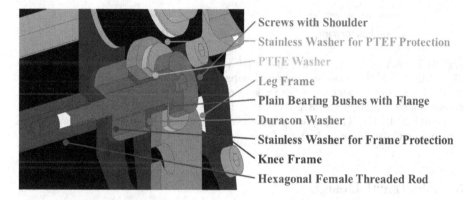

Fig. 5. Cross-sectional view of the sliding bearing structure for the leg pitch and roll axes in the SUSTAINA-OP^{TM}.

4.5   Structure to Reduce Impact of Falls

Damage to hardware caused by falls during competition not only disrupts cooperative play but also demands additional resources for repair and maintenance. In soccer, not only self-falls but also falls due to collisions with opponents are common. To mitigate the impact of this fall, the SUSTAINA-OP^{TM} has installed eight bumpers made of 3D-printed TPU material. These bumpers have succeeded in reducing the impact force by more than 80%, as shown in Fig. 6.

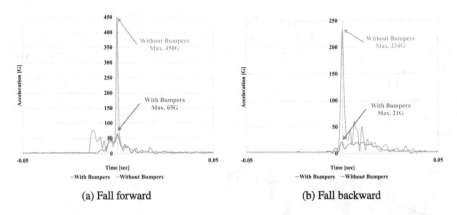

(a) Fall forward   (b) Fall backward

Fig. 6. Impact of falling with (blue) and without (orange) TPU bumpers on the SUSTAINA-OP^{TM}. These are measured impact forces when falling forward and backward with no initial velocity in the walking position. To measure the impact force, an accelerometer (MicroStone MA3-1000AD-RDB-SS) was retrofitted to the trunk and measured at 1 kHz. The impact acceleration (G) shows the norm of forces in three directions. (Color figure online)

5 Electrical Design

The control circuit and the electrical components of the SUSTAINA-OP^{TM} consist of a single-board computer (SBC) connected to various devices via USB I/F, as shown in Fig. 7. USB I/F is highly versatile as it is independent of the specification of the SBC used. For the camera, the MIPI SCI-2 I/F is used for real-time

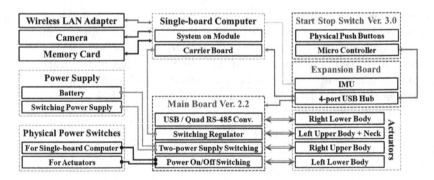

Fig. 7. System block diagram of the electrical components and connections in the SUSTAINA-OP^{TM}. The electrical components boards were developed originally (red). One of the two power supplies is supplied to each device (orange). The camera is connected to the SBC via a MIPI SCI-2 I/F (purple). The wireless LAN adapter and the USB-HUB are connected to the SBC via USB I/F (green). The USB-HUB is further connected to the USB/RS-485 Conv. and the Microcontroller. The IMU is connected to the SBC via I2C I/F (yellow). Actuators are connected to the MainBoard via RS-485 I/F (blue) and power supply (orange). (Color figure online)

image processing at a lower cost than the USB I/F. The control circuits, including the SBC, are integrated into a box that is stored in the robot's abdomen and can be easily removed from the robot. This design offers the advantage of enabling independent software development and the ability to replace the robot with another in case of failure.

5.1   Single-Board Computer

In the Humanoid League, a SoM with a Graphics Processing Unit (GPU) is desirable to perform real-time walking control and object recognition. The SUSTAINA-OP^{TM} employs an SoM equipped with an NVIDIA® Jetson Xavier^{TM} NX and an AVerMedia EN715 carrier board to enable various I/Fs to be connected. The carrier board is equipped with a USB I/F wireless LAN adapter for receiving instructions from the referee during competitions, as well as EN715 Expansion Board Ver. 1.1 [16], which further expands the carrier board's functions. This board includes a 4-port USB 2.0-HUB and a TDK MPU-9250 inertial measurement device.

5.2   Power Supply

The SUSTAINA-OP^{TM} is equipped with two power supply outlets. The first outlet is for a battery to enable independent soccer competitions, and with an 11.4 V 2,800 mAh Li-Hv battery, it enables one to walk continuously for up to 30 min. The second outlet is intended for connecting a switching power supply when a long-time power source is required for software development. These two power sources can be connected concurrently, facilitating seamless switching without powering off the computer. This design feature allows for effortless battery replacement during the five-minute halftime interval in competitions. In addition, a buck-boost DC/DC switching regulator is incorporated to ensure a stable voltage supply to the SBC unit. These functions are implemented in Main Board Ver. 2.2 [17].

5.3   High-Speed Communication Board for Actuator Control

The SUSTAINA-OP^{TM} is equipped with 19 RS485 I/F daisy-chained command servo motors throughout its body. These servo motors incorporate encoders, voltage, and current sensors for body control and status logging. When controlling numerous servo motors, acquiring sensor values within a control cycle can be difficult if all the servo motors are daisy-chained in series. To address this issue, a method that enables simultaneous communication and control of 19 servo motors in 4-parallel using a single USB 2.0 Full Speed port has been implemented. This control circuit was developed based on QUADDXL [18] and is integrated into Main Board Ver. 2.2 [17], which also includes other functions. The Main Board supports a maximum baud rate of 4.5 Mbps and is also compatible with 3 Mbps, the maximum baud rate of the B3M series employed in the SUSTAINA-OP^{TM}.

5.4 Versatile Control Buttons Device

According to the Humanoid League competition rules, robots can be equipped with two buttons to start/stop their movements, in addition to the emergency stop button. The SUSTAINA-OP^{TM} incorporates Start Stop Switch Ver. 3.0 [19], a control button module equipped with two tactile switches. Recognized as a USB-HID (Human Interface Device), this module is designed for compatibility with various SBCs.

6 Development Result

The development of this platform resulted in material costs (excluding machining expenses) of approximately 7,000 EUR (1,000,000 JPY), which is low in comparison to other platform robots such as the Wolfgang-OP. During the RoboCup2022, six SUSTAINA-OP^{TM}s were utilized in nine matches, experiencing 47 falls in total. Despite these falls, none of the robots had to leave the field due to hardware failures. This indicates that the robot successfully achieved its objectives of "enhancing robustness and minimizing the resources required for repair and maintenance." Moreover, the robot won the RoboCup2022 Humanoid League Soccer Competition for KidSize, showcasing its potential as a hardware platform humanoid robots.

7 Conclusion and Future Work

This paper presents a novel hardware platform humanoid robot, SUSTAINA-OP^{TM}, which adheres to the competition rules of the RoboCup Humanoid League. Developed under the concept of "sustainability," this platform is designed for ease of use and long-term viability. The primary objectives are enhancing robustness, minimizing resources required for repair and maintenance, and increasing flexibility to adapt to evolving competition regulations. As a result, the robot won the RoboCup2022, is relatively low cost, and endured 47 falls without hardware failure. Data to comply with the competition rules is also available.

For the future, to reflect the results obtained in the competition and to accelerate software development and humanoid research, plans are being made to add various sensors and comply with the competition rules, which are updated in annually. In addition, as an open hardware platform, we plan to maintain publicly available materials.

Acknowledgement. In the development of a novel hardware platform humanoid robot, SUSTAINA-OP^{TM}, we would like to thank the members of CIT Brains for their great cooperation. In particular, Mr. Hiroki Noguchi was in charge of the system development by introducing NVIDIA® Jetson Xavier^{TM} NX, Mr. Riku Yokoo was in charge of introducing the MIPI SCI-2 I/F camera, and Mr. Satoshi Inoue was in charge of the 4-parallel servo motor communication control, for which we express our profound appreciation. We would also like to thank Mr. Gaku Kuwano for constructing a strategy in soccer competitions that fully demonstrates the capabilities of SUSTAINA-OP^{TM}. In addition, we would like to thank Mr. Naoki Iwasawa and Mr. Kiyoshiro Kawanabe, who manufactured the mechanical components of SUSTAINA-OP^{TM} with us and provided us with feedback on the design.

References

1. Ha, I., et al.: Development of open humanoid platform DARwIn-OP. In: SICE Annual Conference 2011, pp. 2178–2181 (2011)
2. The rules of the Humanoid League. https://humanoid.robocup.org/materials/rules/. Accessed 23 June 2023
3. RoboCup Soccer: Humanoid League DRAFT Roadmap from 2022 to 2050. http://humanoid.robocup.org/wp-content/uploads/roadmap_2022.pdf. Accessed 23 June 2023
4. Ficht, G., et al.: NimbRo-OP2X: adult-sized open-source 3D printed humanoid robot. In: 2018 IEEE-RAS 18th International Conference on Humanoid Robots (Humanoids), pp. 1–9 (2018)
5. Bestmann, M., et al.: Wolfgang-OP: a robust humanoid robot platform for research and competitions. In: 2020 IEEE-RAS 20th International Conference on Humanoid Robots (Humanoids), pp. 90–97 (2021)
6. SUSTAINA-OP^{TM} Open Hardware Platform website. https://github.com/SUSTAINA-OP. Accessed 23 June 2023
7. CIT Brains website. http://www.cit-brains.net/en/. Accessed 23 June 2023
8. Hayashibara, Y., et al.: RoboCup2022 KidSize league winner CIT brains: open platform hardware SUSTAINA-OP and software. In: Eguchi, A., Lau, N., Paetzel-Prusmann, M., Wanichanon, T. (eds.) RoboCup 2022:. RoboCup 2022. LNCS, vol. 13561, pp. 215–227. Springer, Cham (2023). https://doi.org/10.1007/978-3-031-28469-4_18
9. Gerndt, R., et al.: Humanoid robots in soccer - robots versus humans in RoboCup 2050. IEEE Robot. Autom. Mag. **22**(3), 147–154 (2015)
10. Rhoban Football Club - Robot Specification Humanoid Kid-Size League, Robocup 2023 Bordeaux. https://submission.robocuphumanoid.com/uploads//Rhoban_Football_Club-specs-6396ffb295003.pdf. Accessed 23 June 2023
11. Gondry, L., et al.: Rhoban football club: RoboCup Humanoid KidSize 2019 champion team paper. In: Chalup, S., Niemueller, T., Suthakorn, J., Williams, M.A. (eds.) RoboCup 2019: Robot World Cup XXIII. RoboCup 2019. LNCS, vol. 11531, pp. 491–503. Springer, Cham (2019). https://doi.org/10.1007/978-3-030-35699-6_40
12. Allali, J., et al.: Rhoban football club: RoboCup humanoid Kid-Size 2017 champion team paper. In: Behnke, S., Sheh, R., Sariel, S., Lee, D. (eds.) RoboCup 2016: Robot World Cup XX. RoboCup 2016. LNCS, vol. 9776, pp. 423–434. Springer, Cham (2018). https://doi.org/10.1007/978-3-319-68792-6_41
13. Schwarz, M., et al.: NimbRo-OP humanoid TeenSize open platform. In: RoboCup 2013: Robot World Cup XVII, pp. 568–575 (2014)
14. SUSTAINA-OP's 3D-CAD model viewing website. https://sustaina-op.com/autodesk_viewer. Accessed 23 June 2023
15. Robot Specifications of CIT Brains in RoboCup2019. https://submission.robocuphumanoid.com/uploads//CIT_Brains-specs-5c052b8625d1a.pdf. Accessed 23 June 2023

16. EN715 Expansion Board Ver. 1.1 website. https://github.com/SUSTAINA-OP/ EN715_ExpansionBoard_ver1_1. Accessed 23 June 2023
17. Main Board Ver. 2.2 website. https://github.com/SUSTAINA-OP/MainBoard_ ver2_2. Accessed 23 June 2023
18. Bestmann, M., et al.: High-frequency multi bus servo and sensor communication using the dynamixel protocol. In: Chalup, S., Niemueller, T., Suthakorn, J., Williams, M.A. (eds.) RoboCup 2019: Robot World Cup XXIII. RoboCup 2019. LNCS, vol. 11531, pp. 16–29. Springer, Cham (2019). https://doi.org/10.1007/978-3-030-35699-6_2
19. Start Stop Switch Ver. 3.0 website. https://github.com/SUSTAINA-OP/ StartStopSwitch_ver3_0. Accessed 23 June 2023

An Opponent Formation Classifier for Simulated Robot Soccer

Davi M. Vasconcelos[✉][iD], Marcos R. O. A. Maximo[iD],
and Paulo M. Tasinaffo[iD]

Aeronautics Institute of Technology, São José dos Campos, Brazil
davi.muniz41@gmail.com, {mmaximo,tasinaffo}@ita.br

Abstract. This paper contributes with a novel opponent formation classifier for simulated robot soccer. Modeling opponent positioning strategy can help the development of dynamic soccer behaviors and increase the team's performance. We used tools from RoboCup 2D Soccer Simulation League (RoboCup 2D) for running soccer matches. Several researchers of RoboCup 2D developed classifiers for soccer formations but were limited to defense or preestablished formations. To acquire the formation categories of the opponents, we obtained positioning data from game logs against 11 opponents and detected mean formation patterns with the Gaussian Mixture Model clustering algorithm. Later, we trained a neural network and a random forest to predict four formation categories. The random forest outperformed the neural networks on average for unseen teams during training. However, the neural network achieved the lowest error rate for four unseen teams during training. Last, we introduced a method to decrease the number of game cycles required for correct classification by choosing the predicted label with the highest frequency over time.

Keywords: Soccer simulation · Soccer formation · Opponent modelling · Neural network

1 Introduction

Developing successful dynamic behaviors against different teams is a leading challenge in RoboCup 2D Soccer Simulation League (RoboCup 2D). We should identify the opponent's strategy for efficiently changing an agent's playing style. Although we can address team strategy in many ways, we can approximate it to the team formation strategy since team positioning is a dominant factor in the team strategy.

Akiyama and Noda [2] developed a multi-agent positioning mechanism for RoboCup 2D. The authors defined the position of the players as a function of the ball's location. They created formation configuration files containing the position of each player for a finite number of ball locations. Next, they run a Delaunay

Supported by CNPq.

Triangulation for the set of points defined by the ball's positions in the formation configuration files. Lastly, the authors computed the team's positioning when the ball was not on a triangle vertex with the Gouraud shading interpolation algorithm. Furthermore, most researchers of RoboCup 2D use the suggested positioning mechanism in [2] because it has a low computational budget and is part of the agent2d team [1], the most popular base team in the league.

Fukushima, Nakashima, and Akiyama [6] developed a classifier for defense formations of selected opponents. The authors chose opponents with a considerable defensive performance against their team. Later, they obtained the positioning data from game logs and converted the players' positions to a formation representation. A tabular soccer field was used as formation representation, where each cell contained the cumulative mean of the number of players on it over time. Next, the authors defined formation labels by applying a clustering algorithm on the mean defense formations of opponents. Last, they trained several supervised learning models to in-game predict the defense formations of opponents.

Almeida, Reis, and Jorge [3] showed that preestablished soccer formations, for instance, 4-3-3, 3-5-2, can be identified by training a classifier with positioning data of their team. The authors generated the data by adjusting the formation configuration files. The formation representation comprised the players' positions and the team's center of mass (CoM). Compared to this work, the authors did not develop an in-game classifier but measured the performance of multiple classifiers on different training scenarios.

Faria et al. [5] compared four opponent formation classifiers and complemented the work made in [3]. The authors identified preestablished soccer formations by modifying the formation configuration files similarly to [3]. Later, they collected game logs and applied Principal Component Analysis (PCA) to the positioning data. Next, the authors obtained the following accuracy sequence in ascending order when evaluating the classifiers in the test set: Kernel Naive Bayes, Artificial Neural Network, 3-Nearest Neighbor, and Support Vector Machine. The 3-Nearest Neighbor outperformed the other classifiers considering a trade-off between computational time and accuracy.

Shaw and Glickman [9] developed a formation classifier for professional soccer using Bayesian model selection criteria. The formation representation at a given time was computed by incrementally adding the relative position between a player and his nearest teammate that has not been added to the formation yet. Furthermore, the authors represented a player's position as a two-dimensional Gaussian distribution. They found similar formations by applying hierarchical clustering with similarity measure as the minimum sum of the Wasserstein metric [8] between players of two different formations.

The contribution of this work is the development of an in-game opponent formation classifier not limited to defensive formations or preestablished formations. We also analyze the classifier performance for unseen teams during training, which was indicated as future work in [6]. Furthermore, we introduce a method to decrease the number of game cycles required for correct classification by memorizing the classifier output over time.

The remainder of this paper is organized as follows. Section 2 presents the methodologies applied to determine the formation categories and to train the classifiers. Section 3 shows the types of opponent formations and the performance of the classifiers. Section 4 describes conclusions and future work.

2   Methodology

In this section, we describe the formation representations used in this work. Then, we clarify the formation clustering step, which finds similar mean formations between opponents. Finally, we explain the training and testing methodologies for the classifiers.

2.1   Formation Representations

A soccer formation has properties that may cause classification errors if we do not select a proper formation representation. A permutation of the uniform number of players should not change a formation. We can remove the uniform number dependency by defining an enumeration that does not depend on the player's uniform number or discretizing the soccer field as in [6].

We tested two formation representations. The representations at game cycle k had statistics computed over positioning data from game cycle 1 to k. The first formation representation is a continuous representation, where we used the players' positions in the soccer field's center frame. To remove the uniform number dependency, we numbered the players in ascending order by the angle between the player's position in the CoM frame and the x-axis. Moreover, the formation at game cycle k contained the cumulative mean of the players' positions over time. We also added variance and skewness of each player's position to distinguish formations more appropriately, which resulted in a vector with 66 elements.

The second formation representation is a discrete representation, where we discretized the soccer field in a uniform grid of dimensions $(30, 20)$. In this case, we defined the formation at game cycle k as the cumulative mean of the number of players on each cell from cycles 1 to k. Moreover, this formation representation was selected in [6], which surpassed classifiers trained using grids with other dimensions.

2.2   Formation Labels

Teams of RoboCup 2D can modify their formations as they wish by adjusting the formation configuration files. If we previously defined which soccer formations we want to classify as in [3], then we do not include the wide range of positionings of RoboCup 2D. Therefore, we can cover a wider range of formations by applying data mining techniques to game logs.

Similar to the approach in [6], we obtained the formation categories from the positioning data of opponents. We run 140 half-matches of ITAndroids playing against each one of the following opponents: Persepolis (2021), RoboCIn (2021), Ri-one (2021), Titans (2020), HELIOS (2018), CYRUS (2021), Futvasf (2021), ThunderLeague (2021), JyoSen (2021), Hades2D (2021), and Alice (2021). The game log files were converted to a tabular format with `rcg2csv`, which is available in librcsc [1]. Later, we removed positioning data when the play mode was not `play_on`. The play mode is `play_on` when the soccer game runs freely. For example, the players are not moving to take a free kick or a corner kick. The play modes in RoboCup 2D are described in [10].

Although teams may change their formations during the game, we are interested in finding similarities between the mean positioning of the teams. This simplification was made in previous works [6] and achieved notable results. For this reason, we compared the mean formations to establish the formation categories. The definition of a mean formation follows from the formation representations: a mean formation is a formation at the last `play_on` game cycle. This property holds because we defined the formation representations cumulatively: a formation at game cycle k has positioning statistics computed over all the previous game cycles. In the following sections, we use this definition when referring to mean formations.

We used Gaussian Mixture Model (GMM) clustering algorithm to find similar opponent mean formations. Since GMM is sensitive to its initial parameters, we run 2,000 clustering rounds with different random seeds. We modified the number of clusters from 2 to 15 in each clustering round. Furthermore, we applied the Calinski-Harabasz Index [4] to select the optimal number of clusters in each clustering round. Table 1 shows the parameters of the clustering algorithm.

Table 1. Parameters used in GMM clustering algorithm.

Parameter	Value
Maximum number of iterations	150
Convergence threshold	0.001
Parameters initialization	k-means
Covariance type	full

2.3   Classifier

RoboCup 2D establishes constraints on computational time and storage consumption for teams. A team shall make decisions in less than 100 ms in a game cycle and have a size below 200 MB. Therefore, we selected a neural network and a random forest to perform classifications. These models are known to generalize well in classification tasks, even with a small computational budget. For instance, a KNN classifier would not scale for large formation data sets due to high storage usage. The scikit-learn framework [7] was used to train the model.

Table 2 shows the training parameters for the neural network and random forest. The training stops for the neural network when the norm of the final projected gradient in the L-BFGS method is less than the tolerance value.

After determining the categories of mean formations, the label of the formation at game cycle k was assigned to the respective mean formation label of the match. The classifier input is a formation after the formation representation transform. It has positioning statistics computed over previous game cycles. Therefore, the classifier output for the formation at game cycle k should converge to the correct label as k increases.

The training and test sets contain formation data from 100 and 40 half-matches per team, respectively. Furthermore, we chose one opponent of each formation label to be removed from the training. Hence, we evaluated the classifier generalization performance for unseen teams during training in 140 half-matches per team.

Table 2. Parameters in scikit-learn used for training the classifiers.

Model	Parameter	Value
Neural network	Optimizer	lbfgs
	Tolerance	0.0001
	Learning rate	0.0001
	Activation function	logistic
	Hidden layer size	10
Random forest	Number of trees	100
	Criterion	gini
	Bootstrap	true

3   Results

This section exhibits the clustering step results for each formation representation. We also compare the ability of the two formation representations to distinguish mean formations. Last, we discuss the performance of the classifiers.

3.1   Clustering with Continuous Representation

After performing 2,000 clustering rounds, we obtained the most probable optimal number of clusters equals three. Table 3 provides the distribution of the optimal number of clusters. Thus, we selected the final clustering result as the clusters with the highest Calinski-Harabasz Index among clustering rounds with an optimal number of clusters equal to three.

The label distribution from the final clustering result is in Table 4, where l_i^c represents label i. All the teams but Ri-one have a single label for their mean formations. However, we set the Ri-one label as l_0^c since it contains almost all the mean formations from Ri-one.

Figure 1 exhibits the mean formations of each team divided by clustering labels. Distinct colors represent players with different numbers in the formation representation. The axes follow the conventions of RoboCup 2D: the origin is the soccer field's center, x-axis values increase to the right, and y-axis values increase downwards. Figure 1a shows that teams with label l_0^c move towards the positive y-axis. Figure 1b shows that teams with label l_1^c have a symmetric pattern, i.e., players are symmetric with the horizontal axis. Figure 1c shows that teams with label l_2^c also have a symmetric arrangement, but the team's center of mass is moved to the right. Therefore, our players can stay for a longer time on the opponent's field side when playing against teams with the label l_2^c.

Table 3. Distribution of the optimal number of clusters in 2,000 clustering rounds with the continuous formation representation.

Number of clusters	Percentage
2	1.6%
3	70.4%
4	27.3%
5	0.5%
6	0.2%

Table 4. Label distribution of the mean formations in the final clustering result with the continuous formation representation.

Team	Percentage (l_0^c)	Percentage (l_1^c)	Percentage (l_2^c)
Persepolis (2021)	100.0%	0.0%	0.0%
RoboCIn (2021)	0.0%	100.0%	0.0%
Ri-one (2021)	98.6%	1.4%	0.0%
Titans (2020)	0.0%	100.0%	0.0%
HELIOS (2018)	0.0%	100.0%	0.0%
CYRUS (2021)	100.0%	0.0%	0.0%
Futvasf (2021)	0.0%	100.0%	0.0%
ThunderLeague (2021)	0.0%	100.0%	0.0%
JyoSen (2021)	0.0%	100.0%	0.0%
Hades2D (2021)	0.0%	0.0%	100.0%
Alice (2021)	0.0%	100.0%	0.0%

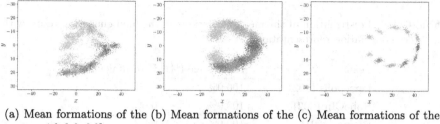

(a) Mean formations of the teams with label l_0^c.

(b) Mean formations of the teams with label l_1^c.

(c) Mean formations of the teams with label l_2^c.

Fig. 1. Mean formations divided by each label obtained in the final clustering result.

3.2 Clustering with Discrete Representation

After running novel 2,000 clustering rounds for the discrete formation representation, we discuss the obtained results. Table 5 gives the most probable optimal number of clusters equal to two. Hence, we selected the final clustering result as the clusters with the highest Calinski-Harabasz Index among clustering rounds with the optimal number of clusters equal to two. The final label distribution is in Table 6, where l_i^d represents label i.

Figure 2 and 3 illustrate the average of the mean formations for each team with labels l_0^d and l_1^d, respectively. All mean formations but CYRUS and Persepolis are symmetric with respect to the horizontal axis. CYRUS and Persepolis mostly move downwards when playing against us. Moreover, the positioning of Hades2D is different from all the teams.

Table 5. Distribution of the optimal number of clusters in 2,000 clustering rounds with the discrete formation representation.

Number of clusters	Percentage
2	89.4%
3	9.8%
4	0.8%

3.3 Comparison Between Formation Representations

Since most RoboCup 2D teams are built on the agent2d team [1], the continuous formation representation could not distinguish the formations well. We only captured broad differences between mean formations. Most positioning statistics were close because players nearly visited the same positions in a half-match.

Nonetheless, the discrete representation exhibited distinctive differences. The soccer field grid holds the positioning trace of the players during a full half-match. The continuous representation did not show a positioning path but a

Table 6. Label distribution of the mean formations in the final clustering result with the discrete formation representation.

Team	Percentage (l_0^d)	Percentage (l_1^d)
Persepolis (2021)	100.0%	0.0%
RoboCIn (2021)	100.0%	0.0%
Ri-one (2021)	100.0%	0.0%
Titans (2020)	100.0%	0.0%
HELIOS (2018)	100.0%	0.0%
CYRUS (2021)	100.0%	0.0%
Futvasf (2021)	0.0%	100.0%
ThunderLeague (2021)	0.0%	100.0%
JyoSen (2021)	0.0%	100.0%
Hades2D (2021)	0.0%	100.0%
Alice (2021)	0.0%	100.0%

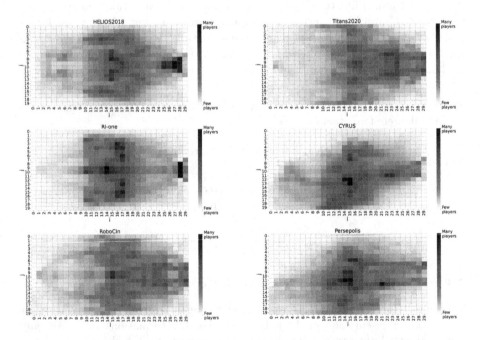

Fig. 2. Average of the mean formations for each team with label l_0^d. We computed a mean formation by averaging the positioning grids of a half-match, where a positioning grid contains the number of players on each cell at a given game cycle.

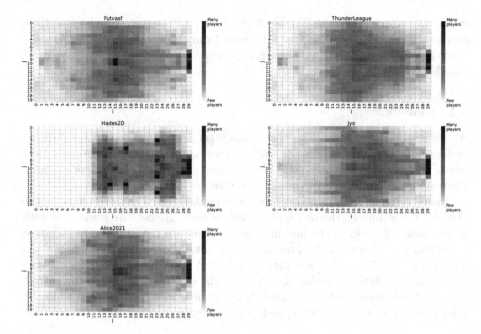

Fig. 3. Average of the mean formations for each team with label l_1^d. We computed a mean formation by averaging the positioning grids of a half-match, where a positioning grid contains the number of players on each cell at a given game cycle.

Table 7. Formation label of each team after adjustments using expert knowledge.

Team	Formation label
HELIOS (2018)	l_0^d
Titans (2020)	l_0^d
Ri-one (2021)	l_0^d
RoboCIn (2021)	l_0^d
Futvasf (2021)	l_1^d
ThunderLeague (2021)	l_1^d
JyoSen (2021)	l_1^d
Alice (2021)	l_1^d
CYRUS (2021)	l_2^d
Persepolis (2021)	l_2^d
Hades2D (2021)	l_3^d

single positioning instance. Thus, we chose the discrete formation representation to train the classifiers as it provided additional information.

We changed the labels of CYRUS and Persepolis teams to a novel category l_2^d. The players of both teams mostly move to the positive y-axis without symmetry. We also changed the label of the Hades2D team to a new class l_3^d as its mean formations are essentially different from all previous mean formations. Table 7 presents the category of each opponent after adjustments using expert knowledge.

3.4   Classifier

We removed three teams from the training set to measure the generalization performance of the classifier: RoboCIn, Alice, and CYRUS. The teams have labels l_0^d, l_1^d, and l_2^d, respectively. We also removed HELIOS and JyoSen from the training set to reduce the label imbalance.

Figure 4 depicts the misclassification probability of both classifiers in the test set. We estimated the probability over 40 half-matches. We resampled with replacement 1000 times the half-matches to compute the probability standard error. Samples of novel 40 half-matches were not obtained due to the high computational cost. The classifiers rapidly achieved an error probability near zero for teams seen during training. In addition, the classifiers predicted the correct label with low error probability after fewer game cycles than in [6]. The lowest error probabilities are almost equal to the results in [3,5].

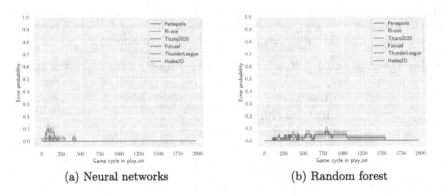

(a) Neural networks   (b) Random forest

Fig. 4. Misclassification probability in the test set. The width of a shaded region is two times the probability standard error.

Figure 5 shows the misclassification probability for five unseen teams during training. We computed the probability over 140 half-matches. We also performed the resampling approach used in Fig. 4. The neural networks achieved an approximately zero error probability for four teams after 700 game cycles. Nonetheless, the model misclassified the CYRUS team with a considerable probability. Moreover, the random forest outperformed the neural networks classifier on average. Previous works did not measure the generalization performance for teams not selected for training [3,5,6].

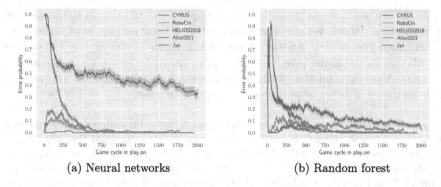

(a) Neural networks   (b) Random forest

Fig. 5. Misclassification probability for five unseen teams during training. The width of a shaded region is two times the probability standard error.

We can improve the classification accuracy by saving the output labels for n consecutive play_on game cycles and choosing the label with the highest frequency. If the classifier achieved an error probability of less than 0.5 for every play_on game cycle $t \geq t_0$, then we can estimate how many outputs to save after t_0 so the highest frequency label corresponds to the correct label. We can compute n to all lines in Fig. 5. The worst-case success probability is

$$P(\text{success}) = \sum_{k=\lfloor \frac{n}{2} \rfloor + 1}^{n} \binom{n}{k} (1 - p_0)^k p_0^{n-k}, \qquad (1)$$

where k is the number of play_on game cycles where the classifier correctly identified and $p_0 < 0.5$ is the worst-case error probability.

For instance, the random forest classifier had an error probability lesser than 0.3 for game cycles greater than $t_0 = 250$ for unseen teams during training. A worst-case success probability of 0.99 with $p_0 = 0.3$ can be achieved by choosing $n = 20$. Hence, we can correctly predict the teams in Fig. 5b at play_on game cycle 270, which is n play_on game cycles after t_0. Although we need to specify the parameters before matches, this technique can tremendously improve the performance of the classifiers.

4 Conclusion

We developed a novel opponent formation classifier for RoboCup 2D. We determined categories of opponent formations with data mining techniques on positioning data from game logs. After testing two formation representations to cluster positioning data, we selected the most descriptive formation representation and trained two classifiers: neural networks and random forest. Both classifiers could identify teams seen during training with a low error probability. The random forest surpassed the neural networks for unseen teams during training.

For future work, we suggest including temporal information in the formation representation. Hence, we may find novel patterns between opponent formations and enhance the model. Another research direction is identifying formations that change as the game progresses. We also intend to adapt the behaviors of our team depending on the identified opponent formation, so we can evaluate the advantages of being able to determine the opponent.

Acknowledgments. D. M. Vasconcelos thanks CNPq for his undergraduate research scholarship. Marcos Maximo is partially funded by CNPq - National Research Council of Brazil through grant 307525/2022-8. The authors acknowledge the sponsors of ITAndroids: Altium, Cenic, Intel, ITAEx, Mathworks, Metinjo, Micropress, Neofield, Polimold, Rapid, SIATT, Solidworks, STMicroelectronics, WildLife, and Virtual Pyxis.

References

1. Akiyama, H., Nakashima, T.: Helios base: an open source package for the robocup soccer 2D simulation. In: The 17th Annual RoboCup International Symposium, July 2013
2. Akiyama, H., Noda, I.: Multi-agent positioning mechanism in the dynamic environment. In: Visser, U., Ribeiro, F., Ohashi, T., Dellaert, F. (eds.) RoboCup 2007: Robot Soccer World Cup XI. RoboCup 2007. LNCS, vol. 5001, pp. 377–384. Springer, Berlin, Heidelberg (2008). https://doi.org/10.1007/978-3-540-68847-1_38
3. Almeida, R., Reis, L.P., Jorge, A.M.: Analysis and forecast of team formation in the simulated robotic soccer domain. In: Lopes, L.S., Lau, N., Mariano, P., Rocha, L.M. (eds.) Progress in Artificial Intelligence. EPIA 2009. LNCS, vol. 5816, pp. 239–250. Springer, Berlin, Heidelberg (2009). https://doi.org/10.1007/978-3-642-04686-5_20
4. Caliński, T., Harabasz, J.: A dendrite method for cluster analysis. Commun. Stat. **3**(1), 1–27 (1974). https://doi.org/10.1080/03610927408827101, https://www.tandfonline.com/doi/abs/10.1080/03610927408827101
5. Faria, B., Reis, L., Lau, N., Castillo, G.: Machine learning algorithms applied to the classification of robotic soccer formations and opponent teams, pp. 344–349, July 2010. https://doi.org/10.1109/ICCIS.2010.5518540
6. Fukushima, T., Nakashima, T., Akiyama, H.: Online opponent formation identification based on position information. In: Akiyama, H., Obst, O., Sammut, C., Tonidandel, F. (eds.) RoboCup 2017: Robot World Cup XXI. RoboCup 2017. LNCS, vol. 11175, pp. 241–251. Springer, Cham (2018). https://doi.org/10.1007/978-3-030-00308-1_20
7. Pedregosa, F., et al.: Scikit-learn: machine learning in Python. J. Mach. Learn. Res. **12**, 2825–2830 (2011)
8. Ramdas, A., Trillos, N.G., Cuturi, M.: On wasserstein two-sample testing and related families of nonparametric tests. Entropy **19**, 47 (2017)
9. Shaw, L., Glickman, M.: Dynamic analysis of team strategy in professional football. Barça Sports Analytics Summit (2019)
10. The RoboCup Soccer Simulator Maintenance Committee: The robocup soccer simulator users manual. https://rcsoccersim.github.io/manual/. Accessed March 2023

Swing Foot Pose Control Disturbance Overcoming Algorithm Based on Reference ZMP Preview Controller for Improving Humanoid Walking Stability

Eunsoo Chung[1], Haewon Jung[2], Yeonghun Chun[1], Wonyong Lee[2], Jangwon Lee[2], Minsung Ahn[3], and Jeakweon Han[4(✉)]

[1] Department of Convergence Robot System, Hanyang University, 15588 Ansan, Republic of Korea
{dmstn1257,arirang2067}@hanyang.ac.kr
[2] Department of Robotics, Hanyang University, 15588 Ansan, Republic of Korea
{eking158,wonyong0928,wkddnjs8527}@naver.com
[3] Mechanical and Aerospace Engineering, University of California,, CA Los Angeles 90095, USA
aminsung@ucla.edu
[4] Department of Robotics, Hanyang University, 15588 Ansan, Republic of Korea
jkhan@hanyang.ac.kr

Abstract. To improve the walking stability of humanoid robots, it is necessary to increase the performance of overcoming external disturbance. In this paper, step modification strategy based on the predicted Zero Moment Point (ZMP) is applied to the Reference ZMP Preview Controller to increase the overcoming disturbance performance of humanoid robots. It also uses a Horizon Swing Foot strategy that can keep the ankle of the Swing phase parallel to the ground to increase stability when changing the Step. The proposed algorithm was verified through experiments and confirmed that the Horizon Swing Foot strategy can overcome up to 14.85 kg·m/s of impact. By applying the proposed algorithm to humanoid robots, it is expected to increase bipedal walking stability and prevent damage and safety accidents caused by the robot falling.

Keywords: Overcoming Disturbance · Humanoid Robot · Preview Controller · Bipedal Walking

1 Introduction

Humanoid robots are designed to assist humans in environments optimized for humans. Therefore, it is designed in a structure similar to humans and adopts

C. Buche et al. (Eds.): RoboCup 2023, LNAI 14140, pp. 191–202, 2024.
https://doi.org/10.1007/978-3-031-55015-7_16

a bipedal walking method. Bipedal walking has higher mobility in real environments compared to the moving method that utilizes wheels. But it has the disadvantage of being more difficult to maintain balance. Especially, if unexpected disturbances are applied during walking, humanoid robots easily become unstable [1].

Material damage and safety accidents can occur if the robot loses balance and falls in a disturbance situation. To prevent this, it is essential to have disturbance overcoming technology that can maintain balance even in situations where disturbance is applied.

For stable bipedal walking, Vukobratovićé and Stepanenko proposed the ZMP theory [2]. The area created when a robot's foot touches the ground is called support polygon. And ZMP means to the point on the support polygon where the moment sum at that point is zero [3]. If the zmp is located outside the support polygon area, the robot quickly becomes unstable. Conversely, if the zmp is within the support polygon, the robot can remain stable.

Based on this ZMP theory, researchers such as Kamioka, T. [4] and Feng, S. [5] presented a step modification strategy to overcome disturbance. The strategy that they proposed is to change the robot's support polygon by controlling the landing point of the foot in the swing phase when disturbance is applied to the robot while walking.

In addition to the ZMP theory, techniques for modeling robots with Linear Inverted Pendulum Model (LIPM) are also used to implement stable walking. Seekircher, A. [6] presents a strategy to implement dynamic walking based on LIPM and optimize the parameters used by utilizing covariance matrix adaptation. Also, Graf, C. [7] presented a strategy using LIPM to control the robot's center of mass, improve the stability and agility of walking, and reduce joint loads.

The humanoid robot being developed in our laboratory is modeled using LIPM and applied with a walking algorithm based on the Reference ZMP Preview Controller [8]. The Reference ZMP Preview Controller controls the robot's Center of Mass (CoM) to follow the ZMP that serves as a reference. To improve the disturbance overcome performance of the humanoid robot, we apply a ZMP prediction-based step modification strategy to the Reference ZMP Preview Controller. Additionally, we plan to supplement the step modification strategy with an ankle strategy.

This paper aims to improve the disturbance overcoming performance of humanoid robots through the presented disturbance overcoming algorithm. The algorithm allows balance to be maintained by stretching the landing point of the foot in the swing phase further forward or backward in the situation of disturbance to the walking robot.

2   Related Work

Researchers at [9–11] are proposing a step change strategy as one of the strategies to improve the performance of humanoid robots to overcome disturbance. They made it possible to overcome the disturbance stably by changing the landing position of the foot when external disturbances act on the robot. In particular, [10] argued that a step change strategy is necessary for disturbances larger than a certain size because the larger the size of the disturbance, the larger the size of the resilience required.

Another strategy to overcome disturbance is the ankle strategy to control the ankle angle. Ankle strategies can be divided into two main categories according to the purpose. The first is a strategy to increase walking stability by controlling the ankle of the foot in the swing phase at an angle that can maximize the contact area between the foot and the ground based on topographic information [12–15]. In particular, [13] found that the tip of the foot collided with the ground when the robot tilted forward while walking, and solved this through the swing phase ankle control strategy. [14] and [15] additionally used proximity sensors and Force Sensitive Resistor (FSR) sensors to implement the corresponding algorithm, respectively. All of these prior studies were said to have been able to increase the safety of walking by allowing the foot to secure the maximum contact area with the ground. The second is a strategy to control the support phase ankle, enabling the robot to maintain stability even when a disturbance applied [16–21]. Researchers [16] and [17] utilized not only support phase ankle control strategy but also pelvis strategies to enhance overcoming disturbance performance. In addition, in the study by [18], they successfully implemented a support phase ankle control algorithm based on Inertia Measurement Unit (IMU) sensor data. In the study of [21], the support phase ankle control strategy was judged to be an effective strategy to improve the performance of overcoming disturbance. All of these prior studies are said to have helped keep robots from losing their balance due to disturbances.

Based on the study of [9–11], we aim to increase the performance of overcoming disturbance by adding a predictive ZMP-based step change strategy to the Reference ZMP Preview Controller. In addition, we plan to supplement the problems that may arise in the Step strategy by adding an ankle strategy. As shown in [16–21], the ankle of the supporting phase will be controlled to allow the robot to maintain balance while executing the step strategy, even in the presence of external disturbances. However, with this control method, the foot may hit the ground during the step strategy like [13], which may reduce the safety of walking. To achieve this, we will also add ankle control strategies that increase the contact area of the foot, similar [12–15]. To increase the contact area of the foot, the robot will maintain an angle parallel to the ground, and we will define this as the Horizon Swing Foot strategy.

3   Disturbance Overcoming Algorithm

3.1   ZMP Prediction

ZMP is calculated through force-torque sensors located on both feet, and the predicted future ZMP value is obtained by differentiating the calculated ZMP value over time in Eq. (1). In addition, The predicted value is mitigated by using the moving average filter.

$$x_{future} = (\Delta x / \Delta t) * t + x_{curr} \tag{1}$$

3.2 Change Step Strategy

In this paper, we design the algorithm by considering disturbance only applied in the x-axis direction. So we consider only the ZMP and foot positions in x-axis direction. The entire sequence of the step modification strategy can be expressed by Algorithm 1.

The ZMP error value in the x-axis direction is calculated through the difference between the predicted ZMP in the x-axis direction and the x-axis position when the swing phase foot lands on the ground, which is presented in Eq. (2).

$$P_x^{Error} = \lambda * (P_x^{Predict} - P_x^{End}) \tag{2}$$

At Eq. (2), P_x^{Error} represents the ZMP error in the x-direction, and λ is a gain value that determines how much the swing foot will be stretched in proportion to the ZMP error. Also $P_x^{Predict}$ represents the predicted ZMP in the x-axis direction after n seconds, P_x^{End} means the x-axis position at the moment when the swing phase foot lands on the ground.

If absolute value of P_x^{Error} exceeds the threshold, it suggests an external disturbance, and a step modification strategy is required. At this point, the step adjustment strategy determines how much further the foot of the swing phase should stretch forward or backward on the x-axis compared to the expected landing point in proportion to the ZMP error. Here, the modified landing point in the x-axis direction of the foot is expressed as $\acute{P}_x^{End}$ and calculated through Eq. (3).

$$\acute{P}_x^{End} = P_x^{End} + P_x^{Error} \tag{3}$$

Finally, walking controller of ALICE adjusts the position of the foot in the swing phase by the value obtained in Eq. (3) to help restore balance against disturbance.

Algorithm 1. Step Modification Strategy Algorithm

Require: P_x^{Error}, P_x^{End}, threshold
1: $P_x^{Error} = \lambda * (P_x^{Predict} - P_x^{End})$
2: $\acute{P}_x^{End} = P_x^{End} + P_x^{Error}$
3: **if** $P_x^{Error} >$ threshold **then**
4:     Modify the position where the foot lands in the swing phase to $\acute{P}_x^{End}$
5: **end if**

---

4   Horizon Swing Foot Strategy

The walking controller of the humanoid robot developed by our laboratory includes a balance recovery algorithm that changes the CoM by controlling the ankle angle based on IMU sensor data. When using the step change strategy, the balance recovery algorithm can create a problem where the foot digs into the ground and attempts to move forward while stretching out in the swing phase. This is expressed through (b) and (c) of Fig. 1.

In Fig. 1, the robot is shown in a walking position with the left foot on the ground (support phase) and the right foot in the air (swing phase). The ankle angle of the swing phase is indicated by a red line. When the robot is walking normally without any disturbance, the ankle of the swing phase is parallel to the ground as shown in (a). However, when the robot experiences a disturbance, it tilts in the direction of the disturbance as shown in (b). In this case, Because the balance recovery algorithm continuously adjusts the ankle angle during the swing phase, the red line in (b) forms a non-parallel angle with the ground. When applying the step modification strategy as shown in (c), the foot of the swing phase digs into the ground while stretching forward. As a result, the foot in the support phase is pushed back. To solve this problem, we use the Horizon Swing Foot strategy that can keep the ankle of the Swing phase parallel to the ground. In order to combine with the existing balance recovery algorithm, the Horizon Swing Foot strategy will include an algorithm that distinguishes between the support phase and the swing phase of each foot during walking.

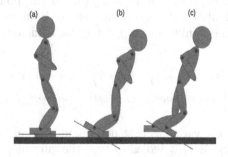

Fig. 1. (a): Ankle angle under normal circumstances (b): Ankle angle when the robot is tilted due to disturbance behind the robot (c): Robot movement when using step change strategy in situations of (b)

4.1   Ankle Control Algorithm for Swing Phase

The ankle of the swing phase is controlled by a controller in the form Fig. 2 using the elements presented in Table 1. Figure 2 Controller controls the ankle of the swing phase to be at an angle parallel to the ground.

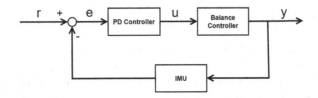

Fig. 2. Controller that allows the ankle of the swing phase to always be parallel to the ground

Table 1. Elements used in the controller

Symbols	Elements
r (Control target figure)	Pelvis Pitch Angle of Reference Motion
e (error)	Target pitch of the pelvis - Pelvis pitch measured by IMU
u (System Input)	Swing Phase Ankle angle control data
y (System Output)	Output to ankle pitch motor

4.2 Distinguish Between Support and Swing Phases

The control angle of each foot is calculated using linear interpolation to apply different ankle strategies depending on whether the foot is in the support phase or in the swing phase. The reason why linear interpolation is used at this time is to ensure that the ankle control strategy is smoothly switched when it changes to each phase. This is expressed through Eq. (4). At this point, θ_y^{Right} and θ_y^{Left} means the finally calculated Pitch control angle of both feet. Also the control angle of the swing phase ankle and support phase ankle are expressed through θ_y^{Swing} and $\theta_y^{Support}$.

$$\theta_y^{Right} = \theta_y^{Swing}(1 - \alpha^{Right}) + \theta_y^{support}\alpha^{Right}$$
$$\theta_y^{Left} = \theta_y^{Swing}(1 - \alpha^{Left}) + \theta_y^{support}\alpha^{Left} \tag{4}$$

α^{Right} and α^{Left} are variables that determine what phase each foot is currently in. If that value is 1, it indicates that the current phase is fully in the support phase. Conversely, if that value is 0, it indicates that the current phase is fully in the swing phase. If α^{Right} and α^{Left} are values between 0 and 1, it means that we are currently linearly interpolating between the swing phase and the support phase.

α^{Right} and α^{Left} are calculated from the Z-axis positions of the robot's feet (Z^{Right}, Z^{Left}). This is expressed in Eq. (5). If the difference in the Z-axis position between both feet is less than λ^{min}, then the α value becomes greater than or equal to 1, and this is defined as the support phase. In addition, if the difference in the Z-axis position between both feet is greater than λ^{max}, then the α value becomes less than or equal to 0, and this is defined as the swing phase. And if the difference in the Z-axis position of both feet is between λ^{min}

and λ^{max}, the α value is between 0 and 1, which is the interval where the foot state changes.

$$\alpha^{Right} = 1 - (Z^{Right} - Z^{Left} - \lambda^{min})/(\lambda^{max} - \lambda^{min})$$
$$\alpha^{Left} = 1 - (Z^{Left} - Z^{Right} - \lambda^{min})/(\lambda^{max} - \lambda^{min})$$
$$(\alpha > 1 \Rightarrow \alpha = 1, \alpha < 0 \Rightarrow \alpha = 0) \tag{5}$$

The α^{Right} and α^{Left} are converted to 1 for all values greater than 1 and 0 for all values less than 0, so that they can be used in the linear interpolation of Eq. (4).

5 Hardware and Experiment

5.1 Hardware

In this paper, we conduct an experiment using the previously developed humanoid robot ALICE. The overall design appearance of ALICE is presented in Fig. 3. The total length of ALICE's leg is approximately 662 mm, and in this experiment, a weight will be used at approximately 700 mm, the center of the pelvis, to apply an impact. We are balancing the robot with the angle and gyro data of the 3DM-GX5-AHRS IMU sensor mounted on the Pelvis. ZMP is calculated using force (Fx, Fy, Fz) and torque (Tx, Ty, Tz) measured from two Robotic RFT82-HA02 force-torque sensors located on both feet.

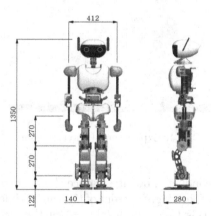

Fig. 3. ALICE's 3D CAD model (overall dimensions version) (Unit: mm)

5.2   Outline of Experiment

The performance of each algorithm is evaluated by comparing the maximum height that succeeded in overcoming disturbance and the amount of impact at that time. At this time, the impact amount is changed by changing the height h of the weight when disturbance is given with a weight of 5 kg.

There are a total of three control methods used in the experiment: Default Control of ALICE without Disturbance Overcoming Algorithm (default), Disturbance Overcoming Algorithm without Horizon Swing Foot Strategy (No Horizon Swing), Overcoming Disturbance Algorithm with Horizon Swing Foot Strategy (Horizon Swing)

Experimental environment is configured as shown in Fig. 4. The mass (m) of the weight used in the experiment is 5 kg and the height of the weight from the center of mass to the bottom is 70 cm. The weight is suspended from a 2-meter-long line. The height of the weight (h) is defined as the difference in height between the center of mass of the weight when it is lifted and the center of mass of the weight when it is collided to the robot.

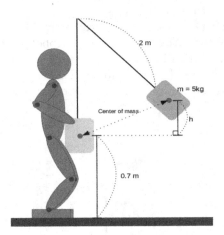

Fig. 4. Experimental Environment

The experiment is conducted by hitting once the 70 cm high part of the robot from the ground with a 5 kg weight in front of the robot while the robot is walking 50 steps in place. At this time, the height (h) of the weight is 10 cm, 20 cm, 25 cm, 30 cm, 35 cm, 40 cm, and 45 cm in total. Experiments for each height are conducted three times and are considered to have succeeded in overcoming disturbance only if all three times have been restored. At this time, whether the robot recovers its balance is defined as the case where there is no movement of the pelvis for 5 s after the impact is applied to the robot.

5.3   Set ZMP Predict Time

The duration of the Double Stance phase during one step in the ALICE basic walking motion is 0.1 s. Therefore, it is necessary to predict the ZMP at least 0.1 s after to determine how further the leg will be stretched. However, when predicting 0.1 s later, it reacted slowly to disturbance. Therefore, in this experiment, we predict the ZMP after 0.2 s, which is twice the value of 0.1 s.

6   Experimental Results

The experimental results are summarized in Table 2, and if overcoming disturbance is successful, the impact amount at the corresponding height is also written. The empty part of Table 2 is the case where the experiment was not conducted because it was judged that the experiment result was clear. In the table, h refers to the value obtained by subtracting 70 cm from the height from the ground to the weight center of the weight.

Table 2. Experiment Result (h: Height of Weight (cm)) (I: Impulse (kg·m/s))

Control Method	Default	No Horizon Swing	Horizon Swing
h = 10	Success (I = 7.00)	-	-
h = 20	Success (I = 9.90)	Success (I = 9.90)	Success (I = 9.90)
h = 25	Success (I = 11.07)	-	-
h = 30	Fail	Success (I = 12.12)	Success (I = 12.12)
h = 35	Fail	Fail	Success (I = 13.10)
h = 40	Fail	Fail	Success (I = 14.00)
h = 45	Fail	Fail	Success (I = 14.85)

Figure 5 is what it looks like when experimented with a default control method at a height of 30 cm. (3) in Fig. 5 is the appearance immediately after the impact on the robot, and (4) shows that the robot no longer maintains balance and tilts backward. As shown in Table 2, it was possible to withstand up to 11.07 kg·m/s impact with the default control method.

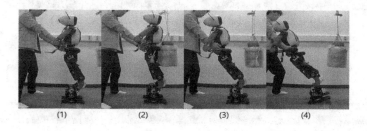

(1)   (2)   (3)   (4)

Fig. 5. Default experiment result (h: 30 cm)

As can be seen in Table 2, the disturbance overcoming algorithm without applying the Horizon Swing Foot strategy was able to overcome disturbance up to 12.12 kg·m/s impact. However, it showed that the balance was completely lost at more than that amount of impact, which can be confirmed through Fig. 6.

Figure 6 is what it looks like when experimented with a disturbance overcoming algorithm without applying the Horizon Swing Foot strategy at a height of 35 cm. (2) of Fig. 6 is the appearance immediately after the impact is applied to the robot, and it can be seen that the swing phase foot forms a certain angle with the ground. As a result, as soon as the foot stretches backward, it pushes the ground, and the foot of the opposite support phase is also pushed out. This is shown in (3) of Fig. 6. Due to this problem, as shown in the picture of (4), the robot no longer maintains balance and falls.

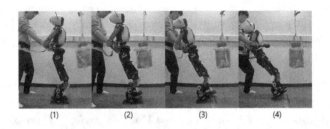

Fig. 6. No Horizon Swing experiment result (h: 35 cm)

Figure 7 is what it looks like when experimented with a disturbance overcoming algorithm applying the Horizon Swing Foot strategy at a height of 45 cm. the picture in (2) is immediately after the impact is applied. Looking at the photo of (4) in Fig. 7, the ankle of the left foot in the swing phase is parallel to the ground. Thanks to this, it is possible to stretch foot backward without colliding with the ground. This solved the problem that occurred in Fig. 6 and allowed the highest performance to be recorded as shown in Table 2.

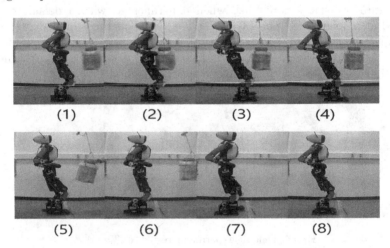

Fig. 7. Horizon Swing experiment result (h: 45 cm)

7   Conclusion and Future Work

For humanoid robots to be used in a real environment, they must be able to stably maintain their walking even in situations of disturbance. To improve disturbance overcoming performance, we present a disturbance overcoming algorithm that combines a step modification strategy based on the predicted ZMP in the Reference ZMP Preview Controller. In addition, the Horizon Swing Foot strategy was introduced to compensate for the shortcomings of the Step modification strategy.

Experiments have confirmed that applying the disturbance overcoming algorithm can restore balance even with up to 34.15% higher impact than before. In particular, it was confirmed that the introduction of the Horizon Swing Foot strategy could overcome disturbance even with 22.52% higher impact than the disturbance overcoming algorithm in which the strategy was not introduced.

If the proposed algorithm is applied to the humanoid robot, Stable walking will be possible even in situations of disturbance. It is expected that this will prevent damage and safety accidents that may occur when the humanoid robot loses balance and collapses, so that the robot can be operated stably in the real environment.

When ZMP is calculated with a force-torque sensor, accuracy is reduced in situations where the feet are in the air. So to solve this problem, we will calculate ZMP based on the IMU sensor. And we plan to add pelvis' movement to the algorithm so that it can overcome disturbance even with higher impact.

Acknowledgements. This research was supported by the MOTIE (Ministry of Trade, Industry, and Energy) in Korea, under (global) (P0017311) supervised by the Korea Institute for Advancement of Technology (KIAT).

References

1. Huang, Q., et al.: Planning walking patterns for a biped robot. IEEE Trans. Robot. Autom. **17**(3), 280–289 (2001)
2. Vukobratović, M., Stepanenko, J.: On the stability of anthropomorphic systems. Math. Biosci. **15**(1–2), 1–37 (1972)
3. Kajita, S., Hirukawa, H., Harada, K., Yokoi, K.: Introduction to Humanoid Robotics, vol. 101, p. 2014. Springer, Heidelberg (2014). https://doi.org/10.1007/978-3-642-54536-8
4. Kamioka, T., Kaneko, H., Takenaka, T., Yoshiike, T.: Simultaneous optimization of ZMP and footsteps based on the analytical solution of divergent component of motion. In: 2018 IEEE International Conference on Robotics and Automation (ICRA), pp. 1763–1770. IEEE (2018)
5. Feng, S., Xinjilefu, X., Atkeson, C.G., Kim, J.: Robust dynamic walking using online foot step optimization. In: 2016 IEEE/RSJ International Conference on Intelligent Robots and Systems (IROS), pp. 5373–5378. IEEE (2016)
6. Seekircher, A., Visser, U.: An adaptive lipm-based dynamic walk using model parameter optimization on humanoid robots. KI-Künstliche Intelligenz **30**(3–4), 233–244 (2016)

7. Graf, C., Röfer, T.: A center of mass observing 3D-LIPM gait for the RoboCup Standard Platform League humanoid. In: Röfer, T., Mayer, N.M., Savage, J., Saranli, U. (eds.) RoboCup 2011. LNCS, vol. 7416, pp. 102–113. Springer, Heidelberg (2012). https://doi.org/10.1007/978-3-642-32060-6_9

8. YITAEK KIM. (2019). The Development of the Preview-Control walking method for a stable bipedal walking of an adult size humanoid robot (Master dissertation, Hanyang Univ)

9. Urata, J., Nshiwaki, K., Nakanishi, Y., Okada, K., Kagami, S., Inaba, M.: Online decision of foot placement using singular LQ preview regulation. In: 2011 11th IEEE-RAS International Conference on Humanoid Robots, pp. 13–18. IEEE (2011)

10. Stephens, B.: Humanoid push recovery. In: 2007 7th IEEE-RAS International Conference on Humanoid Robots, pp. 589–595. IEEE (2010)

11. Mesesan, G., Englsberger, J., Ott, C.: Online DCM trajectory adaptation for push and stumble recovery during humanoid locomotion. In: 2021 IEEE International Conference on Robotics and Automation (ICRA), pp. 12780–12786. IEEE (2021)

12. Han, L., Chen, X., Yu, Z., Li, Q., Meng, L., Huang, Q.: Ankle torque control for steady walking of humanoid robot. In: 2019 IEEE 9th Annual International Conference on CYBER Technology in Automation, Control, and Intelligent Systems (CYBER), pp. 395–400. IEEE (2019)

13. Reichenberg, P., Röfer, T.: Step adjustment for a robust humanoid walk. In: : Alami, R., Biswas, J., Cakmak, M., Obst, O. (eds.) RoboCup 2021. LNCS, vol. 13132, pp. 28–39. Springer, Cham (2022). https://doi.org/10.1007/978-3-030-98682-7_3

14. Guadarrama-Olvera, J.R., Kajita, S., Cheng, G.: Preemptive foot compliance to lower impact during biped robot walking over unknown terrain. IEEE Robot. Autom. Lett. **7**(3), 8006–8011 (2022)

15. Yoo, S.M., Hwang, S.W., Kim, D.H., Park, J.H.: Biped robot walking on uneven terrain using impedance control and terrain recognition algorithm. In: 2018 IEEE-RAS 18th International Conference on Humanoid Robots (Humanoids), pp. 293–298. IEEE (2018)

16. Jeong, H., Lee, I., Oh, J., Lee, K.K., Oh, J.H.: A robust walking controller based on online optimization of ankle, hip, and stepping strategies. IEEE Trans. Rob. **35**(6), 1367–1386 (2019)

17. Mousavi, F.S., Masouleh, M.T., Kalhor, A., Ghassemi, P.: Push recovery methods based on admittance control strategies for a NAO-H25 humanoid. In: 2018 6th RSI International Conference on Robotics and Mechatronics (IcRoM), pp. 451–457. IEEE (2018)

18. Shafiee-Ashtiani, M., Yousefi-Koma, A., Mirjalili, R., Maleki, H., Karimi, M.: Push recovery of a position-controlled humanoid robot based on capture point feedback control. In: 2017 5th RSI International Conference on Robotics and Mechatronics (ICRoM), pp. 126–131. IEEE (2017)

19. Kim, J., Park, B., Lee, H., Park, J.: Hybrid position/torque ankle controller for minimizing ZMP error of humanoid robot. In: 2021 18th International Conference on Ubiquitous Robots (UR), pp. 211–216. IEEE (2021)

20. Li, Q., Yu, Z., Chen, X., Meng, F., Meng, L., Huang, Q.: Dynamic torso posture compliance control for standing balance of position-controlled humanoid robots. In: 2020 5th International Conference on Advanced Robotics and Mechatronics (ICARM), pp. 529–534. IEEE (2020)

21. Aslan, E., Arserim, M.A., Uçar, A.: Development of Push-Recovery control system for humanoid robots using deep reinforcement learning. Ain Shams Eng. J. **14**, 102167 (2023)

Structural Pruning for Real-Time Multi-object Detection on NAO Robots

G. Specchi[1], V. Suriani[1(✉)], M. Brienza[2], F. Laus[2], F. Maiorana[1],
A. Pennisi[2], D. Nardi[1], and D. D. Bloisi[2]

[1] Department of Computer, Control, and Management Engineering, Sapienza
University of Rome, Rome, Italy
{specchi,suriani,maiorana,nardi}@diag.uniroma1.it
[2] School of Engineering, University of Basilicata, Potenza, Italy
domenico.bloisi@unibas.it

Abstract. In this paper, we propose a real-time multi-class detection
system for the NAO V6 robot in the context of RoboCup SPL (Standard Platform League) using state-of-the-art structural pruning techniques on neural networks derived from YOLOv7-tiny. Our approach
combines structural pruning and fine-tuning, to obtain a pruned network
that maintains high accuracy while reducing the number of parameters
and the computational complexity of the network. The system is capable of detecting various objects, including the ball, goalposts, and other
robots, using the cameras of the robot. The goal has been to guarantee
high speed and accuracy trade-offs suitable for the limited computational resources of the NAO robot. Moreover, we demonstrate that our
system can run in real-time on the NAO robot with a frame rate of
32 frames per second on 224×224 input images, which is sufficient for
soccer competitions. Our results show that our pruned networks achieve
comparable accuracy to the original network while significantly reducing
the computational complexity and memory requirements. We release our
annotated dataset, which consists of over 4000 images of various objects
in the RoboCup SPL soccer field.

Keywords: Deep Neural Networks · Pruning · Embedded Systems ·
Robot Soccer

1 Introduction

RoboCup SPL is an annual international competition where teams of humanoid
robots play soccer against each other. The competition requires robots to have
advanced perception, decision-making, and motor control capabilities to succeed
in the fast-paced and dynamic game of soccer. One critical component of a
robot's perception system is object detection, which enables the robot to identify
and track relevant objects, such as the ball, teammates, and opponents (Fig. 1).

In recent years, deep learning-based object detection has emerged as a popular approach due to its ability to achieve high accuracy and robustness in complex environments. However, deploying deep learning-based object detection on

© The Author(s), under exclusive license to Springer Nature Switzerland AG 2024
C. Buche et al. (Eds.): RoboCup 2023, LNAI 14140, pp. 203–214, 2024.
https://doi.org/10.1007/978-3-031-55015-7_17

Fig. 1. An example of an annotated image with a labeled bounding box for each class: robot, center-spot, goal-spot, goal-post, and ball. The images are taken with natural light and shadows, and noisy backgrounds.

resource-constrained platforms such as humanoid robots is challenging due to their limited computational power and memory. Therefore, developing an efficient object detection pipeline that can run in real-time on these platforms is crucial. In this paper, we present a study on building a Deep Vision pipeline for the RoboCup SPL using end-to-end trainable object detection. Specifically, we focus on ball, robots, goal posts, and landmark detection, which are critical for a robot to perceive the game state and make decisions accordingly. We explored two popular detection architectures, YOLO (You Look Only Once) and SSD (Single Shot Detector). From those, we created derived models using commercial tools and structural pruning techniques in order to achieve accuracy comparable to state-of-the-art approaches but with improvement in the execution time enabling the deployment of such technologies on the NAO architecture. We created a dataset from logs collected by the SPQR team during official and unofficial events, that is publicly released. We demonstrated the effectiveness of our approach by developing a practical, multi-class object detector that can run at 32 frames per second on 224 × 224 input images while maintaining good detection performance on the Aldebaran NAO V6 robots.

The contribution of this work is three-fold.

1. A methodology for SSD neural network structural pruning that can be applied iteratively to obtain a greatly reduced model.
2. A quantitative comparison of different SSD approaches on NAO robots for detecting four different object classes.
3. A novel publicly available annotated dataset containing five different object classes.

The code and the additional material mentioned in this paper can be found on the following webpage: https://sites.google.com/diag.uniroma1.it/spqr-multi-object-ssd-pruning.

The rest of the paper is organized as follows. Section 2 contains a brief survey of the state-of-the-art and compares it to our approach; in Sect. 3, we expose a brief background to fully understand the concepts expressed in the paper; in Sect. 5 we show more in detail the proposed method; in Sect. 6 we discuss the experimental results obtained comparing different network models sizes inputs; and, finally, in Sect. 7 we discuss the conclusion obtained and the possible future developments of this work.

2   Related Work

Playing soccer with limited hardware in Standard Platform League has always represented a challenge also in the computer vision pipeline that each robot has to carry out onboard. With the adoption of more challenging field elements, for example, the black and white ball, the use of classic computer vision techniques has shown its limitations. The introduction of deep learning frameworks helped in migrating the classic computer vision pipelines to deep learning architectures. One of the first attempts in deploying neural networks on the NAO robot has been carried out in [1] with a two-stage approach to reduce the search space and then, a validation phase based on Convolutional Neural Networks, for multi-class classification.

To reduce the computational requirements several approaches have been proposed in literature with classic computer vision and neural network approaches. For example, several teams have explored the use of grayscale images to speed up their detectors: in [2], the team used a classical computer vision pipeline based on HAAR classifier to detect the ball on OpenCV taking advantage of the TBB library. The same idea is exploited in [4] where a whole vision pipeline for RoboCup SPL is presented that takes as input only a grayscale image to reduce the computational load. These findings suggest that grayscale images may be a promising approach for improving the efficiency of ball detection algorithms in the RoboCup SPL.

Existing deep learning frameworks usually target GPU-equipped devices and multi-core CPUs but do not perform very well on low-end hardware. Since the NAO V5 version, several approaches tackled the speed-up of the network inference on the NAO CPU. Among those, some of them have been presented to work efficiently on CPU, such as RoboDNN and the JIT Compiler [7] from the B-Human team. The former presents an approach based on the Darknet library, behaving like interpreters of neural networks built in Tensorflow and taking advantage of XLA instructions. To improve the performance, the B-Human team presents a C++ library that compiles neural network models into machine code that performs inference, targeting the Intel Atom processor of the NAO robots and outperforming the existing approaches. Both approaches are not able to manage all the layers and activations of the commercial neural networks.

Pruning techniques have been adopted in order to work efficiently with ready-to-use neural networks. In fact, in [6], the ROBO architecture uses the *weighted pruning* technique, starting from the tiny YOLO model. In the Humanoid

League, a YOLO architecture is used as a base for a multi-class real-time detector. In SPL, [8] presents a wide evaluation of latency and mean Average Precision (mAP) of several model architectures from the YOLO and SSD families on a range of devices representative of robot and edge device capabilities. Recently, in [5] the authors present an object detector that is robust to lighting conditions, and is able to work at 35 Hz for both cameras. This performance usually does not scale very well when passing from single to multi-class detectors and our goal was to preserve the performance of the ball perceptor, guaranteeing comparability with the single-class detector.

A more efficient way of pruning is represented by structural pruning. In [3], a general and automatic procedure for pruning is presented, which explicitly models the dependency between layers and comprehensively groups coupled parameters for pruning.

3   Pruning

Pruning is a technique used in neural networks to reduce the size of a trained model by removing unnecessary connections or weights. The goal of pruning is to improve the efficiency of the model by reducing its complexity without sacrificing performance. The pruning technique involves iteratively removing the connections or weights with the least impact on the model's output. The process of pruning can be done in different ways:

- *Weight pruning*: this method involves removing small weights or connections that are deemed unimportant. Weights with low absolute values are typically considered insignificant and can be removed.
- *Neuron pruning*: this method involves removing entire neurons from the network. Neurons with little or no impact on the model's output can be pruned.
- *Filter pruning*: this method involves removing entire filters or feature maps from a convolutional neural network. Filters that have little or no effect on the output can be removed.
- *Structural pruning*: removing entire sets of weights, neurons, or filters based on their structure in the network.

Pruning can be done at different stages of the neural network training, such as during initialization, after the first few epochs of training, or after the network has been fully trained. The most common approach is to prune the network after it has been fully trained. This allows for a more fine-grained evaluation of the model's performance. One popular approach is to use a technique called "magnitude-based pruning", which involves ranking the weights or activations by the magnitude and then removing the smallest ones.

Overall, pruning can help reduce the size of a neural network, improve its computational efficiency, and reduce the risk of overfitting.

3.1   Structural Pruning

Structural pruning is a type of neural network pruning that involves removing entire channels, filters, or layers from the neural network to reduce its computational and memory requirements. Unlike weight pruning, which sets individual weights to zero based on their magnitude, structural pruning targets entire structural components of the network. It can achieve higher levels of sparsity than weight pruning, as it can remove entire channels or filters that are redundant or not contributing significantly to the network's performance. However, structural pruning requires careful design and analysis to ensure that the pruned network maintains the necessary representational capacity to perform the desired task with high accuracy. In order to preserve as much as possible the accuracy of the unpruned network, we used an automatic pruning routine.

We adopted structural pruning as presented in [3] in order to reduce the memory requirements and have faster inference time on the NAO robot hardware.

The main concept behind structural pruning is the dependency between neurons. More specifically, if a neuron of a fully-connected neural network must be pruned, then the row of the previous weight matrix and the column of the next weight matrix corresponding to that neuron will be removed. This concept is easy to be analyzed and implemented for such a simple structure built by only fully-connected layers, but it can be complex in case of residual, concatenation, and reduction dependencies that are indeed in the YoloV7 structure. In order to keep track of the dependency of each neuron with the other neurons in the model, the approach in [3], builds a dependency graph. This graph represents the dependencies in the network and allows the execution of the pruning of any architecture in a fully automatic manner.

4   SPQR Dataset

The SPQR dataset consists of images acquired during friendly matches at Maker Faire 2022 in an outdoor scenario, and it includes images both from the lower and upper camera of the NAO robot. The dataset is used for training networks that have to detect robots, balls, goalposts (representing the goalposts), goal-spots (representing the penalty spot), and center-spots (representing the center circle). At the SPL Open Research Challenge at RoboCup 2022, MARIO was presented. It is a modular and extensible architecture for computing visual statistics. Two different datasets have been used, respectively one for robot and ball detection for statistics processing, and one for identifying robot poses.

The dataset for the detection task consists of 35000 images divided into 24000 for training, 3000 for validation, and 8000 for testing, and used for detecting the robots and ball. The second dataset, used for pose estimation, was created using the COCO Annotator tool, a web-based image annotation tool designed for efficiently labeling images for image localization and object detection. All annotations share the same basic data structure. The pose consists of up to 18 key points: ears, eyes, nose, neck, shoulders, elbows, wrists, hips, knees, and ankles. The annotations are stored using a JSON structure. It can be found at the following link https://shorturl.at/uBKS3.

To evaluate the presented approach, we chose a standard SPL dataset [8] released by the RoboEireann team, which ensures comparison with techniques developed in other works. Specifically, the dataset includes four classes, namely: robot, ball, goal-spot, and goal-post, and it has been divided into 3924 images for training, 491 images for validation, and 491 images for testing (Fig. 2).

Fig. 2. Examples of labeled images taken from SPQR Dataset. The images also include samples with natural light conditions and noisy backgrounds, which make the detection more challenging for lightweight neural networks.

The novel dataset we released includes robots with the jersey colors yellow and red. It can be found at the following link https://shorturl.at/biJK3. It consists of more than 4000 images including an extra class with respect to the dataset in [8], namely the center-spot, representing the center circle. Some images are shown in Figure 3.

5   Proposed Approach

In RoboCup scenarios and on-edge devices, it is often hard to reach a trade-off between accuracy and performance in execution time. Often the approaches rely on the manual adaptation of the neural network by changing layers and activation functions. This becomes harder when the pruning affects a high number of network parameters.

To tackle this, we proposed a pipeline to shrink a Pytorch Neural Network in several steps, relying on an automated approach to structural pruning:

1. We start with a neural network architecture derived from YOLOv7-tiny, a popular object detection model. This network has a small footprint but it is still too heavy for real-time execution on the NAO hardware. We train this network on the RoboEireann dataset, which consists of images and annotations of soccer fields and robots used in SPL RoboCup. We manipulate the dataset with data augmentation, using the following techniques: mosaic, flip left-right, scaling, and HSV (saturation, value, and hue).
2. We apply structural pruning to the trained network to reduce its size while preserving its accuracy. Our pruning algorithm works by iteratively ranking the channels/filters according to their importance and removing the least important ones. We use a combination of L2 regularization and sensitivity-based ranking to ensure that the pruned network maintains its performance.
3. After pruning, we fine-tune the pruned network on the RoboEireann dataset to recover any loss in accuracy caused by pruning. We repeat this process of pruning and fine-tuning until we reach a desired network size that is small enough to run in real-time on a NAO robot, but still preserving accuracy in a multi-class fashion. The results of this procedure are highlighted in Table 1 and Table 2.

Combining structural pruning and fine-tuning, it has been possible to obtain a pruned network that maintains high accuracy while reducing the number of parameters and the computational complexity of the network.

To evaluate the effectiveness of our approach, we compare the performance of our pruned network with an unpruned network and with the iteratively pruned networks. The iterative pruning process consists of many iterations where fine-tune steps are followed by pruning procedure. The process stops when reaching the best trade-off between computational time and mAP.

As can be seen, our approach offers a promising solution to designing efficient neural networks for robotics applications. By using structural pruning, we are able to reduce the network size while maintaining accuracy, which is critical for real-time applications like SPL RoboCup.

5.1 Experimental Setup

Software Environments. In order to deploy efficiently the Network on the robot, we performed several experiments using combinations of deep learning frameworks and optimization tools.

Firstly, we used the YOLOv7-tiny object detection network as a base network for our experiments. YOLOv7-tiny is a variant of the YOLO object detection algorithm, which uses a single neural network to simultaneously predict object classes and bounding boxes.

We performed preliminary experiments by running our PyTorch models using the Python 3.8 interpreter. Then, in order to optimize our networks, we used the ONNX (Open Neural Network Exchange)[1] framework. ONNX is an open-source framework that allows for the interoperability of deep learning models

---

[1] https://github.com/onnx/onnx.

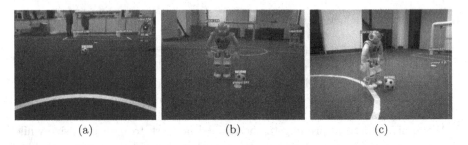

         (a)   (b)   (c)

Fig. 3. Three examples of inference performed on images from the RoboEireann dataset. The model used for the predictions is YTv7_47K, which is a pruned version of YTv7_177K.

between different frameworks. We used ONNX to convert our PyTorch models to the ONNX format, which allows for efficient inference on different hardware platforms.

Finally, we used the OpenVINO (Open Visual Inference and Neural Network Optimization) toolkit[2] to optimize our networks for inference on Intel CPUs. OpenVINO is an open-source toolkit that provides a set of pre-trained models, optimized libraries, and tools to accelerate deep learning inference on Intel hardware. We used OpenVINO to optimize our ONNX models for inference on the NAO V6 robot.

Used Platforms. The images in the used datasets and in the released one are acquired by the NAO V6 cameras and are saved in two different resolutions: 640 × 480 for the upper camera and 320 × 240 for the lower. For inference, the onboard computation unit of the NAO is represented by the quadcore Intel Atom E3845 CPU with 4 GB of RAM. The NAO CPU is also provided with an integrated GPU, but, as demonstrated in [5], it cannot perform better than the CPU on inference tasks.

6   Experimental Evaluation

To evaluate the effectiveness of our proposed approach, we conducted experiments on the NAO V6 robot equipped with the Atom E3845 CPU. We also tested networks with different input sizes and parameter sizes, ranging from 37M parameters to 7K parameters.

In fact, we trained and tested several models, as reported in the tables below. Only the model Yv7_37M is derived from YOLOv7. The model YTv7_177K is derived from YOLOv7-tiny (here denoted as YTv7_7M), that originally has 263 layers and 7M params. The name of each model represents the number of parameters of that model. The model YTv7_177K contains 177K parameters and 140 layers. The model YTv7_47K is a pruned version obtained by removing

---

[2] https://docs.openvino.ai/latest/home.html.

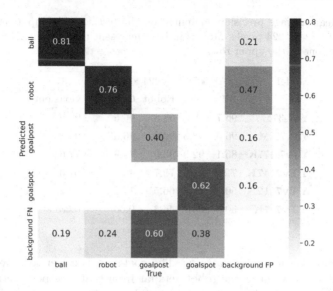

Fig. 4. Confusion matrix for the multi-class detector YTv7_47K on images with size of 224 × 224 pixels

half of the channels from the model YTv7_177K. The pruned model exhibited initially too low performance, due to a drop in the mAP. Then, we fine-tuned it for 371 epochs on the same training set used for training before the pruning, and it reached the performance shown in Table 1 and Table 2. The approach was applied for three iterations by pruning and then fine-tuning, obtaining the model YTv7_12K from the already pruned YTv7_47K, and we obtained YTv7_7K by applying the same approach to the model YTv7_12K.

Table 1 and Table 2 show the results of the experiments taking into account the different network and input sizes.

We report the mAP and execution time in milliseconds per image on the test set of the chosen dataset. As expected, the performance of the network improves as the input size and parameter size increase. For instance, the network YTv7_47K with an input size of 224 × 224 achieves the mAP of **72.1** on the NAO V6 platform.

Table 1 shows the results of the experiments for the unpruned and pruned networks executed on the NAO V6. We report the mAP and execution time for the pruned networks compared to the unpruned network. As expected, the pruned network maintains a high accuracy by reducing the size of the network. It is important to notice how the fine-tuning and pruning cycle allows us to reduce the loss of mAP while reducing the number of parameters.

Figure 4 depicts the confusion matrix for the multi-class detector YTv7_47K. We can notice that the less confused classes are ball and robot. This is due to the fact that they have particular patterns easy to learn. On the other hand, the goalpost and the goal-spot can be confused very easily with other objects in the

Table 1. Mean average precision computed on the test set. The input images have been scaled to 224 × 224 pixels. Models in bold represent that the model is a pruned version of the one in the upper row.

Model	mAP@.5(%) - 224 × 224				
	All	Ball	Robot	Goalpost	Goalspot
Yv7_37M	96.7	99.5	98.8	96.5	92.0
YTv7_7M	96.3	98.6	99.0	96.6	90.8
YTv7_177K	85.1	92.5	93.6	76.9	77.6
YTv7_47K	**72.1**	81.0	75.7	40.6	61.6
YTv7_12K	50.5	78.2	66.5	17.2	40.2
YTv7_7K	30.0	65.7	46.3	0.00	0.08

scene, because of their poor patterns. The goal-spot is easier to be recognized when close, but as soon as the robot gets far from that, the perspective makes the typical cross thin and the detector must take this into account, leading to the possibility to confuse other thin objects. It is worth noting that often, the mistakes of the detector are performed on patches that are outside the field, maybe because of a confusing background. This is usually solved in SPL by detecting the field borders and discarding perception out of them. Our approach provides an effective way to design compact and efficient neural networks for playing SPL RoboCup. The experiments show that the pruned network can achieve high accuracy while reducing the network size by several orders of magnitude. The best trade-off of accuracy and mAP are the models YTv7_47K with input dimension 224 × 224 pixels and YTv7_177K that for input dimension 160 × 160 pixels, that show similar results in terms of both latency and mAP. Although the performance is similar, we prefer to keep the input size as large as possible in order to have more details in the image, which are crucial when performing classification on objects that are far from the robot. Then the model we present is YTv7_47K with input dimension 224 × 224, that reaches a mAP of 81 even

Table 2. Average inference timing computed on the NAO CPU using PyTorch and on the test set of the RoboEireann dataset. Input images were resized to be squared. Smaller input sizes have been not considered to avoid a high drop in the mean average precision.

Model	PyTorch (ms)				OpenVINO (ms)			
	320px	224px	160px	128px	320px	224px	160px	128px
YTv7_177K	164	106	67	51	121	56	30	20
YTv7_47K	114	79	54	41	65	**32**	20	15
YTv7_12K	44	39	27	21	49	28	14	10
YTv7_7K	32	22	17	14	45	23	13	9

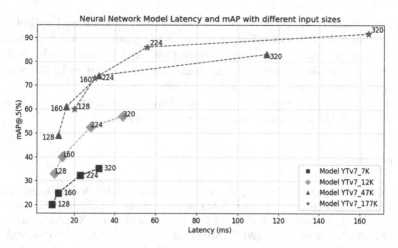

Fig. 5. Plot of relationship among latency, mAP, and input size. Each color corresponds to a specific model. For each model, we plotted four spots, one for each input size, written in the plot. Latencies were computed on the NAO V6 CPU.

on the single-class ball, being comparable to the single-class detector previously presented in literature [5]. The performance of the network depends on the input size and parameter size, as well as the hardware platform used. In fact, in Fig. 5 there is the plot of Latency, mAP, and input size of the models, related to four different input sizes. The most promising size in terms of accuracy is the highest one, but it is also the slowest. We can notice the smallest drop in performance is achieved when switching from an input image size of 320×320 to 224×224. This is due to the fact that for the specific purpose of the soccer robot, there exists a minimum requirement for the image in order to contain the visual information needed by the neural network.

7   Conclusions

In this paper, we presented a pipeline for pruning structural neural networks derived from YOLOv7-tiny to efficiently detect objects in the context of SPL RoboCup matches. Our approach combines structural pruning, fine-tuning, and iterative training to obtain a pruned network that maintains high accuracy while reducing the number of parameters and the computational complexity of the network. We conducted experiments on the NAO V6 robot, and we tested networks derived from YOLOv7-tiny with different input sizes and parameter sizes and measured their performance on a public SPL test set. The results show that the networks pruned with this approach achieve admissible accuracy to the original networks but significantly reduce the computational complexity and memory requirements. With a model of 47K parameters, we can achieve real-time performance (more than 30 Hz) and preserve a mAP@0.5(%) greater than 70. Such a performance is obtained thanks to the combination of deep learning frameworks and optimization tools, i.e. ONNX and OpenVINO, to train and optimize our neural networks for efficient inference on the NAO hardware. Our approach can be useful also for other robotics applications that require real-time object detection and tracking, as happened in the context of RoboCup SPL. We publicly released datasets, models, and code for iterative pruning.

As future work, we intend to prune skeleton detection approaches in order to run on the NAO algorithms to recognize game actions.

References

1. Albani, D., Youssef, A., Suriani, V., Nardi, D., Bloisi, D.D.: A deep learning approach for object recognition with NAO soccer robots. In: Behnke, S., Sheh, R., Sariel, S., Lee, D. (eds.) RoboCup 2016: Robot World Cup XX. LNCS, vol. 9776, pp. 392–403. Springer, Cham (2017). https://doi.org/10.1007/978-3-319-68792-6_33
2. Bloisi, D., Duchetto, F.D., Manoni, T., Suriani, V.: Machine learning for realisticball detection in RoboCup SPL (2017)
3. Fang, G., Ma, X., Song, M., Mi, M.B., Wang, X.: Depgraph: towards any structural pruning (2023)
4. Leiva, F., Cruz, N., Bugueño, I., Ruiz-del Solar, J.: Playing soccer without colors in the SPL: a convolutional neural network approach. In: Holz, D., Genter, K., Saad, M., von Stryk, O. (eds.) RoboCup 2018. LNCS, pp. 122–134. Springer, Cham (2019). https://doi.org/10.1007/978-3-030-27544-0_10
5. Narayanaswami, S.K., et al.: Towards a real-time, low-resource, end-to-end object detection pipeline for robot soccer. In: Eguchi, A., Lau, N., Paetzel-Prüsmann, M., Wanichanon, T. (eds.) RoboCup 2022. LNCS, vol. 13561, pp. 62–74. Springer, Cham (2023). https://doi.org/10.1007/978-3-031-28469-4_6
6. Szemenyei, M., Estivill-Castro, V.: Robo: robust, fully neural object detection for robot soccer. In: Chalup, S., Niemueller, T., Suthakorn, J., Williams, M.A. (eds.) RoboCup 2019. LNCS, vol. 11531, pp. 309–322. Springer, Cham (2019). https://doi.org/10.1007/978-3-030-35699-6_24
7. Thielke, F., Hasselbring, A.: A JIT compiler for neural network inference. In: Chalup, S., Niemueller, T., Suthakorn, J., Williams, M.A. (eds.) RoboCup 2019. LNCS, vol. 11531, pp. 448–456. Springer, Cham (2019). https://doi.org/10.1007/978-3-030-35699-6_36
8. Yao, Z., Douglas, W., O'Keeffe, S., Villing, R.: Faster yolo-lite: faster object detection on robot and edge devices. In: Alami, R., Biswas, J., Cakmak, M., Obst, O. (eds.) RoboCup 2021. LNCS, vol. 13132, pp. 226–237. Springer, Cham (2022). https://doi.org/10.1007/978-3-030-98682-7_19

Dynamic Joint Control for a Humanoid Walk

Philip Reichenberg[1] and Thomas Röfer[2,3(✉)]

[1] JUST ADD AI GmbH, Konsul-Smidt-Straße 8p, 28217 Bremen, Germany
philip.reichenberg@justadd.ai
[2] Deutsches Forschungszentrum für Künstliche Intelligenz, Cyber-Physical Systems,
Enrique-Schmidt-Str. 5, 28359 Bremen, Germany
[3] Universität Bremen, Fachbereich 3 – Mathematik und Informatik, Postfach 330
440, 28334 Bremen, Germany
thomas.roefer@dfki.de

Abstract. Worn-out robots are a topic that is often overlooked when developing approaches for walking with humanoid robots. When robots get older, their joints get more and more play, resulting in control commands being not executed as intended. In this paper, we present a novel approach for modifying the target joint angles of the leg joints of the humanoid robot NAO to bring its performance closer to a robot without considerable wear and tear. Based on the estimated center of mass and an estimated rotation error of the support foot, the joint velocities are adapted to handle stuck joints that result from the weight and movement of the robot. Moreover, the differences of the commanded joint angles and the measured ones are used to bring worn-out robots closer to the state of good ones by reducing such errors.

1 Introduction

In the RoboCup Standard Platform League (SPL), all participating teams use the humanoid robot NAO manufactured by Aldebaran. NAO's joints are position-controlled, i.e. target joint angles are commanded and motor controllers with unknown parameters try to execute these commands. With this system, most teams reach similar walking speeds, but with varying degrees of stability. Our team B-Human participates in the SPL and became world champion nine times. Our previous paper [7] describes a step adjustment to let the robot walk in the direction of a probable fall as well as correct the swing foot rotation to prevent premature collisions with the ground. In this follow-up paper, we present our newest approaches in achieving a smoother walk that can compete with our previous walk and makes better use of worn-out robots.

In Sect. 2, we first discuss the related work. Afterwards in Sect. 3, we present the current state of our robots and the problems we face with it. Section 4 describes the old approach from our previous paper [7] and shows our new refinements. As the main focus for this paper, Sect. 5 presents our balancing approach to achieve a better synchronization between the different joints of the

C. Buche et al. (Eds.): RoboCup 2023, LNAI 14140, pp. 215–227, 2024.
https://doi.org/10.1007/978-3-031-55015-7_18

Table 1. Fall statistics of the top 4 teams at RoboCup 2019 and 2022 (Due to missing video footage, the number of games per team varies. The numbers in parentheses include falls due to already broken gears, the regular numbers do not.)

Team	Robo-Cup	Avg. #Falls per Game		
		Overall	Collision	Walking
B-Human	2019	10.1	9.4	0.7
	2022	9.3 (14.3)	6.0	3.3 (8.3)
HTWK	2019	18.5	14.1	4.4
Robots	2022	21.9	16.0	5.9
rUNSWift	2019	16.6	14.0	2.6
	2022	22.2	14.7	7.5
Nao Devils	2019	18.3	12.6	5.7
	2022	31.5	21.2	10.3

legs with the help of a neural-network-based prediction. As an addition in Sect. 6, we present a novel idea on how to also use such prediction to reduce the differences between the requested and measured joint positions. The resulting walk is evaluated in Sect. 7. Finally, we conclude the paper in Sect. 9.

2   Related Work

Rodriguez and Behnke [8] use a deep neural network to learn omnidirectional locomotion, with first learning in simulation and using sim-to-real transfers to apply the result to the real robot. Such an approach would be interesting for us as well, but our simulator SimRobot [5] does not represent the NAO's physics good enough, in particular not the behavior of the motors, and we are not aware of a simulator with a sufficiently realistic model of the robot.

This issue could be resolved using the so called *grounded simulation learning* (GLS) by Farchy *et al.* [2]. They optimize the parameters for their walk in simulation and then evaluate them afterwards on the real robot. Afterwards the simulation is modified to match the results on the real robots more closely. Then, the cycle is repeated. However, on the level of wear and tear of robots, the simulation needs to get much more expressive in terms of the effects simulated, so that its parameters could be adapted in such a learning approach.

Similar to our approach described in Sect. 3.3, the team Nao Devils [6] also automatically controls the walking speed of their robots. They use criteria such as the number of falls and oscillations of the torso's orientation to determine when to reduce the speed.

Another typical solution to gain more stability that is proposed is the introduction of additional controllers. Ashar *et al.* [1] and Schwarz *et al.* [10] use PID controllers to stabilize the walk. Due to our analysis that we present in Sect. 3.2, we decided against such a solution, as it is not sufficient enough.

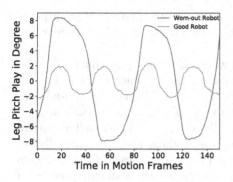

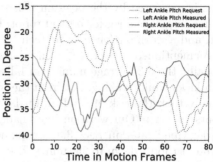

Fig. 1. The summed-up play of the three pitch joints of a leg of a good robot (in orange) and a worn-out one (in blue). The leg was moved by hand in both directions. (Color figure online)

Fig. 2. The ankle pitch requests and measurements while a robot is catching itself from a backwards fall.

3 State of the Robots

3.1 Fall Statistics

The robots used by the team B-Human are mostly from the year 2019. Since then, they participated in five soccer competitions with actual 5v5 games. Those events alone sum up to 30 full games, with over 40 additional practice matches against empty fields, other teams, or our own robots. Outside of games the robots have been heavily used for motion related developments. All of this results in noticeable wear and tear of the robots. Despite these hardware downsides, Table 1 shows our improvements between the last two RoboCup events in 2019 and 2022. The average number of falls per game increased by a lot for all top four teams. As we can not know the reasons behind it, it is still remarkable that the team B-Human managed to lower the number of average falls per game from 10.1 to 9.3. One reason could be broken robots, which we cannot know from the video footage alone. That is why we also counted our falls including broken robots. We had a few instances where ankle pitch joints were broken, but the robots could still walk mostly stable, except for one game. Here one robot fell in a span of three minutes 16 times but was not taken out of the game, because the robot mostly walked sideways. This caused the broken gear to not have a high enough influence in the walking and the robot could still play to be a threat to the opponent team in that game. But despite when counting those falls in, B-Human had still 35 % to 45 % less falls than other teams. Excluding this one robot, we had 58 % to 70 % less falls than the other top teams.

3.2 Wear and Tear of the Robots

To analyze the state of the robots, we place them in their default standing position, hold them in the air and move the joints by hand. The play from the gears is measured by the position sensors. In Fig. 1, the play of all pitch joints summed up of one leg for a good robot, i. e. one without considerable wear and tear, and a worn-out one can be seen.

As mentioned in Sect. 3.1, even robots with a high joint play could still walk. Actually, the 3.3 average number of falls while walking shown in Table 1 result from kicks while walking, not from the walking itself. This is because we intentionally took the risk of a fall in duels with an opponent. Here even our good robots fell often. Our worn-out ones had a different problem: low walking speed. As described later in Sect. 3.3, we reduce the walking speed dynamically for worn-out robots down to 250 mm/s. But from the video footage of the RoboCup and the log files of those robots, we can clearly see the walking speed is on average close to 135 mm/s, nearly 50 % less than intended.

Another problem is the increasing number of broken gears. In 2019, our team had no broken gears, only a few instances of damaged electronics. In 2022, more than ten times a gear broke, all leg joints, mostly ankle pitches with some knee pitches. Also the wear and tear accelerated, with multiple robots having worn-out hip pitches. In particular the broken robot with 16 falls within three minutes can give us some insights about what the joints and motors are capable of, as seen in Fig. 3. The right ankle pitch gear was damaged, which caused the joint to be unable to follow the target trajectory correctly. While the foot is in the air, this is not much of a problem, but with every second step, it is the supporting one. Therefore, having a consistent error of 5° to 15° results in a forward torso rotation of also about 10°. However, even with this damaged gear, the robot hold out for seven walking steps, about 1.7 s. For this time window, we can see two interesting observations:

Even though the gear is broken and the robot is tilted forward with the whole weight on the foot, the right ankle pitch can still hold its position. The same applies for the healthy left ankle pitch, which can execute the target command much more precisely, but still with some deviation due the weight of the robot.

The other observation is that the motor controller weights changes in the target position much more than absolute positional errors. This can be seen for the right ankle pitch in Fig. 3. The position error is several times close to 10°, but as the change is in the same direction as the robot is already trying to fall, the joint is able to execute it with ease. One would expect from the motors to at least still hold the position for longer, but as those are as given and can not be changed, whether hardware nor software, we are forced to work with them.

Interestingly, all those 16 falls were to the front. When looking into walking steps meant to catch a robot from a fall backwards, another observation can be made. Such situation is shown in Fig. 2. Here the requests for the ankle pitches seem to oscillate. This is the result of the walk step adjustment [7] and the swing foot leveling. Since our team had no broken gears back in 2019, the assumption is reasonable that those oscillation could be a cause of broken gears.

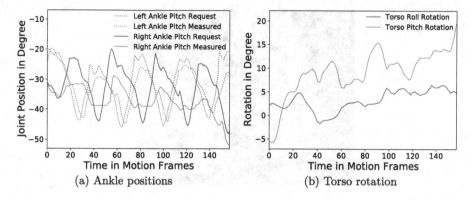

Fig. 3. The ankle positions and torso rotation of a robot with a broken right ankle pitch, closely before it fell.

3.3 Joint Play Rating

In the 2022 SPL competition, one of the challenges were 7v7 games, with the possibility of using robots from pool and thereby foreign robots. As the they could range from a very good to very worn-out state and the time window to adjust their walking speed was quite narrow, we opted for an automatic calibration, which regulated the walking speed, i. e. the maximum forward, sideways, and rotation speeds. For this automatic procedure, we calculate a quality measure α between 1 and 0, with 1 representing a good robot and 0 a worn-out one [9]. α was then used to interpolate the walking speed of the robot, given a configured maximum and minimum walking speed.

4   Swing Foot Leveling

In our previous paper [7] we described one consequence of the limited strength of the motors is that the support foot will tilt in the direction of the motion, because some joints are stuck while others are not. This in turn causes the swing foot to prematurely collide with the ground and often results in a fall. Our proposed solution back then had the downside that if the robot tilted more, e. g. when lifting off of the support foot as seen in Fig. 4 no correction could be made. Moreover as mentioned in Sect. 3.2 the swing foot leveling causes some oscillation in the ankle pitches, which further stresses for another approach.

For our new implementation we do not use the support foot rotation anymore, instead use the predicted torso rotation [7] and still interpolate the compensation down to a lower value at the end of the walking step, to prevent too much compensation. Additionally the measured rotation of the swing foot is used to reduce or increase the compensation. Moreover the roll rotation is compensated too.

Fig. 4. Examples of a robot tilting more backwards or forwards than it is measurable from the support foot rotation alone.

Throughout the paper, we often need to map values from an input range $[x_{min}, x_{max}]$ to an output range of $[0, 1]$, calculated by the following function:

$$\text{normalize}_{x_{min}}^{x_{max}}(x) = \text{clamp}_0^1\left(\frac{x - x_{min}}{x_{max} - x_{min}}\right) \tag{1}$$

The target swing foot pitch angle Γ^{p} is determined as follows:

$$\hat{t}^{\text{p}} = \begin{cases} 0.5 & , \ \theta^{\text{p}} > \theta_{\text{actual}}^{\text{p}} \\ 1 - 0.5 \cdot \text{normalize}_{t_{min}^{\text{p}}}^{t_{max}^{\text{p}}}(t) & , \ \text{otherwise} \end{cases} \tag{2}$$

$$\Gamma^{\text{p}} = \gamma^{\text{p}} + \text{clamp}_{-v_{max}}^{v_{max}}(\hat{t}^{\text{p}} \cdot (\theta^{\text{p}} - \theta_{\text{actual}}^{\text{p}}) + f \cdot (\theta^{\text{p}} - \gamma_{\text{actual}}^{\text{p}}) - \gamma^{\text{p}}) \tag{3}$$

The target swing foot roll angle Γ^{r} is determined slightly different:

$$\hat{t}^{\text{r}} = \begin{cases} 0 & , \ \theta_{\text{actual}}^{\text{r}} > 0 \ \text{and left is swing foot} \\ 0 & , \ \theta_{\text{actual}}^{\text{r}} < 0 \ \text{and right is swing foot} \\ 1 - 0.5 \cdot \text{normalize}_{t_{min}^{\text{r}}}^{t_{max}^{\text{r}}}(t) & , \ \text{otherwise} \end{cases} \tag{4}$$

$$\hat{\Upsilon} = \text{normalize}_{\Upsilon_{min}}^{\Upsilon_{max}}(\Upsilon) \tag{5}$$

$$\Gamma^{\text{r}} = \gamma^{\text{r}} + \text{clamp}_{-v_{max}}^{v_{max}}(\hat{\Upsilon} \cdot (\hat{t}^{\text{r}} \cdot (\theta^{\text{r}} - \theta_{\text{actual}}^{\text{r}}) + f \cdot (\theta^{\text{r}} - \gamma_{\text{actual}}^{\text{r}})) - \gamma^{\text{r}}) \tag{6}$$

In both cases, θ is the target torso angle (by default $0°$ for the pitch direction and always $0°$ for the roll direction) and θ_{actual} the estimated one. Similarly, γ is the target swing foot angle and γ_{actual} is the measured one. t is a value between 0 and 1 that defines where the walk is in the current step phase. $\hat{t}$ stretches the middle part of that interval so that there are two plateaus at both ends of the step phase. Since the compensation is weighted by this value and it should be maximal at the beginning of the step and minimal at its end, the phase is inverted. However, it is constant if the torso is tilted backwards. f is a factor that defines how much the actual swing foot angle influences the result. The amount of compensation is then limited to a maximum velocity v_{max} that reflects how much the swing foot rotation can be changed in a single 12 ms frame.

For the swing foot roll angle, a compensation is only applied if the robot is actually moving sideways. Based on the side step size Υ and given thresholds Υ_{min} and Υ_{max}, another factor $\hat{\Upsilon}$ is calculated. With $\hat{\Upsilon}$, the roll compensation is interpolated to 0 for small side steps and to full for larger ones.

5 Joint Speed Control

A major downside of typical balancing approaches applied to individual joints is that it is difficult to consider the movement that the joints can actually execute in a specific moment. For instance, in extreme situations the joints of the NAO can only hold a given position, but the motors are not powerful enough to change them against the gravity anymore, as shown in Fig. 3.

One aspect of our walk is the ankle pitch balancing. It stems from the walk by Hengst [4]. It scales the pitch measurements of NAO's gyroscope by a factor and adds them to the target ankle pitch of the support foot. One could argue that in extreme situations increasing the factor could help, but as seen in Fig. 3, the joints do not reach the target position. Instead they get stuck and start moving in the opposite direction once the request does so, too. Increasing the factor would widen the gap between the target angle and actual angle and would only let the joint move more quickly when not working against the gravity.

Instead, we introduce a different balancing idea: Reduce the allowed rotation speed of a given joint for directions that would destabilize the robot even further, scaled based on the center of mass (CoM) position in the supporting foot and a predicted measured rotation error of the supporting foot.

So if the robot is tilting forward, the ankle pitch will contract slower; if the robot is tilting backward, the hip pitch will stretch slower. In case the robot stabilizes itself afterwards, the joints can move a small amount faster than originally needed for the step to catch up again.

To calculate the rotation error of the supporting foot ϵ, a neural network developed by Fiedler and Laue [3] is used to predict the joint positions for the legs two frames into the future. Since real measurements are usually delayed by three frames, the output of the network reduces this delay to a single frame. Those positions can be converted with forward kinematic to determine the rotation of the foot. Then, the difference to the request rotation can be calculated. The CoM is projected into the support foot area to get the ratio λ. We use the same prediction as we do in our original paper [7]. We calculate two ratios based on the position of the CoM. For the pitch direction, the ratio ranges from the heel (0) to the tip (1) of the foot. The CoM and ϵ are then converted into two ratios $r_b, r_f \in [0, 1]$ for the pitch direction:

$$r_b = \min(1 - \text{normalize}_{p_{min}}^{p_{max}}(\epsilon), \text{normalize}_{b_{min}}^{b_{max}}(\lambda)) \tag{7}$$

$$r_f = \min(\text{normalize}_{n_{min}}^{n_{max}}(\epsilon), 1 - \text{normalize}_{f_{min}}^{f_{max}}(\lambda)) \tag{8}$$

For the roll direction, 0 is defined as the origin point of the robot projected on the ground, 0.5 at the inner edge of the supporting foot, 0.75 at the origin of the foot, and 1 at the outer edge. A ratio $r_s \in [0, 1]$ is calculated for the current support foot.

Those ratios are used to determine the rotational velocity allowed for each leg joint, by calculating the minimum and maximum position of the given joint based on the last requested one. The parameters p, n, b, and f denote ranges for the rotation error (p and n) and the CoM position (b and f). The range p interpolates r_b to 1 if ϵ is low and to 0 if ϵ is high. n does the same for r_f, but for high negative ϵ values. The range n itself is also interpolated by the rating value from Sect. 3.3 to use a more narrow range for worn-out robots, as those need a more aggressive control. The ranges b and f do the same based on the CoM ratio. r_b is 1 for CoM positions more forward and 0 for those closer to the heel. r_f is 1 for CoM positions more backward and 1 for those closer to the tip of the foot.

For each joint j, the control is applied by using an interpolation on the currently intended target position Φ_t^j, which is the target position determined by the base walk and the walk step adjustment, to compute the target position ϕ_t^j that will be forwarded further in the walk generation:

$$\phi_t^j = \text{clamp}_{\phi_{\min}^j}^{\phi_{\max}^j}(\Phi_t^j) \tag{9}$$

For joints $j \in P$ (P is the set of pitch joints), the limits are computed in the following way:

$$\phi_{\min}^j = \psi_{t-1}^j - \left(s_{\max}^j \cdot r_b + s_{\min}^j \cdot (1 - r_b)\right), j \in P \tag{10}$$

$$\phi_{\max}^j = \psi_{t-1}^j + \left(s_{\max}^j \cdot r_f + s_{\min}^j \cdot (1 - r_f)\right), j \in P \tag{11}$$

ψ_{t-1}^j denotes the last commanded target of joint j, $s_{\min}^j$ and $s_{\max}^j$ the minimum and maximum positional change allowed for joint j. $s_{\min}^j$ is a static value while $s_{\max}^j$ is calculated at the beginning of a walking step based on the needed change to execute the requested walk step size.

In contrast, for roll joints, the rotation error is currently not used, only the CoM position, transformed into a ratio in roll direction, as described before. The limits are joint-specific to be mirrored between the left and the right leg, although all roll joints have the same rotation direction:

$$\phi_{\min}^j = \psi_{t-1}^j - \begin{cases} s_{\max} & , j \in \{\text{lHipRoll}, \text{rAnkleRoll}\} \\ s_{\max} \cdot r_s + s_{\min} \cdot (1 - r_s) & , j \in \{\text{rHipRoll}, \text{lAnkleRoll}\} \end{cases} \tag{12}$$

$$\phi_{\max}^j = \psi_{t-1}^j + \begin{cases} s_{\max} & , j \in \{\text{rHipRoll}, \text{lAnkleRoll}\} \\ s_{\max} \cdot r_s + s_{\min} \cdot (1 - r_s) & , j \in \{\text{lHipRoll}, \text{rAnkleRoll}\} \end{cases} \tag{13}$$

The idea is that movements that push the CoM away from the support leg are not controlled, but movements that bring the CoM closer to the support leg are reduced to prevent a potential sideways fall.

Fig. 5. The course used for the evaluation.

Moreover, as a consequence of the kinematics of the robot, a joint speed control is necessary for turn steps, too. To do a turn step, the feet need to rotate on the yaw direction. This can only be achieved with the so-called hip-yaw-pitch joint. This joint connects both legs and is rotated by 45° around the roll axis. This not only creates a dependency between the yaw angles of both feet (they are always mirrored), but it also requires other joints to compensate for the actually diagonal rotations the joint can only create. This comes with a problem: worn-out robots will no execute this correction correctly and the same effect of stuck joints can occur here, too. Therefore we apply the same equations from Eqs. (10) and (11), but for the desired yaw rotation of the current step. So if the robot rotates the legs outward (i. e. positive yaw rotation), the rotation is slowed down if the robot risks tilting more forward, and for inward rotation if the robot risks tilting more backward.

6   Joint Position Compensation

The approach from Sect. 5 is good at handling the observed state of the robot, but still has a major problem: ignoring what the joints are actually doing in any given moment. Figure 3 shows the deviation between the target joint angles and the measured ones. Assuming that the right ankle pitch request would hold its position for longer, the measured one would still have an offset of the observed 5° to 15°. In addition, a good robot would also behave differently from a worn-out one, as a result of less joint play. To more accurately handle the different amounts of play, a joint position compensation is applied:

$$\delta^j = m_{\text{pred}}^j - \psi_{t-1}^j - \text{clamp}_{\min(m_t^j - m_{t-1}^j,0)}^{\max(m_t^j - m_{t-1}^j,0)} (m_{\text{pred}}^j - \psi_{t-1}^j) \qquad (14)$$

An offset between the target joint angle ψ_{t-1}^j and a predicted measurement m_{pred}^j is calculated, with the help of the neural network already mentioned in Sect. 5. The measured position change is then subtracted from this offset (if it is smaller), i. e. the difference between the current measurement m_t^j and the previous one m_{t-1}^j, to gain δ^j. Afterwards it is further filtered with a low-pass filter.

δ^j is then used to hold the requested position ϕ_t^j, i. e. the request after the joint speed control, of the support leg joints, in case the measured position is already at the target or even further away. Equation (15) is applied after all other parts of the walking are calculated. The changes determined by the joint

Table 2. Results of the evaluation (significantly better values in bold)

Walk	Robot State	Walking Speed	1st Part	2nd Part	3rd Part	Ball Contacts	Falls
old	worn-out	default	$170\ \frac{mm}{s}$	$78\ \frac{mm}{s}$	$134\ \frac{mm}{s}$	2	1
new	worn-out	default	$\mathbf{190\ \frac{mm}{s}}$	$86\ \frac{mm}{s}$	$\mathbf{159\ \frac{mm}{s}}$	1	0
old	good	default	$211\ \frac{mm}{s}$	$\mathbf{108\ \frac{mm}{s}}$	$158\ \frac{mm}{s}$	1	2
new	good	default	$\mathbf{264\ \frac{mm}{s}}$	$77\ \frac{mm}{s}$	$\mathbf{180\ \frac{mm}{s}}$	1	$\mathbf{0}$
old	worn-out	fast	$\mathbf{264\ \frac{mm}{s}}$	$125\ \frac{mm}{s}$	$164\ \frac{mm}{s}$	3	0
new	worn-out	fast	$234\ \frac{mm}{s}$	$116\ \frac{mm}{s}$	$159\ \frac{mm}{s}$	1	0
old	good	fast	$\mathbf{310\ \frac{mm}{s}}$	$116\ \frac{mm}{s}$	$173\ \frac{mm}{s}$	1	0
new	good	fast	$261\ \frac{mm}{s}$	$\mathbf{152\ \frac{mm}{s}}$	$172\ \frac{mm}{s}$	1	0

speed control $\phi_t^j - \varPhi_t^j$ are also used to prevent applying their offsets a second time. ψ_{t-1} is the final request from the previous calculation cycle and ρ^j a factor, by which the offset shall be applied:

$$\psi_t^j = \phi_t^j - \rho^j \cdot \text{clamp}_{\min(\delta^j,0)}^{\max(\delta^j,0)} (\phi_t^j - \psi_{t-1}^j - \text{clamp}_{\min(\phi_t^j - \varPhi_t^j,0)}^{\max(\phi_t^j - \varPhi_t^j,0)} (\phi_t^j - \psi_{t-1}^j)) \quad (15)$$

7   Evaluation

To evaluate the new walk compared to the previous 2022 version, we use a course which tests the robots in omnidirectional speed, stability in the forward walking direction, and walking around a ball. For the experiments, a soccer field was prepared as seen in Fig. 5.

The test consists of three parts. First the robots walk 2 m under normal conditions from the goal to the end of the penalty area. Afterwards they need to walk over a few obstacles: two 4 mm thick and 4 cm wide planks, a few 4 mm thick and 8 × 8 cm pieces and a ramp at the end with at first a 4 mm thick and 16 cm wide area followed by a 6 mm thick and 16 cm area. Those are similar obstacles as used in our previous paper [7]. As third part, the robots need to walk around balls and sideways between them multiple times, as shown in Fig. 5, to evaluate the full omnidirectional capabilities of the walk.

To let the robots walk as close as they would in a real soccer game, the actual soccer behavior is used to let the robots walk to the different destination points based on their own world model and perception, but with the obstacle detection disabled. Besides the measured speed for each part of the course, falls and ball contacts are counted, too. To allow a comparison, the balls will be hold by a human in place while the robots will walk around it. Otherwise the ball would roll away from an unintentional contact by up to 1 m and make a comparison between the different tries impossible.

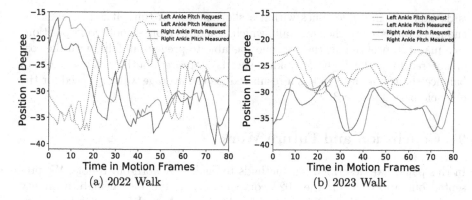

Fig. 6. Requested and measured ankle pitches when a robot is catching itself backwards, compared old and new walk.

The evaluation was carried out with two robots, a good one and a worn-out one, each once with our default walking speed and a forced fast one. The default walking speed allows for a rotational speed of $120°/s$, $250\,mm/s$ forward and $200\,mm/s$ sideways. Worn-out robots are scaled down to $100°/s$, $220\,mm/s$ forward and $180\,mm/s$ sideways. For the fast walking speed, both robots are forced to use $120°/s$, $300\,mm/s$ forward and $230\,mm/s$ sideways.

8 Results

The results are shown in Table 2. Overall, both walks are similar and none showed significant improvements over the other on average. Note that the time for a fall and getting up again was not counted for the walking speed, to allow for a better comparison. From the first part, we see that the old walk has problems to reach the actual commanded default walking speed, which should be near $220\,mm/s$ to $250\,mm/s$ for the default walking, while the new walk goes close or even overshoots it a bit. For the fast walk, which should reach $300\,mm/s$, only the old walk achieves that goal with a good robot. There are two reasons, why robots can fail to reach the intended walking speed. On one hand, the robots unintentionally rotate while walking. Afterwards the robots need to intentionally rotate back, which wastes one walking step and the robots need to accelerate again to reach the maximum allowed forward speed. This happened for the old walk on the good robot with default walking speed and for the new walk on the good robot with fast walking speed. On the other hand, once the robot is tilted too much forward, it takes a few walking steps to get upright again, which also waste some time. This mostly occurred on the worn-out robot.

Stability-wise both walks had their issues. The old walk is more aggressive, as seen in Fig. 6.[1] This helped in the past to prevent falls, but when a robot

---

[1] A comparison between the old and the new walk when tilting backwards is shown here: https://youtu.be/-_wJXzCVCg0.

is destabilized multiple times within a short period of time, it is not sufficient enough. Compared to the new walk, which generates more smooth joint positions as a major improvement, the new one was able to prevent all falls, with the cost of not reaching the highest walking speed. Moreover, both walks struggle to balance the robots fast and as a result reduce the average walking speed for the obstacle part down to 30%.

9   Conclusion and Future Work

In this paper, we described our methods to deal with worn-out robots. We presented our approach for the 2022 competitions, where we calculate a quality measure to control the walking speed for different robots. We proposed two control approaches. On one hand, a joint speed control, which allows the leg joints to move in the desired direction, but with a controlled speed. On the other hand, a joint position compensation, to bring the measured joint positions closer to the requested ones. Both approaches use a neural network to predict more recent actual joint positions. The evaluation showed similar results in speed as the previous walk on average and a slight improvement in stability for the new walk. Moreover even though the higher walking speeds do not seem to be usable for the worn-out robots, reaching the default walking speed is already a huge improvement. The new approach also results in smoother joint commands, which has the potential to reduce the wear and tear of the gears over time. We will monitor this over the upcoming competitions. A major problem the evaluation showed for both walks is that the robots slow down unintentionally by experiencing rotations while walking. Those need to be corrected by intentionally rotating back with walk steps and result in an overall slower walk, even though the robots could walk faster. This will be further investigated in the future.

References

1. Ashar, J., et al.: rUNSWift team report 2019 (2019). https://github.com/UNSWComputing/rUNSWift-2019-release/blob/main/rUNSWift_Team_Report.pdf
2. Farchy, A., Barrett, S., MacAlpine, P., Stone, P.: Humanoid robots learning to walk faster: from the real world to simulation and back. In: Proceedings of the 2013 International Conference on Autonomous Agents and Multi-agent Systems, pp. 39–46 (2013)
3. Fiedler, J., Laue, T.: Neural network-based joint angle prediction for the NAO robot. In: RoboCup 2023: Robot World Cup XXVI. Lecture Notes in Artificial Intelligence, Springer (2023). to appear
4. Hengst, B.: rUNSWift Walk 2014 report. Technical report, School of Computer Science & Engineering University of New South Wales, Sydney 2052, Australia (2014). http://cgi.cse.unsw.edu.au/robocup/2014ChampionTeamPaperReports/20140930-Bernhard.Hengst-Walk2014Report.pdf

5. Laue, T., Spiess, K., Röfer, T.: SimRobot - a general physical robot simulator and its application in RoboCup. In: Bredenfeld, A., Jacoff, A., Noda, I., Takahashi, Y. (eds.) RoboCup 2005. LNAI, vol. 4020, pp. 173–183. Springer, Heidelberg (2006). https://doi.org/10.1007/11780519_16

6. Moos, A., Larisch, A.: Nao Devils team description paper for RoboCup 2023 Standard Platform League (2023). https://spl.robocup.org/wp-content/uploads/SPL2023_TDP_Nao_Devils.pdf

7. Reichenberg, P., Röfer, T.: Step adjustment for a robust humanoid walk. In: Alami, R., Biswas, J., Cakmak, M., Obst, O. (eds.) RoboCup 2021. LNAI, vol. 13132, pp. 28–39. Springer, Cham (2022). https://doi.org/10.1007/978-3-030-98682-7_3

8. Rodriguez, D., Behnke, S.: Deepwalk: omnidirectional bipedal gait by deep reinforcement learning. In: 2021 IEEE International Conference on Robotics and Automation (ICRA), pp. 3033–3039. IEEE (2021)

9. Röfer, T., et al.: B-Human team report and code release 2022 (2022). https://github.com/bhuman/BHumanCodeRelease/raw/coderelease2022/CodeRelease2022.pdf

10. Schwarz, I., Urbann, O., Larisch, A., Brämer, D.: Nao Devils team report 2019 (2019). https://raw.githubusercontent.com/NaoDevils/CodeRelease/CodeRelease2019/TeamReport2019.pdf

RL-X: A Deep Reinforcement Learning Library (Not Only) for RoboCup

Nico Bohlinger[(✉)] and Klaus Dorer

Hochschule Offenburg, Institute for Machine Learning and Analytics,
Offenburg, Germany
`nico.bohlinger@gmail.com` , `klaus.dorer@hs-offenburg.de`

Abstract. This paper presents the new Deep Reinforcement Learning
(DRL) library RL-X and its application to the RoboCup Soccer Simulation 3D League and classic DRL benchmarks. RL-X provides a flexible
and easy-to-extend codebase with self-contained single directory algorithms. Through the fast JAX-based implementations, RL-X can reach
up to 4.5× speedups compared to well-known frameworks like Stable-
Baselines3.

1 Introduction

Research in Reinforcement Learning (RL) continues to produce promising algo-
rithmic advances. Those new algorithms keep pushing the results on complex
environments and benchmarks. But to implement them, it is often not enough
to simply follow the instructions of the accompanying papers. Deep RL algorithms are notoriously brittle and their performance strongly depend on nuanced
implementation choices [1]. To tackle this problem big open-source frameworks,
like Stable-Baselines3 (SB3) [2], offer community-proven implementations with
robust hyperparameter choices. For RL practitioners it is key to have such sound
implementations but having the newest algorithms at their disposal is just as
necessary for them. Unfortunately the big frameworks, developed during the rise
of Deep RL algorithms like SAC [3] and PPO [4], became stale over time and
cannot keep up with the rapid development of new algorithms.

On the other spectrum, RL researchers need flexible frameworks to allow
for easy and fast prototyping. Convoluted directory and file structures, which
are used for code reuse, can harm the early development process of algorithms.
Moreover, deeply understanding an algorithm for the first time is easier with a
compact implementation, that is straightforward to overview and not entangled
with other algorithms.

What combines practitioners and researchers is the benefit of a better runtime for their algorithms. Most Machine Learning papers still use Tensorflow [5]
or plain PyTorch [6] as the underlying Deep Learning library. While they are
reliable and have big communities with continuing development behind them,
they are not necessarily the fastest options. Deep Learning libraries that build

C. Buche et al. (Eds.): RoboCup 2023, LNAI 14140, pp. 228–239, 2024.
https://doi.org/10.1007/978-3-031-55015-7_19

on JAX [7] can utilize features like Just-In-Time (JIT) compilation or vector-ization mappings to reach higher throughput on GPUs and TPUs. Furthermore, RL actually benefits the most from those features, because the training loop for RL algorithms is more involved than for other categories of Machine Learning.

To combat those challenges, we developed RL-X, a flexible and fast frame-work for Deep RL research and development. It is perfect to understand and pro-totype new algorithms, through compact single directory implementations. RL-X provides some of those implementations in PyTorch and TorchScript (PyTorch + JIT) but every algorithm has a JAX version available for maximum compu-tational performance. A generic interface between the algorithms and the envi-ronments, advanced logging, experiment tracking capabilities and a simple to use command line interface (CLI) to set hyperparameters are just some of the features that make RL-X a great tool for RL practitioners and researchers alike.

For the RoboCup community RL-X makes it easy to hook up any kind of new environment and test it with the latest algorithms or custom implementations. We test RL-X in the RoboCup Soccer Simulation 3D League but non-simulation leagues can benefit just as much through the high performance gains of RL-X with the typically used off-policy algorithms, like SAC, for such non-parallelized environments.

2   Related Work

Over the last years, many frameworks for DRL have been developed. Each of them focusing on either different kinds of algorithms (on-policy vs. off-policy, multi-agent vs. single-agent, online vs. offline, model-free vs model-based, etc.), different use cases (simulation vs. real world, robotics vs. games, etc.) or different implementation complexities (distributed and scalable vs. single machine and simple, etc.). All of the following listed frameworks are open-source and written in Python and use either Tensorflow, PyTorch or a JAX-based library as the underlying Deep Learning library.

Stable-Baselines3 is the improved and in PyTorch rewritten successor of Stable-Baselines [8], which in itself is a more stable fork of the OpenAI Baselines repository [9]. SB3 offers 13 classic online model-free RL algorithms, like PPO, SAC, DQN [10] etc. It is one of the most popular DRL frameworks for practition-ers because of its extensive documentation, test coverage and active community. Extending SB3 with new algorithms is possible but not as easy as with other frameworks, because of the modular directory structure inherited from OpenAI Baselines, that grew over time.

RLlib [11] is the RL component of the Ray framework, which is a distributed computing framework for Python. Therefore it focuses on scalable distributed training for production-ready applications. It provides PyTorch and Tensorflow implementations of a wide range of algorithms in all categories of RL. RLlib's codebase is big and complex, which can make it hard to understand and extend.

Acme [12] and Dopamine [13] are both Tensorflow and JAX-based frame-works from DeepMind and Google Brain respectively. Besides algorithm imple-mentations, Acme defines also more general functions that can act as building blocks for RL research, like different loss calculations. Dopamine on the other hand focuses fully on DQN-based algorithms.

CleanRL [14] is a PyTorch and JAX-based collection of single-file implementations of RL algorithms, that are easy to understand and build upon. It is a great resource for research and development but it needs to provide the same algorithm multiple times to support different environment types, e.g. PPO is implemented 12 times in small variations.

Lastly we want to highlight Ilya Kostrikov's JAXRL repository [15], which provides a small range of simple and high quality implementations of off-policy algorithms with JAX.

This work tries to combine the advantages of all the mentioned frameworks but focuses on the needs of RL researchers. The completely independent single directory implementations of RL-X remind of CleanRL's simplicity but are supported by generic interfaces for environments and algorithms, which is similar to the other more traditional modular frameworks. JAXRL's high quality implementations are used as a reference for the implementations of the SAC-based algorithms in RL-X. Whereas Acme is used as a reference for efficient JAX code and for its official MPO [16] implementation.

In regards to the Deep Learning frameworks, PyTorch is well established in the Machine Learning community and TorchScript allows for minor improvements by adding (limited) JIT compilation. JAX on the hand is a relatively new library, that can automatically differentiate and JIT compile Python/NumPy code, which then can be run on CPUs, GPUs and TPUs. On its own, JAX doesn't provide any high-level abstractions for Neural Networks, which is why Deep Learning frameworks were developed on top of it. The most popular ones are Flax [17], developed by Google Brain and Haiku [18], developed by DeepMind. Both frameworks are really similar in their API and only differ marginally in their design choices. For RL-X we chose Flax, because of its bigger community and the subsequently larger amount of examples online.

3   RL-X

The codebase of RL-X is divided into three main directories:

Algorithms: This directory contains the implementations of the algorithms listed in Table 1. Each algorithm version provides a `__init__.py` that registers the algorithm, a `default_config.py` that defines the hyperparameters, a `<algorithm_name>.py` that implements the algorithm and further helper files that contain utility code, e.g. neural network modules or replay buffers.

Environments: This directory contains the implementations of the environments listed in Table 2. Each environment version provides a `__init__.py` that registers the environment, a `default_config.py` that defines hyperparameters, a `create_env.py` that instantiates the environment(s) and a `wrappers.py` that provides properties and functions for the generic interface between algorithms and environments, e.g. the action and observation space types, handling of terminal observations etc. This interfaces makes it possible to freely mix and match registered algorithms and environments, as long as the algorithm supports the environment's action and observation space type.

Runner: This directory contains the runner class, which takes the chosen algorithm and environment, parses the hyperparameter configurations set through the CLI and starts the training or testing loop.

Table 1. Algorithms in RL-X

Algorithm	Deep Learning framework	Category	Reference
AQE	Flax	Off-policy	[19]
DroQ	Flax	Off-policy	[20]
ESPO	PyTorch, TorchScript, Flax	On-policy	[21]
MPO	Flax	Off-policy	[16]
PPO	PyTorch, TorchScript, Flax	On-policy	[4]
REDQ	Flax	Off-policy	[22]
SAC	PyTorch, TorchScript, Flax	Off-policy	[3]
TQC	Flax	Off-policy	[23]

Table 2. Environments in RL-X

Environment type	Providing framework	References
Atari	EnvPool	[24,25]
Classic control	EnvPool	[25,26]
DeepMind Control Suite	EnvPool	[25,27]
MuJoCo	Gym, EnvPool	[25,26,28]
Custom environments with socket communication		

Experiments are started from the `experiments` directory inside the root of the RL-X repository. The directory contains a `experiment.py` to quickly start experiments and instructions on how to use the CLI to set hyperparameters and how to structure multiple experiments with bash scripts. Tracking of experiments is done with Tensorboard and Weights & Biases integrations and all logs and models are stored in an automatically generated "project/experiment/run" directory structure. Classic console logging is also supported.

RL-X is made for easily extending the framework with new algorithms and environments by following the code structure described above. Even copying the algorithms out of RL-X in new projects is super simple through the self-contained single directory implementations. RL-X also provides a generic prototype for a custom environment interface with a simple socket communication layer. We used this interface to run experiments in the RoboCup Soccer Simulation 3D League and easily train our Java-based agents with RL-X. In comparison to

BahiaRT-GYM [29], which provides a 3D Soccer Simulation specific environment wrapper for high level trainer commands, our interface is fully generic and can be used by any league in RoboCup, as it leaves high level commands to the agent. We made RL-X fully open-source with the MIT license and it can be found on GitHub under the following link: https://github.com/nico-bohlinger/RL-X.

4   Results

To make sure that RL-X is a viable alternative to other frameworks, we compare its results to SB3. PPO and SAC are well known DRL algorithms and are therefore used for this comparison. Both algorithms are implemented with PyTorch, TorchScript and Flax in RL-X. All three versions are compared to the SB3 baseline, which uses PyTorch. As on-policy algorithms profit from running multiple environments in parallel, we use 24 environments in all PPO experiments and one environment in the SAC case. All used hyperparameters are the same as in the SB3 baseline and can be found in Table 3 in the appendix.

We use two different environments to test the algorithms. The first one is a custom RoboCup Soccer Simulation 3D running task. A Nao robot has to run as fast as possible towards a goal 30m away. An episodes stops after 8 s or when the robot falls over. In this time, it is not possible to reach the goal, but the agent gets continuous reward every timestep based on its current distance to the goal subtracted by the distance in the previous timestep. The action space is continuous and consists of 14 joints in the lower body of the robot. The observation space is made up of 120 values, which are mostly the joint angles and velocities and the goal position.

The second environment is the Gym MuJoCo Humanoid-v4 environment [26], which is a standard benchmark for DRL algorithms. Here the agent controls a humanoid robot with 17 joints and a observation space of 376 values. The agent gets reward based on its forward movement and not falling over and is penalized for too large joint actuations and too large contact forces. We use the EnvPool [25] implementation of the environment, as it is faster than the original one.

A short showcase of the two environments can be found under the following link: https://youtu.be/H4fw_cqBFDU

4.1   Reward Performance

The reward performance of the RL-X implementations for PPO and SAC should be indistinguishable from the SB3 baseline. There can be small differences due to different initialization schemes and random number generations in the underlying Deep Learning libraries. To compensate for those differences, we run each version of the two algorithms six times with different seeds and plot the average and standard deviation for the reward collected during training.

SB3 logs the reward in off-policy algorithms by default as a running average over the last 100 episodes. To ensure a fair comparison, we also log the reward in RL-X in the same way for the experiments with SAC.

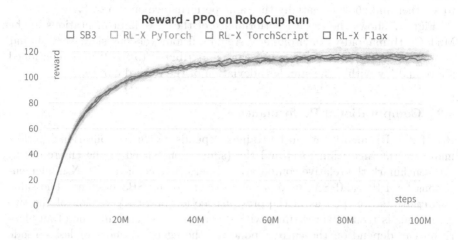

Fig. 1. Comparison of the reward performance in the RoboCup Run environment of the RL-X implementations for PPO in PyTorch, TorchScript and Flax to the SB3 baseline.

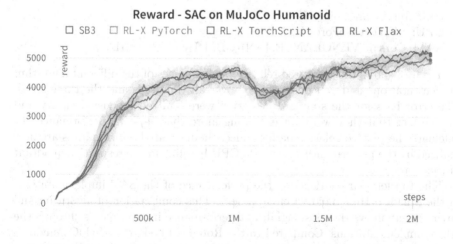

Fig. 2. Comparison of the reward performance in the MuJoCo Humanoid-v4 environment of the RL-X implementations for SAC in PyTorch, TorchScript and Flax to the SB3 baseline.

Figure 1 shows the reward performance of the PPO implementations in the RoboCup Run environment. As expected, all four reward curves are very similar to another and show essentially the same performance on the task.

Figure 2 shows the reward performance of the SAC implementations in the MuJoCo Humanoid-v4 environment. Again, all four versions show very similar performance. The minor differences can be attributed to the factors mentioned above and lay within the standard deviation of the reward curves.

4.2   Computational Performance

How fast a RL algorithm can be trained depends on the computational performance of the algorithm itself and the (simulation) speed of the environment. We benchmark the relative computational performance of the RL-X implementations for PPO and SAC and compare them to the SB3 baseline. The same environments are used as in the previous section and each version of the two algorithms is trained three times with different seeds. The runtime of an algorithm can depend on the current policy of the agent, as more or less episode resets can be triggered, various actions can consume various processing time and different parts of the environment can be different in their computational complexity. To limit the influence of those factors, the experiments only last for 500k steps with PPO and 50k steps with SAC to ensure that the agents policies don't diverge too much from each other.

Hardware components do naturally have a huge impact on the runtime. Therefore each experiment in this section is run on the same hardware to ensure a fair comparison. We used the following hardware setup:

- CPU: Intel Core i9-9900K
- GPU: NVIDIA GeForce RTX 2080 Ti
- RAM: Corsair VENGEANCE 4 × 16 GB, DDR4, 3200 MHz

Figure 3 shows the measured relative performances of the different algorithm implementations and versions averaged over all timesteps and the three seeds. The error bars for the standard deviation were omitted for visual clarity and for the fact that they were not exceeding more than +/- 1% performance. To calculate the plotted relative performance, the measured performances are normalized by the performance of the SB3 CPU baseline in the respective quadrant of the chart.

The top left bar chart shows the performance of the SAC implementations in the MuJoCo Humanoid-v4 environment. This combination of algorithm and environment shows the most significant performance improvements through the RL-X implementations. Compared to the RoboCup task, the MuJoCo environment is much less computationally demanding and resembles less of a computational bottleneck in the RL training loop. A step in the MuJoCo environment takes around 0.001 s on average, which is 25 times less than the average step time of 0.025 s in the RoboCup environment. This means that improvements in the computational performance of the algorithm are more noticeable. Off-policy algorithms like SAC compute their loss and update their parameters in every timestep by sampling the used batch from a replay buffer, whereas on-policy algorithms like PPO only do so after a full batch of newly collected trajectories is available. This optimization in every step is the reason why SAC undergoes a much bigger performance improvement than PPO. PPO's performance is more dependent on the runtime of the environment and on over how many parallel agents it can distribute the data collection.

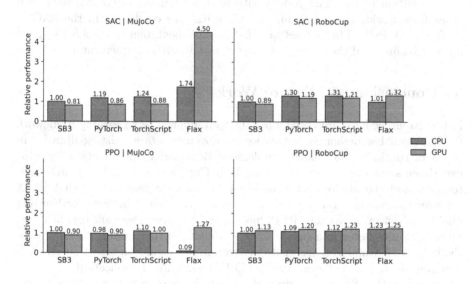

Fig. 3. Comparison of the relative computational performance of the RL-X implementations for PPO and SAC in PyTorch, TorchScript and Flax to the SB3 baseline.

In the ideal case of using a fast simulated environment (here MuJoCo) and an off-policy algorithm (here SAC), Flax can speed up the training by a factor of 4.5× with the help of a GPU compared to SB3's PyTorch implementation running on CPU. For the more infrequent updating PPO the speedup with Flax is not as drastic but still noticeable with a factor of 1.27 and 1.25 on the MuJoCo and RoboCup environments respectively. In the case of the slower RoboCup environment, RL-X's PyTorch, TorchScript and Flax implementations achieve all roughly the same performance and are around 1.2–1.3× faster than SB3. In all our experiments, the Flax GPU versions achieved the best computational performance, especially when the acting in the environment is not the bottleneck. The TorchScript versions offer a consist boost in performance over the pure PyTorch implementations, which is great as it barely requires additional code changes. Noticeable is that using the GPU with PyTorch and TorchScript had a negative impact on the performance, with the PPO + RoboCup setup being the exception. This is most likely due to the small batch sizes we used. In this regime the cost of copying the data to the GPU is higher than the performance gain from its fast processing capabilities. On the contrary, Flax handles this better, as its GPU version outperforms the CPU version in all our experiments. Unfortunately, the JIT compilation with JAX can suffer from high initial compilation times on the CPU. This is not the case for TorchScript's JIT. Additionally the poor performance of the Flax CPU version on the MuJoCo environment should be noted, but we have not yet found the reason for this. Finally we do not yet have results on the performance of JAX on TPUs and leave this for future work.

In addition to the main results with SB3, a small set of comparisons with other frameworks, namely RLlib and CleanRL, are conducted in the SAC + PyTorch + GPU + MuJoCo setup. RL-X's implementation shows a 5.1× speed up over RLlib's and the same performance as CleanRL's implementation.

5 Conclusion and Future Work

In this paper we have presented a new Deep Reinforcement Learning framework RL-X, which has demonstrated major improvements over existing libraries in terms of runtime performance, implementation clarity and extensibility. Our experiments conducted on a custom RoboCup Soccer Simulation 3D environment and the MuJoCo Humanoid-v4 environment have shown that RL-X achieves comparable training results to Stable-Baselines3 in terms of learning quality, as expected. Notably, RL-X has showcased impressive walltime efficiency, up to 4.5 times faster in a classic SAC + MuJoCo setup running on GPU with the help of JAX and JIT compilation. Overall, our results suggest that RL-X is a highly effective and efficient tool for DRL research and applications.

To ensure that RL-X stays up to date with the latest developments in RL, we plan to regularly add new algorithms and features to the library. Especially newer state-of-the-art algorithms like Muesli [30] and V-MPO [31], which completely lack open-source implementations, are on our roadmap. Additionally, we will soon add support for offline RL datasets and implementations of algorithms in the field of intrinsic motivation, as RL-X is already in full use in multiple research projects in those areas. A separate evaluation loop during training is the first feature extension we plan to add to RL-X.

While we provide the framework documentation and further literature on all algorithms in extensive readme files, we plan to further improve the documentation and add more examples and tutorials for our users. More Python type hints and a broad test coverage are also on our list.

To enable further performance improvements, we want to benchmark RL-X on TPUs, as JAX was developed with this hardware in mind. PyTorch 2.0 did also just release with a new JIT compile system, which might improve over TorchScript's JIT and would allow for a merge of both implementation versions.

Acknowledgement. Thanks to the magmaOffenburg team for providing the tools used in this paper.

Appendix

Table 3. Hyperparameter settings used in the experiments

Algorithm	Parameter	Value
PPO	clip_range	0.2
	critic_coef	0.5
	entropy_coef	0.0
	gae_lambda	0.95
	max_grad_norm	0.5
	minibatch_size	1536
	nr_epochs	10
	nr_steps	2048
	std_dev	0.3
	environment.nr_envs	24
SAC	batch_size	256
	buffer_size	1000000
	learning_starts	5000
	log_std_min	-20
	log_std_max	2
	target_entropy	"auto"
	tau	0.005
	environment.nr_envs	1
Both	anneal_learning_rate	False
	gamma	0.99
	learning_rate	0.0003
	nr_hidden_units	64

References

1. Andrychowicz, M., et al.: What matters for on-policy deep actor-critic methods? In: A Large-Scale Study International Conference on Learning Representations (2021)
2. Raffin, A., Hill, A., Gleave, A., Kanervisto, A., Ernestus, M., Dormann, N.: Stable-baselines3: reliable reinforcement learning implementations. J. Mach. Learn. Res. **22**, 268 (2021)
3. Haarnoja, T., Zhou, A., Abbeel, P., Levine, S.: Soft actor-critic: off-policy maximum entropy deep reinforcement learning with a stochastic actor. In: International Conference on Machine Learning, pp. 1861–1870 (2018)

4. Schulman, J., Wolski, F., Dhariwal, P., Radford, A., Klimov, O.: Proximal policy optimization algorithms arXiv preprint arXiv:1707.06347 (2017)
5. Abadi, M., et al.: Tensorflow: a system for large-scale machine learning. In: OSDI, vol. 16, pp. 265–283 (2016)
6. Paszke, A., et al.: Pytorch: an imperative style, high-performance deep learning library. In: Advances in Neural Information Processing Systems, vol. 32 (2019)
7. Bradbury, J., et al.: JAX: composable transformations of Python+NumPy programs (2018). http://github.com/google/jax. Version 0.4.9
8. Hill, A., et al.: Stable Baselines (2018). https://github.com/hill-a/stable-baselines
9. Dhariwal, P., et al.: OpenAI Baselines (2017). https://github.com/openai/baselines
10. Mnih, V., et al.: Human-level control through deep reinforcement learning. Nature **518**, 529–533 (2015)
11. Liang, E., et al.: RLlib: abstractions for distributed reinforcement learning. In: International Conference on Machine Learning, pp. 3053–3062 (2018)
12. Hoffman, M.W., et al.: Acme: a research framework for distributed reinforcement learning arXiv preprint arXiv:2006.00979 (2020)
13. Castro, P.S., Moitra, S., Gelada, C., Kumar, S., Bellemare, M.G.: Dopamine: a research framework for deep reinforcement learning arXiv preprint arXiv:1812.06110 (2018)
14. Huang, S., et al.: CleanRL: high-quality single-file implementations of deep reinforcement learning algorithms. J. Mach. Learn. Res. **23**, 12585–12602 (2022)
15. Kostrikov, I.: JAXRL: implementations of reinforcement learning algorithms in JAX (2021). https://github.com/ikostrikov/jaxrl
16. Abdolmaleki, A., Springenberg, J.T., Tassa, Y., Munos, R., Heess, N., Riedmiller, M.: Maximum a posteriori policy optimisation. In: International Conference on Learning Representations (2018)
17. Heek, J., et al: Flax: a neural network library and ecosystem for JAX (2023). http://github.com/google/flax. Version 0.6.8
18. Hennigan, T., Cai, T., Norman, T., Babuschkin, I.: Haiku: sonnet for JAX (2020). http://github.com/deepmind/dm-haiku. Version 0.0.9
19. Wu, Y., Chen, X., Wang, C., Zhang, Y., Ross, K.W.: Aggressive Q-Learning with Ensembles: Achieving Both High Sample Efficiency and High Asymptotic Performance Deep Reinforcement Learning Workshop NeurIPS (2022)
20. Hiraoka, T., Imagawa, T., Hashimoto, T., Onishi, T., Tsuruoka, Y.: Dropout Q-functions for doubly efficient reinforcement learning. In: International Conference on Learning Representations (2021)
21. Sun, M., et al.: You may not need ratio clipping in PPO arXiv preprint arXiv:2202.00079 (2022)
22. Chen, X., Wang, C., Zhou, Z., Ross, K.: Randomized ensembled double q-learning. In: Learning fast Without a Model International Conference on Learning Representations (2021)
23. Kuznetsov, A., Shvechikov, P., Grishin ,A., Vetrov, D., Hofmann, K., Whiteson S.: Controlling overestimation bias with truncated mixture of continuous distributional quantile critics. In: International Conference on Machine Learning, pp. 5556–5566 (2020)
24. Bellemare, M.G., Naddaf, Y., Veness, J., Bowling, M.: The arcade learning environment: an evaluation platform for general agents. J. Artif. Intell. Res. **47**, 253–279 (2013)

25. Weng, J., et al.: Envpool: a highly parallel reinforcement learning environment execution engine. In: Thirty-Sixth Conference on Neural Information Processing Systems Datasets and Benchmarks Track (2022)
26. Brockman, G., et al.: Openai gym arXiv preprint arXiv:1606.01540 (2016)
27. Tassa, Y., et al.: Deepmind control suite arXiv preprint arXiv:1801.00690 (2018)
28. Todorov, E., Erez, T., Tassa, Y.: Mujoco: a physics engine for model-based control IEEE/RSJ International Conference on Intelligent Robots and Systems, pp. 5026–5033 (2012)
29. Simoes, M., Mascarenhas, G., Fonseca, R., dos Santos, V., Mascarhenas, F., Nogueira, T.: BahiaRT Setplays Collecting Toolkit and BahiaRT Gym Software Impacts, vol 14. Elsevier (2022)
30. Hessel, M., et al.: Muesli: combining improvements in policy optimization. In: International Conference on Machine Learning, pp. 4214–4226 (2021)
31. Song, H.F., et al.: V-mpo: on-policy maximum a posteriori policy optimization for discrete and continuous control. In: International Conference on Learning Representations (2019)

Orienting a Humanoid Robot in a Soccer Field Based on the Background

Eric Guerra Ribeiro$^{(\boxtimes)}$ (ID) and Marcos R. O. A. Máximo (ID)

Autonomous Computational Systems Lab (LAB-SCA), Computer Science Division,
Aeronautics Institute of Technology, Praça Marechal Eduardo Gomes 50, Vila das
Acácias, 12228-900 São José dos Campos, SP, Brazil
{guerra,mmaximo}@ita.br

Abstract. RoboCup Humanoid League Kid Size is an international soccer competition of humanoid robots. As the field is symmetric, you can't know which side you are on based on the field features alone. This work contributes by proposing an algorithm to estimate the robot's orientation based on the background. To do it, we use a feature detector to match the features between the image and reference images. Then, as we know the reference images' orientation, we can calculate the current orientation based on their difference. We searched for parameters to optimize the algorithm. Using the parameters found, we can run the algorithm on 101 ms on average, while having a mean absolute error of 6.9°.

Keywords: orientation · feature detector · robot soccer

1 Introduction

RoboCup is an international robotics competition created to foster research in artificial intelligence and robotics [10]. It created the ambitious goal to have a team of autonomous humanoid robots win against the World Cup Champions by 2050. Many leagues with different rules and constraints focus on various aspects, which need to be developed to conclude the competition's objective. ITAndroids, Aeronautics Institute of Technology (ITA)'s robotics team, participates in the Humanoid League Kid Size, in which humanoid robots play soccer. The robot must be able to estimate its position to play well. We do this by using the camera's vision to observe the field features (goal posts, field lines, etc.) [19] and to use this information in a particle filter (Monte Carlo Localization) [5,15].

However, as the field is symmetric, there is an ambiguity problem: the robot cannot determine the side of the field that it is on based on features alone. On the particle filter's initialization, the robot knows which side it starts on. However,

Supported by ITAndroids and its sponsors: Altium, SIATT, Intel, ITAEx, Mathworks, Metinjo, Micropress, Neofield, Polimold, Rapid, Solidworks, STMicroelectronics, WildLife, e Virtual Pyxis. Marcos Maximo is partially funded by CNPq - National Research Council of Brazil through the grant 307525/2022-8.

C. Buche et al. (Eds.): RoboCup 2023, LNAI 14140, pp. 240–251, 2024.
https://doi.org/10.1007/978-3-031-55015-7_20

if the localization is hampered, *e.g.*, the robot falling near the field center, it is impossible to determine the side of the field of the robot only with this method. This may cause the robot to score own goals by thinking it is on the wrong side of the field. Other teams calculate the orientation using visual odometry [7] or an open loop approach with the robot's inertial sensors [13]. Nevertheless, these approaches are subject to drift in long soccer matches. The background colors have also been used [1], instead of the features, which may not work on venues with few colors.

The contribution of this work is to solve this ambiguity problem by using the background of the camera images. Soccer matches happen in venues that are not symmetric. Therefore, by knowing how the background looks from different reference angles, you can infer the orientation, *i.e.*, the angle at which the camera is pointed, using the background. This approach is drift-free, as it only depends on the current position. Moreover, during a competition, there is a limited number of fields, whose background does not change significantly after the venue has been built. Hence, this method is practical to use in competitions.

If it is fast, precise, and reliable enough, this technique could be used to yield another observation to the particle filter, improving localization. Otherwise, it could still be used to solve the ambiguity problem.

We used the ORB feature detector [18] to automatically detect the features in the reference images. That way, to estimate the robot's orientation at a given position, we compare the features in the reference images to the image that it sees. We use a FLANN feature matcher [14] to compare the features and use OpenCV's [3] recover pose function to estimate the robot's orientation.

This paper is organized as follows. Section 2 provides theoretical background. Section 3 describes the methodology used to collect the dataset and to tune the algorithm's parameters. In Sect. 4, results for calculating the orientation are shown. Finally, Sect. 5 concludes and shares our ideas for future work.

2   Theoretical Background

This section explains the algorithms used by the feature detector and matcher. It also presents how structure-from-motion techniques can be used to estimate the robot's orientation in the field.

2.1   Feature Detector

We used the ORB (Orientated FAST and Rotated BRIEF) feature detector [18]. It combines FAST's (Features from Accelerated Segment Test) [17] key points with the BRIEF (Binary robust independent elementary feature) [4] descriptor to compare different key points, and it optimizes the algorithms' performance. FAST is first used to find the N best key points, according to the Harris corner filter [9], where N is the desired number of key points. However, FAST is modified to become rotation and scale invariant. The image is scaled a set number of times using a scale factor, creating a pyramid scale, to make ORB more scale invariant [18]. To assure rotation invariance, we use the a canonical rotation for both Orientated FAST and Rotated BRIEF [18].

2.2 Feature Matcher

We used the FLANN (Fast Library for Approximate Nearest Neighbors) matcher [14] to find the correspondence between features. It finds the two nearest neighbors to a feature using the Hamming distance, *i.e.*, the number of different entries between the binary vectors. To accept the matching, the ratio of the distances has to be less than a threshold, to avoid ambiguous features.

2.3 Intrinsic Matrix

The intrinsic matrix converts points from the camera coordinate system to the image pixels coordinate system. It depends on f_x and f_y, which are the focal lengths of the camera in the x and y axes, respectively, and on c_x and c_y, which are the center of the sensor in the x and y axes, respectively. The intrinsic matrix is described by

$$K = \begin{bmatrix} f_x & 0 & c_x \\ 0 & f_y & c_y \\ 0 & 0 & 1 \end{bmatrix}. \tag{1}$$

These constants can be measured or estimated by the proprieties of the image and the camera, assuming ideal conditions. As long as the sensor is perfectly centered on the optical axis of the camera, c_x, and c_y are given by

$$c_x = \frac{W}{2}, \quad c_y = \frac{H}{2}, \tag{2}$$

respectively, where H and W are the height and width of the image. If the object is far away, f_x and f_y can be estimated by

$$f_x = \frac{c_x}{\tan\left(\frac{FoV}{2}\right)}, \quad f_y = \frac{c_y}{\tan\left(\frac{FoV}{2}\right)}, \tag{3}$$

respectively, where FoV is the field of view.

2.4 Recover Pose

Recover pose, an OpenCV method, solves the five-point relative pose problem, which consists of the possible solutions for relative camera motion between two calibrated views – views are not distorted and whose camera's intrinsic matrix is known – given five corresponding points [16]. For reliable performance, more than five points are used, and for that, RANSAC (Random Sample Consensus) [6] may be used.

RANSAC will choose five random points and find the relative pose given by the solution of the five-point relative pose problem. Then, it checks if this solution correctly predicts where the other points would be given that relative pose, counting the inliers, *i.e.*, whether the prediction is within a threshold or not (outliers). It does this for many iterations to find the answer that predicts the most points. The amount of iterations depends on the chosen probability to find the right solution.

3   Methodology

This section describes the methodology used in this work, including the datasets used and how the experiments were conducted.

3.1   Camera Properties

We used a camera with a field of view of 58°, capturing an image of 640 × 480 pixels. We assumed the ideal conditions to be able to use all the equations in Sect. 2.3. Using (2) and (3), respectively, we estimate that $c_x = 320$ px, $c_y = 240$ px, $f_x = 577.29$ px, and $f_y = 432.97$ px. Then, by (1), the intrinsic matrix in this conditions is given by

$$K = \begin{bmatrix} 577.29 & 0 & 320 \\ 0 & 432.97 & 240 \\ 0 & 0 & 1 \end{bmatrix}. \tag{4}$$

3.2   Algorithm's Parameters

Section 2 refers to the many parameters used by the algorithms. In particular, the ORB feature detector uses the number of key points, the pyramid scale factor, and the BRIEF patch size. The FLANN matcher uses the distance ratio threshold, and it also uses the number of checks. Finally, the recover pose function uses the RANSAC's threshold and probability of success. There are default values for each of these parameters, in their OpenCV implementation. However, we looked for parameters with better performance in our setup, i.e., camera and robot.

Many of the parameters – the number of key features, number of checks, and RANSAC probability – increase both accuracy and processing time when they are incremented. So there is a trade-off between speed and accuracy. Other parameters – patch size and RANSAC threshold – have an optimal value with the most accuracy, while not affecting the speed. If the scale factor is close to 1, the algorithm would not be reliable for different scales, or more pyramid levels would be needed, requiring more time. On the other hand, values close to 2 can degrade the feature matching scores, as the scale change too much between each level. As the set of parameters affect the results of the algorithm in a nonlinear fashion, searching for the optimal parameters is not straightforward.

Each iteration takes around five minutes, so we decided to use a random search for the best parameters due to the high computational cost, with 500 iterations in total. This is a common approach to tune hyper-parameters in Deep Learning due to the cost [2]. We will refer this process of looking for the best parameters as training. We defined a minimum and maximum value for each of these parameters, besides the distance ratio threshold which was set to 0.7, as default. Then, for each iteration, we chose a random uniform value for the parameters between its minimum and maximum values and calculated the cost according to

$$ J = \begin{cases} \bar{e} + \sigma_e & \text{if } \bar{t} \leq 100\,\text{ms} \\ \bar{e} + \sigma_e + \bar{t} + \sigma_t & \text{if } \bar{t} > 100\,\text{ms} \end{cases}, \tag{5} $$

where $\bar{e}$ is the mean error, σ_e is the error standard deviation, $\bar{t}$ is the mean iteration time, and σ_t is the time standard deviation. This cost function was chosen, because we allotted around 100 ms to run the algorithm. It does not need to be run at the same frequency as the decision making algorithms, so it can be run only when needed to clear ambiguities in the localization.

Table 1 gives the minimum, maximum, and default values for each parameter. The processing times were measured using an Intel NUC i5 D54250WYK – the computer embedded in the Chape humanoid robot, used by ITAndroids [11].

Table 1. Minimum, maximum, and default values for each parameter.

Parameter	Minimum	Maximum	Default
Number of Key points	100	5000	500
Scale Factor	1.01	2	1.2
Patch Size	10	50	31
Number of Checks	1	100	50
RANSAC Probability	0.95	0.9999	0.999
RANSAC Threshold	1	10	1

3.3   Datasets

All the datasets consist of photos from the same robot's perspective on different positions of the field, and with eight different backgrounds, seven from the Webots simulator [12], and one from the robot soccer field at ITA. For each position and in each background, 24 pictures were taken: different rotations offset by 15° from the previous, starting from the 0° reference.

The images were separated into three datasets: the simulation training dataset, the simulation testing dataset, and the real field testing dataset. All datasets included the reference images, which are the photos in the center of the field. During the experiment, we can choose how many reference images to use. Figure 1 shows the different field positions from which photos were taken, in the simulated and real fields. The reference-labeled position images were also used in training and testing the algorithm.

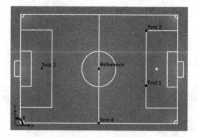

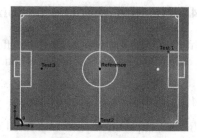

(a) Positions in the Webots field from which pictures were taken and a label for each positions.

(b) Positions in the real field from which pictures were taken and a label for each positions.

Fig. 1. Soccer field diagrams for the simulation and real fields. Shows the positions from where photos were taken. These photos were used for training and evaluation.

Simulation Dataset. We used the Webots simulator, which can have different backgrounds for the field. The dataset contains pictures from all the backgrounds available by default on the RoboCup soccer field. Figure 3 shows an example image. We separated the images into training and testing data, to better evaluate the accuracy of the algorithm. For each position, 12 random pictures were assigned to the testing dataset and the remaining 12 pictures were assigned to the training dataset. Figure 1a shows the positions from which the pictures were taken. Webots allows translating the simulated robot to the desired positions and to rotate in increments of 15°, making the placement of the robot precise.

Real Field Dataset. We also took pictures from the robot soccer field at ITA. However, this environment is unfavorable for the algorithm as the field is a room surrounded by white walls on four sides. So in some pictures, no distinguishable features may be seen. Figure 5 shows an example image. For this reason, this dataset was only used to evaluate the algorithm's performance, not to train it. To measure the rotations, 15°–75°, 30°–60°, and 45°–45° set squares were used with the field lines as reference. However, this method is not very precise.

3.4 Calculating the Orientation

First, we choose the reference images whose angles are known. Then, we use the feature detector at the reference images and save their detected features. At last, we extract the features of another image, compare them with the references, and find the best reference as the one with the most valid features matches. Using the best reference, we can apply OpenCV's recover pose with the reference and the image to find the rotation matrix between them. From the rotation matrix, we find the yaw offset and add the reference angle to it to find the orientation. We also compared this approach with using the angle of the best reference.

4 Results and Discussions

In this section, we analyze the effects of the algorithm's parameters. We also compare the results of the methods of calculating the orientation.

4.1 Number of References

In this experiment, we evaluated the performance of the algorithms using a different number of reference images. As we took 24 equally spaced reference images, we can use any divisor of 24 as the actual number of reference images. So we can have 24 reference images (spaced 15° from each other), 12 (spaced 30°), 8 (spaced 45°), 6 (spaced 60°), 3 (spaced 120°), 4 (spaced 90°), 2 (spaced 180°), or 1 reference image (spaced 360° from itself). We used the default parameters to explore the optimal number of reference images.

As the field of view is around 58°, if we use less than 8 reference images, there will be parts of the background not visible from any of the reference images. So the error should decrease with the increase of the number of images, as more background features can be seen, but with diminishing gains past 8 reference images. Moreover, as the algorithm checks the number of features matches between the image and all the used reference images, the processing time is expected to be $\mathcal{O}(N_{ref})$, where N_{ref} is the number of reference images.

Figure 2 shows the results of this experiment. As we predicted, the error decreases with more reference images, while the processing time increases. The relation between processing times and the number of references is affine as can be seen in Fig. 2a. The r^2 of the linear regression on the recover pose case is 0.9996, while for the best reference case, it is even higher at 0.9999, so it is an excellent fit. From Fig. 2b, we can see that error decreases sharply at first, when the number of reference images is lesser than 8. However, increasing further the number of reference images reduces the error with diminishing returns, as no new background features become visible while taking as much as twice as long.

With that in mind, we found that the optimal number of reference images is 8 due to striking the best balance of accuracy and processing time. From Fig. 2a, we can notice that the processing time for the recover pose and best reference points are offset by an approximately constant amount. Using the linear fit, we have that the lines are almost parallel, with a difference of 0.15° between them, and that the offset value is approximately 8.4 ms. The angular coefficient of the fits is approximately 2.2 ms, which means it takes around that time to see if the image matches with each reference. From Fig. 2b, we can also notice that, in general, the recover pose method is more accurate than just using the best reference. The only exception is when using all 24 reference images. This probably happens, because the best reference method has a bias towards angles multiples of 15° and all the test angles have this propriety. Although the error standard deviation is significant, it might be mitigated by incorporating it into a filter.

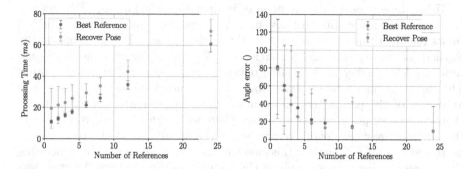

(a) The processing times for different number of reference images.

(b) The errors for a different number of
reference images.

Fig. 2. Processing time and error for a different number of reference images. The blue dots refer to only using the best reference as the angle. The orange dots refer to using the recover pose function based on the best reference. The bars represent one standard deviation. (Color figure online)

4.2   Random Search

In this experiment, we applied the method described in Sect. 3.2 to find better parameters. We analyzed the results of the algorithm with those parameters in different situations. The best parameters we found were 1230 as the number of key points, 1.885 as the scale factor, 44 as the patch size, 18 as the number of checks, 0.983 as the RANSAC probability, and 7 as the RANSAC threshold. A threshold close to the maximum indicates that the recover pose, in this case, is not very precise, as to consider the inliers the threshold is fairly high. This may also indicate that there are not many false positives that would be considered valid with a high threshold, which could be due to the simulation environment being well behaved. The other parameters involve a speed-accuracy trade-off and their effects are intertwined.

Fig. 3. The orange and blue points are the features detected and matched in the reference image and test image, respectively. Green lines connecting features mean inliers, while red lines mean outliers. The error in this case was 0.4° (Color figure online).

Using these parameters, the processing time was of 96±30 ms, with an error of mean 4.5°, and of standard deviation 15.4° on the training dataset. Table 2 shows the algorithm's performance on the testing dataset. It also compares the methods of recover pose and best reference. We can notice that the processing time was 5.2% higher in the testing dataset, compared to the training dataset. The difference in the mean error was 53.3%, which indicates that there was an overfit of the parameters. Once more, the best reference method is faster than the recover pose but less accurate. There were significant improvements in the accuracy over the default parameters – the mean error in the recover pose decreased by 47.7%. However, this came at the cost of an increase in processing time. Figure 3 shows an example of the feature matching, where the error was only 0.4°.

Table 2. The processing time, the mean, and the standard deviation of the error for the testing dataset using the parameters found and the default ones.

Method	Time (ms)	Mean Error (°)	Std Error (°)
Recover Pose (Default)	33.9 ± 5.4	13.2	31.5
Best Reference (Default)	26.0 ± 2.2	18.4	25.1
Recover Pose (Random Search)	101 ± 31	6.9	23.8
Best Reference (Random Search)	88 ± 26	15.1	16.7

We also analyzed the distribution of the angle errors to better understand the algorithm's capabilities. Figure 4 shows histograms with the angle errors using the methods recover pose and best reference with the found parameters. We can see from these histograms that the error is frequently low, but in some cases, it can be high enough to not solve correctly the ambiguity problem. Figure 4b shows that in over 88% of cases, the errors are smaller than 5°. Moreover, in less than 5% of the cases, the error is greater than 45°. Figure 4a also shows that using the best reference method, in less than 4% of the cases, the error is greater than 45°.

4.3   Real Soccer Field

As the available field is surrounded by white walls, there was a lack of features to detect. In six cases, which were looking at a close wall, not enough features were detected for the algorithm to work at all. On one side of the field, there were objects that could be used as features. Figure 5 shows an example of the feature matching. Notice that the amount of features is lower than in Fig. 3. Moreover, there still an outlier counted as an inlier, indicating that the threshold might be too large for realistic scenarios. Nevertheless, the error was low at 4.3°. Figure 6 shows that even so, the most frequent angle error is less than 5°, corresponding to 25% of the cases. Due to the lack of features, the processing time was much shorter: 11±11 ms. The mean and standard deviation errors were larger at 56° and 53°, respectively, due to the difficulties in this case.

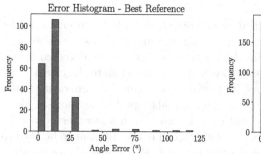
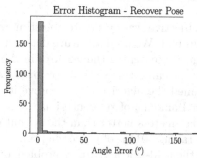

(a) Histogram of the error of the algorithm using the testing dataset, with the best reference method and the found parameters.

(b) Histogram of the error of the algorithm using the testing dataset, with the recover pose method and the found parameters.

Fig. 4. Histograms of the processing times and errors of the algorithm using the testing dataset, with both methods (best reference and recover pose) and the found parameters. Each bin represents a range of 5°.

Fig. 5. The orange and blue points are the features detected and matched in the reference image and test image, respectively. Green lines connecting features mean inliers, while red lines mean outliers. The error in this case was 4.3° (Color figure online).

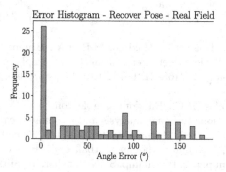

Fig. 6. Histogram of the error of the algorithm using the real dataset, the recover pose method and the found parameters. Each bin represents a range of 5°.

5   Conclusion

Our objective was to create to estimate the orientation of the robot using the background. We used a feature detector to reference images whose orientation is known. By matching the features in the reference images to the detected in one image, we can estimate the rotation between them and calculate the orientation. We tuned the algorithm to improve its performance. For the camera used, the optimal amount of reference images is eight. We also used a random search to find parameters better than the default ones. It resulted in a mean error of $6.9°$, while taking 101 ms of processing time, on average. This is sufficient to be used to solve the field-side ambiguity problem on most cases. We applied the parameters found using a simulator dataset to real images with mixed results.

This work can be extended by improving the method of searching parameters, using the algorithm in the localization estimated by the particle filter, and by testing in realistic situations. CMA-ES [8] can be used to find even better parameters. A new dataset containing images from competitions could be created to better validate the work's proposed algorithm in real-life situations, including changes in the background due to spectators or other players obstructing it, and changes in the lighting. Using images from another camera, with different aspect ratio or resolution, is another possibility to extend this study.

Code Availability. The source code is available at: https://gitlab.com/itandroids/open-projects/orientation-in-field.

References

1. Bader, M., Prankl, J., Vincze, M.: Visual room-awareness for humanoid robot self-localization (2013)
2. Bergstra, J., Bengio, Y.: Random search for hyper-parameter optimization. J. Mach. Learn. Res. **13**(null), 281–305 (2012)
3. Bradski, G.: The OpenCV Library. Dr. Dobb's Journal of Software Tools (2000)
4. Calonder, M., Lepetit, V., et al.: Brief: binary robust independent elementary features. In: Daniilidis, K., Maragos, P., Paragios, N. (eds.) ECCV 2010. LNCS, vol. 6314, pp. 778–792. Springer, Heidelberg (2010). https://doi.org/10.1007/978-3-642-15561-1_56
5. Fernandes, G.C.G., Dias, S.S., Maximo, M.R.O.A., Bruno, M.G.S.: Cooperative localization for multiple soccer agents using factor graphs and sequential monte Carlo. IEEE Access **8**, 213168–213184 (2020). https://doi.org/10.1109/ACCESS.2020.3040602
6. Fischler, M.A., Bolles, R.C.: Random sample consensus: a paradigm for model fitting with applications to image analysis and automated cartography. Commun. ACM **24**(6), 381–395 (1981). https://doi.org/10.1145/358669.358692
7. Gondry, L., Hofer, L., et al.: Rhoban football club: Robocup humanoid kidsize 2019 champion team paper. In: Chalup, S., Niemueller, T., Suthakorn, J., Williams, M.A. (eds.) RoboCup 2019. LNCS, vol. 11531, pp. 491–503. Springer, Cham (2019). https://doi.org/10.1007/978-3-030-35699-6_40
8. Hansen, N.: The CMA evolution strategy: a tutorial. ArXiv abs/1604.00772 (2016)

9. Harris, C.G., Stephens, M.J.: A combined corner and edge detector. In: Alvey Vision Conference (1988)
10. Kitano, H., Asada, M., Kuniyoshi, Y., Noda, I., Osawa, E., Matsubara, H.: Robocup: a challenge problem for AI. AI Mag. **18**(1), 73 (1997). https://doi.org/10.1609/aimag.v18i1.1276, https://ojs.aaai.org/aimagazine/index.php/aimagazine/article/view/1276
11. Maximo, M.R.O.A., Ribeiro, C.H.C., Afonso, R.J.M.: Real-time walking step timing adaptation by restricting duration decision for the first footstep. Adv. Robot. **34**(21–22), 1420–1441 (2020). https://doi.org/10.1080/01691864.2020.1821769
12. Michel, O.: Webots: professional mobile robot simulation. J. Adv. Robot. Syst. **1**(1), 39–42 (2004). http://www.ars-journal.com/International-Journal-of-Advanced-Robotic-Systems/Volume-1/39-42.pdf
13. Muhtad, Ulya, A.R.A., Wimansyah, M.R.Z.: Ichiro its team - extended abstract humanoid kid-size league, robocup 2023 france (2023)
14. Muja, M., Lowe, D.: Fast approximate nearest neighbors with automatic algorithm configuration, vol. 1, pp. 331–340 (2009)
15. Muzio, A., Aguiar, L., Maximo, M., Pinto, S.: Monte Carlo localization with field lines observations for simulated humanoid robotic soccer. In: Latin American Robotics Symposium. In: Proceedings of the the 2016 Latin American Robotics Symposium (LARS) (2016)
16. Nister, D.: An efficient solution to the five-point relative pose problem. IEEE Trans. Pattern Anal. Mach. Intell. **26**(6), 756–770 (2004). https://doi.org/10.1109/TPAMI.2004.17
17. Rosten, E., Drummond, T.: Machine learning for high-speed corner detection. In: Leonardis, A., Bischof, H., Pinz, A. (eds.) ECCV 2006. LNCS, pp. 430–443. Springer, Berlin Heidelberg, Berlin, Heidelberg (2006)
18. Rublee, E., Rabaud, V., Konolige, K., Bradski, G.: ORB: an efficient alternative to sift or surf. In: 2011 International Conference on Computer Vision, pp. 2564–2571 (2011). https://doi.org/10.1109/ICCV.2011.6126544
19. Steuernagel, L., Maximo, M.R.O.A., Pereira, L.A., Sanches, C.A.A.: Convolutional neural network with inception-like module for ball and goalpost detection in a small humanoid soccer robot. In: 2020 Latin American Robotics Symposium (LARS), 2020 Brazilian Symposium on Robotics (SBR) and 2020 Workshop on Robotics in Education (WRE), pp. 1–6 (2020). https://doi.org/10.1109/LARS/SBR/WRE51543.2020.9307038

Autonomous Waiter Robot System for Recognizing Customers, Taking Orders, and Serving Food

Yuga Yano[1]([✉]), Kosei Isomoto[1], Tomohiro Ono[2], and Hakaru Tamukoh[1,3]

[1] Graduate School of Life Science and Systems Engineering, Kyushu Institute of Technology, 2-4 Hibikino, Wakamatsu-ku, Kitakyushu-shi 808-0196, Japan
yano.yuuga158@mail.kyutech.jp
[2] Toyota Motor Corporation, 543 Kirigabora, Nishihirose-cho, Toyota-shi 470-0309, Japan
[3] Research Center for Neuromorphic AI Hardware, Kyushu Institute of Technology, 2-4 Hibikino, Wakamatsu-ku, Kitakyushu-shi 808-0196, Japan

Abstract. Existing food delivery robots are not fully autonomous and require human guidance for their movements. Although they can perform simple human-robot interaction (HRI) tasks, they cannot find waving customers or take orders. In this paper, we propose an autonomous robot system that performs waiter tasks, such as finding customers, taking orders, and serving food. The proposed method uses a human support robot with human and action recognition to identify waving customers. It estimates the chair position of the customer using semantic mapping. The robot moves toward the customer and takes orders through speech recognition. Finally, the robot takes the order to the kitchen and delivers it to the customer. The proposed method was implemented in an actual restaurant, and it received high customer evaluation. The experimental results are available at https://youtu.be/KOu9h3tjzDI.

Keywords: Human-robot interaction · Food delivery robot · Restaurant · RoboCup@Home

1 Introduction

Food delivery robots are being widely employed in restaurants owing to labor shortages and the impact of COVID-19. Typical food delivery robots can reduce the workload of employees in a restaurant and improve restaurant sales by simultaneously serving multiple dishes using the trays attached onto them. Therefore, the demand for food delivery robots is expected to grow [4]. However, most food delivery robots are not fully autonomous, and restaurant employees are required to guide their movements [5,6,16]. Furthermore, they can perform simple Human-Robot Interaction (HRI) tasks but cannot find waving customers or take orders.

To address this issue, RoboCup@Home conducts a benchmark test called Restaurant, which can evaluate the performance of waiter tasks using Toyota Human Support Robot(HSR) [17] as shown in Fig. 1. In this task, a robot

C. Buche et al. (Eds.): RoboCup 2023, LNAI 14140, pp. 252–261, 2024.
https://doi.org/10.1007/978-3-031-55015-7_21

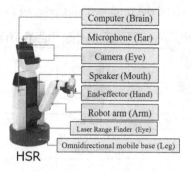

Fig. 1. Human support robot (HSR); main sensors and actuators with the corresponding metaphorical comparison with a human body are provided.

autonomously finds customers, takes orders, and serves items in a restaurant. This task is challenging because it requires complex HRI techniques, including human recognition, action recognition, and speech recognition. Several teams have partially accomplished this task in recent years, but there has yet to be a social implementation of these technologies. Therefore, we implemented our proposed method for accomplishing this task in an actual restaurant and evaluated the performance of a waiter robot targeting ordinary customers. Our main contributions are as follows.

- Realization of a waiter robot that achieves complex HRI, which is not possible with conventional catering robots.
- Social implementation and evaluation of waiter robots for ordinary customers.

2   Related Work

Several companies are actively developing food delivery robots. Reeman [10], which develops domestic service robots, has recently developed several food delivery robots [9]. The robots' onboard touch screens allow waiters to instruct the delivery location to the robot. However, these robots cannot find waving customers and take orders because they are not capable of human or voice recognition. Pudo Robotics [12] has developed many food delivery robots for restaurants and hotels, including BellaBot [11] and HolaBot [13]. BellaBot has been used by more than 2,000 international companies and can serve food and perform simple HRI tasks based on voice and action recognition, whereas HolaBot can be operated from a remote seat using a smartphone.

Table 1 presents a performance comparison of existing robots and the proposed robot system. The proposed robot can find waving customers and take orders using speech recognition. However, its payload is smaller than that of other robots.

Table 1. Comparison of the proposed and existing food delivery robots.

	REEMAN's robot[9]	HolaBot[13]	BelaBot[11]	HSR with our system
Appearance				
Payload	~10 kg	~60 kg	~40 kg	~1 kg
Find waving customers		need another devices	✓	✓
Taking orders				✓

3   Proposed Method

HSR with our proposed method can operate a sequence of waiter tasks such as finding waving customers, taking orders, and serving ordered food. Figure 2 shows the sequence tasks when using our proposed method. First, the robot finds a waving customer using human and action recognition. Simultaneously, the robot identifies the table of the waving customer using a predefined semantic map. Next, it moves toward the customer and takes orders through speech recognition. Finally, it takes the order to the kitchen and delivers the ordered food to the customer. In this study, we use an external PC to control HSR.

3.1   Finding Waving Customers

This section describes our proposed method for finding waving customers using human and action recognition and semantic mapping. Figure 3 shows an overview of the method. First, the robot finds a waving customer using the human action recognition method proposed by Ono et al. [8]. The method detects the 3-dimensional (3D) human location and waving action simultaneously. Next, the

Fig. 2. Flow of our proposed method.

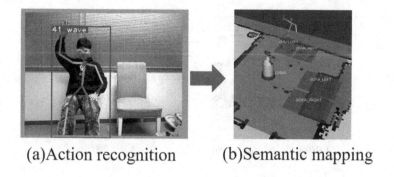

(a)Action recognition   (b)Semantic mapping

Fig. 3. Find a waving customer and estimate the chair position of the customer.

robot estimates the chair position of the customer using semantic mapping. The semantic map is created based on an environmental map using simultaneous localization and mapping (SLAM) and real-time appearance-based mapping (RTAB-MAP) [7]. Next, the semantic map is updated by manually mapping the furniture location to the coordinates in the environment map. Manual mapping is effortless and fast because it requires only two diagonal coordinates for each object. For example, a semantic map for a standard room can be created in less than an hour. Figure 3(b) shows the semantic map. In this case, the robot estimates that the waving customer is sitting in the left chair.

3.2   Taking Orders

This section describes how the robot takes orders through speech recognition. Figure 4 illustrates the process. First, the robot asks for the customer's order and records the sound of the customer's order for a fixed time. The robot transfers the audio file to the external PC using the robot operating system (ROS) topic [14]. However, binary data such as audio files cannot be communicated as a ROS topic. Therefore, we first convert the binary data to a sequence of decimal numbers before transmission. Next, we use the noise reduction method proposed by Sainburg et al. [15] to filter out the noise in the audio files. The method is easily adjustable and can be applied to various situations. Finally, we use speech recognition using Vosk [1]. Vosk is an offline method used in environments with unstable internet, such as a restaurant. In addition, Vosk registers a list of words to be recognized (dictionary) and excludes other words from recognition. Thus, names of food items and drinks in the dictionary to improve recognition accuracy.

3.3   Serving Orders

After taking orders, the robot takes orders to the kitchen and receives the ordered food. Conventional food delivery robots can serve many food items using trays, but HSR can serve only one item at a time because of the unavailability of a tray.

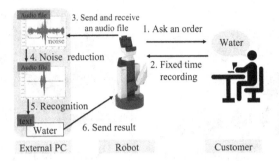

Fig. 4. Overview of our order-taking method.

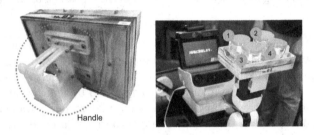

Fig. 5. Proposed tray. (a) Tray viewed from the handle side. (b) Robot serving four drinks using our proposed tray.

Therefore, we prepared a tray that could serve multiple items simultaneously. Figure 5(a) shows the tray's handle. HSR grasps this handle upward with an end effector. Because the top of our tray has drink holders, HSR can carry up to four drinks simultaneously. Figure 5(b) shows how HSR delivers four drinks.

4   Experiments

We conducted experiments in an actual restaurant with 12 customers for approximately one hour using HSR with our proposed method. Figure 6 shows the experimental environment. HSR served only four kinds of drinks (beer, lemon sour, sake, and water) due to its low payload. In addition, we recorded the audio of customers' orders with noise from the restaurant environment and evaluated the speech recognition accuracy. The PC specifications to control HSR are as follows: CPU: Intel core i7-7820HK, GPU: Geforce RTX 1080, Memory: 32 GB, OS: Ubuntu18.04.

4.1   Speech Recognition

We evaluated the speech recognition accuracy using 81 audio files recorded at the restaurant, containing names of drinks or numbers, namely beer, lemon sour,

Fig. 6. Experimental environment (HSR finds customers).

Table 2. Speech recognition accuracy.

	without dictionary	with dictionary
without noise reduction	48%	98%
with noise reduction	29%	81%

sake, water, 1, 2, 3, and 4. Table 2 shows the recognition accuracy with and without the dictionary and noise reduction. The highest accuracy was 98% when only dictionary specification was used. However, the accuracy decreased by 17 points to 81% with noise reduction. In addition, the processing time for our proposed speech recognition system was 2.74 s. The communication time for the audio file was 0.31 s, the noise reduction time was 0.10 s, and the recognition time was 2.33 s.

4.2 Semantic Mapping

Figure 7 shows the semantic map of the restaurant where the experiment was conducted. We mapped the five tables and the kitchen in the restaurant on an

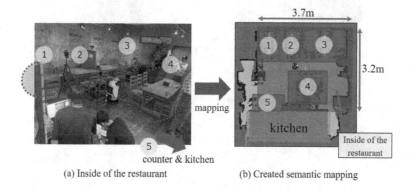

(a) Inside of the restaurant   (b) Created semantic mapping

Fig. 7. Semantic map of the restaurant.

environmental map. The time required to create the semantic map was approximately 30 min. Furthermore, HSR completed the sequence of waiter tasks by accurately estimating the customer's table.

4.3 Questionnaire

After the experiment, we asked six customers and five waiters to answer a questionnaire about our robot service on a five-point scale. Figure 8 shows the questionnaire results. We received 3.5 and 4.0 points for questions, "Could HSR work as a waiter?" and "Would you like to use HSR with our proposed method in the future?", respectively. However, we received a relatively low score of 2.7 points for the question, "Did you think our order-taking flow was smooth?".

Some customers were satisfied with the robot's behavior but gave feedback for smoother movement and speech recognition. Some waiters commented that HSR with our proposed method reduced their workload by taking orders and serving the drinks. Regarding suggestions, three customers said they would like to talk with HSR about food or drinks, whereas two waiters wanted HSR to clean the tables.

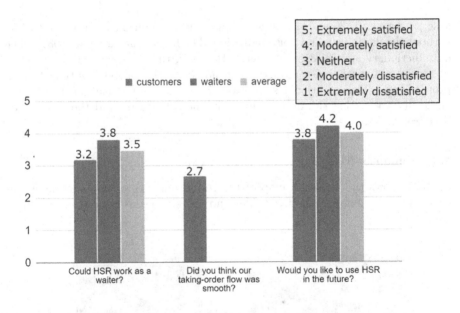

Fig. 8. Questionnaire result from customer and waiter.

5   Discussion and Future Works

5.1   Questionnaire

Many customers and waiters gave feedback that the robot's order-taking method was slow. One of the reasons is that the proposed speech recognition method records the sound of the customer's order for a fixed time regardless of the customer's state. Therefore, we will consider employing a voice activity detection method [3], which requires real-time processing of an audio file. However, real-time processing is challenging because our proposed method requires converting the audio file to communicate with the external PC. Therefore, in the future, we will consider methods for real-time communication with the external PC or detection using the robot's internal resources.

This study focused on the food serving process comprising finding customers, taking orders, and serving food using a tray. However, some waiters wanted HSR to clean the tables. Unlike conventional food delivery robots, HSR can clean the tables with its robot arm. Earlier, we studied object recognition and grasping using HSR and won a competition targeting room tidying [8]. In the future, we will apply these techniques to realize a waiter robot equivalent to a human waiter.

5.2   Speech Recognition

Figure 9 shows the speech waves before and after applying noise reduction to the audio file recorded at the restaurant. However, noise reduction reduces the amplitude of the speech section, reducing the recognition accuracy. Since the recognition accuracy is high with raw audio data, we will investigate a faster order-taking method using raw audio data.

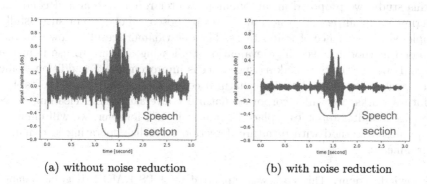

(a) without noise reduction   (b) with noise reduction

Fig. 9. Wave signal amplitude.

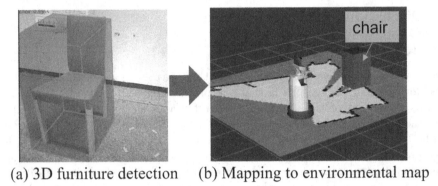

(a) 3D furniture detection   (b) Mapping to environmental map

Fig. 10. Developing semantic map using furniture detection.

5.3   Semantic Mapping

The experimental results in an actual restaurant setting revealed that our semantic map is effective in waiter tasks. However, our semantic map cannot operate in a dynamic environment where the location of objects keeps changing. Because our proposed map is created manually, real-time updating is challenging. In future works, we will enhance the proposed semantic map to operate in dynamic environments using furniture detection. Figure 10 shows our enhanced semantic map with 3D object detection. We use omni3d [2] as a furniture detection method capable of 3D detection and tracking the detected furniture.

6   Conclusion

In this study, we proposed an autonomous waiter robot system and conducts experiments in an actual restaurant. The proposed robot system successfully completed the sequence of waiter tasks. The questionnaire results show that our proposed method received high evaluation, indicating a desire to use it in the future; however, the order-taking speed needs improvements. In addition, some participants wanted HSR to have natural conversations and clean the tables. In future works, we will incorporate natural conversation and cleaning tasks to realize a waiter robot to replace human waiters. Moreover, we will enhance our proposed method with furniture detection to realize operating in dynamic environments.

Acknowledgement. This work was supported by JSPS KAKENHI grant number 23H03468. This paper is based on results obtained from a project, JPNP16007, commissioned by the New Energy and Industrial Technology Development Organization (NEDO).

References

1. alpha: Vosk offline speech recognition (2022), https://alphacephei.com/vosk/
2. Brazil, G., Straub, J., Ravi, N., Johnson, J., Gkioxari, G.: Omni3D: a large benchmark and model for 3D object detection in the wild. arXiv:2207.10660 (2022)
3. Chen, Y., Dinkel, H., Wu, M., Yu, K.: Voice activity detection in the wild via weakly supervised sound event detection, pp. 3665–3669 (2020)
4. Deloitte: Forecasting for service robot market in 2022 (2022). https://mic-r.co.jp/mr/02360/
5. KEENON: catering robot T-2 (2022). https://www.keenonrobot.com/jp/index/Page/index/catid/5.html
6. KEENON: catering robot T-8 (2022). https://www.keenonrobot.com/jp/index/Page/index/catid/32.html
7. Labbé, M., Michaud, F.: Rtab-map as an open-source lidar and visual simultaneous localization and mapping library for large-scale and long-term online operation. J. Field Rob. 36(2), 416–446 (2019)
8. Ono, T., et al.: Solution of world robot challenge 2020 partner robot challenge (Real Space). Adv. Rob. 36(17), 1–18 (2022)
9. REEMAN: Autonomous food delivery robot waiter restaurant robot hotel robot service robot (2022). https://www.reemanrobot.com/delivery-robot/food-delivery-robot/autonomous-delivery-robot.html
10. REEMAN: Reeman homepage (2022). https://www.reemanrobot.com/
11. Robotics, P.: Bella bot (2022). https://www.pudurobotics.com/products/pudubot2
12. Robotics, P.: Pudo robotics homepage (2022). https://www.pudurobotics.com/
13. Robotics, P.: Pudo robotics homepage (2022). https://www.pudurobotics.com/products/holabot
14. ROS.org: Ros wiki (2022). https://wiki.ros.org/
15. Sainburg, T., Thielk, M., Gentner, T.Q.: Finding, visualizing, and quantifying latent structure across diverse animal vocal repertoires. PLoS Comput. Biol. 16, e1008228 (2020)
16. SoftBank: catering robot servi (2022). https://www.softbankrobotics.com/jp/product/servi/
17. Yamamoto, T., Terada, K., Ochiai, A., Saito, F., Asahara, Y., Murase, K.: Development of human support robot as the research platform of a domestic mobile manipulator. ROBOMECH J. 6(1), 1–15 (2019)

Anthropomorphic Human-Robot Interaction Framework: Attention Based Approach

Natnael Wondimu[2,5]($\boxtimes$), Maëlic Neau[1,2,4,5], Antoine Dizet[2,5], Ubbo Visser[3], and Cédric Buche[2,5]

[1] CROSSING, CNRS IRL 2010, Adelaide, Australia
[2] Lab-STICC, CNRS UMR 6285, Brest, France
[3] University of Miami, Coral Gables, USA
visser@cs.miami.edu
[4] Flinders University, Adelaide, Australia
{natnael.wondimu,antoine.dizet,cedric.buche}@enib.fr
[5] ENIB, Plouzané, France
neau@enib.fr

Abstract. Robots need to identify environmental cues like humans do for effective human-robot interaction (HRI). Human attention models simulate the way humans process visual information, making them useful for identifying important regions in images/videos. In this paper, we explore the use of human attention models in developing intuitive and anthropomorphic HRI. Our approach combines a saliency model and a moving object detection model. The framework is implemented using the ROS framework on Pepper, a humanoid robot. To evaluate the effectiveness of our system, we conducted both subjective and qualitative measures, including subjective rating measures to evaluate intuitiveness, trust, engagement, and user satisfaction, and quantitative measures of our human attention subsystem against state-of-the-art models. Our extensive experiments demonstrate the significant impact of our framework in enabling intuitive and anthropomorphic human-robot interaction.

Keywords: HRI · human attention · intuitive HRI · anthropomorphic

1 Introduction

AI agents are frequently described as having the capacity to reason and behave in a manner that resembles human and rational thinking [16]. Human-robot interaction (HRI) is improved by agents that can emulate human thinking and behavior because HRI is primarily defined by the observable actions and results of human thought in behaviorism [10].

Human attention models enable robots to respond to visual stimuli like humans [24]. By integrating these models into their behavior, robots can identify relevant visual information, make informed decisions, and interact more naturally with humans. This human-like allocation of visual attention helps robots

C. Buche et al. (Eds.): RoboCup 2023, LNAI 14140, pp. 262–274, 2024.
https://doi.org/10.1007/978-3-031-55015-7_22

perform tasks effectively and efficiently, improving the user experience. Specifically, saliency prediction [24] and moving object detection models [25] simulate human attention in computer vision. Saliency prediction models identify attention-grabbing regions in an image using low and high-level features while moving object detection models identify motion in a scene. Humans attend to moving objects more than static ones. Combining these models can simulate different aspects of human attention, creating more complex attentional simulations that resemble how humans attend to the visual world in complex anthropomorphic behavior.

Human-robot interaction is an essential aspect of the RoboCup@Home competition, where robots are tasked with performing various domestic tasks. Anthropomorphic behaviors, which mimic human characteristics and mannerisms, are highly valued in this competition. These behaviors may include social cues such as maintaining eye contact, appropriate gesturing, and active listening skills. In particular, two of the most challenging tasks in the competition are the Receptionist and General Purpose Service Robot tasks. In these tasks, the robot must be able to autonomously identify and engage with human beings, determining which individual wants to interact and focusing its attention on the speaker for the duration of the conversation. To succeed in these tasks, the robot must possess advanced sensory and cognitive capabilities, including the ability to recognize and interpret saliency and other verbal and nonverbal cues.

In this paper, we propose a framework for anthropomorphic human-robot interaction based on human attention. Our framework comprises a human attention sub-system that uses state-of-the-art video saliency prediction [24] and moving object detection and segmentation [25] models, as well as the Robot Operating System (ROS) framework. Finally, the behavior manager sub-system that controls the behavior of the Pepper robot based on inputs from the human attention sub-system is implemented.

The paper is structured in the following manner. The second section provides a concise overview of the state-of-the-art, followed by the third section which delves into the research methodology. The fourth section presents the experimental findings, while the concluding section offers a summary of the research work and highlights potential areas for future investigation.

2 Related Works

Currently, there is a vast and varied research and design effort focused on human-robot interaction [19]. HRI research can be broadly categorized into three areas: human-supervised HRI [11], autonomous HRI [2], and human-robot social interaction [1], where social robots engage with humans to accomplish specific objectives.

Human-supervised HRI involves human guidance to control robots during interactions. It's used in industrial settings for repetitive and dangerous tasks. The goal is to develop robots that can work alongside humans safely and efficiently [11]. Autonomous HRI, on the other hand, focuses on independent robot operation [2]. Both types of research focus on efficiency [19], while HRSI research aims for anthropomorphic and intuitive robot behavior [3]. This involves designing robots with human-like characteristics for social interaction and communication [5].

Human attention models are crucial for effective human-robot social interaction. The Attentional Intensity Model (AIM) [15] propose that attentional focus intensity determines perception efficiency and accuracy, while the integration of perceptual and action processes is essential for generating intuitive and adaptive behavior [6].

In the field of HRI, research has focused on improving social interaction through emotional expressions and intuitive recognition of human gestures. Emotional expressions can enhance social intelligence and naturalness of robot behavior [1], while recognizing and responding to human gestures is important for building a friendly and natural relationship [13]. Although these models have been studied to enhance HRI, they may not be sufficient to address all intuitiveness challenges associated with it. Emotions and gestures can be ambiguous and not always reflect a person's intentions or needs, creating communication barriers.

Research has shown that human attention-based systems are a reliable and effective approach to improving HRI [25, 26]. These systems track a person's gaze, attention, and movement to better understand their needs and intentions, leading to more intuitive interactions. They are also more universal since they are less reliant on cultural or individual differences in emotional or gestural expression. Approaches include using pointing gestures and saliency maps [18], tracking gaze in real time with deep learning [17], and predicting intentions based on gaze cues [7]. Computer vision is used to understand objects, humans, and the environment for proactive collaboration in HRI [4]. Moreover, a paper by Li et al. shows that combining saliency prediction and moving object detection can improve robot understanding of human attention, leading to more intuitive interactions [12]. Consequently, we propose a novel framework for anthropomorphic HRI based on human attention, specifically saliency prediction [24] and moving object detection [25]. Our approach aims to enhance the robot's understanding of potential user's focus of attention, which can facilitate more intuitive and anthropomorphic communication. By leveraging the latest advances in computer vision and machine learning, our framework can enable the robot to anticipate and respond to the user's needs, leading to a more seamless and personalized interaction. In the following section, we describe the key components of our framework and demonstrate its effectiveness through experiments and evaluations.

3   Proposal

3.1   Overview

Our anthropomorphic HRI framework is a sophisticated system that enables robots to interact with humans in a more natural and intuitive way. As it is shown in Fig. 1, the framework consists of several key components that work together to create a seamless interaction between the robot and the human user.

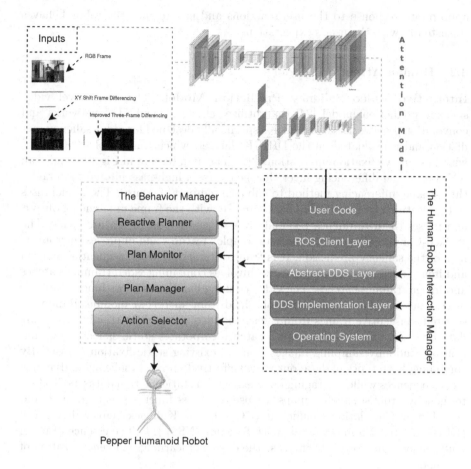

Fig. 1. Anthropomorphic human-robot interaction framework

At the heart of the system is a human attention model, that detects and highlights important regions and moving objects in the video feed, helping the robot understand the user's focus. State-of-the-art interactive video saliency prediction [24] and moving object detection and segmentation [25] models were adapted for this purpose.

The human-robot interaction manager is responsible for managing the interaction between the robot and the human. It uses a ROS framework to enable communication between modules, robots, and humans. ROS provides various tools for building complex robotic systems, allowing the robot to receive commands and respond naturally.

The behavior manager manages perception and action of the robot based on the human attention model. It uses this information to determine the most appropriate response to the user's actions and ensure that the robot behaves consistently with the user's expectations.

3.2   Human Attention Model

Interactive Video Saliency Prediction Model. This is a novel video saliency prediction model [24] that utilizes stacked-ConvLSTM networks and convolutional networks. The model is specifically designed for video saliency prediction and is evaluated on the DHF1K dataset, which consists of 1,000 videos with human eye fixation annotations [22]. The architecture in Fig. 2 includes an XY-shift frame differencing layer that generates a high-pass filtered map and a three-frame differencing method to enhance temporal features. The model fuses spatial features from a VGG16 backbone [20] with the frame differencing output and passes them through a residual layer to create a single feature space. The stacked-ConvLSTM network extracts complex features and improves the robustness of the saliency prediction. It is trained iteratively using sequential fixation and image data. The training process involves combining video training batches and image training batches. The video training batch uses a loss function on the final dynamic saliency prediction obtained from an LSTM module. Randomly selected consecutive frames from the same video are used for training, ensuring data diversity. The image training batch incorporates static saliency information by randomly sampling images from an existing static fixation dataset. By combining both types of data, our model effectively predicts saliency in dynamic video sequences while leveraging knowledge from static fixation datasets. To better generate robust saliency maps, we use three loss functions as used in [8] and [22]. Linear Correlation Coefficient (CC) [9], the Kullback-Leibler divergence (KLD) [21] and Normalized Scanpath Saliency (NSS) [14]. The essence of using multiple loss functions is to increase the degree of learning and generalization of the model.

A Moving Object Detection and Segmentation Model. This is a novel XY-shift frame differencing technique and a three-stream encoder-decoder architecture for moving object detection and segmentation [25]. As shown in Fig. 2, the XY-shift frame differencing reduces irrelevant background objects and exposes foreground objects, while the improved three-frame differencing extracts temporal features in the spatio-temporal domain. The three-stream encoder-decoder network consists of a VGG16-based encoder and decoder and uses binary cross-entropy as the loss function for training. We used a Binary Cross Entropy loss function due to the nature of the problem. The model is trained using the CDNet-2014 dataset [23] with 4-fold cross-validation and early stopping to prevent overfitting. Adaptive Moment Estimation (Adam) is used to optimize the network during training.

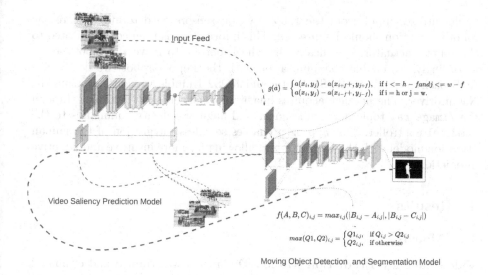

$$g(a) = \begin{cases} a(x_i, y_j) - a(x_{i+f}+, y_{j+f}), & \text{if } i <= h - f and j <= w - f \\ a(x_i, y_j) - a(x_{i-f}+, y_{j-f}), & \text{if } i = h \text{ or } j = w. \end{cases}$$

$$f(A, B, C)_{i,j} = max_{i,j}(|B_{i,j} - A_{i,j}|, |B_{i,j} - C_{i,j}|)$$

$$max(Q1, Q2)_{i,j} = \begin{cases} Q1_{i,j}, & \text{if } Q_{i,j} > Q2_{i,j} \\ Q2_{i,j}, & \text{if otherwise} \end{cases}$$

Moving Object Detection and Segmentation Model

Fig. 2. Human Attention Model Architecture

3.3 Simulation Environment

The proposed framework is evaluated in two different settings: the Gazebo environment with ROS and the real Pepper robot. The experiment was conducted using a 3D model of the Pepper robot in the Gazebo environment, providing a realistic simulation to test the interactive video saliency prediction and moving object detection and segmentation models in a controlled environment. The process flow includes setting up the Gazebo environment, implementing the computer vision models as ROS nodes, developing a behavior manager module to control the virtual robot's camera movements, and evaluating the system's performance in different scenarios. This approach enables the testing and refinement of human attention models in a simulated environment before deploying them on a real Pepper robot.

3.4 Real Environment

The integration of the Pepper robot with ROS (Robot Operating System) was made possible through the use of the ROSBridge protocol, which enables seamless communication between the robot and external systems. This integration was facilitated by the Naoqi driver, which enabled the Pepper robot to interact with ROS and utilize its vast array of tools and functionalities. The integration is accomplished through the ROS message protocol, enabling data exchange in a standardized format that is native to ROS. This approach offers several benefits including a more streamlined and efficient communication process and greater compatibility with ROS-based tools and functionalities.

We developed our human attention model using ROS nodes, dedicating nodes to computer vision, navigation, and the model itself. The human attention model utilizes input from the robot's vision sensors to determine where the robot's attention should be directed. This information is then communicated to the robot's actuator, specifically the wheel motors, to move the robot's body accordingly. To enable communication with the Pepper robot, we designed a ROS package for both ROS1 Noetic and ROS2 Humble versions, utilizing the Naoqi_driver. The package acquires image information in RGB format through the /image_raw topic and sends linear and angular velocity commands to the /cmd_vel controller. This approach enables seamless integration of the human attention model with the Pepper robot, allowing for more intuitive and adaptive interactions.

4   Results

4.1   Models

Video Saliency Prediction Model. Our model was trained and evaluated on the DHF1K dataset, with the first 70% of the dataset used for training and evaluation. We used a 60/10/30 split ratio for training, validation, and testing, respectively, and randomly selected 420 and 70 videos for training and validation, respectively. To measure the model's performance, we employed five evaluation metrics, including Normalized Scanpath Saliency, Similarity Metric, Linear Correlation Coefficient, AUC-Judd, and shuffled AUC. Our video saliency prediction model exhibited an outstanding performance in all evaluation metrics when compared against 6 static saliency models adapted for video saliency prediction and 10 dynamic saliency models, demonstrating its effectiveness. For more detailed results on our proposed video saliency prediction model, we invite readers to refer to [24].

Moving Object Detection and Segmentation. We used a dataset called CDNet-2014 [23] for training and evaluating our model. The dataset contains over 160,000 annotated frames in 53 video sequences, divided into 11 categories and two spectra: visible and thermal infrared. The scenes in the dataset include urban environments with people and cars, both indoor and outdoor, and with real-world challenges such as shadows, dynamic backgrounds, and camera motion. The ground truth for each image is a gray-scale image that describes four motion classes: static, hard shadow, unknown motion, and motion. An additional class is used for areas outside the region of interest. We evaluated our model on the testing sets of CDNet-2014, which contains 11 video sequences with almost 39,820 frames. We focused on the Recall, Precision, and F1-score metrics as they were deemed sufficient for the problem at hand. We evaluated our model against five state-of-the-art moving object detection and segmentation models. Consequently, our model outperformed all models in all evaluation metrics. For more detailed results on our proposed video saliency prediction model, we invite readers to refer to [25].

4.2   Simulation Environment

In order to assess the performance of the Pepper robot in various human-robot interaction scenarios, we designed and conducted an evaluation study using Gazebo platform. The study consisted of four distinct scenarios that aimed to simulate different real-world situations. The scenarios were as follows:

Moving Objects in a Closed Room. In this scenario, we exposed the Pepper robot to a closed room environment where it encountered moving objects.

Interaction with Multiple Humans/Figures. Pepper interacted with a combination of multiple humans and figures, some of which were moving and some interacted directly with the robot.

Operating in an Open Space with Visual Variations. Pepper operated in an open space with various visual variations over time, simulating a dynamic environment.

Dynamic Environment with Humans and Moving Objects. Pepper was left in a dynamic environment where it encountered both humans and other moving objects.

To ensure a diverse participant pool, we selected seven individuals from Addis Ababa University, considering their relevance to the discipline while also preserving gender variety. Each participant had the opportunity to observe the responses of the Pepper robot when it was placed in an environment relevant to each scenario. Moreover, to evaluate the performance of the Pepper robot, we employed the following metrics: Intuitiveness, Trust, Engagement, and User Satisfaction. To put the metrics into context,

Intuitiveness. Intuitiveness refers to the ease with which users can understand and interact with the Pepper robot. This metric is important because a robot that is intuitive to interact with can enhance user acceptance and engagement.

Trust. Trust evaluates the level of confidence and reliance that users place in the robot. Trust is crucial in human-robot interaction as it influences user willingness to engage and collaborate with the robot.

Engagement. Engagement measures the extent to which users are actively involved and interested in the interaction with the Pepper robot. High engagement levels indicate a successful interaction that keeps users engaged and attentive.

User Satisfaction. User Satisfaction measures users' overall contentment and fulfillment with the interaction experience. User Satisfaction is a crucial metric as it provides insight into the overall acceptability and desirability of the human-robot interaction.

We chose these specific metrics to comprehensively evaluate the human-robot interaction experience, including Intuitiveness, Trust, Engagement, and User Satisfaction. These metrics provide insights into ease of use, perceived reliability, user involvement, and overall satisfaction. They allow us to assess the performance of the Pepper robot, identify areas for improvement, and guide future enhancements in human-robot interaction systems. The data was collected through a single form using a rating scale from 1 to 10. Participants rated the robot's performance based on predefined metrics.

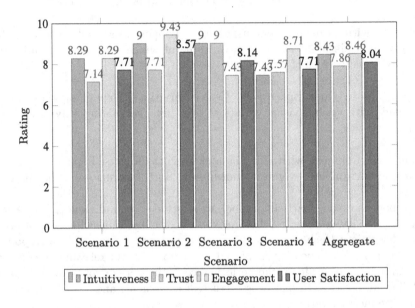

Fig. 3. Evaluation Ratings for Scenarios

Figure 3 presents the evaluations conducted by participants across four scenarios, using four metrics: Intuitiveness, Trust, Engagement, and User Satisfaction. The ratings varied for each metric across scenarios.

In terms of Intuitiveness, participants consistently rated the scenarios highly, indicating ease of understanding and use. This suggests well-designed scenarios. Participants demonstrated moderate to high levels of Trust, with positive ratings indicating confidence and reliance on the scenarios, albeit with some variations. Regarding engagement, ratings were consistently high, indicating active involvement and interaction with the scenarios. Finally, User Satisfaction ratings were positive, reflecting overall satisfaction and meeting or exceeding participants' expectations in terms of user experience.

To provide a visual representation of these scenarios, we included screenshots in Fig. 4a[1], Fig. 4b[2], Fig. 4c[3], and Fig. 4d[4].

---

[1] Pepper paying attention to moving bodies.
[2] Pepper interacting with temporarily salient body.
[3] Pepper acting humanly in a still environment.
[4] Pepper attending a very dynamic environment and on the move.

(a) Moving Object Detection Scenario

(b) User Interaction Scenario

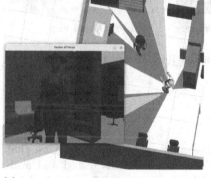

(c) Anthropomorphic Robot Behaviour Scenario

(d) Dynamic space Interaction Scenario

Fig. 4. Pepper Humanoid Robot Operating in Simulated Environment

According to the results, our human attention based anthropomorphic human-robot interaction framework enabled intuitive, trustworthy, and fairly satisfying interaction capabilities with the virtual environment.

4.3   Real-Time Embedded Strategy

Although we conducted an extensive evaluation in a simulated environment, we also performed a qualitative analysis of our HRI framework using a Pepper humanoid robot. The tests we conducted involved moving object detection using a moving object detection model, user interaction saliency model, and anthropomorphic robot action using both saliency and moving object detection models.

To demonstrate the efficiency of our approach in the real-time and low-resources constraints of the RoboCup@Home, we employed ourselves to optimize and deploy the architecture onboard the Pepper robot. To do so, models weights are first converted to Tensorflow Lite[5] format for lightweight inference on the

---

[5] https://www.tensorflow.org/lite/guide?hl=en.

robot CPU[6]. Then, a synchronizer is added to ensure low-latency communication between the attention module, moving object module, and behavior module.

Figure 5 displays a screenshot of the Pepper humanoid robot operating with our anthropomorphic HRI framework.

| (a) Pepper view | (b) Real-time saliency | (c) Global view |

Fig. 5. Pepper Humanoid Robot Operating in the Real World: Human Interaction Scenario.

5   Conclusion and Future Work

In conclusion, this paper presented an Anthropomorphic HRI framework that is based on the human attention model. The framework was tested and evaluated using subjective ratings from 7 participants in four different scenarios, assessing intuitiveness, trust, engagement, and user satisfaction. The framework was extensively tested in a simulated environment and underwent functionality tests on the real humanoid robot Pepper. This work contributes to the field of HRI and human attention models by providing a framework that can be used to guide robots on how to act based on human attention. Future research problems that might interest the research community in the area of HRI and human attention models were also highlighted. Overall, this work provides a significant step towards developing more efficient and intuitive HRI systems.

Acknowledgment. This work would not have been possible without the financial support of the Brittany region administration, French Embassy in Ethiopia and the Ethiopia Ministry of Education (MoE). We are also indebted to Brest National School of Engineering (ENIB) and specifically LAB-STICC for creating such a conducive research environment.

References

1. Andreasson, R., Alenljung, B., Billing, E., Lowe, R.: Affective touch in human-robot interaction: conveying emotion to the nao robot. Int. J. Soc. Robot. **10**, 473–491 (2018)

---

[6] Intel Atom™ E3845 @ 1.91GHz x 4.

2. Beer, J.M., Fisk, A.D., Rogers, W.A.: Toward a framework for levels of robot autonomy in human-robot interaction. J. Hum.-Robot Interact. **3**(2), 74 (2014)

3. Duchaine, V., Gosselin, C.: Safe, stable and intuitive control for physical human-robot interaction. In: 2009 IEEE International Conference on Robotics and Automation, pp. 3383–3388. IEEE (2009)

4. Fan, J., Zheng, P., Li, S.: Vision-based holistic scene understanding towards proactive human-robot collaboration. Robot. Comput.-Integr. Manuf. **75**, 102304 (2022)

5. Fong, T., Nourbakhsh, I., Dautenhahn, K.: A survey of socially interactive robots. Robot. Auton. Syst. **42**(3–4), 143–166 (2003)

6. Hommel, B., Müsseler, J., Aschersleben, G., Prinz, W.: The theory of event coding (TEC): a framework for perception and action planning. Behav. Brain Sci. **24**(5), 849–878 (2001)

7. Huang, C.M., Andrist, S., Sauppé, A., Mutlu, B.: Using gaze patterns to predict task intent in collaboration. Front. Psychol. **6**, 1049 (2015)

8. Jiang, L., Xu, M., Liu, T., Qiao, M., Wang, Z.: Deepvs: a deep learning based video saliency prediction approach. In: Proceedings of the European Conference on Computer Vision (ECCV), pp. 602–617 (2018)

9. Jost, T., Ouerhani, N., Von Wartburg, R., Müri, R., Hügli, H.: Assessing the contribution of color in visual attention. Comput. Vis. Image Underst. **100**(1–2), 107–123 (2005)

10. Kahn, P.H., Jr., et al.: What is a human?: toward psychological benchmarks in the field of human-robot interaction. Interact. Stud. **8**(3), 363–390 (2007)

11. Kiesler, S., Powers, A., Fussell, S.R., Torrey, C.: Anthropomorphic interactions with a robot and robot-like agent. Soc. Cogn. **26**(2), 169–181 (2008)

12. Li, H., Chen, G., Li, G., Yu, Y.: Motion guided attention for video salient object detection. In: Proceedings of the IEEE/CVF International Conference on Computer Vision, pp. 7274–7283 (2019)

13. Li, X.: Human-robot interaction based on gesture and movement recognition. Signal Process. Image Commun. **81**, 115686 (2020)

14. Peters, R.J., Iyer, A., Itti, L., Koch, C.: Components of bottom-up gaze allocation in natural images. Vision. Res. **45**(18), 2397–2416 (2005)

15. Petersen, S.E., Posner, M.I.: The attention system of the human brain: 20 years after. Annu. Rev. Neurosci. **35**, 73–89 (2012)

16. Russell, S., Norvig, P.: Artificial Intelligence: A Modern Approach. Pearson Education Limited, London (2016)

17. Saran, A., Majumdar, S., Short, E.S., Thomaz, A., Niekum, S.: Human gaze following for human-robot interaction. In: 2018 IEEE/RSJ International Conference on Intelligent Robots and Systems (IROS), pp. 8615–8621. IEEE (2018)

18. Schauerte, B., Fink, G.A.: Focusing computational visual attention in multi-modal human-robot interaction. In: International Conference on Multimodal Interfaces and the Workshop on Machine Learning for Multimodal Interaction, pp. 1–8 (2010)

19. Sheridan, T.B.: Human-robot interaction: status and challenges. Hum. Factors **58**(4), 525–532 (2016)

20. Simonyan, K., Zisserman, A.: Very deep convolutional networks for large-scale image recognition. arXiv preprint arXiv:1409.1556 (2014)

21. Tatler, B.W., Baddeley, R.J., Gilchrist, I.D.: Visual correlates of fixation selection: effects of scale and time. Vision. Res. **45**(5), 643–659 (2005)

22. Wang, W., Shen, J., Guo, F., Cheng, M.M., Borji, A.: Revisiting video saliency: a large-scale benchmark and a new model. In: Proceedings of the IEEE Conference on Computer Vision and Pattern Recognition, pp. 4894–4903 (2018)

23. Wang, Y., Jodoin, P.M., Porikli, F., Konrad, J., Benezeth, Y., Ishwar, P.: CDnet 2014: an expanded change detection benchmark dataset. In: Proceedings of the IEEE Conference on Computer Vision and Pattern Recognition Workshops, pp. 387–394 (2014)

24. Wondimu, N., Visser, U., Buche, C.: Interactive video saliency prediction: the stacked-ConvLSTM approach. In: 15th International Conference on Agents and Artificial Intelligence, pp. 157–168. SCITEPRESS-Science and Technology Publications (2023)

25. Wondimu, N., Visser, U., Buche, C.: A new approach to moving object detection and segmentation: the XY-shift frame differencing. In: 15th International Conference on Agents and Artificial Intelligence, pp. 309–318. SCITEPRESS-Science and Technology Publications; SCITEPRESS-Science and ... (2023)

26. Wondimu, N.A., Buche, C., Visser, U.: Interactive machine learning: a state of the art review. arXiv preprint arXiv:2207.06196 (2022)

Crossing Real and Virtual: Pepper Robot as an Interactive Digital Twin

Louis Li[1(✉)], Maëlic Neau[1,2,3,4], Thomas Ung[1], and Cédric Buche[1,4]

[1] CROSSING, CNRS IRL 2010, Adelaide, Australia
manhim1218@gmail.com
[2] Lab-STICC, CNRS UMR 6285, Brest, France
[3] Flinders University, Adelaide, Australia
[4] ENIB, Plouzané, France
buche@enib.fr

Abstract. This paper proposes a practical framework for implementing a Digital Twin (DT) application in Unity Engine, aimed at simulating the Softbank Pepper robot for testing interactive tasks in the RoboCup@Home (https://www.robocup.org/) competition using virtual reality. The proposed framework employs a versatile robotic middleware integrating open-source ZeroMQ (ZMQ) websocket and Qi API, which enables researchers to implement the framework in various simulations. This paper also provides a short insight into setting up the DT framework in Unity Engine to enable real-time communication between the virtual and physical robot. The framework can be used by future researchers to simulate Pepper robots in diverse 3D game engines for testing interactive tasks.

Keywords: Digital Twin · Human-Robot Interaction · Virtual Reality · Unity Engine · Robotic Middleware · Open Source · RoboCup@Home

1 Introduction

The development of behaviors in robotics requires a large number of trials and errors. Classical approach [2] uses physical robots in real environments. This is problematic when the most efficient algorithms, derived from machine learning (ML), require a growing number of tests. In addition, tests in a real situation can be dangerous for the robot (e.g. navigation) or the human (e.g. grasping) as far as the behaviors are not finalized. To address these limitations, simulators such as Gazebo[1] are utilized, representing the prevailing robotic simulation application that supports ROS (Robot Operating System).

Despite the existing alternative software and tools available in robotics applications [6], the use of simulation for testing remains limited among developers due to challenges such as inadequate realism and complex setup requirements [1]. Conventional simulation tools like Gazebo pose a disadvantage as

---

[1] https://gazebosim.org/.

C. Buche et al. (Eds.): RoboCup 2023, LNAI 14140, pp. 275–286, 2024.
https://doi.org/10.1007/978-3-031-55015-7_23

they are unable to accurately replicate real-world behaviors, despite their simple installation process [15]. The lack of high-fidelity environments in such simulations is a crucial limitation for advanced robotics research, particularly in the RoboCup@Home competition that involves testing tasks for human-robot-interaction (HRI), where a high-quality rendering is essential in the virtual arena. The resolution of these challenges will enable the development of a real-time digital twins (DT) application in simulation to evaluate the performance of interactive tasks involving the Pepper robot and human participants.

In the context of HRI, DT further extends its capabilities by integrating the human element into the simulated environment [8,14], creating a dynamic platform for human-robot collaboration. DT has emerged as a promising paradigm in the field of robotics, enabling the creation of a simulated environment that accurately represents the physical robot and its behavior in the real world. By facilitating a communication pipeline between humans and robots, DT allows for real-time data and feedback exchange [10], thereby providing an opportunity to seamlessly blend the real and virtual worlds.

Prior research has attempted to simulate Pepper robot in a virtual world using various simulation platforms such as qiBullet [4], MORSE [11], and Unity Engine [5]. However, these studies have not addressed the integration of the subsequent technical obstacles:

1. high fidelity simulation, including graphics and physics, necessary for vision and machine learning purposes
2. interaction with users in the simulated environment using virtual reality (VR) technologies
3. integrate a versatile robotic middleware in the simulation, in order to emulate the real robot behavior
4. develop a real-time communication pipeline that enables bidirectional control between virtual and real robots. The pipeline facilitates concurrent task execution with virtual and real robots, as well as direct communication between both robots.

The main focus of this paper is to design a DT application for Softbank Pepper, a humanoid robot employed in the Social Standard Platform League (SSPL) of RoboCup@Home. RoboCup@Home stands as the largest annual competition dedicated to the field of service robotics, with a primary focus on fostering technological advancements in domestic robotic applications intended for personal usage. The competition encompasses various domains, including but not limited to navigation, computer vision, and human-robot interaction. This paper is structured into several sections. Section 2 presents a review of the relevant literature on the topic of robotic simulation, VR, and DT. Section 3 describes our contribution, which includes the development of a DT architecture designed to establish a flexible and robust robotic integration middleware between virtual and real Pepper robots. Furthermore, we introduce a state-of-the-art high-fidelity simulation integration that is specifically aimed at user interaction purposes. In Sect. 4, we demonstrate an application of our architecture in the context of the

RoboCup@Home competition, highlighting the effectiveness of our approach in a practical setting. Finally, in Sect. 5, we provide a summary of the key findings of our research and discuss the potential implications of our work for future research in the domain of robotic simulation and DT. The source code is publicly available for the community[2].

2   Related Work

This section will review relevant previous studies regarding utilizing robotic middleware in a 3D game engine, the implementation of VR for HRI, and the application of DT framework with Softbank Pepper robot in real-life scenarios.

ROS (Robot Operating System) [16] has been widely used by earlier studies [9,12] as a middleware to communicate with Unity Engine. In the context of integrating ROS modules with virtual environments developed in high-fidelity 3D game engines such as Unity Engine and Unreal Engine, a direct integration cannot be easily established due to divergences in dependencies and programming languages [7]. For instance, the absence of sufficient open-source community support for integrating ROS packages and communication protocols in Unreal Engine imposes limitations on the ease of robotic development. To overcome this challenge, in [3], authors utilize the ZeroMQ websocket (ZMQ) as a middleware to transfer data between ROS and Unity Engine. However, utilizing ROS middleware in Unity Engine to transfer large sensory messages like image data can result in performance limitations [9]. The limitations have been observed to have a negative impact on the transfer speed of the system. In the context of digital twin development, it is not essential to incorporate ROS middleware within the simulation itself. The primary requirement is to have a virtual robot that exhibits similar behaviors in terms of vision, joint movement, speech, and navigation. Researchers can leverage ROS packages outside the simulation for other purposes, such as utilizing the navigation stack for Simultaneous Localization and Mapping (SLAM). Thus, a more flexible robotic middleware framework is needed for bridging between a 3D game engine and robots. The proposed framework serves as a resolution to this issue by facilitating communication between disparate systems and enabling seamless integration in different game engines.

In [13], the authors present a study that showcases the practicality and reliability of VR technology for human-robot collaboration in a simulated environment. The authors created a virtual setting using Siemens NX simulation software and employed the HTC Vive as their experimental VR device. The study concluded that VR technology facilitates an improved understanding of how collaborative interaction between humans and robots can occur in a virtual space before developing a physical human-robot system. As a result, incorporating VR technology in a real-time DT (data-driven) application could prove advantageous in evaluating interactive tasks for the RoboCup@Home competition.

Cascone et al. [5] introduce a DT application utilizing a virtual Pepper in Unity Game Engine and a physical Pepper equipped with external IoT smart

---

[2] https://github.com/RoboBreizh-RoboCup-Home/NaoqiUnityWrapper-PepperDT.

objects to identify hazardous conditions in the living environment of the elderly. The simulated robot emulated concurrent behaviors with its physical counterpart and transmitted alerts to remote caregivers in the event of an emergency. This approach demonstrated the successful integration of DT techniques with humanoid robots in the healthcare domain. However, the use of external third-party devices on Pepper was not viable within the RoboCup@Home framework, highlighting the need for an adaptable DT solution that does not rely on external hardware.

3   Digital Twins Architecture

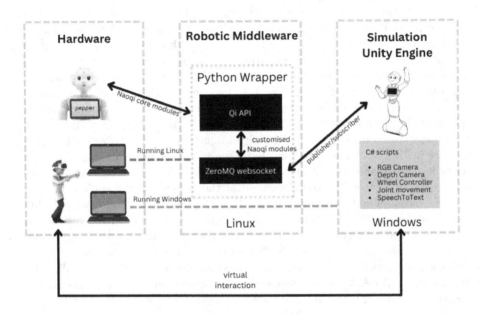

Fig. 1. Digital Twins Framework

The use of socket connections for inter-process communication between game engines and external robotic modules is common [7]. However, the management of such connections can become cumbersome in complex software architectures. To address this issue, the adoption of ROS middleware has been widely used as a means of simplifying management and increasing the reusability of intricate robotic software architectures. Despite the availability of ROS middleware plugins for Unity Engine, the performance limitation of low transferring speed is deemed to be a setback for certain sensory data, such as transmitting RGB and depth images. Therefore, this research suggests a novel framework to establish a means of communication between virtual Pepper in Unity Engine and physical Pepper using open-source APIs. The proposed DT architecture, illustrated in Fig. 1, consists of three primary components: hardware (left), a virtual environment in a game engine (right), and a bridging middleware (middle). The hardware component includes a Pepper robot, an Oculus Quest 2 VR device worn by the user, and two computers running on separate operating systems, namely Windows and Linux. The Linux computer acts as middleware, facilitating communication between the Unity Game Engine running on Windows on the other computer and the physical Pepper robot, leveraging the ZeroMQ websocket (ZMQ)[3] software and the Qi API[4] of the robot. ZeroMQ is an open-source websocket library that enables the communication between Python scripts running on the Linux computer and C# scripts in Unity Engine. The Qi API is a software development kit (SDK) used to create a Client/Server communication pipeline with the Naoqi OS in Pepper. To simplify the communication process between the ZMQ websocket and the Qi API, we have developed a Python wrapper to encapsulate all functions that run using these interfaces. This wrapper simplifies the codebase, reducing the complexity of the implementation while enhancing the overall robustness of the system. By abstracting the underlying functionality of the ZMQ and Qi API, the wrapper makes it easier to develop, test, and maintain the system, ensuring a smoother integration of the various components in the DT architecture.

3.1   Robotic Integration Middleware

ZeroMQ Websocket. ZMQ, an open-source networking library, offers a robust websocket that supports multiple connection patterns such as regular interval connection and asynchronous I/O. It also provides libraries for Python, C#, and C++, allowing the development of a bidirectional communication pipeline between two platforms that use different programming languages. This capability enables the creation of a publisher-subscriber communication bridge between Unity Engine, running with C# scripts, and Linux computers running Naoqi modules in Python with Qi API, as illustrated in Fig. 1.

Naoqi/Qi API Framework. The Python bindings of the Qi API framework are installed on the Linux laptop. Qi API registers a session service to the Naoqi OS, containing a variety of core modules that allow access to the Naoqi robot, such as camera subscription, joint movement control, and motion control. The Qi API can be implemented in both C++ and Python, as described in the Aldebaran documentation. After installing the API in Python, we initialized the connection between the Qi API running on the Linux laptop and the Pepper robot via the local network. To implement virtual Pepper in Unity, we utilized the Qi API to register a separate service to various customized Naoqi modules. These customized Naoqi modules consist of Python classes with multiple functions to access the virtual Pepper in Unity Engine. The function names of the customized modules were written with the same names used in the default Naoqi Core

---

[3] https://zeromq.org/.

[4] http://doc.aldebaran.com/2-5/naoqi/index.html.

Modules. For example, we created a function named *getImageRemote()* in the Camera class of our customized module to retrieve an RGB image from Unity Engine. This approach enabled the use of our framework to control both virtual Pepper and real Pepper without requiring extensive modifications.

3.2 High Fidelity Interactive Simulation for User's Interactivity

We choose Unity Game Engine as our primary simulation to create our DT application. Unity is a widely adopted game engine that offers an intuitive interface and a wide array of development resources. Notably, Unity's capability of constructing multiplayer simulations and its versatility across various operating systems, such as Windows and Linux, have been the primary drivers behind choosing it as the preferred engine for this research. Moreover, Unity Engine provides functions supporting interaction with a virtual object or agent via virtual reality, augmented reality, and mixed reality. Our project uses an Oculus Quest 2 VR device, which has been widely supported by the community of Unity Engine. In addition to its versatility and VR supporting compatibility, another compelling reason for selecting Unity Engine is its advanced built-in 3D physics settings, as documented by Unity[5]. Given these settings, we were able to create realistic and accurate simulations of real-world physical interactions between the virtual Pepper and virtual objects. This capability is crucial for testing and refining interactive tasks between the robot and humans, as it enables one to accurately replicate complex real-world scenarios.

4   Design of an Interactive Digital Twin for RoboCup@Home

In this section, we provide a comprehensive overview of the key steps involved in configuring our proposed Digital Twins (DT) application using the Softbank Pepper robot and Unity Engine.

4.1   Virtual Environment Setup

Our research team utilizes Blender[6] as a 3D software tool for designing a virtual arena based on our lab environment. Real measurements of the lab environment are taken to create identical 3D objects in Blender accordingly. Some open-source 3D furniture models are obtained online from websites like TurboSquid[7], and edited in Blender according to the real measurement before being exported to Unity Engine. Figure 2 visually represents a comparison between the environment in reality and the virtual environment that has been exported to Unity Engine.

---

[5] https://docs.unity3d.com/Manual/PhysicsOverview.html.

[6] https://www.blender.org/.

[7] https://www.turbosquid.com/.

4.2   Virtual Pepper Setup

URDF File. Our team acquires a Unified Robotics Description Format (URDF) file of a 3D virtual Pepper robot from a Naoqi git repository[8]. The Unity Technology framework[9] provides a URDF importer package that allows users to import URDF file into Unity Engine. Subsequently, adjustments are made to the virtual Pepper's physics to ensure that its behaviors in the virtual environment are consistent with those of the physical Pepper. For example, the mesh collider of Pepper's wheels is modified, as the original mesh is not a perfect sphere and can cause unbalanced motion in Unity Engine. In addition to the adjustments made to the mesh collider, we also noted that the moving XYZ axis from the original URDF file is not aligned with the axis in Unity Engine. As a result, we made further adjustments to the joint moving axis based on the joint movement described in the Aldebaran documentation. These adjustments ensure that the virtual Pepper is able to move and behave in a manner consistent with the physical robot, further enhancing the accuracy and reliability of the DT application in the simulation environment.

Fig. 2. Arena setting in reality (top) and Unity Engine (bottom)

Camera. We developed virtual RGB and depth cameras in Unity Engine that emulate the specifications of the physical cameras, such as the field of view (FOV), resolution, and the range of the depth camera, etc. The position of the virtual cameras was set to match their physical counterparts on the real Pepper. During runtime, Unity Engine generates a render texture that produces an encoded image in either JPG or PNG format. The rendered JPG image is then transmitted via a ZMQ websocket and received by a subscriber on the Linux laptop. The image is then integrated into a customized Naoqi module using the Qi API, allowing our team to access the virtual and physical Pepper's camera within the Naoqi framework. The virtual camera in Unity is utilized to conduct vision tests before exporting the final model to the physical Pepper. These tests involve tasks that require vision, tracking, and navigation. Using the

---

[8] https://github.com/ros-naoqi/pepper_robot.
[9] https://github.com/Unity-Technologies/URDF-Importer.

image obtained from the virtual Pepper's camera, we can implement tracking algorithms to track humans using pose detection. This approach is more feasible than testing it in a real-life setting and enhances the training efficiency by reducing the time required for testing on the physical Pepper. Additionally, the virtual robot can be used to test object detection models based on identical camera specifications and positions. Figure 3 illustrated an example of a testing result from our custom Yolov8[10] object detection model training on the YCB dataset[11] in Unity Engine (left) and reality (right).

Fig. 3. Object detection using YOLOV8 trained on the YCB dataset in Unity Engine (left) and reality (right).

Motion. A wheel controller C# script is developed in Unity Engine to simulate the motion behavior of a physical Pepper robot. The controller script receives velocity commands published via ZMQ websocket and controls the rotational speed of the virtual Pepper's wheels. Parameters such as linear and angular velocity, wheel radius, and damping are adjustable in the controller script to fine-tune the motion behavior. We conducted several trials to optimize the physics properties of the wheels and robot physics, resulting in the virtual Pepper that moves and behaves similarly to its physical counterpart. The wheel properties of the virtual Pepper robot in Unity are derived from the URDF file, as mentioned earlier in Sect. 4.2. In order to enable rotation in Unity, adjustments have been made to the collision and mesh data. However, it should be noted that one constraint of our modification is that the virtual wheel of the virtual Pepper is not omni-directional. As a result, the virtual robot is capable of moving only forward, backward, and in the angular axis. Despite this limitation, the implemented setup serves as an effective testing platform for navigation and movement-related tasks. It reduces the testing time required on the physical robot and enhances training efficiency.

---

[10] https://github.com/ultralytics/ultralytics.
[11] https://www.ycbbenchmarks.com/.

Joint Movement. We developed a motion planning script in Unity Engine to simulate the joint movement behavior of a physical Pepper robot. The joint movements are based on a hierarchical tree structure as defined in the URDF file. The rotation axis and joint moving limited derived from the URDF file is similar to the real Pepper's limitation written in the Aldebaran documentation. Articulation physics in Unity Engine is utilized to simulate realistic joint movement behaviors for the virtual robot. The C# script of the motion planning system allows for the customization of joint movements by tweaking physics parameters such as stiffness, damping, speed, and acceleration. Our team has made some modifications to these physic parameters for the virtual Pepper to imitate the similar joint motion delivered from the real Pepper. The required joint name and joint angle are sent from the Python wrapper and the message is handled in the motion planning C# script to move the required joint to the target based on the physics. A DT application of virtual and real Pepper simultaneously raising their arms for a grasping task is shown in Fig. 4.

Speech Communication. In addition to basic vision and motion behaviors, we present an implementation of a VOSK-based speech-to-text model integrated into the Unity Engine with a virtual Pepper robot. The aim is to enable bidirectional communication between virtual Pepper and users wearing VR headsets, allowing for natural and interactive conversations. The VOSK model is loaded into a Python wrapper, enabling speech messages to be converted to string-type data and published to the subscriber side of a ZMQ websocket in Unity Engine. We also created a virtual microphone and speaker in Unity, allowing it to receive and send string data messages via websockets, creating a bidirectional communication pipeline. This implementation allows us to deliver an interactive conversation with virtual Pepper in Unity to test interactive tasks for RoboCup@Home.

4.3 Virtual Reality Setup

The Oculus Quest 2 VR device is utilized for interacting with a virtual robot in Unity. The VR device is composed of a head-mounted display (HMD) and handheld controllers. Unity offers a suite of pre-built SDKs, including the Extended Reality (XR) application, which supports development in VR, AR, and MR. A virtual character is developed in the Unity Engine to enable interaction with virtual Pepper using XR applications. For example, the handheld controllers of the Oculus device allow users to control the virtual character's movement in the virtual arena and interact with virtual objects, such as grabbing. Figure 4 depicts a real-world example of passing a tennis ball to Pepper, as well as simultaneously passing a virtual tennis ball to the virtual robot using XR applications.

4.4 Python Wrapper Setup for Real-Time Communication

A Python wrapper was developed to facilitate the integration of essential components required for connecting real and virtual Pepper via QiAPI and ZMQ

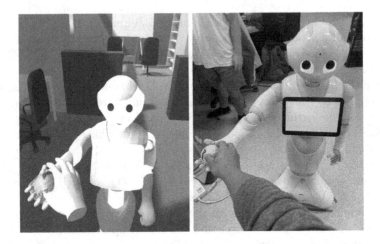

Fig. 4. Demonstration of passing a tennis ball from human to virtual/real Pepper.

websocket. The inspiration for creating the wrapper was derived from the Naoqi wrapper, which simulates virtual Pepper on QiBullet[12] [4], a bullet-based simulation platform designed for simulating Softbank Robotics' robots in a 3D virtual environment. Our wrapper contains a set of functions that enables to access the complete functionality of virtual Pepper, such as subscribing to RGB and depth cameras, controlling joint movements, managing motion, and facilitating speech communication. Figure 5 illustrates the wrapper's framework that uses Qi API to establish a connection session with both virtual and real Pepper. As explained in Sect. 3.1, our customized Naoqi modules consist of several Python classes with multiple functions that allow to access the virtual robot. Here we refer to the Naoqi core modules as default modules used in the Naoqi OS to control the Softbank Pepper robot. Our wrapper facilitates the simultaneous publication of joint angles, wheel rotational speeds, and subscription to RGB or depth images from both robots via a local network. This framework gives instantaneous feedback from Unity during testing, providing valuable insights into how actual tasks can be performed more effectively by the physical Pepper. Furthermore, this bidirectional pipeline enables the direct exchange of information between virtual and physical robots.

---

[12] https://github.com/softbankrobotics-research/qibullet.

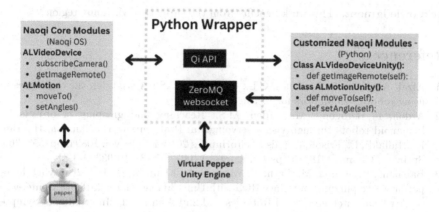

Fig. 5. Diagram representation of our wrapper framework, allowing efficient communication between the Naoqi Modules and the Unity Engine.

5 Conclusion and Future Work

This research proposes a digital twins framework that provides a secure environment for Pepper to perform testing in tasks of the RoboCup@Home competition. Our proposed framework integrates a VR implementation to enable human and robot interaction in the simulation. We used Unity Engine as the primary simulation for delivering digital twin applications, as it provides high-fidelity and interactive simulation with strong community support for robotic and VR functions. Our research also outlines the steps for setting up an interactive digital twins application in robotics. The communication pipeline in our framework is real-time and bidirectional, allowing users to obtain immediate feedback from both virtual Pepper in Unity and physical Pepper during testing. Our proposed robotic middleware is flexible and can be implemented in various simulations. Future researchers can work on our framework in other 3D game engines, such as Unreal Engine, for future robotic development. In future work, we consider rewriting the Qi API in C# or C++ languages and implementing the API directly in the 3D game engine, further simplifying the communication pipeline in the wrapper between virtual and real Pepper. In addition, the use of haptic gloves to implement tangible touch in the simulation will be deployed. This last point should enable synchronized interactive tasks for users and robots in both the virtual environment and reality.

6 Supplemental Materials

Supplemental material is available in our git repository[13] including a video[14] showing digital twins demonstration in vision, motion control, joint movement and VR interaction with Pepper.

---

[13] https://github.com/RoboBreizh-RoboCup-Home/NaoqiUnityWrapper-PepperDT.
[14] https://youtu.be/j-0Rkxu1bwI.

Acknowledgment. This work benefits from the support of Britanny region.

References

1. Afzal, A., Katz, D.S., Goues, C.L., Timperley, C.S.: A study on the challenges of using robotics simulators for testing (2020)
2. Ardón, P., Dragone, M., Erden, M.S.: Reaching and grasping of objects by humanoid robots through visual servoing. In: Prattichizzo, D., Shinoda, H., Tan, H., Ruffaldi, E., Frisoli, A. (eds.) EuroHaptics 2018. LNCS, vol. 10894, pp. 353–365. Springer, Cham (2018). https://doi.org/10.1007/978-3-319-93399-3_31
3. Babaians, E., Tamiz, M., Sarfi, Y., Mogoei, A., Mehrabi, E.: ROS2Unity3D; high-performance plugin to interface ROS with Unity3d engine. In: 2018 9th Conference on Artificial Intelligence and Robotics and 2nd Asia-Pacific International Symposium, pp. 59–64 (2018). https://doi.org/10.1109/AIAR.2018.8769798
4. Busy, M., Caniot, M.: qiBullet, a bullet-based simulator for the pepper and nao robots (2019)
5. Cascone, L., Nappi, M., Narducci, F., Passero, I.: DTPAAL: digital twinning pepper and ambient assisted living. IEEE Trans. Industr. Inf. 18(2), 1397–1404 (2022)
6. Christiansen, M., Larsen, P., Jørgensen, R.: Robotic design choice overview using co-simulation and design space exploration. Robotics 4(4), 398–420 (2015)
7. Coronado, E., Itadera, S., Ramirez-Alpizar, I.G.: Integrating virtual, mixed, and augmented reality to human-robot interaction applications using game engines: a brief review of accessible software tools and frameworks. Appl. Sci. 13(3), 1292 (2023)
8. Hagmann, K., Hellings-Kuß, A., Klodmann, J., Richter, R., Stulp, F., Leidner, D.: A digital twin approach for contextual assistance for surgeons during surgical robotics training. Front. Robot. AI 8, 735566–735566 (2021)
9. Inamura, T., Mizuchi, Y.: SIGVerse: a cloud-based VR platform for research on multimodal human-robot interaction. Front. Robot. AI 8, 549360–549360 (2021)
10. Kuts, V., et al.: Digital twin as industrial robots manipulation validation tool. Robotics 11(5), 113 (2022)
11. Lier, F., Wachsmuth, S.: Towards an open simulation environment for the pepper robot. In: Companion of the 2018 ACM/IEEE International Conference on human-robot interaction, HRI 2018, pp. 175–176. ACM (2018)
12. Liu, Y., Novotny, G., Smirnov, N., Morales-Alvarez, W., Olaverri-Monreal, C.: Mobile delivery robots: mixed reality-based simulation relying on ROS and unity 3D. In: 2020 IEEE Intelligent Vehicles Symposium (IV), Ithaca, pp. 15–20. IEEE (2020)
13. Malik, A.A., Masood, T., Bilberg, A.: Virtual reality in manufacturing: immersive and collaborative artificial-reality in design of human-robot workspace. Int. J. Comput. Integr. Manuf. 33(1), 22–37 (2020)
14. Oyekan, J., Farnsworth, M., Hutabarat, W., Miller, D., Tiwari, A.: Applying a 6 DoF robotic arm and digital twin to automate fan-blade reconditioning for aerospace maintenance, repair, and overhaul. Sensors 20(16), 4637 (2020)
15. Rizzardo, C., Katyara, S., Fernandes, M., Chen, F.: The importance and the limitations of sim2real for robotic manipulation in precision agriculture (2020)
16. Stanford Artificial Intelligence Laboratory: Robotic operating system. https://www.ros.org

Improving Applicability of Planning in the RoboCup Logistics League Using Macro-actions Refinement

Marco De Bortoli[1][(✉)], Lukáš Chrpa[2], Martin Gebser[1,3],
and Gerald Steinbauer-Wagner[1]

[1] Graz University of Technology, Graz, Austria
`mbortoli@ist.tugraz.at`
[2] Czech Technical University in Prague, Prague, Czech Republic
[3] University of Klagenfurt, Klagenfurt, Austria

Abstract. This paper focuses on improving the action plans obtained through the use of sequential macro-actions in temporal planning. Macro-actions are a way to address the high complexity of temporal planning in challenging domains. Investigating the Robocup Logistics League (RCLL), a testbed for logistics scenarios in the area of Industry 4.0, we introduce a method to unfold the macro-actions of an obtained abstract plan back into their original atomic actions in an improved plan. This allows to extract potentially better solutions in terms of makespan from the Simple Temporal Network (STN) representing the abstract plan. The proposed method is evaluated on a macro-based modeling of the RCLL domain and is shown to yield improved plans over those obtained using either the original atomic actions or the macro-actions without refinement.

1 Introduction

Industry 4.0, also known as Flexible Production, addresses the demand for more flexibility and autonomy in production and logistics. In this regards, the RoboCup Logistics League (RCLL) [25] was established with the goal of providing an appealing showcase for teaching and research in the area of Flexible Production within the RoboCup Initiative [16]. In order to deal with complex logistics and production problems, classical and temporal planning can be used to automatize the decision making of the involved agents. Classical planning is a technique that derives a sequence of actions aiming to achieve a specified goal, given a description of the domain [23]. Temporal planning enhances such capabilities by introducing concurrent execution of actions and management of time [18]. For this reason, it is particularly suitable for complex logistics domains where multiple agents need to coordinate and cooperate. However, as the number of tasks and resources increases, the capability of temporal planning engines to deliver suitable plans in short time tends to deteriorate rapidly, thereby limiting their practical deployment in solving complex logistical problems.

One of the techniques used to mitigate the high computational complexity of planning problems, both in classical and temporal planning, consists of the introduction of sequential macro-actions. Such a macro-action is a merging of two atomic actions, which are constrained to be executed sequentially. Macro-actions encode some kind of domain knowledge about actions often used in sequence. Due to the fact that the overall number of actions involved in a plan decreases, so does the planning time. In temporal planning, macro-actions are more difficult to formalize and incorporate in view of the constraints related to the parallel execution of actions [19]. However, some properties of an obtained temporal plan can be exploited to further improve it. In fact, a solution to a temporal planning problem can be seen as a temporal-constrained partial order, instead of a total order like in classical planning. This allows some temporal flexibility in the execution of the plan's actions. Moreover, as macro-actions abstract away the preconditions and effects of their atomic actions into a compound, their concurrent execution with other actions is limited as a price for more efficient planning. But when macro-actions are unfolded into their original atomic actions, some of the latter's flexibility can be regained. This paper proposes an automated method to refine temporal plans, namely the solutions of temporal planning processes using macro-actions, that unfolds the macro-actions into the original atomic actions, maintains the basic temporal order of the obtained plan and extracts a potentially better solution in terms of makespan from the resulting partial order by exploiting the regained flexibility of the atomic actions.

In the next section, we give an overview on related research in planning with macro-actions. Section 3 provides the necessary background on durative actions for temporal planning, introduced in the PDDL 2.1 standard [18], the RCLL, and the concept of sequential temporal macro-actions. The main contribution is elaborated in Sect. 4, where the procedure for refining temporal plans with macro-actions is described. Finally, the experimental evaluation using the RCLL domain is presented in Sect. 5, followed by Sect. 6, drawing the conclusions of our work.

2   Related Work

A huge corpus of research exists on the definition of macro-actions in classical planning. First studies date back to the 1970s, with the STRIPS [17] and REFLECTS systems [11]. There macro-actions are defined either as a preprocessing technique that modifies the original domain, or generated on-the-fly during planning as an heuristic technique. Regarding the former, interesting works present techniques to automatically identify macro-actions by means of a genetic algorithm [24] or a plan database [21]. Furthermore, in a work from Miura et al. [22] axioms are derived to reduce the number of actions, and in 2019 MUM is presented [6], a technique that extracts macro-actions from sample plans calculated over small instances. More recent works [4,5] focus on mutual-exclusion properties of some atoms in specific types of domains. Approaches using macro-actions for solving include the planners Marvin [9,10] and MACRO-FF [2]. Unlike for classical planning, there is less research on macro-actions in the realm of temporal planning. Wullinger et al. [31] have introduced a method that involves deriving macro-actions from partially overlapping temporal actions. However, it should be noted that their macro-actions are not always executable and require a separate consistency check. The most recent approach to temporal macro-actions, to the best of our knowledge, has been presented in a master's thesis [19]. This approach outlines procedures for creating sequential and parallel macro-actions, including support for numeric fluents. However, the underlying action definition does not adhere to the PDDL 2.1 specifications. Regarding techniques used for post-processing in planning, a method to parallelize some parts of a classical sequential plan is proposed in a work from Veloso et al. [29]. Part of the work presented in this paper can be viewed as an extension of that technique to temporal plans.

3 Background

In order to understand the concepts and definitions presented in this paper, like unfolded and refined plans, it is important to be familiar with the notions of durative actions and temporal plans. The former are introduced in PDDL 2.1 [18], and enable simultaneous execution and efficient time management. Unlike regular actions, which have preconditions that must hold for an action to be executable and effects that modify the state of the world after the execution, durative actions specify conditions and effects for both the starting and ending timepoints of the actions, with the option of adding invariants that must hold during their execution. Formally, a durative *action* a is defined by a *duration* $dur(a) \in \mathbb{R}^+$, the sets $pre^\vdash(a)$, $pre^\leftrightarrow(a)$, and $pre^\dashv(a)$ of atoms specifying *preconditions* that must hold at the start, as invariants during, or at the end of the action a, respectively, as well as the sets $eff^\vdash(a)$ and $eff^\dashv(a)$ of literals determining *effects* that apply at the start or the end of a. Let $add^\vdash(a)$ (or $add^\dashv(a)$) and $del^\vdash(a)$ (or $del^\dashv(a)$) denote the sets of atoms occurring as positive or negative literals, respectively, in $eff^\vdash(a)$ (or $eff^\dashv(a)$). Negative preconditions are not considered for this work. A temporal *plan* π consists of a finite collection of events that are associated with durative actions whose execution is scheduled at a given time such that the preconditions of all actions are met. Specifically, the collection is defined such that, if an action a is scheduled to be executed at time t, then π contains a pair of events in the form $(t, a^\vdash)$ and $(t + dur(a), a^\dashv)$. Note that $a^\vdash$ (resp. $a^\dashv$) refers to the event happening when a starts (resp. when a ends).

3.1 The RoboCup Logistics League

The objective of the league is to promote the advancement of Robotics and AI through the organization of robotics competitions. In a real-world setting, a team of autonomous mobile robots collaborates to manufacture a variety of products by interacting with production stations. The orders for specific products, including the desired configuration and delivery schedule, are generated incrementally during the game. The products are composed of a base, up to three rings, and a cap, with the number of rings indicating the product's complexity (ranging from C0 to C3). Special stations are designated for each of the intermediate production steps, and additional pieces are required to attach some of the rings, which must be provided to the corresponding station. The assembly of the products typically requires several stages of refinement by different machines. The complexity of a delivered product determines the number of points awarded. Details about how the participating teams tackle the competition can be found in the champion papers of the Carologistics [20] and GRIPS [28] teams.

3.2 Sequential Temporal Macro-actions

In our earlier work [12], we demonstrated that combining certain PDDL durative actions to macro-like actions in the RCLL domain results in a faster planning process and better plans in terms of makespan. These combined actions are referred to as *sequential macro-actions*.

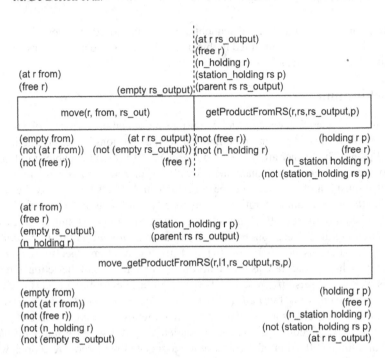

Fig. 1. Macro-action in the *GRIPS* domain, obtained by merging the *move* and *getProductFromRS* actions from the native *GRIPS_MOVE* domain. The effects of the actions are represented by the literals located below them, whereas the literals located above indicate the preconditions that are required at the start, end, or during the action, depending on their respective positions.

Example 1. We consider a common scenario in the RCLL as running example, which involves one robot delivering a product to a station for processing. In many obtained plans, another agent is responsible for retrieving the product from the output side of the station after processing. The encoding for the *move* and *get* actions from the native domain, along with the resulting macro, can be seen in Fig. 1. The native domain used in the experiments corresponds to the *GRIPS_MOVE* domain, which was evaluated in [12], together with the *GRIPS* macro-based domain. In the latter, the *move* action was merged with other actions involved in retrieving or delivering a product from or to a station. A macro-based plan obtained for this scenario is presented in Listing 1.

Listing 1. Macro-based plan for mounting a ring. We consider 15 seconds for movement and 30 seconds for retrieving or delivering a product from or to the ring station (RS).

```
[0.000]   move_and_deliverProductToRS_start(r1,loc1,rs1_input,rs1,p1)
[45.000]  move_and_deliverProductToRS_end(r1,loc1,rs1_input,rs1,p1)
[45.001]  move_and_getProductFromRS_start(r2,loc2,rs1_output,rs1,p1)
[90.001]  move_and_getProductFromRS_end(r2,loc2,rs1_output,rs1,p1)
```

Listing 2. Unfolded plan for mounting a ring.

```
[0.000]     move_start(r1,loc1,rs1_input)
[15.000]    move_end(r1,loc1,rs1_input)
[15.0001]   deliverProductToRS_start(r1,rs1_input,rs1,p1)
[45.0001]   deliverProductToRS_end(r1,rs1_input,rs1,p1)
[45.001]    move_start(r2,loc2,rs1_output)
[60.001]    move_end(r2,loc2,rs1_output)
[60.0011]   getProductFromRS_start(r2,rs1_output,rs1,p1)
[90.0011]   getProductFromRS_end(r2,rs1_output,rs1,p1)
```

Upon obtaining a macro-based plan, the initial step involves the process of unfolding it, wherein the macro-actions $a = a_1 \circ a_2$ are replaced with their respective original atomic actions a_1 and a_2. In order to adhere to the *no moving targets* requirement of PDDL 2.1, a small time unit δ is introduced to ensure the existence of mutually exclusive starting and ending timepoints of the atomic actions.

Definition 1. *(Unfolded Plan) Given a macro-based plan MP as a finite collection of timed events $(t, a^{\vdash})$ and $(t + dur(a), a^{\dashv})$, let $UP = \{(t, a_1^{\vdash}), (t + dur(a_1), a_1^{\dashv}), (t + dur(a_1) + \delta, a_2^{\vdash}), (t + dur(a) + \delta, a_2^{\dashv}) \mid (t, a^{\vdash}) \in MP, a = a_1 \circ a_2\} \cup MP \setminus \{(t, a^{\vdash}), (t + dur(a), a^{\dashv}) \mid (t, a^{\vdash}) \in MP, a = a_1 \circ a_2\}$, with δ small enough to guarantee the "no moving targets" requirement without changing the order of starting and ending timepoints of actions of the plan, be the unfolded plan.*

Going back to the running example, the unfolded plan UP obtained by unfolding the macro-based in Listing 1 is shown in Listing 2.

In order to use macro-actions in practice, we have to ensure that they are sound, i.e., an unfolded plan is still a solution of the original planning problem.

Definition 2. *(Soundness of Macro-actions). A macro-action composition $a = a_1 \circ a_2$ is sound if each solution for a planning problem using the domain involving the macro-action can be mapped to a solution for the same planning problem using the original domain, just by replacing the macro-action in the plan with the original atomic actions.*

Let us also note that a domain with sequential temporal macro-actions may be incomplete when original atomic actions are dropped, as the latter can then only be applied in the sequence determined by a macro-action, which restricts the solution space.

4   Refinement of Macro-actions

Since the straightforward unfolding of a macro-based plan might lead to suboptimally timed atomic actions, we perform an additional step that refines the unfolded plan by addressing the suboptimalities (at least to some extent). The refinement step consists of building a Simple Temporal Network (STN) [13] based on the unfolded plan. STNs provide a useful representation for temporal plans as they offer greater flexibility during plan execution. Rather than mapping each action to absolute time points, which can be difficult to adhere to in real-world scenarios, STNs represent the relationship between actions using a partial temporal order. In essence, STN nodes represent temporal events, such as the start or end of an action, while direct edges encode a partial temporal order between them. Additionally, temporal constraints are encoded by labeling each edge with a pair of values $[lb, ub]$, where both lb and ub are either a natural number or $+\infty$. The numbers lb and ub represent a lower bound or an upper bound, respectively, between the two timepoints associated with the source and target node of the edge. If $+\infty$ is used, the target node can occur at any time after the source node.

Given a temporal plan, it is possible to build the corresponding STN by adapting the algorithm from Veloso et al. [29] to lift a total order in classical planning to a partial order as seen in ROSPlan [3,27] and, to some extent, in a work from Cimatti et al. [7]. The adaptation to the temporal case is shown in Algorithm 1. For each action a in the plan (lines 4–10), two nodes are added to the STN, identifying the start and end of the action, along with an edge between them with $lb = ub = dur(a)$. An extra node that corresponds to the start of the plan is also included, which is connected to every other starting node via an edge. Then, we iterate over each node in descending order of assigned time in the input plan (line 12). For each node, we identify the supporting edges (or causal links) and the interference edges (or threats) going into that node. We use different names for the edges to better explain their roles, but they have the same semantics inside an STN. For each precondition of the current node (lines 13–17), a supporting edge is defined from the latest previous node enabling that precondition to the current node. In lines 18–31, an interference edge is added from every previous node to the current node in case the latter interferes with the former. A node interferes with another one if it disables one of its preconditions or if it is adding/deleting an atom deleted/added by the other. Invariants must also be taken into consideration. We treat them as preconditions of a starting node in the case of supporting edges and as postconditions of an ending node in the case of interference edges. This makes sure that no node can be scheduled between the start and end of an action if it interferes with the invariant.

The algorithm is greedy and does not guarantee to find the best possible partial order in terms of concurrency [8], but it is polynomial ($\mathcal{O}(n^2)$ with n the number of events in a temporal plan) and runs in negligible time compared to the planning time.

Figure 2 and Fig. 3 display the two STNs built for the macro-based plan and its unfolded version, respectively. One can easily identify the key aspect: the (red) causal link that initially led to a macro-action is shifted to the second sub-action after the macro is unfolded. The aim of the proposed method is to utilize such opportunities for concurrency, which are quite common after macro unfolding. Although it cannot be guaranteed that this approach will always result in an improved makespan, either because the edges still refer to the first sub-action or because the target nodes of shifted links may not contribute to the overall makespan, the experimental results presented in the following section indicate that it provides benefits for almost all RCLL instances.

The final step involves extracting a potentially improved plan from the STN that was obtained during the unfolding process. A solution of the STN is characterized by an assignment of timepoints to the network nodes while satisfying the temporal constraints specified by the edges. As each node in the network represents the start or end of an action, any solution of the STN provides a valid temporal plan. Although the unfolded plan is a feasible solution of the STN (by construction), it may not necessarily be an optimal one such that the timepoint for the latest event(s), determining the overall makespan, is smallest.

Algorithm 1: Building an STN from temporal plan TP. We let $pre(e_i)$ refer to the starting (or ending) precondition if e_i is a starting (or ending) event, and similarly for $add(e_i)$ and $del(e_i)$; $preInv(e_i) = pre^\vdash(e_i)$ (or $preInv(e_i) = \emptyset$) if e_i is a starting (or ending) event, and oppositely for $postInv(e_i)$.

Input : List of n timed events e_i (start and end of actions a_i), ordered by timepoints t_i, in temporal plan $TP = \{e_1 = (t_1, a_1^{x_1}), e_2 = (t_2, a_2^{x_2}), \dots\}$ with $x_i \in \{\vdash, \dashv\}$

Output: STN

1 STN $\leftarrow \emptyset$;
2 $plan\_start \leftarrow (0, start)$;
3 STN.addAsNode($plan\_start$)   // adding a start node for the plan;
4 **for** $i \leftarrow 1$ **to** n **do**
5   STN.addAsNode(e_i);
6   **if** $isStartingNode(e_i)$ **then**
7   STN.addEdge($plan\_start, e_i, 0, +\infty$)   // (source, target, lb, ub);
8   **else**
9   STN.addEdge($findStartNode(e_i), e_i, dur(a_i), dur(a_i)$);
10   **end if**
11 **end for**
12 **for** $i \leftarrow n$ **down-to** 1 **do**
13   **foreach** $p \in pre(e_i) \cup preInv(e_i)$ **do**
14   /* For each precondition p, look for the latest previous node e_j s.t. $p \in add(e_j)$ */
15         $supporting\_node \leftarrow findLastSupportingNode(p, i)$;
16   STN.addEdge($supporting\_node, e_i, 0, +\infty$) ;
17   **end foreach**
18   **foreach** $p \in del(e_i)$ **do**
19   /* For each delete effect p, look for all previous nodes e_j s.t. $p \in pre(e_j) \cup postInv(e_j) \cup add(e_j)$ */
20         $interfering\_nodes \leftarrow$ $findAllNodesNeedingEffect(p, i) \cup findAllNodesAddingEffect(p, i)$;
21   **foreach** $interfering\_node \in interfering\_nodes$ **do**
22   STN.addEdge($interfering\_node, e_i, 0, +\infty$) ;
23   **end foreach**
24   **end foreach**
25   **foreach** $p \in add(e_i)$ **do**
26   /* For each add effect p, look for all previous nodes e_j s.t. $p \in del(e_j)$ */
27         $interfering\_nodes \leftarrow findAllNodesDeletingEffect(p, i)$;
28   **foreach** $interfering\_node \in interfering\_nodes$ **do**
29   STN.addEdge($interfering\_node, e_i, 0, +\infty$) ;
30   **end foreach**
31   **end foreach**
32 **end for**
33 **return** STN;

Definition 3. *(Refined Plan) Given an unfolded plan UP and its STN $G = (V, E)$, let $\sigma : V \to \mathbb{R}$ be the best solution for the STN, mapping each node to its earliest possible*

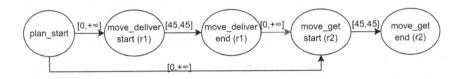

Fig. 2. STN of the macro-based plan, with most action attributes omitted for better readability.

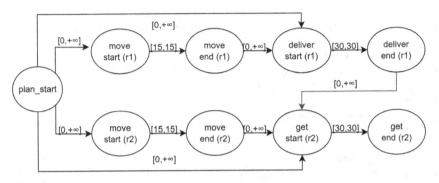

Fig. 3. STN of the unfolded plan, with most action attributes omitted for better readability. (Color figure online)

time. The refined plan RP is defined as $RP = \{(\sigma(a^{\vdash}), a^{\vdash}), (\sigma(a^{\vdash}) + dur(a), a^{\dashv}) \mid a^{\vdash} \in V\}.$

Note that, in Definition 3, we are only interested in timepoints assigned to starting nodes. Since in this work we are only considering durative actions with fixed durations, the constraints specified by the generated STN fix the timepoint of each ending node to the sum of the corresponding starting node's timepoint and the action's duration.

The computation of an optimal solution σ for an STN can be achieved in polynomial time by applying Dijkstra's algorithm for shortest paths [14]. A detailed explanation of this procedure is provided in the Dechter et al. paper about STNs [13]. To summarize, the STN is converted into a distance graph: for each edge, a reversed copy is created, whose weight is the negative of the edge's lower bound. The original edge's weight is its upper bound. Then, the shortest paths (in terms of edges' weights) from each node to the *plan_start* node are calculated, where the negatives of the obtained values provide the earliest timepoints for the nodes. The computational complexity of the entire process remains $\mathcal{O}(n^2)$.

A refined plan is presented in Listing 3. Thanks to the rearrangement of some edges w.r.t. to the STN of the macro-based plan, it is possible to anticipate the *move* action related to the second robot, resulting in a 15-seconds improvement over the macro-based plan. It is important to note that the requirement of "no moving targets" is still met since the two *move* actions do not have any shared attributes.

Listing 3. Refined Plan for mounting a ring.

```
[0.000]     move_start(r1,loc1,rs1_input)
[0.000]     move_start(r2,loc2,rs1_output)
[15.000]    move_end(r1,loc1,rs1_input)
[15.000]    move_end(r2,loc2,rs1_output)
[15.0001]   deliverProductToRS_start(r1,rs1,rs1_input,p1)
[45.0001]   deliverProductToRS_end(r1,rs1,rs1_input,p1)
[45.0011]   getProductFromRS_start(r2,rs1,rs1_output,p1)
[75.0011]   getProductFromRS_end(r2,rs1,rs1_output,p1)
```

5 Evaluation

We conducted experiments with the two RCLL domains *GRIPS* and *GRIPS_MOVE* from our previous planners evaluation paper [12]. As already mentioned in Example 1, *GRIPS_MOVE* is the original domain with atomic actions, while *GRIPS* is based on macro-actions only, obtained by merging the *move* action such that it (implicitly) occurs immediately before other actions. The macro-actions in *GRIPS* are sound and complete w.r.t. the actions defined in *GRIPS_MOVE*. Therefore, an unfolded or refined solution from *GRIPS* is also a valid solution for *GRIPS_MOVE*. While improvements in terms of planning time and total time have already been discussed in the planners evaluation paper [12], we focus in this paper on the further improvement of the makespan obtained by refining macro-based plans from *GRIPS*. We compare the refined plans with both the macro-based plans from which they originate and the plans found for the same instances with the *GRIPS_MOVE* domain, in order to provide a comprehensive assessment of the benefits of using macro-actions with refinement. Since our focus is on the makespan and not total time, and since the RCLL is an online domain, we set a 60 s timeout for the planning time. We ran each instance with three different planners: Optic [1], Temporal Fast Downward (TFD) [15], and YAHSP3 [30]. All tests were conducted on a machine with 16 GB RAM and an Intel i5 10300u CPU under Ubuntu 18.06. We used the same set of 50 instances used in the past [12], involving 10 different game configurations generated by the official software suite of the league, each with 5 different product configurations of increasing complexity.

The results are shown in Table 1. For each instance, we compare three different plans: (1) the one obtained from the native domain (*GRIPS_MOVE*) denoted as "native", (2) the one related to the *GRIPS* macro domain denoted as "macro", and (3) the latter refined through the procedure presented in this paper denoted as "refined". We cal-

Table 1. Average makespan improvement (positive numbers represent a reduction), measured in percentage. In each column, given three types of plans (native, macro and refined), the entries provide the relative makespan improvement achieved by the planners for a pair of encodings. Please note that TFD could only solve 11 out of 50 instances for the macro vs. native pairing.

planner	macro vs. native	refined vs. native	refined vs. macro
Optic	−6.0%	+3.3%	+9.2%
TFD	−30.5%	−13.1%	+12.7%
YAHSP3	+36.6%	+43.6%	+11.1%

culate the difference in percentage between the makespan of every type of plan for each instance and planner, and report the average makespan improvement in Table 1. For example, a value of −6.0% in the first cell indicates that with Optic, on average, the macro-based plans are 6.0% worse (longer) than the native ones. In contrast, with YAHSP3, the macro-based plans are 36.6% better (shorter) on average, which increases to 43.6% if we consider the refined plans instead of the macro-based plans.

The results provide valuable insights. For Optic, the use of macro-actions without refinement led to a decline in plan quality compared to the native domain. However, after refinement (which improved the macro-based plans by an average of 9.2%), the plans obtained were on average 3.3% better than the native ones. This improvement was accompanied by a significant boost in planning performance due to macro-actions, as observed in our evaluation paper. Thus, the use of macro-actions and plan refinement can result in an overall improvement in both planning time and makespan for Optic.

For TFD, the results may be misleading as it was only able to solve 11 out of the 50 instances with the native domain, which were the easiest ones. Please note that the difficulty in solving large instances was exactly the reason for the introduction of macro-actions in our previous work [12]. Interestingly, for the 11 simple instances, TFD found much better solutions with the native domain, and results with the macro domain were on average 30.5% worse. However, refining these solutions reduced the gap to 13.1%. Among the three planners, TFD thus benefits the most from plan refinement, with an average makespan improvement of 12.7%.

YAHSP3 is a planner that, unlike its competitors, adopts heuristics that sacrifice plan quality for coverage (i.e., the ability to find at least one solution). As observed in our evaluation paper [12], it is one of the planners with the best percentage of solved instances. However, the difficulty of solving the native domain is reflected in the significant difference between the makespan with the native and the macro domain, which is 36.6% better. This gap increases to even 43.6% when the macro-based plans are refined.

Overall, the makespan improvements obtained through the refinement of macro-based plans are consistent across the three planners. Moreover, since the computing time for refinement is negligible compared to the rest of the planning process, this procedure provides a further benefit to the use of macro-actions in temporal planning. The results show that the proposed plan refinement method can be beneficial and lead to a reduction of the makespan of plans for complex logistics domains like the RCLL.

Additionally, the technique presented in this paper has been deployed by the GRIPS team in the RCLL German Open 2023 [26]. The refinement enabled the anticipation of certain move actions during the execution, which was clearly observed in the real field. This resulted in a better production rate, helping the GRIPS team to win the league.

6   Conclusion

Using temporal planning to manage complex logistics domains such as the RCLL presents challenges regarding scalability. One way to tackle the combinatorial explosion of the planing process is to define macro-actions that restrict certain actions to be executed sequentially, thereby restricting the solution space. As a consequence, better solutions might be excluded. In this paper, we propose a post-processing refinement procedure for plans obtained using macro-actions. The macro-actions are unfolded into atomic actions, generating a corresponding STN, and then the best possible solution for such an STN in terms of makespan is calculated. Our experimental evaluation shows that, on average, the refined solutions improve the original macro-based plans by 9% to 13%, depending on the planner used. These refined solutions are not part of the macro domain solution space, but they are valid solutions for the native domain, providing access to previously excluded parts of the solution space. With the Optic planner, the macro-action refinement allowed to go from an average deterioration of the plans' makespan when macro-actions are used to an average improvement w.r.t. the native domain. Given the fact that our procedure runs in polynomial time, which in practice is negligible in comparison to the planning time, and can consistently improve the solutions found for a domain featuring macro-actions, it provides a valuable and efficient addition to the handling of complex temporal planning problems by using macro-actions.

Acknowledgements. M. De Bortoli and M. Gebser were funded by Kärntner Wirtschaftsförderungs Fonds (project no. 28472), cms electronics GmbH, FunderMax GmbH, Hirsch Armbänder GmbH, incubed IT GmbH, Infineon Technologies Austria AG, Isovolta AG, Kostwein Holding GmbH, and Privatstiftung Kärntner Sparkasse. L. Chrpa was funded by the Czech Science Foundation (project no. 23-05575S). M. De Bortoli's and M. Gebser's visit to CTU in Prague was funded by the OP VVV project no. EF15_003/0000470 "Robotics 4 Industry 4.0" and by the Czech Ministry of Education, Youth and Sports under the Czech-Austrian Mobility programme (project no. 8J22AT003), respectively. L. Chrpa's visits to University of Klagenfurt were funded by OeAD, Austria's Agency for Education and Internationalisation (project no. CZ 15/2022).

References

1. Benton, J., Coles, A., Coles, A.: Temporal planning with preferences and time-dependent continuous costs (2012)
2. Botea, A., Enzenberger, M., Müller, M., Schaeffer, J.: Macro-FF: improving AI planning with automatically learned macro-operators. J. Artif. Intell. Res. **24**, 581–621 (2005)
3. Cashmore, M., et al.: ROSPlan: planning in the robot operating system. In: Proceedings of the International Conference on Automated Planning and Scheduling, vol. 25 (2015)
4. Chrpa, L., Vallati, M.: Improving domain-independent planning via critical section macro-operators. In: Proceedings of the AAAI Conference on Artificial Intelligence, vol. 33 (2019)
5. Chrpa, L., Vallati, M.: Planning with critical section macros: theory and practice. J. Artif. Intell. Res. **74**, 691–732 (2022). https://doi.org/10.1613/jair.1.13269
6. Chrpa, L., Vallati, M., McCluskey, T.L.: MUM: a technique for maximising the utility of macro-operators by constrained generation and use. In: Twenty-Fourth ICAPS (2014)
7. Cimatti, A., Do, M., Micheli, A., Roveri, M., Smith, D.E.: Strong temporal planning with uncontrollable durations. Artif. Intell. **256**, 1–34 (2018)
8. Coles, A., Coles, A., Fox, M., Long, D.: Forward-chaining partial-order planning. In: Proceedings of the International Conference on Automated Planning and Scheduling, vol. 20 (2010)
9. Coles, A., Smith, A.: On the inference and management of macro-actions in forward-chaining planning. In: Twenty-Fourth UK Planning and Scheduling SIG (2005)
10. Coles, A.I., Smith, A.J.: Marvin: a heuristic search planner with online macro-action learning. J. Artif. Intell. Res. **28**, 119–156 (2007)

11. Dawson, C., Siklossy, L.: The role of preprocessing in problem solving systems: "an ounce of reflection is worth a pound of backtracking". In: Proceedings of the 5th International Joint Conference on Artificial Intelligence, vol. 1, pp. 465–471 (1977)

12. De Bortoli, M., Steinbauer-Wagner, G.: Evaluating action-based temporal planners performance in the robocup logistics league. In: Eguchi, A., Lau, N., Paetzel-Prüsmann, M., Wanichanon, T. (eds.) RoboCup 2022. LNCS, vol. 13561, pp. 87–99. Springer, Cham (2023). https://doi.org/10.1007/978-3-031-28469-4_8

13. Dechter, R., Meiri, I., Pearl, J.: Temporal constraint networks. Artif. Intell. **49**(1), 61–95 (1991). https://doi.org/10.1016/0004-3702(91)90006-6

14. Dijkstra, E.W.: A note on two problems in connexion with graphs. In: Edsger Wybe Dijkstra: His Life, Work, and Legacy, pp. 287–290 (2022)

15. Eyerich, P., Mattmüller, R., Röger, G.: Using the context-enhanced additive heuristic for temporal and numeric planning. In: Proceedings of the Nineteenth International Conference on Automated Planning and Scheduling (ICAPS 2009). AAAI Press (2009)

16. Ferrein, A., Steinbauer, G.: 20 years of RoboCup: a subjective retrospection. KI-Künstliche Intelligenz **30**, 225–232 (2016)

17. Fikes, R., Nilsson, N.J.: STRIPS: a new approach to the application of theorem proving to problem solving. Artif. Intell. **2**(3/4), 189–208 (1971)

18. Fox, M., Long, D.: PDDL2.1: an extension to PDDL for expressing temporal planning domains. J. Artif. Intell. Res. (JAIR) **20**, 61–124 (2003)

19. Hansson, E.: Temporal task and motion plans: Planning and plan repair: repairing temporal task and motion plans using replanning with temporal macro operators (2018)

20. Hofmann, T., Limpert, N., Mataré, V., Ferrein, A., Lakemeyer, G.: Winning the robocup logistics league with fast navigation, precise manipulation, and robust goal reasoning. In: RoboCup 2019: Robot World Cup XXIII, pp. 504–516 (2019)

21. Hofmann, T., Niemueller, T., Lakemeyer, G.: Initial results on generating macro actions from a plan database for planning on autonomous mobile robots. In: Twenty-Seventh International Conference on Automated Planning and Scheduling (2017)

22. Miura, S., Fukunaga, A.: Automatic extraction of axioms for planning. In: Twenty-Seventh International Conference on Automated Planning and Scheduling (2017)

23. Nau, D., Ghallab, M., Traverso, P.: Automated Planning: Theory & Practice. Morgan Kaufmann Publishers Inc., San Francisco (2004)

24. Newton, M.A.H., Levine, J., Fox, M., Long, D.: Learning macro-actions for arbitrary planners and domains. In: ICAPS, vol. 2007, pp. 256–263 (2007)

25. Niemueller, T., Ewert, D., Reuter, S., Ferrein, A., Jeschke, S., Lakemeyer, G.: RoboCup Logistics League Sponsored by Festo: A Competitive Factory Automation Testbed, pp. 605–618 (2016)

26. RoboCup: RoboCup Logistics League - German Open Aachen 2023 (2023). https://robocup-logistics.github.io/go2023/. Accessed 01 May 2023

27. ROSPlan: ROSPlan Esteral Plan (2021). https://kcl-planning.github.io/ROSPlan//tutorials/tutorial_05. Accessed 12 Apr 2023

28. Ulz, T., Ludwiger, J., Steinbauer, G.: A robust and flexible system architecture for facing the robocup logistics league challenge. In: RoboCup 2018: Robot World Cup XXII (2019)

29. Veloso, M.M., Pérez, A., Carbonell, J.G.: Nonlinear planning with parallel resource allocation (1990)

30. Vidal, V.: YAHSP3 and YAHSP3-MT in the 8th International Planning Competition. In: Proceedings of the 8th International Planning Competition (IPC-2014), pp. 64–65 (2014)

31. Wullinger, P., Schmid, U., Scholz, U.: Spanning the middle ground between classical and temporal planning. In: Proceedings of the 22nd Workshop on Planen, Scheduling und Konfigurieren (2008)

In Defense of Scene Graph Generation for Human-Robot Open-Ended Interaction in Service Robotics

Maëlic Neau[1,2,3(✉)], Paulo Santos[3], Anne-Gwenn Bosser[2], and Cédric Buche[1,2]

[1] CROSSING CNRS IRL 2010, Adelaide, Australia
[2] Lab-STICC CNRS UMR 6285/ENIB, Brest, France
[3] Flinders University, Adelaide, Australia
{neau0001,paulo.santos}@flinders.edu.au

Abstract. Compositional relations represent a good source of information in the task of scene understanding. However, current approaches in domestic service robotics only scratch the surface of the benefits of compositional relations by leveraging only their spatial component. In this position paper, we propose a new perspective on the use of compositional relations as a means to extract meaning from context in open-ended interactions. We especially design a multi-layer representation based on scene graphs that encapsulates four different dimensions of knowledge. To exploit this new representation, we introduce a new large-scale dataset for indoor service robots with high-quality scene graph annotations. We then argue for the opportunities of using this representation to easily extract a wide range of fine-grained information about human interaction with context (All data and code are available at https://github. com/Maelic/IndoorVG).

Keywords: Scene Graph Generation · Service Robotics · Human-Robot Interaction

1 Introduction

As Service Robotics is moving forward to domestic applications, the need for reasoning engines to support open-ended interactions with humans will soon become critical. An Open-Ended Human-Robot Interaction (OE-HRI) happens when an autonomous agent is given as the only goal to assist humans in their everyday life. In such scenarios, the human is not expected to explicitly address the robot or give any sort of details on the activity he wants to perform (i.e. intentions) or what sort of assistive actions he could require (i.e. needs). A first consideration when designing reasoning engines to address this problem is the efficient representation of acquired knowledge. As with many Human-in-the-Loop systems, a comprehensive and symbolic representation is preferred over neural approaches of Deep Neural Networks, as the former provides a readable (and, thus, accountable) output [18]. In this work, we are interested in scenarios

C. Buche et al. (Eds.): RoboCup 2023, LNAI 14140, pp. 299–310, 2024.
https://doi.org/10.1007/978-3-031-55015-7_25

where the autonomous agent has to intuitively collaborate with the human during open-ended interactions in domestic environments. In such scenarios, traditional goal-directed representations [3,11,16,19] used in service robotics would be inefficient as the scope of their representation only extends to the robot capabilities. This work presents a new type of general symbolic representation that supports open-ended reasoning in domestic contexts. Especially, we are interested in representing context information as Scene Graphs and extracting this representation from image features directly using Scene Graph Generation (SGG) [23].

SGG aims at generating a complete abstract representation of the scene, including both the static context (as spatial relations and dynamic context), as well as functional relations between agents and the environment. From a bottom-up perspective, SGG leverages image features to infer object regions, object pairs, and relations in the form of $< subject, predicate, object >$ triplets. The connection of those triplets forms a directed graph where each vertex contains information about the object's location coordinates and label. From a semantic perspective, these relations can be of different types such as spatial (e.g. $< person, next\ to, table >$), functional (e.g. $< person, eating, pizza >$), part- whole (e.g. $< person, has, head >$) or attributive (e.g. $< person, wearing, shirt >$). Spatial relations can be useful to model a semantic map of the environment and help the agent to share a common space with the human. Functional relations can be used to infer human mental states such as intentions or needs. Traditional approaches in SGG do not model these relations separately, instead, all kinds of relations are learned and predicted together. While this is reasonable for general purposes, it is unsuited for Service Robotics where spatial information needs to be treated apart from functional ones. In this work, we present a novel approach to the task of SGG, oriented toward applications in Domestic Service Robotics. (1) we introduce a new task of Scene Understanding for Human-Robot Open-Ended Interaction and show the opportunities and challenges of SGG in these settings; (2) we detail the collection and refinement of a new dataset containing high-quality scene graphs annotations of indoor scenes and (3) provides a set of preliminary experiments that outline the advantages of this new dataset in a real-world evaluation scenario.

2   Motivations

In OE-HRI, no explicit details are given about the activity that the human wants to perform nor the assistive actions he may require to achieve it. Modeling humans' intentions and goals is a complex task even in simple scenarios, since it is contextually dependent. Specifically, relations between spatial and semantic context are necessary for a holistic scene understanding [8]. In contrast to traditional activity recognition methods, which reason mostly on temporal features, holistic scene understanding aims to understand human behaviors through context modeling [6]. To address real-world scenarios, this context needs to be as large and extensive as possible. The present paper focus on this new direction by proposing a novel meta-representation that encapsulates the global context of the scene in the form of knowledge graph triplets. Traditional Knowledge Representation approaches to service robotics can be classified into symbolic representations [9,16], ontologies [11], or hybrid representations [3,19]. Despite their effectiveness in representing knowledge in a comprehensive manner, these approaches' rule-based design hinders their ability to exploit large unstructured data. In addition, these representations are not linked to the perception pipeline, posing a significant challenge to transferring real-time acquired data, such as object features, into the database's specific representation. These frameworks are also goal-directed only, as they are primarily designed to cater to the robot's actions and capabilities in the real world. In this work, we argue that these issues make this type of representation not optimal to support complex reasoning in OE-HRI where a maximum of information needs to be extracted from the scene. On the other hand, advances in Scene Graph Generation [15] tackle these bottlenecks and propose to extract complex holistic representations from image features directly. Popular approaches combine object detection backbones such as the popular Faster-RCNN [17] with a graph generation model in a two-stage pipeline [20,22,23]. More recently there has been an emergence of scene graph generation for embodied agents, especially in autonomous exploration and navigation. Graphs representing spatial relations between static objects are leveraged from 2D image features [7] or from 3D sensors using PointCloud [13] during the navigation of an embodied agent. This representation can then be used for planning and exploration of the environment [1,2]. Approaches in robotics are actually goal-directed for specific navigation tasks and only take into account the *topological* level of the relations between objects while approaches in SGG make no difference between relation types. This work aims to bridge the gap between those approaches by proposing a new paradigm that leverages image features to produce a multi-layer graph structure composed of 4 different relation types that are of specific use in OE-HRI. We believe that this new type of symbolic representation will facilitate the localization of objects and agents as well as the description of their interaction within the environment. Moreover, a symbolic representation of this sort will enhance the explainability of the system, while the scene graph format facilitates the learning and discovery of new relations.

The proposed meta-representation represents every entity (agents or objects) in the form of a single label associated with a 2D image region. This type of approach has the advantage of ensuring the consistency of relations across different domains while being more efficient for real-time processing. Our representation encapsulates different types of knowledge that can be used at different steps of reasoning. Four categories, or dimensions, are introduced in this paper:

- **Functional**: dynamic relations between entities;
- **Topological**: static spatial relation between any pair of entities;
- **Physical Part-Whole**: hierarchical and invariant relation between a defined entity (i.e. "whole") and one of its building blocks (i.e. "part");
- **Attributive**: relation between a physical entity and a non-invariant attribute.

Table 1. Example of relations for each category.

Category	Examples
Functional	person reading book, coat hanging on rack, cat sleeping on bed
Topological	phone on table, person next to window, paper on top of keyboard
Physical part-whole	person has head, key on keyboard, window on building
Attributive	person wearing jacket, frame has painting, writing on sign

We provide a few examples of these four categories in Table 1. **Functional** relations encompass temporal dependencies of events between entities in the scene, it can be atomic actions from agents or discrete changes in the domain. This dimension can be used to reason about the sequentiality of events. Next is the **Topological** dimension that builds a spatial abstract map of the scene and supports qualitative spatial reasoning. The **Physical Part-Whole** dimension relates to components of agents or objects and how they are assembled. Finally, the **Attributive** dimension can be used to describe entities. Altogether, these four dimensions may support complex reasoning about the purpose and consequences of actions, object affordances, and, ultimately, the actors' intentions and goals. It is important to notice here that categories are not uni-directional, i.e. both triplets $< flowers, painted\ on, towel >$ and $< towel, has, flowers >$ will be similarly classified as attributive. The design of this meta-representation and choice of dimensions has been made aiming at providing useful information to an autonomous agent in the understanding of the scene. As annotating scene graph data is a time-consuming task, this choice has also been made by taking into consideration existing large-scale scene graph datasets such as Visual Genome (VG) [10]. The next section elaborates on the strategy to select and refine scene graph annotations in a novel large-scale indoor scene graph dataset.

3 Dataset Creation

Annotating data for the SGG task is very time-consuming as not only bounding boxes and labels need to be annotated but also object pairs and predicates in every image. Noticing that VG contains densely annotated indoor scene snapshots, we focused on leveraging the original annotations provided by authors [10]. Annotations in Visual Genome were collected by annotators in the form of region captions, then various parsing techniques have been applied to retrieve $< subject, predicate, object >$ triplets for each region. This resulted in a noisy dataset that contains 53K object classes and 27K predicate classes, where more than 50% of them only have one sample. The process of selecting a subset of indoor images, curating the annotations, and adding new annotations for relation categories, is presented below.

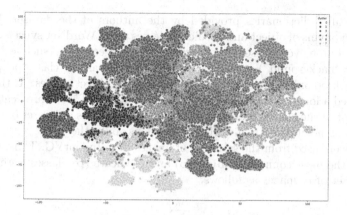

Fig. 1. T-SNE visualization of Visual Genome image clusters, with k clusters = 9.

3.1 Leveraging Existing Data

As highlighted in previous work [25], several coarse to fine-grained motifs can be mined from the Visual Genome dataset annotations. This makes sense because relations are highly inter-dependent and images from Visual Genome can be easily clustered by higher-level semantic frames. The hint here is that Visual Genome images represent different contexts, such as *food*, *sports*, or *streets* that can be clustered by looking at the semantics of regions annotations. Our method uses Sentence Embeddings to compute each region caption using the MpNet sentence transformers pre-trained model[1], then region embeddings are averaged per image and clusters are computed using the *k-means* algorithm. We ran experiments with different cluster sizes, ranging from 2 to 30. We found out that 9 was the best value, in regard to the average silhouette score. In the T-SNE visualization from Fig. 1, we can see a clear distinction between image cluster, that shows clear patterns or motifs [25], in regard to the context of the scene. The obtained clusters have a size ranging from 3,927 to 20,698 images. For analysis and experiments in this study, we selected a cluster that encapsulates indoor scenes with a size of 17,740 images. We call the new distribution extracted from this cluster the **IndoorVG** split.

3.2 Refining Annotations

As stated in numerous works (e.g. [12,25]), annotations from Visual Genome are noisy and contain duplicate bounding boxes, ambiguous classes, or synonyms. For all images in the IndoorVG subset, annotations were processed as follows: for object regions, we replicated the approach proposed by [23] to merge bounding boxes with an Intersection over Union (IoU) greater than or equal to 0.9. For the textual annotations, we also followed [23] to remove stop-words and punctuation

---

[1] https://huggingface.co/sentence-transformers/all-mpnet-base-v2.

using the alias dictionaries provided by the authors of the dataset. We then merged synonyms of object and predicate classes using WordNet synsets. Finally, we manually removed classes that represent abstract concepts (such as "object", "edge" or "background") or groups of entities (such as the class "people" and "food") to keep only physical, tangible, and unitary object classes. At this point, we obtained a long-tailed data split of 11,620 objects and 5,407 predicate classes where most of the classes still possess only one sample. As a dataset of this scale would be of no use for real-world applications, only the most representative relations were used from the selection of images from IndoorVG. Thus, for every graph G, the most connected object ($\hat{o}$) and predicate ($\hat{p}$) classes were selected from the set of n images as follows:

$$\theta(\hat{o}, \hat{p}) = \max_{\hat{o}, \hat{p}} \sum_{k=1}^{n} \text{Conn}(\hat{o}, \hat{p}, G_k) \tag{1}$$

$$\text{Conn}(\hat{o}, \hat{p}, G) = |G(u, v, w)|, w \in \hat{p} \vee [u, v] \in \hat{o} \tag{2}$$

To encourage diversity of object classes and variety of relations, we set $|\hat{o}| = 130$ and $|\hat{p}| = 50$. This split between the number of object and predicate classes is similar to the most used versions of Visual Genome in SGG [23]. As this is a complex optimization problem, a satisfying solution can be found by first optimizing $\theta(\hat{o})$ and then $\theta(\hat{o}, \hat{p})$ with a fixed set of classes $\hat{o}$. By doing so, we ensure to keep the maximum of relations that describe every scene in fine-grained detail. Finally, a data split of 149,020 relations was obtained with an average of 9.18 relations per image across 16,221 images.

3.3   Relations Categories

To classify relations by semantic categories, previous approaches relied on hand-crafted predicate categories [25]. However, this categorization only takes into account the semantics of predicates, which assumes the consistency of annotations in the dataset. This assumption, however, is far from true, given the semantic ambiguity of annotations introduced in [26]. We give a clear example given the following two triplets from Visual Genome:

$$man \xrightarrow{\text{has}} nose \tag{3}$$

$$man \xrightarrow{\text{has}} surfboard \tag{4}$$

When we look at image samples that contain these relations, we see that Formula 3 refers to a `part-whole` relation that would be described as *nose is part of man* while in Formula 4, the relation is `functional` and could be described as *man is carrying surfboard*, even though they share the same predicate *has*. To alleviate this issue, we categorized the relations based on the entire triplets. We first manually annotated a set of 500 random triplets between the four categories `topological`, `functional`, `part-whole`, and `attributive`. Then, we used these samples to fine-tune OpenAI's GPT3 [4] large language model to give an effective classification of all triplets in the dataset. Here, we used GPT3 to benefit from its pre-training on a large corpus of data that showed some abilities in making inferences about commonsense knowledge [5]. Commonsense knowledge is needed to differentiate between ambiguous cases, such as $< man, on, phone >$ (which is a `functionnal` relation, even though the predicate "on" is usually used in `topological` relations). We fine-tuned the *ada*, *curie*, and *davinci* versions of GPT3 using a training set of 400 triplets and a validation set of 100, results are displayed in Table 2. We observed that *davinci* showed the best performance on correctly classifying misleading triplets, such as the `part-whole` triplet $< key, on, keyboard >$; which was misclassified as `topological` by *ada* and *curie*.

Table 2. Fine-tuning of GPT3 for classification of triplet categories.

Model	Accuracy	Weighted F1
Ada	0.8	0.792589
Curie	0.85	0.855134
Davinci	0.86	0.858542

The present approach is more efficient than the traditional methods, but not optimal. The triplet-level classification applied is still too general to disambiguate rare and complex cases. For instance, we noticed that the triplet $< arm, on top of, man >$ could even be a `part-whole` relation or `topological` relation, depending on the visual features. To solve this issue, future work should consider annotating the relation triplets per image and training a classifier based on the union of the visual features and the triplet embedding.

3.4 Data Augmentation

The effect of selecting a subset of the original annotations and then splitting relations into different categories led to sparse annotations per relation category. In fact, we observed that only a small percentage of images contained annotations from the 4 different categories at once. To alleviate this issue, data augmentation was used to enlarge the number of annotated relations between existing object pairs. We leveraged the external data-transfer method proposed in [26]. This approach aims at re-labeling missed annotations on the training set by ranking new predictions on the set of overlapping bounding boxes. The hint here is that overlapping object regions have a higher probability to form a compositional relation than non-overlapping ones. Considering U as the set of unannotated relations where $U = P \cup N$, with P as the set of missed true positives and N true negatives, the external transfer T is defined as, for every triplet $(s, \theta, o) \in U$:

$$T(s, \theta, o) = \{p | (p \in R) \wedge (\beta(c_s, p, c_o) > 0) \wedge (IoU(b_s, b_o) > 0)\} \quad (5)$$

with R being the set of possible predicates between (s, o) and the IoU of b bounding boxes. β denotes the set of existing relations in the original dataset. This new set of T possible relations is then ranked by confidence and the top predicate θ is selected, following [26]. As it is, this method cannot discover any zero-shot triplet but can still relabel a consequent amount of missed true positive annotations. This process created a set of 42,356 new relations that enlarge the total number of samples to 191,599. We introduced these new annotations and the associated images as the **IndoorVG** dataset. Table 3 displays statistics on the collected data as well as the distribution of relations categories.

Table 3. Statistics of the **IndoorVG** dataset, Rels/Image is an average of all annotated samples. # Objects represent the total number of bounding boxes. The Train/Val/Test split is larger for objects to allow object detection training on the full original dataset.

# Rels	# Triplets	Rels/Image	Categories			
			Topo.	Func.	Part.	Attr.
191,599	20,122	11.8	59.2%	23.0%	10.0%	7.7%
Classes		# Objects	Train/Val/Test			
Obj.	Pred.		Objects		Rels	
130	50	858,149	64,982/5,199/30,094		10,826/782/4,615	

4 Experiments

Scene Graph Generation. The aim of our approach is similar to traditional two-stage methods in SGG [21,25]. It first leverages the use of the Faster-RCNN [17] backbone to generate objects and object-union features. Then, a relation head takes as input the concatenation of those features with predicate features and learns the predicate representation. We represent the generation of a graph T from a visual scene S as follows:

$$p(T_S|S) = p(B_S|S)p(O_S|B_S, S)p(R_S|O_S, B_S, S) \qquad (6)$$

with B referring to the set of bounding boxes, O the set of object classes, and R the set of possible predicates. It is worth noticing here that all relations are modeled jointly, this is due to the fact that relations on the same scene are highly dependent on each other and can benefit from context learning. In addition to SGG, our objective also integrates relation classification. However, the learning of triplets categories at the image level is not currently supported, which is a task for future work. Instead, this work modified the inference process, allowing the prediction of multiple predicates for every object pair. This type of inference is usually referred to as *No-graph constraint* in SGG [22]. A filter was further applied to ensure that no predicate from the same category can be inferred. Thus, any $< subject, object >$ pair could be associated with up to 4 different predicates.

Metrics. The standard way of assessing SGG is to use **Recall@K** (R@K) at the image level. This measures how often the correct relationship is predicted in the top K confident relationship predictions, traditional approaches use R@20, R@50, and R@100. SGG models trained on biased datasets like VG are known to have lower performance for infrequent categories. To address this, a metric called **Mean Recall@K** (mR@K) was used [20]. This metric calculates recall for each predicate category independently and then takes the average of the results, giving equal weight to each category. By doing so, it reduces the impact of some frequently occurring predicates such as "on" and "of," while placing more emphasis on infrequent predicates like "reading" and "carrying", which are more valuable for high-level reasoning.

Table 4. Results of Scene Graph Generation training on a set of baseline models using our new dataset IndoorVG. Numbers are in %.

Model	Recall			meanRecall		
	@20	@50	@100	@20	@50	@100
Motifs [25]	13.17	17.96	21.74	8.82	11.30	13.34
Transformer [22]	12.05	17.04	20.65	9.84	12.58	14.71
GPS-Net [14]	14.38	17.16	18.74	11.26	14.21	15.83

Results. We first trained the Faster-RCNN on our new dataset for object detection. As this step does not involve the use of predicates annotations, we trained the backbone on the full Visual Genome dataset with the set of object classes of IndoorVG. This way, we enlarged considerably the number of annotations and ensured a better generalization. Faster-RCNN was trained for 50,000 iterations with a batch size of 12 and a base learning rate of 0,001 on one Nvidia RTX3090, following [25]. The accuracy of the final model was 23.8 mAP, which is not far from previous results reported with this architecture [25]. We then trained three different popular baseline models on the task of Scene Graph Generation (SGGen), namely Neural-Motifs [25], Transformer [22] and GPS-Net model [14] using code from authors[2]. Even after carefully selecting predicate classes and performing data augmentation, the predicate distribution of IndoorVG still suffered from a long-tail distribution. Thus, we also used the re-weighting strategy introduced in [24] that assigns different loss weights for every predicate class during training. This strategy has been shown to further boost the meanRecall@K metric while not deteriorating Recall@K [26]. Every model was trained using one Nvidia RTX3090 GPU for 40,000 iterations with a batch size of 12. For training,

---

[2] https://github.com/waxnkw/IETrans-SGG.pytorch.

the dataset was split using the 0.6/0.1/0.3 ratio scheme for train/val/test splits, respectively (see Table 3). Results are displayed in Table 4 where we can see that the Motifs and Transformer architectures had very similar overall performance while GPS-Net presented better in meanRecal@K, ensuring better learning of tail classes. In our paradigm, performance in these tail classes is very important because they mostly encapsulate fine-grained *functional* information, such as `eating` or `reading`, that are essential for Scene Understanding and Reasoning.

Real-World Usage. We further demonstrated the interest and opportunities of our approach in real-life scenarios. We equipped the Softbank Pepper robot with the GPS-Net model trained on the IndoorVG dataset and let it operate in real-world environments, as represented in Fig. 2. First, we see that even on out-of-distribution images with bad lightning conditions the model was still able to detect relevant regions. Then, we observed that our novel inference process was able to correctly split relations per categories, leading to a multi-layer graph, represented as four different graphs here. We saw that the `topological` category had more relations than the others, this can be explained with respect to the original distribution of the data, where topological relations count for more than 50% of the total annotated relations. We are planning to add a further step of data re-sampling to alleviate this issue in future work. From the example below, by adding simple axioms such as `handle` is a `graspable` object, simple inferences on possible human actions can be made by looking at the interconnection between the part-whole and topological graph. Finally, this representation could also ease the robot to answer complex user commands such as "Find the person watching the television that is located on top of two cabinets".

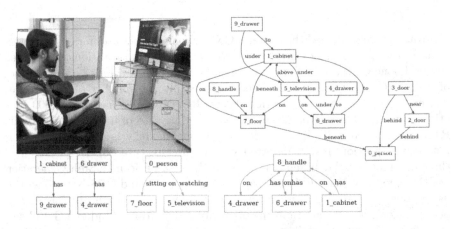

Fig. 2. Real-world inference using our architecture, colors indicate the functional, part-whole, topological and attributive layers, respectively. (Color figure online)

5   Conclusion and Future Work

Our work presents a novel approach to Knowledge Representation in service robotics that addresses open-ended Human-Robot Interaction. This paradigm introduces the use of multi-layer Scene Graphs to model four different knowledge dimensions in a single representation. This novel type of representation alleviates the close-domain bottleneck of current knowledge representations in service robotics while at the same time satisfying the constraints of real-world applications. To further encourage the use of this type of representation in the community, we introduce a novel large-scale dataset: IndoorVG. This dataset contains 16,221 images of indoor scenes annotated with diverse high-quality scene graphs and relations categories. Finally, we use this dataset to train different Scene Graph Generation approaches and demonstrate the opportunities and interest of such representation in real-world settings. We believe that this work could help bridge the gap between scene perception and robust reasoning for service robots in open-ended interactions. In future work, we are planning to train different SGG models to predict relation categories using image features. To do so, we will manually refine current categories annotations and add a new classification head to the models. Going forward, we plan to extend this representation for deep reasoning of autonomous agents by creating an inference process that leverages commonsense knowledge bases to extract human activities and intentions from fine-grained contexts.

Acknowledgment. This work benefits from the support of Britanny region.

References

1. Agia, C., et al.: Taskography: evaluating robot task planning over large 3D scene graphs. In: Conference on Robot Learning. PMLR (2022)
2. Amiri, S., Chandan, K., Zhang, S.: Reasoning with scene graphs for robot planning under partial observability. IEEE Robot. Autom. Lett. **7**(2), 5560–5567 (2022)
3. Beetz, M., et al.: Know rob 2.0: a 2nd generation knowledge processing framework for cognition-enabled robotic agents. In: 2018 IEEE International Conference on Robotics and Automation (ICRA). IEEE (2018)
4. Brown, T., et al.: Language models are few-shot learners. In: Advances in Neural Information Processing Systems, vol. 33, pp. 1877–1901 (2020)
5. Chatpatanasiri, R.: GPT3 and commonsense reasoning (2021). https://agi.miraheze.org/wiki/GPT3_and_Commonsense_Reasoning. Accessed 30 Apr 2023
6. De Magistris, G., et al.: Vision-based holistic scene understanding for context-aware human-robot interaction. In: Bandini, S., Gasparini, F., Mascardi, V., Palmonari, M., Vizzari, G. (eds.) AIxIA 2021. LNCS, vol. 13196, pp. 310–325. Springer, Cham (2022). https://doi.org/10.1007/978-3-031-08421-8_21
7. Gadre, S.Y., et al.: Continuous scene representations for embodied AI. In: Proceedings of the IEEE/CVF Conference on Computer Vision and Pattern Recognition, pp. 14849–14859 (2022)
8. Graf, F., et al.: Toward holistic scene understanding: a transfer of human scene perception to mobile robots. IEEE Robot. Autom. Mag. **29**(4), 36–49 (2022)

9. Gupta, R., et al.: Common sense data acquisition for indoor mobile robots. In: AAAI, pp. 605–610 (2004)
10. Krishna, R., et al.: Visual genome: connecting language and vision using crowd-sourced dense image annotations. Int. J. Comput. Vision **123**(1), 32–73 (2017)
11. Lemaignan, S., et al.: Oro, a knowledge management platform for cognitive architectures in robotics. In: 2010 IEEE/RSJ International Conference on Intelligent Robots and Systems, pp. 3548–3553. IEEE (2010)
12. Li, L., et al.: The devil is in the labels: Noisy label correction for robust scene graph generation. In: Proceedings of the IEEE/CVF Conference on Computer Vision and Pattern Recognition, pp. 18869–18878 (2022)
13. Li, X., et al.: Embodied semantic scene graph generation. In: Proceedings of the 5th Conference on Robot Learning, pp. 1585–1594. PMLR (2022). ISSN 2640-3498
14. Lin, X., et al.: GPS-Net: graph property sensing network for scene graph generation. In: Proceedings of the IEEE/CVF Conference on Computer Vision and Pattern Recognition, pp. 3746–3753 (2020)
15. Cewu, L., Krishna, R., Bernstein, M., Fei-Fei, L.: Visual relationship detection with language priors. In: Leibe, B., Matas, J., Sebe, N., Welling, M. (eds.) ECCV 2016. LNCS, vol. 9905, pp. 852–869. Springer, Cham (2016). https://doi.org/10.1007/978-3-319-46448-0_51
16. Paulius, D., Jelodar, A.B., Sun, Y.: Functional object-oriented network: construction & expansion. In: 2018 IEEE International Conference on Robotics and Automation (ICRA), pp. 5935–5941 (2018)
17. Ren, S., et al.: Faster R-CNN: towards real-time object detection with region proposal networks. In: Advances in Neural Information Processing Systems, vol. 28 (2015)
18. Sado, F., et al.: Explainable goal-driven agents and robots-a comprehensive review. ACM Comput. Surv. **55**(10), 1–41 (2023)
19. Saxena, A., et al.: Robobrain: large-scale knowledge engine for robots (2015)
20. Tang, K., et al.: Learning to compose dynamic tree structures for visual contexts. In: Proceedings of the IEEE/CVF Conference on Computer Vision and Pattern Recognition, pp. 6619–6628 (2019)
21. Tang, K., et al.: Unbiased scene graph generation from biased training. In: Proceedings of the IEEE/CVF Conference on Computer Vision and Pattern Recognition, pp. 3716–3725 (2020)
22. Tang, K., et al.: Unbiased scene graph generation from biased training. In: 2020 IEEE/CVF Conference on Computer Vision and Pattern Recognition (CVPR), Seattle, WA, USA, pp. 3713–3722. IEEE (2020)
23. Xu, D., et al.: Scene graph generation by iterative message passing. In: Proceedings of the IEEE Conference on Computer Vision and Pattern Recognition, pp. 5410–5419 (2017)
24. Yan, S., et al.: PCPL: predicate-correlation perception learning for unbiased scene graph generation. In: Proceedings of the 28th ACM International Conference on Multimedia, pp. 265–273 (2020)
25. Zellers, R., et al.: Neural motifs: scene graph parsing with global context. In: Proceedings of the IEEE Conference on Computer Vision and Pattern Recognition, pp. 5831–5840 (2018)
26. Zhang, A., et al.: Fine-grained scene graph generation with data transfer. In: Avidan, S., Brostow, G., Cissé, M., Farinella, G.M., Hassner, T. (eds.) ECCV 2022. LNCS, vol. 13687, pp. 409–424. Springer, Cham (2022). https://doi.org/10.1007/978-3-031-19812-0_24

Champion Papers

RobôCIn SSL-Unification: A Modular Software Architecture for Dynamic Multi-robot Systems

Victor Araújo[✉], Riei Rodrigues, José Cruz, Lucas Cavalcanti,
Matheus Andrade, Matheus Santos, João Melo, Pedro Oliveira, Ryan Morais,
and Edna Barros

Centro de Informática, Universidade Federal de Pernambuco, Av. Prof. Moraes Rego,
1235 - Cidade Universitária, Recife, Pernambuco, Brazil
{vhssa,rjmr,jvsc,lhcs,mvtna,mpgs,jgocm,ppso,rvsm,ensb}@cin.ufpe.br
https://robocin.com.br/

Abstract. RobôCIn robotics team has participated in the RoboCup
Small Size League since 2019 and is currently a two-time world champion (Division B) and four-time Latin-American champion. This paper
presents our improvements to defend the Small Size League (SSL) division B title in RoboCup 2023 in Bordeaux, France. In this paper, we
present the academic research that our team developed over the past
year. We migrated from our legacy architecture to a novel modular approach called SSL-Unification, designed for parallel execution of multi-
robot systems in dynamic environments. Results show that the new software architecture overcomes the Division B SSL team's average in 2023
competition in key metrics such as 300% more scored goals and 19.4%
less number of fouls.

Keywords: Software Architecture · Multi-robot Systems · Mobile
Robots

1 Introduction

When developing an architecture and software to coordinate multiple cooperative agents, as in SSL, one of the main concerns is defining a clear execution flow
with responsibilities correctly distributed, preventing the complexity of maintaining and evolving the system from becoming prohibitive. Furthermore, cooperation between agents is essential for good performance, like in human football.
Therefore, the architecture must support explicit cooperation and coordination
of multiple agents.

From these architectural concerns, STP (Skill, Tactics, and Plays) [1]
emerged. The main idea is to hierarchize an agent and integrate it with others:
A skill is a basic ability, such as moving to a point. A tactic is the application
of a skill sequence to execute an activity, such as a shot on goal, and a play is

C. Buche et al. (Eds.): RoboCup 2023, LNAI 14140, pp. 313–324, 2024.
https://doi.org/10.1007/978-3-031-55015-7_26

the coordination of multiple tactics to generate cooperation between agents, as in a rehearsed play.

In SSL, we have a huge scenario of the evolution of game strategies over the years, whether seeking to evolve the level of the game or respond to strategies from rival teams. As the software evolves, great architectural pressure is imposed, with new demands for architectures that are not flexible and expandable, the system's complexity escalates absurdly. This creates anomalous software components outside the already consolidated principles of clean architecture, for example, components that now have undue responsibilities either for accessing objects from other components or for coupling external business rules, breaking the Single-Responsibility Principle (SRP) [2].

During software development, including new requirements is a major challenge for preserving the architecture. At this point, the application of the principle that new functionalities should extend the existing components and not modify them, the Open-closed Principle (OCP) [2], the non-application of this principle degrades the architecture, and as this process is repeated, complexity scales and can lead to the point of complete refactoring if necessary.

Applying the visitor behavioral design pattern [3] in the architecture guarantees that the OCP will be followed. By separating algorithms from the base structure of the object, new operations only expand the base structure and create new nodes to be visited. Thus, contacting the new component with existing ones is minimized. Furthermore, as each algorithm is on a separate node, this allows broad modularization, segregation of access and directs maintenance.

Regarding trajectory planning, correlated planning and control guarantee a robust process of moving a mobile robot through space. It keeps the flow of inputs and outputs and the interface contract between the modules. Otherwise, the system will be stuck with just one algorithm/implementation.

Path planning algorithms such as visibility graph and RRT-based algorithms (RRT*, RRT-Connect, ERRT) [4] are widely used within the SSL category, as are navigation algorithms. Trajectory Planning appears as an intermediate component to meet the demand for compliance with the geometric path [4], defined by the path planner, taking into account the dynamics and kinematics of the robot, as well as their movement restrictions. The path planner seeks to create the optimal sequence of states, generating as output a sequence of robot states over time, starting from the current state (position, speed, acceleration) to the final state (position, speed, acceleration, time). With this, the control now has a well-defined function of synchronizing the state expected by trajectory planning with the current state of the robot over time.

In SSL, having a trajectory planner in the navigation flow represents a great performance gain, reducing total movement time and system stress, but as the other team's robots move, generating moving obstacles and the robot kicks, leading to target position changes abruptly, we need optimized algorithms to run in real-time. Following the restrictions and scope, keeping in mind that the robot has an acceleration, deceleration and maximum speed, that with changes in objectives, it may need to change states accelerating or decelerating and more importantly, for performance, the robot will always apply the most significant effort possible in this change of state.

This work aims to present the software architecture called SSL-Unification, full modular, which comprises an enhanced architecture for coordinating multiple cooperative robots. This work also discusses applying design principles such as the Single-Responsibility Principle (SRP) and the Open-closed Principle (OCP) to maintain a clean and extensible architecture. The paper also addresses trajectory planning, emphasizing the importance of a robust flow of inputs and outputs between modules and the need for optimized real-time algorithms in the dynamic SSL environment.

2   SSL-Unification Modular Architecture

The first version of the team's software architecture was presented in [5]. It was inspired by the STP (Skill, Tactics, and Plays) [1], and was a combination of the team's previous experience in the software development for robot soccer in the VSSS (IEEE Very Small Size Soccer) category and the STP approach. However, the software presented issues in previous competitions, such as data flow anomalies, strong dependencies between software components, and uncertainty about decision-making stages. All these issues were created due to the short time for development in order for the team's first participation in RoboCup 2019 in Sydney, Australia.

Over the last four years of software development, the team accumulated many technical debts in the architecture and development infrastructure, making it extremely difficult to create more collaborative plays among robots, as proposed in the STP approach. For example, to include new information flows and functionalities on the attacker side, we had to change critical parts of code that bring side effects in the defensive plays. Another issue was that during the integration of new team members, the time to ramp up the software team increased over the years due to increased code complexity. Therefore, we decided to concentrate on building a new modular software architecture to reduce the complexity and failure points presented in the previous one.

In this paper, we propose creating a modular, modern and flexible architecture with the possibility of reuse by the other categories in which the team competes. We also propose an open-source library called Soccer-common[1] as a shared library which aims to concentrate all common code among different competitions, providing a separation between User Interface (UI) and back-end. The main components of the Soccer-common library are a library of geometric functions, a graphical interface with drawing support at any point, debugs, and the design of a module on the SSL-Unification architecture. A module in the new architecture consists of the major abstraction capable of executing parallel logic, providing support for communication with the UI and other modules. The modules are the core of our architecture, which we will describe in the next section.

---

[1] https://github.com/robocin/soccer-common.

2.1 Architecture Overview

The proposed SSL-Unification modular architecture is shown in Fig. 1. The information flow starts with the vision system (VisionClient) that sends robot position information. At the same time, the referee system (Referee) sends stage and command updates. The software then applies the filtering process to the vision data. It makes it available in the vision pipeline (VisionWorldPipeline), parses the referee information, and makes it available in the referee pipeline (RefereeStatusPipeline). The proposed architecture comprises four modules: decision, behavior, planning, and navigation.

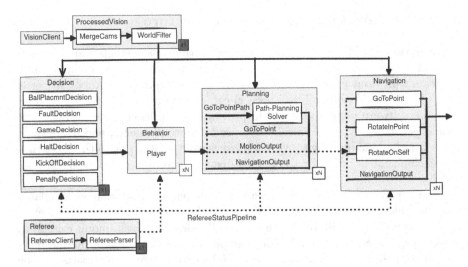

Fig. 1. Overview of SSL-Unification software architecture detailed dataflow. With dashed lines is the data with variant group type, each module has a notation of the number of threads, in gray modules with one thread running and in white modules with execution in the function of the number of available robots, N.

The decision module is responsible for determining the players' behaviors according to the referee data, which determines which submodule will be activated using the vision data to identify which player should perform a particular action, such as goalkeeper, forward, defender, or support. The behavior module receives the decision assignments for each player to execute the intended behavior that each player must execute using separate threads. The output of each thread is a tactic that the planning and navigation modules will process. The planning module seeks to plan a trajectory to be followed by the robot, avoiding obstacles and collisions. In contrast, the navigation module indicates which movements the robot will perform to execute the planned trajectory successfully.

One of the main issues of the previous architecture was the communication between modules. Each module was represented by a static global object with a unique instance, commonly called a singleton. The information exchange between the modules was done through direct connections with set and get commands, violating the SRP principle presented in Sect. 1. In order to solve these issues, the execution flow was changed to an event-based flow, using callbacks to enable a coordinated execution of each thread.

The callback infrastructure was done using QT Signals & Slots[2]. This infrastructure was initially intended to communicate objects linked to the UI in the QT framework. However, it has a robust and easy-to-use system for callbacks in C++, which consists of implementing an Observer Pattern to facilitate communication between modules of the Framework.

Thus, the communication of our modules was implemented as a cascaded publisher-consumer system, where each emitter function is connected to receivers during the creation of modules, ensuring that each requirement is met. When a module receives the input, the information is stored in a critical region and waits for the subsequent execution to be effectively consumed.

With this new infrastructure, we have also improved the communication between modules using more flexible data packages. Previously, the shared information was an extensive data structure with all the relevant information to be transmitted. The distinction of its use was made using an enumerator, and the filling of this structure was only sometimes fully complete, making the messages difficult to understand. To solve this issue, we started using a variant type, introduced in C++17[3], which consists of a type-safe union, capable of aggregating different structures into a single type, enumerating each one of them.

2.2   Modular Architecture Implementation

This subsection presents how the SSL-Unification was implemented, highlighting the changes between the previous and the new architecture according to our technical debts. The main goal is to reduce the number of flags and remove boilerplate code.

In our previous architecture, there was a component called DataWorld [5]. This component was responsible for receiving vision information from the vision software, processing image processing and receiving commands from the referee's software. We split this component into three modules: parser tree, trainer, and behavior.

Parser Tree: vision and the previous context, aiming at the specialization of game situations, simplifying the strategy carried out later, so each leaf situation at parser tree output, started to be treated isolated.

Figure 2 shows the complete referee parser tree. It starts from the game's command and the state received from the external referee. The Game Action division decides if the robots must halt or not. Then, the Game Status transition defines if we are dealing with an in-game situation or a positioning one, such

---

[2] https://doc.qt.io/qt-6/signalsandslots.html.
[3] https://en.cppreference.com/w/cpp/utility/variant.

as a preparation for kick-off. Lastly, at the Planning Game division, the parser chooses between states whether the robots must move without touching the ball (Dynamic Formation), execute a predefined play (Planned Tactic), or play the game normally (Game Tactic).

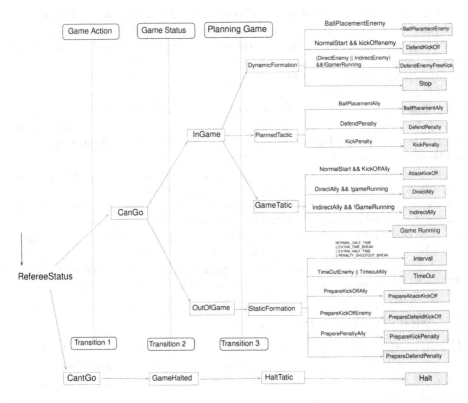

Fig. 2. Complete referee parser tree, showing all possible game states.

Trainer: the Parser tree module is dedicated to receiving arbitration software commands. We have developed our parser[4] based on the Stage and Command received, allied to the analysis of internal flags, information from One of the key abilities for a successful team in robot soccer is the ability to make quick changes depending on the applied game state and the opponents state. Over the years, we have evolved players' formation within the decision component. The Trainer module, formerly called Decision, is responsible for the team setup during game states.

We started with a static team of 3 Defenders, 1 Support, and 1 Forward in 2019, and now we have a dynamic allocation based on the ball's position and risk offered by the enemies' positions. Therefore, we can be an adaptable team, trying

[4] https://github.com/robocin/soccer-common/wiki/Referee-Parser.

to be highly offensive by pushing the game to the enemy half and exchanging passes, looking for an opportunity for a clear shoot on the goal.

Our offensive tactics are made up of a forward, who is the player closest to the ball, and of a variable number of supporters according to the position of the opposing team's robots, where each supporter seeks to stay in optimal positions, the best within our heuristics to receive a pass from forward and perform a successful play. Once the ball is passed to the supporter, it will become the new forward, switching position with the previous forward, keeping the attack cycle performed by our team.

Behavior: one of the main goals of the SSL-Unification was to decouple functionalities and simplify state machines. In our previous architecture, we had behaviors with Finite State Machines (FSM) of many states and with similar logic functions, needing help understanding the transitions and being hard to debug during testing. Before, each state corresponded to an enumerator, and the state processing node functions, which were incapable of storing contexts, switched by many conditionals. The input for each processing node was a pair $< state, context >$, with the information needed for all existing states, making it challenging to distinguish information relating only to specific states.

With the introduction of SSL-Unification, we implemented improvements to our FSMs using the previously mentioned variant types. This concept is similar to the messages used for communication between modules, where the machine states started to consist of a variant. In contrast, the processing nodes of these states became classes. With this change, the state processing nodes are now more independent, where the context restarts when a transition to a new state occurs.

Also, the SSL-Unification architecture applies the concept of SkillBook coming from the STP [1], which defines the attacker as a set of tactics that involve interacting with the ball, either passing a ball or shooting. Previously, all these commands were present inside a single FSM, making it complex to change or fix any situation inside it.

2.3 Path-Planning and Navigation

The Planning and Navigation modules were removed from the Behavior component from the previous architecture to enable the implementation of new algorithms more easily. Therefore, we created a dedicated module for path-planning and another for navigation, enabling us to change the path-planning algorithm and optimize our low-level control.

Issues from Past Competitions: we previously used an evolved version of the visibility graph presented in [5], optimised to handle corner cases over the following years. However, it became tough to maintain due to its code complexity. One of our major issues in past competitions was the high number of fouls due to crashing and robot distance to forbidden locations, as shown in Table 1. Due to the yellow cards arising from those fouls, we were frequently forced to remove robots from the field to carry out punishments for fouls, which massively reduced our offensive power, given the reduced number of players to compose the attack. This analysis led us to believe that improving the path-planning algorithm would increase the chances of scoring goals since most of those fouls would be avoided, and we would attack with all our resources.

Table 1. Collision and invasion detected during matches at RoboCup 2019, 2021 and 2022.

Referee foul event	# Occurences
ATTACKER_TOO_CLOSE_TO_DEFENSE_AREA	22
BOT_CRASH_UNIQUE	93
DEFENDER_TOO_CLOSE_TO_KICK_POINT	69

Despite using the shortest Euclidean path as a parameter, Visibility Graph's approach does not prove time-optimal for omnidirectional robots when an abrupt change in direction and velocity occurs [6]. Furthermore, the Visibility Graph's algorithm does not consider the agent's momentum or direction. Only its position is being considered. Therefore, there is a difference between the calculated path and the robot's real trajectory, as shown in Fig. 3. When the robot moves, we need to consider its state with position, velocity and acceleration instead of its position only. Additionally, the available margin for navigation error with the Visibility Graph's approach is minimal due to the generated path being tangential to the obstacles. Hence, combining all these factors culminates in a high amount of collision and invasion.

Considering all the issues shown in this subsection, we listed the following desired key improvements for the new planning algorithm:

- Fewer number of collisions, allowing better velocity and movement.
- A generated path harmonic to the real robot's trajectory.
- Robust algorithm for real-time and dynamic scenarios as those of SSL.
- Possibility of an obstacle model that appraises the movement's dynamic, considering time as a factor to determine possible collisions.
- Obstacles that can be differentiated from each other for a greater fidelity of representation of the world.
- Possibility of simulating the robot's movement to feed estimate the robot reaching range.

Bang-Bang Trajectory: despite the popularity of RRT-based algorithms (RRT-Connect, RRT*, ERRT) among SSL teams, we noticed that Bang-bang trajectory-based path-plannings were studied and adopted by two successful teams in the league: Tigers Mannheim [7] and Er-Force [8]. Therefore, we chose the Bang trajectory [9] given that its traditional implementation already met

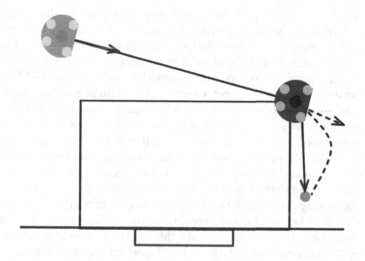

Fig. 3. The difference between the planned path and the trajectory executed in dashed line, emphasises the forces acting in the change of edge of the graph.

our stated requirements. Both Tigers' and ER-Force's implementations are open-source and demonstrate distinct ways of dealing with the implementation of the algorithm. While Tigers' approach consists of selecting intermediate points from a constellation of points around a given origin connected by trajectory segments to the target, the Er-Force approach goes with a more open search approach, seeking through the trajectory time and orientation.

Each implementation has its advantages and drawbacks, and we tried to validate both approaches and their code bases. We converted Tigers' implementation to C++, but the lack of performance compared to the Java version made us adopt Er-Force's base, which was already developed in C++ and had an execution time of less than 1 ms. In order to achieve this execution time, the presented ER-Force algorithm has a reduced number of search iterations and a large search bias around previously found solutions. Thus, when the previous path is no longer possible, and a large deviation is required to reach the target, the search for paths fails in creating a trajectory.

With that in mind, we modified the ER-Force algorithm with new features, such as an additional validation of the robot's movement reset to prevent the speed in one direction from distorting the trajectory. Another feature added was the constellation of points around the robot to force further exploration of obstacle contour direction brought from the Tigers' solution, at the cost of increased complexity but still fitting in a time frame.

Navigation: path planning and navigation are inherently related. A path planning that does not consider the robot's dynamics results in a different trajectory. The previous Visibility Graph approach had sharp changes in the velocity and direction of the generated path because it only considers the distance changes (ΔS). The navigation needs to predict the output for the robot that fulfils and generates all the movements that affect the planning result. However, this information was propagated to the next path-planning calculation cycle.

On the other hand, trajectory-based algorithms close this control loop, feeding the next iteration with the robot's current state with its position and velocity. However, the software relies on data from the vision system where this current state corresponds to a robot's past state captured by the currently received frame. Furthermore, an SSL robot can change its velocity, making it difficult for vision processing to keep up. Therefore, vision-only approaches limit the robot state transition update by the camera frame rate, typically 60 Hz.

This limitation of detection of the robot's current state by the vision mainly impacts the ability to control the acceleration and deceleration of the robot when the path is being adjusted throughout the cycles since it cannot reach the expected state. In order to mitigate this effect, we developed methods for estimating the current state of the robot based on the vision frame current information using Extended Kalman Filter (EKF) [10], the vision processing delay and the speed commands sent to the robot during this delay, starting from the state seen in the vision. We apply the commands sent to the robot by replicating its performance time, thus estimating its current state.

3   Results and Discussion

The implementation was validated during the RoboCup 2023 competition. The hardware specification for the robot in use is shown in Table 2, with no electronic changes from the version presented in [5]. The results were evaluated using the competition match statistics comparing the team's 2023 results with the average data from all participating teams in division B in 2023, which used similar hardware, including our team, available in[5]. Table 3 compares essential competition metrics.

Table 2. Robot Hardware Specifications.

Robot Version	v2023
Driving motors	Maxon EC-45 flat - 50W
Microcontroller	STM32F767ZI
Gear Transmission	Direct transmission
Wheels	3D Printed
Total Weight	2.42 kg
Communication Link	nRF24L01+
Battery	LiPo 2200mah 4S 35C

---

[5] https://ssl.robocup.org/match-statistics/.

Table 3. Metrics evaluation between the average of all Division B teams in 2023 and the RobôCIn team.

Metric	Team's Average in 2023	RobôCIn 2023
Scored goals	15	60
Conceded goals	15	0
Total number fouls	67	54
Total number of Yellow Cards	18	16
Total number of Red Cards	2	0
Total number of Ball Placements	57	240

The number of scored goals from the team was 300% higher than the average, which shows a successful rate of tactics and plays executed. Also, the team did not suffer a goal in the competition, which shows that the defensive system was the best among all teams. The average number of fouls (19.4% lower than average) and yellow cards (11.1% lower than average) were still an excellent indicator as the team played more matches than the teams' average since we reached the finals. The absence of red cards indicates the team is not committing many fouls in a row, and a high number of ball placements indicates the team is successfully acquiring ball possession during the matches.

Part of this dominance during games comes from the team's speed of response and movement. With improvements in planning and control, it was possible to increase the operating limits of robot movement, increasing the maximum speed from 2.2 m/s to 2.5 m/s and the acceleration from 3.1 m/s^2 to 3.8 m/s^2. Even with these increases, the number of fouls received by RobôCIn during the games was below the average of other teams. As shown in the Table 4, there was a reduction in the number of fouls committed by invasions of the kicking point and collisions. However, the number of invasions in the enemy's defensive area remains high.

Table 4. Collision and invasion detected during matches at RoboCup 2023.

Referee foul event	# Occurences
ATTACKER_TOO_CLOSE_TO_DEFENSE_AREA	32
BOT_CRASH_UNIQUE	10
DEFENDER_TOO_CLOSE_TO_KICK_POINT	8

4   Conclusion and Further Work

In this work, we proposed a modular software architecture called SSL-Unification. The complete architecture was presented with its main advantages regarding the previous STP-based approach, and its implementation details were shared. This approach uses a shared library to reuse geometric, drawing and debug functions and improved path-planning and navigation modules using the Bang-bang Trajectory approach. We also emphasise the importance of clear execution flow and responsibility distribution to prevent system complexity from becoming prohibitive.

Further works include separating modules into services, moving away from a monolithic architecture, and seeking to take advantage of the best performance and facilities that other languages can offer for software evolution. Another work would be the investigation of effective approaches to the navigation module to eliminate assumptions about the current state of the robot to calculate its current trajectory segment performing embedded navigation, similar to solutions adopted by Division A teams.

References

1. Browning, B., Bruce, J., Bowling, M., Veloso, M.: STP: skills, tactics, and plays for multi-robot control in adversarial environments. Proc. Inst. Mech. Eng. Part I J. Syst. Control Eng. **219**(1), 33–52 (2005)
2. Martin, R.: Clean Architecture: A Craftsman's Guide to Software Structure and Design, 1st edn. Prentice Hall Press, Hoboken (2017)
3. Oliveira, B., Wang, M., Gibbons, J.: The visitor pattern as a reusable, generic, type-safe component. In: Proceedings of the 23rd ACM SIGPLAN Conference on Object-Oriented Programming Systems Languages and Applications, OOPSLA 2008, pp. 439–456. Association for Computing Machinery, New York (2008)
4. Gasparetto, A., Boscariol, P., Lanzutti, A., Vidoni, R.: Path planning and trajectory planning algorithms: a general overview. In: Carbone, G., Gomez-Bravo, F. (eds.) Motion and Operation Planning of Robotic Systems, pp. 3–27. Springer, Cham (2015). https://doi.org/10.1007/978-3-319-14705-5_1
5. Silva, C., et al.: Robôcin 2019 team description paper. In: RoboCup 2019 Symposium and Competitions: Team Description Papers, 2019. Robocup Small Size League, Sydney, Australia (2019)
6. Balkcom, D., Kavathekar, P., Mason, M.: Time-optimal trajectories for an omnidirectional vehicle. Int. J. Robot. Res. **25**(10), 985–999 (2006)
7. Ommer, N., Ryll, A., Geiger, M.: Tigers mannheim (team interacting and game evolving robots) extended team description for robocup 2019. In: RoboCup 2019 Symposium and Competitions: Team Description Papers, 2019. RoboCup Small Size League, Mannheim, Germany (2019)
8. Wendler, A., Heineken, T.: ER-Force 2020 extended team description paper. In: RoboCup 2021 Symposium and Competitions: Team Description Papers, 2020. RoboCup Small Size League, Erlangen, Germany (2021)
9. Purwin, O., D'Andrea, R.: Trajectory generation for four wheeled omnidirectional vehicles. In: Proceedings of the 2005, American Control Conference, vol. 7, pp. 4979–4984 (2005)
10. Yang, S., Baum, M.: Extended kalman filter for extended object tracking. In: 2017 IEEE International Conference on Acoustics, Speech and Signal Processing (ICASSP), pp. 4386–4390 (2017)

Rhoban Football Club: RoboCup Humanoid Kid-Size 2023 Champion Team Paper

Julien Allali, Adrien Boussicault, Cyprien Brocaire, Céline Dobigeon, Marc Duclusaud, Clément Gaspard, Hugo Gimbert, Loïc Gondry, Olivier Ly, Grégoire Passault[✉], and Antoine Pirrone

Rhoban Football Club Team, LaBRI, University of Bordeaux, Bordeaux, France
team@rhoban.com, gregoire.passault@u-bordeaux.fr

Abstract. In 2023, Rhoban Football Club reached the first place of the KidSize soccer competition for the fifth time, and received the *best humanoid award*. This paper presents and reviews important points in robots architecture and workflow, with hindsights from the competition.

1 Introduction

During the 2023 RoboCup kid-size soccer competition, Rhoban played 8 games, scored 95 goals, and took a total of 2 goals (both during the final against CIT Brains, Japan), reached the first place for drop-in games, technical challenges and software challenge. Those achievements resulted in obtaining the *best humanoid award* for Sigmaban, Rhoban's kid-size humanoid robot.

This paper presents the main aspects of our robots, focusing on the recent improvements. Section 2 gives a short overview of the robots architecture, along with recent mechanical upgrades, Sect. 3 presents our vision and perception system, Sect. 4 details our new walk engine and Sect. 5 describes the strategy and monitoring system.

2 Robots Architecture

2.1 Overview

Sigmaban has 20 degrees of freedom, 3 per arm (MX-64), 2 for the head (MX-64) and 6 per leg (1xMX-64 + 5xMX-106). The legs are fully serial (no parallel kinematics). Parts are mostly milled in 2017 aluminium alloy. They are equipped with Intel NUC (i5) running a (non real-time) Debian and a low-level custom board with STM32 (72Mhz) to interface devices communication with the computer. We use BNO055 IMU (Accelerometer+Gyroscope) and each foot is equipped with four strain jauges to measure the pressure. More details can be found in the public team description paper and specifications[1].

---

[1] https://humanoid.robocup.org/previous-editions/robocup-2023/teams/.

C. Buche et al. (Eds.): RoboCup 2023, LNAI 14140, pp. 325–336, 2024.
https://doi.org/10.1007/978-3-031-55015-7_27

OnShape[2] is used as CAD software, which allows us a seamless CAD-to-URDF conversion using OnShape-to-robot [9], our own open-source tool (winner of the 2023 RoboCup software challenge).

2.2 Software

Most of the software running on the robots is written in C++. We factored out core components such as motion planning, control and strategy to separate modules and using Python bindings, allowing us to test, visualize, plot, run physics simulation in a faster workflow than C++, while keeping the same code running on the robot. We switched from RBDL [3] to *pinocchio* [2] as rigid body dynamics library, because of its state-of-the-art performances and active development.

2.3 Recent Mechanical Upgrades

Bumpers. Shocks with other robots and the ground are very common during the games, and mechanical breaks are frequent during the competition. Our previous design was relying on bent piano wires to dampen the shocks, which has proven to be efficient, but was not easy to reproduce, cumbersome and could create some obstruction with the vision. We switched to 3D (filament) printed TPU bumpers on the torso and the shoulders for 2023. This approach led to similar damping during lab tests.

Hip Yaw Bearings. In the leg architecture, the hip yaw degrees of freedom are typically highly stressed radially. In our previous design, the whole leg was fixed at this point with one unique (M3) screw, with no easy possibility to use a passive horn. We added cross roller bearings to this joint, and significantly reduced the backlash and possible screw loosening or damage.

3 Vision, Perception and Localisation

3.1 Lenses and Field of View

When selecting a lens for a robot camera, a natural trade-off arises between the field of view and the resolution/distortion of the image. Our previous lens had a field of view of 68°(H), 54°(V), which required too many head movements to scan the field. We switched to a higher field of view, keeping the same image processed resolution (644×482) because we wanted to keep the same computational power in order to still process the images at 30fps in real-time. Our new lens (BF5M2023S23C[3]) has a field of view of 100°(H), 83°(V). The time taken for a look-around scan was reduced from 3.2 s to 2 s to cover the same observation space. In the future, we can consider removing the *head pan*, which is arguably useless in the current architecture.

[2] https://www.onshape.com/.
[3] Technical Documentation of BF5M2023S23C Lens.

3.2   Camera Calibration

Intrinsic calibration was done for each camera using ChArUco boards, enabling tangential and radial distortions. We found better results by imposing $k_3 = 0$ for radial coefficients during the calibration. Since we are using mobile robots, the extrinsic calibration is not relevant and is replaced with pose estimation produced by whole body forward kinematics.

In hindsight, the distortion on the border of the image is still high, which makes some part of the image barely usable. We also notice significant reprojection errors that we countered by adjusting the optical center of the camera, especially to ensure proper positioning when the ball is close to the robot. Even if we had satisfying reprojection results with such adjustment, we need to investigate whether it is caused to extrinsic errors (e.g. bent parts) or intrinsic errors (e.g. errors in intrinsic calibration).

3.3   Image Processing

We have switched from an approach based on Multi-class ROI and classification [5] to the state-of-the-art end-to-end YoloV8 [6] algorithm for object detection, in order to detect different points of interest (POI, cf. Sect. 3.3) in the image. Camera extrinsic estimation allows for the projection of the POI in the world frame and feeding a particle filter [5] for localisation.

Thanks to pressure sensors and the robot kinematics model, we also use extensively the odometry to adjust the localisation.

Training: In order to train the neural network, we need to have a dataset of images with the features labeled. The HTC Vive auto-labeling described in [5] was not enough accurate to train the neural network. We manually labeled a set of 400 images to train a first version of the neural network in order to pre-label the rest of the dataset. Correcting such pre-labeled image was considered two times faster than labeling an image from scratch.

We used Label-Studio [11] as labeling tool because it is open-source, comes with a user-friendly web-based interface that can be shared through the network.

Yolo is trained with our dataset (see Sect. 3.3) based on the pre-trained YoloV8n weights (3.2M parameters). It takes 48 min on an Intel Core^{TM} i7-9700K, 32Go of RAM, a Nvidia RTX 2070 and a SSD to train the neural network for 407 epochs.

On-Robot Inference: Robots are running Intel Core^{TM} i5-7260U with integrated GPU, 8 GB of RAM and a SSD. YoloV8n is translated to an OpenVINO[4] IR model, which is then loaded and run on the robot. We apply our own post-processing (Non-Maximum Suppression) to the output, and also some custom filtering such as removing unrealistic bounding boxes based on extrinsic information.

The robot runs the neural network online at approximately 48fps on integrated GPU instead of 5fps on CPU only (without OpenVINO).

---

[4] https://www.openvino.ai/.

3.4 Dataset

Images Selection and Data Augmentation: Our dataset is composed of 1794 images. We arbitrarily split it into the usual three parts to evaluate the performance of a machine learning model: Train set: 1462 images (80%)|Evaluation set: 166 images (10%)|Test set: 166 images (10%).

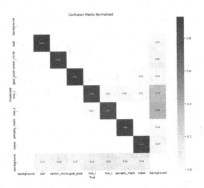

Fig. 1. Inference on a frame with our trained neural network

Fig. 2. Normalized confusion matrix of our neural network (confidence threshold = 0.25)

The majority of these images (∼80%) were captured at Rhoban lab with different brightness conditions and variations of the shutter speed and white balance of the camera. The rest of it was taken during the RoboCup 2022 and 2023 competition. We had to train the network not only on images extracted from video (as in 2019 [5]) but also on raw images, because the network tends to learn compression artefacts and the onboard performances on the raw camera stream was diminished. We also used data augmentation to make our network more robust with the following transformations: HSV modification, rotation, vertical flip, translation and rescaling.

Detected Features: We use 5 main localisation features: The lines "L" and "T" patterns (4500 and 3500 instances), the center circle (700 its.), the penalty mark (800 its.) and the bottom of the goal posts (2000 its.). We also detect the ball (1500 its.) and the other robots (1500 its.). Figure 1 displays an example of detection.

The normalized confusion matrix of the neural network training is depicted on Fig. 2. The L an T corners have a relatively high false positive rate (confused with background). Note that this matrix is computed with a confidence threshold (0.25) lower than the one we use on the robot (0.6) The rest of the matrix shows us that the neural network is able to detect the features with a high accuracy.

4 Walk

4.1 Overview

Our walk engine was almost entirely reworked in 2023. The previous walk engine
[5] was based on cubic splines and analytic inverse kinematics for the legs. This
approach lacked a preview on the dynamics of the center of mass and versatility
in the tasks that can be used to define the trajectories. This section describes
the three main stages of this new walk engine, as depicted on Fig. 3: planning
the footsteps, planning the center of mass trajectory and finally computing the
whole body inverse kinematics to produce the joint trajectories that are sent to
position-controlled actuators. Note that kicking and standing-up are, however
still achieved with hand-tuned keyframe animation, which gives efficient results,
but is tedious and not satisfying.

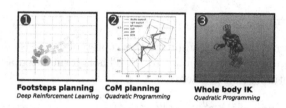

Footsteps planning
Deep Reinforcement Learning

CoM planning
Quadratic Programming

Whole body IK
Quadratic Programming

Fig. 3. Overview of the stages of the walk engine

4.2 Footsteps Planning

In the past, we relied on extensively hand-tuned approaches (based for example
on potential fields) to plan the footsteps. On the one hand, this has proven
to be efficient but relied on many hyper-parameters to be adjusted manually,
especially when the robot walking abilities are updated, which is not satisfying.

Reinforcement learning, on the other hand, rely on simulated environments
directly parametrized by the robot abilities along with a reward signal that can
be adjusted to exactly match the desired outcome (in this case, minimizing the
number of footsteps). It can embrace non-linearity and, thanks to Deep Reinforcement Learning and the use of neural networks as functions approximators,
continuous actions and observations space to produce a policy with a fast on-line
inference. We thus formulated the footsteps planning as a reinforcement learning
problem.

This RL environment is based on different parameters defined by our robot's
structure: maximum step sizes for the robot's movement (Δx_{max}, Δy_{max}, and
$\Delta\theta_{max}$), the feet spacing (l_f) and tolerances for reaching the target (t_x and t_θ
in meters and radians, respectively).

The actions in this environment are represented as tuples of ($\Delta x, \Delta y, \Delta\theta$),
with the step sizes in meters and radians. These actions are clipped to ensure
that they fall within an ellipsoid, rather than a box, to encourage more natural

movement patterns. Footsteps are simulated using purely geometrical displacements. The observation space consists of the position and orientation of the currently considered neutral support foot, along with information about the current support foot (left or right). These values are expressed in the target frame to represent "errors".

The reward function in this RL environment is shaped as a cost function, which includes factors like the cost of taking additional steps, a reward shaping factor (α), and penalties for collisions with the ball.

Technically, the environment is implemented as an OpenAI gym, and trained using TD3 [4] algorithm (implementation from [8]). The policy is then exported to OpenVINO IR model for inference, where the inference of one footstep takes about $100\,\mu s$ on the robot.

Extensive details about this work will be published later in a separate paper, and the environment is intended to be open-sourced.

4.3   CoM Planning

In order to ensure the robot stability, the center of mass is planned with a preview horizon, on a scheme similar to [7]. This is formulated as the following discrete time optimization problem:

$$
\begin{aligned}
&\min_{c,\dot{c},\ddot{c},\dddot{c},z} \|z - z^d\|^2 + \epsilon\|\dddot{c}\|^2 \\
&s.t \quad
\begin{bmatrix} c_{k+1} \\ \dot{c}_{k+1} \\ \ddot{c}_{k+1} \end{bmatrix}
=
\begin{bmatrix} 1 & \Delta t & \frac{\Delta t^2}{2} \\ 0 & 1 & \Delta t \\ 0 & 0 & 1 \end{bmatrix}
\begin{bmatrix} c_k \\ \dot{c}_k \\ \ddot{c}_k \end{bmatrix}
+
\begin{bmatrix} \frac{\Delta t^3}{6} \\ \frac{\Delta t^2}{2} \\ \Delta t \end{bmatrix}
\dddot{c}_k \\
&\qquad z_k = c_k - \frac{h}{g}\ddot{c}_k, z_k \in S_k \\
&\qquad c_0, \dot{c}_0, \ddot{c}_0 = c_{init}, \dot{c}_{init}, \ddot{c}_{init} \\
&\qquad c_f, \dot{c}_f, \ddot{c}_f = c_{final}, \dot{c}_{final}, \ddot{c}_{final}
\end{aligned}
\tag{1}
$$

where:

- $c_k, \dot{c}_k, \ddot{c}_k, \dddot{c}_k$ are respectively the (2D) center of mass position, velocity, acceleration and jerk at step k,
- z_k is ZMP approximation under the LIPM model at step k, h being the (assumed constant) height of the center of mass and g the gravity,
- z^d is a the desired ZMP trajectory,
- S_k is the support polygon at step k, given by the current support footprint or by the convex hull of the two support footprints in the double support phase,
- Initial and final center of mass positions are given by the current state of the robot and the state at the end of the preview horizon.

The objective function is quadratic. The only constraint that is not an equality is $z \in S$, which can be turned into inequalities because S are convex polygons. This can then be translated into a quadratic programming (QP) problem.

In practice, we used *eiquadprog* [1] solver. Note that $c, \dot{c}, \ddot{c}, \dddot{c}$ and z are all coupled with equality constraints, the problem can be rewritten (with less clarity) so that $\dddot{c}$ is the only decision variable.

The reference trajectory for the ZMP (z^d) is in our case a target that is constant in the current support foot. This offset can then be tuned to adjust the walk, with for example the effect of increasing or reducing the lateral swing. During the competition, this target was set to zero (i.e. we try to have the ZMP as close as possible to the center of the support foot).

Because our single support duration was tuned to 360 ms, our value for Δt is 36 ms, we plan 48 steps ahead which implies 96 decision variables ($\dddot{c}$) to optimize. The preview horizon is then 1.7 s (roughly 5 walk steps). Solving this optimization problem takes about 2 ms on the robot and was done with a constant period of 25 ms.

Equation 1 can be integrated as a smooth $\mathcal{C}^2$ trajectory for $c(t)$.

4.4 Swing Foot Trajectory

The swing foot trajectory is a trade-off between the risk of applying tangential forces on the ground while taking off or landing and the need to limiting the speed that is required to reach the target. Even if more thoughtful work can be considered in the future, we tried empirically different trajectories and settled on the most efficient one.

z being the vertical axis, $x(t)$ and $y(t)$ are simply cubic splines defined by initial and final positions, and zero initial and final velocities (a similar approach is used for the yaw of the foot). The vertical trajectory $z(t)$ is a piecewise cubic splines with a taking off, a plateau (tuned to 30% of the duration) and a landing phase (see Fig. 4).

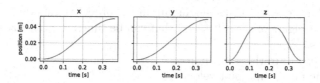

Fig. 4. Cartesian trajectory of a swinging foot of 5 cm along x axis and 5 cm along y axis

4.5 Whole Body Inverse Kinematics

The planning for the center of mass, along with the swing foot spline provides the following task-space trajectories to be followed by the robot:

1. **Center of mass**: output of the optimization problem from the previous stage and a constant height h,

2. **Trunk orientation**: constant pitch/roll (tuned to leaning 11.5° forward), and a yaw following the swing foot,
3. **Support foot**: not moving in the world,
4. **Swing foot**: following the spline described in the previous section and remaining parallel to the ground.

Kinematically, task 1. is a position task (3D), task 2. an orientation task (3D) and tasks 3. and 4. are frame tasks (6D). This results in assigning 18 degrees of freedom, which are exactly the degrees of the legs (12) plus the floating base (6).

To find the corresponding joint-space trajectories $q(t)$, we need to solve the inverse kinematics problem. Formally, tasks can be written as errors $e(q)$ that we want to take to zero. Since $e(q)$ is highly non-linear, it is approximated by a first order Taylor expansion around the current state q_0: $e(q) \approx e(q_0) + J(q_0)\Delta q$ where $J(q_0)$ is the Jacobian matrix of e at q_0. The problem is then to find Δq such that $e(q_0) + J(q_0)\Delta q = 0$. Again, we formulate this as a QP problem:

$$\min_{\Delta q} \sum_i w_i \| J_i^s(q_0)\Delta q + e_i^s(q_0)\|^2 + \epsilon\|\Delta q\|^2$$

$$s.t \ J_i^h(q_0)\Delta q + e_i^h(q_0) = 0 \tag{2}$$

$$q_{min} < q_0 + \Delta q < q_{max}$$

$$-\Delta t.\dot{q}_{max} < \Delta q < \Delta t.\dot{q}_{max}$$

Here:

- q_0 is the current joint state of the (reference) robot, around which linear approximation is made, and Δq is the variation of the joint state that we want to find,
- J^h and e^h are the *hard* tasks (equality constraints)
- J^s and e^s are the *soft* tasks, ending up in the objective function to minimize
- w_i are the weights of the soft tasks, that can be tuned to prioritize some tasks over others,
- q_{min} and q_{max} are the joint limits,
- $\dot{q}_{max}$ is the maximum joint velocity.

All the tasks are expressed in the world frame, and the Jacobian are computed locally for numerical stability. The $j\epsilon\|\Delta q\|^2$ term is a regularization term that is used to ensure that the solution is not too far from the current state, and ensure that the problem is well-posed.

In practice, we also used *eiquadprog* [1] solver, relying on *pinocchio* [2] to compute efficiently the transformation matrices and Jacobians from the URDF model that is kept consistent with CAD updates tanks to Onshape-To-Robot [9]. This optimization problem was solved at the control frequency (about 200 Hz, $\Delta t = 5$ ms), and takes approximately 100 μs on the robot.

4.6   Open-Source

Efforts were made to get the previously mentioned optimization problems convenient to formulate and solve from a software engineering point of view. Our mid-term objective is to document and open-source all the parts of the walk engine.

4.7   Limitations

The trajectories were not planned in accordance with the actuators limitations, which resulted in some of them reaching their velocity limit during the walk. This was especially true for the knee, and ankle actuators which are the ones that experience the more torque during the walk. This is illustrated in Fig. 5.

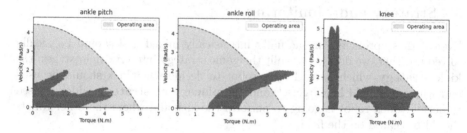

Fig. 5. Planned velocities during the walk for the knee and ankle actuators. The red area represent the operational range of the actuators given by the ROBOTIS for MX-106 [10]. (Color figure online).

To avoid extra velocity solicitations of high torque-providing actuators, we decided to substitute the center of mass by the trunk position while resolving the whole-body kinematics. This "trunk mode" (as opposed to the "CoM mode") is motivated by the fact that most of the mass is located in the trunk, and by the fact that the constant CoM height constraint is the source the targeted velocity solicitations. As a result, the target velocities of the support leg actuators are lower (cf. Fig. 6), which allows to stay in the operational range.

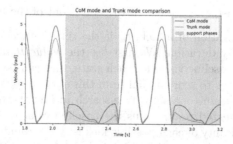

Fig. 6. Comparison of the planned velocity for the knee actuator during the CoM-walk (blue) and the walk in trunk mode (orange). (Color figure online)

Taking in account the true ability of the actuators when planning and controlling is really important in a competitive scenario where the robot is pushed to its limits of operation.

The only feedback we currently use to ensure the stability of the robot is a detection of the support using the pressure sensors of the feet. In the case of a light instability, the robot will take more time to touch the ground with the swing foot. Thus, we delay the trajectory reading to ensure that the real state of the robot match the planned one. Another objective is thus to implement a proper model predictive control (MPC) to be resilient to greater instabilities.

Facing the limitations of the Sigmaban platform, in particular the difficulty to use the actuators with torque control, we are considering to move to a new architecture.

5 Strategy and Monitoring

Even if those problems are actually intrinsically mixed and should be ideally solved together, we decided to split the game strategy into two main stages: the **kick strategy** which is used by a robot to decide what kick should be used and where it should be targeted, and the **placement strategy** which is used to decide which robot is going to perform the kick and where the other robots should be placed on the field.

5.1 Kick Strategy

Four different kick motions are currently implemented in the robot: a forward kick (*classic*), a short forward kick (*small*), a lateral kick (*lateral*) and a diagonal one (*diag*). For all of them, we estimated the optimal relative positioning, and the distribution of kick length and angle. We also model the effect of kicking against the grass blades as a reduction of 70% of the kick length. We first formalize the problem as a Markov Decision Process where the state s is the position of the ball on the field, the action a the kick type and yaw, and the reward:

$$r = \begin{cases} -t_k & \text{if the ball is in the goal} \\ -t_k - t_w(s, s') & \text{if the ball is on the field} \\ -t_p & \text{if the ball is out of the field} \end{cases} \tag{3}$$

Here, t_k is the duration of a kick, t_w is the time it takes to walk from s to s', and t_p is a penalty duration. We first use the *Value Iteration* algorithm to (off-line) compute a baseline value for each state, that can be interpreted as the (negative) time it takes to score a goal from this state.

On-line, we perform a (one step) tree-search to find the best action to perform, using an augmented reward plus the baseline value of the next state. At this stage, the uncertainty of each possible kick is still accounted for by sampling the kick length and angle from the estimated distribution. The following extra information are added to the reward:

- If the kick would **collide** an ally or an opponent, we recursively compute the reward for the two possible state using a collision probability,
- If we are **not allowed to score** (because of indirect free kick) and the kick would score, we add extra penalty,
- Instead of $t_w(s, s')$, we use the time it would take to the **closest ally** to walk to the ball,
- We add extra penalty if the ball would reach a position where the **opponents are closer to the ball**,
- We add extra penalty if the robot is targeting a position that **obstructs our goals** to perform its kick.

We used a graphical drag-and-drop representation as depicted on Fig. 7 to hand-tune the reward according to our preferences and across a playbook of multiple standard situations. The top 10% of those possible actions are then passed to the footsteps generator, which uses its value function (see Sect. 4.1) in inference to estimate the number of steps required for each action and select the best one accordingly.

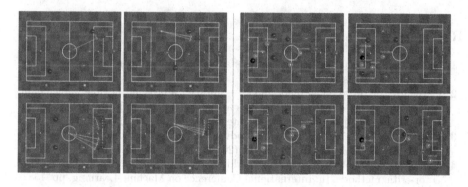

Fig. 7. On the left: examples of situations for the kicking strategy problem. On the right: situations for the placement strategy problem.

5.2 Placement Strategy

The robots are distributed autonomous agents that need to agree on a common team strategy. To simplify this problem, we leverage the WiFi communication between robots to elect a Captain that is responsible for computing and broadcasting a global team roles assignment. The captain listens to robots information such as estimated location on field, location of the ball and allies opponents detection (Protobuf-encoded packets over UDP broadcast). Next, the captain applies clustering algorithm to aggreagate robots observations and infer common opponents detection. A kicker is selected among robots using a simple scoring (bonus for previous kicker to avoid oscillation, distance to ball and robot orientation). The remaining robots are placed over a set of interesting positions (empirically selected).

5.3   Monitoring and Replay

We designed a new monitoring system written entirely in Python for convenience. It listens over the network for the *Game Controller*, robot communication, records a video from an external webcam to keep a ground truth overview. Such a tool allows real time debugging during development phases, but also to replay a game and analyze the strategy (Fig. 8).

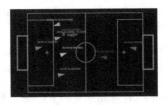

Fig. 8. Monitoring system

References

1. Buondonno, G.: Github repository: stack-of-tasks/eiquadprog. https://github.com/stack-of-tasks/eiquadprog
2. Carpentier, J., et al.: The pinocchio c++ library - a fast and flexible implementation of rigid body dynamics algorithms and their analytical derivatives. In: IEEE International Symposium on System Integrations (SII) (2019)
3. Felis, M.L.: Rbdl: an efficient rigid-body dynamics library using recursive algorithms. Auton. Robot. **41**(2), 495–511 (2017)
4. Fujimoto, S., Hoof, H., Meger, D.: Addressing function approximation error in actor-critic methods. In: International Conference on Machine Learning, pp. 1587–1596. PMLR (2018)
5. Gondry, L., et al.: Rhoban Football Club: RoboCup humanoid KidSize 2019 champion team paper. In: Chalup, S., Niemueller, T., Suthakorn, J., Williams, M.-A. (eds.) RoboCup 2019. LNCS (LNAI), vol. 11531, pp. 491–503. Springer, Cham (2019). https://doi.org/10.1007/978-3-030-35699-6_40
6. Jocher, G., Chaurasia, A., Qiu, J.: YOLO by Ultralytics (2023). https://github.com/ultralytics/ultralytics
7. Kajita, S., et al.: Biped walking pattern generation by using preview control of zero-moment point. In: 2003 IEEE International Conference on Robotics and Automation (Cat. No. 03CH37422), vol. 2, pp. 1620–1626. IEEE (2003)
8. Raffin, A., Hill, A., Ernestus, M., Gleave, A., Kanervisto, A., Dormann, N.: Stable baselines3 (2019)
9. Rhoban: Github repository: rhoban/onshape-to-robot. https://github.com/rhoban/onshape-to-robot
10. ROBOTIS: ROBOTIS e-Manual. https://emanual.robotis.com/docs/en/dxl/mx/mx-106-2/
11. Tkachenko, M., Malyuk, M., Holmanyuk, A., Liubimov, N.: Label Studio: Data labeling software (2020–2022). Open source software https://github.com/heartexlabs/label-studio

RoboCup 2023 Humanoid AdultSize Winner NimbRo: NimbRoNet3 Visual Perception and Responsive Gait with Waveform In-Walk Kicks

Dmytro Pavlichenko[✉], Grzegorz Ficht, Angel Villar-Corrales,
Luis Denninger, Julia Brocker, Tim Sinen, Michael Schreiber, and Sven Behnke

Autonomous Intelligent Systems, Computer Science Institute VI,
University of Bonn, Bonn, Germany
pavlichenko@ais.uni-bonn.de
https://ais.uni-bonn.de

Abstract. The RoboCup Humanoid League holds annual soccer robot world championships towards the long-term objective of winning against the FIFA world champions by 2050. The participating teams continuously improve their systems. This paper presents the upgrades to our humanoid soccer system, leading our team NimbRo to win the Soccer Tournament in the Humanoid AdultSize League at RoboCup 2023 in Bordeaux, France. The mentioned upgrades consist of: an updated model architecture for visual perception, extended fused angles feedback mechanisms and an additional COM-ZMP controller for walking robustness, and parametric in-walk kicks through waveforms.

1 Introduction

The Humanoid AdultSize League actively pursues the vision of RoboCup, i.e. by 2050 fully autonomous humanoid robot soccer players shall win against the FIFA world champion. Participating teams continuously improve their systems towards this ambitious objective.

For RoboCup 2023, we upgraded our perception pipeline with a new model capable of opponent robot pose estimation. Further, we extended the fused angle feedback mechanism for footstep adjustment and introduced an additional COM-ZMP controller to facilitate walking with higher stability. A novel gait based on a five-mass control principle was introduced for the push recovery technical challenge, improving resilience against pushes in the sagittal plane. Finally, we developed a parametric in-walk kick formulation through waveforms which enabled stronger kicks and easier tuning.

These updates lead to an improved performance at RoboCup 2023, compared to the previous year [21] and resulted in our team, shown in Fig. 1, winning the AdultSize soccer competition of the Humanoid League. A video of the highlights of our performance during RoboCup 2023 is available online[1].

---

[1] RoboCup 2023 NimbRo highlights video: https://youtu.be/hKLC0Vz1GmM.

C. Buche et al. (Eds.): RoboCup 2023, LNAI 14140, pp. 337–349, 2024.
https://doi.org/10.1007/978-3-031-55015-7_28

Fig. 1. RoboCup 2023 in Bordeaux. Left: Team NimbRo AdultSize with NimbRo-OP2(X) robots, Right: Scene from the Final soccer game vs. HERoEHS (Korea).

2   3D-Printed NimbRo-OP2(X) Humanoid Soccer Robots

For the 2023 competition held in Bordeaux, we continued using our well-established NimbRo-OP2 [11] and NimbRo-OP2X [16,17] humanoid robot platforms.

The robots possess 18 Degrees of Freedom (DoF), with 5 DoF per leg, 3 DoF per arm, and 2 DoF in the neck, driven by a total of 34 Robotis Dynamixel actuators. Their 4-bar leg parallel linkage increases stiffness in the sagittal plane—at the cost of locking the pitch of the foot relative to the trunk [13]. Synchronized actuation of the parallelogram with multiple actuators increases joint torques.

Our robots are equipped with a strong Intel quadcore CPU with Nvidia GPU and a CM740 microcontroller board, with a 6-axis IMU (3-axis accelerometer & 3-axis gyro). Their control architecture is based on ROS. By using off-the-shelf components, a single type of actuator, and 3D printing, the robots are affordable and their maintenance is significantly easier than that of custom solutions [13].

Both the NimbRo-OP2 and NimbRo-OP2X humanoid soccer robot are open-source in terms of hardware[2] and software[3], with detailed documentation.

3   Deep-Learning Based Visual Perception: NimbRoNet3

Our humanoid NimbRo robots perceive the environment using a single 5 MP Logitech C930e camera equipped with a wide-angle lens, providing a wide field-of-view in high-resolution.

To successfully perceive the environment in progressively larger soccer fields and more challenging game situations, we enhance our visual perception pipeline with respect to our previous NimbRoNet2 [22] model. Our improved NimbRoNet3 perception model, depicted in Fig. 2, is a new convolutional neural

---

[2] NimbRo-OP2X hardware: https://github.com/NimbRo/nimbro-op2.

[3] NimbRo-OP2X software: https://github.com/AIS-Bonn/humanoid_op_ros.

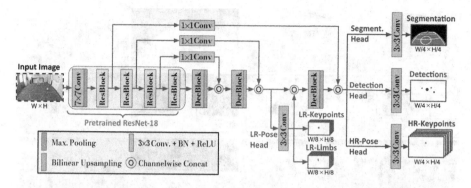

Fig. 2. NimbRoNet3 model. Our model employs an encoder-decoder architecture with a pretrained ResNet-18 backbone, and four different network heads for **field segmentation**, object detection, and **HR/LR robot pose estimation**.

network that simultaneously detects objects relevant to the soccer game, including the ball, goalposts, and robots; segments the field boundaries and lines; and estimates the pose of nearby robots. Our visual perception pipeline, including a forward-pass through the model and post-processing steps, processes high-resolution input images ($3 \times 540 \times 960$) at a rate of 33.3 fps on the robot hardware, thus providing for real-time perception of the game environment.

Inspired by our previous works [21,22], our perception model is a deep convolutional neural network employing an asymmetric encoder-decoder architecture with three skip connections, similar to UNet [23]. To minimize annotation efforts, we utilize a pretrained ResNet-18 [19] backbone as encoder, after removing the final fully-connected and global average pooling layers. Our decoder is formed by three convolutional blocks followed by bilinear upsampling, in contrast to the transposed convolution blocks employed in our previous work [22]. Additionally, our decoder produces outputs with 1/4th of the input resolution, thus drastically reducing the number of required operations. Three different skip connections bridge from the encoder to the decoder, thus maintaining high-resolution information, improving the spatial precision of the outputs [23]. These skip connections contain a 1×1 convolution to align the number of feature maps.

Our model is simultaneously trained to perform object detection, field segmentation, and robot pose estimation using four distinct output heads:

- **Object Detection:** The detection head predicts the location of goalposts, soccer balls and robots, represented by Gaussian heatmaps centered at the ball center and bottom-middle point of goalposts and robots. The exact object locations are retrieved from the predicted heatmaps in a post-processing step./
- **Field Segmentation:** The segmentation head predicts a semantic category, e.g. background, field or line, for every pixel of the input image in order to obtain the segmentation of the soccer field.
- **Robot Pose Estimation:** Inspired by recent work on human- and robot-pose estimation [3,6], our model employs two convolutional output heads

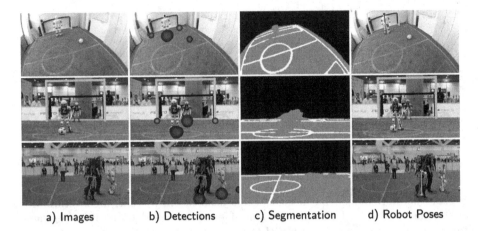

a) Images   b) Detections   c) Segmentation   d) Robot Poses

Fig. 3. Qualitative results for NimbRoNet3. a) Captured images. b) Predicted object heatmaps for soccer balls (red), robots (blue) and goalposts (green). c) Semantic segmentation of the field with lines (white), field (gray) and background (black). d) Predicted robot poses. We depict the predicted joint locations with a circle and connect all joints corresponding to a single robot. (Color figure online)

operating at different spatial resolution for the task of robot pose estimation. To estimate the robot poses, our model predicts six different keypoints (i.e. head, trunk, left hand, right hand, left foot, and right foot) at high and low resolutions. Additionally, following [3], the low-resolution pose head also predicts the limbs connecting such keypoints. During post-processing, the predicted keypoints and limbs are associated into robot poses following a greedy matching algorithm [5].

Our model is trained to minimize the combined loss function:

$$\mathcal{L} = \lambda_1 \mathcal{L}_{Det} + \lambda_2 \mathcal{L}_{Seg} + \lambda_3 \mathcal{L}_{Pose} + \lambda_4 \mathcal{L}_{TV}, \qquad (1)$$

where $\mathcal{L}_{Det}$ is the mean-squared error between predicted and target object heatmaps, $\mathcal{L}_{Seg}$ is the cross entropy loss between predicted and ground-truth segmentation maps, $\mathcal{L}_{Pose}$ is the mean-squared error between predicted and target joint keypoints and limb heatmaps, and $\mathcal{L}_{TV}$ is a total variation regularization loss that enforces the model to predict smooth heatmaps. The hyper-parameters $\lambda_{1,...,4}$ weight the loss terms.

We train and evaluate our models with a dataset consisting of around 8000 images with annotations for object detection, 1100 samples with ground truth segmentation masks, and 1150 images with annotated robot poses; which are divided 80/20 for training and testing. Our data annotation process follows a semi-automatic approach. First, a small set of images was manually annotated using existing annotation tools[4]. Then, a trained NimbRoNet3 model is used to generate pseudo-labels for the remaining images, and the user simply has to

---

[4] https://supervise.ly, https://github.com/bit-bots/imagetagger.

manually correct those labels that contain errors. This semi-automatic annotation process allowed us to quickly gather and annotate data of unseen robots and game balls during the RoboCup 2023 competition.

Qualitative results obtained by NimbRoNet3 on test images are shown in Fig. 3. Our model simultaneously detects the soccer-related objects, accurately segments the soccer field, and estimates the pose of diverse robots. Additionally, we see how our model generalizes to different viewpoints, lighting conditions, ball designs, and robot appearances.

Our improved perception pipeline allows our humanoid robots to accurately perceive the game environment in real time, being able to detect relevant objects across the soccer field, segment the field lines and boundaries, and to estimate the pose of the opponent robots. In the future, we plan to employ the estimated robot poses to develop advanced soccer behaviors, such as recognizing and anticipating the actions from our opponents [8].

4   Core Motion Components for Walking and Kicking

The soccer skills presented by our robots are all combined into a framework, which extends our previous approaches [21,22]. The following subsections summarize all of the necessary features for robust and flexible dynamic walking and in-walk kicking that contributed to the dynamic soccer play demonstrated in the RoboCup 2023 Humanoid League AdultSize soccer tournament.

4.1   Gait Motion Generation

The core of our walking scheme remained unchanged to the previous years [21,22] and revolves around a Central Pattern Generator (CPG). Joint trajectories are computed with inverse kinematics from end-effector positions, obtained by waveforms designed in the *abstract space* and progressing with the *gait phase*.

The *abstract space* is a convenient partitioning of humanoid movement into meaningful components e.g. limb swinging, shifting and extension as presented in [4] and further extended in [2]. By manually tuning such easily quantifiable variables, we obtain a *self-stable* and omnidirectional gait, to which feedforward and feedback mechanisms are added for rejecting disturbances.

As the approach is model-less and the quantities of the abstract space are bounded, we do not need to artificially keep a certain height of the hips or Center of Mass (CoM). In fact, we allow our NimbRo-OP2(X) robots to walk with nearly fully extended legs, which increases their stride length and simultaneously reduces the necessary knee torque.

4.2   State Estimation

Despite limited sensing capabilities of the NimbRo-OP2(X) robots, we are still able of sufficiently reconstructing the robot's state to close the control loop. By using the kinematic model, absolute joint encoder readings, and torso orientation, we obtain the robot's current spatial configuration.

The torso orientation is estimated with a non-linear passive complementary filter and represented in the form of *Fused Angles* [1]. Using *Fused Angles*, we can split the tilt of the robot into uniform sagittal and lateral components, and apply PID-like feedback on tilt deviations.

Furthermore, by knowing that the soccer field is flat, we assume the lower leg to be the supporting one. To prevent rapid support exchanges and assess how much support is provided by each of the legs, we apply a height hysteresis. Finally, we track the whole state of a pseudo CoM $\mathbf{c} = \begin{bmatrix} c & \dot{c} & \ddot{c} \end{bmatrix}$ in both sagittal and lateral planes. The pseudo CoM position is calculated as a fixed offset from the torso frame, when the robot is in the nominal gait pose. Due to the symmetry of the limb movement, this is a sufficiently accurate approximation of where the actual CoM is. This is then fused in a Kalman filter [14] with $\ddot{c}$—the unrotated trunk acceleration measured with the IMU, with gravity g removed— and used to provide a pseudo Zero Moment Point (ZMP) $\widehat{p}_z$:

$$\widehat{p}_z = \widehat{c} - \frac{\widehat{c}_z}{g}\,\widehat{\ddot{c}}. \tag{2}$$

4.3   Feedforward and Feedback Control

Before RoboCup 2023, our feedback scheme was based on the Capture Step Framework [20], which fitted a Linear Inverted Pendulum Model (LIPM) to the observed robot movement using the CPG-based gait. Using the observed state of the fitted LIPM, step-timing and step-size feedback based on a predicted state would then be determined and applied to the robot, thus closing the loop.

Despite its impressive push rejection capabilities, it has a caveat in the form of decreased responsiveness to commands. As the approach welcomes compliant low-gain control to smoothly dissipate a certain level of disturbances, it requires overly exaggerated commands to achieve desired effects. This essentially equates to embedding non-descriptive feedforward compensation for both the lower-level joint trajectories and higher-level gait commands. In consequence, the actuators are always actively tracking a moving target, which results in increased power consumption and generated heat.

A unified feedforward controller on the joint level could potentially alleviate this problem, but it introduces non-linear behavior which decreases predictability by disrupting the initial assumption of the robot behaving like an LIPM.

For the 2023 competition, we extended our Fused Angle Feedback Mechanisms gait, previously used in the 2019 competition [22] to achieve a similar level of balancing capabilities without compromising responsiveness. A feedforward compensation scheme is included, integrating RBDL-based Inverse Dynamics [10] and a servo-model, which compensates for joint torque, friction and supply voltage [24]. Due to the combination of multiple actuators, and external gearing, the model coefficients had to be manually adjusted to improve joint position tracking. The gait was also extended with two feedback mechanisms:

○ *Swing-leg feedback:* Tilt-dependent offsets are applied to the abstract swing-leg swing angle (e.g. tilting the robot forward induces a forward swing of the non-supporting leg, to ensure that the foot lands approximately at the desired location with respect to the CoM). The offsets are faded out linearly just after the leg begins to transition into the supporting leg. As such, the offset is applied only during the respective expected swing phase. The scheme is repeated if the tilt progresses into the next step.

∘ *Pseudo-CoM-ZMP feedback:* Despite the lack of a model controlling the movement of the robot, it still physically behaves like an inverted pendulum during its gait cycle and pivots its CoM around the Center of Pressure (CoP). As the open-loop trajectories were designed to be self-stable, experimentally observed that the pseudo CoM and pseudo ZMP do in fact approximate the LIPM. On this basis, we employ a CoM-ZMP controller [7] acting on the pseudo states, which realizes input-to-state stability by adjusting $\dot{c}$ to steer c to the reference value.

To generate the reference pseudo CoM and pseudo ZMP values, a second CPG generates purely reference motions and assumes nominal CPG-execution and upright torso orientation. We match the reference pseudo ZMP location to the observed one on the robot by adjusting an offset from the center of the supporting foot.

We adopted the Direct Centroidal Control (DCC) concept [14] to incorporate leaky integration and applied the integrated pseudo CoM-offset to shift the hips of the robot, replacing the fused angle hip-shift feedback. Additionally, a high-pass rate-limiting scheme [9] was used to provide smooth velocity changes, necessary for the inverse dynamics calculation in the feedforward compensation.

4.4   Flexible Waveform-Based Kicking

For RoboCup 2019 in Sydney, we introduced the in-walk kicking technique [22] integrated seamlessly into the gait. This was a subtle yet effective change that greatly increased our performance and made the game pace more dynamic. In-walk kicking was extended in 2022, where the kicks became more robust to the alignment of the robot and allowed for directional kicking [21].

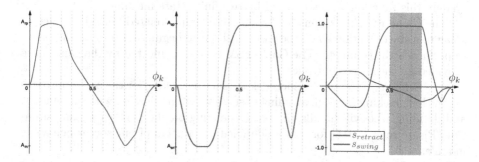

Fig. 4. In-walk kick waveforms. Left: Isolated design of the retraction waveform. Middle: Isolated design of the swing waveform. Right: Absolute applied values with scaling to the abstract gait pose. ϕ_k is the kick phase (like x_K in Fig. 6 of [22]). s_{swing} and $s_{retract}$ are the experimentally achieved swing and retract waveforms, the gray area depicts the time-window where momentum is the highest, e.g. leg is being fully extended and swung forward.

However, the distance achieved with each kick would vary largely, barely reaching 4 m. Sometimes four to five kicks would be necessary to score a goal, which gave opponents more opportunities to take ball possession. Having stronger kicks would not only reduce the number of necessary contacts and make goal attempts quicker, but also help clear the ball from the goal in the attempts of opponents.

To achieve stronger kicks, we implemented a waveform designer to modify the kick parameters on-line. Two waveforms designed in the abstract space responsible for leg retraction and the swing angle are superimposed with the CPG gait trajectories. The waveform editor allows for modifying 12 keypoint values scaled by the positive and negative maximum amplitudes of the allowed retraction and angle. This allows for a resolution of approx. 30 ms with our current step duration. The keypoints are linearly interpolated and low-pass filtered for smooth transitions. With the kicking waveforms shown in Fig. 4, we aimed to maximize the momentum transmitted to the ball during contact, which happens when both the thigh and shank reach their maximum velocity.

Designing the waveforms on-line allowed for quick iteration of the kicks directly on the robot. The operator can then quickly iterate and receive feedback on the attempt, to the point where a single 1-hour manual tuning session was enough to exceed the previous approach. Tuning directly on the robot ensured that the kicks would be feasible on the physical system by striking a balance between kick strength and stability, omitting simulation efforts entirely. By parameterizing the positive and negative amplitudes of the waveforms, we can vary the kick strength depending on the game situation. The presented approach effectively doubled our kicking distance from an average of 2.5 m to 5 m, and quite often surpassing 7 m allowing us to even score goals from our own half.

5   Higher-Level Game Control and Soccer Behaviors

The decision process for playing soccer is referred to as soccer behaviors. In our system, this functionality is realized by two finite state machines (FSM).

The Game FSM is responsible for high-level game-related behaviors, such as going to a start position when the game is about to begin, awaiting the opponent to perform a throw-in, etc. The Game FSM is mostly affected by the game state provided by the game controller.

The Behavior FSM defines soccer skills, such as looking for the ball, approaching the ball, kicking the ball, avoiding obstacles, communicating with teammates, and deciding who will handle the ball depending on the perceived game situation. Please refer to [18] for a more detailed description of our soccer behaviors module.

6   Technical Challenges

Technical Challenges are a separate competition in the RoboCup AdultSize League where the robots compete in performing four predefined tasks in a 25 min

Fig. 5. Technical Challenge: Push Recovery. The robot successfully recovers from a frontal push of 10 kg pendulum, which is more than half of the robot's weight.

timeslot. The limited time available forces the teams to design robust and reliable solutions. In this section, we present our approaches to the three challenges: Push Recovery, High Kick, and Goal Kick from Moving Ball.

6.1 Push Recovery

The Push Recovery challenge is the most relevant for Humanoid Soccer, as it tests the robot's ability to withstand a set of three pushes while walking on the spot: from the front, from the back, and any of the two. Each push is applied by a free-falling pendulum which impacts the robot at its CoM. The final score achieved depends on how far the pendulum was retracted and the ratio of its mass to that of the robot. For this challenge we used a novel gait, which unifies centroidal state estimation, feedforward and feedback control techniques through a five-mass representation of a humanoid robot [12].

For the NimbRo-OP2X it was particularly important to compensate for the limitations arising from the 4-bar parallel linkage mechanism in the legs, and generate tilt-based step-feedback [15]. Using this approach, the robot completed several trials with a 3 kg and 5 kg pendulum. Our robot won the challenge by sustaining pushes from a 5 kg pendulum, let go at a horizontal distance of 90 cm, more than doubling the result of the second-best team. This also superseded our results obtained previously with the Capture Steps Framework. NimbRo-OP2X was also able to withstand two consecutive pushes from a 10 kg pendulum (at 40 cm), which is more than half of its own weight (see Fig. 5).

Fig. 6. Technical Challenge: High Kick. First, the robot moves the ball closer to the obstacle by making a weak kick. Second, the robot approaches the re-positioned ball and kicks it over the obstacle.

Fig. 7. Technical Challenge: Goal Kick from Moving Ball.

6.2 High Kick

The objective of this challenge is to score a goal such that the ball flies over an obstacle placed at the goal line. The challenge starts with the ball on the penalty mark. To maximize the height which we can kick over, we first move the ball closer to the obstacle by performing a weak kick, defined as a predesigned motion. After this, we approach the ball and perform a predesigned high kick motion, which aims at kicking the ball at a closest-to-the-ground point, thus directing the ball upward. Our robot successfully scored a goal over a 20 cm obstacle (Fig. 6), coming in second in this challenge. Team HERoEHS won this challenge, kicking over a 21 cm obstacle.

6.3 Goal Kick from Moving Ball

The objective of this challenge is to score a goal by kicking a ball which is moving towards the robot. The robot starts at the penalty mark and the pass is performed by a human. To reliably kick at the right moment, we use ball detections from our visual perception module to estimate its velocity and acceleration, which then enables us to estimate the time of arrival to the region in front of the foot. Finally, knowing the time needed for a kick motion to be executed, we identify the moment when the kick has to be triggered. Our robot managed to score two goals out of three passes (Fig. 7), coming in second in this challenge. Team HERoEHS won this challenge, scoring three goals in a row.

7 Soccer Game Performance

At the RoboCup 2023 AdultSize soccer competition, teams consisting of two autonomous humanoid robots played matches against each other. This year, four teams participated in the AdultSize League.

Prior to the main soccer tournament, a Drop-In competition, where robots from different teams had to collaborate during 3 vs. 3 matches, took place. In this competition, our robots played four games with a cumulative score of 26:0. All these goals were scored by our robots.

During the round-robin of the main soccer tournament, our robots won all their three matches with a total score of 22:0. In the semifinals, our team played against team RoMeLa from UCLA (USA), winning the match with a score of 10:0. In the final, we met team HERoEHS from Hanyang University (Korea).

Our robots played well and won the final game with the score of 8:0, becoming the champions in the AdultSize League for the fifth year in a row. Overall, our robots demonstrated a solid performance throughout all the matches they played without losing a single goal, achieving a total score of 66:0.

8   Conclusions

In this paper, we presented the improvements to our previous-year RoboCup-winning humanoid soccer system. The improvements enabled us to win again the main soccer tournament as well as Drop-In competition in the Humanoid AdultSize League at RoboCup 2023 in Bordeaux.

In particular, we introduced an updated visual perception model NimbRoNet3 capable of estimating poses of the opponent robots. Further, we proposed an extended fused angles feedback mechanism for footstep adjustment and an additional COM-ZMP controller. These updates improved walking stability which contributed to our robots staying in the game without falling for extended periods of time, including episodes of intense whole-body contacts with much heavier robots. The introduced waveform-based formulation for parametric in-walk kicks enabled our robots to reliably score goals from greater distances, including goals from our own half of the field. Finally, a newly introduced gait helped us to win the Push Recovery technical challenge, outperforming our results from previous years.

Acknowledgments. This work was partially funded by H2020 project EUROBENCH, GA 779963.

References

1. Allgeuer, P., Behnke, S.: Fused angles: a representation of body orientation for balance. In: IEEE/RSJ International Conference on Intelligent Robots and Systems (IROS), pp. 366–373 (2015)
2. Allgeuer, P., Behnke, S.: Omnidirectional bipedal walking with direct fused angle feedback mechanisms. In: 16th IEEE-RAS International Conference on Humanoid Robots (Humanoids), pp. 834–841 (2016)
3. Amini, A., Farazi, H., Behnke, S.: Real-time pose estimation from images for multiple humanoid robots. In: Alami, R., Biswas, J., Cakmak, M., Obst, O. (eds.) RoboCup 2021. LNCS (LNAI), vol. 13132, pp. 91–102. Springer, Cham (2022). https://doi.org/10.1007/978-3-030-98682-7_8
4. Behnke, S.: Online trajectory generation for omnidirectional biped walking. In: IEEE International Conference on Robotics and Automation (ICRA), pp. 1597–1603 (2006)
5. Cao, Z., Simon, T., Wei, S.E., Sheikh, Y.: Realtime multi-person 2D pose estimation using part affinity fields. In: IEEE/CVF Conference on Computer Vision and Pattern Recognition (CVPR), pp. 7291–7299 (2017)
6. Cheng, B., Xiao, B., Wang, J., Shi, H., Huang, T.S., Zhang, L.: HigherHRNet: scale-aware representation learning for bottom-up human pose estimation. In: IEEE/CVF Conference on Computer Vision and Pattern Recognition (CVPR), pp. 5386–5395 (2020)

7. Choi, Y., Kim, D., Oh, Y., You, B.J.: Posture/walking control for humanoid robot based on kinematic resolution of CoM Jacobian with embedded motion. IEEE Trans. Rob. **23**(6), 1285–1293 (2007)
8. Duan, H., Zhao, Y., Chen, K., Lin, D., Dai, B.: Revisiting skeleton-based action recognition. In: IEEE/CVF Conference on Computer Vision and Pattern Recognition (CVPR), pp. 2969–2978 (2022)
9. Englsberger, J., Mesesan, G., Werner, A., Ott, C.: Torque-based dynamic walking- a long way from simulation to experiment. In: IEEE International Conference on Robotics and Automation (ICRA), pp. 440–447 (2018)
10. Felis, M.L.: RBDL: an efficient rigid-body dynamics library using recursive algorithms. Auton. Robot. **41**(2), 495–511 (2017)
11. Ficht, G., Allgeuer, P., Farazi, H., Behnke, S.: NimbRo-OP2: grown-up 3D printed open humanoid platform for research. In: 17th IEEE-RAS International Conference on Humanoid Robots (Humanoids), pp. 669–675 (2017)
12. Ficht, G., Behnke, S.: Fast whole-body motion control of humanoid robots with inertia constraints. In: IEEE International Conference on Robotics and Automation (ICRA), pp. 6597–6603 (2020)
13. Ficht, G., Behnke, S.: Bipedal humanoid hardware design: a technology review. Curr. Rob. Rep. **2**(2), 201–210 (2021)
14. Ficht, G., Behnke, S.: Direct centroidal control for balanced humanoid locomotion. In: 25th International Conference on Climbing and Walking Robots (CLAWAR), pp. 242–255 (2022)
15. Ficht, G., Behnke, S.: Centroidal state estimation and control for hardware-constrained humanoid robots. In: 22nd IEEE-RAS International Conference on Humanoid Robots (Humanoids) (2023)
16. Ficht, G., et al.: NimbRo-OP2X: adult-sized open-source 3D printed humanoid robot. In: 18th IEEE-RAS International Conference on Humanoid Robots (Humanoids), pp. 1–9 (2018)
17. Ficht, G., et al.: NimbRo-OP2X: affordable adult-sized 3D-printed open-source humanoid robot for research. In: J. Humanoid Rob. **17**(05), 2050021:1–2050021:35 (2020)
18. Ficht, G., et al.: Grown-Up NimbRo robots winning RoboCup 2017 humanoid AdultSize soccer competitions. In: Akiyama, H., Obst, O., Sammut, C., Tonidandel, F. (eds.) RoboCup 2017. LNCS (LNAI), vol. 11175, pp. 448–460. Springer, Cham (2018). https://doi.org/10.1007/978-3-030-00308-1_37
19. He, K., Zhang, X., Ren, S., Sun, J.: Deep residual learning for image recognition. In: IEEE/CVF Conference on Computer Vision and Pattern Recognition (CVPR), pp. 770–778 (2016)
20. Missura, M., Bennewitz, M., Behnke, S.: Capture steps: robust walking for humanoid robots. Int. J. Humanoid Rob. **16**(6), 1950032:1–1950032:28 (2019)
21. Pavlichenko, D., et al.: RoboCup 2022 AdultSize winner NimbRo: upgraded perception, capture steps gait and phase-based in-walk kicks. In: Eguchi, A., Lau, N., Paetzel-Prusmann, M., Wanichanon, T. (eds.) RoboCup 2022: Robot World Cup XXV. Lecture Notes in Computer Science, vol. 13561, pp. 240–252. Springer, Heidelberg (2023). https://doi.org/10.1007/978-3-031-28469-4_20
22. Rodriguez, D., et al.: RoboCup 2019 AdultSize winner NimbRo: deep learning perception, in-walk kick, push recovery, and team play capabilities. In: Chalup, S., Niemueller, T., Suthakorn, J., Williams, M.-A. (eds.) RoboCup 2019. LNCS (LNAI), vol. 11531, pp. 631–645. Springer, Cham (2019). https://doi.org/10.1007/978-3-030-35699-6_51

23. Ronneberger, O., Fischer, P., Brox, T.: U-Net: convolutional networks for biomedical image segmentation. In: Navab, N., Hornegger, J., Wells, W.M., Frangi, A.F. (eds.) MICCAI 2015. LNCS, vol. 9351, pp. 234–241. Springer, Cham (2015). https://doi.org/10.1007/978-3-319-24574-4_28

24. Schwarz, M., Behnke, S.: Compliant robot behavior using servo actuator models identified by iterative learning control. In: Behnke, S., Veloso, M., Visser, A., Xiong, R. (eds.) RoboCup 2013. LNCS (LNAI), vol. 8371, pp. 207–218. Springer, Heidelberg (2014). https://doi.org/10.1007/978-3-662-44468-9_19

b-it-bots: Winners of RoboCup@Work 2023

Gokul Chenchani, Kevin Patel[✉], Ravisankar Selvaraju, Shubham Shinde,
Vamsi Kalagaturu, Vivek Mannava, Deebul Nair, Iman Awaad,
Mohammad Wasil, Santosh Thoduka, Sven Schneider, Nico Hochgeschwender,
and Paul G. Plöger

Institute for AI and Autonomous Systems, Hochschule Bonn-Rhein-Sieg,
53757 Sankt Augustin, Germany
{gokul.chenchani,kevin.patel,ravisankar.selvaraju,shubham.shinde,
vamsi.kalagaturu,vivek.mannava,deebul.nair,iman.awaad,
mohammad.wasil, santosh.thoduka,sven.schneider,
nico.hochgeschwender,paul.ploger}@inf.h-brs.de

Abstract. This paper outlines the approach used by the b-it-bots team
to win the 2023 RoboCup@Work World Championship in Bordeaux. We
describe the updates in hardware and software since the last competition. We explain how we addressed the challenges in perception, grasping,
and task planning resulting from new rules and an Advanced Object set.
The main changes include an updated camera position, a new gripper, 2D
object, and cavity detection, and point cloud-based free space detection.
We discuss the advantages of our modifications and explain how it helped
in solving the different tasks robustly. Our code and datasets are made
public.

1 Introduction

The RoboCup@Work competition [5] focuses on autonomous mobile robots
operating within industrial environments, performing transportation tasks with
objects such as nuts, bolts, metal profiles, screwdrivers, etc. The tasks require
perception of objects on arbitrary workstation surfaces, navigation in a known
environment with unseen obstacles, and manipulation of small and textureless
objects. In addition to flat workstations, special workstations such as shelves, a
rotating table, and a precision placement workstation with cavities for specific
objects are part of the environment.

Our team, b-it-bots, has been an active participant in this league since 2012
and has competed in both the RoboCup World Championship and German Open
throughout the years, placing in the top three in most years. Having previously
won the world championship title in 2019, we reclaimed the title this year in our
first in-person competition since 2019[1]. We were also winners of the technical
challenge *Coworker Assembly Test*. The team is composed of students pursuing

---

[1] https://atwork.robocup.org/rc2023/.

C. Buche et al. (Eds.): RoboCup 2023, LNAI 14140, pp. 350–361, 2024.
https://doi.org/10.1007/978-3-031-55015-7_29

their Master's degrees in Autonomous Systems at Hochschule Bonn-Rhein-Sieg, who are guided by Ph.D. students and professors.

The overall hardware and software architecture for our robot remains the same as in 2019 [6]. Therefore, in this paper, we mainly present updates to the individual components by starting with the challenges introduced by new changes in the competition in Sect. 2, our robot platform in Sect. 3, perception capabilities in Sect. 4.1, object manipulation in Sect. 5, task planning in Sect. 6, and conclude by describing our current activities in preparing for the next competition in Sect. 7. In line with our commitment to open-source development, the code for our robot's systems, reflecting the updates and advancements described in this paper, is made available on our GitHub repository: https://github.com/b-it-bots/mas_industrial_robotics.

2 New Challenges

This year's competition introduced the *Advanced Transportation Task* (ATT), which integrated the previously stand-alone tasks, Precision Placement and Rotating Table Test. ATT also includes the new Advanced Object set, since the old "RoCKIn" object set has been removed from the competition. The advanced objects were introduced in 2022, but only as a separate technical challenge; in 2023 they were integrated into the ATTs and the finals. The new objects introduced challenges in perception, grasping, and task planning. Objects such as the Allen key and wrench (see Fig. 1) are challenging to grasp since they are quite small. Their small size also means that 3D perception is challenging since the objects blend into the noisy 3D point cloud. The motor, which weighs 350 g, is the heaviest of the objects and requires an adjustment of the gripper design to reliably grasp it. The staging area for objects on the robot had to be redesigned for the longer objects, such as the allen key and screwdriver. Although the technical challenge Coworker Assembly Test had been introduced previously, this was our first time attempting it, and thus new functionalities were developed for it.

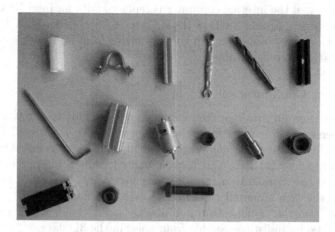

Fig. 1. A selection of some of the objects to be manipulated. The new objects, such as the wrench, Allen key, and drill bit are challenging to grasp.

3   Robot Platform

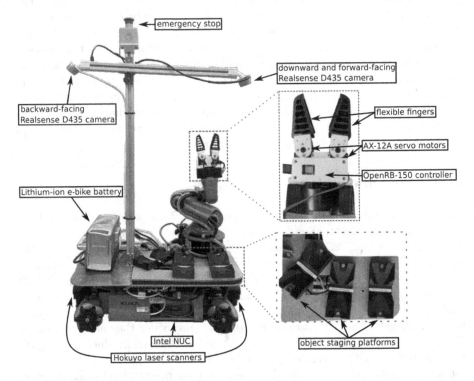

Fig. 2. Modified youBot platform

We use the KUKA youBot (see Fig. 2), which is an omnidirectional platform with a 5-DoF manipulator. The original gripper is replaced with a flexible two-finger gripper, and the internal computer is replaced with an Intel NUC with an Intel Core i7 processor and 8 GB of RAM. Two Hokuyo URG-04LX laser range finders are mounted upside down in the platform's front and back so that even 5 cm workstations are detectable.

3.1   Camera Configuration

We switched from an arm-mounted camera (eye-in-hand) to a tower-mounted Intel RealSense D435 camera for object perception. An additional backward-facing Intel RealSense D435 camera is used for black and yellow barrier-tape detection during navigation. The tower-mounted camera allows the robot to observe the entire workstation from a single viewpoint, instead of three viewpoints with the arm-mounted camera. However, the increased distance of the workstation from the camera results in a noisy point cloud, which means that smaller objects are indistinguishable from noise in the 3D data.

3.2   Penguin Gripper Finger

The flexible gripper fingers are based on the adaptive FinRay finger design by Festo[2]. To address the challenges of grasping some of the advanced objects, we modified the original finger to include a curved tip, which allows the robot to grasp small, flat objects like the wrench and Allen key by scooping them from the platform surface (see Fig. 3 and 4). The flexibility of the new finger, which we call the *Penguin* finger, is achieved by 3D printing it using the ThermoPlastic Polyurethane (TPU) filament. The fingers are actuated by individual Dynamixel AX-12A servo motors, which provide a position interface and force-feedback information and are controlled using the OpenRB-150 controller[3] by Robotis.

Fig. 3. The curved tip of the Penguin fingers allows the gripper to grasp thin objects, while the adaptivity from the original Festo design still allows it to wrap around larger objects.

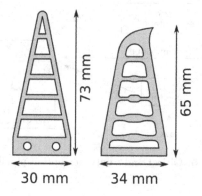

Fig. 4. 2D profile of the original gripper finger (left) and revised Penguin gripper finger (right)

---

[2] https://www.festo.com/us/en/a/3998967/.

[3] https://emanual.robotis.com/docs/en/parts/controller/openrb-150/.

3.3 Arm Mount and Object Staging Platforms

Based on the configuration of team robOTTO [10], we place the arm in the front-left corner of the base such that the staging platform for the objects can be placed beside the arm, thus reducing arm motions while staging and unstaging objects. The arm, staging platforms, camera tower, and battery are all mounted on an aluminum plate on the base, allowing most cabling to be concealed below the plate.

3.4 Battery

The original dry lead acid batteries of the youBot are heavy and have a capacity of 5 Ah, which limits the run time of the robot without external power. We thus decided to upgrade the battery to a 26 V lithium-ion (Li-ion) e-bike battery[4]. We plan to replace the entire power management system with a new one that can allow hot-swapping and better battery management and move from Li-ion to safer, more reliable, and long-lasting lithium iron phosphate (LiFePO$_4$) batteries.

4 Perception

The RGB-D cameras are used for detecting objects and cavities, detecting barrier tapes, identifying free space on workstations for placing objects, and tracking objects on the rotating table. In the following sections, we describe our current approach for some of these perception tasks.

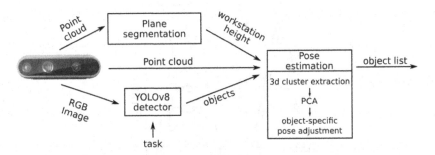

Fig. 5. Object and cavity perception pipeline

4.1 Object and Cavity Detection

Previously we used both 2D image and 3D point cloud-based object detection and recognition approaches. This year, due to the newly introduced objects, we use only 2D image-based detection. Nevertheless, we still use the 3D point cloud

---

[4] https://akku4bikes.de/produkt/e-bike-akku-26v-13-2ah-fuer-flyer-kalkhoff-und-kettler-2/..

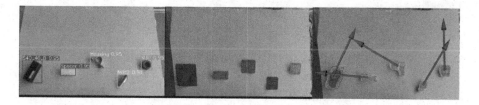

Fig. 6. 2D object detection and corresponding poses in 3D

for pose estimation after 2D detection. We use YOLOv8 [3] for object detection, which is a single-stage deep learning-based detector. It predicts the axis-aligned bounding boxes and the class probabilities for each bounding box. The training data consists of approximately 1500 annotated images on varying backgrounds, with an average of 300 instances of each object, except for a few object pairs that are similar in color and texture and only differ in size, for which we collected 500 instances per object. Rather than manually annotating bounding boxes, we use the Segment Anything Model (SAM) [4] to semi-automatically annotate bounding boxes[5], thus reducing the effort and time for annotation. In addition to images collected in our lab, we also collected and annotated images in the competition arena in order to bias the model to the environmental conditions there. We use YOLOv8's [3] small model of 10M parameters, which can run at 10 FPS on the CPU. Our dataset is made public and is accessible here [7].

Our object detection model achieves a 92% mean average precision (mAP) across IoU thresholds from 0.5 to 0.95 in increments of 0.05 on our test set. We adhere to an 8:1.5:0.5 ratio for training, validation, and testing datasets, respectively. Table 1 lists the class-wise results on the test set, using standard metrics including precision, recall, and mAP.

In order to generate a grasping pose for a detected object, we first extract the 3D points from the point cloud corresponding to each pixel in the 2D bounding box. The workstation height is determined by using random sample consensus (RANSAC) to segment the dominant horizontal plane. After applying a pass-through filter on the object cluster based on the workstation height, we use the centroid of the filtered cluster as the grasp position. For yaw, we apply Principal Component Analysis (PCA) to the cluster such that the gripper is aligned along the principal axis. Roll and pitch are set to zero since we assume a horizontal workstation surface. This entire process is visualized in Fig. 6 from object detection to pose generation (left to right). For asymmetric objects, such as the screwdriver and bolt, the grasp pose is adjusted along the principal axis such that it is closer to the heavier part of the object for a more stable grasp, as illustrated in Fig. 7.

---

[5] The annotator has to click on an object, and potentially make minor modifications to the generated bounding box.

Table 1. Class-wise object detection performance on the test set

Class	mAP(0.5-0.95)
AllenKey	0.90
Axis2	0.91
Bearing2	0.88
Drill	0.97
F20_20_B	0.91
F20_20_G	0.93
Housing	0.91
M20	0.87
M20_100	0.88
M30	0.89
Motor2	0.93
S40_40_B	0.96
S40_40_G	0.96
Screwdriver	0.92
Spacer	0.88
Wrench	0.90
Container_box_blue	0.99
Container_box_red	0.97

For precision placement of objects into cavities in the Advanced Transportation Task 1, the same perception pipeline as in Fig. 5 is used with a *task* configuration parameter selecting a different YOLOv8 model trained on the cavities, as seen in Fig. 8. For the pose, the 3D cavity clusters are extracted by only considering points *below* the workstation, since they are points from the floor below in the shape of the cavities. These points are first projected back onto the workstation plane before computing their pose using the same method as for object clusters.

Currently, the YOLOv8 object detector is running as a separate Python node; thus inter-process communication via ROS is necessary to coordinate with the pose estimation. In the future, we plan to convert all models to the Open Neural Network Exchange (ONNX) format so that inference can be run in C++ in the same node. Additionally, we plan to switch to a semantic segmentation model to improve the orientation estimation for diagonally oriented objects (Fig. 9).

4.2   Free Space Detection

Due to a new rule introduced in 2022, objects must be placed within a specified *Manipulation Zone* on a workstation, such that no other object on the workstation is touched during placement. Therefore, the robot first perceives the

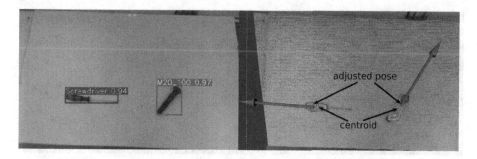

Fig. 7. Pose adjustment for asymmetric objects

Fig. 8. The pose for cavities detected in the RGB image is computed based on the 3D point cloud projected from the floor to the workstation

workstation to identify free spaces where the object can be placed. This replaces our previous approach of using pre-defined arm poses for placing objects. The free space detection is based on the 3D point cloud data from the RGB-D camera. The dominant horizontal plane is segmented using RANSAC, and all plane inliers are considered to be candidate free points if they are within the manipulation zone. Random candidates are selected and discarded if the number of neighboring free points within a certain radius is below a threshold. The process is repeated until at least two candidates with sufficient free neighbors are found.

In case of poor lighting conditions, glare from overhead lights, or shiny workstation surfaces, the point cloud of the workstation might contain "holes" that are incorrectly categorized as occupied. Additionally, the current approach does not consider the size and shape of the object to be placed; addressing both these issues are potential area for improvement.

4.3 Rotating Table

In the Advanced Transportation Task 2 and final, the robot is required to pick up an object from a rotating table. In our current approach, object detection is performed using YOLOv8 on a sequence of 15 frames from the camera. Centroids and orientations for the target object are transformed to the robot's base frame for all images, and stored along with their timestamps. A circular model is fit to the sequence of centroids (see Fig. 10) and used to estimate the direction and rotation speed of the rotating table. To measure the accuracy of the estimated radius and rotation speed, we used four objects (S40_40_B, M20, Housing, and

Fig. 9. Free space detection for safe object placement

AllenKey) at eight radii (32 to 46 cm in 2 cm increments), yielding 32 readings. We found a Mean Absolute Error (MAE) of 5 mm for the estimated radius and 6×10^{-3} rad/sec for rotational speed, compared to the ground truth, which was estimated by manually measuring the time for 10 rotations.

The point on the circle that is closest to the robot is chosen as the grasp position (see Fig. 10), and the predicted time when the object will reach the selected location is determined by taking into account the last known position of the object and the rotation speed of the table.

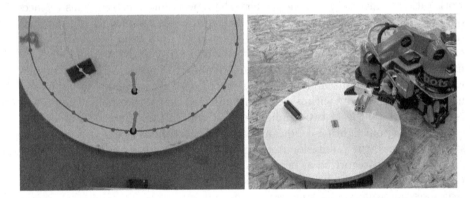

Fig. 10. Left: Circles fit to detected object poses with anticipated grasp location (black dot) and orientation (red arrow) in the image frame. Right: Robot picking an object during the competition. (Color figure online)

4.4 Technical Challenge - Coworker Assembly Test

In the Coworker Assembly Test, the goal is for the robot to collaborate with a human to create an assembled product. The robot is responsible for fetching the parts of the assembly for the human and for delivering the assembled product to its final destination after the human assembles the product. The robot waits for a signal from the person before detecting and grasping the assembled product. We chose the hand gesture of a two-finger victory sign as the signal for task completion since it is quite distinct. We again used YOLOv8 models to detect the hand gesture and to detect the assembled object.

5 Manipulation

Without extensive tuning, the trajectories planned with MoveIt! have lower joint velocities compared to the position command interface of the youBot driver. To speed up arm motions, we switched to the position command interface for motions from and to fixed pre-defined positions where safety is guaranteed, such as moving to the object staging platforms. For motions to variable positions, such as for grasping an object, we continue to use MoveIt! for trajectory planning.

For grasping objects, the robot approaches the object from above, such that the end-effector is perpendicular to the workstation. However, this reduces the workspace of the arm, causing inverse kinematics (IK) failures for objects that are further away from the robot. In case of an IK failure with the default approach, we use an orientation-independent approach that samples poses at different angles so that the arm can reach the object. While this approach increases the robot's workspace and improves the grasping success rate, it is also prone to failure when the objects are approached at an angle that is too horizontal. When grasping from a workstation with an overhanging shelf, the normal top-down approach is unsafe due to potential collisions with the shelf, especially during the approach and retract phases. Therefore, base motions are used to align the robot with the object with the arm in a safe, pre-grasp position. After grasping, base motions are used again to retreat from the workstation.

To perform grasp verification, we rely on the feedback from the gripper controller, which constantly emits the current state of the gripper, which can be `open`, `closed`, `grasped`, or `moving`. These states are computed based on the fully open and fully closed motor angles and the current action the gripper is executing. The controller computes the relative difference between the positions of the motors for each finger to determine the current state of the gripper. While this works well for large objects, the relative difference is not sufficiently large for thin objects for a reliable grasp verification.

6 Task Planning

In our system, automated task planning is combined with finite state machines (FSMs) as a means to both improve tractability as well as facilitate plan execution. This choice is ideal given that the environment in the @Work league is well-defined - meaning that there is full observability with regard to the initial state as well as the precise locations and goal destinations of all of the objects. The LAMA planner [8] is used to generate the plans whose actions constitute the high-level control required. Actions are implemented as state machines represented as SMACH[6] scripts, making each action modular and easy to test and maintain.

Seven operators are defined in the planning domain which correspond to the following actions: `move base`, `perceive`, `pick`, `place`, `stage`, `unstage`, and `insert`. As an example, the definition of the `place` operator is shown in Listing 1.1. These carefully defined operators allow for traceability and restrict the number of constraints to be considered during planning. They require predicates and literals that represent knowledge such as the robot's location, the status of the gripper, and the object staging area.

Listing 1.1. PDDL example for *place*

```
(:action place
    :parameters (?r − robot ?l − location ?o −
        object)
    :precondition  (and (at ?r ?l)
                        (holding ?r ?o)
                        (not (on ?o ?l))
                        (not (insertable ?o ))
                        (not ( gripper_is_free  ?r))
                    )
    :effect  (and  (on ?o ?l)
                    (not (holding ?r ?o))
                    ( gripper_is_free  ?r)
                    (not (perceived ?l))
                    (increase (total−cost) 2)
                )
)
```

Listing 1.2. Sample generated plan

```
(move_base youbot−brsu start ws01)
(perceive youbot−brsu ws01)
(pick youbot−brsu ws01 axis−00)
(stage youbot−brsu platform_left axis−00)
(move base youbot−brsu ws01 ws03)
(unstage youbot−brsu platform_left axis−00)
(place youbot−brsu ws03 axis−00)
```

During a run, the referee box sends the current locations of objects and their target destinations. The task planning module adds these facts and goals to a knowledge base (KB) implemented in the ROSPlan [2] framework. Generating an optimal plan for all of the goals is considered a time-intensive task given the total allotted time for a run. Therefore, only three goals are selected for inclusion in the PDDL problem file that is sent to the LAMA planner. A maximum of 20 s is allotted to the planner to come up with the best-generated plan given this limit.

The plan, consisting of a sequence of actions, is sent to the plan executor. Listing 1.2 shows a sample plan generated to move an object from workstation 01 to workstation 03. As the respective SMACH script gets executed, the KB is updated to reflect the changes made in the real world. This ensures that the current state of the world is always available in case re-planning is needed - either due to the failure of an action or the successful completion of all of the actions.

In the process of migrating from ROS to ROS 2, we plan to adopt the Unified Planning Library (UPL) [1] to replace our current task planning framework. While we intend to continue utilizing the LAMA planner within this framework, the transition to UPL in ROS 2 offers the flexibility for future exploration and testing of alternative planners.

---

[6] http://wiki.ros.org/smach.

7 Current Activities

For the next championship, we are in the process of porting our code to use ROS 2. We would like to make use of managed lifecycle nodes so that components can be activated and deactivated based on the action being performed. We are also exploring the use of behavior trees to replace SMACH state machines. In the future, we plan to utilize formal models of robot software and hardware to automate development activities such as the generation of motion control architectures [9].

Acknowledgement. We acknowledge the financial support of the Vice President of International Affairs and Diversity at Hochschule Bonn-Rhein-Sieg (H-BRS), the Computer Science department at H-BRS, the Student Committee (AStA) at H-BRS and the b-it Bonn-Aachen International Center for Information Technology. We would also like the acknowledge Chaitanya Gumudula, Kishan Sawant, Michał Stolarz, and Ibrahim Shakir Syed for their contribution to various aspects of the hardware and software development.

References

1. Unified Planning Library. https://github.com/aiplan4eu/unified-planning. Accessed 13 Oct 2023
2. Cashmore, M., et al.: ROSPlan: planning in the robot operating system. In: Proceedings of the International Conference on Automated Planning and Scheduling, vol. 25, pp. 333–341 (2015)
3. Jocher, G., Chaurasia, A., Qiu, J.: Ultralytics YOLOv8 (2023). https://github.com/ultralytics/ultralytics. Accessed 13 Oct 2023
4. Kirillov, A., et al.: Segment Anything. arXiv:2304.02643 (2023)
5. Kraetzschmar, G.K., et al.: RoboCup@Work: competing for the factory of the future. In: Bianchi, R., Akin, H., Ramamoorthy, S., Sugiura, K. (eds.) RoboCup 2014: Robot World Cup XVIII 18. LNCS, vol. 8992, pp. 171–182. Springer, Cham (2015). https://doi.org/10.1007/978-3-319-18615-3_14
6. Padalkar, A., et al.: b-it-bots: our approach for autonomous robotics in industrial environments. In: Proceedings of the 23rd RoboCup International Symposium, Sydney, Australia (2019)
7. Patel, K., et al.: RoboCup @Work 2023 dataset (2023). https://doi.org/10.5281/zenodo.10003915
8. Richter, S., Westphal, M., Helmert, M.: Lama 2008 and 2011. In: International Planning Competition, pp. 117–124 (2011)
9. Schneider, S., Hochgeschwender, N., Bruyninckx, H.: Domain-specific languages for kinematic chains and their solver algorithms: lessons learned for composable models. In: 2023 IEEE International Conference on Robotics and Automation (ICRA), pp. 9104–9110. IEEE (2023)
10. Steup, C., et al.: Team Description Paper robOTTO RoboCup@Work 2022 (2022). https://www.robotto.ovgu.de/robotto_media/Downloads/TDPs/tdp_robotto_2022.pdf

Robust Integration of Planning, Execution, Recovery and Testing to Win the RoboCup Logistics League

David Beikircher, Marco De Bortoli[✉], Leo Fürbaß, Thomas Kernbauer,
Peter Kohout, Dominik Lampel, Anna Masiero, Stefan Moser, Martin Nagele,
and Gerald Steinbauer-Wagner

Graz University of Technology, Graz, Austria
mbortoli@ist.tugraz.at

Abstract. This paper presents the evolution of the software architecture developed by the GRIPS team from Graz University of Technology for the RoboCup Logistics League (RCLL) competition, to the point of winning the 2023 RoboCup Logistics League. The RCLL simulates a flexible production environment, and the team's software addresses the challenges of automation, planning, and execution in this dynamic setting. The software architecture consists of three main layers: planning and dispatching, mid-level execution, and low-level control. Key features include temporal planning for optimization, Behavior Trees for fine-grained control, and robust recovery strategies. Testing methods encompass real field testing and simulations.

1 Introduction

Due to the surge in e-commerce and the increasing demand for highly customizable products with swift delivery, there is a pressing need for enhanced flexibility in production processes. This emerging trend, often referred to as flexible production or Industry 4.0, calls for a higher degree of automation to ensure competitive pricing, consistent product quality, and rapid availability. However, the growing demand for flexibility poses a significant challenge to traditional rigid automation systems, thereby raising novel research questions in fields such as Robotics, Internet of Things (IoT), multi-agent systems, planning, and scheduling.

To address these challenges and establish a platform for both research and educational purposes in the field of flexible production, the RoboCup Logistics League (RCLL) competition was instituted [12]. The RCLL provides a simulated environment that emulates a flexible production facility, serving as an attractive arena for the development and assessment of innovative production concepts.

The GRIPS team, comprising students and researchers from Graz University of Technology, has actively engaged in the RCLL since 2016. In recent years, significant advancements have been made in enhancing the software. These improvements encompass the deployment of new technologies as well as further refinement of existing ones, ultimately resulting in the team's victory in the 2023

© The Author(s), under exclusive license to Springer Nature Switzerland AG 2024
C. Buche et al. (Eds.): RoboCup 2023, LNAI 14140, pp. 362–373, 2024.
https://doi.org/10.1007/978-3-031-55015-7_30

RoboCup Logistics League. In this paper, the main components and techniques adopted by the team are presented, ranging from low level topic as navigation and manipulation to high level technologies like planning and scheduling.

2   Software Architecture

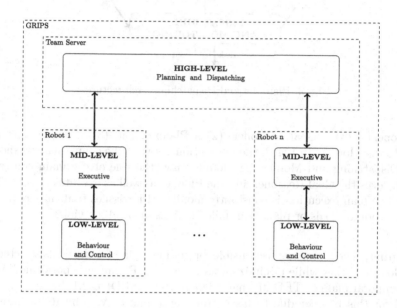

Fig. 1. GRIPS distributed software architecture.

In this section we present the main components of our software architecture, which present some changes w.r.t. to the one presented in [9]. The general architecture, depicted in Fig. 1, is based on three main layers, namely (1) planning and dispatching (high-level), (2) plan refinement and execution (mid-level), (3) behavior, control and further low-level functionality. In order to gain more flexibility and optimality a new high-level planning layer was introduced. The planning and dispatching top layer relies on temporal planning, in order to pursue long-term optimality. The difference between the high-level dispatching module and the mid-level executive module implemented on the robots are that, while the former has a wider view and dispatches intermediate actions of the derived general plan to the corresponding robots, the latter refine such actions into into behaviour trees [2]. Then, correspondingly to some of trees' node the ROS-based low-level is triggered for skill execution.

2.1   Planning and Dispatching

The Planning and Dispatching layers implements a centralized control strategy for multi-agent system in a dynamic domain. It is based on three main

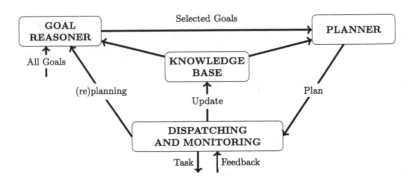

Fig. 2. Planning and Dispatching Architecture.

components: (1) a Goal Reasoner, (2) a Planner, and (3) a Dispatching and Monitoring Module. In Fig. 2, the interaction between the components is shown. The Dispatching and Monitoring module plays the role of the main controller that invokes the Goal Reasoner and the Planner as well as executes the obtained plan. The plan execution is constantly monitored for issues that may require a regeneration of goals or plans, e.g. failed actions or deadline violations.

Planning. The planner is responsible for finding a plan for the goals selected by the Goal Reasoner while minimizing its makespan. Planning is performed using the temporal planner TFD [6] that offers numerous PDDL 2.1 features [7]. We opted for this planner due to his overall performance over the RCLL domain [5]. We chose temporal planning for its ability to handle temporal deadlines and coordinate multiple agents. The downside is the high planning costs. In order to address this issue for the RCLL domain, we abstracted the domain model and introduced an online goal selection. The domain is modeled in PDDL by representing the two main interactions with a station as abstract action: *get* or *delivery* only. The former retrieves a workpiece from a station after processing, while the latter delivers the workpiece to a station for processing. In the RCLL robots can not carry more than one piece at a time, so every *get* o *delivery* action is interleaved with a *move* action. For this reason, both *get* and *delivered* already include costs and constraints related to the previous *move* action: a *get* action actually models a *move_and_get* macro-action. This significantly speed-up the planning process [4]. Figure 3 gives an insight of the process.

The result of planning is a temporal plan, which is represented by the schedule σ, formed by triples $\langle a, t_a, d_a \rangle$, where a is an action, t_a is the time when the action a needs to be started, and d_a is the duration of the action. Listing 1 shows a temporal plan to build and deliver a simple product in the RCLL. However, as a following improvement step, such plan based on macro-actions is refined into a new one, where every macro is unfolded into its original sub-actions. Then, the underlying Simple Temporal Network is rebuilt upon these sub-actions, improving the makespan in many cases [3]. An example is shown in

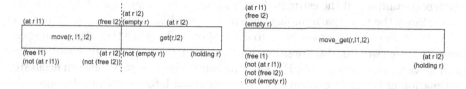

Fig. 3. Description of two actions and the resulting macro. Literals below each action represent effects, while the literals above them provide preconditions (at the start, end, or during an action, as indicated by their positions).

Listing 1 Macro Temporal plan for the simplest product. Parameters (except for the agent) have been omitted for better readability.

```
1   0.000:(move_getBaseFromBS  r1)[51.000]
2   0.000:(move_bufferCapBaseFromCS  r2)[89.000]
3   89.001:(move_getBaseFromCS  r2)[52.000]
4   141.002:(move_deliverProducttoCS  r1)[85.000]
5   226.003:(move_getProductFromCS  r1)[52.000]
6   278.004:(move_deliverProductToDS  r1)[73.000]
```

Listing 2, depicting the result of this refinement process applied over the macro plan of Listing 1. The makespan improved by 55 s.

This representation poorly supports action dispatching, since it is not easy to determine how delays in the execution of an action, affect the other triples of the plan. To address this, we represent the plan as a temporal graph (Simple Temporal Network), which encodes the temporal dependencies and the partial order of actions, without constraining the start of actions to specific time points. An accurate estimation of action durations is crucial for appropriate planning and monitoring plan execution. The interaction time of a robot with a station has been estimated empirically. Regarding the traveling time, we precompute a

Listing 2 Refined Temporal plan for the simplest product.

```
1    0.000:(move r1 bs_output) [21.000]
2    0.000:(move r2 cs_input) [44.000]
3    21.001:(getBaseFromBS r1)[30.000]
4    44.001:(bufferCapBaseFromCS r2)[45.000]
5    89.002:(move r2 cs_output) [22.000]
6    89.003:(move r1 cs_input) [55.000]
7    111.004:(getBaseFromCS r2)[30.000]
8    141.005:(deliverProducttoCS r1)[30.000]
9    171.006:(move r1 cs_output) [22.00]
10   193.007:(getProductFromCS r1)[30.000]
11   223.008:(move r1 ds) [43]
12   266.009:(deliverProductToDS r1)[30.000]
```

matrix containing all the estimated costs for traveling between each pair of locations. Since the same path finding algorithm is used as in the robot's navigation skill, the estimated times are close to the real ones. To make the estimation even more precise, we are also considering orientation costs at the start and at the end of each movement action. By adopting this procedure we achieve an accurate estimation of actions duration that is incorporated into the PDDL domain.

Goal Reasoner. As we are interested in dynamic domains, planning needs to be fast, to be able to react to changes and new opportunities in the environment in time. For this reason, the Goal Reasoner selects the most rewarding set of goals P the planner may be able to obtain a plan for with a given time (e.g., 1 min.). For RCLL a single goal is an individual order. In general, planning for all received orders is not possible within a reasonable time window. Thus, we follow the idea of partial satisfactory planning [13]. The Goal Reasoner solves a relaxed version of the domain, assuming that each goal can be achieved by a single agent individually, ignoring cooperation or resource management. Giving this setting, the goals selection is formulated as a simple task allocation problem with an overall deadline. We employ the ASP solver CLINGO [8] to compute this optimization task, which consists of finding a subset of goals such that the awarded points are maximized within the given constraints. A drawback of the goal selection heuristic is that the solution of the relaxed problem may be too optimistic. Thus, the planner may not able to find a plan achieving all selected goals while respecting the given deadlines. To mitigate this we exploit parallel planning over multiple sets of goals. The sets are the original set plus sets obtained by either dropping goals or replacing goals with less complex ones. Initially, 3 threads were deployed. In the actual setup, such number has been double, in order to be able to better cope with the stricter soft deadlines of the last editions of the RCLL. Every order is assigned a soft deadline, and failing to meet it incurs a point penalty. In recent editions, this penalty has significantly increased, underscoring the importance of adhering to these deadlines. Consequently, we have implemented the following strategy: for each set, a duplicate is generated in which each order is replaced with others of equivalent complexity but with extended soft deadlines, when available. For each of these 6 sets, a planning thread is ran for 1 min. The rational behind this approach is that in general it is more likely to find a feasible plan for simplified goal sets with a bounded time budget. Among the returned feasible plans, we select and dispatch the one with the highest reward per time value.

Plan Execution and Deadline Estimation. The Dispatching and Monitoring module dispatches the actions of the obtained plan in time, monitors proper execution (in terms of state and time), and initiates replanning if necessary. These three events may trigger replanning: (1) failed skill execution, (2) successful execution of the actual plan, (3) impossibility to achieve a goal in time.

We use a dedicated approach to check the temporal constraint of the temporal network representing the plan, in order to allow an earlier detection of deadline violations. Two types of edges are involved: (1) action duration edges $[d_a, d_a]$ between start and end of the action a, and (2) partial order edges $[0, +\infty)$ between the end of an action and the start of the following one. Nodes corresponding to start actions are dispatched by sending the action to the robot for execution, while end nodes are dispatched when a feedback for the successful execution of the corresponding action is received. The partial order encoded through the edges is ensured by the dispatching. Unfortunately, it can not be expected that the execution in the real world perfectly respects the temporal constraint $[d_a, d_a]$ (interval between min and max time). The approach presented in [1] propagates the detected delay by fixing the execution times of already executed actions and updating the remaining deadlines using constraint propagation. In our approach, violations of such edges are tolerated, since our early deadline detection strategy immediately recognizes if such delays will cause a deadline violation in the future. Thus, we use the opposite approach, propagating back the deadlines from the goal nodes to the rest of the network, labeling each node with a relative deadline $rdl(x)$. This represents the latest time point we can dispatch that node without violating the deadline x. Starting from the *goal* vertices, we calculate the relative deadlines rdl of each vertex by traversing the edges in the opposite direction, subtracting the lower bound of the edge at each step. If there are more paths from a normal vertex to a *goal* vertex, we keep the more restrictive relative deadline. Every time a node is dispatched, we check if all its relative deadlines are respected, otherwise we trigger replanning. In Fig. 4 a partial result of this approach applied to a temporal graph is shown.

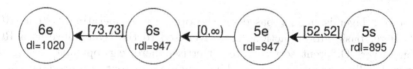

Fig. 4. The deadline propagation process on a part of a temporal network. 1020 is the final deadline for the entire network.

2.2   Mid-Level Executive

In order to ensure reliable execution of tasks, Behavior Trees [2] are deployed for action execution. Each dispatched action is divided into smaller, atomic low-level skills, such as moving the gripper or placing an object on a station. This allows for the decomposition of each action into executable skills. The execution of routines is represented as a tree structure composed of different types of nodes. Control nodes are used to alter the program flow, while execution nodes initiate actions. These nodes exchange data through blackboards implemented by the Behavior Tree library. ROS action clients are used to trigger action on the PLC, the robot platform or to gather sensing information. The high-level receives notifications about the execution outcomes. If a tree fails to execute, control is returned to the high-level, and the robot waits for the next action to be assigned. The key advantage of this approach is the user-friendly nature of behavior trees, while still enabling the encoding of complex behaviors.

One notable improvement over the previous system, described in [9], is the introduction of on-the-fly alignment for the robot's interaction with machines. In the previous system, the robot would first navigate towards the closest zone on the correct side of the machine, followed by a separate alignment step with the conveyor. In contrast, the updated system enables the robots to initiate alignment immediately upon detecting the presence of a machine while moving towards the designated zone. For its implementation, a multiplexer-based mechanism is employed, which switches between the velocity provided by the navigation planner to the robot platform and a feedback controller utilized for precise alignments. A proportional controller was chosen as control algorithm. We can reach reference tracking and a low settling time due to the high gain of the controller and a velocity constraint. The velocity constraint is calculated based on the maximum acceptable error divergence $(2\,\mathrm{cm})$ and the acceleration of the move base $(3\,\mathrm{m/s^2})$. The error calculation for the controller determines the signal for selecting the multiplexer values. Once a threshold is reached, indicating that the robot can safely align with the machine, the multiplexer switches from the move base velocity to the alignment velocity. This on-the-fly alignment approach significantly reduces skill transition delays by minimizing network interactions and tree initializations.

2.3 Low-Level

The lowest layer is mainly based on the open robot operating system (ROS [11]). Here, basic atomic actions are advertised to the layer above as a ROS action server. Different services are advertised here, e.g. opening/closing the gripper, locally navigating to a machine, aligning in front of a machine and so on. Performing these actions, all the error detection and a possible error recovery is made by the ROS service. In the following part of this subsection we will briefly discuss the most important parts of the low-level functions.

Way-Point Navigation. In order to retrieve or deliver objects, the robot moves between defined way-points. These way-points are stored in the mid-level as abstract identifiers e.g. a defined zone of the playing field is stored as M_Z22. In order to move to a given way-point, the low-level uses a table to look up the real world coordinates for the abstract identifier and afterwards plan to move to this way-point. To move to the given coordinates, we use the move_base package of ROS. This package comprises a global planner that uses the map to find a path between the current robot position and the desired final position. In order to avoid the different production machines, these machines are added to the navigation map. Furthermore, after finding a global plan a local planner is used to move along the path by considering and avoiding detected objects on the planned path.

Conveyor Alignment. During the production phase the robot needs to deliver and retrieve products from the conveyor multiple times. This is done through a way-point that is in close proximity to the desired conveyor. Thus, a robot is able to move near the intended machine. After that, the QR-Code and the laser scanner is used to approach the machine and to align the robot close to the conveyor belt. However, as explained in the Mid-Level Executive Section, the alignment starts from the close way-point only if the machine has not been previously detected during the robot movement towards the way-point. Otherwise, the robots is able to align on-the-fly.

Fig. 5. Robot grasping a piece from a machine.

Gripper Control. Since quick and reliable manipulation is a key factor for an efficient production process, a new gripper system shown in Fig. 5 was developed. All processing related to the gripping procedure is now handled by a programmable logic controller (PLC), using Structure Text (ST) as programming language. It communicates with the Mid-Level of the Software Architecture (see Sect. 2.2) via Open Platform Communications Unified Architecture (OPC UA). Moreover, it exposes an interface to the gripper ROS-node for accepting commands and sending sensor measurements. A command for the gripper can be fine-grained like opening or closing the gripper for grabbing a product, but the interface also allows for more complex commands. A more complex command sequence is for example grabbing a product from the shelf and directly delivering it to the input of the Cap Station. The gripper is mounted on a 3-axis positioning system that is equipped with two distance sensors, one facing to the front and one to the bottom. When picking up a product the front sensor scans a profile in the approximate area, from which the actual position of the product can then be estimated. The initial scanning area can be tuned to the accuracy of the alignment between robot and the machine and if no plausible object is found the scanning is repeated at a wider angle. The placing of the product is done in a similar fashion but using the sensor facing down.

Most problems related to grasping arise due to the robots not being identical to each other and relatively flexible in their geometry. A slight tilt or a height difference in the robot structure can have an effect on the grasping precision, where the tolerance is in the mm range. For this purpose, the robots are checked and some calibrations are set before each competition.

3   Testing Pipeline and Environments

The GRIPS team comprises individuals of varying expertise, including students and researchers, with diverse proficiencies across different subject areas. As described in the preceding section, the comprehensive software stack is extensive, encompassing a multitude of distinct frameworks and programming languages distributed across three layers of abstraction. The practical execution of this system occurs within both the robots themselves and a central server, necessitating a reliable communication infrastructure. Given the multitude of components involved, in conjunction with the considerable scale of the stack, occurrences of bugs and errors of varying types manifest with notable frequency. In order to effectively address these issues, the team has adopted the ensuing strategic approach:

- periodic code revision and refactoring from software engineers;
- intensive testing on both real field and simulations;
- robust recovering strategy;
- testing pipeline executed on the actual competition field before official games;

Testing Pipeline on the Field. In our team's experience during RoboCup competitions, we often encountered challenges during actual games on the field that were impossible to replicate in our controlled laboratory environment. These challenges typically stemmed from environmental factors specific to the competition field, such as room lighting, the type of flooring, and the assembly variations of the stations, including minor differences in conveyor height and cable management. Our testing process begins with the creation of a map, which involves allowing the robot to navigate the field. This step helps us identify issues related to both navigation and sensing capabilities. The second phase involves each robot performing grasping and delivery tasks at all 14 stations, on both sides of each station. While this process is time-consuming, as it entails a total of $3 \times 14 \times 2$ tasks, it has consistently enabled the team to detect problems related to the gripper or alignment with the station. Finally, we conduct a demo game to ensure that all components function correctly and that communication between them operates smoothly.

Light-Weighted Event-Based Simulations. Testing all the software components together poses several challenges, often making it impractical. This comprehensive testing approach requires the entire field and the presence of multiple individuals to maneuver the robots, making it time-consuming and frequently unnecessary. Typically, when modifications are made to specific parts of the software, such as the planning component, it suffices to test that particular portion in isolation before proceeding to integration testing with the rest of the software stack. To address these testing needs, two simulations have been developed. The first simulation, based on Gazebo [14], incorporates physics and can evaluate a substantial portion, if not the entirety, of the software stack. This simulation permits teams to run a game when physical robots and fields are unavailable, significantly reducing the time required for field setup. However, it does have its limitations; task execution times are tethered to real-world counterparts, and it demands significant computational resources. In response to these limitations, we have crafted a Lightweight Event-Based simulation [10]. Figure 6 depicts the architecture. This simulation is tailored to assess the top layer of the software stack, focusing on planning and execution. Additionally, it facilitates the customization of task durations, enabling the simulation of an entire game in just a few minutes. Thanks to this tool, numerous bugs related to planning, execution, and high-level failure handling have been identified and fixed.

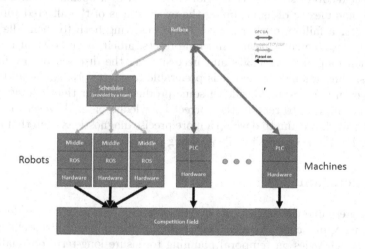

Fig. 6. Overview of the Light-Weighted simulation system. All components of the simulation are shown in grey, in orange the refbox provided by the league and in blue the scheduler of a team. (Color figure online)

Testing on the Real Field. While it is crucial to possess the tools for separate component testing, it becomes equally imperative to evaluate their integration. Until early 2023, the Laboratory for Autonomous Agents at Graz University of

Technology, the home base of the GRIPS team, primarily employed robots and stations for testing individual tasks. This practice was necessitated by spatial constraints that prevented the execution of full games. However, a significant change occurred with the rearrangement of laboratory furnishings, providing the team with the capacity to conduct games on a near full-field scale. The ability to replicate complete games without resorting to simulation has enabled the team to unearth a substantial number of previously hidden bugs spanning across all components.

Recovering Strategy. Based on the extensive experience gained over many years in RoboCup, it becomes evident that robustness is the pivotal attribute required to secure victory in the RCLL. The critical aspect involves maintaining continuous robot operation and preventing situations of deadlock. It is not uncommon to encounter scenarios where an undetected, erroneously diagnosed, or mismanaged error obstructs a robot from further functionality. For instance, in our framework, we employ long-term planning, necessitating a consistent knowledge base to recover from failures through replanning. When a failure has not been accurately diagnosed, resulting in a plan based on a false representation of the world, most actions within the new plan are bound to fail, perpetuating a loop of failures and wrong recoveries. To ensure a cautious approach, we adopt a stringent recovery strategy that prioritizes safety over optimization. Given the potential complexity of ascertaining the exact status of the affected robot and station after a failure, our strategy involves resetting both to their idle states. Indeed, the league rules permit machine resets, albeit at the cost of rendering the station inoperative for 30 s and necessitating the disposal of any involved products. Our rationale is that it is preferable to effectively handle all types of failures, even if it entails sacrificing some products, rather than risking a deadlock by attempting to rebuild the correct knowledge base. However, as part of our future work, we aim to develop a more precise diagnostic system that ensures a similar level of robustness while avoiding product wastage.

4   Conclusion

We have presented the key aspects of our software, together with our developing and testing approaches. We have discussed our planning and dispatching architecture, which relies on temporal planning to ensure long-term optimality and goal selection heuristics to adapt to dynamic environments. We have also highlighted the use of Behavior Trees in our mid-level executive layer, which allows for fine-grained control of robot actions and on-the-fly alignment with production machines. Additionally, we have described our low-level control, including waypoint navigation, conveyor alignment, and gripper control. Our testing pipeline includes a combination of real field testing, lightweight event-based simulations and physics-based simulations. These testing approaches allow us to identify and address issues at different levels of the software stack, from individual components to integrated systems. Our commitment to robustness and recovery strategies ensures that our robots can handle unforeseen challenges and continue operating effectively during competitions.

In conclusion, the GRIPS team's participation in the RCLL and the continuous development of our software architecture demonstrate our dedication to advancing the field of flexible production. As we look to the future, we will continue to refine our software, enhance our diagnostic capabilities, and strive for excellence in the world of autonomous production systems.

References

1. Castillo, L., Fdez-Olivares, J., González-Muñoz, A.: A temporal constraint network based temporal planner (2002)
2. Colledanchise, M., Ögren, P.: Behavior Trees in Robotics and AI: An Introduction. CRC Press, Boca Raton (2018)
3. De Bortoli, M., Chrpa, L., Gebser, M., Steinbauer-Wagner, G.: Improving applicability of planning in the robocup logistics league using macro-actions refinement. In: RoboCup 2023. Springer, Cham (2023)
4. De Bortoli, M., Chrpa, L., Gebser, M., Steinbauer-Wagner, G.: Enhancing temporal planning by sequential macro-actions. In: Logics in Artificial Intelligence, pp. 595–604. Springer, Cham (2023). https://doi.org/10.1007/978-3-031-43619-2_40
5. De Bortoli, M., Steinbauer-Wagner, G.: Evaluating action-based temporal planners performance in the robocup logistics league. In: RoboCup 2022, pp. 87–99 (2023)
6. Eyerich, P., Mattmüller, R., Röger, G.: Using the context-enhanced additive heuristic for temporal and numeric planning (2012)
7. Fox, M., Long, D.: PDDL2.1: an extension to PDDL for expressing temporal planning domains. J. Artif. Intell. Res. **20**, 61–124 (2003)
8. Gebser, M., Kaminski, R., Kaufmann, B., Schaub, T.: Clingo= asp+ control. arXiv preprint arXiv:1405.3694 (2014)
9. Kohout, P., De Bortoli, M., Ludwiger, J., Ulz, T., Steinbauer, G.: A multi-robot architecture for the RoboCup Logistics League. e & i Elektrotechnik und Informationstechnik **137**, 291–296 (2020)
10. Lampel, D.: An Agent-Based Simulation for the RoboCup Logistics League. Master's thesis, Faculty of Computer Science and Biomedical Engineering, Graz University of Technology (2023)
11. Quigley, M., et al.: Ros: an open-source robot operating system, vol. 3 (2009)
12. Steinbauer, G., Niemueller, T., Karras, U.: The RoboCup logistics league - a testbed for novel concepts in flexible production. In: Robotic Assembly - Recent Advancements and Opportunities for Challenging R&D: Workshop IEEE International Conference on Automation Science and Engineering (2018)
13. Van Den Briel, M., Sanchez, R., Do, M., Kambhampati, S.: Effective approaches for partial satisfaction (over-subscription) planning. In: Proceedings of the National Conference on Artificial Intelligence (AAAI), pp. 562–569 (2004)
14. Zwilling, F., Niemueller, T., Lakemeyer, G.: Simulation for the RoboCup logistics league with real-world environment agency and multi-level abstraction. In: Bianchi, R.A.C., Akin, H.L., Ramamoorthy, S., Sugiura, K. (eds.) RoboCup 2014. LNCS (LNAI), vol. 8992, pp. 220–232. Springer, Cham (2015). https://doi.org/10.1007/978-3-319-18615-3_18

RoboCup@Home SSPL Champion 2023: RoboBreizh, a Fully Embedded Approach

Cédric Buche[1,4(✉)], Maëlic Neau[1,2,3,4], Thomas Ung[1], Louis Li[1], Sinuo Wang[1], and Cédric Le Bono[2]

[1] CROSSING, CNRS IRL 2010, Adelaide, Australia
buche@enib.fr
[2] Lab-STICC, CNRS UMR 6285, Brest, France
[3] College of Science and Engineering, Flinders University of South Australia, Adelaide, Australia
[4] ENIB, Plouzané, France

Abstract. This paper presents the approach employed by the team RoboBreizh to win the championship in the 2023 RoboCup@Home Social Standard Platform League (SSPL). RoboBreizh decided to limit itself to an entirely embedded system with no connection to the internet and external devices. This article describes the design of embedded solutions including the global architecture, perception, navigation, interaction, reasoning and digital twin.

1 Introduction

RoboBreizh's team made the decision to focus only on embedded systems, depriving Pepper of internet connectivity and the myriad of AI options available online, particularly from well-known tech companies. The fully embedded strategy was implemented for a number of reasons, not just the restricted conditions in the arena. In fact, it was also influenced by the practical uses of these robots, which are frequently created for elderly or dependent individuals who may not have an adequate internet connection. Additionally, there are significant energy and environmental costs associated with the ongoing transmission of data for online analysis. Finally, since images and sounds are processed locally in the robot rather than being transferred to the cloud, a complete embedded system provides the primary advantage of data privacy.

This document describes the software used, the suggested architecture, and the connections between the modules in order to fulfill the competition's requirements. Reader will find the description of the overall functional architecture in [3], including connection between subsystems. The structure of the article is as follows. First, Sect. 2 goes into detail about how to use Pepper by employing embedded software architecture instead of the traditional NaoQi API. The embedded perception module is covered in the next Sect. 3. The Sect. 4 presents the embedded navigation module. In Sect. 5, the embedded dialogue module is explained. Section 6 details knowledge representation and reasoning mechanisms. Last, in Sect. 7, new simulation tools are presented as digital twin.

C. Buche et al. (Eds.): RoboCup 2023, LNAI 14140, pp. 374–385, 2024.
https://doi.org/10.1007/978-3-031-55015-7_31

2 Architecture

When working with the Pepper robot, the main limitation is the integrated Operating System (OS), NaoQi2.5.5, based on a 32bits version of Linux Gentoo that restricts and limits the number of libraries that can be installed (for instance no ROS version is officially supported on Gentoo). The second limitation is the root access to the OS that is not available on the robot. To overcome those two limitations, we created a continuous integration pipeline based on the work from [11]. Even if Gentoo is an old system, it offers some interesting solutions such as the *Gentoo Prefix Project* [2]. A prefix is an offset version of Gentoo that can be installed alongside another OS (preferably another Gentoo) without root permission. To make it work, we used a Docker Image of a 32bits gentoo prefix[1] and then built on top of it our full architecture. At runtime, the required components of the prefix are extracted from the Docker Image and pushed directly to the robot, alongside the NaoQi OS. This solution resolved the root access problem but the limitations of the 32bit OS are still here. As a workaround, we decided to cross-compile ROS and other libraries in Docker using a dump of the Pepper OS[2] and our Gentoo prefix. First, to cross-compile ROS Noetic we used the ros-overlay project[3]. As we decided to use exclusively Python3, the native Python API from Pepper was not available anymore. Thus, we built on top of the LibQi API a version that can run onboard and allow us to still have access to the resources of the robot[4]. Latest Machine Learning Python tools such as Tensorflow Lite [1], ONNX[5], OpenCV[6] or Kaldi[7] have also been cross-compiled for Pepper.

3 Perception

Embedded Computer Vision: Embedded perception in robotics is always a trade-off between speed and accuracy, as models with higher accuracy tend to be more resource-intensive. On a constraint platform such as the Pepper robot and with a real-time goal in hand, we had to find the best solution for inference with the hardware specification (32-bit OS and 4-core Intel ATOM CPU). We leveraged different inference methods for the different capabilities needed in the competition. For efficiency, we retrieve images from the Pepper top camera in 640 × 480 px resolution and run all models either directly on this input size (dynamic size input) or by reshaping them to 640 × 640 or 320 × 320. For face detection, we used a pre-trained lightweight YuNet model [16] that achieves very low latency onboard (300 ms). This model runs with the OpenCV4.7 DNN

---

[1] https://github.com/awesomebytes/gentoo_prefix_ci_32b.
[2] https://hub.docker.com/r/awesomebytes/pepper_2.5.5.5.
[3] https://github.com/ros/ros-overlay.
[4] https://github.com/Maelic/libqi-python.
[5] https://github.com/onnx/onnx.
[6] https://github.com/itseez/opencv.
[7] https://github.com/kaldi-asr/kaldi.

backend and ONNX file format. For age and gender detection, we used a pre-trained MobileNetV1 model with 4 Million parameters[8] that perform well while being very fast to run on Pepper's CPU (900 ms). For this part, we leveraged the Tensorflow Lite library to run both age and gender classification on the cropped face image detected by our YuNet backbone.

Pose Estimation: For pose detection, we used two different pre-trained models for different scenarios. For multiple pose detection (for instance in the Receptionist scenario), we used the MoveNet MultiPose by the Tensorflow team[9] in float16 precision with the Tensorflow Lite inference engine. For single-pose detection, we used the MoveNet SinglePose Lightning model[10] in float16 precision with the Tensorflow Lite inference engine. MoveNet is a MobileNetV2-based architecture that reports to outperform other real-time models such as OpenPose or PoseNet [6]. MoveNet Lightning (single pose) runs with a latency of 200 ms onboard whereas MoveNet Multipose with 1500 ms.

Object Detection: Finally, for object detection, we fine-tuned different YOLOV8 models[11] depending on the use case. For the Receptionist task, we extracted the `person`, `chair`, and `couch` classes from the COCO dataset and retrained the nano model (YOLOV8n). Regarding other tasks, we decided to implement a custom few-shot learning strategy as objects are not known in advance. This strategy was as follows:

1. During setup days, we took 300 pictures of the objects in context
2. Images were then annotated using Roboflow[12] (4 people during 4–5 h)
3. Data augmentation was performed to enlarge the dataset and make the model more robust to lighting conditions (4 augmentation has been performed: shear, saturation, brightness, and exposure) for a total of 900 images
4. The dataset is then split between train (80%) and validation (20%) sets (no test set as we want to use the maximum of images for learning)
5. Hyper-parameter tuning is then done using the Ray Tune library, this helps the model to converge faster and slightly improve accuracy
6. Finally, we fine-tuned YOLOV8 (pre-trained on COCO) using the official Ultralytics implementation[13].

We display the results of this strategy in Fig. 1. We can see that the hyperparameter tuning makes the loss very stable. The model already converges after 200 epochs (around 5 min of fine-tuning) which is impressive for quick, on-the-spot

[8] https://github.com/radualexandrub/Age-Gender-Classification-on-RaspberryPi4-with-TFLite-PyQt5.
[9] https://tfhub.dev/google/lite-model/movenet/multipose/lightning/tflite/float16/1.
[10] https://tfhub.dev/google/lite-model/movenet/singlepose/lightning/tflite/float16/4.
[11] https://github.com/ultralytics/ultralytics.
[12] https://roboflow.com/.
[13] https://github.com/ultralytics/ultralytics.

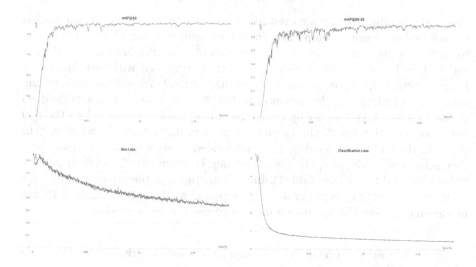

Fig. 1. Mean Average Precision and training Loss for Object Detection. The model is YOLOV8n with 320×320 image size as input fine-tuned for 2,000 epochs (around 1h) on one RTX3080 GPU with 16 GB VRAM.

adjustments in the context of the competition. The final model obtains 91.32% in mAP@50 and 68.76% in mAP@50–95 on the validation set. As the validation set is minimal, the high metrics mostly show some overfitting but this is an expected behavior as the background as well as object size and shape are most likely to not change between the setup days and competition days. As YOLOV8 is a very new architecture (only a few months old at the time of the competition this year), no clear advantage for any inference engine has been demonstrated by the community. We thus decided to run our own evaluation using three different popular frameworks onboard the Pepper robot: ONNXRuntime[14], OpenCV[15], and Tensorflow Lite (TFLite)[16]. We experimented with different model sizes (nano and small[17]) as well as different input sizes (640 px or 320 px) to find the best trade-off between speed and accuracy. Results are displayed in Table 1 where we can see that the YOLOV8n 320 px version with OpenCV inference engine possesses the lowest latency (323 ms). Higher values for ONNX engine can be explained by an old version of the library (1.4), the only one available for a 32-bit OS. The difference between latency on Pepper CPU and the computer CPU is significant, with an average of 50.44 times slower on Pepper, showing the clear limit of the platform for embedded real-time computer vision. In addition to the model size and inference engine, we experimented with model quantiza-

---

[14] https://github.com/microsoft/onnxruntime/releases/tag/v1.4.0.

[15] https://github.com/opencv/opencv/tree/4.7.0.

[16] https://www.tensorflow.org/lite.

[17] The Small version of YOLOV8 (YOLOV8s) has 11.2 million parameters and YOLOV8n 3.2 million.

tion with the aim of reducing even more the latency. We quantized all models to int8 and we show a comparison in Table 2. However, we observed very low to no improvement with the int8 quantization of YOLOV8 onboard the Pepper robot. The TfLite inference engine is especially very bad with int8 models as it is on average 1.82 slower than with traditional fp32. We did not observe any accuracy drops by using the int8 models. However, we observed an average drop of 1.3 to 1.9% mAP@50–95 by using the 320 px models compared to the 640 ones. On the other hand, the latency drops from 0.91 s to 6.11 s when switching from the 640 to 320 models, thus we decided to stick to the 320 resolution. Regarding the model size, the lowest latency is 323 ms for YOLOV8n against 980 ms for YOLOV8s (see Table 1). In our experiments, the accuracy difference with few-shot settings is under 3% after a period of 100 epochs (around 10 min in fine-tuning), see Fig. 2, thus we decided to use the Nano version.

Table 1. Comparison of YOLOV8 inference latency onboard the Pepper robot and with classical CPUs, in second.

Model	Res.	Engine	Latency$_{Pepper}$[a]	Latency$_{CPU}$[b]	Mult.
Small	640	ONNX	6.674819	0.077126	86.54
		OpenCV	3.767041	0.075650	49.79
		TFlite	3.909041	0.256922	15.21
	320	ONNX	1.603461	0.020387	78.64
		OpenCV	1.013117	0.023091	43.87
		TFlite	0.980744	0.067226	14.59
Nano	640	ONNX	3,022189	0.027367	110.43
		OpenCV	1.581089	0.036503	43.31
		TFlite	1.903541	0.086502	22.01
	320	ONNX	0.783669	**0.008307**	94.34
		OpenCV	**0.323400**	0.010952	29.52
		TFlite	0.389299	0.022777	17.09

[a] Intel Atom™ E3845 @ 1.91 GHz × 4
[b] 11th Gen Intel Core™ i7-11800H @ 2.30 GHz × 16

Table 2. Comparison of the latency of the quantized models onboard, with resolution 640. The difference is a comparison with values obtained in Table 1

Model	Size	Engine	Latency$_{Pepper}$	Diff.
Small int8	11.3 mb	ONNX	6.667678	−0.007141
		OpenCV	4.247251	+0.480210
		TfLite	8.127156	+4.218115
Nano int8	3.1 mb	ONNX	3.020009	−0.002180
		OpenCV	1.237249	−0.343840
		TfLite	2.968650	+1.065109

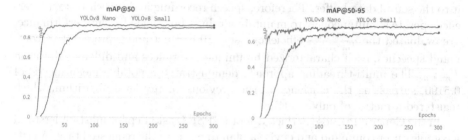

Fig. 2. Comparison of the fine-tuning of YOLOv8 Small and Nano in few-shot settings. The final difference after 300 epochs is 2.52% in mAP@50.

4 Navigation

The ROS navigation stack with AMCL[18] for localisation, the Dijkstra algorithm as a global planner over the global costmap, and the Dynamic Window Approach (DWA)[19] as a local planner over the local costmap, are used by the navigation module. To retrieve data from depth cameras and lidars, we use an updated version of the naoqi_driver ROS package. Since the data from Pepper's lidar is insufficient for accurately computing costmaps, the depth camera's PointClouds are added as inputs. This enables Pepper to detect more fine-grained obstacles such as tables or chairs. In order to reduce the computational cost for pointcloud data processing, obstacles are represented using voxels. In addition, RoboBreizh uses Spatio-Temporal Voxel Layer [9] as a 2D local costmap plugin that continuously adds a new dynamic obstacle layer to the costmap. With the contribution of the voxel layer and DWA, our Pepper robot is able to safely navigate in a known environment and avoid dynamics obstacles.

---

18 http://wiki.ros.org/amcl.

19 http://wiki.ros.org/dwa_local_planner?distro=noetic.

5 Interaction

The embedded dialogue module enables Pepper to recognize spoken language and examine its semantic content. The native API of Robot offers a grammar parsing library and a tool for recording sound. However, the versatility and maintainability of these technologies are constrained. RoboBreizh customizes an embedded dialogue system as a result. The initial step in the process is sound processing, which entails listening to the sound and identifying and recording human voices. Regarding Automatic Speech Recognition (ASR) we use the lightest Vosk[20] model ("vosk-model-small-en-us-0.15") with the Kaldi recognizer[21] for noise suppression. To prevent the cases of sound recording early stopping or late recording, we created a thread to record the sound all the time and append it to the sound data buffer. Therefore, speech recording and speech-to-text inference operate simultaneously to maintain a robust but time-efficient performance. We evaluated the $\frac{T_{speech}}{T_{inference}}$ efficiency using 10 distinct and representative command speeches, each characterized by unique utterances and different duration T_{speech}. The multi-threading approach demonstrated a notable mean metric of 0.5190, surpassing the efficiency of the previous energy level algorithm, which registered a metric of only 0.3047.

In the General Purpose Service Robot (GPSR) task, Pepper must understand a complex user command and devise a plan to perform the requested task. A critical component of this process is Joint-Slot Filling, which facilitates downstream modules by providing structured and unequivocal information, thus allowing for the formulation and execution of a precise action plan. The inherent challenge in Natural Language Understanding (NLU) for GPSR is twofold: (1) classifying multiple intents encapsulated within a single sentence, and (2) resolving the antecedents of ambiguous pronouns, a problem akin to the Winograd Schema Challenge [7]. For instance, given the following utterance:

Go to the kitchen, leave a bowl on the storage table and a spoon in it.   (1)

A proficient NLU system is anticipated to identify the intents such as go and put, and the task-related arguments (or slots) such as destination: kitchen and destination: storage table, object: bowl, spoon. This example further showcases the nuanced complexities of GPSR command understanding. Particularly, 1) the demand to perceive a spoon in it as a distinct user intent, even in the absence of a verb within this span of sub-task. 2) The interpretation of the correct antecedent for the pronoun it, wherein the correct association pertains to the bowl, contrarily to a potentially misleading association with the storage table. In response to the aforementioned challenges, we proposed RoboNLU [15], a novel approach to NLU tailored for service robots. This approach harnesses the capabilities of a pre-trained language model and couples them with task-specific classifiers to interpret user commands effectively. At its core, the model incorporates the Bidirectional Encoder Representations from Transformers (BERT) [4]

---

[20] https://github.com/alphacep/vosk.
[21] https://github.com/kaldi-asr/kaldi.

model as the base encoder and is combined with 3 Multilayer Perceptron (MLP) heads dedicated to slot filling, intent span recognition, and pronoun resolution. We trained the model on our newly created, large-scale, and high-quality GPSR command dataset, yielding impressive results in all the intent classification, slot filling, and pronoun resolution tasks. Additionally, to facilitate real-time processing on the Pepper robot, we employed smaller, quantized versions of the BERT base model and integrated the system through the ONNXruntime[22] framework. We experimented with various BERT variants, assessing their sentence accuracy and mean inference time across 50 randomly selected commands from the unseen test set. As shown in Table 3, our findings indicate that RoboNLU, when powered by DistilBERT [12] as its foundational encoder, stands out as the most efficient, clocking an average inference time of 0.65 s while upholding a 100% GPSR command understanding accuracy rate.

Table 3. Inference time comparison between the different BERT models. Sentence accuracy has been computed on the full test set of our dataset.

Model	Model Size (mb)	Latency (ms)			Sen. Acc. (%)
		GPU[a]	CPU[b]	Pepper CPU[c]	
BERT [4]	440	2.63	71.98	–	100
–quant. fp16	275	6.75	176.37	5525.21	100
–quant. int8	105	21.98	47.73	3185.37	98.3
DistillBERT [12]	264	**1.66**	34.71	**654.57**	100
–quant. fp16	153	10.84	96.55	2774.27	100
–quant. int8	64	11.87	33.91	1768.53	100
MobileBERT [14]	101	8.23	35.88	1032.95	100
–quant. fp16	49	16.44	56.29	4569.35	100
–quant. int8	**25**	28.01	**33.63**	1767.89	98.3

[a] Nvidia GeForce RTX3080 8 GB
[b] 11th Gen Intel Core^{TM}i7-11800H @ 2.30 GHz × 16
[c] Intel Atom^{TM}E3845 @ 1.91 GHz × 4

6   Reasoning

6.1   Manager

The manager is viewed as the one that makes decisions about what actions to take and when to activate the necessary elements to accomplish the desired goal. For instance, the manager's actions can include finding a specific area, interacting with people, and spotting and controlling things in the immediate surroundings. Using a Petri Net approach, the manager is put into action. It is a directed network of nodes and connections that supports flexible finite-state machines and parallel processing. Pros and cons of Petri nets approach in the context of

---

[22] https://onnxruntime.ai/.

RoboCup@Home have been already discussed [3]. A plan was established for each activity to outline the many steps of action that would be encountered as well as the sub-plans that would be triggered under specific circumstances. The use of sub-plans enables a clear and modular strategy. To execute our Petri Net with ROS, we use a package named Petri Net Plans [17], which allows linking a set of places and transitions to the reference of C++ functions. Each function could then act as an independent process firing one or multiple ROS nodes and returning a state to the Petri Net to change state. Important data about the environment are stored in an onboard SQLite file.

6.2   Knowledge Representation

In RoboCup, the Knowledge Representation and Reasoning framework often solely relies on visual low-level inputs. Instead of representing objects and persons as static disjoint entities in a scene, we are interested in representing the abundant dynamic of the context in the form of $< subject, predicate, object >$ semantic relationships. This representation encompasses four different types of relations that we can infuse with external commonsense knowledge of object affordances and temporal dependencies of events. This is done by extracting a Scene Graph using Scene Graph Generation models [10] and then matching it with external knowledge from ConceptNet [13] and ATOMIC [5] databases. The outcome of this process will create an extended graph representing the objects and relations between them in the scene as well as their relations with prior knowledge [10]. This data could be used to infer the latent context of the scene in different downstream tasks such as activity recognition. An example of this knowledge representation is shown in Fig. 3.

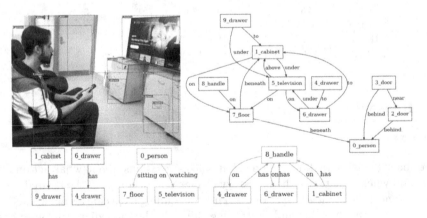

Fig. 3. Detected relationships grounded to object regions: colors indicate the functional, part-whole, topological and attributive layers, respectively. (Color figure online)

7   Digital Twin

Our team has successfully developed a robust digital twins framework with the primary goal of creating secure testing environments tailored for Pepper robots within the highly competitive context of the RoboCup@Home competition. Our innovative framework seamlessly integrates cutting-edge virtual reality (VR) technology, empowering intricate human-robot interactions within the simulation [8]. Leveraging the Unity Engine[23], we have crafted simulations that offer a remarkable level of fidelity and interactivity, harnessing the support of a vibrant community dedicated to both robotics and VR functionalities.

At the heart of our framework lies a real-time bidirectional communication system, powered by ZMQ Websockets[24], ensuring instant and seamless communication between Unity and the robot. This communication pipeline, in conjunction with the Qi API[25], facilitates immediate feedback from both virtual and physical Pepper robots during testing, enabling precise control and monitoring of robot behavior within the digital twin environment. To simplify and streamline the communication process between the ZMQ websocket and the Qi API, we have developed a Python wrapper that encapsulates all functions running using these interfaces. This wrapper reduces the complexity of the implementation, making it easier to develop, test, and maintain the system, while enhancing overall robustness.

Additionally, our framework enables users to interact with the robot through hand controllers, effectively allowing them to grasp virtual objects and pass them to the virtual robot. This remarkable feature enhances the immersive experience, enabling users to simulate real-world interactions with Pepper in both virtual and physical environments. This interactive capability proves particularly invaluable for testing and refining competition-specific challenges, such as the GPSR task and the serve breakfast task, within the RoboCup@Home competition.

Furthermore, our adaptable robotic middleware possesses versatility, making it well-suited for diverse simulation scenarios, with potential future integration into alternative 3D game engines such as Unreal Engine (see Fig. 4). The compelling demonstration of our framework at the RoboCup@Home final showcased its capabilities, featuring simulations of robot joint movements and navigation within a virtual replication of the competition arena, initially created using Blender and then seamlessly imported into Unity. This represents a substantial leap forward in the domain of human-robot interaction and robotics simulation, with the added dimension of tangible interaction through hand controllers.

---

[23] https://unity.com/.
[24] https://zeromq.org/.
[25] http://doc.aldebaran.com/2-4/dev/libqi/index.html.

Fig. 4. Digital twin in Unreal

8   Conclusion and Future Work

In this paper, we offered an overview of the architecture developed by the team RoboBreizh to perform at the SSPL RoboCup@Home contest. This wasn't the full extent of our research. Some approaches were considered before the competition but were scrapped due to time-constraints. Some of our work was judged too experimental to be properly implemented before the competition.

Our future activities will first examine work in computer vision, and in particular object detection, is an ever-evolving field. YOLOv8 Nano was used in the competition as it offered a solid trade-of between accuracy and speed on our robot with limited resources. YOLO-NAS (Neural Architecture Approach) was also tested and would have an alternative solution. In some minor experimentation done before the competition, the smallest YOLO-NAS modal was more confident and able to detect more objects (higher recall) than yolov8n while maintaining similar computation times. However, YOLO-NAS was released only one month prior the event and would have required too much work and time to be thoroughly tested and implemented on all our models before the competition.

Our future works will also examine the architecture. ROS Noetic was used in the competition and cross-compiling it on gentoo was a tricky task. After the competition, we were able to build ROS2 Humble on our 32bits gentoo environment from source and test in on Pepper. ROS2 has several advantages over ROS1 that could prove useful in future competitions. First, the communication protocol between nodes is based on DDS (Distributed Data Service) instead of the TCP/UDP protocol used by ROS1. As a consequence, ROS2 works better in environments where the network is saturated or lossy. This is especially important at the RoboCup as a single network error can, at worst, cause an entire task to fail. Secondly, whereas ROS1 only supports cpp and python, the ROS2 api supports more language such c or rust. This could prove vital in future to be more resource efficient and lessen the burden on the CPU.

Acknowledgments. This article benefited from the support of CERVVAL and Brittany Region.

References

1. Abadi, M., et al.: TensorFlow: a system for Large-Scale machine learning. In: 12th USENIX Symposium on Operating Systems Design and Implementation (OSDI 2016), pp. 265–283 (2016)
2. Amadio, G., Xu, B.: Portage: bringing hackers' wisdom to science. arXiv preprint arXiv:1610.02742 (2016)
3. Buche, C.: RoboBreizh, RoboCup@Home SSPL Champion 2022. Springer, Heidelberg (2023)
4. Devlin, J., Chang, M.W., Lee, K., Toutanova, K.: Bert: pre-training of deep bidirectional transformers for language understanding. arXiv preprint arXiv:1810.04805 (2018)
5. Hwang, J.D., et al.: (comet-) atomic 2020: On symbolic and neural commonsense knowledge graphs. In: Proceedings of the AAAI Conference on Artificial Intelligence, vol. 35, pp. 6384–6392 (2021)
6. Jo, B., Kim, S.: Comparative Analysis of OpenPose, PoseNet, and MoveNet models for pose estimation in mobile devices. Traitement du Signal **39**(1), 119–124 (2022)
7. Levesque, H., Davis, E., Morgenstern, L.: The winograd schema challenge. In: Thirteenth International Conference on the Principles of Knowledge Representation and Reasoning (2012)
8. Li, L., Neau, M., Ung, T., Buche, C.: Crossing real and virtual: pepper robot as an interactive digital twin. In: Proceedings of RoboCup Symposium (2023)
9. Macenski, S., Tsai, D., Feinberg, M.: Spatio-temporal voxel layer: a view on robot perception for the dynamic world. Int. J. Adv. Rob. Syst. **17**(2) (2020)
10. Neau, M., Santos, P., Bossser, A., Buche, C.: In defense of scene graph generation for human-robot open-ended interaction in service robotics. In: Proceedings of RoboCup Symposium (2023)
11. Pfeiffer, S., et al.: UTS unleashed! RoboCup@Home SSPL champions 2019. In: Chalup, S., Niemueller, T., Suthakorn, J., Williams, M.-A. (eds.) RoboCup 2019. LNCS (LNAI), vol. 11531, pp. 603–615. Springer, Cham (2019). https://doi.org/10.1007/978-3-030-35699-6_49
12. Sanh, V., Debut, L., Chaumond, J., Wolf, T.: Distilbert, a distilled version of bert: smaller, faster, cheaper and lighter. arXiv preprint arXiv:1910.01108 (2019)
13. Speer, R., Chin, J., Havasi, C.: Conceptnet 5.5: An open multilingual graph of general knowledge. In: Thirty-First AAAI Conference on Artificial Intelligence (2017)
14. Sun, Z., Yu, H., Song, X., Liu, R., Yang, Y., Zhou, D.: Mobilebert: a compact task-agnostic bert for resource-limited devices. arXiv preprint arXiv:2004.02984 (2020)
15. Wang, S., Neau, M., Buche, C.: RoboNLU: advancing command understanding with a novel lightweight bert-based approach for service robotics. In: Proceedings of RoboCup Symposium (2023)
16. Wu, W., Peng, H., Yu, S.: YuNet: a tiny millisecond-level face detector. Mach. Intell. Res. (2023)
17. Ziparo, V.A., Iocchi, L., Nardi, D.: Petri net plans. In: Fourth International Workshop on Modelling of Objects, Components, and Agents, pp. 267–290 (2006)

HELIOS2023: RoboCup 2023 Soccer Simulation 2D Competition Champion

Hidehisa Akiyama[1]([📧])[iD], Tomoharu Nakashima[2][iD], Kyo Hatakeyama[2], Takumi Fujikawa[2], and Akei Hishiki[2]

[1] Okayama University of Science, Okayama, Japan
hidehisa.akiyama@ous.ac.jp
[2] Osaka Metropolitan University, Osaka, Japan
tomoharu.nakashima@omu.ac.jp

Abstract. The RoboCup Soccer Simulation 2D Competition is the oldest of the RoboCup competitions. The 2D soccer simulator enables two teams of simulated autonomous agents to play a game of soccer with realistic rules and sophisticated game play. This paper introduces the RoboCup 2023 Soccer Simulation 2D Competition champion team, HELIOS2023, a united team from Okayama University of Science and Osaka Metropolitan University. The overview of the team's recent efforts is also described. The first one is the enhancement of the visual debugger. The second is an approach about applying learning to rank to decision making.

Keywords: Multiagent systems · Visual Debugging · Evaluation function · Learning to Rank

1 Introduction

This paper introduces the RoboCup 2023 Soccer Simulation 2D Competition champion team, HELIOS2023, a united team from Okayama University of Science and Osaka Metropolitan University. This is the sixth time the team has won the championship, and the team has won consecutively since 2022. In 2023, we enhanced our viewer application to improve the quality of training data. We then incorporated some of the machine learning results using that functionality into our team.

The team released several software for developing a simulated soccer team using the RoboCup Soccer 2D simulator. A team base code and a visual debugger integrated with a formation editor are available as an open source software[1]. The details can be found in [2].

The organization of this paper is as follows. Section 2 introduces the league and the overview of this year's competition. Section 3 describes how our visual debugger has been enhanced to promote our machine learning approach. Section 4 describes our recent approach to obtaining evaluation functions for action selection and some of its results. We present our conclusions in Sect. 5.

---

[1] Available at: https://github.com/helios-base.

C. Buche et al. (Eds.): RoboCup 2023, LNAI 14140, pp. 386–394, 2024.
https://doi.org/10.1007/978-3-031-55015-7_32

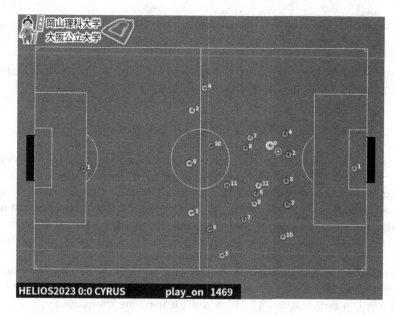

Fig. 1. A scene from the final of RoboCup2023, a match between HELIOS2023 (Okayama University of Science and Osaka Metropolitan University, Japan) and CYRUS (Dalhousie University and Memorial University, Canada).

2   Soccer Simulation 2D Competition

The RoboCup Soccer Simulation 2D Competition, one of the oldest of the RoboCup competitions, is designed as a simulated soccer robot competition on a virtual soccer field. [8]. The simulation system[2] enables two teams of 11 autonomous player agents and an autonomous coach agent to play a game of soccer with realistic rules and game play. Figure 1 shows a scene from the final of RoboCup2023. Player agents receive a visual sensor message, an aural sensor message, and a body sensor message from the simulation server, and can send a few types of abstract action commands (kick, dash, turn, turn_neck, and so on). In the game of RoboCup Soccer Simulation 2D Competition, player agents make a decision at each simulation cycle in real time. In 2023, a new observation model was introduced in the simulation server. This model allows players to move the focus position within their field of view. This change requires more realistic active sensing behavior in the player's recognition process. The new model is still experimental and is expected to be refined over the next few years.

In RoboCup2023, 16 teams qualified for the tournament and 14 teams participated in the competition. The competition consisted of five round-robin rounds and a final tournament. HELIOS2023 won the championship with all 35 wins, scoring 182 goals and conceding 10 goals. CYRUS from Dalhousie University and

---

[2] Available at: https://github.com/rcsoccersim.

Memorial University won the second place, and YuShan2023 from Anhui University of Technology won the third place. Two types of challenge competitions were also held. Oxsy won the Cooperation Challenge, a challenge competition that mixes players from two different teams to form one team, and EMPEROR won the Starter Challenge, a challenge competition by newbie teams.

3   Enhancement of the Visual Debugger

This year, we made some enhancements to our viewer application, soccerwindow2. soccerwindow2 is a viewer application for the 2D soccer simulation, developed by our team. soccerwindow2 can work not only as a monitor client and a log player but also as a visual debugger. This means soccerwindow2 can visualize not only the actual simulation state but also the agents' internal state on the virtual soccer field. This feature helps us to observe a gap between the actual simulation state and the agents' internal state.

To make team development more efficient, we added the two functions to soccerwindow2. The first one is the integration of the formation editor. The second one is a new feature, a label editor for machine learning.

3.1   Integration of Formation Editor

The formation editor, fedit2, was also a GUI application that we had been continuously developing. fedit2 supported the formation framework provided by HELIOS base [1] and enabled us to edit the formation data graphically. Until 2022, the formation editing function has been implemented as a stand-alone application, without the ability to connect to a simulation server or playback logs. This means game information from the soccer simulator could not be displayed during formation editing, therefore it was difficult for us to edit the formation while comparing it to the actual game situation. To solve this problem, we integrated the formation editing function into soccerwindow2.

Figure 2 shows a screenshot of the integrated formation editor function. Now, we can edit the formation data while comparing it to the game situation on the same canvas. This feature makes team formation adjustments more efficient.

3.2   Annotation Tool for Machine Learning

To enable us to create training data for machine learning efficiently, we implemented new operation panels, Label Editor and Simple Label Selector, to soccerwindow2 as an annotation tool. Figure 3 shows screenshots of these two operation panels.

Label Editor enables us to edit the label values for each feature, usually state variables at some game state. Label Editor is mainly used to edit training data for Learning to Rank, which will be explained later. Label Editor has 3 columns. The first column lists the game time. If users select the value on this column, the game state on the main window is automatically moved to that time and

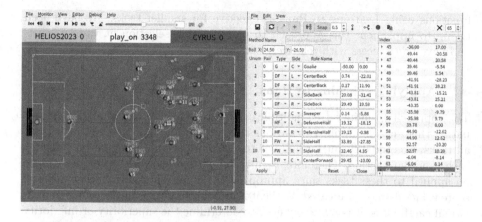

Fig. 2. screenshot of the formation editor function integrated into soccerwindow2.

Fig. 3. Screenshots of Label Editor and Simple Label Selector.

the values on the second column are also updated. The second column lists the candidates, usually the action to be selected, and their values (labels), in the first column game time. The last column lists the feature values if users select the specific row on the second column. Users can edit the label value on the second column, then the updated labels can be saved as CSV files.

Simple Label Selector enables us to change the label value for each game state. This panel simply shows the list of the pair of game time and its label value. If users select a row, the game state on the main window is automatically moved to that time. Users can change several label values all at once by clicking the label value button after selecting the target pairs. The updated labels can be saved as CSV files.

4 Evaluation Function Using Learning to Rank

Acquiring a practical evaluation function for action selection is still a problem to be solved. We tried to apply machine learning methods to this problem (such as in [3,6]). Unfortunately, it has not yet been possible so far to obtain an evaluation function for ball kicking behavior for cooperative behavior that has practical performance. However, it is becoming clear that acquiring evaluation functions using Learning to Rank is effective for smaller tasks. We have been trying to implement this approach to player action selection at various levels and have had success with relatively small tasks.

4.1 Applying Learning to Rank

The approach of enumerating multiple candidate behaviors and numerically evaluating them can be applied to various sub-tasks in soccer. However, for almost all tasks, it is too difficult for humans to assign an accurate evaluation value for each candidate action. Therefore, regular supervised learning techniques cannot be applied to these tasks since appropriate training data with such numerical score values cannot be created. While it is difficult to give accurate scores to individual candidates, it is relatively easy to determine the superiority or inferiority of candidates. Learning to Rank approach seems promising for these characteristics. Learning to Rank is one of the machine learning techniques that is widely used in the information retrieval domain. That approach is used to sort and prioritize items, such as search results or product recommendations, based on their relevance to user queries or preferences.

Currently, we are applying Learning to Rank with Gradient Boosting Decision Trees (GBDT) as the internal learning model. GBDT is an ensemble learning method based on decision trees and has demonstrated practical performance in ranking tasks [4,7]. We employ CatBoost [5] as the implementation of the learning-to-rank model. CatBoost is a well-established library that belongs to GBDT family and is widely used in machine learning competitions.

4.2 Case Study: Ball Chasing Behavior

Problem Overview. We explain an example of applying Learning to Rank to the ball-chasing behavior. The ball-chasing behavior is a frequently occurring behavior in soccer games. Usually, individual players estimate the predictions of the future ball positions based on the simulator's physics model. When it comes to catching up with the ball in the shortest distance, optimizing the ball-chasing behavior is not so difficult. If the objective is to reach the ball in the shortest distance, optimizing the ball-chasing behavior is not challenging. However, for a pass receiver player, chasing the ball in the shortest distance is insufficient when considering team tactics and making a more significant contribution to the overall team performance. In such cases, the receiver must identify a ball-trap position and corresponding posture that provide greater advantages to the team and select the appropriate movement accordingly. Determining a more advantageous position and posture for the team in the context of ball-chasing behavior, while taking into account the current game situation, is not a straightforward task.

Ball Chasing Behavior in the Soccer Simulation. Figure 4 shows an example of the ball trap position predicted by Player #10. Each player predicts the

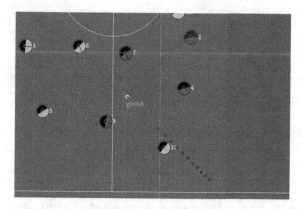

Fig. 4. Example scene showing the future ball positions predicted by Player #10 and candidate positions where it is possible to trap the ball.

position of the ball based on its observed information and predicts whether or not he can reach those positions. The figure shows the ball trajectory predicted by Player #10 and the possible positions where Player #10 can trap the ball as circles. It is easy to predict the future ball position and find the position to trap it with the shortest distance. However, Player #10 is playing an offensive role who attacks from left to right, so trapping the ball more toward the opposition, i.e., more to the right, is expected to give his team an advantage. As shown in this case, the most effective ball trap position is not clear because it is necessary to consider the positional relationship with other players and the team's tactics. Conventional team development approaches commonly rely on manually designed rules and hand-coded evaluation functions to tackle this challenge.

Numerical Experiments. In order to assess the learning method, we conducted experiments using the players' decision logs. The assessment will be performed using training data that is assumed to be created by humans.

Figure 5 shows an excerpt of the training data. Each line represents an action candidate. The leftmost column indicates the score of each action, the second column represents the ID of the corresponding situation, and the remaining columns denote feature values. A total of 15 feature values were employed in our experiments. They were manually selected and were used by HELIOS2023 in the actual competitions. In this example, 10 candidates were generated and ranked from 1 to 10, which are then used as the score. In this way, the training dataset is generated from the game situations, with each situation having a unique ID value.

The data in Fig. 5 represents accurately ranked candidate actions as recorded by the player program. We call this type of training data AllRank. We also generate pseudo training data, which simulates the data that a human supervisor would generate, by converting from AllRank. An example of the pseudo training data is shown in Fig. 6. In this example, the data consists of the list of pairs

```
10,1,0,0,8,8,0.288107,6246.58,13.5868,23.4031,48.2747,23,30,3.7709,1.06471,2.04423,1.2461
9,1,1,2,4,6,6.10623e-16,6717.68,12.4835,23.4031,47.7571,23,30,1.44939,1.06471,2.04423,1.41025
8,1,1,2,5,7,4.96507e-16,6620.49,13.0522,23.4031,48.0051,23,30,2.76357,1.06471,2.04423,1.32563
7,1,0,0,10,10,0.615877,6082.23,14.5616,23.4031,48.8551,23,30,5.83604,1.06471,2.04423,1.10105
6,1,1,2,6,8,2.77556e-16,6529.68,13.5868,23.4031,48.2747,23,30,4.05813,1.06471,2.04423,1.2461
5,1,1,0,3,3,0.884642,6460.66,10.5503,23.4031,47.2201,23,30,2.72605,1.06471,2.04423,1.6979
4,1,1,2,7,9,3.33067e-16,6448.38,14.0892,23.4031,48.5597,23,30,5.28908,1.06471,2.04423,1.17133
3,1,1,2,8,10,4.996e-16,6373.44,14.5616,23.4031,48.8551,23,30,6.45147,1.06471,2.04423,1.10105
2,1,1,2,9,11,2.16493e-15,6305.42,15.0056,23.4031,49.1566,23,30,7.54664,1.06471,2.04423,1.03499
1,1,1,2,10,12,1.4988e-15,6248.9,15.4229,23.4031,49.4607,23,30,8.57748,1.06471,2.04423,0.972889
0,1,0,0,9,9,0.817467,6190.35,14.0892,23.4031,48.5597,23,30,4.47252,1.06471,2.04423,1.17133
```

Fig. 5. Example of training data (AllRank). The exact ranking information for all candidate actions in the same situation is recorded.

```
1,1,0,0,5,5,0.369284,6568.78,11.8785,23.4031,47.5377,23,30,0.393129,1.06471,2.04423,1.50027
0,1,0,0,4,4,0.46181,6541.35,11.2349,23.4031,47.3555,23,30,1.51267,1.06471,2.04423,1.59603
1,2,0,0,5,5,0.369284,6568.78,11.8785,23.4031,47.5377,23,30,0.393129,1.06471,2.04423,1.50027
0,2,1,0,4,4,0.319704,6651.13,11.2349,23.4031,47.3555,23,30,1.92135,1.06471,2.04423,1.59603
1,3,0,0,5,5,0.369284,6568.78,11.8785,23.4031,47.5377,23,30,0.393129,1.06471,2.04423,1.50027
0,3,0,0,6,6,0.812594,6514.72,12.4835,23.4031,47.7571,23,30,0.658325,1.06471,2.04423,1.41025
1,4,0,0,5,5,0.369284,6568.78,11.8785,23.4031,47.5377,23,30,0.393129,1.06471,2.04423,1.50027
0,4,0,0,7,7,0.374891,6365.38,13.0522,23.4031,48.0051,23,30,2.39057,1.06471,2.04423,1.32563
1,5,0,0,5,5,0.369284,6568.78,11.8785,23.4031,47.5377,23,30,0.393129,1.06471,2.04423,1.50027
0,5,0,0,8,8,0.288107,6246.58,13.5868,23.4031,48.2747,23,30,3.7709,1.06471,2.04423,1.2461
```

Fig. 6. Example of pseudo training data (VSTop). The data consists of pairs of the best candidate and others.

of the best candidates and others contained in AllRank. A value of 1 in the leftmost column indicates the best action candidate in the given situation, while a value of 0 indicates other candidates. For example, if AllRank has 10 ranked candidates, it will generate 9 pairs of top and other combinations. We call this pseudo training data VSTop.

The training is performed by varying the number of situations: 10, 100, 1000, 10000, and 40000 for AllRank and VSTop, respectively. For instance, AllRank10 represents having complete ranking information for 10 situations, while VSTop10 signifies pseudo data generated based on AllRank10. For this experiment, we specifically focused on the logs recorded by the offensive role players within the team. We collected data from a total of 100 games, resulting in a grand total of 49,096 situations, by running the latest HELIOS team. From the complete dataset, we extracted subsets for training purposes and for evaluation purposes.

The depth of each decision tree in the boosted trees is limited to 6, and the total number of iterations is set to 2000. YetiRankPairwise is used as the loss function. The model is trained using the training subset and evaluated using the evaluation subset. Normalized discounted cumulative gain (NDCG) is employed as the performance indicator for the acquired models. NDCG is a widely used metric for evaluating ranking models. If the predicted ranking by the model perfectly matches the ground truth, the NDCG value becomes 1.0.

Results. Figure 7 shows the learning curve for 2000 training iterations. It is evident that VSTop exhibits lower performance compared to AllRank. With 10 situations, VSTop achieves an NDCG of approximately 0.91, while AllRank converges at around 0.94. However, as the number of situations surpasses 1000,

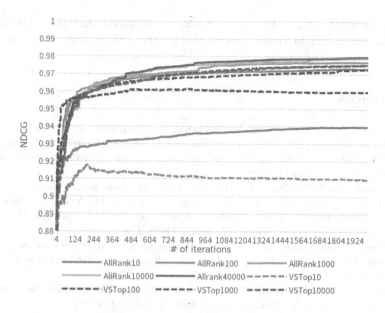

Fig. 7. The change in NDCG value during the training iterations.

the performance gap between AllRank and VSTop becomes smaller. This result shows that while VSTop consistently underperforms AllRank, the difference between the two approaches decreases rapidly when the number of situations exceeds about 1000.

The experimental result indicates that even with human-created training data like VSTop, comparable performance to fully ranked training data can be achieved when the number of situations exceeds approximately 1000. It should be noted that the necessary number of situations may vary depending on the task complexity and the size of the feature vectors. Nonetheless, it is feasible for a human supervisor to select the best action for 1000 to 10000 situations. In the case of ball chasing behavior, it may be plausible to consider an approach where humans train the player program.

5   Conclusion

This paper introduced the champion team of RoboCup 2023 Soccer Simulation 2D Competition. First, the overview of the competition is described. Then, we described our recent effort, enhancements of the visual debugger, and applying learning to rank to decision making. The HELIOS team won 6 championships in the past RoboCup competitions. Currently, our released software is widely used in the 2D community not only for competition but for research.

Although our released software has not yet supported the new observation model, we plan to model an active visual search behavior performed by humans and apply it to agents. We are developing applications that allow humans to immerse themselves in virtual spaces, observe the environment, and make decisions.

References

1. Akiyama, H., Noda, I.: Multi-agent positioning mechanism in the dynamic environment. In: Visser, U., Ribeiro, F., Ohashi, T., Dellaert, F. (eds.) RoboCup 2007. LNCS (LNAI), vol. 5001, pp. 377–384. Springer, Heidelberg (2008). https://doi.org/10.1007/978-3-540-68847-1_38
2. Akiyama, H., Nakashima, T.: HELIOS base: an open source package for the RoboCup soccer 2D simulation. In: Behnke, S., Veloso, M., Visser, A., Xiong, R. (eds.) RoboCup 2013. LNCS (LNAI), vol. 8371, pp. 528–535. Springer, Heidelberg (2014). https://doi.org/10.1007/978-3-662-44468-9_46
3. Akiyama, H., Fukuyado, M., Gochou, T., Aramaki, S.: Learning evaluation function for RoboCup soccer simulation using humans' choice. In: Proceedings of SCIS & ISIS 2018 (2018)
4. Burges, C.J.C.: From RankNet to LambdaRank to LambdaMART: an overview. Microsoft Research Technical Report, MSR-TR-2010-82 (2010)
5. Dorogush, A.V., Ershov, V., Gulin, A.: CatBoost: gradient boosting with categorical features support. In: Workshop on ML Systems at NIPS 2017 (2017)
6. Fukushima, T., Nakashima, T., Akiyama, H.: Evaluation-function modeling with multi-layered perceptron for RoboCup soccer 2D simulation. Artif. Life Rob. **25**(3), 440–445 (2020)
7. Ke, G., et al.: LightGBM: a highly efficient gradient boosting decision tree. Adv. Neural Inf. Process. Syst. 3147–3155 (2017)
8. Noda, I., Matsubara, H.: Soccer server and researches on multi-agent systems. In: Proceedings of IROS-1996 Workshop on RoboCup, pp. 1–7 (1996)

B-Human 2023 – Object and Gesture Detection

Thomas Röfer[1,2]([✉]), Tim Laue[2], Arne Hasselbring[2], Fynn Böse[2],
Lukas Malte Monnerjahn[2], and Kelke van Lessen[2]

[1] Deutsches Forschungszentrum für Künstliche Intelligenz, Cyber-Physical Systems,
Enrique-Schmidt-Str. 5, 28359 Bremen, Germany
thomas.roefer@dfki.de
[2] Universität Bremen, Fachbereich 3 – Mathematik und Informatik, Postfach 330
440, 28334 Bremen, Germany
{tlaue,arha,fboese,lumo,kelke}@uni-bremen.de

Abstract. For winning a RoboCup Standard Platform League competition, a team needs to have sophisticated solutions for a number of robotics subproblems, ranging from the fields of computer vision and state estimation to decision-making and motion control. In this paper, we focus on three new solutions for different computer vision tasks that are based on Deep Learning. We do not provide an overview of the complete B-Human system. Such an overview is given in [14].

1 Introduction

The B-Human team has successfully participated in RoboCup Standard Platform League competitions for several years. During this time, an elaborate modular code base, which has become released as open source after each RoboCup year, has emerged. As our approach is to make continuous progress, major rewrites or any restart from scratch have never occurred. Instead, major parts of the system remain almost untouched between two competitions and only a subset of our software components becomes replaced. In general, this happens when rule changes require different approaches or when scientific progress allows for more sophisticated solutions of certain subproblems.

In recent years, the field of Deep Learning-based computer vision made great progress and offers solutions for many typical RoboCup vision problems. That's why we started to gradually replace our classic computer vision components by Deep Learning solutions. In the past, this have been, for instance, a new robot detector [8] or a new detection approach for the field border [4]. In this champion paper, we focus on three further Deep Learning-based contributions that were developed for the 2023 competitions: a new approach for object detection in the lower NAO camera (see Sect. 2), our updated robot detection network (see Sect. 3), and a solution for the technical challenge task of human referee gesture detection (see Sect. 4).

Further major improvements for 2023 that are not described in this paper have been made in the areas of team behavior and robot motion. At this

C. Buche et al. (Eds.): RoboCup 2023, LNAI 14140, pp. 395–406, 2024.
https://doi.org/10.1007/978-3-031-55015-7_33

RoboCup, games with seven robots per team were held for the first time. Thus, the overall team coordination, including our intensive passing [15], was refined. Furthermore, a more sophisticated approach for retrieving a lost ball was developed. A majority of our robots is already some years old. Thus, many of their joints are worn out, which makes stable walking more difficult. Two major developments that counteract this problem have been published at this year's RoboCup symposium: "Dynamic Joint Control For A Humanoid Walk" [10] and "Neural Network-based Joint Angle Prediction for the NAO Robot" [2].

2   CNN-Based Preprocessing for the Lower Camera

The NAO robot has two cameras in the head which are arranged above each other and do not overlap. While this prohibits stereo processing, it is useful for playing soccer since it allows observing close and far objects simultaneously despite the small field of view of each camera. This results in different image characteristics. Especially, objects in the lower camera vary much less in size and are generally bigger. The fact that knowledge of the camera perspective is useful to efficiently subsample the image is one of the reasons we have still been using scanline-based region proposal algorithms for the ball and the penalty mark, followed by convolutional neural network (CNN) classifiers for which the input is scaled according to the expected size. Also, since other players take diverse shapes in the lower camera that are not described well by a bounding box, the obstacle detection on the lower camera was previously based on analytic features (in contrast to the deep neural network for the upper camera). This motivates a special model to preprocess the lower camera image for ball, penalty mark, and obstacle detection. The model operates on the raw 320×240 YUYV images as obtained from the camera and outputs proposal heatmaps for the ball and penalty mark and a binary low-resolution segmentation mask for obstacles. The ball and penalty mark proposals are still postprocessed by the same classifiers as on the upper camera, mainly because we already have good solutions for that of which we know the characteristics and to which our remaining system is tuned. Since only the highest response proposals are passed on, the runtime overhead is minimal.

The particular kind of architecture we use is inspired by works from the RoboCup Humanoid League [1,16]. However, those platforms have significantly more processing power than the NAO and can thus afford more expensive models.

2.1   Dataset

A custom dataset has been created from 15 JPEG log files (3 of them kept as validation set) recorded by the NAO's lower camera during games between 2019 and 2023. Images are sampled once per second, excluding phases in which the robot's image processing does not run (e. g. when serving a penalty). The resulting training set has 11361 images, of which 3198 contain at least one of the relevant objects. Specifically, there are 1301 balls, 761 penalty marks, and

Fig. 1. Sample images from the training set, conditioned on the presence of at least one object. Ground truth ball and penalty mark centers are annotated as red and blue dots, respectively, and the obstacle mask is shaded yellow. (Color figure online)

1952 images contain at least one obstacle cell. The area ratio covered by obstacle cells is 2.4% overall or 14.1% among the images that contain at least one obstacle cell. Labels are imported from the log files as well (given by the output of the perception modules at the time when the log has been recorded), which accelerates the following manual annotation process. Balls and penalty marks are represented by their center point, while obstacles are binary-segmented on a 20×15 grid (matching the output resolution of the network). The own body of the observing robot is not labeled as obstacle. Figure 1 shows a few samples from the training set.

2.2   Model and Training

The model we use is derived from ResNet-18 [5]. However, due to computational constraints and the desired output shape, we use fewer filters, separable convolutions in all but the first and last layers, and cut off the lowest resolution layers without a subsequent decoder, such that the output remains at a 16th of the input resolution. The output is thus a 20×15 map for each object class. One peculiarity pertains to the YUYV input format: The image is represented with resolution 320×240 and two channels, which the first convolution with a large (7×7) filter and stride 2 rectifies. The targets for the model are unnormalized object-centered Gaussians with a constant standard deviation for the ball and the penalty mark channels, and the raw annotated binary mask for the obstacle channel. We use the mean squared error as loss function as in [1,16], however binary crossentropy with a sigmoid activation works, too. Optimization is performed by Adam [6] for 100 epochs with batches of 16 elements. When sampling a batch, each input image is randomly perturbed by global scaling/shifting, pointwise noise addition, blur, and left/right flipping.

Fig. 2. Sample images from the validation set with predicted heatmaps

2.3 Results

Since the ball and penalty mark outputs from the model are used as proposals which are filtered by another classifier, recall is a more meaningful metric than precision here. It can be defined without a threshold by counting how often the highest response location is compatible to the annotated object. This recall is 94% for the ball and 59% for the penalty mark on the validation set. Sample images with predicted heatmaps are shown in Fig. 2. The neural network runs in 16 ms using a custom data parallel code generator [17], which is fast enough for real-time processing at the camera's frame rate of 30 Hz.

A particular failure mode is the center mark which is occasionally detected as penalty mark. The ball detector also often responds to the heels of robots, although the previous scanline-based approach would do this too. The obstacle detection performance is clearly better than before, especially in hard lighting conditions. It is weakened by the existing post-processing that clusters the segmentation mask to bounding boxes and discards typical failure modes of the previous analytic approach. This will be improved in the future by integrating the segmentation mask directly into a probabilistic grid representation.

3   Robot Detection

Since 2018, we have used the convolutional neural network JET-Net [8] for detecting robots in images of the robot's upper camera. This network uses downscaled grayscale images as inputs and outputs bounding boxes of detected robots within these images. Grayscale images, however, lack information about the color of the detected robots, so the aforementioned network is not able to determine the jersey color and thus the team affiliation of the detected robots. Consequently, we had to use additional image recognition modules to identify robot jerseys. Over the years, we have tried multiple approaches, but none of them achieved our desired reliability. To overcome this situation, we aim to develop an improved neural network for robust robot recognition that includes jersey classification. Although the jersey classification part has not been finished yet, a first major step has been done: the implementation of a network that works on color images.

3.1 Network Architecture and Data

The network architecture we chose closely resembles that of the previous detection module [8]. It is a YOLOv2 type network as described in [9], but the classification step is omitted since the only type of objects our network needs to detect are NAO robots. We use multiple convolutional layers with ReLU activation interspersed by max-pooling layers, which is the typical structure of many image recognition networks. Our bounding box prediction utilizes anchor boxes, a concept first introduced in Faster R-CNN [11]. The idea of this approach is to avoid having the network predict actual bounding box coordinates and instead predict only an offset to a fixed reference.

One major area that we reworked was the dataset used for training, which we created using a total of 8333 images. 1959 of these images were downloaded from the open-source labeling platform *ImageTagger* [3] while all other images were extracted from log files of B-Human games. Within our 8333 images, we manually labeled 18968 robots, each with a bounding box and their appropriate jersey color. As a labeling platform, we chose Label Studio[1], as it enabled us to easily collaborate while labeling. We hope that the addition of jersey colors to our dataset will help in the development of future jersey color classification.

Unlike the previous robot detector, we decided against generating training material from simulated images and only used natural images with augmentations instead. These augmentations included mirroring and zooming, as well as adjustments in brightness.

The image input resolution stayed the same as with the old network. We scale images down by a factor of 8 in both width and height, to 80×60 pixels. Since we labeled all robots in their original resolution of 640×480 pixels, a lot of robots are unrecognizably small in their downscaled version. For this reason, we set a minimum size of 64 pixels that a bounding box has to cover. Otherwise, it is removed from the training dataset (see Fig. 3).

For training our network, we also implemented an Intersection over Union loss, that makes a single predictor responsible for each robot in the ground truth

---

[1] https://labelstud.io/.

(a) Resolution of: 640 × 480 pixels   (b) Resolution of: 80 × 60 pixels

Fig. 3. A sample image from the NAO's upper camera in its original quality (left) and downscaled to the resolution our robot detector network processes (right)

and, in contrast to the previous implementation, incurs an increased loss for detecting the same robot multiple times.

3.2 Results

We evaluated the detection performance of our networks on the evaluation datasets using two types of network structures: first, a simple network based entirely on separable convolution layers with a comparatively low number of trainable parameters (6794 on grayscale input/7086 on YUV). Second, we tested the same network structure as used for JET-Net [8], with a high number of trainable parameters (26938 on grayscale/27230 on YUV) while maintaining a similar number of floating point operations needed to execute it.

By also looking at different confidence thresholds, we get the precision-recall curves in Fig. 4. The curves for the simple models are very close to each other, showing no big difference in detection accuracy regardless of using color or grayscale input. In contrast, the curves for the more complex color models reach better precision-recall trade-offs when using higher confidence thresholds. Again, the more complex grayscale model shows significantly worse performance.

No systematic evaluation of the actual detection performance was performed after post-processing. However, the simple color model was extensively field tested by using it throughout all of RoboCup 2023. No obvious problems arose when using the new network and the detection performance appeared to be at least as good as with the old detector.

4   Detecting Human Referee Gestures

In 2022 and 2023, the Standard Platform League held technical challenges on detecting human referee gestures. In 2022, twelve different gestures had to be detected. Eleven of them were static and one was dynamic, i.e. it included motion. A NAO robot standing on the center of the field looked at a referee

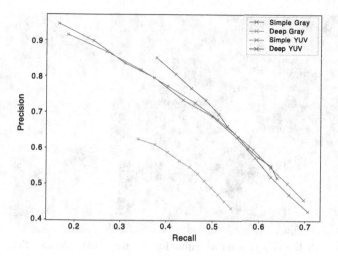

Fig. 4. Precision-Recall curves of the evaluated models

standing at the end of the halfway line and had to detect a gesture the referee showed after he/she whistled. In 2023, another dynamic gesture was added and the whole challenge was conducted during all games of the preliminary rounds of the soccer competition [13, section 2]. After the whistle for kick-offs, goals, and the end of a half, a gesture was shown the robots had to detect. In both challenges, we used a two-step approach for gesture detection. A neural network detects keypoints on the referee's body and then the spatial relations between some of these keypoints are checked to detect the actual gestures.

4.1 Keypoint Detection

MoveNet [18] is used to detect 17 so-called keypoints in the images taken by the upper camera in NAO's head. Most of these keypoints are located on a person's joints, but some mark attributes of a person's face, such as ears, eyes, and the nose. The single pose version of MoveNet is used to detect these keypoints. The network delivers 17 triples of x and y coordinates and a confidence, one for each type of keypoint. There are two versions available that both use RGB images as input: The *Lightning* variant processes an input of 192 × 192 pixels and runs at around 13.5 Hz on the NAO. The *Thunder* version processes an input of 256 × 256 pixels and subsequently runs slower (3.5 Hz on the NAO). We used the latter version, because the detections proved to be more reliable.

A quadratic region around the center of the upper camera image is used as the input for the MoveNet network (see Fig. 5a). The region has a fixed size of 384 × 384 pixels. It is scaled down to the required input size using bilinear interpolation. It is also converted from the YUYV color space to the RGB color space MoveNet expects. Using self-localization, the NAO looks at the position the referee should stand on the field at the fixed height, thereby centering the referee in the region used for detection.

(a) Camera with the region used as input for the net-work. Parts of that region are recolored in magenta to mask them out. The red dots mark the keypoints found.

(b) Bloom effect and low contrast make the arms hard to detect.

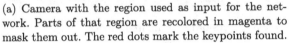

Fig. 5. Images taken during the visual referee challenges

The single pose version of MoveNet is supposed to detect keypoints on a single person. It is not defined what will happen if several people are visible in the image. As there can be spectators present in the background during the execution of the challenge, we try to increase the likelihood that the actual referee is marked with the keypoints. In the part of the image that is used as input for the network, we define a mask to exclude regions where the referee could not be visible. The idea is that the network will prefer a person more of which is visible over one, e. g., the legs of which are hidden. The mask consists of a rectangular region representing the area where the legs of the referee could be and a circular region that represents the area the arms can reach. Everything outside these two regions is recolored to magenta. We also tried to color it black, which was less effective, probably because the network simply considers these parts to be in the shadow and still places keypoints into them. This setup was used for the detection from a fixed position in 2022. For the detection in actual games in 2023, the mask was also scaled based on the distance to the referee and the horizontal angle between the observing robot and the referee.

4.2   Gesture Detection

The gesture detection is performed by defining a set of constraints for each of the gestures. Each constraint defines valid ranges for the distance between two keypoints and the direction one of these keypoints is located relative to the other one. The constraints for all gestures are checked in a fixed order. The first one that satisfies all constraints is accepted. The ordering allows to use less constraints for gestures that are checked later. For instance, the gesture for *goal* consists of one arm pointing to the side and the other arm pointing at the center of the field, i. e. basically in the direction of the observing robot. MoveNet struggles with correctly placing the keypoints on the latter arm. Therefore, an arm pointing to the side is accepted as *goal* without checking the second arm if none of the other gestures was accepted.

Similar to the mask presented in the previous section, the keypoints are scaled based on the distance and the direction to the referee before the constraints are checked. To suppress noise and to avoid detecting intermediate gestures the referee goes through while lifting the arms, detections are buffered. A gesture is only accepted if at least 40% of the detections within the last ten images are the same. A special handling was implemented for dynamic gestures, where different phases of these gestures are counted as the same gesture.

4.3   Behavior

At RoboCup 2023, the referee gesture detection had to be perform during actual games. A gesture was continuously shown 5–15 s after the referee whistled. The robots had to report the gesture they detected through the wireless network no later than 20 s after the whistle. The first network packet received from a team after the whistle was the one that counted. We used this setup to implement a coordination without communication between the robots of our team. Any robot that is not playing the ball and is located within a circular sector of 2.5–6 m and ±35° relative to the referee turns towards the referee. It then tries to detect the gesture. If it is not successful within 6 s, it will step sideways in the direction of the halfway line to get a different perspective. Robots closer to the halfway line will report their findings earlier than robots that observe the referee under a more acute angle, assuming that the detections of the latter are more error-prone. Gestures that rely on detecting a single arm are reported even later. In addition, robots that are not able to detect a gesture, even if they have not tried to do so, report a default gesture shortly before the time window closes. The default gesture was selected to maximize the expected result for just guessing (≈30% of the achievable points). Part of the challenge is also to actually detect the whistle. In case it was missed, the robots receive the change in game state by the league's referee application 15 s after the whistle, which is still early enough to send a guessed gesture.

4.4   Discussion

Although we won the challenges both in 2022 and 2023, our approach is not the one we would choose if the success in soccer games would actually depend on the detection of the referee gestures. On the one hand, MoveNet is designed to solve a more complex problem than just detecting a few predefined gestures, and therefore, it is unnecessarily complex and thus slow. On the other hand, it lacks the information that only these gestures should be detected. It would be better to detect a gesture as a whole and provide a confidence for the whole detection rather than for each individual keypoint, as MoveNet does. Lukas Molnar [7]

404   T. Röfer et al.

Table 1. B-Human's game results in RoboCup competitions in 2023

(a) German Open 2023

Home	Away	Score
R-ZWEI Kickers	**B-Human**	0:6
B-Human	HTWK Robots	7:0
B-Human	HULKs	7:0
B-Human	Dutch Nao Team	10:0
B-Human	Bembelbots	10:0
B-Human	Naova	10:0
B-Human	Nao Devils	10:0
B-Human	HTWK Robots	7:0

(b) RoboCup 2023

Home	Away	Score
Nao Devils	**B-Human**	0:10
B-Human	HTWK Robots	8:0
B-Human	NomadZ	10:0
B-Human	HULKs	9:0
B-Human	SPQR Team	10:0
B-Human	Bembelbots	10:0
B-Human	rUNSWift	10:0
B-Human	HTWK Robots	9:0

uses such an approach. In 2023, our approach ran into some problems. To look at the referee, the NAO robots have to look up. As a result, the ceiling lights come into view. During the RoboCup in Bangkok, we basically used the whole image as input for the auto exposure of the camera, which worked fine (see Fig. 5a). However, in Bordeaux, the ceiling lights were so strong that the whole image would become very dark. Therefore, we only used the lower half for the auto exposure. Under these conditions, the camera images have a low contrast and contain a bloom effect around bright lights. If these are close to the referee, parts of the body might actually disappear, preventing MoveNet from placing keypoints onto them (see Fig. 5b).

5   Results

In 2023, B-Human won the RoboCup German Open as well as the Champions Cup and the overall Technical Challenges at the World Cup in Bordeaux. This section presents our results and briefly describes our approaches for the different Technical Challenges. The detailed results of all teams are given at [12].

5.1   Soccer Competitions

As in the previous year, the B-Human team was able to win all its games without conceding a single goal. The detailed results of all official games are listed in Table 1. This clearly shows that our intensive passing approach is still effective in games that involve 7 robots per team. Furthermore, attention should be paid to the fact that B-Human successfully participated in two in-game technical challenges (see Sect. 4 and Sect. 5.2) which both have the potential to affect the playing performance.

5.2   Technical Challenges

At RoboCup 2023, three different Technical Challenges were held. B-Human won the *In-Game Visual Referee Challenge* as well as the *Dynamic Ball Handling*

Challenge and became runner-up in the *Data Minimization Challenge*, resulting in a total challenge score of 74.5 out of 75 possible points. The rules of the different challenges are described in [13].

All relevant details about the *In-Game Visual Referee Challenge* have already been given in Sect. 4. It remains to be mentioned that only three other teams were able to score in this challenge.

The *Dynamic Ball Handling Challenge* had a similar setup as in 2022, when we became the runner-up in this challenge. Its overall goal is defined as "Score a goal as the attacking team after two or more passes without letting the defending players touch the ball". To solve this challenge, we were able to use our passing approaches for the normal games, as described in [15]. However, several minor adaptions were necessary to fulfill the challenge-specific constraints, above all to prevent the opponent from touching the ball. Eventually, at RoboCup 2023, we were the only team that scored in each of its three attempts after playing at least two passes.

We were not aiming to win the *Data Minimization Challenge* but to achieve a result in the top third. The reason for this was that it is defined as an in-game challenge, in which all teams have to communicate as few bytes as possible during their official games. Our team strategy highly benefits from a proper distribution of the players on the pitch and from passes between them. This kind of cooperation currently still relies on communication among the robots. We decided not to weaken our team in favor of a technical challenge. Thus, we kept our communication scheme as described in [15], which aims to communicate as many messages as safely possible within the given limit. To minimize the overall amount of communicated bytes, we removed some data, which we considered to be dispensable, from the packets and slightly compressed the remaining data, for instance by using a lower precision of some position information. Overall, becoming second in this challenge after the Dutch Nao Team can be considered as a great success.

References

1. Ficht, G., et al.: NimbRo-OP2X: adult-sized open-source 3D printed humanoid robot. In: Proceedings of the 18th IEEE-RAS International Conference on Humanoid Robots, Beijing, China (2018)
2. Fiedler, J., Laue, T.: Neural network-based joint angle prediction for the NAO robot. In: Buche, C., et al. (eds.) RoboCup 2023. LNAI, vol. 14140, pp. 66–77. Springer, Cham (2024)
3. Fiedler, N., Bestmann, M., Hendrich, N.: ImageTagger: an open source online platform for collaborative image labeling. In: Holz, D., Genter, K., Saad, M., von Stryk, O. (eds.) RoboCup 2018. LNCS (LNAI), vol. 11374, pp. 162–169. Springer, Cham (2019). https://doi.org/10.1007/978-3-030-27544-0_13
4. Hasselbring, A., Baude, A.: Soccer field boundary detection using convolutional neural networks. In: Alami, R., Biswas, J., Cakmak, M., Obst, O. (eds.) RoboCup 2021. LNCS (LNAI), vol. 13132, pp. 202–213. Springer, Cham (2022). https://doi.org/10.1007/978-3-030-98682-7_17

5. He, K., Zhang, X., Ren, S., Sun, J.: Deep residual learning for image recognition. In: Proceedings of the 29th IEEE Conference on Computer Vision and Pattern Recognition, Las Vegas, NV, USA (2016)
6. Kingma, D.P., Ba, J.: Adam: a method for stochastic optimization. In: Proceedings of the 3rd International Conference for Learning Representations, San Diego, CA, USA (2015)
7. Molnar, L.: Visual referee detection on NAO robots for RoboCup SPL 2022. Bachelor thesis, ETH Zürich (2022)
8. Poppinga, B., Laue, T.: JET-net: real-time object detection for mobile robots. In: Chalup, S., Niemueller, T., Suthakorn, J., Williams, M.-A. (eds.) RoboCup 2019. LNCS (LNAI), vol. 11531, pp. 227–240. Springer, Cham (2019). https://doi.org/10.1007/978-3-030-35699-6_18
9. Redmon, J., Farhadi, A.: YOLO9000: better, faster, stronger. In: 2017 IEEE Conference on Computer Vision and Pattern Recognition (CVPR), pp. 6517–6525. IEEE, Honolulu, HI (Jul 2017). https://doi.org/10.1109/CVPR.2017.690
10. Reichenberg, P., Röfer, T.: Dynamic joint control for a humanoid walk. In: Buche, C., et al. (eds.) RoboCup 2023. LNAI, vol. 14140, pp. 125–227. Springer, Cham (2024)
11. Ren, S., He, K., Girshick, R., Sun, J.: Faster R-CNN: towards real-time object detection with region proposal networks. IEEE Trans. Pattern Anal. Mach. Intell. **39**(6), 1137–1149 (2017). https://doi.org/10.1109/TPAMI.2016.2577031
12. RoboCup Technical Committee: Standard Platform League results (2023). https://spl.robocup.org/results-2023/
13. RoboCup Technical Committee: RoboCup Standard Platform League (NAO) Technical Challenges (2023). https://spl.robocup.org/wp-content/uploads/SPL-Challenges-2023.pdf
14. Röfer, T., et al.: B-Human code release documentation 2023 (2023). https://wiki.b-human.de/coderelease2023/
15. Röfer, T., Laue, T., Hasselbring, A., Lienhoop, J., Meinken, Y., Reichenberg, P.: B-Human 2022 - more team play with less communication. In: Eguchi, A., Lau, N., Paetzel-Prüsmann, M., Wanichanon, T. (eds.) RoboCup 2022. LNAI, vol. 13561, pp. 287–299. Springer, Cham (2023). https://doi.org/10.1007/978-3-031-28469-4_24
16. Schnekenburger, F., Scharffenberg, M., Wülker, M., Hochberg, U., Dorer, K.: Detection and localization of features on a soccer field with feedforward fully convolutional neural networks (FCNN) for the adult-size humanoid robot Sweaty. In: Proceedings of the 12th Workshop on Humanoid Soccer Robots at the 17th IEEE-RAS International Conference on Humanoid Robots, Birmingham, UK (2017)
17. Thielke, F., Hasselbring, A.: A JIT compiler for neural network inference. In: Chalup, S., Niemueller, T., Suthakorn, J., Williams, M.-A. (eds.) RoboCup 2019. LNCS (LNAI), vol. 11531, pp. 448–456. Springer, Cham (2019). https://doi.org/10.1007/978-3-030-35699-6_36
18. Votel, R., Li, N.: Next-generation pose detection with MoveNet and TensorFlow.js (2021). https://blog.tensorflow.org/2021/05/next-generation-pose-detection-with-movenet-and-tensorflowjs.html

RoboCup 2023 SSL Champion TIGERs Mannheim - Improved Ball Interception Trajectories

Michael Ratzel[✉], Mark Geiger, and André Ryll

Department of Information Technology, Baden-Württemberg Cooperative State
University, Coblitzallee 1-9, 68163 Mannheim, Germany
info@tigers-mannheim.de
https://tigers-mannheim.de

Abstract. In 2023, TIGERs Mannheim won the RoboCup Small Size
League competition with individual success in the division A tournament, and the chip pass technical challenge. Given only one conceded
goal during the Robocup 2023, in addition to the focus of last year's
champion's paper on the offense parts of the strategy, this year will focus
on an important improvement for the goalkeeper: An improved trajectory
generator for goal shot interceptions. The current time-optimal second-
order BangBang trajectories include a complete stop at the intercept
destination, wasting valuable time. This is overcome by generating virtual destinations for the robot, that overshoot the intercept point and
avoid the preliminary braking, while ensuring the keeper will reach the
intercept point at the same time as the ball.

1 Introduction

RoboCup Small Size League (SSL) games stand out with their highly dynamic
games and a fast pace. With 11v11 fully autonomous and omnidirectionally moving robots, fast decision-making and efficiently trajectories are a key component
for success. This paper will focus solely on an extension to the current system
for generating 2D trajectories that improves the goalkeeper performance when
catching shots on the goal, as our last champion papers focused on the hardware development of our robots [1] and the offensive part of our strategy [2].
The currently generated second-order trajectories are time-optimal with constant acceleration and include a full stop to reach zero velocity at the specified
destination position. However, this full stop wastes valuable time when intercepting goal kicks, and as long as the goalie and the ball are at the interception
point at the same time, it is irrelevant that the goalie comes to a full stop at the
intersection point in a time-optimal manner.

Since the TIGERs robots are controlled only by specifying the final destination at which the robot should stop, we present an extension algorithm that can
provide virtual destination positions such that the actual destination is reached
at a given time by an actual trajectory created to the virtual destination. Since

C. Buche et al. (Eds.): RoboCup 2023, LNAI 14140, pp. 407–415, 2024.
https://doi.org/10.1007/978-3-031-55015-7_34

this problem is overdetermined, as the robot is not always able to reach the destination in the given time, a best possible virtual position is generated that brings the robot as close as possible to the destination in the given time.

2 Related Work

The SSL is a fast paced robot soccer league, and due to the high power of the motors compared to size and weight, the omnidirectional drive system of the robots is mainly limited by friction. Therefore, the Cornell Big Red team has presented an approach that generates second-order time-optimal trajectories with constant acceleration and a complete stop at a given target destination [3]. The current implementation is based on this approach and is discussed in more detail in Sect. 3.

The work of Hove et al. [4] presents a problem similar to intercepting a goal shot: Catching a ball with a robotic arm. However, they must impose more stringent requirements on the trajectory of the arm's end effector as they attempt to match the position, velocity, and acceleration of the ball at the interception point to reduce the risk of the ball bouncing off the arm. For future offensive applications, such as receiving a pass with a moving robot, these requirements may also be imposed, but for simply intercepting a shot on the goal, whether the ball bounces off the goalkeeper is irrelevant, and trying to match velocity and acceleration wastes valuable interception time.

In the "Mousebuster" work, an attempt is made to catch a mouse with a robotic arm. Here, the end effector of the robot does not have to match the velocity of the mouse, so the problem is closer; instead, an attempt is made to catch the mouse by placing a cup over it on the floor. Therefore, the velocity of the robot at the point of contact must be 0 to avoid hitting the ground. As mentioned earlier, this full stop again wastes valuable time. Furthermore, the trajectory presented in the paper is a third-order jerk-limited trajectory. The TIGERs use only second-order acceleration-limited trajectories because the robots are built to withstand very high jerks in collisions with other robots, and the motors are powerful enough to generate the large acceleration jumps. More details on the TIGERs robots can be found in the team's latest publications [1,5,6].

3 Current Approach: Untimed Trajectories

As mentioned earlier, our current approach for time-optimal 2D BangBang trajectories is based on the approach presented by Cornell Big Red [3,7]. It consists of two 1D trajectories for the two orthogonal axes x and y in the plane of the field. Each 1D trajectory consists of up to 3 phases with constant acceleration. An acceleration phase, an optional plateau phase with maximum velocity and an second acceleration phase. Each phase is described by the following equations of motion, with the position $s(t)$, the initial position of the phase s_0, the velocity

$v(t)$, the initial velocity of the phase v_0 and the constant acceleration a is either zero or the positive or negative limit $\pm a_{\max}$.

$$s(t) = s_0 + v_0 t + \frac{1}{2}at^2$$
$$v(t) = v_0 + at \tag{1}$$
$$a = \text{const}$$

A 2D trajectory is shown in Fig. 1 that starts at $S_0 = (0\,\text{m}, 0\,\text{m})^T$ with an initial velocity of $V_0 = (0\,\text{m s}^{-1}, 1\,\text{m s}^{-1})^T$, ends at the given destination $S_t = (1.5\,\text{m}, 0.5\,\text{m})^T$, and has a maximum velocity of $v_{\max} = 2\,\text{m s}^{-1}$ and a maximum acceleration of $a_{\max} = 3\,\text{m s}^{-2}$. The bottom two rows of the figure show the position, velocity, and acceleration of the 1D trajectories of the x and y axes, with the target destination marked as a horizontal solid black line in the position graph. The 1D graphs have time stamps marked with a vertical dashed line: the transition times of the phases $t_0, t_1, t_2[, t_3]$. These are used in the following to assign variables to specific time points or time intervals. A position, velocity, or

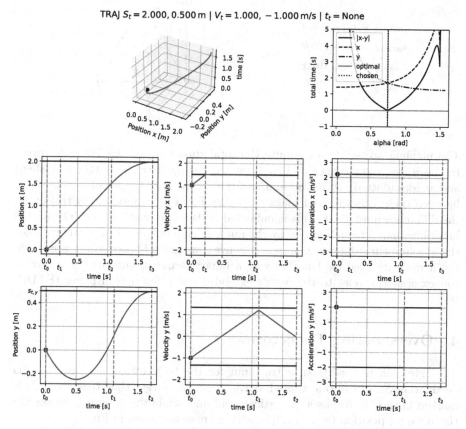

Fig. 1. 2D-Trajectory without Ball Interception Improvements

acceleration with a single index specifies its value at the exact time stamp, e.g., $s_i = s(t_i)$ is the position exactly at t_i. Variables with two indices describe the difference, e.g., $s_{i,j} = s(t_j) - s(t_i)$, or $t_{i,j} = t_j - t_i$.

The velocity profile of the x-axis in the middle clearly shows all three possible phases: $t_{0,1}$ the acceleration phase one, $t_{1,2}$ constant velocity phase and $t_{2,3}$ acceleration phase two. Overall, the velocity resembles a trapezoidal shape. The y axis has only the two acceleration phases $t_{0,1}$ and $t_{1,2}$, which resembles a triangular velocity shape. The constant velocity phase is omitted for the triangular shape because the distance on the y-axis is not long enough to accelerate to v_{max} and decelerate back to 0.

In order to enforce the maximum velocity and acceleration that the robot's hardware can achieve, we need to solve the optimization problem of what fraction of the total maximum velocity and acceleration can be assigned to each 1D trajectory. We can formulate the problem as finding the optimal angle α and computing from it the respective velocity and acceleration maxima using the following equations:

$$
\begin{aligned}
v_{max,x} &= v_{max} \cos \alpha \\
a_{max,x} &= a_{max} \cos \alpha \\
v_{max,y} &= v_{max} \sin \alpha \\
a_{max,y} &= a_{max} \sin \alpha
\end{aligned}
\tag{2}
$$

The maxima are used to compute the total time t_{total} of the 1D trajectories. In the upper right corner of Fig. 1 we see the total times of the x (dashed) and y (dashdotted) trajectories in relation to α, and the absolute difference between these times in as a black solid line. For a time-optimal 2D trajectory, the difference must be 0. This is indicated by the gray vertical line. The dotted black line marks the α^* chosen by the implemented optimization strategy. Since the absolute time difference is mostly convex, we use a binary search approach. For a more detailed explanation why a binary search is sufficient in a mostly convex scenario, refer to this year's extended team description paper (ETDP) [8].

4   Overshooting Trajectories

The extension now adds an extra input for the trajectories, not only the 2D destination S_t, but also a wanted arrival time, the target time t_t is given. It is marked in the 1D graphs as a vertical solid line, while the 2D graph marks the timed target position $(s_{t,x}, s_{t,y}, t_t)^T$ with a cross, as shown in Fig. 2.

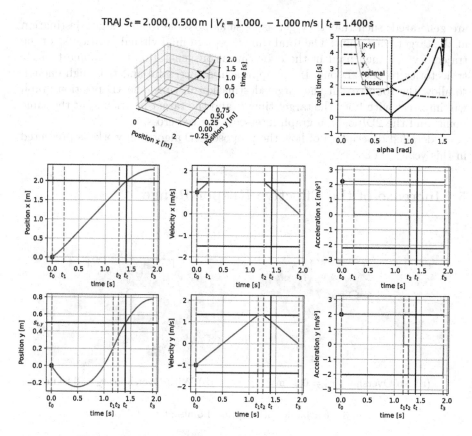

Fig. 2. 2D-Trajectory with Ball Interception Improvements

The new output of the extension are virtual destinations S_t^*, so s_3 of the x and y graphs in Fig. 2. This virtual position $S_t^* = (s_{3,x}, s_{3,y})^T = (s_{t,x}^*, s_{t,y}^*)^T$ is then sent to the robot as a normal target destination, and the robot will drive there with a trajectory generated by the current approach, as the virtual position is created such that the robot passes the target destination at the target time. The virtual destinations can be placed behind the actual destination S_t to avoid the unnecessary breaking before reaching S_t, or exactly at S_t if t_t is large enough to allow for a full stop. We call trajectories where the robot drives further than the actually wanted destination overshooting trajectories, and they can be either a forced overshoot: The robot is too fast and passes the destination before the target time, so it overshoots and has to recover. Or they can overshoot deliberately, so that the robot heads for a virtual destination in order to reach the actual destination just in time.

For the generation of 2D virtual positions, the extension reuses the same α optimization strategy used in the existing approach, but replaces how 1D trajectories are generated. The new 1D trajectories to the virtual destination are generated, such that they get as close as possible to the target destination at the target time point. The total time t^*_{total} and final virtual position s^*_t of the trajectory are then used in the α optimization generation to combine two 1D trajectories to one 2D one. If the approach is successful and t_t is high enough to allow the robot to hit the target destination in time, the 1D position graph will intersect with both the target time t_t and the target position s_t at the same point, and the 2D position graph intersects the red cross.

A detailed description of how the proposed 1D algorithm works is presented in this year's ETDP [8].

5   Increase of the Effective Keeper Range

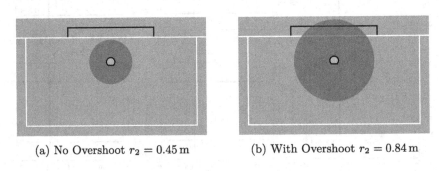

(a) No Overshoot $r_2 = 0.45\,\text{m}$ (b) With Overshoot $r_2 = 0.84\,\text{m}$

Fig. 3. Reachable Interception Points at $t = 0.75\,\text{s}$

To compare the effect of the overshoot, the situation of a goal shot with $6.5\,\text{m}\,\text{s}^{-1}$ and a distance of $4\,\text{m}$ is constructed. Resulting in travel times for the ball of roughly $0.75\,\text{s}$ depending on the carpet and ball model. The distances the keeper can travel within those $0.75\,\text{s}$ are drawn around a keeper in front of a Division A goal in Fig. 3. Within the $0.75\,\text{s}$ the keeper travels without overshooting $0.452\,\text{m}$ and with $0.835\,\text{m}$, such that the keeper with overshooting can block all goal shots, that are further away than $4\,\text{m}$. The keeper without overshooting will need $1.055\,\text{s}$ to reach the same distance of $0.835\,\text{m}$ as the overshooting keeper, which translates to a kick distance of roughly $5.3\,\text{m}$. As mentioned above, these numbers are certainly not completely accurate, as they vary depending on the carpet and also goal shots cannot be detected immediately by the image processing system, but as a rough estimate, over-shooting significantly improves the performance of the goalkeeper.

6   Optimal Ball Interception Point Selection

The selection of the optimal ball interception point is not trivial, the simplest estimate with the foot of the perpendicular of the robot's position and the ball flight line can be improved. If the goalkeeper is standing still and the interception point is moved slightly towards the goal, the distance the goalkeeper has to travel increases only slightly, while the distance the ball travels increases significantly. Knowing how fast the ball and the robot will be at the interception point, it is possible to calculate how far the interception point should be optimally shifted towards the goal. However, the TIGERs keeper rarely stands still during a match and constantly updates its blocking position. Therefore, the calculation becomes more complex as the initial velocity of the robot strongly influences the optimal interception point. We decided to use a sampling approach because the entire trajectory generation process is very performant and can be executed many thousands of times per second. Every ten millimeters along the ball flight line and within the penalty area, a position is sampled. At each position the time it takes for the ball to reach the position is calculated and with this information a trajectory to a virtual destination is generated.

Trajectories are then selected via the following criteria: first distance to the intersection point, velocity at the intersection point, distance to the goal line, and finally time remaining. Thus, if the goalkeeper cannot reach the destination within the remaining time at any interception point, the trajectory with the smallest distance to the ball at its intersection time is selected. If there are multiple locations where the ball can be reached, the one where the goalie is slowest is selected, as this increases both accuracy and the margin for adjustments to the destination in the next frame. If there are multiple positions where the goalie can come to a stop in time, we prefer positions farther from the goal line. However, only within the first $0.27\,m$ (3 bot radii), since we consider any interception point farther away to be safe. If there are multiple positions where the ball can be intercepted with a full stop that are further than $0.27\,m$ from the goal line, the final decision criterion is to maximize the time between the goalkeeper's arrival and the ball to maximize the margin for future adjustments.

7 Results During the RoboCup

With Sect. 5 highlighting the theoretical benefits of the presented extension, the practical proof is still missing that it is usable and works in a real tournament environment together with the interception point selection presented in Sect. 6. The extension was added to the goalkeeper prior to the 2022 RoboCup, but in 2022 the goalkeeper had to block only two goal shots, of which none required any movement and successively no overshooting as the keeper was already positioned correctly before the shots were fired. Therefore, this section will focus only on the four goal shots during the 2023 RoboCup. Table 1 gives an overview about the shots and information to judge the interception. The first columns provide information to find the actual situation in the official game logs[1]. The keeper velocity mentioned is the absolute-measured velocity of the goalkeeper at the interception point, and the intercept constellation diagrams show the situation of the intercept. The flattened circle shows the outer shape of the keeper, and

---

[1] https://ssl.robocup.org/game-logs/.

the point is the ball. The arrows pointing away from the shapes are their velocity directions at the interception point.

Table 1. Goal Shots at TIGERs Goal durign RoboCup 2023

#	Opponent	Game	Timestamp	Keeper Velocity	Intercept Constellation
1	Immortals	Upper 4	1st 00:02	$1.8\,\mathrm{m\,s^{-1}}$	
2	Immortals	Upper 4	1st -00:36	-	Not Intercepted
3	ZJUNlict	Upper Final	2nd 00:19	$1.2\,\mathrm{m\,s^{-1}}$	
4	ZJUNlict	Grand Final	1st 03:16	$0.8\,\mathrm{m\,s^{-1}}$	

To analyze the shots more deeply, the first one is shot number 2, which was a long shot over half of the field. It was deflected by our own robots close to our penalty area, which mislead the keeper and the keeper was too slow no matter the overshoot. For the other three shots, the keeper used the overshoot extension, as the keeper velocity was not zero or close to zero at the interception point. But especially for shot 1 and 3 the intercept constellation shows, that the ball was not intercepted optimally with the center of the keeper, and it were rather close calls. This is caused due to inaccuracies and latencies within the whole control setup, which complicates the task of ensuring that the robots follow exactly the calculated path. Between the Upper Final and Grand Final this system was tweaked, which can be seen in the interception constellation, as the keeper hits the ball more central.

8 Conclusion

This paper describes an extension to the existing system for generating 2D trajectories. Unlike the existing approach, this extension does not guarantee that the robot will reach a destination point in an optimal time manner, including a full stop. This additional freedom allows the robot to reach the actual destination faster by removing the full stop constraint, while the extended algorithm ensures that the robot reaches the destination at a desired time, such as when intercepting a goal kick.

During the 2023 RoboCup, this extension was successfully used to defend 3 goal shots, and a deeper analysis showed, that the TIGERs system to control the robots is sufficiently accurate to follow the calculated trajectories and intercept goal shots.

References

1. Ryll, A., Ommer, N., Geiger, M.: RoboCup 2021 SSL champion TIGERs Mannheim - a decade of open-source robot evolution. In: Alami, R., Biswas, J., Cakmak, M., Obst, O. (eds.) RoboCup 2021. LNCS (LNAI), vol. 13132, pp. 241–257. Springer, Cham (2022). https://doi.org/10.1007/978-3-030-98682-7_20
2. Geiger, M., Ommer, N., Ryll, A.: RoboCup 2022 SSL champion TIGERs Mannheim - ball-centric dynamic pass-and-score patterns. In: Eguchi, A., Lau, N., Paetzel-Prüsmann, M., Wanichanon, T. (eds.) RoboCup 2022. LNCS, vol. 13561, pp. 276–286. Springer, Cham (2023). https://doi.org/10.1007/978-3-031-28469-4_23
3. Purwin, O., D'Andrea, R.: Trajectory generation and control for four wheeled omnidirectional vehicles. Robot. Auton. Syst. **54**(1), 13–22 (2006). https://doi.org/10.1016/j.robot.2005.10.002
4. Hove, B., Slotine, J.J.E.: Experiments in robotic catching. In: 1991 American Control Conference, pp. 380–386 (1991). https://doi.org/10.23919/ACC.1991.4791395
5. Ryll, A., Jut, S.: TIGERs Mannheim - extended team description for RoboCup 2020 (2020)
6. Ommer, N., Ryll, A., Geiger, M.: TIGERs Mannheim - extended team description for RoboCup 2022 (2022)
7. Kalmár-Nagy, T., D'Andrea, R., Ganguly, P.: Near-optimal dynamic trajectory generation and control of an omnidirectional vehicle. Robot. Auton. Syst. **46**(1), 47–64 (2004)
8. Ratzel, M., Geiger, M., Ryll, A.: TIGERs Mannheim - extended team description for RoboCup 2023 (2023)

FC Portugal: RoboCup 2023 3D
Simulation League Champions

Miguel Abreu[1]([⊠])(iD), Pedro Mota[2](iD), Luís Paulo Reis[1](iD), Nuno Lau[3](iD),
and Mário Florido[2](iD)

[1] LIACC/LASI/FEUP, Artificial Intelligence and Computer Science Lab,
Faculty of Engineering of the University of Porto, University of Porto, Porto, Portugal
{m.abreu,lpreis}@fe.up.pt
[2] LIACC/LASI/FCUP, Artificial Intelligence and Computer Science Lab,
Faculty of Sciences of the University of Porto, University of Porto, Porto, Portugal
{pedro.mota,amflorid}@fc.up.pt
[3] IEETA/LASI/DETI, Institute of Electronics and Informatics Engineering
of Aveiro, Department of Electronics, Telecommunications and Informatics,
University of Aveiro, Aveiro, Portugal
nunolau@ua.pt

Abstract. FC Portugal, a team from the universities of Porto and
Aveiro, achieved the second consecutive victory in the main competition of the 2023 RoboCup 3D Simulation League. The team registered
18 wins, 1 tie, and 3 losses, scoring a total of 109 goals while conceding
only 13. The codebase used in this competition was developed in Python
after RoboCup 2021. This paper presents a brief overview of its structure
along with the new features developed for this year's competition. The
key developments include a revised dribble technique, designed to keep
the ball further from the robot to prevent ball-holding fouls in compliance
with new rules, and the introduction of a new programming language
called TSAL. TSAL enables the creation of high-level team strategies
in robotic soccer, combining deep symbolic reinforcement learning with
human sub-optimal knowledge to optimize team tactics.

1 Introduction

FC Portugal won the 2023 RoboCup 3D Soccer Simulation League (3DSSL)
in Bordeaux, France, marking the second consecutive victory after the 2022 tri-
umph [2]. The last victory before that was in 2006 when the league was composed
of spherical agents. Throughout the competition, the team registered 18 wins, 3
losses, and 1 tie, scoring a total of 109 goals, while only conceding 13.

Over recent years, FC Portugal has contributed to the simulation league
through low-level skills for walking, running, kicking and dribbling the ball [1–
3,5,12,14,26]. Moreover, it contributed with skill development methodologies
[13], high-level strategies [4,20,24] and reinforcement learning techniques [6,11].

C. Buche et al. (Eds.): RoboCup 2023, LNAI 14140, pp. 416–427, 2024.
https://doi.org/10.1007/978-3-031-55015-7_35

After RoboCup 2021, the team's code was written from the ground up in Python, leading to a victory in the 2022 RoboCup 3DSSL in Bangkok, Thailand [2]. The current iteration of our agent is based on this Python codebase. Certain updates were made in response to the introduction of the ball-holding foul in the league's new rules[1]. These changes encompass the modification of the dribbling behavior, and the removal of the push skill, employed in the local RoboCup competitions in Brazil, in 2022, and Portugal, in 2023.

FC Portugal also introduced a new programming language called TSAL for defining high-level team strategies in robotic soccer, while exploring the use of deep symbolic reinforcement learning along with human sub-optimal knowledge to optimize team strategies. Other changes to the current team include a new goalkeeper defending strategy, and fine-tuning several modules.

The remainder of this paper is organized as follows. Section 2 introduces the league and the new rules for RoboCup 2023. Section 3 provides an overview of FC Portugal's codebase with the most recent updates. Section 4 presents the new programming language called TSAL. Section 5 describes the Kick Rolling Ball Challenge and the skill developed to participate in the challenge. Section 6 presents the results obtained in the main competition as well as the technical challenge and its constituent events. Lastly, we conclude and outline future research directions in Sect. 7.

2   3D Simulation League

The RoboCup 3D simulation league uses SimSpark [9, 27] as its physical multi-agent simulator, which is based on the Open Dynamics Engine library. The league's environment is a 30 m by 20 m soccer field containing several landmarks that can be used for self-localization: goalposts, corner flags, and lines. Each team consists of 11 humanoid robots modeled after the NAO robot, created by Soft-Bank Robotics[2]. Agents get internal data (joints, accelerometer, gyroscope, and foot pressure sensors) with a 1-step delay every 0.02 s and visual data (restricted to a 120° vision cone) every 0.04 s. Agents can send joint commands every 0.02 s and message teammates every 0.04 s. There are 5 humanoid robot types with 22 to 24 controllable joints, and slightly different physical characteristics. Each team must use at least three different robot types during an official game, with a maximum of seven agents of any one robot type and a maximum of nine agents of any two robot types.

2.1   New Rules for RoboCup 2023

For RoboCup 2023, the Technical Committee has approved three new rules. First, the introduction of a ball-holding foul, triggered when a player keeps the ball within 0.12 m of itself for over 5.0 s, with no opponents closer than 0.75 m.

---

[1] The official rules can be found at https://ssim.robocup.org/3d-simulation/3d-rules/.
[2] https://us.softbankrobotics.com/nao.

Second, the addition of a catch command that allows goalkeepers to grip the ball. The command's success rate is inversely related to the ball's distance and speed. Finally, the league introduced a new penalty format, where each team takes a single shot from 6 m away from the goal in an attempt to score and determine the winner.

3   Team Codebase

This section provides an overview of the code structure used in this year's competition. Please refer to previous work for additional information [2]. Figure 1 illustrates the internal decision flow of the agent and server. The white and orange modules are implemented in Python and C++, respectively. The agent is mainly written in Python, except for the most resource-intensive components such as the 6D pose estimator, role manager, and A* pathfinding algorithm.

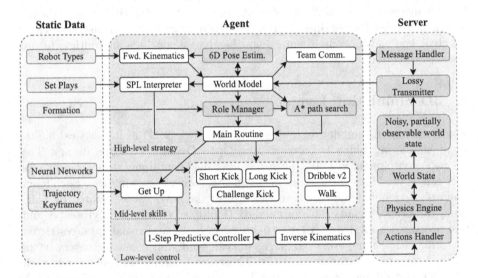

Fig. 1. Overview of the internal decision flow of agent and server, and their external interaction. White modules are implemented in Python while orange modules are implemented in C++. Gray blocks represent static data. (Color figure online)

The server updates the soccer environment based on agent actions, introducing various types of noise. This includes a constant calibration error affecting the robot's vision sensor, a perception error following a normal distribution that alters object coordinates based on distance, and rounding errors due to a lossy transmitter, rounding all numbers to the nearest hundredth.

3.1 High-Level Strategy

As previously stated, agents receive internal data from the server every 20 ms and visual data every 40 ms, consisting of a noisy partial view of the world state. That information is then used to build a world model and devise a common strategy. The main high-level components are briefly described as follows:

- 6D Pose estimator—updates the robot's position and orientation in 3D space. The algorithm uses known noise models to enhance the accuracy of perceived objects, iteratively adjusting the robot's pose [7];
- Forward Kinematics—allows the computation of body part poses for each robot type specification;
- Team communication—ensures all teammates possess a reliable representation of the world state. Messages are limited to 20 characters and are split into three groups, each conveying different game-related information, with specific synchronization and broadcast rules. This protocol ensures efficient communication among agents during a soccer match while adapting to varying visibility conditions;
- TSAL interpreter—manages set plays based on statically specified trigger conditions (see Sect. 4 for a detailed explanation);
- A* path search—divides the soccer field into 70941 nodes (32m x 22m, 10cm grid), mapping the position of goalposts, goal nets, players, and the ball. Role precedence among teammates ensures space allocation for higher-priority roles. The algorithm computes the best path that avoids all obstacles within the time limit of 5 ms;
- Role manager—assigns dynamic roles to players based on the game situation, by considering the position of every player and the ball trajectory. Roles are assigned according to their priority and the agents' distance to the objective, depending on whether the team is attacking or defending;
- Main routine—starts by selecting an intention, such as moving somewhere, dribbling, kicking, or starting a set play. Then, the agent decides the current low-level skill and computes the best way of reaching the chosen target. Shooting is favored if likely to succeed; otherwise, passing is chosen if it aids game progression over dribbling. Information is shared with teammates to synchronize the world model and the execution of set plays.

3.2 Mid-Level Skills

FC Portugal has five major skills, as depicted in Fig. 1:

- Kick—encompasses two distinct kicks: a short kick offering precise control over distance, spanning 3 to 9 m, and a long kick capable of reaching a maximum distance of 21 m. The latter variation is typically utilized for aiming shots at the goal;
- Challenge Kick—developed for the Kick Rolling Ball Challenge, where the agent must kick a ball that is rolling towards the player, with the goal of propelling it as far as possible in a fixed direction;

- Walk—omnidirectional walk, able to sustain an average linear speed between 0.70 and 0.90 m/s, depending on robot type and walking direction;
- Dribble v2—second version of the dribble behavior presented in 2022 [2], adapted to keep the ball further away from the robot to prevent ball-holding fouls;
- Get Up—used to get up after falling to the ground. There are three variations of the skill per robot type depending on the falling direction (front, back, side).

Dribble v2. The first iteration of this behavior, used in RoboCup 2022, kept the ball between both feet, usually at less than 0.12 m from the robot's center. This meant that it could not be used this year, due to the ball-holding foul described in Sect. 2.1. Consequently, a new dribble skill was trained using the initial setup [2], with a new condition that sets the reward to zero if the ball is within 0.115 m.

4   Set Plays

Previously, a complete framework for the specification and execution of set plays was designed and developed by FC Portugal [16–19,21], and later adopted by other teams in the RoboCup Simulation League [25]. Set plays were represented through a programming language based on S-expressions. Due to the minimalism of S-expressions, and consequent lack of syntactic constructs, the set plays were cumbersome and inconvenient to write by hand, as the programs would get large and difficult to understand. Thus, a graphical tool was developed [22], which later evolved into a complete environment named *SPlanner* (Strategic Planner) [10], allowing the graphical definition of complex set plays.

In 2023, FC Portugal introduced TSAL—a new programming language for the specification of set plays [20]. In TSAL, each set play has a name, active roles, and a body. The body consists of an initial condition, designated the trigger condition, followed by a set of steps that form the set play itself.

Initially, all agents are regarded as potential candidates for the set play roles. However, they are gradually eliminated as additional constraints are introduced.

The trigger condition defines the initial conditions that must be held in order to start the set play. It is also during the evaluation of the trigger condition, as we test new constraints, that we filter out the agents that do not satisfy the imposed conditions. If we reach a situation where there are no viable candidates for a role, the trigger condition will evaluate to false and the set play will not be executed.

Ultimately, a valid combination of agents is selected, and the set play is started. Every step of the set play includes a set of concurrent actions, each accompanied by a timer for action delay, another timer to establish the set play timeout, and a post-condition that must be satisfied upon completion. Should a timeout or post-condition violation occur, the set play is immediately terminated.

Example in Listing 1.1 implements a triangulation set play where three agents pass the ball between them in order.

```
def setplay 'Triangulation' with agents 'P1', 'P2', 'P3':
    {
        iam(agent='P1') and
        pos(agent='P1', xy = P1Pos, tol = Tol) and
        pos(agent='P2', xy = P2Pos, tol = Tol) and
        pos(agent='P3', xy = P3Pos, tol = Tol)
    }

    pass(agent='P1', to='P2')
        with WaitTime = Time
    {
        has_ball(agent='P2')
    }

    pass(agent='P2', to='P3')
        with WaitTime = Time
    {
        has_ball(agent='P3')
    }

    pass(agent='P3', to='P1')
        with WaitTime = Time
    {
        has_ball(agent='P1')
    }

    where
        P1Pos = (-13, 0);
        P2Pos = (-8, -4);
        P3Pos = (-8, 4);
        Tol = 2.5;
        Time = 1.5
```

Listing 1.1. Triangulation set play

In this set play, three agents, with names P1, P2, and P3, are involved. Once the team has ball possession, the agent holding the ball starts evaluating the triggering condition of the set play, which, in this case, is a conjunction of four predicates.

The initial test is iam(agent='P1'). This predicate narrows down the potential agents for P1 from all uniform numbers (1 to 11) to only the agent holding the ball. In this case, this predicate always returns true since it binds P1 to the player holding the ball and P1 is still unassigned.

The second test is pos(agent='P1', xy=P1Pos, tol=Tol) with P1Pos, and Tol equal to $(-13, 0)$, and 2.5, respectively. This predicate filters agents that are within the circle with center $(-6, 5)$ and radius 2. In this case, we have already filtered the role P1 to be just the agent holding the ball, therefore this predicate will just test if the player holding the ball is within that circle. The third and fourth conditions are similar to the second one, but, in both cases, the roles can still be any player, so they will just filter out agents that do not satisfy the restriction.

Currently, there are 8 predicates and 6 actions implemented, which are completely described in Table 1 and Table 2, respectively. Some parameters are optional and may have default values. Both these lists are easily extensible. All predicates filter possible candidates for a specific role. If after filtering, there are no possible candidates, the predicate returns false. Otherwise, it returns true.

Table 1. Implemented predicates

Predicate	Arguments	Description
iam	*agent*: str	E.g., *iam(agent* = "*P1*") The *iam* predicate tries to bind the role defined in the named argument *agent* to the player evaluating, returning true on success, or false otherwise
game	*play_mode*: str *winning_by*: str *losing_by*: int	E.g., *game(play_mode* = "*play_on*", *winning_by* = 3) The game predicate is used to verify the game state, such as the current play mode or the current score
has_ball	*agent*: str	E.g., *has_ball(agent* = "*P1*") The *has_ball* predicate filters all candidate agents to the role named in *agent* to the agent holding the ball
pos	*agent*: str *xy*: [double, double] *tol*: double	E.g., *pos(agent* = "*P1*", *xy* = (−5, 0), *tol* = 6.5) The *pos* predicate filters all candidate agents to the role named in *agent* that are within the circle with center *xy* and radius *tol*
xcoord	*agent*: str *min*: double *max*: double *is_abs*: bool	E.g., *xcoord(agent* = "*P1*", *min* = 3, *max* = 6) The *xcoord* predicate filters all candidate agents to the role named in *agent* that have their x-coordinate greater or equal than *min*, and less or equal than *max*. When *is_abs* is set to true, these comparisons are conducted using absolute values
ycoord	*agent*: str *min*: double *max*: double *is_abs*: bool	E.g., *ycoord(agent* = "*P4*", *min* = −2, *max* = 2) The *ycoord* predicate filters all candidate agents to the role named in *agent* that have their y-coordinate greater or equal than *min*, and less or equal than *max*. When *is_abs* is set to true, these comparisons are conducted using absolute values
in_front	*agent*: str *min*: double *max*: double	E.g., *in_front(agent* = "*P4*", *min* = −2, *max* = 2) The *in_front* predicate filters all candidate agents in role *agent* that have x-coordinate in the range [*min*, *max*]
dist	*agent_1*: str *agent_2*: str *min*: double *max*: double	E.g., *dist(agent_1* = "*P1*", *agent_2* = "*P2*", *min* = 0, *max* = 2) The *dist* predicate filters all candidate agents in role *P2* that are within a minimum distance *min* meters and maximum distance *max* meters
free	*agent*: str *radius*: double	The *free* predicate filters all candidate agents to the role named in *agent* that are free (i.e., not near opponents) from a distance, at least, *radius* meters

In the end, after evaluating all conditions, we will have, for each role, a set of possible agents that can fulfill that role. Note that there is always, at least, one agent for each role since if there was none, the predicate that caused that, would return false, making the trigger condition also immediately false. Then, we simply choose a random candidate player for each role, and start the set play.

The assignment of the players to the roles is not complete, i.e., our approach to filtering candidates may miss some combination that would make the trigger condition true, as the search is done in a greedy way. The only reason for this design decision is due to time constraints.

The successful execution of the set play by all participating agents is ensured through the simulator's communication medium. When an agent initiates a set play, it announces this intention via the communication channel using a message that starts with 's' (indicating the start), followed by the set play's ID and the uniform numbers of the participating agents. This allows all agents to be informed about the ongoing set play and their potential involvement.

Table 2. Implemented actions

Action	Arguments	Description
kick	*xy*: (double, double)	E.g., $kick(agent = \text{"}P1\text{"}, xy = (2, -1*2)$ Instructs the agent in role *P1* to kick the ball to position given by *xy*
pass	*to*: str	E.g., $pass(agent = \text{"}P1\text{"}, to = \text{"}P2\text{"})$ Instructs the agent in role *P1* to pass the ball to agent in role *P2*
pass_in_depth	*to*: str	E.g., $pass\_in\_depth(agent = \text{"}P1\text{"}, to = \text{"}P2\text{"})$ Instructs the agent in role *P1* to pass the ball forwarded to agent in role *P2*
move	*xy*: (double, double) *tol*: double *wait*: bool	E.g., $move(agent = \text{"}P4\text{"}, xy = (10,4), wait = false)$ Instructs the agent in role *P1* to move to position *xy*. If *wait* is set to true, the step does not advance until the player reaches the position, otherwise, the step immediately advances
dribble	*xy*: (double, double)	E.g., $dribble(agent = \text{"}P1\text{"}, xy = (3,1))$ Instructs the agent in role *P1* to move to position *xy*
shoot		E.g., $shoot(agent = \text{"}P1\text{"})$ Instructs the agent in role *P1* to shoot in direction of the opponent's goal

After completing their actions, the agents notify other agents of their progress by sending a message starting with 'a' (indicating advancement), along with the set play's ID. This communication ensures that all participating agents are aware that the set play has moved to the next step and allows them to verify if they have any specific tasks to carry out. If the action being executed is the final step of the set play, the agent signals its completion using a message that starts with 'e' (indicating the end), followed by the set play's ID. This way, all agents involved are informed that the set play has concluded.

If a set play ends due to a timeout or post-condition violation, there is no requirement to announce it through the communication medium, as all participating agents will detect it.

5   Kick Rolling Ball Challenge

The magmaOffenburg team introduced the Kick Rolling Ball Challenge, included in their magmaChallenge tool, accessible on GitHub[3]. The challenge consists in kicking a ball that is rolling towards the player as far as possible in a fixed direction. The ball begins at a random distance between 1 and 4 m from the player, positioned at a random angle between -90 and $90°$. The player is given a 5-second window to locate the ball. After this time, the ball is propelled to a predetermined location in front of the player, with slight random directional variations. Then, the player must kick the ball and wait without falling until the ball speed drops below 0.01 m per cycle.

The final score is computed as $\max(0, dx) - |dy| - fallen \times 3$, where dx is the displacement of the ball in the x-axis after being kicked, dy is analogous to dx in the y-axis, and $fallen$ is 1 if the player falls or 0 otherwise.

[3] 3D magmaChallenge tool https://github.com/magmaOffenburg/magmaChallenge.

5.1   Challenge Kick

A new skill was developed specifically for this challenge using reinforcement learning. The Challenge Kick follows the model architecture shown in Fig. 2. An underlying bias model is used to guide the optimization at an early stage, expediting the learning process. The bias model has two stages: a back swing that lasts for 0.06 s and consists in swinging the right leg backward and rotating the hip to counterbalance the movement, and a forward acceleration stage that lasts until the end and consists in swinging the right leg forward to perform a powerful kick.

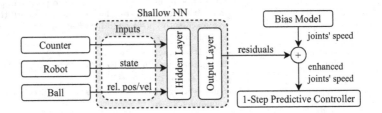

Fig. 2. Model architecture for the Challenge Kick

The state of the bias model is conveyed to the neural network with a counter variable. The state of the robot comprises its internal sensors, position and velocity of joints, and head height. Additionally, the state space also includes the position and velocity of the ball. The episode setup closely mirrors the challenge conditions, with the reinforcement learning reward being given by the challenge score. The player must kick the ball within 0.28 s, after which the agent reverts to using the Walk skill while waiting for the ball to stop.

The output of the shallow neural network (single hidden layer with 64 neurons) is added to the output of the bias model to generate a target speed for 16 joints, excluding the head, toes and 4 elbow joints. The optimization is performed by the Proximal Policy Optimization algorithm [23].

6   Results

The results of the main competition are summarized in Fig. 3. FC Portugal finished in first place with 18 wins, 3 losses and 1 tie. During the course of the competition, the team scored 109 goals while conceding only 13. In the final, it defeated the strong magmaOffenburg team by 3-2, a team that defeated UT Austin Villa, the 2021 champion [15], in the semi-finals by 4-0.

Fig. 3. Main competition results

In addition to the main competition, there was a Technical Challenge, which was composed of three events: the Free/Scientific Challenge, where competing teams presented their research work in the context of the 3D simulation league; the Kick Rolling Ball Challenge presented in Sect. 5; and the Fat Proxy Challenge, which was played in a single round-robin tournament using the magmaFatProxy [8]. The purpose of the proxy is to provide the same skills to all teams, preventing the agent from controlling the joints of the robot, thus making the competition exclusively about high-level strategies.

Table 3 shows the scores obtained in each event per participating team. The Technical Challenge ranks teams based on their cumulative points across all challenges. magmaOffenburg won the Technical Challenge and its three constituent events.

Table 3. Technical Challenge results based on accumulated points in the Kick Rolling Ball Challenge, the Fat Proxy Challenge, and the Free/Scientific Challenge

Team	Overall		Kick R. Ball		Fat Proxy		Free/Scientific	
	Rank	Points	Rank	Points	Rank	Points	Rank	Points
magmaOffenburg	1	75	1	25	1	25	1	25
UT Austin Villa	2	50	3	15	2	20	3	15
FC Portugal	**3**	**45**	**2**	**20**	**3**	**15**	**4**	**10**
BahiaRT	4	40	4	10	4	10	2	20
Wits FC	5	5	–	–	5	5	–	–

7   Conclusion

FC Portugal has developed numerous skills and methodologies concerning the NAO humanoid robot and the simulation league in general. Currently, the team has a very robust code base developed from scratch after RoboCup 2021, which led to the second consecutive victory in the RoboCup 3D Soccer Simulation League. In the main competition, the team registered 18 wins, 1 tie, and 3 losses. It scored 109 goals and conceded only 13.

This year's key developments included a revised dribble technique, designed to keep the ball further from the robot to prevent ball-holding fouls in compliance with new rules, and the introduction of a new programming language called TSAL. TSAL enables the creation of high-level team strategies in robotic soccer, combining deep symbolic reinforcement learning with human sub-optimal knowledge to optimize team tactics. Despite the good results, there are still many improvement opportunities. Future research directions include high-level multi-agent coordination strategies, opponent modeling, goalkeeper skills, omnidirectional kicks, optimization algorithms, and more.

Acknowledgments. The first author was supported by the Foundation for Science and Technology (FCT) under grant SFRH/BD/139926/2018. Additionally, this research was financially supported by FCT/MCTES (PIDDAC), under projects UIDB/00027/2020 (LIACC) and UIDB/00127/2020 (IEETA).

References

1. Abdolmaleki, A., Simões, D., Lau, N., Reis, L.P., Neumann, G.: Learning a humanoid kick with controlled distance. In: Behnke, S., Sheh, R., Sarıel, S., Lee, D.D. (eds.) RoboCup 2016. LNCS (LNAI), vol. 9776, pp. 45–57. Springer, Cham (2017). https://doi.org/10.1007/978-3-319-68792-6_4
2. Abreu, M., Kasaei, M., Reis, L.P., Lau, N.: FC Portugal: RoboCup 2022 3D simulation league and technical challenge champions. In: Eguchi, A., Lau, N., Paetzel-Prüsmann, M., Wanichanon, T. (eds.) RoboCup 2022. LNCS, vol. 13561, pp. 313–324. Springer, Cham (2022). https://doi.org/10.1007/978-3-031-28469-4_26
3. Abreu, M., Lau, N., Sousa, A., Reis, L.P.: Learning low level skills from scratch for humanoid robot soccer using deep reinforcement learning. In: 2019 IEEE International Conference on Autonomous Robot Systems and Competitions (ICARSC), pp. 256–263. IEEE (2019)
4. Abreu, M., Reis, L.P., Cardoso, H.L.: Learning high-level robotic soccer strategies from scratch through reinforcement learning. In: 2019 IEEE International Conference on Autonomous Robot Systems and Competitions, pp. 128–134. IEEE (2019)
5. Abreu, M., Reis, L.P., Lau, N.: Learning to run faster in a humanoid robot soccer environment through reinforcement learning. In: Chalup, S., Niemueller, T., Suthakorn, J., Williams, M.-A. (eds.) RoboCup 2019. LNCS (LNAI), vol. 11531, pp. 3–15. Springer, Cham (2019). https://doi.org/10.1007/978-3-030-35699-6_1
6. Abreu, M., Reis, L.P., Lau, N.: Addressing imperfect symmetry: a novel symmetry-learning actor-critic extension. arXiv preprint arXiv:2309.02711 (2023)
7. Abreu, M., Silva, T., Teixeira, H., Reis, L.P., Lau, N.: 6D localization and kicking for humanoid robotic soccer. J. Intell. Robot. Syst. **102**(2), 1–25 (2021)
8. Amelia, E., et al.: magmaFatProxy (2023). https://github.com/magmaOffenburg/magmaFatProxy
9. Boedecker, J., Asada, M.: SimSpark-concepts and application in the robocup 3D soccer simulation league. In: Proceedings of the SIMPAR-2008 Workshop on The Universe of RoboCup Simulators, Venice, Italy (2008)
10. Cravo, J.: SPlanner: Uma Aplicação Gráfica de Definição Flexível de Jogadas Estudadas no RoboCup. Master's thesis, University of Porto, Porto, Portugal (2011)
11. Kasaei, M., Abreu, M., Lau, N., Pereira, A., Reis, L.P.: A CPG-based agile and versatile locomotion framework using proximal symmetry loss. arXiv preprint arXiv:2103.00928 (2021)

12. Kasaei, M., Abreu, M., Lau, N., Pereira, A., Reis, L.P.: Robust biped locomotion using deep reinforcement learning on top of an analytical control approach. Robot. Auton. Syst. **146**, 103900 (2021)
13. Kasaei, M., Abreu, M., Lau, N., Pereira, A., Reis, L.P., Li, Z.: Learning hybrid locomotion skills - learn to exploit residual actions and modulate model-based gait control. Front. Robot. AI **10** (2023)
14. Kasaei, S.M., Simões, D., Lau, N., Pereira, A.: A hybrid ZMP-CPG based walk engine for biped robots. In: Ollero, A., Sanfeliu, A., Montano, L., Lau, N., Cardeira, C. (eds.) ROBOT 2017. AISC, vol. 694, pp. 743–755. Springer, Cham (2018). https://doi.org/10.1007/978-3-319-70836-2_61
15. MacAlpine, P., Liu, B., Macke, W., Wang, C., Stone, P.: UT Austin villa: RoboCup 2021 3D simulation league competition champions. In: Alami, R., Biswas, J., Cakmak, M., Obst, O. (eds.) RoboCup 2021. LNCS (LNAI), vol. 13132, pp. 314–326. Springer, Cham (2022). https://doi.org/10.1007/978-3-030-98682-7_26
16. Mota, L.: Multi-robot coordination using flexible setplays: applications in RoboCup's simulation and middle-size leagues. Ph.D. thesis, University of Porto (2011)
17. Mota, L., Lau, N., Reis, L.P.: Co-ordination in RoboCup's 2D simulation league: Setplays as flexible, multi-robot plans. In: 2010 IEEE Conference on Robotics, Automation and Mechatronics, pp. 362–367 (2010)
18. Mota, L., Reis, L.P.: Setplays: achieving coordination by the appropriate use of arbitrary pre-defined flexible plans and inter-robot communication. In: 1st International ICST Conference on Robot Communication and Coordination (2007)
19. Mota, L., Reis, L.P., Lau, N.: Multi-robot coordination using setplays in the middle size and simulation leagues. Mechatronics **21**(2), 434–444 (2011)
20. Mota, P.: A team strategy programming language applied to robotic soccer. Master's thesis, University of Porto, Porto, Portugal (2023)
21. Reis, L.P., Almeida, F., Mota, L., Lau, N.: Coordination in multi-robot systems: applications in robotic soccer. In: Filipe, J., Fred, A. (eds.) ICAART 2012. CCIS, vol. 358, pp. 3–21. Springer, Heidelberg (2013). https://doi.org/10.1007/978-3-642-36907-0_1
22. Reis, L.P., Lopes, R., Mota, L., Lau, N.: Playmaker: graphical definition of formations and setplays. In: 5th Iberian Conference on Information Systems and Technologies, pp. 1–6 (2010)
23. Schulman, J., Wolski, F., Dhariwal, P., Radford, A., Klimov, O.: Proximal policy optimization algorithms. arXiv preprint arXiv:1707.06347 (2017)
24. Simões, D., Amaro, P., Silva, T., Lau, N., Reis, L.P.: Learning low-level behaviors and high-level strategies in humanoid soccer. In: Silva, M.F., Luís Lima, J., Reis, L.P., Sanfeliu, A., Tardioli, D. (eds.) ROBOT 2019. AISC, vol. 1093, pp. 537–548. Springer, Cham (2020). https://doi.org/10.1007/978-3-030-36150-1_44
25. Simões, M.A., Mascarenhas, G., Fonseca, R., dos Santos, V.M., Mascarenhas, F., Nogueira, T.: Bahiart setplays collecting toolkit and BahiaRT gym. Softw. Impacts **14**, 100401 (2022)
26. Teixeira, H., Silva, T., Abreu, M., Reis, L.P.: Humanoid robot kick in motion ability for playing robotic soccer. In: 2020 IEEE International Conference on Autonomous Robot Systems and Competitions (ICARSC), pp. 34–39. IEEE (2020)
27. Xu, Y., Vatankhah, H.: SimSpark: an open source robot simulator developed by the RoboCup community. In: Behnke, S., Veloso, M., Visser, A., Xiong, R. (eds.) RoboCup 2013. LNCS (LNAI), vol. 8371, pp. 632–639. Springer, Heidelberg (2014). https://doi.org/10.1007/978-3-662-44468-9_59

Tech United Eindhoven Middle Size League Winner 2023

Ruben M. Beumer[✉], Stefan Kempers, Jorrit Olthuis, Aneesh Deogan,
Sander Doodeman, Wouter Aangenent, Ruud van den Bogaert,
Patrick van Brakel, Matthias Briegel, Dennis Bruijnen, Hao Liang Chen,
Yanick Douven, Danny Hameeteman, Gerard van Hattum, Kayden Knapik,
Johan Kon, Harrie van de Loo, Ferry Schoenmakers, Jaap van der Stoel,
Peter Teurlings, and René van de Molengraft[iD]

Tech United Eindhoven, De Rondom 70, P.O. Box 513,
5600 MB Eindhoven, The Netherlands
{techunited,techunited}@tue.nl
https://www.techunited.nl/

Abstract. The RoboCup Middle Size League (MSL) aims to promote
robotics research through robots playing autonomous soccer. In this
league, robots play 5 vs 5 on a field of 22 by 14 m. The research in
the MSL focuses on distributed multi-agent systems that exclusively
have on-board sensors. At RoboCup 2023 in Bordeaux, France, Tech
United Eindhoven of the Eindhoven University of Technology won the
MSL competition. This paper reflects on the tournament and the developments that led to the victory of Tech United. Specifically, we discuss
three developments. Firstly, the concept of a 'sweeper keeper', where the
goalkeeper more actively participates in the match, is applied to robotic
soccer. Secondly, the developments of Tech United towards a human dribble, where the robots release the ball from the ball handling mechanism
during dribbling to gain a higher speed and more freedom of movement,
are discussed. Finally, the evolution of using the Skills, Tactics and Plays
(STP) framework in MSL is presented.

Keywords: RoboCup Soccer · Middle Size League · Multi-robot ·
Human Dribble · Sweeper Keeper

1 Introduction

Tech United Eindhoven is the RoboCup team representing the Eindhoven University of Technology (TU/e), competing in the Middle Size League (MSL).
RoboCup is an international initiative to advance the state of the art of intelligent robots. The MSL realises this, for example, through contributions to distributed multi-agent systems and novel motion control solutions. Since 2006,
Tech United has participated in thirteen world championship finals, emerging
victorious on seven occasions. The MSL team comprises five PhD students, two

C. Buche et al. (Eds.): RoboCup 2023, LNAI 14140, pp. 428–439, 2024.
https://doi.org/10.1007/978-3-031-55015-7_36

MSc students, one BSc student, six former TU/e students, six TU/e staff members, and one member not affiliated with TU/e. In this paper, we discuss the significant scientific advancements made by the Tech United soccer robots in the past year, as well as outline key developments for upcoming RoboCup tournaments.

Section 2 of this paper provides a comprehensive overview of the fifth generation soccer robot utilised mainly in the RoboCup 2023 competition. Next, Sect. 3 presents relevant statistics regarding the performance of these robots throughout the tournament. In Sect. 4 we show our work on a more offensive strategy where the goalkeeper is included during attacking plays. This is followed by Sect. 5, in which the work on implementing the human dribble is presented. Section 6 then gives an overview of the improvements made to the Skills, Tactics and Plays (STP) framework. Finally, the paper is concluded in Sect. 7, which presents our outlook for the coming years.

2 Robot Platform

The soccer robots of Tech United are called TURTLEs, which is an acronym for Tech United Robocup Team: Limited Edition. Their development started in 2005, and through years of iterations and experience they have evolved into the fifth generation TURTLE, shown in Fig. 1. A schematic representation of the robot design can be found in [6]. A detailed list of hardware specifications, along with CAD files of the base, upper-body, ball handling mechanism (BHM) and shooting mechanism, is published on the Robotic Open Platform wiki[1].

Fig. 1. Fifth generation TURTLE robots, with the goalkeeper on the left-hand side. (Photo by Bart van Overbeeke)

---

[1] http://roboticopenplatform.org/wiki/TURTLE.

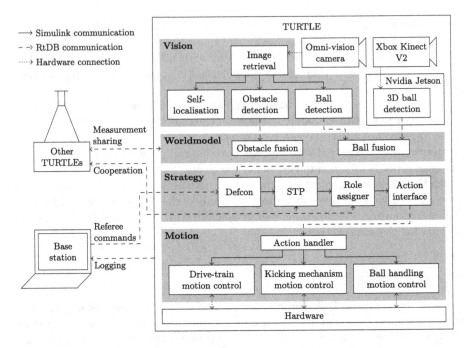

Fig. 2. A simplified, logical overview of the Tech United software architecture.

Figure 2 shows a high-level schematic of the Tech United software architecture. The software controlling the robots consists of four main modules: Vision, Worldmodel, Strategy, and Motion. These parts of the software communicate with each other through a real-time database (RtDB) designed by the CAMBADA team [1], depicted by dashed arrows. The data flows within these four executables are governed by Simulink as shown by solid arrows.

The Vision module processes the omni-vision camera data to obtain the locations of the ball, opponents, and the robot itself. The Xbox Kinect V2 camera is connected to an Nvidia Jetson board, which is used to track airborne balls that are out of view for the omni-vision module.

The position information from both Vision and the Jetson is fed into the Worldmodel module, where this data is combined with data from all other team members to form a unified representation of the world. Based on this representation, strategical choices are made by the team.

The Strategy module first makes high-level decisions in the Defcon submodule. This module determines if we need to perform certain actions (e.g., free kick) ordered by the referee, or what the play should be (e.g., offensive, defensive, neutral). This analysis is forwarded to the STP framework, which is discussed in more detail in Sect. 6.1. The roles in the play chosen by STP are distributed over the available robots. Every robot executes the tasks corresponding to its role. These tasks prescribe low-level actions (e.g., pass, intercept the ball, shoot).

Finally, the Motion module takes these actions as input and uses motion control algorithms for driving, ball handling, and shooting respectively to operate the motors. The driving motion control system has been configured to be able to support different driving systems [4].

3   RoboCup 2023 Statistics

Six teams participated at RoboCup 2023 in the MSL: Falcons, LAR@MSL, Robot Club Toulon, Tech United Eindhoven, UM Croatia, and VDL Robot Sports.[2] Five of them participated in the soccer competition, which resulted in a total of thirty-four scheduled matches. Tech United played in eleven of these matches (plus three that were not played due to technical issues of an opponent), during which we were able to score 107 times out of 172 attempts at target (plus twelve regulatory goals), while only conceding three goals. That means that this year our robots scored 9.7 goals per match on average, compared to 12.3 goals per match during the previous tournament in 2022. According to odometry data, the robots collectively drove 50.7 km over the course of the tournament, of which 1.2 km was covered by the goalkeeper.

4   Sweeper Keeper

In the RoboCup MSL, robots play 5 vs 5. One robot per team can be a goal-keeper, which means that it is the only robot allowed to be in the goal area [7]. In addition, it is the only robot allowed to use extendable frames when it is within its own penalty area, similar to a human goalkeeper being the only player allowed to touch the ball with his arms and hands there. Until this year, goalkeepers in the MSL have always remained within their goal area and have only been used to prevent balls from entering the goal. Therefore, teams effectively play with only four robots when they are in possession of the ball. In human soccer and futsal however, goalkeepers often actively contribute to the game. They some-times leave their goal area to intercept balls from the opponents that are behind their own defensive players, and serve as an additional (defensive) field player when their team has the ball. Goalkeepers who show this behaviour are often called rush goalies or sweeper keepers. Doing this is for instance in line with the vision of the late Johan Cruijff, a famous Dutch soccer player and coach with a large influence on the historic development of soccer strategies, who said: "In my teams, the goalie is the first attacker, and the striker is the first defender". Besides that it is reasonable to assume that playing with an additional field player is an advantage, it is also supported by statistics. For example, it was found that the expected impact of a sending-off 30 min before the end of a soc-cer match, is approximately 0.39 or 0.50 goals (depending on whether the sent-off player is on the visiting or home team, respectively) [2]. In futsal and RoboCup

---

[2] For detailed results see https://msl.robocup.org/history/2023-detailed-results.

Fig. 3. Example of the sweeper keeper (robot 2) in a match at RoboCup 2023, For a video see https://youtu.be/_fCUDPPtgLM?t=75.

MSL, the relative advantage of having an additional field player is even larger than in human outdoor soccer, because there are fewer players.

This year, Tech United applied the sweeper keeper behaviour for the first time in an official RoboCup MSL match. To enable it, the robot with goalkeeper hardware (extendable frames and no ball handling and shooting mechanism) was replaced by a 'normal' substitute robot, either already at the start of a match, at half-time, or by means of an autonomous substitution [7]. Two different versions of strategies using a sweeper keeper were applied.

The first version mainly served as a proof of concept. Every time Tech United got in possession of the ball, the goalkeeper moved several metres forward out of its goal area, while still staying in between the ball and the centre of its goal. As soon as possession of the ball was lost, the goalkeeper quickly returned to its goal area. An example of this version being applied in a match is shown in Fig. 3, where the sweeper keeper (robot 2) serves as a fifth field player for Tech United (black with blue robots, playing towards the right side), making it impossible for the four opponent field players (black robots with red number plates) to defend every robot. As a result, robot 4 could receive a pass and score a goal.

Whereas the first version was a proof of concept having only a small impact on the gameplay, the second version improved on this and showed the advantages of having a sweeper keeper. In this version, instead of staying close to the goal and in line with the ball, the sweeper keeper moved forward, joining the attack in the same way as the other TURTLEs.

The current goalkeeper robot of Tech United does not have a ball handling and kicking mechanism and is not even allowed to play as a field player because of its larger dimensions [7]. Therefore, this robot had to be replaced by another (normal) robot in order to apply the sweeper keeper behaviour during the matches. The consequence of using a goalkeeper without extendable frames is that it is less suitable to stop shots by the opponent. In the future, we aim to develop a robot with the same ball handling and kicking mechanism as the field player robots, and additionally the goalkeeper's extendable frames with adapted dimensions. It should be designed such, that it still adheres to the rules allowing it to play as a field player when desired. In that way, when applied at the appropriate occurrences, we can benefit from the advantages of the sweeper keeper while not suffering from the disadvantages.

5   Human Dribble

In view of the 2050 goal, in which fully autonomous humanoid robots will beat the winners of the most recent world cup, we want to move away from wheel-based robots. When we make this transition, the way the robots handle the ball will change since they will no longer have a ball handling mechanism (BHM). Therefore, the way the robots dribble will change. The first step is the so-called human dribble. Essentially, this mimics how a human or quadruped would dribble. This allows a more natural gameplay with humans, so this development is beneficial to the goal in 2050. Additionally, there are immediate benefits to teams who implement this skill. It enables the robot to bypass the 3 m rule, which states that once the ball is held by the BHM of a robot, the robot may not dribble further than a 3 m radius about the point where it gained control over the ball [7]. However, once the ball is released from the BHM and caught again, the 3 m rule begins anew, meaning that there is no longer a limit to how far the robot can move with the ball if the human dribble skill is used. This is shown in Fig. 4, where the robot performs the human dribble skill to displace the 3 m rule; the robot in possession of the ball in step 1 and bounded by the 3 m rule, it pushes the ball in step 2, and in step 3 it catches the ball, restarting the 3 m rule at this new position.

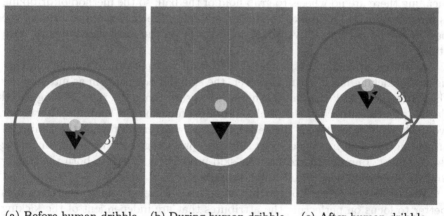

(a) Before human dribble   (b) During human dribble   (c) After human dribble

Fig. 4. How the human dribble skill can overcome the 3 m rule. The black triangle represents the robot and the yellow circle is the ball.

The flowchart of the skill is shown in Fig. 5, which explains the different steps in the human dribble skill: first rotating to the target, dribbling for a distance

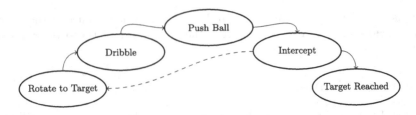

Fig. 5. Flowchart of the human dribble skill.

of less than 3 m to build up speed, pushing the ball, and intercepting the ball, after which either the target can be reached within 3 m or the human dribble skill needs to be performed again before reaching the target.

We have implemented the kicking skill into the human dribble. So far, only the BHM has been used by other teams in the MSL, to push the ball during the human dribble skill. However, this is more difficult for newer teams, meaning they would be in more of a disadvantage against teams who have a more developed ball handling. By using the kicking mechanism, this previously advanced skill also becomes feasible for newer teams. Kicking and the BHM provide two options for pushing the ball. Testing has shown that kicking is better for higher driving speeds, while the BHM performs better at lower driving speeds.

In addition, we have also generalised this skill to include curved trajectories, where the path of the human dribble does not have to be in a straight line. Teams using their active BHM have only shown human dribbles in straight lines. Even though curved paths have been seen in the past, these were with a passive BHM, meaning there are no wheels to grab hold of the ball; so the method of dribbling is for the robot to bump into the ball. Combining the curved trajectories of the past with the current active BHM would provide the ideal attributes of both styles.

At RoboCup 2023, the human dribble skill was performed during matches using the kicking mechanism. However, the skill did not perform as intended, as the robot would kick the ball too hard or too soft. Since the right kicking speed depends on the surface of the pitch, additional focus on the tuning of this factor would have been required. Instead, the focus was on improving the timing of triggering the skill in the strategy software, providing a robust basis for future development. In order to execute this skill properly in matches, both the trigger and the execution need to be tuned properly.

We are in the process of moving away from wheeled robots, therefore it is better to focus on perfecting the attributes that are independent of the kicking or pushing method. For future work, perfecting the trajectory planner is crucial as that can be used for quadrupeds as well as wheeled robots. Only the manner in which the kicking is performed changes.

6 STP Review

At RoboCup 2017, De Koning et al. [5] presented their work on transferring the Skills, Tactics and Plays (STP) framework from the Small Size League (SSL) to the MSL. Following this, Tech United Eindhoven started implementing the STP framework in their software. In January 2019, all Tech United strategy was rewritten into this format, and Tech United won their 2019 MSL world title [3] while using STP.

Some differences between the SSL and MSL were covered by De Koning et al. [5]. However, one of the main problems, the difference in game speed, is not investigated. This section presents the changes made to the STP framework by Tech United Eindhoven in the period from January 2019 until RoboCup 2023 and planned changes in the near future.

6.1 STP Concept

The goal of STP is to make the strategy more easily configurable and reusable. It does this by splitting the strategy up into several layers as shown in Fig. 6.

When using STP, the human coach chooses a *playbook* before the match to define the possible behaviours of the team available during the game. A playbook contains a set of plays.

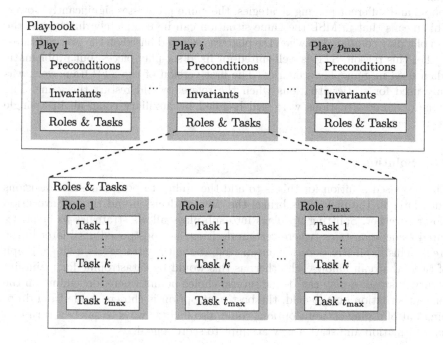

Fig. 6. A simplified overview of the STP framework as used by Tech United.

Each *play* has preconditions and invariants to indicate when it can be used. The *play selector* decides if the current play is applicable, and chooses a different play when necessary based on these conditions. Furthermore, each play contains a list of *roles*. Roles are dynamically distributed over the robots by the *role assigner*. In the Tech United software this means that the physical goalkeeper always becomes the goalkeeper of the team, and the other roles are distributed such that all robots reach their target as quickly as possible.

The selected roles are then processed by the *play executer*. It ensures that the *tasks* of each role are executed in order, and that all robots are executing the same index of task at the same time. Tasks describe simple actions, that may be tailored to the specific point in the play where they are used. Tasks are a translational layer between the STP framework and the *actions* of the Motion process.

6.2 Limitations of the Original Framework

Several differences between the SSL and MSL are discussed by De Koning et al. [5]. The primary differences are the distributed computational capabilities of the robots in the MSL.

A difference that was not discussed is the time variability. Where a play in SSL takes at most several seconds, plays in MSL generally take significantly longer. Due to the slower robots in relation to field size, physical size of the robots and different playing strategies, the game progresses significantly slower. This means that in MSL the game situation can be completely different at the end of a play compared to when the play was selected based on the preconditions.

For this reason, STP is well-suited for fixed set-play pieces, but problematic when used in gameplay scenarios. The first version of the STP framework was only used for static situations when the referee would restart the game. The dynamic game situations were still handled by auxiliary code, all in a single task.

6.3 Solution

The proposed solution for this is to add the ability to postpone some decisions until later in the play. This brings the time of decision and time of execution closer together. Splitting up plays into sub-plays allows strategies to be structured as decision trees (where certain decisions are postponed until later in the tree). This explicitly does not mean that the entire strategy is a single graph of tasks that can follow each other, as this would be catastrophic for maintainability. Instead, a play can define several choice points where, depending on the current situation on the field, the best next option is chosen. Aside from dropping out of a play entirely, options could also include ways to safely return to a base formation and start a new attempt to score a goal.

6.4   Other Extensions

Several other additions were made to the STP framework to improve the user-friendliness and performance. Some of these improvements are highlighted.

Position-Based Strategies. Looking at human football or futsal strategies, the exact coordinates of players are most often irrelevant for the execution of the strategy as seen from a high level perspective. In most cases, the coordinates relative to the ball, opponents and teammates are more important than the exact absolute coordinates. For example, the same idea behind a play can often be applied if we start with the ball 1 m closer and a teammate 1.5 m more to the left of the goal. Instead of defining absolute coordinates in a play, we can define formations (as also used in human soccer and futsal) in which every role corresponds to one position in the formation. These positions can be described as regions in which the player has some freedom to execute its task. The regions can either be defined as fixed with respect to the field lines or relative to, for example, the ball or opponents. In this way, Position-Based Strategies allow easy configurations of strategies that can operate with varying conditions on the field. The aforementioned regions can even be defined and used to construct preconditions and invariants of plays.

Role Assignment. Before STP was employed in the Tech United software, roles were assigned based on distance to the target: the idea is that in this way every TURTLE reaches their target as soon as possible. In order to prevent doubly and not assigned roles, TURTLEs would optimise the role assignment by switching roles with each other. The problem with this approach in STP is that the set of targets is not known when continuing to the next task. To resolve this, every time the team continues to the next task, each TURTLE computes the target for each role. Using this result, an initial distribution of roles over the TURTLEs can be made. After the initial distribution, it is still possible for TURTLEs to switch roles and achieve a better role distribution.

Synchronisation. One of the crucial properties that the STP framework has to ensure, is that all robots are executing the correct play and task at the same time. Due to communication delays and varying field conditions, this has proven to be more difficult than it appears at first glance. Selection of a play happens by one of the TURTLEs: the team leader[3]. The team leader is put in charge of evaluating the preconditions. Based on this, they select a play for the entire team. A similar process runs continuously to check the invariants.

We continue to the next task in a play when all roles have finished their current task. Due to communication delays all roles will keep signalling during several samples that they have finished their task, when in fact they are still

---

[3] Every TURTLE is ready at any time to take over the team leader role. For example, it can be the active TURTLE with the lowest ID.

referring to the previous task. Therefore, in addition to their task execution status, they also indicate to which task this status refers, to prevent skipping through several tasks in an instant. The team leader keeps track of every TUR-TLE's progress. Once the team leader has received from all TURTLEs that they finished their task k, it is the trigger for the team leader to signal to continue to the next task $k+1$, or to select a new play if k was the last task.

Success Criteria. A major advantage of STP is to have multiple alternative plays for a single situation. This ensures that the team is always unpredictable, and difficult to defend against using fixed tricks. To this end, Tech United Eindhoven has implemented probability preconditions and success criteria. A probability precondition is a precondition based on a sample from a probability distribution that is true or false with a probability that can be set. These probabilities can be set in advance by the human team members, or adjusted automatically by means of success criteria.

Each play defines a success criterion to indicate when it is considered to have been executed successfully. For example, when the team has regained control over the ball (for a defensive play), or when the ball progresses forward and is still in our possession (for an offensive play). During all matches the robots record how often certain plays were completed successfully and unsuccessfully. These results can be used to (automatically) tune the probabilities that influence the likelihood with which the plays are selected. If there is sufficient data, this may even be decided on a per-opponent basis.

7   Conclusion

This paper described the major scientific and technological developments of Tech United in preparation of RoboCup 2023. Part of the work has not actively contributed to the result of winning RoboCup 2023, but creates a strong foundation to build upon for the coming tournaments. On the other hand, Sect. 6 of this paper reviewed the strategy overhaul that we started some years ago.

One of the major recent contributions to the strategy aspect, is to let the goalkeeper actively participate during gameplay. This year the sweeper keeper played its first few matches. Including an extra player, in the form of a sweeper keeper, increases the scope of possible strategies that can be incorporated, similar to human football and futsal. Furthermore, the extra player gives the corresponding team the upper hand over teams with a passive goalkeeper.

We elaborated on our work on the human dribble, an important skill when playing on a large field against human players. Letting go of the ball to reset the 3 m rule can be achieved either by pushing with the BHM or by gently kicking the ball forward. Since the league is expected to eventually move away from wheeled robots, we emphasised on making the skill hardware independent, and thus opted for using the kicking mechanism, which all types of soccer robots have.

In this work we also reviewed our implementation of the STP framework from the SSL to the MSL, which was started in 2017. The majority of the framework could be transferred to the MSL. However, some limitations arose during the first few tournaments, which were the reasons to make adjustments. One adjustment to the original framework is the transition to Position-Based Strategies, which allows for easy configuration of strategies that are more robust to changes on the field. Another improvement made in the last few years, is the addition of success criteria. The weights of different plays can now be tuned based on how well the play is performing, allowing for a more dynamic and unpredictable strategy. Furthermore, the difference in time variability compared to the SSL turned out to be an important aspect: similar plays in the MSL typically last significantly longer. We therefore plan to add the possibility to postpone some decisions until later on in the play. This allows the play itself to adapt, to some extent, to the varying game conditions.

Altogether, the discussed work not only advances the state of the art of the MSL, but also that of intelligent robots in general. This should make robot soccer more dynamic and more attractive to watch, while maintaining the scientific foundation. The continued developments hopefully allow us to stay with the top of the MSL and contribute to the long term goal of beating the human world champion in soccer in 2050.

References

1. Almeida, L., Santos, F., Facchinetti, T., Pedreiras, P., Silva, V., Lopes, L.S.: Coordinating distributed autonomous agents with a real-time database: the CAMBADA project. In: Aykanat, C., Dayar, T., Körpeoğlu, İ (eds.) ISCIS 2004. LNCS, vol. 3280, pp. 876–886. Springer, Heidelberg (2004). https://doi.org/10.1007/978-3-540-30182-0_88

2. Badiella, L., Puig, P., Lago-Peñas, C., Casals, M.: Influence of red and yellow cards on team performance in elite soccer. Ann. Oper. Res. 325, 149–165 (2023). https://doi.org/10.1007/s10479-022-04733-0

3. Houtman, W., et al.: Tech united Eindhoven middle-size league winner 2019. In: Chalup, S., Niemueller, T., Suthakorn, J., Williams, M.-A. (eds.) RoboCup 2019. LNCS (LNAI), vol. 11531, pp. 517–528. Springer, Cham (2019). https://doi.org/10.1007/978-3-030-35699-6_42

4. Kempers, S.T., et al.: Tech united Eindhoven middle size league winner 2022. In: Eguchi, A., Lau, N., Paetzel-Prüsmann, M., Wanichanon, T. (eds.) RoboCup 2022. LNCS, vol. 13561, pp. 337–348. Springer, Cham (2023). https://doi.org/10.1007/978-3-031-28469-4_28

5. de Koning, L., Mendoza, J.P., Veloso, M., van de Molengraft, R.: Skills, tactics and plays for distributed multi-robot control in adversarial environments. In: Akiyama, H., Obst, O., Sammut, C., Tonidandel, F. (eds.) RoboCup 2017. LNCS (LNAI), vol. 11175, pp. 277–289. Springer, Cham (2018). https://doi.org/10.1007/978-3-030-00308-1_23

6. Lopez Martinez, C., et al.: Tech United Eindhoven team description (2014). https://www.techunited.nl/media/files/TDP2014.pdf

7. Middle Size League Technical Committee: Middle Size Robot League rules and regulations for 2023 - version 24.2. https://msl.robocup.org/wp-content/uploads/2023/06/Rulebook_MSL2023_v24.2.pdf

Author Index

Printed in the United States
by Baker & Taylor Publisher Services